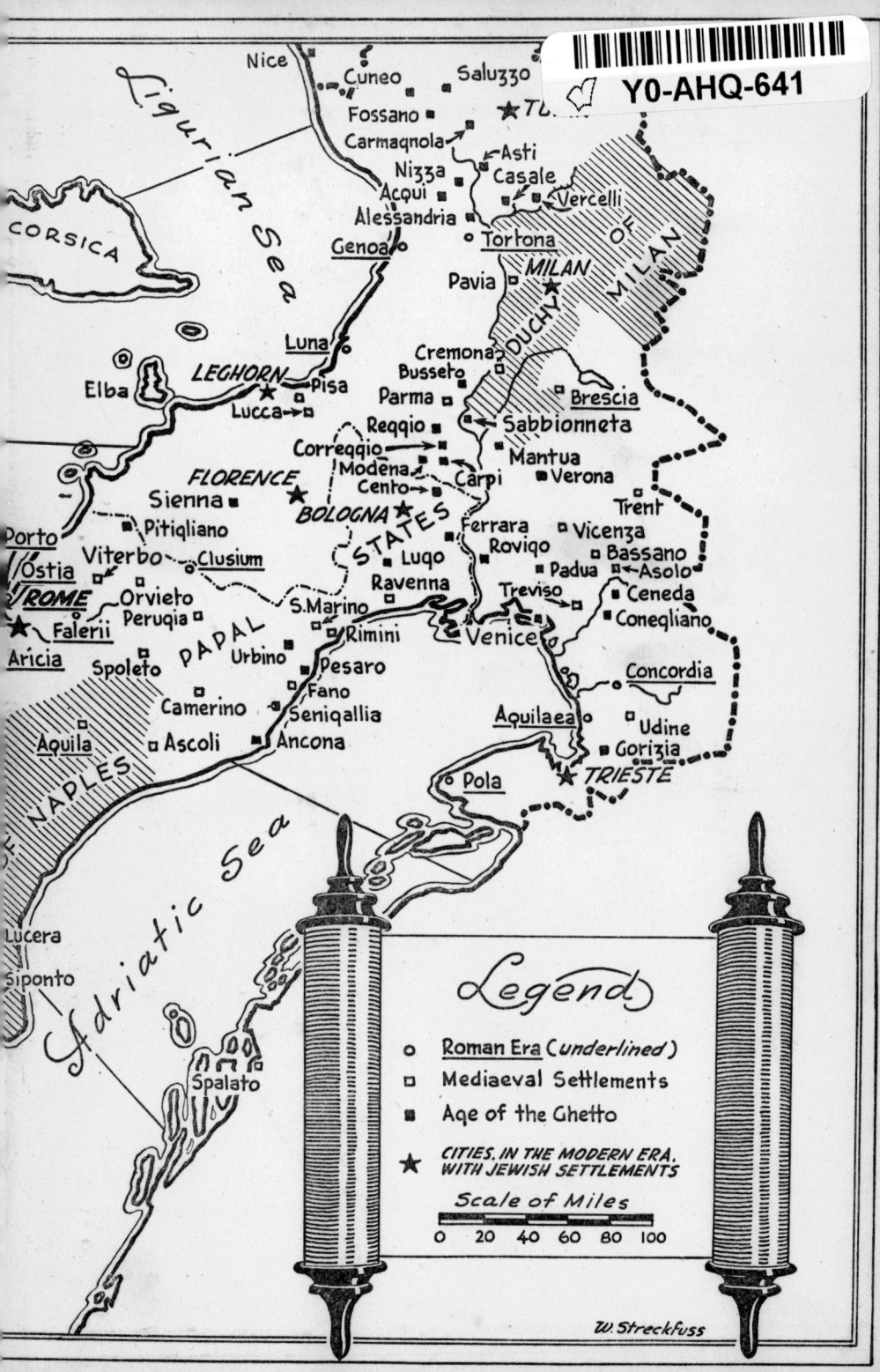

The History of the Jews of Italy

SOME OTHER BOOKS BY THE SAME AUTHOR

THE LAST FLORENTINE REPUBLIC, 1925
THE CASALE PILGRIM, 1929
HISTORY OF THE JEWS IN VENICE, 1930
A JEWISH BOOK OF DAYS, 1931
A HISTORY OF THE MARRANOS, 1932
THE NEPHEW OF THE ALMIGHTY, 1933
A LIFE OF MENASSEH BEN ISRAEL, 1934
A BIRD'S-EYE VIEW OF JEWISH HISTORY, 1935
THE RITUAL MURDER LIBEL AND THE JEW, 1935
THE JEWISH CONTRIBUTION TO CIVILIZATION, 1938
ANGLO-JEWISH LETTERS, 1938
HISTORY OF THE ROTHSCHILD FAMILY, 1939
THE SASSOON DYNASTY, 1941
A HISTORY OF THE JEWS IN ENGLAND, 1941

The History of the Jews of Italy

by
CECIL ROTH

PHILADELPHIA
The Jewish Publication Society of America
5706–1946

Copyright, 1946, by

THE JEWISH PUBLICATION SOCIETY OF AMERICA

All rights reserved. No part of this book may be reproduced in any form without permission in writing from the publisher: except by a reviewer who may quote brief passages in a review to be printed in a magazine or newspaper.

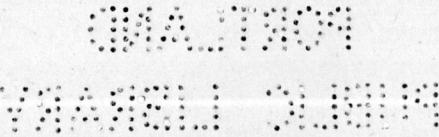

 60

PRINTED IN THE UNITED STATES OF AMERICA
PRESS OF THE JEWISH PUBLICATION SOCIETY
PHILADELPHIA, PENNA.

PREFACE

SURPRISING though it may appear, this is the first history of the Jews in Italy to be written in any language. The difficulties of the task are obvious enough. The subject covers over twenty centuries and half a dozen successive civilizations. It is bound up with the history of the Roman Empire and of the Papacy, of the Renaissance and the Counter-Reformation, of the medieval city republics and modern totalitarianism. Apart from the repercussions of ecclesiastical, economic and intellectual history in their broader aspects, it reflects every aspect of Italian as well as of Jewish life. On the other hand, notwithstanding the notable amount of research devoted to the subject during the past century (I have in my own collection upwards of 300 monographs, large and small), the preparatory work has been unevenly performed. Out of the scores of Italian Jewish communities, only two — Rome and Venice — have received the honor of full-dress monographs covering their entire history and paying attention to Hebrew sources and to intellectual life; and while there is a very great deal of disconnected material on individual cities and regions, there is very little indeed which deals with the country as a whole.

In the preparation of this volume, therefore, the author has not even had an older ground-plan to work upon, and (if the metaphor may be continued) has frequently found himself compelled to lay the foundations as well as build the structure. It has been necessary to discover general tendencies in apparently unrelated happenings in widely separated places, to piece together isolated episodes so as to form a coherent picture, and, in a word, to transform anecdotes into history. Though the result may sometimes seem simple, the process has not been easy. The task has been rather like that of writing a history of England for the first time, with nothing to go upon but fairly adequate accounts of a couple of the larger towns and a host of articles in the local antiquarian journals written mainly by theologians, most of them failing to take account of anything but selected melodramatic episodes, occasional rioting, and the work of the local savants.

On the other hand, in view of the vast amount of scattered material that is available, a very great deal of compression has been necessary. On the community of Florence alone, for example, Umberto Cassuto has written a classical work of at least twice the length of the present volume, covering with masterly skill a mere 150 years at the time of the Renaissance. The present writer has himself published one volume and some scores of "scientific" studies on Italian Jewish history, all from original sources, running to perhaps half a million words all told. All this, and a vast amount besides, has had to be compressed rigorously and without regard to personal predilections. It has been exceptionally difficult to refrain from introducing at every turn the picturesque detail which exists in connection with Italian Jewish history in such peculiar abundance. To include it would doubtless have made the work more readable, but would utterly have destroyed its balance. Critics often suggest that an author has "overlooked" some point, not realizing that the aspect to which they attach such importance may have been weighed in the balance and found wanting, or may be summed up by the inclusion (or even the omission) of a single line. In some cases, in order to forestall such criticism, I have spent dismal hours in rereading recent monographs, with purely negative results. The builder is not necessarily to be blamed for rejecting what the mason intended to be the headstone of the corner. It would have been easy for me to multiply names, especially of the savants who flourished in such profusion all over Italy from the thirteenth century onwards; but I have deliberately restricted myself to the handful of outstanding personalities. Even in these cases, the scale of my work has imposed extreme moderation; thus my half-dozen articles on that picturesque literary adventurer, Leone da Modena, have had to be condensed into as many lines, while the scholar who formed the subject of my first monograph has not even been mentioned. If I have treated my own favorites in this way, I can hardly have been expected to be more generous with the reader's, or the critic's; and the same applies to familiar episodes.

Now and then, my account may differ from what has generally been accepted hitherto. Though this may be due to Johnsonian "ignorance, pure ignorance," it is not always the case. The data are sometimes based on archivistic material, official broadsides, contemporary ephemeral literature, manuscripts and documents in my own collection, and notes compiled over a long period of years both in Italy and abroad; and conclusions which do not tally with those in the standard histories may nevertheless be correct. Some misunderstandings might have been removed had circumstances permitted me to furnish the text with a full panoply of footnotes and references; this would have given my work a far greater appearance of erudition, but such was not my object. In general, the student who may desire fuller information will find it in the monographic literature on the place mentioned, easily traceable in Gabrieli's *Italia Judaica* and in Salo W. Baron's superb bibliographical material, which has now become the historian's stand-by. In a generation of fluid international boundaries, it has been a little difficult to decide whether certain frontier towns should be included in the scope of this volume or no. With no political axe to grind, I can testify that all the Jewish communities spoken of belonged to the historic Italian nexus, whatever the present or future circumstances of the places in question.

There has been some difficulty in deciding what form

should be given to names the English and Italian forms of which differ. Isaaco for Isaac, or Davide for David, seems incongruous in an English work; but Caesar for Cesare, or Lewis for Ludovico, or James for Giacomo, is out of the question; there is no doubt that the name "Florentia" rather than "Florence" should be applied to the Roman city, but in that case why should not "Roma" replace "Rome"? It has seemed best in the circumstances to abandon the attempt at consistency and to use those forms which seem best suited to the context. At many points, I have referred to the state of affairs as it applies in Italy *today*: this refers, alas, to the period before the tragedy of 1943–5, the subject of my last chapter.

I must end on a personal note. I have received more from Italy than I can ever hope to repay, known more happiness there than in any other land, have joyous recollections of scenes and places and persons there such as I have of nowhere else. At one time, the writing of these pages could have been a sheer joy to me. Under the shadow of the recent tragedy, it has been sheer agony. I would inscribe this work to the memory of those dear Italian friends who have fallen victim to the Nazi fury.

Cecil Roth

Oxford, October, 1945.

BIBLIOGRAPHICAL NOTE

In view of the fact that a classified Bibliography of Italian Jewish history exists (G. Gabrieli, *Italia Judaica*, Rome, 1924) it is unnecessary to give here a list of books consulted in the writing of this work. They have included, of course, a number of more recent articles and monographs, e. g., by A. Ottolenghi (Venice), R. Pacifici (Venice, Genoa), H. Rosenberg (Ancona), I. Sonne (Verona, Papal States, etc.) A. Milano (Rome), V. Colorni (Mantua), F. R. Salter (Florence), J. Starr (Naples, Byzantine Italy), and others. In addition, R. Bachi has published various monographs on Italian-Jewish statistics. The present writer's scattered papers on the subject deal with Venice, Rome, Leghorn, Florence, Ferrara, Verona, Urbino, Sienna, and others. In addition to the above, the *Rassegna Mensile di Israel*, published between 1925 and 1938, contains many admirable historical articles by various hands. The researches of Umberto Cassuto, by no means confined to his masterly volume on the Jews of Florence at the time of the Renaissance, must receive special mention, as also J.-B. Frey's superb *Corpus* of Jewish inscriptions (vol. I, Rome, 1936). Most recently, E. Munkácsi has published a richly-illustrated monograph in German on the communities of Apulia, V. Colorni an important work on the application of Jewish law in Italy in the past, and M. Grilli a series of articles on the role of the Jews in modern Italy. In English, very little is available, except H. Vogelstein's volume on Rome and the present author's on Venice.

NOTE ON CURRENCY

Up to the middle of the 19th century, every Italian state minted its own currency, the value and denomination differing from place to place and from period to period. In the early Middle Ages, the silver penny (*denarius*), of which there were many local varieties, was the coin most generally used. In 1234, Florence issued a new unit of currency, the silver *solidus* or *soldo* of 12 *denarii* (*piccoli*) and then, in 1252, boldly went over to gold, issuing the gold "florin" (named after the city) containing in small volume the value of 20 *soldi*. This, carefully minted and of a high standard of purity, was henceforth generally accepted and was imitated elsewhere under different names — e. g., as the ducat or *zecchino* in Venice, the *scudo* or crown (divided into 10 *baiocchi* each of 10 *paoli*) in the Papal States, and so on. The gold content of the pure florin or ducat was 3.42 grams, corresponding to 12.65 gold Italian lire (gold) in contemporary value: the papal *scudo*, much debased, was worth about half of this (6¾ lire in the 16th century, 5½ lire in the 19th). Very roughly, it may be said that the Florentine *florin* or Venetian *ducat* was equivalent to about 10 English shillings or $2.50, and the papal *scudo* about half that amount, with a purchasing power of two to three times as much in 1939 values.

CONTENTS

	PAGE
PREFACE	v
BIBLIOGRAPHICAL NOTE	ix
NOTE ON CURRENCY	x
LIST OF ILLUSTRATIONS	xiii

CHAPTER

I. THE CLASSICAL PERIOD 1
    i. The Beginnings 1
    ii. The Early Empire 7
    iii. Vespasian to Constantine 15
    iv. Life under the Emperors 20
    v. The Christian Empire 29

II. THE DARK AGES 38
    vi. The Teutons 38
    vii. The Popes 42
    viii. The Byzantine South 48
    ix. Saracenic Sicily 55
    x. The Literary Revival 58

III. THE HIGH MIDDLE AGES 66
    xi. The Communities of Upper Italy 66
    xii. Jews in Italy in the Twelfth Century ... 74
    xiii. The Craftsmen 84
    xiv. Scholars and Translators 90
    xv. Southern Twilight 96

IV. THE RISE OF THE NORTHERN COMMUNITIES 103
    xvi. The Loan Banks 103
    xvii. The New Communities 117
    xviii. Light and Shade 137
    xix. The New Literary School 143

V. THE RENAISSANCE 153
    xx. Councils, Pontiffs and Friars 153
    xxi. The *Monti di Pietà* 166
    xxii. The Communities in the Sixteenth Century ... 177
    xxiii. The Jews and the Renaissance 193
    xxiv. Books and Authors 216

Chapter		Page
VI.	The Islands and the South	228
	xxv. Sicilian Jewry	228
	xxvi. Reaction and Expulsion	245
	xxvii. Sardinia	262
	xxviii. The Kingdom of Naples	269
VII.	The Catholic Reaction	289
	xxix. Prelude	289
	xxx. *Cum Nimis Absurdum*	294
	xxxi. The Extension	309
VIII.	The Age of the Ghetto	329
	xxxii. The Italian Ghettos	329
	xxxiii. Life in the Ghetto	353
	xxxiv. The Houses of Study	394
	xxxv. De Profundis	406
IX.	The Breaking of the Bonds	421
	xxxvi. Revolution and Napoleon	421
	xxxvii. The Recoil	445
	xxxviii. Enfranchisement	463
X.	The Age of Emancipation	474
	xxxix. Italian Jewry under Emancipation	474
	xl. The Impact of Emancipation	489
	xli. The New Hope	506
XI.	Downfall	509
	xlii. The Totalitarian State	509
	xliii. The Betrayal	517
	xliv. The Catastrophe	536

LIST OF ILLUSTRATIONS

                                                           FACING PAGE

1. Titus' Triumphal Procession.
   From the Arch of Titus..................................... 20

2. The Interior of a Catacomb.
   From Hans Lietzmann and Hermann Beyer, *Die Katakombe Torlonia*, plate 12.. 21

3. Entrance to the Former Jewish Quarter in Trani.
   From Ernst Munkácsi, *Der Jude von Neapel*, illustration no. 18 80

4. The Synagogue in Trani, built in 1247 (now the Church of S. Anna).
   From Ernst Munkácsi, *Der Jude von Neapel*, illustration no. 22 81

5. The Last Page of the First Printed Hebrew Book (Rashi, Reggio di Calabria, 1475).
   From A. Freimann's *Thesaurus Typographiae Saeculi XV*, plate A 1, 3... 174

6. Daniel Norsa and his Household — An Italian Jewish Family of the Fifteenth Century.
   From a painting formerly in the Church of the Madonna della Vittoria, Mantua... 174

7. An Italian Jewish Wedding (Renaissance Period).
   From Cecil Roth, *The Jewish Museum*, plate no. 5............ 175

8. A Corner of the Roman Ghetto.............................. 304

9. Scene at a Conversionist Sermon.
   From an engraving... 305

10. Scenes in the Venetian Ghetto: a) Marriage; b) Circumcision.
    From panels attributed to Pietro Longhi..................... 358

11. Scenes in the Venetian Ghetto: a) Funeral; b) Interment.
    From panels attributed to Pietro Longhi..................... 359

12. Leone da Modena.
    From *Rite Ebraici*, Paris, 1637............................. 400

13. Samson Morpurgo.
    From an oil painting in the possession of the Morpurgo family 401

14. The Great Synagogue at Leghorn.
    From Ernst Munkácsi, *Livorno Regisegek*.................... 450

LIST OF ILLUSTRATIONS

FACING PAGE

15. Interior of the Synagogue at Leghorn.
    From an engraving reproduced in Ernst Munkácsi, *Livorno Regisegek*... 450

16. The *Cuccagna* of the "Jewish Nation" at Leghorn (see page 385).
    From an engraving.. 451

17. Synagogue of Rome....................................... 538

18. The Mole Antonelliana in Turin, built for a Synagogue........ 538

19. Synagogue of Florence.................................... 538

20. Liberation Scene in Modern Rome.
    From *The National Jewish Monthly*, Washington, D. C., July–August, 1944.. 539

The History of the Jews of Italy

CHAPTER I

The Classical Period

i

THE BEGINNINGS

A QUAINT, but in its way profound, talmudic fable tells how, when King Solomon sinned, an angel planted a reed in the Great Sea; the mud that gathered round it became in due course dry land, and thereon in fullness of time was built the great city of Rome. The intention of the parable is plain. The lots of Jerusalem and of Rome, of Israel and of Italy, are inextricably interwoven. The one exists in history, the rabbis thought, as corrective to the other.

The history of the Jews in Italy is indeed of profound antiquity. It is the only land — except Palestine and the regions bordering on it — the Jewish connections of which have been unbroken from remote times down to the present day. The continuity of Italian life is one of that country's most remarkable features. But its Jewish communities are older than even its most venerable corporations; and if there is now in Rome any institution more ancient than the Papacy, it is the Synagogue. Compared with this record, the few centuries that some other Jewish groups of the Western world can boast would seem almost insignificant.

For there is no need to resort to legend or hypothesis to demonstrate the antiquity of Italian Jewry. Recent discoveries have made it appear more and more probable that the settlement of the Jews in Europe goes back into the second, or perhaps even the third, century before the beginning of the Christian era. It may be that Jews penetrated to the southern part of the Peninsula, *Magna Graecia,* and even to the destined capital, at this early period. The recorded settlement is very little younger. In the year 168 B.C.E., the Jews of Palestine rose in revolt under the Hasmonaean brothers against the religious oppression of Antiochus Epiphanes. It was one of the decisive events in human history. Never before had men been convinced, as they were then, that an Idea was something to fight for and to die for; and the success of the revolt saved for mankind the ethical monotheism which lies at the basis not only of Judaism but also of Christianity and Islam, as yet unborn, and of Western civilization in its true sense. Before his assault on Jewish liberties, Antiochus had come into conflict with the growing might of Rome, already vitally interested in the balance of power in the Eastern Mediterranean. It may in fact have been his discomfiture in Egypt, through the intervention of the Roman envoy, that led him to attempt a compensatory triumph, on his way home, by imposing his will on Jerusalem. Hence, when the Hasmonaeans established their precarious independence, endangered for a long time by their powerful Syrian neighbor to the north, it was natural to solicit the sympathy and support of the great new Power in the west. According to the very ancient record preserved in the Books of Maccabees, immediately after his decisive victory against Nicanor in 161, Judas Maccabaeus sent a mission to establish friendly relations with Rome. The names of the ambassadors have been preserved: Jason (Joshua) ben Eleazar and Eupolemos (Ephraim?) ben Johanan, whose father had once represented his people at the Syrian court. The account tells how they appeared before the Senate and received written assurances of friendship and protection — today we might term it a "guarantee." These details are by no means insignificant. These are the first Jews to be in Italy, or to visit Europe, who are known to us by name, and the spiritual ancestors of Western Jewry as a whole.

Some critics, incredulous on principle of any written statement regarding ancient Jewish history, question whether this record can be authentic, though it is so plausible and accords so fully with current political conditions and with diplomatic wisdom. They doubt, too, the story of a similar mission said to have been despatched a decade later by Judas' brother and successor, Jonathan, after his investiture as high priest and head of the Jewish state in 150. But before long we are out of the realm of peradventure. In 142, Jonathan was succeeded in turn by Simon, the eldest of the brothers, who founded a dynasty and to whom was mainly due the consolidation of the new Jewish state. He certainly entered into diplomatic relations with Rome, sending an embassy thither in 139 B.C.E., "with a great shield of gold of a thousand pound weight, to confirm the league with them." Not long after, when hard-pressed by his enemies, his son, John Hyrcanus, appealed to Rome for help, in accordance with the terms of the treaty negotiated at this time.

The diplomatic success was qualified by a somewhat unfortunate episode. The details are obscure, but it seems that the Jews became involved in the movement to purge the country of the Levantine cults which had already begun to invade it. According to an almost contemporary record, Cnaius Cornelius Hispalus, the *praetor peregrinus*, who was responsible for the supervision of aliens, banished the Chaldeans from Rome and all Italy, that very year, "because, by their fallacious interpretation of the stars, they made trouble in feeble and light minds for their personal profit;" and at the same time he "forced the Jews, who had endeavored to corrupt Roman morals by the cult of Jupiter Sabazius, to return to their country." According to another recension, the charge was that they had attempted to "deliver their holy things to the Romans." The truth underlying this confused story is very difficult to disentangle, for Sabazius was a Phrygian deity. It is not impossible that the mention of the Jews in this connection is due to a corruption in the text. On the other hand, "Jupiter Sabazius" may be the result of a confusion in the mind of the writer, who knew vaguely that the Sabbath was a distinguishing feature of Jewish religious observance and accordingly thought it to be the name of the God of Israel. Conceivably, pious members of the embassy, flushed with the success of their revolt against idolatry in Judea, courageously but untactfully carried on religious propaganda in the same sense among the temples of Rome. But the phrasing of the record seems to suggest a widespread movement on the part of a more settled section of the population and, if it is taken literally, would imply the existence in Italy, already before 139 B.C.E., of a relatively numerous and distinctly zealous Palestinian colony.

From this period onwards, down to our own day, the record of the Jews in Rome, and in Italy as a whole, is continuous. Since the decrees of the *praetor peregrinus* remained valid only during his year of office, when this was over the exiles could return. As Rome established herself in the Greek archipelago, in Asia Minor, and ultimately in Africa, there came under her sway areas in which old-established Jewish communities were to be found. This was especially the case in Egypt, the granary of the ancient world, where the Jews constituted an important element of the population. Already at this time, Italy was absorbing vast numbers of immigrants from every part of the Mediterranean — slaves who resulted from Rome's numerous campaigns, the merchants who followed the trade-routes to their hub, the members of subjected races on whom the center of Empire exercised an inevitable attraction. In 63 B.C.E. Palestine itself was conquered by Pompey; and the Jewish king, Aristobulus, and numerous Jewish captives walked behind his chariot in the brilliant triumphal procession which celebrated his return to Rome. Thereafter, every period of unrest or distress in Palestine tended to send more and more slaves to Italy; and traders, politicians and adventurers, men in search of a career and men in search of "culture," followed at their heels.

Other immigrants rapidly lost their identity, being absorbed in the general population and becoming forebears of the hybrid, brilliant, Italian people of today. But the Jews, because of their unique religious tradition and their unique religious zeal, could not follow this example. The slaves, moreover, were in many cases not slaves for long. They were strong and they were wiry. But, with their curious religious practices — their refusal to eat what other men ate, and their incomprehensible insistence on resting every seventh day — they were inconvenient servants; while their free compatriots regarded it as a primary ethical duty to ransom those in captivity. Before long, there had been established in Jerusalem a special synagogue for the "Libertines" returned from Italy; but the majority, in all probability, remained in their new home. There is no need to go once again in detail into a process which has so often been described before. It is enough to state that the Jewish population of Italy increased, until by the time of Julius Caesar it was, so far as we are able to judge, well established, numerous and not uninfluential. Rome of course received the overwhelming majority; but there were even at this date, as it seems, a few other settlements, especially along the trade routes and in the seaports which controlled trade with the Eastern Mediterranean.

The importance of the Roman community is attested by a well-known episode. When, in 59 B.C.E., L. Valerius Flaccus was prosecuted for gross corruption during his term of office as propraetor of Asia, one of the charges brought against him was that he had appropriated the money which the Jews of that region had brought together to send to Palestine for the upkeep of the Temple, as their coreligionists did throughout the world. He was defended by the greatest of Roman orators, Cicero. The

Jews of the capital were deeply interested in the issue of the case; they too, as was mentioned in the course of the proceedings, sent their contributions to Jerusalem year by year, and a number of them were in court. This gave the defending counsel his opportunity. He asserted that the venue near the Aurelian Steps had been chosen to suit the convenience of the Jews, whose quarter was situated not far off. He referred to their numerical importance and their influence in the popular assemblies. He asserted that they had come with the intention of intimidating the jury by weight of numbers; and he theatrically lowered his voice almost to a whisper, so that only the judges should hear what he was saying. Obviously, this was in part rhetorical exaggeration; but it would have sounded ridiculous had there not been a considerable Jewish population in Rome at this time — four years only after Pompey's capture of Jerusalem — actively interested in public affairs.

This is attested also by the policy of Julius Caesar, who went to considerable trouble to win the sympathy of the Jews, not only of Palestine, but of the Diaspora as a whole and incidentally of Italy. At one time, during his struggle with Pompey, he planned a military raid on Syria under the command of Aristobulus, ex-king of Judaea, still a prisoner of state; but on his way, the royal exile was poisoned. Julius Caesar safeguarded Jewish interests by a series of regulations which applied no less in Italy than in the provinces. They were exempted from military service, in which their religious observances led to some inconvenience. They were allowed to judge cases amongst themselves in accordance with their own law. They were exempted from the new regulation against private associations (*collegia*), which would have made the establishment of Jewish communities impossible. It is no wonder that, when he was assassinated, in 44 B.C.E., the Italian Jews mourned his death more than any other section of the population; and we are informed that, for a long time after, they continued to visit his tomb and to weep over it, in their exaggerated Oriental fashion, by night as well as by day. Did they have some obscure inkling that, with the Republic, there had passed away something of the former mutual understanding between their people and his, and that the time was coming when mighty Rome and puny Judaea were to be locked together in a struggle the effects of which would still be felt two thousand years after?

ii

THE EARLY EMPIRE

When, with the triumph of Gaius Julius Caesar Octavianus Augustus, the Roman Republic was swept away and the Roman Empire came into being, Jewish communities were to be found solidly established in many Italian cities. In Rome the main settlement was on the right bank of the Tiber, near the docks and landing-stages, where harbor-workers and petty traders from every part of the Mediterranean world swarmed in overcrowded tenements. Two synagogues, founded by former slaves of Augustus and Agrippa respectively, seem to have been established here in this period; the fact that they bore these distinguishing names obviously implies the existence of older congregations. Josephus records that, on the death of Herod, in 4 B.C.E., when a delegation was sent from Palestine to Rome to plead for the abolition of the Herodian monarchy, they were accompanied to their audience in the Temple of Palatine Appollo by no fewer than 8,000 native Jews. Besides the Jewish community, there was at an early date another recruited from their kinsmen and neighbors, the Samaritans, which maintained itself for centuries — not apparently the only one in Italy.

Other Jewish settlements extended southwards, along the trade-routes and in the ports. To reach Rome, travellers from Egypt or Palestine generally disembarked at Puteoli (the modern Pozzuoli), not far from Naples, where there was a considerable colony. When Paul of Tarsus landed here in 63, he found a number of "brethren," the term he used to designate Judaeo-Christian sympathizers. Some years earlier, a claimant to the throne of Judaea, who pretended to be one of the dead Hasmonaean princes, was deliriously greeted by the local Jews, who loaded him with presents and escorted him like a reigning prince on his way to Rome. Here, we are informed, their coreligionists poured out to see him, and vast crowds thronged the narrow streets when he passed. Just outside Naples, there has been discovered a monument erected over the body of a young freedman of the Emperor Tiberius — probably in the reign of Claudius or of Nero — by a female slave, Claudia Aster (i. e., perhaps, Esther) "of Jerusalem" (how pathetic is this description!). Pompeii, too, destroyed by the eruption of Vesuvius in 79, had its Jewish colony, as several fragments of archaeological evidence suggest; the most interesting is a charcoal scrawl of the words "Sodom and Gomorra" on the wall of a house — perhaps made at the beginning of the fatal eruption by a zealous Jew, horrified by the corruptions of the luxurious city. Brundisium — the modern Brindisi, terminus of the Via Appia and second in importance only to Puteoli for maritime connections with the East — must similarly have received a very early settlement, though the extant evidence dates from somewhat later. Sicily certainly knew them at this period; for the Jewish historian and rhetorician Caecilius, who worked in Rome under Augustus and who, from the slender fragments of his work that survive, seems to have been a notable literary figure, hailed from Calacte, one of the smaller cities of the island, where he had perhaps been taken from Palestine as a slave. Without doubt, Jews were to be found by now at many other places in Italy, as was probably the case, as we shall see, before the Empire declined; for, in the nature of things, archaeological and literary evidence is fragmentary and sporadic. The places mentioned are, however, enough to demonstrate that, even before the fall of Jerusalem, the Italian Jewish settlement was relatively widespread.*

Julius Caesar's benevolent policy towards the Jews was continued, as a rule, by the early emperors. Augustus indeed extended it, enjoining that they should not be summoned to courts of law on their Sabbath or even on the Sabbath eve; and that, when free distributions of grain to the populace took place then, the Jews should be given their portion on the following day. That they were permitted to participate at all is significant. Under his successor, Tiberius, an untoward event took place. There was, as will be seen later on, considerable sympathy with Judaism in Italy, especially on the part of the upper classes, wearied with the amoral extravagances of the state idolatry. Among those who felt the fascination was a certain Fulvia, wife of a senator named Saturninus. Her enthusiasm proving greater than her judgment, she fell into the hands of a coterie of swindlers, who defrauded her of a goodly amount in money and valuables on the pretext of sending a votive offering to the Temple in Jerusalem in her name. As it happens, the all-powerful minister Sejanus was engaged at this time in an attempt to suppress the objectionable Egyptian cults which had recently invaded Rome. This episode drew his attention to Judaism as well. An edict was now issued, in the year 19, ordering all Jews to leave Italy, unless they foreswore their fantastic religious practices, on the pain of being reduced to slavery. Moreover, on the pretext of submitting them to military service, 4,000 young freedmen were seized and sent to Sardinia, to be employed in fighting the brigands. The climate was notoriously insalubrious; but if

* It is superfluous to take into account a curious medieval legend according to which Jews were established at Cividale, in North Italy, before the Christian era, though this was solemnly commemorated by the local community in the fifteenth century.

they died, sneered the Roman historian Tacitus, it would be a cheap loss. We may assume that some, at least, survived, and that the introduction of Judaism to the island was due to them. It is certain, in any case, that Jewish communities existed there in imperial times. Curious parallels to Jewish practice, curious relics of Semitic vocabulary, linger there even at the present day; and, though in fact they are most likely of Phoenician origin, it has been suggested that they are due to the unwilling immigrants of nineteen centuries ago.

On Sejanus' fall, twelve years later, Tiberius renewed the privileges granted to the Jews by Caesar and Augustus, thereby legitimatizing once more their settlement in Italy. It is to be imagined that before long the exiles returned, and that those who had ostensibly abandoned the public profession of Judaism threw off their disguise. They did not enjoy their ease for long. Tiberius' successor, the megalomaniac Gaius Caligula, took it into his head to have himself worshipped by all his subjects as a god. Only the Jews opposed him; and throughout the Empire — especially in Palestine and in Egypt — a serious crisis ensued. Though we know nothing of the repercussions in Italy, it is not unlikely that here at least, under his own eyes, with an impotent section of the population to victimize and no experienced local administrator to intervene, he had his own way; and that, if any public synagogues existed at the time, they were either desecrated by the erection of the emperor's statue for adoration or else destroyed.

Under pedantic, unpractical Claudius, Caligula's successor, there was another disturbance, due to completely different causes. Christianity had recently come in being, and in Italy, as throughout the world, zealous missionaries were entering into arguments in the synagogues and trying to persuade the Jews that the anticipated Messiah, the *Christos*, had indeed appeared. The Jews on their side objected vociferously, and from their point of view not unreasonably.

Nothing arouses fiercer passion than religious differences — all the more so when the conflicting principles are relatively close to one another. There were constant disorders and brawlings. The Jews perhaps appealed to the emperor to suppress this innovation. Wearied by a dispute in which he was quite uninterested, and not really understanding what it was all about, he put an end to it by expelling the Jews from the city in the year 49–50. As the historian Suetonius uncomprehendingly phrased it, "he chased from Rome the Jews, who were creating continual disturbances at the instigation of a certain Chrestus."* Some of the exiles, we know, made their way to Greece. But, once more, the period of exclusion must have been brief. There is indeed reason to believe that only the active members of the group had to leave, and that public assemblies were suspended. When, in 61, the Apostle Paul visited Italy, he found in Rome as well as Puteoli prosperous, well-established and fully-organized communities, with some members of which he had already been in touch. Indeed, it is probable that what took place on all these occasions was that Jewish life was driven underground and its public manifestations suspended, rather than anything more drastic. In any case, this interruption was to be, so far as is known, the last.

Throughout this period, color and interest was added to the life of the Jews in Italy — especially, of course, in the capital — by the constant procession of visitors from Palestine and elsewhere. King Herod was there more than once during his reign, currying favor or soliciting support; and his escort inevitably included Palestinian Jews, with the latest news of Jerusalem, of the rabbis, and of the Temple. Members of the old Hasmonaean royal house were there

---

* This seems the most probable interpretation of Suetonius' statement. It is possible however that Chrestus really existed, being a demagogue or missionary who had caused disturbance in the community; or that we have here an otherwise unrecorded pseudo-messiah (*Christos*) whose claims caused a commotion.

living in gilded captivity. Young Judaean princes and nobles were sent there to be educated and, well supplied with money, cut a brilliant figure among the *jeunesse dorée* of the capital. We know in detail the escapades of Herod Agrippa, one of Herod's grandsons, who, after spending a riotous youth in Italy and playing a great part in political affairs under both Caligula and Claudius — for whose accession to the imperial throne his adroitness was very largely responsible — went back to Judaea as king and earned a somewhat incongruous reputation in middle age as defender of his people and a pious votary of the Jewish faith. There would be in Rome deputations from Palestine, asking for new privileges or the redress of some abuse of authority on the part of the local officials. There might be scholars, or representatives of the Jerusalem priesthood, collecting funds for the upkeep of the Temple and other Palestinian institutions, and at the same time organizing religious life, or even carrying out propaganda among the non-Jewish population. ("Ye compass land and sea," the New Testament taunted the Pharisees, "to make one proselyte.") Philo, the great Alexandrian Jewish philosopher, was there in 40 at the head of a deputation of Egyptian Jews who had come to implore the withdrawal of Caligula's edict for desecrating the synagogues, and has left a vivid account of the megalomaniac emperor and his court. In 64, the future historian, Josephus, still a young man, arrived on a mission to secure the liberation of certain priests whom the Roman procurator had sent in chains from Judaea for trial on a trifling charge. Christian propagandists early made their appearance, to be followed, as we have seen, by the Apostle Paul, similarly sent for judgment. A complete record of those who visited Italy in this period is almost a record of Jewish history at large.

The outbreak of the revolt against the Romans in Palestine in 66 and the hard-fought war that succeeded it, culminating in the fall of Jerusalem in 70, seriously affected the position of the Jews in Italy, the center of the Empire.

It is to the credit of the Romans that they did not permit the Palestinian war to involve a universal religious persecution. Nevertheless, though the Jews of Italy were not apparently molested, their position must have been for some time highly uncomfortable. The war proved indeed to be a turning-point in their history. Vast numbers of Palestinian Jews were enslaved, the majority being doubtless brought back to Italy — 97,000, it is stated, to the capital alone. Many were used for public works, the Colosseum being one of the undertakings on which they were employed. But others were sold to private owners, and in many cases, like those who had arrived before them, ultimately recovered their liberty.

Thus the number of the Jews of Italy was enormously increased. A tradition, which goes back to the tenth century at the latest, tells how Titus settled five thousand Jewish captives in Taranto, Otranto, and elsewhere in South Italy — perhaps including Oria, where too there is a legendary report of a Jewish settlement at this time. At Bari, one of the most important seaports of this region, the newcomers, according to rabbinic fancy, found Jews already settled, who succored them so nobly that they were rewarded by God with surpassing beauty, unrivalled in the rest of the land. According to another medieval account of high antiquity, Titus brought back with him from Jerusalem to Rome four noble families — Min ha-Tapuhim, Min ha-Adomim, Min ha-Zekenim and Min ha-Anavim (or Anau). Under the names of De' Pomi, De' Rossi, De' Vecchi, and Delli Mansi or Piattelli, these four families continued to play an important part in Italian Jewish life down to our own day.*

* There is a slight variation in the names in different forms of the legend. It is hardly to be taken literally, but it is clear that when the story is first encountered, nearly a thousand years ago, the families in question were already thought to have been established in Italy from time immemorial.

Jerusalem now lay in ruins, and its Temple, one of the marvels of the ancient world, was destroyed. The last heroes of Jewish independence had been cruelly put to death to make a Roman holiday. The spoils of the Holy of Holies had graced Titus' triumph and were now displayed in the Temple of Peace. Soon there was to rise near the Forum the conqueror's Arch of Triumph, decorated with representations of the captive Jordan, and the holy vessels, and the intractable Jewish prisoners of war. The voluntary yearly tribute of half a shekel, which Jews throughout the world had previously sent for the upkeep of the Temple of Jerusalem, now had to be paid into a special department of the Imperial Treasury in the Temple of Jupiter Capitolinus, the *Fiscus Judaicus*. The sister of the last Jewish king, Bernice, oblivious of the Hasmonaean blood that flowed in her veins, was prostituting herself in the conqueror's bed, and Flavius Josephus, the traitor general who had commanded the patriot forces in Galilee, was chronicling the titanic conflict in alternate bursts of frankness and sycophancy.

According to every precedent, Jewish history was ended. But, as more than one contemporary complained, it was the conquered who gave laws to the conquerors. So far as Italy was concerned, Jewish history was only beginning. But the events of the tragic years 66–70 had made one great difference. The earlier settlement had been, as it were, an ethnic one — a colony of members of a remote part of the Empire, inevitably drawn, as must always be the case, to the capital. Henceforth it had rather a religious basis: it was a settlement of persons, often boasting Roman citizenship, who were distinguished from their neighbors mainly by their beliefs, though never losing the hope that in God's good time, when they had expiated their sins, He would bring them back to their distant fatherland again.

iii

Vespasian to Constantine

Of the external history of Italian Jewry in the period immediately after the fall of the Jewish state, we have only sparse and scattered information. It is known that the new tax devoted to the *Fiscus Judaicus* — the first religious disability in history — was exacted with needless brutality. In Italy, some persons tried to evade payment by denying their Jewish origin, and were submitted to a degrading personal examination to see whether their claim was true. The historian Suetonius tells of the indignities inflicted in his presence on an old man of ninety, in order to discover whether he was a Jew. This obviously gave a special opportunity to the informers who were one of the banes of the age; and when in the reign of Nerva (96–8) there was a return to more humane methods in levying the tax, a medal was struck bearing the emperor's head and the inscription: *Fisci judaici calumnia sublata* ("On the removal of the calumny of the *Fiscus Judaicus*"). Nevertheless, the tax itself continued to be exacted until the fourth century, and indeed provided the prototype for the exceptional levies made on the Jews in the Middle Ages. Italian Jewry must have had to pass through further periods of acute discomfort at the time of the various risings of their coreligionists in Palestine. We know, indeed, no details; but an ultimate result of these outbreaks was the flooding of the Italian slave-markets with yet more Jewish captives, some at least of whom further swelled the communities.

While the number of Jews in Italy was increasing, Italian Judaism was becoming consolidated. This was partly due to the exertions of emissaries from Palestine, who visited Italy from time to time on political missions. One of the most notable occasions was in 95–6, during the reign of Domitian, when Gamaliel II, head of the Academy, led a deputation to secure the withdrawal of an edict against Judaism which, according to a friendly senator, was about to be issued. The other members were Rabbis Akiba, Joshua and Eleazar, the most famous scholars of the day. So urgent was the matter that they travelled during the Feast of Tabernacles, the pious Akiba erecting a booth at the masthead in order to fulfill the religious obligations of the celebration. They landed at Puteoli, where to their joy they found a group of Jewish children playing in the street at a game of separating the tithe in accordance with the biblical precept. In Rome, they were hospitably received in the home of a "philosopher," who has been plausibly identified with the historian Flavius Josephus; and, whether it was as a result of their pleading or of Domitian's death in 96 in a palace revolution, the immediate danger that they feared was averted.

The most prominent member of the Jewish community at Rome, at this time, was a certain Theudas, a man apparently of great enthusiasm but not quite so much learning, who now arranged to collect for the upkeep of the Palestinian schools the self-imposed dues formerly sent to the Temple every year — a practice which was to last in Italy for at least three centuries, and to be revived in a different form later on. It is on record that on one occasion when danger threatened the community, he mounted the pulpit and, after a clumsy prelude, demonstrated how it was the Jew's duty to suffer martyrdom rather than infringe upon the principles of his faith. (The talmudic literature preserves also fragments of the discourses of another Roman Jewish leader of this period, a certain Pelation.) In his well-meaning way, Theudas introduced into the Roman community the practice of sacrificing a lamb on Passover eve in accordance with the biblical injunction, just as had hitherto been done in the Temple of Jerusalem. The authorities in Palestine sent to chide him, firmly but good-naturedly, for this unorthodox innovation, which however seems to have opened their eyes to the fact that the Diaspora in Italy could no longer be left entirely to its own devices.

Not long after, Rabbi Mathia ben Heresh, a promising Palestinian scholar, was sent to Rome to organize the Jewish community; and he introduced apparently a new educational system, in accordance with the principles of teaching the Torah now established in Judaea. The "House of Study of R. Mathia ben Heresh" henceforth enjoyed a certain reputation. His efforts to create a Jewish cultural atmosphere were assisted by occasional visits of other leaders of Palestinian Jewish intellectual life, who were enthusiastically welcomed by their coreligionists, as we may imagine, in every other place through which they passed on their way from the port of disembarkation. We know, for example, how Rabbis Simeon ben Johai and Eleazar ben Jose went to Rome from Palestine at a threatening moment in the middle of the second century, how they were admitted to audience with the emperor, how they gave Rabbi Mathia information on certain points of law and assisted him in his cultural work, and how they visited the Temple of Peace and there saw the spoils brought from Jerusalem. It is some centuries before the consecutive intellectual history of Italian Jewry begins, but it obviously is to these half-revealed episodes that its origins are to be traced.

Despite the uncomprehending contempt with which Judaism was regarded in fashionable circles, it continued to exercise a fascination on some of the more thinking elements in Italian society, particularly in the capital. Numerous persons discarded idolatry, adopted the pure Jewish monotheism and began to observe some of the outstanding Jewish ceremonies, such as the Sabbath: these were known among the Jews as "God-fearing" — in Greek *sebomenoi*, or in Latin *metuentes*. Semi-converts of this description are occasionally mentioned in classical literature, Nero's empress, Poppaea, apparently being one of them. They would normally tend to bring up their children in the full Jewish tradition, the boys being circumcised and the girls formally admitted to Judaism, so that they became full proselytes; and there were many of the first generation too who were not content with the halfway house. A large number of inscriptions which mark the resting-place of such converts have been found, including that, for example, of a Roman knight, and — more interesting still — that of an elderly woman who embraced Judaism at the age of seventy, survived another sixteen years, and enjoyed the honorary title of "Mother of the Synagogue" to two different congregations. In the year 95, Flavius Clemens and his wife Domitilla, cousins of the Emperor Domitian, whose sons might have succeeded to the throne, were arrested with several others on a charge of "atheism," the former being put to death (together with the former consul, Acilius Glabrio) and the latter banished to Pantelleria. Though it was subsequently claimed that they had become Christians, talmudic and other sources render it probable that the charge made against Clemens, at least, was the adoption of Judaism.

The spirit of religious unrest, which manifested itself not only in these conversions but also in the rank growth of newly-imported Oriental cults, some of which imposed self-mutilation upon their votaries, did not fail to impress the authorities. In the end, the Emperor Hadrian categorically prohibited anything of the sort, including circumcision, as a capital offense. This was probably the immediate cause of the Bar Kochba revolt in Palestine of 132–5, which taxed all the power of Roman arms before it was suppressed. The moment must have been a particularly difficult one for Italian Jewry, and it was succeeded moreover by an attempt to suppress all the other outward manifestations and ceremonies of Judaism, such as the Sabbath and even the study of the Torah. This Hadrianic persecution, which lingered long in the memory of Palestinian Jewry, cannot have failed to embitter the lives of those of Italy. At length the Emperor Antoninus Pius (138–161) revoked the legislation, and the even tenor of former days was resumed. There was, however, one significant difference. Circumcision was now permitted as a national and religious rite to the Jews, but it continued to be forbidden as a species of self-mutilation to others. Hence, by implication, conversion to Judaism on the part of males at least became a capital offense. A little while after, in the year 204, the Emperor Septimius Severus, alarmed by the growing prevalence of secession to the monotheistic faiths, specifically forbade conversions whether to Christianity or to Judaism. Thus one of the tendencies that had formerly characterized Italian Jewish life and influenced the composition of Italian Jewry was checked, if not ended.

Normally the Jews — other than the fervid element still remaining in Palestine — had little reason for complaint. In 212, moreover, Caracalla issued the famous edict by which practically all free inhabitants of the Empire were made Roman citizens. It may be true that the underlying reasons were fiscal rather than political, the principal object being to secure general participation in the duties of Roman citizenship. But its privileges, too, were now made universal. Hitherto, only a small group of Jews had enjoyed full citizenship rights. Henceforth, they were extended to the entire body, now on an equal footing with their neighbors in all things save for the fact that they still had to pay their special, though not very onerous, annual tax. The Emperor Alexander Severus (222–235) was so sympathetically inclined to them that he was jeeringly called *Archisynagogus* or "Ruler of the Synagogue" — we might today say, "the *Parnas*" — by some of his subjects. He is said to have had statues of Abraham and of Jesus in his palace, together with those of the Roman emperors; and he began the practice of publishing the names of candidates for office before they were appointed, as was the usage in the Synagogue and the Church. So popular was he apparently among his Jewish subjects that a synagogue in Rome — endowed according to subsequent legend with a scroll of the Pentateuch brought back by Titus from Jerusalem — was given his name.*

The next century in the history of the Roman Empire was taken up by palace revolutions and military anarchy, Caesar after Caesar meeting a bloody end. The Emperor Philip was an Arab by birth — there was no need, henceforth, for Jews to consider themselves in any sense aliens! His successor, Decius, instituted in 250 the persecution of the Christians which was to become a governing factor in Roman politics. Emperor-worship in public was required henceforth as a political test of all loyal subjects. By ancient prescriptive right, the Jews were exempted from this abuse, which was utterly incompatible with their religion as with Christianity. On the other hand, it is not improbable that they suffered sometimes from disturbance at the hands of zealous officials, unable to discriminate between the adherents of the two monotheistic, ethical, and scriptural faiths. The curtain never rises sufficiently to allow us any inkling of the precise course of events on all these occasions; it is certain only that the actors are grouped upon the stage throughout the period, strenuously maintaining their spiritual heritage, and enacting their simple human drama.

iv

Life under the Emperors

In the centuries which have been the subject of the foregoing pages, the Jewish settlements, for which previously we have evidence only from Rome southwards, became established throughout Italy — from the Adriatic sea to the Tyrrhenian and from the Alps down to the islands beyond

* It was also known apparently by the name of his birthplace, Arca of Lebanon; it is hardly conceivable that so many Jews in Rome hailed from this little town that they were able to form their own synagogue.

Titus' Triumphal Procession
(from the Arch of Titus)

The Interior of a Catacomb

Sicily. Definite data for this period are available for something like fifty different centers. The information is frequently archaeological, consisting of inscriptions or burial-places bearing Jewish symbols; even when such details are comparatively late, they presuppose an earlier settlement. Sometimes, our source is literary, generally deriving from the writings of the Church Fathers. We are certainly justified in assuming that, unless for some reason special conditions obtained, every sizeable town in Italy had its Jewish community before the decay of the Roman Empire in the West.

The biggest center — as throughout Italian Jewish history — was of course Rome, and the amount of archaeological evidence relating to this city is very considerable. A subsidiary community, apparently in close relations with that of the capital, existed at Portus Augusti (the later Porto) founded by the Emperor Trajan in 103 — then a harbor, but now some distance inland. A number of epitaphs from this place also have come to light. As regards the great seaport of Ostia, evidence is slight, but an interesting inscription of the first part of the second century testifies how the Jewish community acquired a piece of ground to construct a sepulchral monument for one of its leading members. This was discovered at the present-day Castel Porziano, ten miles to the southeast, where also Jews were apparently to be found. Another place in the neighborhood of Rome where they lived was Aricia, where those expelled by Claudius are said to have settled. North of the capital, we find Jews in the early centuries at Falerii, Clusium (Chiusi) Luna, and perhaps Florentia (Florence) in Etruria; at Janua (Genoa) and Dertona (Tortona) in Liguria; at Milan and Brescia (where an inscription commemorates a "Mother of the Synagogue") in Cisalpine Gaul; and at Concordia, Aquilaea and Pola in Venetia (the evidence for these places is somewhat late). According to hagiographic legend, there was a colony at Bologna in 302, when they reluctantly buried the Christian martyrs Vitale and Agricola. But the most important centers were south of Rome, in the seaports and along the trade-routes; for it was from this direction that Jews from Palestine, Egypt and the Asiatic provinces approached the capital. They were found at an early date, as we have seen, at Naples, Pozzuoli and Pompeii, and there is ancient tradition that they settled shortly after the year 70 in Bari, Oria, Otranto and Taranto, where their presence is attested by some third-century inscriptions. To these places may be added Capua (the epitaph of a Jewess from this place has been found in Jerusalem), Fundi, Terracina, Nola, Venafri, Salerno, Baia, Bacoli, and above all Venosa, the birthplace of Horace, where a veritable Jewish necropolis has been unearthed. One Roman epitaph seems (though this is not quite sure) to refer to a "man of Calabria," which would suggest a settlement in this region at an early date. As has been told, Jews were deported to Sardinia in the year 19, and archaeological evidence proves their presence in two places in the island at the time with which we are now dealing. Sicily, because of its geographical situation, was likely to prove more attractive, and we have seen that Jews were to be found there even in the first century. By the time of the downfall of the Empire, we have evidence of their presence in at least nine places there, including the cities of Syracuse, Palermo, Catania, Messina and Girgenti.* When Paul was shipwrecked on Malta in the year 61, he did not apparently find any Jews there. But a community must have come into being before long, as proved by the discovery of a Jewish burial-place — unfortunately without decipherable inscriptions, but its origin plainly demonstrated by a fine representation of the Temple candelabrum of seven branches, then the recognized symbol of Judaism. It is to be noted that many of these places continued to

---

* I use throughout the medieval name, discarded during the Fascist interlude for the pseudo-classical Agrigento.

figure prominently in Italian Jewish history down to the close of the Middle Ages and even later, so that in some cases there is reason to believe that the record was uninterrupted throughout the centuries.

The number of the Jews in Italy in imperial times cannot have fallen at its peak far short of 50,000. In the aftermath of the various revolts in Palestine, the figure was of course temporarily swollen by consignments of captives, many of whom were speedily exported, or assimilated, or else succumbed. For Rome, estimates vary between 12,000 and as many as 40,000, among a total population which did not probably exceed 1,000,000. The figure, at the lowest, seems extremely high. Nevertheless, since the Jewish immigrants from relatively unimportant places, such as Tripoli and Elaea, were apparently numerous enough to form their own congregations, the city must have attracted such numbers from every corner of the Jewish world as to render this computation at least plausible.

The information we have regarding the economic function of the Jews of Italy at this period, though varied, is far from adequate. It is noteworthy that our sources mention none of the unpopular occupations which are associated with the Jews in later antisemitic propaganda — the result of external pressure in the long night of the Middle Ages. There is no evidence whatsoever of the existence of bankers or moneylenders. Indeed, even merchants are not mentioned specifically, though without doubt they must have existed. One epitaph introduces us to a Jewish painter and another to a Jewish physician; and we know also of Jewish actors, an actress, and a poet, besides the rhetorician who has already been mentioned. Josephus, of course, had cut something of a figure in the literary world. But if there were any callings characteristic of the Italian Jews at this period they were of the lowliest nature. Those specified on epitaphs and similar sources are all humble. There were butchers, tailors, tentmakers and other craftsmen; and there was in Rome a synagogue maintained by the lime-burners' (or perhaps cobblers') guild: *Calcarenses*.* The slaves brought from Palestine, performing the most menial and laborious tasks, were familiar in the cities and on the land. If they were freed, many earned their living as peddlers, crying their wares round the streets — a calling that remained common among the Italian Jewish proletariat down to our own day; there are, indeed, rough statuettes of this period which seem to represent Jewish street traders. Jewish women, profiting by their origin from the even then mysterious Orient, had a reputation as fortune tellers; while others, more frankly, begged outright in the streets. The poet Martial — who incidentally had a Jewish slave in his service — complained that it was impossible to have any sleep in Rome owing to the noise of the street merchants and the Jewish mendicants. The epitaphs of this period that have been preserved in such numbers suggest that, while some Jews were well-to-do, none enjoyed great riches, and the vast majority lived in utter penury. Another contemporary poet, Juvenal, paints a satiric picture of the typical Roman Jew, whose sole furniture was the beggar's livery — a basket and a truss of hay on which he slept at night.

The center of Jewish life, even at this early date, was of course the synagogue, which in Italy as throughout the classical world was often called by the Greek term *proseuche*, or Place of Prayer (*synagoge* signifies rather "place of assembly"). The Jewish community on the other hand was called *schola*, the usual term for a Roman professional corporation, applied also to the place where it met; hence the use later on of the term *scuola* in Italy, as *schul* in Germany, to designate the synagogue. In larger communities, doubtless, more than one place of worship was to be found; but we have certain evidence only as regards Rome itself,

---

* This is not quite certain; the name may designate the district from which the members hailed.

where there were in imperial times not less than twelve or thirteen different congregations. Of these, some were organized on a district basis, some in accordance with the place of origin of their founders, some apparently by the freedmen formerly in the service of a distinguished individual; while others were named, as a token of gratitude, after some prominent public figure who had shown kindly feelings.

Unfortunately, the archaeological remains of no Italian synagogue of the classical era, or even of the early Middle Ages, is now extant. We are nevertheless justified in assuming that they were in the usual style of Jewish places of worship at this period, with mosaic floors, frescoed walls, and the Ark, provided with shelves and pigeon-holes on which the Scrolls were placed horizontally, in a curtained recess at the eastern end of the building: this was flanked with carved lions, seven-branched candelabra, and representations of the sacred vessels of the Temple. This arrangement is depicted on funeral monuments and the gilded glasses found in Rome.

The officials of the community went by Greek, rather than Roman, titles. At its head there was a *gerousia* or Council of Elders (*presbuteroi*) presided over by a *gerousiarch*, who was what we would today call the president. The other responsible officers were termed *archontes* (singular *archon*), a title which may, however, have been used to designate political representatives. The synagogue services were supervised by the *archisynagogos* or "Ruler of the Synagogue" (a term also found in the New Testament). We also know of the *grammateus* or secretary, and *prostates* or patron, and the honorific dignities of Father and Mother of the Synagogue. Many of these offices, at the beginning elective, tended ultimately to become hereditary and thus purely formal, so that we encounter not only an *archon* for life, but even a "child *archon*" of only eight years of age — a clear reflection of the growth of the aristocratic principle in the once democratic community, as might be expected in imperial

Rome. Of the executive officials of the Synagogue we know of the *huperetes* or sexton (presumably the Hebrew *hazzan*); some inscriptions speak of the *hiereus* or priest (sometimes in the feminine) indicating a *cohen*, of Aaronic descent, while there are references, too, to the *nomomathes* or sage (not, so far as we may judge, rabbi in the technical modern sense).

Regarding the burial arrangements we are exceptionally well informed. Where the soil lent itself to this, there was used in Italy a system of underground galleries provided with recesses for receiving the bones of the dead — the so-called catacombs. This system of burial, usually associated with the early Christians, was probably adopted by them from the Jews, by whom it was used widely, if not universally, in the early centuries of the Christian era. Jewish catacombs have been discovered in Italy in Oria, Venosa, Sardinia, Malta, Sicily, and especially Rome, where no fewer than six different systems have been explored — some of them apparently reserved for the use of individual communities or groups of them, as is the case with cemeteries in our own day. The oldest — that of Monteverde — began to be used apparently towards the close of the Republican age. It is to the inscriptions discovered in these burial places — upwards of 500 at Rome, nearly 50 at Venosa — that we owe the greatest part of our knowledge of Jewish life and organization in Italy in classical times. Something like three-quarters of them are in Greek, the international language of the Eastern Mediterranean, especially for trade, and the quasi-sacred tongue of Diaspora Jewry at this period. Most of the remaining 25 per cent are in Latin; only a minority are in Hebrew, and these mainly in stereotyped terms ("Peace" or "Peace upon his resting-place"). On the other hand, nearly one-half of the names are purely Latin (the proportion being rather higher among the women than the men), under one-third Greek, and about one-eighth Semitic. Some of the former, it should be added, embody the names

LIFE UNDER THE EMPERORS 27

of pagan deities: so far had assimilation already progressed! The same impression is conveyed by a long inscription in conventional but not over-elegant Latin hexameters and by certain of the sarcophagi, which bear reliefs embodying the human form and, occasionally, unmistakable pagan motifs; while some of the catacombs include rooms with painted frescos of a type which today would hardly be considered orthodox. It is noteworthy that the greatest freedom is found in the catacombs on the Via Appia outside Rome, which was apparently used by a prosperous and highly Romanized group. The majority of the graves are distinguished by some Jewish religious symbol — the palm-branch, the citron, the ram's horn, and above all the Temple candelabrum of seven branches, which was considered symbolic of Judaism everywhere in the classical world and has continued to the present time to be used as its badge by the Jewish community of Rome, where the famous representation on the Arch of Titus was before everyone's eyes.*

The Italian population — the upper classes at least — were sufficiently conscious of the presence of Jews in their midst to have a vague knowledge, often in an extremely garbled form, of some of their characteristic religious practices. "I would rather be Herod's pig than his son," remarked Augustus, no less aware of the Jewish abstention from pork than of the domestic tragedies in the Palestinian royal house; though contemporaries professed to see in the deprivation a token of gratitude to that animal for a signal service at the time of the Exodus. The amazing practice of giving up — "wasting," as they regarded it — every seventh day for the Sabbath also attracted a great deal of notice, though it was generally believed to be a day of fasting. Ovid thought

* In view of the enormous amount of material available in print on the Jews of Rome in classical times (the last work in English is Vogelstein's *History of the Jews in Rome*, Philadelphia, 1941, which takes some account of the latest literature), I am restricting myself here to a very brief summary of the material.

of the synagogue as a place of assignment. Pliny was aware of the prevailing usage of eating fish at festival meals. The poet Juvenal regretfully drew attention to the phenomenon of the pagan father who was attracted to Judaism and observed the Sabbath, while his son became a full-fledged Jew maintaining the law of Moses in all its "unsocial" details. "What *schul* can I find you in?" (*in qua te quaero proseucha?*), a drunkard asks when he stops him in the street. Horace too — who recommended the "Jew Apella," exemplifying utter credulity, to believe things that he could not — had a friend who was interested in the observance of what he ignorantly termed the "thirteenth Sabbath" (perhaps a confused reference to Pentecost), and alludes to the success of the Jews in winning strangers over to their fold.

At the close of the imperial period, the Italian Jews became more acclimatized. The latest inscriptions of the catacombs, where formerly the greater part had been in Greek, are now mainly in the language of the country. Latin names, always in a majority, now became preponderant. There is some evidence that a vernacular literature had begun to emerge. An Old Testament enthusiast produced about this period a work in which he established a comparison between the Jewish and Roman systems of jurisprudence (*Collatio legum Mosaicarum et Romanarum*); and for educational purposes the Bible was translated into Latin in a version which became current in the western provinces of the Empire and had a noteworthy influence on Jerome's Vulgate. From recent researches, there is reason to believe that these codices were sometimes illuminated, initiating the tradition of Jewish ecclesiastical art in Europe. The language employed displays some characteristic features, perhaps reflecting Jewish linguistic usage of that age, which have been perpetuated down to our own day in the Judaeo-Italian dialect — striking witness to continuity over two millennia.

Generally speaking, the life of the Jews in Italy in imperial times was tranquil. In fashionable circles, they were perhaps regarded with scorn, heightened rather than attenuated by the fact that even in the aristocracy some persons showed a definite inclination towards Judaism. Whenever Palestine was in a state of rebellion, their position must have been delicate, but in every case the danger passed without leaving permanent results. Though they still had to pay the annual tax to the *Fiscus Judaicus*, from some points of view they were actually privileged. They were, as has been mentioned, the only section of the population excused by ancient tradition from the necessity of joining in state worship and offering sacrifice to the state deities, including the emperor — a loyal formality in the eyes of most persons, but one in which Jews could not participate. They were exempted from the universal obligation of filling municipal ("curial") offices, because this would have involved joining in pagan rites. "A highly distinguished religion, of indubitable legality" was the phrase used by jurists of the imperial period to designate Judaism. But the time was now approaching when a different attitude would be adopted, and Italian Jewry would have to encounter a different world.

v

The Christian Empire

In the year 313, Flavius Valerius Constantinus, known to history as Constantine the Great, with his co-Emperor Licinius, issued from Milan an edict establishing in the Roman Empire equal rights for all religions. This did not only stop the persecution of the Christians; it decided, in effect, their domination and sealed the fate of classical paganism. Moreover, seventeen years later the emperor removed his capital to the ancient Byzantium (henceforth to be called Constantinople) on the shores of the Bosporus, the strategic center of the East, thereby ending after four glorious centuries the ascendancy of Rome in the Mediterranean world. There was thus in these years a double breach with the past; and for this reason, it is conventional to regard them as the watershed between the classical period on the one hand and the Middle Ages on the other.

Certainly, this was the case with the Jews, and above all with those of Italy. Their religion had been treated and regarded as legitimate for hundreds of years, notwithstanding the brief periods of reaction. From an early date some, and, since the Edict of Caracalla all, had been full Roman citizens, suffering from no disabilities. But when authority passed into the hands of the zealous and jealous daughter-religion, with its theories of exclusive salvation, the position of Judaism changed. Its adherents, from being in a position almost of privilege, were now reduced to one of inferiority, which ultimately extended not only to the political but also to the economic field. In the end, they were brought down to the level of social outcasts and, in our own day, the attempts made to redress the balance caused the reaction which led to the phenomenon of antisemitism with all its appalling results.

It is true that Constantine, contrary to what is popularly believed, did not himself embrace Christianity at the time of the Edict of Milan; it is true, too, that for some time to come there was no actual legislation against Judaism as such, its position under the pagan emperors being nominally maintained. Nevertheless, the changed atmosphere soon became apparent in the administrative vocabulary, which by now had in mind the Jews of the Diaspora — including Italy — more than those of half-deserted Palestine. The "highly distinguished religion, of indubitable legality" did not become illegal, but it began to be referred to in imperial enactments as a "sacrilegious gathering" or "nefarious sect" — a change of attitude which the executive faithfully maintained. In 315, its adherents were threatened with burning if they dared to persecute those who had deserted their fold for "the faith of the true God." The old imperial legislation against seduction to the monotheistic faiths was renewed, but against them alone, converts and those who won them over being threatened with the death penalty. Even intermarriage between Jews and Christians, unless of course the former abandoned their faith, became a capital offense.

The reaction was not confined to matters connected with spiritual life. Hitherto, for reasons of mutual convenience, the Jews of Italy had been excused, as elsewhere, from serving in municipal office; in 321, Constantine cancelled this arrangement. Notwithstanding the traditional exemption dating back to the times of Julius Caesar, the Jews had of late shown a taste for a military career, to the distress of some of the Fathers of the Church; before the end of the fourth century, and repeatedly afterwards, it was closed to them, and those already enrolled were expelled from the service. From 339, they were forbidden to have Christian slaves in their possession, or to convert to Judaism those who belonged to other faiths; while as a final precaution the Emperor Constantinus went so far as to prohibit them to own pagan slaves as well. In effect, this signified in modern terms an embargo on the employment of any sort of non-Jewish labor, thus virtually involving exclusion from industry and even agriculture on anything but a petty scale. Provisions of this sort do not seem to have been put into effect immediately or universally; yet even if they did nothing more, their existence must have undermined all sense of security among the Jewish population.

When Julian "the Apostate" succeeded to the throne, in 361, it seemed for the moment to Italian Jewry that what had happened had been a fleeting nightmare, and that former conditions could be resumed. Julian was philosophically opposed to both of the monotheistic faiths, but his hatred of the Christian ascendancy made him friendly towards the Jews. His reign began with a proclamation extending freedom and equal rights to all sects and beliefs — Jewish, pagan, and Christian. He abolished the special taxation imposed on the Jews since the days of Vespasian, making assurance surer by destroying the registers on which it was based. The communities of his dominions learned with gratitude of his plan to restore the Temple in Jerusalem, and the zealous Italian Jews doubtless collected money among themselves for this momentous object. But the great plan was forestalled — by the emperor's untimely death, rather than by the supernatural manifestations luridly pictured by Christian writers. For he was killed in a skirmish, hardly more than two years after his accession, during the course of a campaign in the East. Before long, Christianity was restored as the religion of the Empire, and the reaction resumed its course.

This had been tempered at the outset by the universal toleration stipulated by the Edict of Milan. Indeed, long after the emperors had embraced Christianity, paganism remained the state religion of Rome, and its glittering rites continued to be observed. It was only after the accession of the Emperor Gratian, in 375, that the head of the state gave up the title of *Pontifex Maximus*, or "High Priest" of the pagan ritual, that the pagan altar of Victory was removed from the Senate House, and that the public treasury ceased to defray the expenses of the pagan ceremonies and sacrifices. For many years afterwards paganism lingered on among the patrician families, but henceforth it was fighting a lost battle. Notwithstanding the nominal toleration, zealous ecclesiastics often managed to collect a rabble and assault the ancient temples, which they would either destroy or convert into Christian churches — the fate of innumerable [buildings throughout Italy. Theoretically of course there was all the imaginable difference between the pagans, worshippers of idols, and the Jews, worshippers in their own fashion of the true Deity; between a temple dedicated to an amoral image-worship and a synagogue where the God of Moses and of Jesus was revered. Yet in the flush of triumph this was overlooked by the Christian paladins, who put Judaism and paganism on the same plane and were happy at any opportunity that offered of sweeping away the one with the other. Over a long period of years, there was a constant sequence of episodes of violence throughout Italy, the mob, sometimes led by the bishop, attacking the synagogues and pulling them down or else reconsecrating them for Christian worship. A law which forbade new synagogues to be built, under pain of destruction, placed a fresh weapon in the hands of religious fanatics. It was often impossible to define exactly what a new synagogue was: did the term cover extensions to old buildings, or repairs to ruined ones, or the replacement of a temporary by a permanent place of worship? Thus the Jewish communities were more than ever at the mercy of any zealous ecclesiastic or religious demagogue who wished to stir up the rabble.

Assaults of this sort continued sporadically in Italy for two or three hundred years. The earliest instance on record is of about the year 350, when Bishop Innocentius destroyed the synagogue at Tortona (not far from Genoa), erected a chapel on the site, and offered the Jews the alternative of exile or baptism. He was rivalled in zeal and exceeded in range by his contemporary Philaster, who, before his installation as bishop of Brescia, travelled throughout Italy preaching against the Jews and "disputing" with them in matters of faith. It was reported that he had particularly great success in Rome, where large numbers of unbelievers were converted. Something of the physical atmosphere of his propaganda may be realized from an episode of 387-8, when the Roman mob, after systematically destroying heathen temples, turned its attention to the synagogues and burned one of them to the ground. The usurper Maximus, who then controlled central Italy, ordered the culprits to be punished and the damage made good. Obloquy was heaped upon his head in consequence by zealous churchmen, who considered his death next year on the field of battle to be a punishment for this ungodly action. In his sermons in Milan, in 388, the great and learned Bishop Ambrose unsparingly condemned the Emperor Theodosius for ordering the restoration, at the rioters' expense, of a synagogue illegally destroyed in Asia Minor. He himself had no higher ambition, he wrote in one of his letters, than to meet a martyr's death during an assault of this sort; and he regretted that through laziness he had failed to burn down the synagogue of Milan, since destroyed by act of God. We are generally informed of such episodes only when the victims appealed for protection to some conscientious ruler. But this was possible only in a minority of cases; and the sporadic instances of which we know obviously indicate the general tendency all over the country during these obscure centuries. The conversions to Judaism, which had continued notwithstanding legislative enactments, were now increasingly dangerous. On the other hand, apostasy became widely prevalent, for it was enough for a person to be baptized in order to escape automatically from the effects of the growing discrimination and unpopularity. The weaklings, the unconvinced, the indifferent, must have abandoned the Jewish community in large numbers in consequence of this unremitting pressure. The Jewish population of the country dwindled with catastrophic rapidity, proportionately as well as absolutely, for this was a period of general decline. In the succeeding centuries it was relatively insignificant, at least in the north, and perhaps the level reached in the second or third century was never again attained at any subsequent date. Those who fell away from Judaism, on the other hand, must have merged, together with untold thousands and tens of thousands of others, in the general population of the country, recruited from every remote corner of the Mediterranean and the Western world. There is no country of Europe in which racialism is more out of place.

In 395, on the death of the Emperor Theodosius I, his dominions were divided between his two sons, the elder, Arcadius, being recognized as "Augustus" in the East (which he governed from Constantinople) and the younger, Honorius, in the West, including Italy (governed from Rome). This division was to become permanent. It had an important influence on Italian Jewry, which had owed its origin and its growth to the close political association between Italy and Palestine. Henceforth, the two countries were generally under separate administrations, and it was soon made manifest that the two communities had to become independent of one another. At least since the days of Theudas of Rome, at the end of the first century, it had been the practice of the Italian Jewries to collect an annual levy from their members, in imitation of the old half-shekel formerly devoted to the Temple in Jerusalem, for the support of the schools and other religious institutions in Palestine. This became known by the conventional name of "chaplet money" (*aurum coronarium*), like other special taxes at this time. Periodically, the Patriarch or *Nasi* of Palestinian Jewry, who administered the contributions and probably was the principal beneficiary, sent delegates (*apostoloi*) to Italy to organize the collection and encourage the contributors, their visits being a stimulus to local religious life and a further bond between the two countries. The names of two of these learned delegates, both of the early part of the fourth century, are preserved in the Talmud: R. Hiyya ben Abba and R. Judah ben Titus. After the division of the Empire, the emperor of the West objected to the flow of currency to the East which resulted from this levy; and in 399, on the pretext that it was an intolerable burden on his Jewish subjects (it was the only demonstration of his solicitude), Honorius forbade it to be collected henceforth in his dominions. Five years later, relations with his brother having improved, the embargo was lifted; but not long after, the Patriarch died without male issue and the office was abolished. In the East, its former revenues were diverted to the imperial treasury, and it is not improbable that the Western emperors followed the example. Even now, as has indeed been the case throughout Jewish history, Palestinian Jewish institutions and schools continued to receive voluntary contributions from Italy as from other parts of the Jewish world; and an inscription from Venosa of the seventh or eighth century tells with pride how two *apostoloi* had officiated at the funeral of the only child of a prominent communal leader. However that may be, with the abolition of the Patriarchate and the extinction of the *aurum coronarium*, the formal dependence of Italian Jewry on that of Palestine came to an end.

Another imperial pronouncement of this period throws a vivid light on the number and conditions of the Jews of Italy. Though after the death of Constantine they had again been exempted from the general obligation to serve in the onerous "curial" offices, the experiment of including them having apparently been a failure, Honorius insisted, unlike his brother, on the performance of these unpopular functions by all, without distinction of religion. In 398, when he was in South Italy, he was beset by throngs of Jews who implored him to reconsider his decision. "We have found," he wrote, "many citizens of various orders, belonging to the Jewish superstition, wandering about Apulia and Calabria who think that they should be exempted from the obligation of fulfilling their public charges by a certain law recently promulgated in the Eastern provinces." He was of the opinion that such an arrangement would be harmful in his dominions, where all persons of whatever creed must henceforth fulfill their civic obligations. The episode demonstrates how important the communities of this region had become, the Jewish population having spread by now throughout the Peninsula.

Just under a hundred years after Constantine had shorn Rome of its glory by transferring the administration to his resplendent new capital looking towards Asia, the old imperial city received a mortal blow when it was sacked by Alaric and his Visigoths in 410, and then even more ruthlessly by Gaiseric and his Vandals in 455. Italy, swept by wave after wave of barbaric hordes, sometimes in the guise of allies and sometimes of enemies, now knew the horrors of war which she had so often brought on other lands, but had hitherto succeeded in keeping from her own borders. Her cities were sacked, her countryside wasted, and her accumulated treasures — even those that had been brought centuries before from Jerusalem — were looted. The population of Rome was reduced, within a relatively short period, from three-quarters of a million to fifty thousand; and the other cities of the country languished similarly, though not perhaps to a proportionate extent. How the Jews suffered in this period, pre-eminently urban residents as they were, we can imagine by implication, though the only detail that has come down to us is that the synagogue at Syracuse was destroyed during one of the Vandal raids.

On September 4, 476, Romulus Augustulus, last emperor of the West, was deposed; and the Roman Empire came to an end.

CHAPTER II

The Dark Ages

vi

THE TEUTONS

THE so-called "barbarian" rulers, who now controlled Italy, did not differentiate at the outset between the Jews and any other section of the older population. Relatively, therefore, their position vis-à-vis other Roman citizens improved, though the tribulations of both elements were such as to rob the change of significance. The emergence of a more settled system of government barely affected this. Obviously, in areas where the old system was left undisturbed, or ecclesiastical authority became dominant, there was for a time no check on fanaticism and no opportunity of appeal against its excesses. The new ruling caste on the other hand — warlike tillers of the soil, with no reason to resent the economic activities of the Jews — tended to treat them objectively or even with favor so long as they followed the Arian form of Christianity, with its anti-Trinitarian bias. Yet this phase lasted for only a short while. Ultimately, the new masters of the country went over to orthodox beliefs and adopted entirely the Catholic point of view, prejudices and all — sometimes, it may be added, with the extravagance which is so notoriously characteristic of the half-educated and of the proselyte. In any case, it was not long before they succumbed to the cultural influence of the country, above all as regards jurisprudence. Hence the Roman Law, as codified in 438 by Theodosius II, emperor of the East, which systematized the anti-Jewish legislation enacted under Christian influence in the course of the past century, was accepted in the new Italy earlier and more fully than in any other Western land.

The greatest of the barbarian sovereigns was Theodoric the Ostrogoth, who ruled Italy from 487/93 to 526. "We prescribe no religion, for no person can be compelled to profess any faith contrary to his convictions," he declared, in characteristic Arian spirit; and he "gladly" confirmed the Jews' ancient autonomy and free exercise of their religion. "As to the Jews," he wrote, "let the privileges they enjoy be maintained, and let them preserve their own judges." On the other hand, he admonished them time after time to abandon their faith in favor of Christianity, and he strictly enforced the old regulations which forbade the construction of new synagogues or the embellishment of old ones. The need to maintain a fair balance was indeed great, and the number of occasions when he had to intervene in the course of his reign to protect the Jews is itself enough to indicate the abuses from which they must have suffered when a less objective ruler was in control.

For the assault on their position, led by irresponsible ecclesiastics, was unabated. In Milan, where the tradition of Ambrose was all-powerful, they found their rights threatened by the clergy to such an extent that they had to appeal to the king for protection. In Genoa, objections were raised when the community wished to roof over the ruins of their synagogue, destroyed in some previous outbreak. In Rome, the punishment of some Christian slaves for the murder of their master led to a riot, in the course of which the Jews were attacked and a synagogue set in flames; while the Samaritan congregation was summarily deprived of theirs, the site of which had been purchased by a former Pope. Even in Ravenna, now the capital of the country, forced baptisms took place; and when the Jews expressed their contempt of the rite, the Christian rabble burned down their place of worship (near which, it is recorded, the king's murdered predecessor, Odoacer, had been buried in 493). In each case, Theodoric promised protection or restitution in accordance with the law, though he warned the Jews of Genoa not to extend their synagogue when they repaired it, and taunted those of Milan with seeking earthly quiet while neglecting the chance of obtaining it in heaven. Especial resentment was aroused at Ravenna, where the "Roman" population was enjoined to rebuild the synagogue, and those too poor to contribute were flogged. If the Christians did not seek their revenge after Theodoric's death and the fall of his dynasty, their forbearance was unprecedented.

It was not long before their opportunity came. Justinian, the capable, pedantic ruler of the East, embarked upon a grandiose scheme for reconstituting the old Roman Empire. His brilliant general, Belisarius, conquered first Africa, where all the synagogues were converted into churches, then Sicily, and in 537 landed on the Italian mainland and began to besiege Naples. In this city the Jews seem to have been at this time both numerous and influential. They apparently controlled the food market, and there is some evidence that they were admitted to a share in civic life; in Venosa, not far away, Jews were enjoying the rank of *majores civitatis*, or city councillors. They naturally favored resistance, and when the Romanophile section of the populace were about to open the gates to the enemy they intervened and promised to provide the necessary provisions so long as the city held out. The struggle was long and memorable. At last, when Belisarius was on the point of abandoning the siege, one of his followers led a forlorn hope into the city through the aqueduct, while by way of diversion a final assault was delivered on the walls from the direction of the harbor. As it happens, the fortifications here were defended by the Jews, who fought with extreme gallantry. As dawn broke, they were surprised from the rear by another party of assailants, and their resistance was overwhelmed. Naples was captured, and Italy lay open to the invader. Before long, it was reconquered from end to end, the Ostrogoths being driven over the Alps to an unknown fate.

The Byzantines did not remain in control of the entire country for long, and we know nothing of their treatment of its Jewish population; to judge from their policy elsewhere, it must have been intolerant to a degree. In 568, there took place another incursion of barbarians from across the Alps — this time the Lombards, who for a time gave their name to the whole country. Worn out by war, famine and pestilence, the Italians offered little resistance, and in a short while the new invaders were in occupation of the greater part of the peninsula above Rome, and of certain areas below it. They faithfully followed the example of earlier invaders, before long accepting the prevailing culture, the prevailing faith, and the prevailing religious zeal. Once more, the Jews of northern Italy, after going through the agonies of war, must have known a brief intermission from governmentally-organized persecution; once more, this was followed by the conversion of the new arrivals, too, to Christianity, first in its Arian and then in its Catholic form; once more, they ultimately fell victims to the neophyte's zeal, receiving from King Perctarit or Bertarido, in 661, the alternative of baptism or death, after the fashion recently set in the Byzantine Empire and in Spain. But the details are vague. It is not known with any certainty whether this order was carried into effect, or for how long it remained in force, or over what area. At the end of the eighth century, however, it seems that Jews were living under Lombard rule, for a clumsy adaptation of the Theodosian code produced at this time reiterated the old imperial regulations prohibiting intermarriage and the possession or acquisition of Christian slaves by Jews, and permitted those "who were accustomed to consider themselves Romans" to preserve autonomy in internal disputes, though mixed cases were to be submitted to Christian judges.

But, generally speaking, Jewish history at this time, and

for some time to come, is a blank so far as northern Italy is concerned. We are better informed regarding the center of the country, where the Popes of Rome were gradually establishing their influence; and the south, where the Byzantines were as yet supreme.

vii
THE POPES

As the tide of Empire ebbed from Italy and the vestiges of its authority were undermined by successive onslaughts of invasion from every direction, the only stable force left in the central part of the Peninsula was that of the Bishops of Rome, who had managed to vindicate for themselves something of the mystical supremacy of the old Imperial City. Thus ultimately the Popes, as they were termed from the seventh century — earlier, the title *papa* had been applied to all bishops — acquired a unique position as virtual rulers of Rome and the surrounding area, with a vast spiritual influence over the whole of Western Christendom. The history of the Jews in Italy thus becomes in great part a history of their relations with the Papacy, which in a considerable area of the country was immediately, and in nearly the whole of it ultimately, responsible for their fate. As will be seen in the course of these pages, the record was generally speaking a humane one, despite some darker interludes and notwithstanding the fact that over-pious laymen and ignorant ecclesiastics were sometimes guilty of appalling misinterpretations of what the successors of St. Peter declared to be the tenets of the Church. This is demonstrated by one outstanding fact. The only city of the Western world in which the Jewish settlement remained uninterrupted throughout the Middle Ages, from remotest times down to the present day, was that for the rule of which the Popes were themselves immediately responsible — Rome.

Something of this was indeed dimly conveyed in an ancient Jewish legend — one of the many that clustered round Jewish life in the Eternal City. It was said that the first Pope was at heart a loyal Jew, Simon Caipha, who, disquieted at the growth of the new religion and fearing that it might warp Judaism from its right path, pretended to become converted to its principles and organized it as a separate faith under his own direction. It was then that he adopted the name of Peter, because he "absolved" (Hebrew, *ptr*) the Christians from their allegiance to Judaism. Having succeeded in this object, he shut himself up in a tower in Rome (presumably the Lateran), and there composed the superb *Nishmat* prayer included in every Sabbath and festal service of the Synagogue, lauding the universal power of God.

The first successor to Peter who is known to have had personal relations with Jews was Gelasius I (492–296), the Pope who proclaimed the independence of the Papacy in matters of faith.* He had in his service and was on friendly terms with a Jew named Telesinus (the Latin name is worthy of note) one of whose relatives he cordially recommended to a certain bishop. In the next century, successive invasions of Ostrogoths, Lombards and Byzantines all but overwhelmed Italian life, incidentally strengthening the Papacy. We know nothing more bearing on our subject until the days of Gregory the Great (590–604), founder of the modern tradition of the Papacy and formulator of its Jewish policy both in its favorable and its adverse aspects. In his sermons he complained bitterly of the obduracy of the Jews and their stony hearts. He took care that the canonical restrictions against them should be enforced in all their rigor. He

* It is unnecessary to speak of the legendary religious disputation which is said to have taken place in Rome in 312, in the presence of the emperor, between Pope Sylvester I and a number of preposterously-named Jews, headed by Zambri the magician. Sylvester is, however, known to have discussed religious matters with a Jew named Noah.

strongly objected to the observance of any ceremonies that savored of Judaism or tended to obscure the boundaries between Church and Synagogue. But on the other hand, he insisted that they should be treated with humanity, and did what he could to secure them in those rights which were theirs by law. Twenty-four of his eight hundred extant letters deal with the Jews, and enable us to have a glimpse of Jewish life throughout Italy in his day.

We receive the impression of a fairly thick settlement all over the country, but especially in Sicily; though it must be borne in mind that the interest of the Papacy in this island was particularly intense owing to the vast estates which it owned there. Here there was a sprinkling of Samaritans as well as of Jews, as had formerly been the case — and perhaps still was — in Rome. The community of this city naturally enjoyed great prestige, acting when necessary on behalf of their coreligionists of other places; and several of the Pope's letters begin with the statement that they were based on information received from the Roman Jews. Something of a Judaizing tendency was apparently prevalent at the time, which manifested itself in the observance by some persons of the weekly day of rest on Saturday instead of Sunday and the adoption of synagogal vestments by a few of the clergy. On the other hand, the wave of violence against Jewish places of worship, which had been so marked during the past two centuries, was not yet exhausted. It is to Gregory's credit that he was the first Pope known to have thrown the weight of his authority against this abuse, which possibly he checked; though the damage already done was irreparable. In Terracina, for example, an ancient seaport on the coast north of Naples, where a Jewish community existed throughout the Middle Ages, Gregory learned that the bishop not only threatened the Jews with violence if they remained deaf to his theological arguments, but intimated his intention of ejecting them from their place of worship, which was so near a church that the chanting distracted his congregants. The Pope ordered an inquiry to be made by the bishops of two neighboring sees; if the complaint were justified, the synagogue was to be closed and another site within the city walls made available in its place. This in fact happened, but the sequel showed that the bishop was actuated by something more than zeal; for before long he ejected the Jews from the new place of worship that they had set up. The Pope's indignation was now turned against him, and he was ordered to restore the building to its rightful owners and permit them to worship in it without molestation. "We forbid the aforesaid Hebrews to be oppressed and vexed unreasonably," Gregory wrote in this connection. "As in accordance with justice they are permitted to live under the protection of the Roman law, they are to be allowed to keep their observances as they have learned them, without hindrance."

Something of the same sort took place in Palermo, the principal city of Sicily. Here in 598, without the slightest pretext, Bishop Victor seized all the Jewish places of worship and their contents, together with the adjacent guest-chambers. (It is apparent that the term "synagogue" then implied in Italy something in the nature of what one would today term a community center.) The sufferers applied for assistance to their coreligionists in Rome, who petitioned the Pope; and Victor was asked to justify his action before impartial arbitrators or, if they failed to agree, before Gregory himself. Since the confiscated buildings had already been consecrated for Christian worship, the bishop had to pay compensation and to restore the booty that had been carried off. At Cagliari, in Sardinia, a newly-baptized Jew, named Peter, broke into the synagogue on Easter Sunday, 599, with a mob at his heels, and deposited his white baptismal robe, an image of the Virgin, and a crucifix in front of the Ark. The archbishop contented himself with a mild expression of disapproval, and the secular authorities would not permit the offending objects to be removed, with the result that the Jews were unable to continue to hold their religious services. Once again Gregory ordered reparation to be made, "since, in the same manner as the legal definition does not allow the Jews to erect new synagogues, it permits them to enjoy the old ones undisturbed." Similarly, in writing to the bishop of Naples on the occasion of an outbreak in 602, the Pope ordered him to see that the Jews were not molested in future in the performance of their religious rites, and had full liberty to observe their festivals and holy days, as they and their ancestors had done for so long.

This elementary protection did not imply sympathy, and Gregory sternly suppressed any attempt to overstep the boundary of the accepted code, rigorous though it was. There was a Sicilian Jew, for example, Nasas, who had apparently built a synagogue bearing the name of the Prophet Elijah (as many did at this time) which was visited by many Christians. The report reached Gregory's ears in the form that he had "erected an altar to the Blessed Elias and deceived many Christians, impiously inducing them to worship there." In addition, in contravention of the law, he had Christian slaves in his service. For these offenses Gregory requested the prefect of Sicily to see that he received severe corporal punishment; while in a communication to Cagliari, he informed the archbishop that slaves belonging to Jews who took refuge in church were under no circumstances to be returned to their owners.

Though disapproving of the employment of threats or violence in order to make the unbelievers change their faith, Gregory was eager for their conversion and was not averse from reinforcing spiritual argument by material temptation. Thus he instructed the administrators of the papal estates in Sicily, where as is clear the Jews were still landholders and peasants, to reduce by one-third or thereabouts the rent payable by those who were baptized. Even though he questioned the sincerity of persons won over by such means, their children at least would, he hoped, become convinced Christians. This plan seems to have met with some success, and a number of converts are recorded in the subsequent period. At Girgenti, for example, special arrangements had to be made during an outbreak of plague for the baptism of the neophytes from the estates of the Abbess of S. Stefano, and the poor were supplied with baptismal robes at the expense of the Church.

Gregory's correspondence adds some graphic details regarding the economic and general situation of Italian Jewry in his time. Those in the diocese of Luna, around the Gulf of Spezia, were interested in agriculture; and though they were forced to give up their Christian slaves, the latter were allowed to remain in their employment as tenant-laborers. Merchants are more prominent; for at this time a great deal of international trade — especially in the Mediterranean — lay in Jewish hands. Complaints regarding the treatment of the Jews in the south of France by the local authorities were brought to Gregory's notice by merchants who had come from Marseilles to Rome in connection with their business affairs. At Venafri, a Jewish trader imprudently purchased certain Church vessels; but this was against the law, and they had to be restored. A Sicilian Jew had his ship seized by the papal representative in settlement of a debt, but could not get his bond returned to him; another had dealings with the subdeacon of Sicily, who refused to satisfy his claims. There is a good deal of information relating to slave-dealing. This was at this time a perfectly legitimate calling, engaged in largely by Byzantine and Venetian traders, but was objected to in this case out of purely religious motives, the exercise of authority by unbelievers over believers being considered preposterous and unnatural. Gregory exerted himself to the utmost to suppress this "abuse," though he permitted Jewish dealers to retain their Christian slaves for forty days, and ordered them to be compensated for the loss of those who became converted to Christianity within three months of their acquisition. On the other hand, slaves who were circumcised were to be liberated without compensation. One of the main centers of the trade was Naples, where some perplexity was caused by the ingenious plan of a Jew named Basil, who nominally made over to his baptized children those slaves whom he wished to retain for domestic service! From these hasty glimpses, it is possible to reconstruct a general picture, however blurred, of Italian Jewish life in the seventh century. Many generations are to elapse before we have the opportunity again.

viii

The Byzantine South

The decline in the importance of Rome between the fifth and ninth centuries had been apparently responsible for a steady emigration from the once-imperial city and the consequent strengthening of the Jewish settlements in other parts of the country, particularly in the luxuriant south. Here, the forces of the Roman emperors of the East, reigning in Constantinople, had remained in possession, notwithstanding the Lombard invasions and other vicissitudes, their dominions including the "heel" and "toe" of the Peninsula and the island of Sicily. Gaeta, Naples and Amalfi were city-states, now at the height of their prosperity, while Benevento, Capua and Salerno were the capitals of Lombard principalities, rapidly becoming Italianized. This part of the country comprised a number of ancient seaports which carried on a steady trade with Greece, northern Africa and the eastern shores of the Mediterranean, and these in particular attracted flourishing Jewish communities. We happen to be exceptionally well informed about them — partly owing to archaeological finds, partly to the Byzantine records, and partly to recent literary discoveries, which have now made it possible to reconstruct local life in curious and sometimes fantastic detail.

The attitude of the Byzantines towards the Jews, as defined in the sixth century in the legislation of Justinian, founder of the new Empire in Italy, is well known. He developed the anti-Jewish regulations of preceding emperors into a galling code, which hampered every detail even of their religious life to a fantastic extent, loaded them with intolerable burdens and excluded them from all privileges. Particularly famous is his decree of the year 553 in which he forbade the exposition of the biblical lessons in synagogue in accordance with rabbinic tradition, but insisted that they should be translated into the language of the country. Though he specifically ordered this regulation to be communicated to all the provinces of the Empire, it is not known whether it was carried into effect in Italy. The same applies to a reported edict of his successor, Heraclius, about 614, the truth concerning which is not clear, entirely prohibiting the practice of Judaism. Only one piece of evidence bearing upon this matter is extant. The synagogue in Syracuse, destroyed in the course of the Vandal raids in the second half of the fifth century, was not apparently restored, and shortly after Heraclius' death Bishop Zosimus was able to prevent the handful of recent arrivals from constructing a new place of worship.

The period of utter intransigeance on the part of the Byzantine rulers did not last for long, and with the beginning of the ninth century information concerning the Jews in their Italian possessions became relatively plentiful. There were now, it seems, communities in the commercial centers of Lavello, Gaeta, Brindisi, Matera, Taranto, Trani, Oria, Venosa, and Bari, famous apparently for the physical beauty of its Jewish population. Benevento, capital of a Lombard duchy, also had its colony; while at Catania, in Sicily, a curious story tells of a Jewish wizard and his deeds. Oria, about twenty miles from the sea, between Taranto and

Brindisi, was the principal city of Byzantine Italy and the greatest Jewish center after Rome; though now it is not much more than a village in which it is hardly possible to picture its former glory.

The outstanding family of the region was descended from a certain Amittai of Oria, one of whose descendants, named Ahimaaz, wrote a good time afterwards a delightful family chronicle recounting, with a wealth of detail, the vicissitudes and achievements of his forebears and their connections over a period of ten generations and upwards of two centuries. It is a fantastic world into which we are introduced, of students and statesmen and wizards and mystics, of practical jokes by famous scholars and curious superstitions and miraculous deliverances. We are told of an earlier Ahimaaz, who used to go regularly on pilgrimage from Italy to Jerusalem bearing the contributions of his compatriots, and who was instrumental in saving by magical means the life of a boy who accompanied him. A contemporary of his, named Silano, a synagogal poet with an unfortunate wit which got him into trouble on one occasion, also makes his appearance. (He is the earliest European writer in Hebrew known to us by name). Amittai's own family was old-established in southern Italy, its progenitor having been brought from Palestine, according to legend, by Titus. He himself was also a synagogal poet, some of his compositions retaining their place in the liturgy to the present day. He had several sons, "gracious and worthy men, intelligent and learned, poets zealously teaching their disciples, princely persons who were adept in the Mysteries, wisely and discerningly occupied in the study and recital of the Secret Books." Outstanding among them was the poet Shephatiah, who died in the year 886. It was in him that the pride of the family centered. He was inducted into practical mysticism by a certain Aaron — apparently a son of the Exilarch Samuel, Prince of the Captivity and the hero of many remarkable stories — who arrived in South Italy from Bagdad about 850, bringing with him the marvelous lore of the East. Shephatiah proved an apt pupil. It was related how, when Oria was threatened by invaders, he was sent to negotiate with them and saved the city from much misery by a miraculous ride one Sabbath eve, and how, summoned to Constantinople on another occasion by the Emperor Basil, he delivered one of the princesses from the power of a demon and thereby procured the withdrawal, so far as the Italian provinces at least were concerned, of a savage edict enforcing baptism on his coreligionists. His brother Hananel, we are told, inadvertently misinformed the bishop of Oria, in the course of a discussion, as to the time when the New Moon was to appear, but was saved from the consequences by a providential change in the order of nature.

Notwithstanding the highly-colored account that Ahimaaz gives of his forebears and their achievement, there emerges from it the picture that all was not well with the Jews in the Byzantine dominions in Italy, and that persecution was constantly looming even when it was not actual. Indeed, whatever he achieved in Constantinople, it is not certain that Shephatiah succeeded in securing the final abrogation of the intended anti-Jewish legislation, even as far as his own city of Oria was concerned. It is known that in 873-4 Basil embarked upon a determined campaign to break down his Jewish subjects' adherence to their ancestral faith — first by persuasion, then by bribery, and finally by prohibiting the practice of Jewish ceremonies. Perhaps, by demonstrating that special political conditions obtained in southern Italy, or by judiciously-placed gifts, Shephatiah managed to secure the exemption from the scope of the edict of the five local communities referred to in another source or had it reduced to a formality. We are informed, however, that to his last day he did not cease to grieve over the evil decree of forced baptism, which his son Amittai commemorated in two liturgical compositions. In any case, on or shortly after this emperor's death in 886, the attempt to secure the conversion of the Jews was allowed to lapse, and, to the indignation of the Byzantine theologians, those who had succumbed during the period of persecution were allowed to return to their faith.*

In the course of this generation, a new force had made itself felt in South Italy. The astonishing impulse which within a century of Mohammed's death had carried Islam across North Africa and into Spain was not yet spent. In 827, the Emir of Kairouan began the systematic conquest of Sicily (we will have to revert to the history of its Jews in the Moslem period). With the capture of Palermo in 831, a base was available for regular raids on the Italian coast, which henceforth became more and more frequent, more and more violent. In 846, the Crescent was carried to the gates of Rome, where the Basilica of St. Peter was sacked. The coastal towns of the toe and heel of Italy, where Jewish communities lay thick, were especially exposed to attack. In 839, Taranto, one of the oldest centers of the region, was captured, and in the following year Bari, which for the next generation was to be the main Saracen base in this area. For short periods, even Benevento was occupied. In 856 or thereabouts, there was an attack on Oria, under the direction of the "Sultan" Mufarridsh ibn Salim, who had set himself up as an independent ruler. Shephatiah, as it seems, perhaps because of his knowledge of Arabic, was despatched to his camp by the governor in the hope of being able to bribe him off; but he was unsuccessful, for it was on this occasion that he is said to have performed his miraculous ride home on the Sabbath eve to warn the population of their danger. Capua and Naples also suffered in these forays, carried out, according to the Western historians, with incredible barbarity. Ultimately, the Christian

---

* Recent historians question the historicity of the old story that Oria and the surrounding territory were exempted from the persecution, though it is found in more than one source. I find it difficult, however, to credit a major falsification of relatively recent history.

rulers were for once forced to take united action. In 871, Bari was recaptured; in 880, Taranto; and within a few years the last Moslem lairs were uprooted from the mainland. It is safe to assume that the Jews suffered as merchants and householders during the incursions, and as unbelievers at the time of the reconquest, even though in the interval, as was generally the case under Moslem rule, they may have enjoyed a certain degree of well-being. Raids continued intermittently afterwards — especially on the strategic center of Oria, which was so frequently attacked that in the end its Jewish community, once so flourishing, lost all importance. On July 4, 925, for example, the city was plundered by an Arab marauder, and, besides the ten learned and pious Jewish householders who were slain, many persons were seized and carried into captivity. Two years later, a fresh onslaught drove many refugees, with the learned Abraham ben Jehoshaphat at their head, to Bari and Otranto, which henceforth succeeded to Oria's supremacy in Jewish life in South Italy. Yet another raid on the much-tried city took place apparently in 952, when the survivors included the splendid Paltiel, a member of the Amittai family, who entered the service of the conqueror, al-Muiz, and accompanied him as his adviser first to Sicily and then, when he became caliph in 969, to Egypt.*

The intolerance of the Byzantine emperors was brought to a fresh climacteric by the sequence of infidel attacks. Under Romanus Lucapenus orders were again issued for the forcible conversion of the Jews of the Empire (c. 932-6).

* Many attempts have been made to identify Paltiel in the light of the Arabic records, but none is satisfactory: he is perhaps to be brought into relation with the renegade Jew Yakub ibn Killis, for many years vizier to the Egyptian Caliphs al-Muiz and his son al-Aziz, just as Paltiel is said to have been. That he was merely a figment of Ahimaaz's luxuriant imagination is hardly credible, however much allowance must be made for exaggeration; for even the most boastful of chroniclers is unlikely to be guilty of utter fabrication in a matter of major importance, if only from motives of prudence.

This time, there is no story of miraculous intervention, and chance has preserved a pitiful account of what happened in Bari and Otranto. The news of the emperor's decree first reached the former city, where it was interpreted as a signal for an attack on the Jewish quarter. The disorders lasted for two days, and so many prominent Jews were killed that it was found easier to enumerate the living than the dead, while the synagogues were destroyed and the sacred writings burned. At the outset, warning was sent secretly to Otranto, where the community was better prepared. But here, too, there was cause for mourning: one of the leaders of the community killed himself rather than submit to baptism, another died in prison, a third was strangled. An emissary who had been despatched to Italy on a special mission by Hasdai ibn Shaprut, the Jewish physician-adviser to the Caliph Harun-al-Rashid of Cordova, escaped with his life, but only to fall among brigands shortly after. Elsewhere in the region, similar scenes no doubt took place. There is reason to believe that Hasdai, advised in a letter from the community of Bari of what had happened, used his influence at the court of Constantinople to obtain the withdrawal of the intolerant edict, which does not seem to have continued in force for long. For some time, however, Jewish life in Byzantine Italy, though it does not seem to have been interrupted, was driven underground. Doubtless the more zealous migrated now to places where they would be able to observe their faith without fear of interruption, and the Jewish settlement in certain parts of South Italy outside the Byzantine sphere may date to this period. The Amittai family at least — the only one concerning which we have detailed knowledge — was scattered. In the following generation we find two of its members, Sabbatai and Pantaleone, in the service of the Count of Amalfi, who once sent them on a mission to the Moslem ruler of Kairouan; while their brother Samuel administered the finances and mint at Capua, where he built a synagogue.

By now, the Byzantine hold in South Italy was weakening, and before long was to end. There is one further portion of the involved mosaic that is to be considered before we take this development into consideration — Sicily.

ix

SARACENIC SICILY

In 827, the military governor of Syracuse revolted against the rule of Byzantium. Defeated by an imperial army, he appealed for help to the Emir of Kairouan, and a Moslem force landed at Lilybaeum, henceforth called Marset Allah or Marsala. In 831, Palermo was captured and in 878 Syracuse, whence the Jews were brought in chains to the former city to be ransomed by their coreligionists. On the fall of Taormina in 902, seventy-five years after the first landing, serious fighting ended. The Saracen rule was undisputed thereafter, except in some remote places, until 1061, their influence being thus predominant in the island for a little more than two centuries — from some points of view the most brilliant in its history.

We have seen that Jewish communities, some of very great antiquity, were already to be found in Palermo, Catania, Syracuse, Girgenti, and so on. Their lot at the time of the invasion is unchronicled, though the complaint of an orthodox ecclesiastic, that on the capture of Syracuse he was thrown into prison together with a miscellaneous collection of captives who included some Jews, seems to point to the fact that they shared the lot of their neighbors. Once Moslem rule was established, Sicily was in the same position as the other Islamic states along the Mediterranean littoral. The Jews were tolerated — sometimes grudgingly, sometimes generously. Occasionally, they were subjected to degrading regulations. Always, in common with other unbelievers, they had to pay a special tax. There were interludes of benevolence. however, and the treatment they received at Moslem hands seldom compared unfavorably with that to which they were subjected in the lands under Christian rule. The Jewish population thus increased, so that it became an important factor in the island. Quick as always to adopt the dominant culture in external matters, and strongly reinforced perhaps by immigrants from other parts of the Moslem world, they became Arabized very rapidly in dress, in language, and in nomenclature. In Jewish life, as in non-Jewish, Sicily no longer belonged to Europe. It was culturally and politically rather part of Africa; and the communities looked for guidance and comradeship southwards — especially to Egypt — rather than to the Italian mainland. Moreover, the Arabic influences remained long after the Moslem invaders had been ejected, continuing in some details as long as Sicilian Jewish history was to last.

The free Jewish inhabitants of the island enjoyed all civil rights, including that of owning land, and were authorized to have their synagogues, though not indeed to enlarge them or to make proselytes. On the other hand, they could not bear arms and were excluded from the armed forces. The Jewish badge of shame, which afterwards became universal in the Western world, was first introduced into Europe as a measure of discrimination against Christians as well as Jews by the Sicilian ruler Ibrahim in 887-8; the former having to wear and display on the doors of their houses a piece of white stuff designed like a swine, and the latter a piece in the shape of a monkey. Later on, the Jews had to wear a yellow girdle and a special turban. A linguistic relic, which persisted down to a late date, illustrates one aspect of Jewish life under the Moslem rulers. Down to the end, the Jews of the island had to pay a graduated poll tax which went by the name of *gisia*. This term, found nowhere else in Italy, is derived from the Arabic *djizia* — a development of the traditional poll tax levied by the Moslems on all unbelievers as a price of the free exercise of their religion. In addition, they had to pay a special land tax, calculated in accordance with the productivity of the holding, known as the *karadj*. On the whole, therefore, the juridical condition in the Moslem period of the Jews as of the Christians was one of semi-liberty, which, however intolerant in theory, did not leave much cause for complaint in practice. Indeed, the mysterious Paltiel seems to have exercised some authority here when he was vizier to al-Muiz, before his transference to Egypt.

The principal community of the island was, as always, that of Palermo; so much so, that it not only spoke on behalf of the Jewish community of Sicily generally but even arrogated that name to itself in official communications. The Jews now formed the entire population of a suburb outside the walls, first mentioned in 967, which went by their name. Here probably was the home of Mazliah ben Elijah al-Bazak, the *dayyan* or rabbinical judge, who visited Bagdad early in the eleventh century. (It may be that he was the ancestor of the learned family of Busacco, scholars and physicians, who were prominent in communal life in Palermo in a later age.) On his return, he wrote an account of the customs of Hai Gaon, the last great luminary of Jewish learning in Iraq, for presentation to the King of Granada's Jewish vizier, the famous Samuel ibn Nagdela. The latter was revered in Sicily for his princely support of scholars and his gift of manuscripts of the Talmud to eager students, and it is recorded that on one occasion, about 1040, he was able to give the local communities solid assistance in a difficult moment.

Fitful light is thrown on the internal affairs of Sicilian Jewry in the Moslem period by some recently-found documents. Two Spanish Jews, Hayim (Khalah) and his son Nissim, at one time (c. 1030) rendered outstanding service to the local communities — obtaining a remission of burdensome taxation, protecting the interests of the merchants trading with Egypt, and saving a burial-ground from desecration. In gratitude, the community of Palermo, acting on behalf of the Jews of the whole island, wrote to the rabbis of Kairouan asking them to circulate an account of this self-sacrificing action, so that the example should be generally known and followed. The Sicilian Jews subscribed money for the support of the Jewish schools in Palestine, applications for help being read publicly in the synagogue. On one occasion, about 1015 or 1020, the government levied such a heavy impost when the collection was about to be made that many persons were ruined, and the pious duty had to be deferred; though a scholar named Abu'l Hayy promised to see that the loss was made good. When the Sicilian ruler, Samsam ad-Daulah, sent an embassy to Cairo in 1050, it was accompanied by a cultured Jew, Moses the Spaniard, who presumably had some minor office at court. We read of Sicilian Jewish merchants, trading mainly with Egypt; of scholars who went as far afield as Mesopotamia; of silk-exporters and perfumers; and of a Sicilian Jewish colony in Egypt. (There is a curious relic of this in an inscription bearing the name of a Sicilian Jew and his wife which is built into the walls of the famous Mosque of El-Aksa in Cairo.) It is distressingly little to know, over so long a period, of what was indubitably a great center of Jewish life. But intellectual activities are more important to the Jew than political interests; and in these it is certain that the part played by the communities of southern Italy was of exceptional significance.

x

THE LITERARY REVIVAL

During these obscure centuries, something had been happening in Italy which was to be of the greatest imaginable importance in Jewish life — no less than first the development, and then the dissemination, of Hebraic studies in Europe. The story is indeed a fascinating one. Several medieval legends implied that this region had played a vital part in the process, but scholars failed to take them seriously, for nothing more than legend was known. In recent years, however, a series of discoveries have been made which bear out the old tradition to the full, and moreover enable us to place the process in its historical setting. It is noteworthy that it took place at a period when in non-Jewish Italy, as in Europe as a whole, cultural life had touched its lowest level.

That Jewish scholars had visited Italy in the centuries following the fall of Jerusalem is certain (we have seen instances more than once in the foregoing pages) but nothing of their activity or of their literary production — if it existed — is ascertainable. Indeed, from the catacomb inscriptions, mainly extending from the first to the fourth centuries, it would appear that knowledge of Hebrew was scanty among Italian Jews at this time, for only a few scattered and conventional phrases occur in the epitaphs. This was the case, not only at Rome, but also at Venosa in the south, where a considerable number of inscriptions dating from the third to the seventh centuries have been found. Most of these are in Latin or Greek; but some of the later examples demonstrate an awakening interest in and use of Hebrew, still a little stilted, and one refers to the presence of two rabbis (*rebbites*) at the interment. A gap of a couple of centuries follows. Then, by a lucky chance, we have a series of Jewish tombstones from this region — mainly from Venosa itself — bearing long and flowery inscriptions, in choice Hebrew, displaying a wide knowledge of Jewish literature, considerable ability in manipulating the Holy Tongue, and in some cases a distinct poetical gift. These extend from about the year 800 onwards; and they mention, incidentally, Jewish schools, scholars of the academy (e. g., Nathan ben Ephraim of Venosa, who died in

846 — one of the earliest European rabbis known to us by name) and so on.* The views of the Roman savants, and their communications with the ancient seats of learning in Iraq, are referred to a little while later, about 860. It is obvious that in the intervening period — that is, in the seventh or eighth century — there had been a remarkable literary revival among the Jews of South Italy, who began to cultivate Hebrew studies, to become passionately attached to the Hebrew language, and to develop an interest in rabbinic learning.

Before long, this newly-quickened interest began to express itself in the emergence of a school of Hebrew religious poetry — the earliest in Europe, if not the earliest outside Palestine. Recent discoveries have revealed works by a number of its members of the ninth century onwards — Silano of Venosa, perhaps the first of all; Amittai of Oria and his family, including his son Shephatiah; and Menahem Corizzi, known as "the Circumciser," who may have earned that title by venturing his life when he initiated Jewish children to the covenant of Abraham during the Byzantine persecutions. Prose works, too, began to be composed. It is probable that the Hebrew chronicle indirectly modelled on Josephus, known as *Josippon* (so popular among the Jews of the Middle Ages, and in Elizabethan England) is a South Italian composition of the tenth century; the first mention we have of it, in fact, is in a letter written at the time of the persecution at Bari and Otranto about 930. A number of midrashic works, too, comprising rabbinic ethics and legends, possibly owe their origin to this area and this period, such as the midrash on the Song of Songs, the collectanea known as the *Pesikta Rabbati*, and, according to some, the moralizing *Tanna de-Be Elijahu* and the *Abot*

* A characteristic of these inscriptions is that they calculate the year from the Destruction of Jerusalem — a usage which also seems to have obtained locally for other purposes, as, for example, the dating of marriage-contracts.

de-R. Nathan. To these works are probably to be added the mystical *Alphabet of Ben-Sira* and the *Halakhot Kezubot* — one of the oldest handbooks of Jewish religious practice of the post-talmudic period — as well as certain compositions which have entered into the liturgy. Thus a good deal of the early literature, formerly attributed by scholars to Spain, now appears to have originated in this region. With these new discoveries, the importance of South Italy in Jewish scholarship, in the last centuries of the first millennium, is seen to be greater and greater. It is now becoming possible to understand what a twelfth-century scholar meant when he misquoted (it had formerly seemed a preposterous exaggeration) that "from Bari comes forth the Law, and the word of God from Otranto" (cf. Isaiah 2.3).

One of the important figures in this activity has already been mentioned: Sabbatai ben Abraham, called Donnolo (the name, probably a diminutive of *dominus*, in the sense of "Little Master," being the title applied to him as physician) — one of the first European Jewish writers, and one of the first Italian scientists of the Middle Ages. He was taken prisoner in 925, at the age of twelve, when his native Oria was raided by the Saracens and brought to Otranto, the others being taken on to Palermo and Africa. He then turned to the study of medicine and astronomy, subjects in which he claimed to have studied "all the learning of the Greeks, Arabs, Babylonians and Indians." Subsequently, he practiced medicine in various places in South Italy, his clientele including even Church dignitaries. He was in fairly close touch with the famous anchorite, St. Nilus of Rossano, being said indeed to have witnessed one of the saint's miracles, and on another occasion to have received a pointed snub when he offered to keep him in health in his old age. Donnolo composed a well-known commentary on the mystical *Book of the Creation* (he gives in it the earliest medieval description of a burning glass), as well as a medical work the surviving fragments of which display some competence in Greek, Latin and Arabic as well as Hebrew, and knowledge of the medical literature accessible in those tongues.

Donnolo is the only student of the secular sciences at this period whose name is familiar to us, and the only one known to have entered into relations with representatives of non-Jewish thought. There is, however, an ancient and persistent legend which concerns the participation of the Jews in the development of the great medical school at Salerno, the oldest and long the most famous institution of its sort in Christendom. This town, a seaport not far south of Naples, was at one time the capital of an independent Lombard principality; and the records demonstrate the presence in it of Jews in considerable numbers from 872 onwards, including, some time before the year 1000, a certain physician named Judah. It is at about this period that the school of Salerno begins to emerge to light. Ancient legend recounts that it was founded by "four masters"— a Latin, a Greek, a Jew, and a Saracen — and that Jews continued to take a great part in its activities. To interpret the story literally is out of the question; the Salerno school, like other institutions of the sort, was a gradual growth rather than a deliberate creation, and it is impossible to ascribe its establishment to a certain date or to certain individuals. Yet the legend symbolizes the influences under which it came into being, and it is indubitable that a Jewish element was early in evidence, not only in the city, but also in its intellectual life.

More important than any original production of Italian Jewry in the Dark Ages was its importance in the transmission of scholarship, a function which remained, indeed, characteristic of it throughout history. Here, too, recent discoveries tend to give substance to legends once scorned by the learned. One of the best known recounts how in the year 972 — the date may now be fixed with certainty — four scholars set out by sea from Bari in order to collect money for the dowering of brides, perhaps those orphaned by the recent persecutions. They were captured at sea by an Andalusian corsair, Abdullah ibn Riyahin, and were sold as slaves in four different ports, introducing thus to these regions the learning of their native land. In particular, Moses ben Enoch, who was ransomed at Cordova, brought about the development of talmudic studies in Spain, while Hushiel ben Elhanan became the greatest luminary of the rabbinic school of Kairouan. It is now known that the last-named originated in Europe, that intellectual life luxuriated in South Italy at the time, and that the admiral of the Andalusian fleet actually did make a foray in the central Mediterranean in this year; we are justified, therefore, in accepting this account as true in substance if not in detail, with the corollary that South Italy was the pivot for the revival of Jewish learning in the Western world at the end of the first millennium.

Many other fragments of evidence point in the same direction. Another semi-legendary scholar who originated in Apulia was a certain Moses, who, as we are informed, quarreled with the poet Amittai and was constrained to leave Oria about the year 900 — first for Capua and then for Pavia, the old Lombard capital in the north of the country. It seems that he is to be identified with Moses of Pavia, the first known European talmudist of the Middle Ages. The Ahimaaz chronicle also introduces us to the wonder-working Aaron, or Abu Aaron, who, as has been mentioned, arrived in South Italy from Iraq in the middle of the ninth century and was active at Gaeta, Benevento, Oria, Bari and elsewhere, having many disciples. He is obviously identical with the master-cabalist Aaron of Bagdad, who according to medieval tradition was the father of Jewish mysticism in Europe. Among his pupils was [Moses ben] Kalonymus, whose Greek name makes it probable that he originated in Byzantine Italy, but subsequently settled in Lucca. In the second half of the tenth century or thereabouts, he or a member of his family transferred himself to Mainz — apparently with the encouragement of the emperor himself (perhaps he was a physician in addition to his other intellectual attainments). For many generations to come, his descendants are to be traced on the Rhineland. Here he implanted talmudic learning, together with mystical interests and a taste for religious poetry, so that he may be regarded as the father of Jewish learning in Germany. The "Roman Sages" were spoken of with respect in the great Mesopotamian academies before the end of the first millennium, though the Gaon Hai considered them (not without reason, if we are to judge from the Ahimaaz chronicle) to be over-superstitious.

The Jewish scholars of Italy were at all times in particularly close touch with Palestine, as was natural in view of the constant commercial intercourse between the southern ports and the Holy Land and the unceasing stream of pilgrims to Jerusalem. The Ahimaaz chronicle speaks not only of Italian Jewish visitors to Palestine, but also of the presence at Venosa of a Palestinian scholar collecting funds for the schools. We are informed, too, of the bringing of a certain work on biblical hermeneutics from Jerusalem to Bari and thence to Mainz — a symbol of the transference of Jewish scholarship in general. Thus the influence of the schools of Babylonia, so strong in North Africa and Spain — for they were long under the same rule, and continued to be part of the same cultural nexus — was felt here to a relatively minor extent, that of the Holy Land being paramount. From Italy, the Palestinian tradition passed along the historic trade-routes and over the Alps, to France and to Germany. The differentiation long continued to make itself felt — in intellectual interests, in literary style, in synagogal ritual, and so on. Indeed, many standard texts circulated in the Middle Ages in two forms — the one Spanish, and the other Italo-French. In this respect, too, the ancient Apulian Jewish culture long made itself evident.

This digression may perhaps have seemed to some readers over-technical; but the subject is of fundamental interest. If the share taken by the communities of South Italy in the development and the transmission of Jewish culture in the ninth and tenth centuries was so important, it is evident that the Jewish population of the area at this time must have been, not only highly cultivated, but also numerous and influential. We are informed only of the migration of persons of exceptional significance, as scholars were in Jewish life. It is unlikely that they set the fashion; they followed it, being part of a much larger movement which involved hundreds of persons where we are informed only about one. This period was indeed one of rapid expansion in northern Europe — in France, Germany, and ultimately England as well. Before many years had passed, all these lands were the seats of important Jewish communities, distributed in the first instance along the great trade-routes which controlled intercourse with the Mediterranean world. Whence the immigrants came we do not know. But there is every reason to believe that a good number of them belonged to families long established in Italy. The peninsula was an entrepôt not only for merchandise and for ideas, but also — and perhaps to a greater extent — for men.

CHAPTER III

The High Middle Ages

xi

THE COMMUNITIES OF UPPER ITALY

JUST as the essential unity of Italy was shattered, so it was partially restored, by invaders from beyond the Alps. In 774, the Frankish ruler Karl, known to history as Charlemagne, intervened in Italian affairs to protect the Pope from the Lombards, already checked twenty years before by his father Pepin. In a brief campaign, their power was destroyed. Charlemagne was henceforth supreme in the north of the country, and on Christmas Day, 800, he was crowned "Emperor" in St. Peter's. This was the beginning of the Germanic "Holy Roman" Empire, destined to continue in nominal being for a thousand years. It is impossible to describe here in any detail the part it played in Italian history. It is sufficient to say that this somewhat remote overlordship made it possible for the great trading-cities which were now emerging to establish themselves as quasi-independent republics; some of these fell at a later date under the control of local tyrants, becoming sovereign duchies, lordships and so on. Around Rome, the Popes were enabled by the change in circumstances to establish a claim to the direct administration of wide territories, though their rule became generally effective only a long time later. Still further south, Norman invaders of the eleventh century expelled first the Byzantines from the mainland, setting up what was ultimately known as the kingdom of Naples, and then the Saracens from Sicily. Italian history thus regains a certain degree of homogeneity. With the new regimes, moreover, records become more abundant, and so far as the Jewish settlements are concerned it is now possible to present something approaching a consecutive account.*

Those Jews who now come into the picture are, generally speaking, merchants. It is impossible to describe here in detail the economic process to which they had been subjected since the fall of the Roman Empire. In brief, the decay of that remarkable international organization had left them almost the sole element with a consciousness of other countries, a knowledge of other languages, and reliable correspondents in other regions. Hence they had qualifications for importing and exporting which most others lacked. In Italy — an entrepôt for the reception of merchandise from the highly developed Greek and Arabic-speaking lands of the Eastern Mediterranean, and its distribution to the backward areas of northern and western Europe — they had remarkable opportunities. They played a noteworthy role therefore in mercantile activity, until the development of the great Italian maritime republics, with their quasi-cooperative organization and their political backing, made the scale of the operations in which the Jews engaged relatively unimportant. At one time, indeed, the rivalry was intense. Venice, for example, the great trading city, showed an almost spiteful spirit of antagonism. Not content with admitting no Jewish settlers, in 945 she forbade vessels sailing in Oriental waters to take Jews or any other foreign merchants aboard, or even to transport their wares from port to port. When, nearly half a century later, the republic obtained a

* These few lines devoted to a very complex process must not be allowed to oversimplify it in the reader's mind. But the details of the emperor's five-hundred-year struggle to assert his claims in Italy, the fight of the northern cities to vindicate their independence, the long battle of the municipalities against the feudal nobility, and the world-racking controversy between the Papacy and the Empire, do not enter immediately into the story — itself extremely complicated — that I am endeavoring to tell.

reduction of the dues levied on her ships at Abydos, the Byzantine toll-station on the Hellespont, it was stipulated that no similar preferential tariff should be accorded to merchandise belonging to the Jews and other commercial rivals. In addition to excluding her infidel competitors from the Mediterranean sea-routes, the republic attempted to close to them also the alternative land-route across Central Europe, appealing to the Holy Roman Emperor and the Archbishop of Mainz, about the year 932, to take action against those of Germany, and at least to prevent them from touching with their "stained hands" the cross with which merchandise was sealed — that is, in effect, from participating in foreign trade. A similar economic jealousy prevented the establishment of important Jewish settlements, as might have been anticipated, in the other great Italian trading republics, such as Genoa and Pisa.

That the Jews were prominent in commerce did not imply that none was engaged in other callings. They had not, thus far, been excluded completely from agriculture, and scattered records show them as landholders in 967 in the neighborhood of Ancona, throughout the eleventh century at Lucca, in 1025 at Modena, in 1033–9 at Taranto, still under Byzantine rule — to mention only a few instances. As in Spain, their interest was probably in vineyards and olive-orchards rather than in mixed farming, and it is certain that for ritual purposes they manufactured their own wine. In the south of the country on the other hand the majority followed handicrafts, like their coreligionists in the Byzantine Empire. In several places they were engaged in silk manufacture, and they had, it seems, almost a monopoly of the highly technical dyeing industry. More will be said of this later on.

About conditions in northern Italy, in the age of Charlemagne and his immediate successors, not much is known. In 855 his great-grandson, Louis II, is said to have issued a decree expelling the Jews from his Italian dominions. But it does not appear that this was carried into effect, and indeed the dynasty was long remembered in Jewish legend for its consistent generosity of treatment. This attitude was maintained by their successors, the German emperors of the Saxon line. But the services may be considered reciprocal, for it is told how a Jew, named Kalonymus (perhaps connected with the famous family of scholars), saved the life of Emperor Otto II on the battlefield, after his defeat by the Saracens at Cotrone in 982. Though the Jews seem to have been distributed pretty generally at this time, we know of individuals rather than communities, which, where they existed, must have been very small. At Rome (where, to the general scandal, a French archdeacon named Bodo was converted to Judaism in 838) the Jewish community, or *schola*, is recorded to have taken part in the ceremonial reception of the Emperor Otto III in 996. But Rome was then economically unimportant, and its Jewish colony was probably at the lowest numerical level in its history.

There was probably a settlement surviving from an earlier age in the Lombard capital, Pavia, not far from Milan. Here, some time between 761 and 766, a religious discussion took place between a Christian scholar, Peter of Pisa, and a Jew named Lullus or Julius; among those present was the English ecclesiastic Alcuin, who informed Charlemagne about it in one of his letters. It was nearly two centuries later that the mystic named Moses emigrated to Pavia from South Italy, the influence he exercised suggesting that the city was still an important Jewish center. Verona must have been another. Here, it seems, the Jews lived on conspicuously friendly terms with their neighbors and engaged in all branches of commerce without opposition. But Rather, bishop of the see between 931 and 938, and one of the fathers of medieval antisemitism, deliberately set himself to the task of breaking down this cordial tradition, and in the end secured the expulsion of the unbelievers. Venice, Queen of the Adriatic, was outstandingly unfriendly to the Jews, as we have seen. But it was impossible to exclude Jewish traders entirely, whether they came from the Levant or from beyond the Alps; and at least as early as 1090 — presupposing a much older settlement — the large island where they carried on their activities was known after them as the *Giudecca* (this is at least the usually accepted explanation). As early as 905 we read of Jewish traders at Treviso, at the junction of the routes into Germany over the Carnic and Julian Alps, and shortly after of Jewish landowners in the environs. At Imola in the Romagna, between the Apennines and the Adriatic, Jews are said to have lived as early as the seventh century. At Modena, later the seat of an important community, an Ardingus Judaeus (but this may have been a nickname) was receiver of ecclesiastical tithes in 1025. For Milan, we have only the vaguest of information after the persecution at the time of Theodosius, but there is some evidence for the presence of Jewish traders and peasants about the close of the first millennium. Near Ancona, a Jewish landowner is encountered, as has been mentioned, in 967.*

The most important Jewish center in the north of the country at the period with which we are dealing seems to have been Lucca, now a great entrepôt of trade with northern Europe, where Jews are mentioned in numerous documents from the year 1000 onwards. Without doubt the city must have been an important seat of learning to have been associated so persistently in Jewish tradition with the transmission of rabbinical studies to the Rhineland through the family of Kalonymus — which name, incidentally, is encountered in the oldest Latin document dealing with the colony. This is the most northerly Italian city where there is reliable evidence of the presence of Jews in any number,

* There is a picturesque reference to the relations of the bishop of Trieste with David the Jew in 949, but it is probably antedated by four centuries; while the document which records a Jewish landowner at Asti in 812 is now regarded as spurious.

and presumably a Jewish community, during the Dark Ages. On the other hand, such documentation as we have is sporadic, throwing a fitful light on the life of individuals here and there. It is doubtful that they dwelt in isolation, and probably there were many more places, no evidence for which is to hand, where also they had established themselves.

Summing up, we may conclude that at this period small Jewish groups, mainly of traders, with a sprinkling of craftsmen and peasant proprietors, were to be found all over northern Italy, especially in the growing commercial centers; the most important probably were Pavia and Lucca, though not even these two settlements attained any numerical strength. A tendency to discrimination or even exclusion — partly owing to religious prejudice, partly to commercial jealousy — is to be discerned. There is reason to believe that this became more serious with the advance of the Middle Ages and the growth of the native Christian mercantile class, the expulsion from Verona just mentioned being typical of the age; for some of the settlements which are mentioned in the tenth century disappear from view afterwards. But the majority of Italian Jewry was living in the south of the country, below Rome, where the communities which flourished during the Byzantine period — especially but not exclusively in the seaports commanding trade with the Levant — had as yet lost nothing of their importance.

It does not appear that any important change in the condition of Italian Jewry took place in the early years of the second millennium, or that the area of settlement appreciably increased. The revival in the authority of the Papacy, the conquest by the Normans first of Apulia and Calabria and then of Sicily, the rise of the northern communes, all ultimately had a profound influence on the Jews; but we know little or nothing of the immediate effects. The meagerness of our information does not indeed imply that this was in every respect a halcyon period, and now and again there are allusions to local suffering. A Roman synagogal poet of the period, Solomon "the Babylonian" (c. 970–1020), reflects the prevailing conditions in one of his penitential hymns:

> Destroy the Jew! despoil him! is the cry.
>   Thine own true servants are uprooted so.
> To blot us out their aim. They vilify,
>   And tax, and spoil, and fleece, to bring us low.
>
> They strip us and they scorn us, call us "hound"—
>   Each shaveling priest and monk and fool and knave.
> We hear their taunts— unshaming-shamed, tongue-bound.
>   For Thy sake agonized, Thy help we crave.

It is not easy to fill in the details, but occasional glimpses are possible. Legend tells for example of an expulsion from Imola in 976, to avenge which the men of Ravenna were incited to attack the city some time later. After a catastrophic earthquake shock in Rome in 1020 or 1021 and the consequent search for the cause that had provoked the Divine wrath, a number of Jews were savagely punished on an improbable charge of mocking a crucifix. Rabbi Meshullam ben Kalonymus of Lucca, writing to the Babylonian head of the Academy, Hai Gaon, about this time, spoke of an "upheaval" in his native town in terms such as to make one suspect either a local persecution or else sack at the hands of armed forces. In 1062, the community of Aterno (near Pescara) was accused of committing a ritual outrage on an image of Jesus in the synagogue on the eve of Good Friday. Three years later, the ruler of Benevento compelled many of the Jews of that city to become converted to Christianity, though this exposed him to the censure of the Pope. In northern Europe, the religious passions stirred up by the

Crusades led to a succession of savage attacks, beginning in 1096 on the Rhineland. In Italy, interest in the successive expeditions for the recovery of the Holy Sepulcher was predominantly economic, and if anything of the sort took place it was on a small scale. There is, however, a somewhat vague mention of a persecution in "Lombardy" at this time, among the victims being two scholars — a second Moses of Pavia (unless there is some confusion of dates) and Kalonymus of Rome.

A short time after this there took place one of the most colorful and remarkable episodes in the course of Italian Jewish history. In Rome, in the first half of the eleventh century, there lived a Jew named Baruch, who, after amassing a great fortune, had embraced Christianity under the name of Benedict. He married the daughter of a Roman noble and called their son Leo, in honor of the ruling Pope. He, heir to wealth on the one side and rank on the other, became in the disorderly time that followed one of the most powerful grandees in the city, building himself a stronghold in the Trastevere district beyond the Tiber. His son in turn he called Piero (Peter), the family being known thereafter, by a combination of the two names, as Pierleoni. The latter extended the fortified area under his control into a veritable domain, and played a great part in civic life. The climax was reached with his son, Piero Pierleoni, who entered the Church and, backed by the vast family influence, made rapid advances and was created cardinal. On the death of Pope Honorius II, in 1130, one of the two factions then dominant in Rome elevated him to the Papacy, under the name of Anacletus II. His Jewish antecedents, vastly exaggerated by his enemies, who even accused him of practicing Judaism in secret, antagonized many potential adherents, and the majority of Europe supported his rival, Innocent II. The devotion of the Roman populace enabled him nevertheless to maintain his authority at the center of the Christian world; and he thus continued to enjoy the papal dignity, though with only a limited range of obedience, until his death in 1138. It was conceivably because of Anacletus' suspected orthodoxy that, when his rival now entered Rome, he set the example, generally followed afterwards, of telling the Jewish deputation who came to greet him with a scroll of the Pentateuch, that he revered the Law of God but condemned their futile interpretation and the religious practices based on it. It is thought that this remarkable phenomenon, of the elevation to the Papacy of a person the memory of whose Jewish descent was still fresh, may have been the source of the strange fable of Andreas, or Elhanan, the kidnapped Jewish boy who became Pope but continued true at heart to the faith of his fathers — part of the rich store of legend developed in the Middle Ages by Italian Jewry.

xii

JEWS IN ITALY IN THE TWELFTH CENTURY

The first detailed picture of Italian Jewry that we have is in the account of the famous Spanish Jewish traveller, Benjamin of Tudela, who visited the country between 1160 and 1165 on his way to Palestine, and again on his way home in 1173. It is convenient to pause at this point and to describe the scene as it presented itself to this conspicuously accurate observer — the earliest medieval chronicler of travel who generally told the truth.

The first place visited by Benjamin in Italy, arriving thither by sea from Marseilles, was Genoa. Here, where up to the sixth century there had been a flourishing community, he found only two Jews, Rabbi Samuel and his brother, perhaps the "Joseph Judaeus" mentioned in the secular records of the time, recently arrived from Ceuta in North Africa. Some thirty years earlier, the consuls had ordered all Jews, even if they came to the city only on a visit, to pay an annual tribute for the illumination of the high altar in the church of S. Lorenzo, and it may be that an edict of expulsion had been issued in the meanwhile. The republic's jealous policy was to continue. Towards the end of the century, it was forbidden for any Jew to remain in the city longer than three days; and, though there is sporadic mention of merchants and others in the records, it does not seem that any permanent community was established until long afterwards.* Even then, its tenure was precarious; and although — or perhaps because — Genoa was one of the most important commercial centers in Italy, its Jewish community was never a noteworthy one. In the area north of Genoa, the later Piedmont — economically one of the most backward parts of the country — it does not seem that Jews had as yet taken up permanent residence.

From Genoa, Benjamin went on to Pisa, two days' journey distant. It was at this time at the height of its power as a trading republic, with colonies in Syria and Egypt and factories in every part of the Mediterranean. Unlike most of its rivals, Pisa's policy towards the Jews was relatively tolerant, and Benjamin found here twenty Jewish households, presumably participating in the city's active Levantine trade. It may be added that this kindly feeling continued to prevail, the Pisan community being one of the few in Italy which never suffered from any serious interruption or reaction. Not far inland lay the commercial city of Lucca, commanding the overland route into France. The Jewish settlement in this place was important, as we have seen,

---

*I reluctantly follow the local historians in making this statement. I have, however, documents which seem to indicate a pretty intense activity in the middle of the thirteenth century, including the catalogue of a Hebrew library. On the other hand, I see no reason to believe, with some scholars, that the twelfth-century merchant-princes Soliman of Salerno and Solomon Blancard had anything Jewish about them other than their not-unusual biblical names.

even before the year 1000, and still retained something of its reputation for learning; for Abraham ibn Ezra, the encyclopaedic Spanish scholar, was living and writing here in 1145. Benjamin found forty families, implying some 200 souls — not a small number in relation to the conditions of those times.

The places mentioned thus far are the only ones visited by Benjamin in northern Italy. This partial account has therefore to be supplemented from other sources. There were probably a few immigrant traders at Venice, though a report which fixes their number in 1152 at 1,300 is almost certainly unauthentic. At Aquilaea, where Jews had been living in Roman times, a tombstone of 1140 and a casual mention in rabbinical literature in the following century suggest that they were present also in Benjamin's day. An unsubstantiated report speaks of Jews at Ferrara in 1088; that city was in any case a seat of scholarship in the thirteenth century, and probably the tradition went back to the twelfth. Shortly before Benjamin's day, Abraham ibn Ezra was resident for a time, probably as guest or tutor, in a wealthy household in Mantua, and the city is mentioned in various rabbinical sources in the next generation. Verona must have recovered by now from its tenth-century disaster, for at the beginning of the thirteenth century it was the seat of a school of talmudic learning. A document of 1239 speaks, indeed, of the rabbinical courts — not necessarily composed of professionals — at the three cities last mentioned as well as at Cividale in the same region.

The recorded history of the Jews in Padua begins a hundred years after the time with which we are dealing; but in Bologna the community in Benjamin's day was still undisturbed, though in 1171 there was to be a temporary expulsion for unknown reasons. Florence, now on the threshold of her wonderful history, did not as yet have any knowledge of Jews, so far as is ascertainable; but Sienna, at that time perhaps greater in importance, had a community which in 1229 was regarded as old-established. On the Adriatic coast, Jews were still living, as it seems, in Ravenna, while a *mons judaicus* and Jewish harbor-dues are recorded at Rimini; and at Cesena, not far inland, a Jewish bibliophile was to draw up a catalogue of his library in 1205. It is only in the second half of the thirteenth century that we find reliable mention of what was afterwards the important community of Ancona. Nevertheless, in the vicinity of this place, Jews were to be found not long after 1200 in Montegiorgio, Camerino and Recanati; while a rabbinical document informs us of the existence of congregations in 1214 at Fano and Pesaro, which had already produced at least one teacher of distinction.* It is probable that there were settlements also at places such as Cremona, Pavia, and Milan, whence in any case they were ejected in 1225.

Benjamin's account of conditions in North Italy, where he spent only a short while, is thus inadequate. There were probably other communities, besides these, which he did not enumerate; indeed, no major center of commerce is likely to have failed to attract settlers. On the other hand, it is hardly possible that any nucleus of real importance, whether intellectually, economically or numerically, can have escaped mention in his account or some other record of the period. One is justified in concluding that, at this time, the Jewish population of the cities of the north, where Italian Jewish history was afterwards centered and where it was to attain its highest zenith of achievement, was as yet sparse.

Rome was the major attraction in Italy for the Jewish, as for the Christian, pilgrim. Here the traveller found no

---

* These details are from the responsa of R. Eliezer ben Joel ha-Levi of Cologne (c. 1160–1235); R. Isaac *Or Zarua* of Vienna (c. 1180–1260) is another source of information regarding rabbinic scholars of northern Italy at this time, which supplements what we know from secular sources. The reader may find it useful to look up the articles on all these places in the current works of reference.

fewer than two hundred Jewish families, implying at least 1,000 souls — probably some 2% of the total population. Their condition did not seem in Benjamin's eyes to leave much to be desired. They paid no special taxes and were generally honored; they were, moreover, conspicuous for their learning, a certain Rabbi Daniel being the best known scholar and Rabbi Menahem the head of the rabbinical college. Jehiel (grandson of the Rabbi Nathan who was author of the famous talmudical dictionary*) was administrator of the finances of the reigning Pope, Alexander III, who, on the occasion of his state entry in 1165, is recorded to have been greeted jubilantly by the Jews, headed by their rabbis and bearing embroidered banners — a specialty, it seems, of the Jewish craftsmen of the period. But Benjamin had eyes too for the beauties and the monuments of the city, to many of which he managed to attach a Jewish association — for example, the two pillars in St. Peter's, said to have been brought from Solomon's Temple, which, the Roman Jews assured him, ran with sweat year by year on the fast-day which commemorates its destruction.

From Rome, the traveller went by a circuitous route to Otranto, in the "heel" of Italy, where he was to take ship. Not touching Gaeta, where there was a considerable Jewish group, mainly engaged in the dyeing industry, he pushed on to Capua, where he found a community of at least 300,** also, as he informs us, learned and honored. Here he presumably visited the synagogue founded by Samuel ben Hananel (a descendant of Amittai of Oria and controller of the ducal finances in the early part of the eleventh cen-

---

* See pages 90 f.
** I leave it to the reader to decide for himself the vexed question whether he means here 300 souls or families. So far as the north of Italy is concerned, the total is obviously too small in the former case, but in the south it appears exaggerated if the latter is in question. In all probability he was not consistent.

tury), reconstructed not long since by his son and successor, Paltiel. Naples had a community of 500, which probably had maintained its existence without interruption since Roman times. Here, we read in the tenth century of the "Jewish Street" and the synagogue; while a bare dozen years before Benjamin's visit a communal benefactor, named Ahisamekh, had constructed a new synagogue and school. In the next century, the community was to pay about five per cent of the town's taxation, implying perhaps a population of 1,500 out of 30,000. A day's journey to the south lay Salerno, with its medical school and a Jewish population of 600, living mainly in the Jewish quarter (*judaica*) with its wooden houses, which we find mentioned repeatedly from the year 1004 — the oldest specific reference in medieval history to a section of a town reserved for Jewish residents; there is, however, no suggestion of compulsory concentration or of its being walled off from the outside world — the characteristics of the later Ghetto. Shemariah ben Abraham, who had served with distinction in the city's financial administration a generation before, was no doubt dead by now, the leading figure in the community being Rabbi Judah ben Isaac of Siponto.

Thence Benjamin went on to Amalfi, once the rival of Venice and one of the greatest ports of Europe, but now in full decadence; a fact that is reflected in the reduction of its Jewish community to no more than twenty. At Benevento, on the other hand, now under papal rule, there were two hundred, obviously in flourishing circumstances, if at the end of the century no fewer than three parish churches abutted on the Jewish quarter. The next halt was Melfi, the administrative capital of Apulia, where Benjamin found two hundred Jews, at their head being a certain Ahimaaz, perhaps a last survivor of the family so prominent two centuries before. Venosa was by now losing its importance, but it is improbable that the Jewish community, so flourishing not long since, was yet extinct. At Ascoli, there were forty Jews, so significant in commerce that the tolls levied about this time on them, as on their coreligionists in Candela not far off, were considered an important source of revenue. The "heel" of Italy contained a series of ports very active in Levantine trade — especially with Palestine, temporarily in Christian hands. At Trani, "where all the Crusaders gather to go to Jerusalem, for this is the fixed port," Benjamin found two hundred Jews, newly recruited, it is said, by refugees fleeing from the Almoravide persecutions of 1144 in Spain. Here, not long after, there were four synagogues. Taranto, on the border of Calabria, where Greek was still the prevailing language, had a community of three hundred, including many scholars. A document of 1133 refers to them as *affidati*, that is, specially protected non-citizens. Brindisi, a day's journey away, had only ten Jews, dyers by calling. Bari, from which the Torah had once gone forth, now lay in ruins, not having recovered from its total sack at the hands of William the Bad of Sicily in 1156. At Otranto, on the other hand, there was a community of five hundred, obviously attracted by the flourishing trade with the Levant: and it was hence that the traveller set sail.

There were numerous other places in the south of Italy, lying well away from Benjamin's route, where we know Jews to have been living at this time. In Rossano, where a century before Sabbatai Donnolo had been a familiar figure, there was an affluent community whose revenues were worth taking into special consideration; while at Bisignano a special Jewish form of oath had been prescribed in 1150. S. Germano — the later Cassino — had early in the next century a Jewish quarter with its shops, constructed at the expense of the bishop himself and regarded as the property of the famous Benedictine monastery. At Cosenza, where the presence of Jews is attested in the eleventh century,

Entrance to the Former Jewish Quarter in Trani

The Synagogue in Trani, built in 1247
(now the Church of S. Anna)

there was a fresh influx in the twelfth and a new synagogue was built in the thirteenth. An active and industrious colony was to be found in the port of Catanzaro, whither the Jews were invited by the citizens in 1073, with the promise (not destined to be fulfilled) of perpetual rights; and there was another, from 1127 at the latest, at Reggio on the Straits of Messina. At Lecce, too, the city statutes show Jews to have been present in the Norman period. Siponto, an ancient city north of Bari, was the home in the twelfth century of a renowned school of learning, which continued to exist until, in 1256-8, the city was abandoned on account of malaria in favor of the newly-established Manfredonia, named after the ruling sovereign. Candela, Regina, Terlizzi, and so on, also had their nuclei. There had till recently been Jews in Lanciano, in the Abruzzo, who had been driven out in 1156 by the leader of a successful revolt which they had opposed; eighty families were recalled under carefully regulated conditions in 1191. We have seen that in the preceding century a group is reported at Aterno, near Pescara. Mention has been made here only of those places concerning which positive evidence is available. Certainly, many others should be included in this list; for it is highly improbable that Jews were absent from any important city in the south.

On his way home back from the Levant, between 1170 and 1173, Benjamin passed through Sicily. This island had been reconquered for Christianity by the Norman adventurers, Robert and Roger Guiscard, in a series of brilliant campaigns between 1060 and 1090: and from this time we begin to know more about the vicissitudes of its Jewish communities. They continued to show very strongly the influence of the period of Moslem domination. Their synagogues retained the name of *moschea* or *moscheta* (Mosque) and their community was known, as in Spain, by the Arabic name *aljama*, or Assembly (both of these terms were sometimes copied on the adjacent mainland). Many of them had

Arabic names. They long continued to wear Moorish costume. Moorish customs — professional mourners during funerals, bands of music and torchlight processions for marriages — were observed down to the fifteenth century. Even the Arabic language continued to be spoken among them long after the Saracen domination had passed, to the surprise of Jewish visitors from abroad. Late in the thirteenth century, a wandering Spanish scholar, not unaccustomed to a polyglot atmosphere, wrote of them: "But, indeed, most remarkable is what happened to the Jews in all Sicily, who do not speak only Italian or Greek, being the languages of those together with whom they dwell, but have preserved the Arabic tongue, which they learned in former times when the Ishmaelites dwelt there." This linguistic tradition decayed, however, during the course of the following century.

The Arabic influence was still undiminished when, barely a century after the Christian reconquest of the island, Benjamin of Tudela landed at Messina. Here he found a community of 200, living in the midst of such plenty and luxuriance as to amaze even this seasoned traveller, and enjoying the same rights as their neighbors, under a charter of 1129. The vision was outdone when he arrived at Palermo, where he estimated the Jewish population at no fewer than 1,500. Whether it signifies heads or heads of family, this is the largest figure mentioned by Benjamin in relation to any Italian community. Their number had been considerably augmented some twenty years earlier, when Roger II had brought a number of Jews back as prisoners from his expedition of 1147 against Byzantium; and in the following century there was a further immigration from Morocco, the newcomers being allowed to establish their own synagogal organization. We know of Jewish residents, too, at the time of the Norman Conquest at Naso, between Messina and Palermo. There had been twenty-five Jewish families in 1144 at Catania where, five years before Benjamin's visit, the bishop exempted them from special imports and gave them permission to judge internal affairs in accordance with rabbinic law. The Jews of Syracuse (who in 1113 had been preposterously accused of crucifying a ram, in mockery of the Passion!) are known to have submitted a legal problem about this date for the decision of the great Moses Maimonides, who was amazed that he should have been troubled about so elementary a question. At Girgenti, the seat of an old community, the revenues derived from the Jews are mentioned in 1254 as something of old standing.

These are the only places in the island regarding which we have more or less reliable data for the twelfth century. The documents which begin to become exceptionally numerous after the thirteenth testify, however, to the presence of Jews at that time in every city large or small, as well as in the adjacent islands. (In Malta, there were, in 1240, according to an official report, twenty-five Jewish families as against forty-seven Christian, and in Gozzo eight as against two hundred; of course, the majority of the inhabitants were as yet Moslems.) There is every reason to believe that the kingdom of Sicily at this time contained the most numerous, most populous, and most industrious Jewish communities of all Italy. There were also Jews in Sardinia, now under Pisan rule, as there had been in Roman times and as there certainly were in the following century. The island of Corsica, on the other hand, never seems at any time in history to have given hospitality to a Jewish community.

All told, it would appear that the Italian Jews in Benjamin's day may have amounted to as many as 40,000 out of a total population of about 8,000,000. The great majority of them, and all the important communities, were to be found in the south of the country, for which the records extant are amplest by far. The time was not long distant when the picture was to be reversed.

xiii

The Craftsmen

We have seen, in the foregoing few pages, where Jews were to be found when Benjamin of Tudela passed through Italy, in the third quarter of the twelfth century. It remains to be seen — and it is certainly no less important — what they did. For the answer to this question, we are left, as regards some other parts of the world at this time, to rely on conjecture; for Italy, we are fortunate to possess ample and detailed sources of information.

The economic degradation of Jewry had already begun to make headway north of the Alps. In the areas with which we are dealing different conditions obtained, and the process was not felt to any extent. We read as yet little or nothing of Jewish moneylenders, and there is no reason to suspect that they constituted an appreciable element. Merchants on the other hand — in the wide medieval sense of persons engaged in the production, importation and distribution of such commodities as could not be provided locally — were prominent. Even in the intolerant republics of Venice and Genoa, the transactions of Jewish traders and the dues levied on their merchandise are recorded; and it is hardly to be doubted that this was the economic basis of the communities of northern Italy. The earliest papal source after the time of Gregory the Great which mentions individual Jews in Italy is a document of 1255 granting certain Roman Jewish merchants exemption from all tolls in the Patrimony of St. Peter and the kingdom of Sicily — a privilege so welcome that the non-Jewish merchants and citizens of Rome took steps to have it extended to them some weeks later. The Jews of the south of the country had probably been interested in overseas trade ever since Roman times. In the tenth century, they were accustomed to convey their merchandise on vessels belonging to Venetian owners, so as to profit by the concessions that the latter enjoyed at Constantinople; but we have seen that after 962 this was prohibited. On the other hand, it is clear that later on the southern rulers encouraged Jewish traders, their policy being diametrically opposite to that of the jealous northern republics, and it was thus in the harbor towns of their dominions that the largest Jewish communities of the period were to be found. Operations were, of course, on a relatively small scale, and it is probable that the Jews were engaged in every branch of long-shore activity, from ship-owning downwards. Hence they distributed, throughout the region, the various commodities brought from overseas, their agents being generally chosen among their coreligionists, long used to this sort of activity. So great was their importance in trade that in various places, such as Ascoli, the market-dues paid by them were regarded as an important and highly desirable item of revenue, the same being the case in other commercial centers and seaports, at least as far north as Rimini. To be sure, merchants must possess some capital, and must have some competence in handling it; and here and there in the south (for example, at Capua and Salerno) Jews were employed in the financial administration. Yet the part they played in this sort of activity was far from being dominant, or even very important; indeed, when in 1269 the king raised a loan from ten wealthy citizens of Amalfi, only one Jew was of the number. In 1231 the Emperor Frederick authorized the Jews of his dominions in South Italy to lend money at 10% interest, imagining no doubt that they would now follow the example of their German coreligionists, but it does not seem as though there was any response to his invitation. On the other hand, it was no doubt in the capacity of tax-agents that in various places (Bisignano, Salerno, Fondi) the Jews managed the public slaughterhouse, this also having been made by the state a source of profit. That there was a sprinkling of Jewish physicians goes without saying, for the Jews were even then deeply interested in the healing art. Benjamin mentions one who was at the head of the community of Amalfi — by no means the first of a noble succession who distinguished Italian Jewry. Though religious and social causes were now combining to make Jews leave the countryside, they were still found, especially in the south, as landowners and peasants; and there is not infrequent record of the sale of a vineyard or olive-orchard to a Jewish cultivator. Thomas Aquinas was presumably thinking of local conditions when he indicated that Christians were allowed to till land owned by Jews.

More typical was the Jewish interest in handicrafts — especially those requiring special skill. In 1264, we encounter at Genoa a Jewish cheese-maker who, not content with that calling, apprentices himself to learn the secret of soap manufacture. In Salerno, the Jews monopolized not only the dyeing and weaving industries (of which more anon), but also the manufacture of earthenware pottery and of skin-bottles. At Montegiorgio in the Marches of Ancona they engaged in tanning as well as in the linen and woolen industries. In the south, on the other hand, they were associated with two industrial interests in particular — weaving in all its branches, and dyeing: the professions on which, according to Benjamin of Tudela, the communities of Greece and the Byzantine Empire mainly subsisted. Our evidence for this begins only in the tenth century, but the tradition obviously extends far back into the Dark Ages. In Amalfi, the manufacture of silk and woolen brocades and dyed cloths — eagerly sought after, for they were considered to be equal to the finest Venetian weaves — was begun by the Jews in the tenth century, though they lost the monopoly later. At Catanzaro, long an important seat of the industry, they are said to have begun silk-manufacture about 1072. The textile industry was introduced or reintroduced to Palermo by the prisoners, mainly Jews, who were brought back by King Roger from Thebes and other Greek cities in 1147. A great deal more evidence pointing in the same direction might be assembled. The Jewish association with the highly-skilled and laborious craft of dyeing was apparently even more intimate. The Jewish community of Brindisi, according to Benjamin of Tudela, was entirely dependent on it. The proceeds of the "Jews' dye-tax" (*tincta judaeorum*) is recorded at Benevento in the eleventh century, was appropriated by the city treasury at Gaeta in 1129, and is mentioned almost universally as a lucrative and extremely desirable source of revenue in the course of the following few decades. In Sicily too, at Girgenti and elsewhere, the proceeds of the levy from the Jewish dyers is specifically mentioned in various early documents. In the thirteenth century, under the Emperor Frederick, Jews were brought over to the island from Africa and given Crown lands on which to develop plantations of henna and indigo, the plants then used as the basis of the blue and red dye respectively.

So intimate was the association of the Jews of South Italy with these handicrafts that, in 1231, the Emperor Frederick took a memorable step. In modern terms it would be said that he set up a state monopoly over these two branches of activity, the administration of which he entrusted exclusively to Jewish agents. In the summer of that year, he issued letters patent intimating that henceforth all crude silk was to be handled by certain Jewish firms in Trani, each of which was to have the monopoly in a specified area on behalf of the Crown; a maximum rate was fixed for the raw material, now to be sold for the benefit of the Treasury at a minimum profit of one-third on the purchase price, anything received in excess of this being the agents' perquisite. Simultaneously, the Crown took over all the dye-works throughout the kingdom, even in baronial and ecclesiastical domains. Pending the conclusion of new arrangements, all dyeing for the northern region (Terra di Lavoro) was henceforth to be done in Naples or Capua, where two Jews were to reorganize the industry, fix a new scale of charges, and arrange for other establishments to be set up in suitable places. In the Abruzzi, four additional centers were to be organized under the supervision of four reliable Jews, acting in close touch with the others. Though there was some local opposition, both industries, from masters down to operatives, thus became as it were branches of the civil service, working under Jewish technical experts and with the hands largely, if not entirely, recruited among the Jewish population; for it would have been a breach of Canon Law for the unbelievers to be placed in positions of authority over Christians. More than ever, the term "Jew" was quasi-synonymous with "dyer" and "weaver;" though it is obvious that these callings now became less lucrative to those engaged in them than had formerly been the case. On the other hand, the experiment in state socialism must have met with only a qualified success, for ultimately the two industries seem to have reverted to the old system of competitive private enterprise.

Their technical skill and application clearly made the Jews an asset — an asset which was sought after and which could change hands. Hence the revenue derived from them — or, more comprehensively, they themselves, with all potential income — formed a convenient and lucrative gift from a ruler to a subordinate, or baron, or local authority, whom it was desired to gratify. Meanwhile, the theory seems to have been evolved that the Jews, whose toleration was dependent on the sanction of the Church, were to be considered the property of the Church; and in place after place the Jews or the Jewish revenues and the jurisdiction over them — itself a source of profit — were now made over to the bishop or ecclesiastical authorities. The example was set when, shortly after capturing Bari in 1071, Robert Guiscard settled the income deriving from the Jews — obviously very valuable — on his wife Sichelgaita; on his death, in 1085, she and her son Roger made it over to the archbishop. In 1090, those of Salerno, with all the incidental revenues, were conferred on the archbishop of that place by Duke Roger "for the salvation of his mother's soul." The Jewish tithes at Cosenza were settled on the Church by Duke Roger in 1093, those at Otranto about the same date, and those at Rossano (together with certain affluent Hebrews) by the Duchess Adelaide not long after. The jurisdiction and revenues of the community of Reggio were similarly alienated by the Crown in 1127, and about the same time those of Capua and Melfi; the same happened at Trani in 1155, and at Ascoli and Candela under William II (1166–89). The process was introduced into Sicily by Sichelgaita in 1089, when she conferred the fiscal rights over the Jews of Palermo on the archbishop, though reserving five-sixths of the proceeds for herself until her death. By the middle of the twelfth century, a high proportion of the Jews of southern Italy had passed for all essential purposes under the ecclesiastical authority, which exploited them so rigidly that in some places it actually claimed the property of those who died intestate.

It was obvious that the process had gone too far for the welfare of the exchequer as well as for the security of the victims, who found themselves submitted to unremitting pressure to make them abandon their faith. At length, it became necessary to reverse it. In 1195, Henry VI took back into his protection the Jews of Trani, one of the most lucrative of the alienated communities, on the understanding that they paid the archbishop an annual tribute. During the course of the next century, this procedure was repeated elsewhere — especially under the Emperor Frederick, who systematically attempted to restrict the Church's pretensions. Thus the jurisdiction and financial authority over the Jewish communities returned, generally speaking, into the hands of the royal officials. The Church, to be sure, surrendered its rights only reluctantly and persisted in reasserting them at every opportunity, especially when political unrest or royal embarrassment afforded an opening.

A hundred years later, for example, in 1273, the archbishop of Trani was still maintaining extravagant claims over the Jews of his diocese, who had to seek protection from the king; and the question did not by any means end with this. In some places, disputes continued intermittently for another two centuries, down to the last phase of local Jewish life; royal intervention was requisite every now and then; and in practice the Jews often found themselves compelled to pay double taxes to the two eager claimants. But by then their political and economic situation was radically different.

xiv

SCHOLARS AND TRANSLATORS

The remarkable intellectual activity that we have seen in South Italy in the Byzantine period had in due course changed its character and to a considerable extent its scene. From Apulia, the primacy in rabbinic studies, formerly enjoyed by the schools of Bari and Otranto, had passed northwards — particularly to Rome. There is somewhat vague information regarding Roman "sages" and Roman "schools" going back to the ninth century. We know of occasional learned visitors; of the bare names of once-renowned scholars all other details concerning whom are now lacking; of the ambitiously-styled dignitaries who presided over the local academy in 1007; of a composite "Commentary of the Romans," since lost, on various parts of the Talmud; of abstruse inquiries in matters of traditional lore directed to, or transmitted by, the Roman savants. But no single name worthy of permanent record emerges until the middle of the eleventh century, when the Eternal City produced one of the great figures in medieval Jewish intellectual life in Nathan ben Jehiel, of the famous Min ha-

Anavim or Anau* family, which traditionally traced its descent to the Judaean nobility brought to Italy by Titus. Together with two contemporaries — the French commentator Rashi and the Spanish compendist Isaac al-Fasi — he is regarded as the channel through which the key to the complicated talmudic lore was transmitted to later ages, the implement being his great dictionary of post-biblical Hebrew, the *Arukh* (finished in 1101). It is a remarkable work, filled with prodigious erudition, and partaking of the nature of an encyclopaedia as well as of a mere dictionary: with its flashes of philological intuition, its extensive linguistic equipment, its store of oral tradition, its occasional sidelights on folklore, social history and economic life, its industrious amassing of comments and illustrations from a wide literature much of which is now lost. For generations it was the constant companion of the more advanced talmudic student: it exercised a profound influence on the various dictionaries of rabbinic Hebrew and Aramaic produced down to our own day; and it is still to be consulted with interest as well as with profit — a remarkable record for a work of the type which is nearly a thousand years old.

Nathan of Rome was the most prominent, but not the sole, rabbinic scholar of eminence produced by Italian Jewry in his day. There was a famous school of savants, some of whom had studied in the far-famed Mesopotamian academies, at the southern seaport of Siponto; the most noteworthy figures were Anan ben Marinus, a once-famous liturgical poet and casuist of the eleventh century, and Isaac ben Melchizedek, author of a lost commentary on all or part of the Mishnah (the earlier and more strictly legalistic component of the Talmud). At about the same time, Moses ben Halfo presided over the talmudic academy at Bari;

---

* I am using throughout this Hebrew form, preserved for secular purposes too by some branches of the family, as it is impossible to know which of the Italian equivalents — Delli Mansi, Piattelli, Umano, etc. — was applied to any individual in the Middle Ages.

Samuel of Otranto enjoyed great reputation in the world of Jewish learning; and Palermo was graced, as has been told, by Mazliah ibn al-Bazak, who had sat at the feet of the Gaon Hai in Pumbeditha. Nathan of Rome's younger contemporary and fellow townsman, Kalonymus ben Sabbetai, like him a member of a famous family of scholars, enjoyed a reputation as a talmudic expert which extended far beyond the boundaries of Italy, and resulted in the end in his settling at Worms. Another eminent Roman, Menahem ben Solomon, composed in 1139 a diffuse homiletic commentary on the Book of Psalms, known as *Midrash Sekhel Tob* ("Midrash of Good Discernment"), which became very popular; he also, as it seems, first formulated the definitive outline of the liturgy in accordance with what is termed the "Roman" or "Italian" rite as followed by the indigenous communities — differing from both the Spanish (*Sephardi*) and the German (*Ashkenazi*) traditions, though nearer the latter. Pavia seems to have been a seat of talmudic studies in the eleventh century; Verona had, by the end of the twelfth, a flourishing school under Eliezer ben Samuel, who had studied in France and whose opinions were received with deference by his famous contemporaries on the Rhineland; and there were scholars at Ferrara, Pesaro, Cesena and elsewhere in the region about the same time. It was, indeed, mainly the talmudic and associated legal disciplines that engrossed the interests of Italian Jewry; so much so that the great Spanish savant, Abraham ibn Ezra, who traversed the country industriously between 1140 and 1146 from north to south, sneered that some of them could hardly make out the meaning of a simple biblical passage.

But the most significant aspect of Jewish intellectual life in South Italy was of a completely different type. Here, where the Latin, the Italian, the Byzantine, the Moslem and the Jewish influences intermingled, there was at this period a remarkable intellectual ferment. No land — not even Spain — was better fitted to transmit to renascent

Europe both the heritage of antiquity and the great contemporary Islamic culture. From Roger II whose cosmopolitan court produced a brilliant circle of savants, the process was stimulated by a succession of rulers who, though of warring dynasties, were all particularly alive to the new intellectual currents. In this work, as has often been told, Jews played an important part — not only because of their natural acumen, but also because of the wide linguistic knowledge which enabled them to render those works in which interest was now reawakening from one language to another, especially from the Arabic, sometimes *via* Hebrew, to the Latin. In the versions made direct from the Greek they were obviously less qualified to participate. The legendary participation of the Jews in the great medical school of Salerno, to which reference has already been made in these pages, symbolized a process which made itself felt in every intellectual field. It is significant that this city now attracted Jewish scholars with interests as diverse as Solomon Parhon, a Spaniard by birth and pupil of Abraham ibn Ezra, who completed there, in 1160, a long-famous biblical lexicon known as the *Mahberet ha-Arukh*; or, later on, Faraj (Ferragut) ben Solomon of Girgenti, author of a commentary on Maimonides' *Guide to the Perplexed* and of a handbook of religious controversy.

It was above all under the brilliant Frederick, *stupor mundi* ("the world's wonder"), King of Sicily and Apulia, as well as Holy Roman Emperor, that the process attained its fullest development, partly as a result of the intense personal interest that he took in it. It was not only that various Jewish translators were in his employment and in receipt of regular payment for the work they did, but that he was himself in correspondence or personal communication with them on matters of common interest. At his invitation, for example, Jacob Anatoli of Marseilles settled in Naples, where in 1224 he had established a university at which, it is said, Hebrew lectures were at one time given. Anatoli translated the most important philosophical writings of the great Arab thinker Averroes into Hebrew, the standard medieval Latin version being perhaps made from this; in addition, he was responsible for the translation of various Arabic astronomical works. Of his personal relations with the great emperor, there is a curious relic in a volume of philosophical discourses in Hebrew, in which he gives a number of allegorical suggestions — e. g., on the significance of sacrifice — which he received, he says, from "Our Lord, the great King, Emperor Frederick (may he live!)" He also cites with respect a Christian sage with whom he had been on friendly terms, and who is probably to be identified with that almost legendary figure of medieval lore, Michael Scot.

Frederick's wide intellectual interests were inherited by his successor in his Italian possessions, his ill-fated son Manfred (after whom Manfredonia was named) — himself, it seems, a student of Hebrew. Under his direction, too, a number of renderings from Hebrew and Arabic were prepared — among them the famous pseudo-Aristotelian dialogue, *The Book of the Apple*, which was translated from the former tongue under his supervision, and perhaps with his immediate collaboration.

On Manfred's overthrow, the rulers of the house of Anjou, who combined with their eager and sometimes fanatical devotion to the Church a remarkable intellectual alertness and curiosity, renewed the tradition. Charles of Anjou worked on a highly systematic basis, employing more than one professional Jewish translator. The most industrious of these was the Faraj of Girgenti, already mentioned, who is referred to as a member of the royal household. His *magnum opus*, in every sense, was a rendering of the great medical work of Rhazes, known as the *Liber Continens* — one of the most bulky and most famous of all medieval compositions, which had been received by Charles as a personal gift from the king of Tunis. The illuminations in the definitive copy of Faraj's version show him engaged in the work on behalf of his royal patron and handing him the result of his labors. In the Angevin registers many payments made him for his translations are recorded; and when his native city rebelled in 1269, he and his brothers were exonerated, since at the time of the revolt they had been at court in the king's service. He also served as expert in Jewish matters, being, for example, ordered to examine the qualifications of a synagogal functionary to whom Charles wished to give an appointment at Palermo. Another Jew in the service of the court at this time was Moses of Palermo, who received instruction in Latin at the king's expense, so as to be able to translate various Arabic works assembled in the royal library at Naples. He was responsible for rendering into Latin a treatise on the diseases of horses, ascribed to Hippocrates — one of the earliest compositions of the sort to become current in Europe, and the basis of almost all equine veterinary treatment down to the end of the sixteenth century. Meanwhile, in Capua, the Jew Samuel ben Jacob translated from the Arabic the most popular of all medieval books of remedies, which goes by the name of *Mesue*, into the Hebrew version from which it was rendered into Latin. His fellow townsman, the convert Johannes, rendered into the same language the famous *Kalila and Dimna*, source of a great part of the folk-stories of the Middle Ages and fairy tales of modern times; while he collaborated with a Paduan physician in a translation of Avenzoar's *Aid to Health*, another great medical classic of former days.

Robert of Anjou, king of Naples from 1309 to 1343, not only continued the tradition of his house, but was even interested in Hebrew scholarship for its own sake. He is, indeed, said to have studied the entire Bible in the original under the guidance of one of the Jewish scholars in his employment, Judah Romano, known as Leone de Ser Daniel.*

---

* See for him below, page 148.

It was on his commission that Kalonymus ben Kalonymus of Arles, called in the records "the Jew Callo," translated various works of Averroes and others, being brought from the Provence to Italy to continue his labors. He had the run of the royal library, mentions various books which he found there, and refers to his master as a second Solomon. Another illustrious Jewish scholar who worked under Robert's auspices was Shemariah ben Elijah Ikriti of Rome, who had been brought up at Negroponte in Crete. He also was at one time engaged in the work of translation — presumably from the Greek, with which language he was familiar. But his *magnum opus* was a philosophical commentary on the Bible, of enormous bulk, carried out at the Neapolitan court and under the king's auspices, if not on his commission, and dedicated to him in extravagant language. Subsequently, Shemariah voyaged to Spain, hoping to bring about a reconciliation between the Jews and the Karaite sectaries; but his naive hopes seem to have been exaggerated into a claim for Messianic honor, and he died in prison.*

It was on work of this sort that the earlier stage of the great revival of learning, or "Latin" renaissance, which produced its finest flower in Dante, was in great part based; and the participation of the Jews in this vital movement, in Italy and elsewhere, is one of their abiding contributions to the development of European culture.

XV

SOUTHERN TWILIGHT

In the year 1215, a delegation of Jewish notables from southern France made its appearance in Italy. The Fourth Lateran Council had been summoned to meet by the high-

---

* The records introduce us also to a few other translators, such as the ex-Jew known as Paulus Neofidus, who assisted the Dominicans Niccolo da Adria and Guido da Cipro in their versions from the Arabic.

minded and devoted, but not for that reason less fanatical, Pope Innocent III, in order to consider measures to halt the menacing growth of heresy. Already, there had been a foretaste of what might be expected. Towards the end of the eleventh century, Pope Gregory VII had re-enacted, together with other provisions, the old law that Jews might in no circumstances be placed in a position of authority over Christians. More recently, the Third Lateran Council of 1178–9, scared by the advance of Albigensianism, had again prohibited Jews to have Christians in their service or Christians to enter into the employment of Jews even as nurses or midwives, and even forbade true believers to lodge among the infidel. The Council of 1215, however, was flushed with recent triumph in the great struggle against heresy in the south of France, and was clearly likely to go even farther; and in view of this the Provençal communities decided to send a delegation to Rome — not, one may be sure, empty-handed — to see if anything could be done to influence the course of events. But they achieved nothing; and the Council reiterated all the anti-Jewish legislation elaborated centuries before, in the first flush of triumph, by the Church and the early Christian emperors. To this were now added as a corollary some fresh details, such as the obligation on all unbelievers to wear a distinguishing mark and to pay tithes to the Church, as Christians did, on all their property. This code, which became the basis of Jewish persecution in the later Middle Ages, was not immediately carried out — not even so far as is known in Rome, where until a relatively late date the Popes were a good deal more tolerant in practice than in theory. In certain parts of Europe, on the other hand, highly religious or subservient rulers showed themselves tragically compliant. One of the regions in question was southern Italy, where since the beginning of the Norman period the Church had claimed special rights, and where successive rulers, however much they were personally inclined to favor the Jews, found them a useful whipping-boy on which to vindicate their orthodoxy.

This was the case, above all, with the Emperor Frederick II of Hohenstaufen (Holy Roman Emperor 1220–1250; King of Sicily, with Apulia 1197–1250). He was, as has been seen, a man of exceptional culture and breadth of outlook — so much so as to draw suspicion upon him in that generally unenlightened age. He was, however, at loggerheads with the Church, largely because his simultaneous control of Germany and of southern Italy threatened the Pope's temporal possessions from either side. He was suspected moreover — not apparently without reason — of heretical views in matters of religion, and this was a useful weapon for the Popes to brandish against him. He found it absolutely necessary, therefore, to vindicate his orthodoxy in matters which were to him of minor importance; and the Jews were the victims. He favored them personally, protected them against physical molestation, and, as we have seen, was deeply interested in Jewish culture. Nevertheless, he enforced the new Lateran legislation in his Italian dominions, and in 1222 ordered all Jews not only to wear a distinguishing badge of a bluish color in the shape of the Greek letter T (*tau*), but also to grow beards in order to be even more easily distinguishable from non-Jews. It was generations before anything of this sort was generally enforced — the second detail, indeed, proved no more than a momentary exuberance. But it was a premonition of the more extreme reaction that was to follow before long.

In 1265, Pope Clement IV, wishing to rid himself of the menace of the Hohenstaufen in South Italy, induced Charles of Anjou, brother of Louis IX of France, to accept their dominions as a fief of the Church. The conquest, backed with the authority and nominal sanctity of a Crusade, was soon over. In Sicily the new government made itself odious by its exactions and was driven out after the "Sicilian Vespers" of 1282, the island now passing under the house of Aragon. On the mainland, however, the rule of the French dynasty continued for nearly two centuries. Under the Angevin rulers (as they are termed), the influence of the Church in southern Italy increased to a noteworthy extent. Since the new rulers had occupied their realm as a gift of the Papacy, it was natural for them to show particular consideration to ecclesiastical wishes; and generally speaking the lesser church dignitaries were not so discriminating in their religious zeal as the central authority. The ruling house itself was, moreover, inclined to a somewhat unquestioning and primitive piety; it was, indeed, Charles' brother, Louis IX of France (St. Louis), who had recommended a sword driven into the midriff as far as it would go as the best argument to use against a Jew. Hence, from the time of the change of dynasty, there was a change, too, in the atmosphere in which the Jewish communities of the kingdom found themselves. It manifested itself first of all in a greater violence and acerbity in the agitation against Judaism. Neophytes who carried on propaganda against their former coreligionists received special rewards; converts to Christianity found their burden of taxation cancelled or diminished; Dominican friars were subsidized to preach against the Jews in (as they claimed) the Hebrew language. The moving spirit was an apostate from Trani, named Manuforte ("Strong Hand"), who claimed to have been a rabbi before his conversion. This unamiable turncoat secured himself a pension from the revenues of the dye-tax paid by the Jews, procured an edict menacing converts who returned to Judaism with dire penalties, and apparently put pressure on the Jewish communities to compel them to betray penitent apostates. In 1268, the Inquisition was introduced into the kingdom; and though its principal object was the suppression of the heresies that had begun to flourish, backsliding converts also came into its sphere of action. Finally, in 1270, inspired by the example set not long since in France, Manuforte denounced the Talmud and other Jewish literature to the king, on the pretext that it contained blasphemy against Jesus and the Madonna. Orders were forthwith sent to the local authorities throughout the realm, lay and civil, for a search to be made in Jewish homes for copies of the Talmud or even of the liturgy, which were to be sent to Naples. Here, in all probability, they were burned. This episode, though little is known of it, was perhaps responsible in part for the decline of Jewish studies in South Italy at this period. It proved to be the prelude to more drastic action.

In or about 1290, a certain Dominican friar, named Bartolommeo da Capua, prothonotary of the kingdom under Charles II, accused the Jews of Apulia of having put a Christian child to cruel death in imitation and mockery of the Passion of Jesus. This constituted the pretext for the great tragedy. The infidels were given by the king the alternative of embracing Christianity or death.* Large numbers of them fled; thousands accepted baptism; and many more were dragooned into following their example in the succeeding years. The main center of the persecution was Trani, where, according to one account, an outrage deliberately perpetrated on a crucifix by an unscrupulous friar led to a frenzied riot. Thence, the infection spread to Naples, where a grim reminiscence of the methods followed seems to be preserved in the street-name *Via Scannagiudei* ("Kill-the-Jews Street") first found in 1329. From coast to coast there

---

* A Jewish chronicler gives a different story, which is not without a sardonic humor. On his deathbed, he says, Charles I recommended the Jews to his successor, telling him to recompense them for their loyal service. The new ruler could think of no better way of doing so than to secure their eternal felicity! The chronicler goes on to say that they consented to do what was demanded on condition that they were allowed to intermarry with the aristocracy, imagining that this would be refused. Enraged at this impertinence, the king had a lighted candle brought in and ordered them under pain of death to come to a decision before it burned down.

The exact date of these events is unascertainable. There seems to have been a series of onslaughts, beginning in 1290, culminating in 1292-3.

were similar episodes, with devastating results on Jewish life. From the official records, it is known that in the year 1294 no fewer than 1,300 recently-converted Jewish heads of family were exempted from taxation for a period of years as a reward for their apostasy — 310 at Trani, 172 at Taranto, 138 at Naples, 150 at Salerno, 75 at Manfredonia, 72 at Bari, 60 at Aversa, 45 at Capua, and so on — figures which would imply a very considerable total, in addition to those who had perished or had fled to save their lives. Precisely how far the persecution reached is obscure, but the places mentioned extend over the greater part of the kingdom. Everywhere, the synagogues were converted into churches, including four at Trani — one, now S. Anna, still bears the original Hebrew inscription commemorating its construction in 1247 — and the later Church of St. Caterina in Naples.

The precise details of what happened are somewhat vague, and what little is known was rediscovered only recently. But the importance of these events was very great. The old Jewish settlement in South Italy, with its history going back a thousand years and its great contributions to Jewish intellectual life, was so weakened that it ceased for a long time to play any role in history. Its traces were not indeed effaced. Those who had become Christians under stress of violence could not forget their former faith, and, especially in and about Trani, long remained recognizable. For years to come, legislation had to deal with the problem of the "neophytes," who retained their cohesion, their economic interests, and to some extent even their spiritual identity. The *universitas judaeorum* disappears from the records in many cities; but its place is taken by the *universitas neofitorum*, whose origin was notorious. Later on, indeed, as will be seen, the former Jewish communities were reconstituted and new ones set up as the result of subsequent immigration; yet they were never to attain the same significance as their predecessors. Save for the island of Sicily, the ancient, autochthonous, artisan communities of the South lose their importance.

As it happens, this change coincided with the surge of fresh economic currents, which were to result in the formation of new settlements with a completely different background in Upper Italy, where Jewish life was to flourish henceforth with greatest intensity. With the close of the thirteenth century, therefore, our history enters upon a new phase. Hitherto it was principally concerned with the region from Rome southward; henceforth it is principally concerned so far as the mainland is in question, with the region from Rome northward. It is now necessary to turn attention to the new groups that were beginning to emerge and to the circumstances that conditioned them.

CHAPTER IV

The Rise of the Northern Communities

xvi

THE LOAN BANKS

IN classical times and the early Middle Ages, the Jews of Italy, as of Europe generally, had suffered from no explicit economic restrictions, as has already been made clear. They had been farmers, laborers, craftsmen, merchants, artisans, peddlers; and if any occupation were characteristic of them it was wholesale trade on the one hand and certain branches of the textile industry on the other. It was for this reason that they found difficulty in establishing themselves in the great trading and manufacturing cities which were now emerging in the north: for, as was the case beyond the Alps, the inhabitants resented or feared infidel competition. Moreover, the craft guild and the guild merchant, which were now monopolizing industry and commerce respectively, were semi-religious bodies, with spiritual as well as economic functions. They thus had no place for non-Christians; and it was only in those few centers where Jewish craftsmen in some particular branch of activity were to be found in considerable number that they could possibly maintain a guild of their own.

It happens that at this stage a new opening presented itself. Since remote times, there had been some prejudice against the institution of interest. Aristotle insisted that, as money does not breed by any natural process, to extract a profit from it is obviously against nature. Moreover, the

Old Testament, dealing with a close-knit agricultural community, had forbidden the exaction of interest on a loan to a neighbor, presumably meaning thereby a needy neighbor; while, according to the Vulgate version of the New Testament, Jesus enjoined his disciples to lend, expecting nothing (the Greek actually means, "never despairing"). As a result of all this, the Church developed a passionate opposition to the idea of "usury," as it was called, however small the rate might be (the term means simply the charge made for the "use" of money). First it was forbidden to clerics, and then to the laity. The Third Lateran Council in 1179 refused Christian burial to all who followed the heinous calling; and as time went on the attempts to enforce the prohibition became even more determined. The result was not that the practice ended, but rather that it was driven underground. In fact, merchants, princes, even churchmen engaged in it on a vast scale, though as a rule using ingenious fictions and devices to make it appear, on paper, that no interest payment was involved. Nevertheless, open and declared small-scale moneylending was to some extent suppressed.

Ostensibly, this might seem humane and wise. But the problem is not so simple. Most men are sometimes desperately short of money for a time, as the result of illness, or a bad harvest, or domestic misfortune, or some material disappointment. (We need not take into account the merchant who may require a loan in order to engage in some profitable enterprise, or the noble who wishes to anticipate his income for the purpose of building a new house, and cannot expect to use another man's money for the purpose without recompensing him.) To deprive such persons of the opportunity of obtaining the help they need is not humanitarian; indeed, by making the activity illegal, the ecclesiastical policy tended to raise the rate of interest and thereby performed a positive disservice to the poor. It was the presence of the Jews that made the position tolerable. To imagine that they were permitted by the Church to practice usury is incorrect.

They were, in fact, included in the general prohibition, for the offense was considered to be one "against men" as well as "against God." But they could not be touched by the same ecclesiastical penalties which proved superficially effective against Gentile usurers, and the rest followed inevitably. Only one requirement is absolutely essential in a moneylender — that he have money to lend; and of the classes who have money it is the merchant who is most obvious and most accessible to the borrowers. The Jews — or some Jews — had accumulated money during the centuries in which they had been prominent as merchants: and therefore it was to them, among others, that the needy had recourse. Their exclusion from trade becoming more or less effective at this stage, and their exclusion from the soil being now complete, they thus found an outlet for their savings which enabled them to continue to exist. A certain perplexity persisted, indeed, among the casuists over the question, whether according to Canon Law they could be allowed in any circumstances to lend money at usury. Often, initial objections were raised, or qualms would be felt even after the arrangements had been in full swing for some time; and opinions on the subject may be found in various volumes of consultations and correspondence by some of the great Italian theologians of the age, such as Alessandro del Nevo or Panormitano, to mention only two. Later on, the Popes finally settled the question by insisting, in spite of some erudite opposition, that such activities were permissible, provided that an absolution was obtained both for the infidel who lent the money and the local authorities who made the operation possible. Everyone was thus satisfied — the poor man, who was enabled to face his emergency; the city, which found its requirements fulfilled and accumulated a useful profit in the process; the Church, which enjoyed a steady revenue from this source — and for this reason objected vociferously if the legal formalities were neglected — and finally the Jews, who were able to make a living.

The pioneers in this new economic development were the Jews of Rome, who had presumably become accustomed to the manipulation of capital by participation, on however small a scale, in the transmission of the papal revenues from every corner of Christendom, and by their long practice in supplying the needs of pilgrims to the Eternal City and in changing the various currencies brought there. It was no doubt in occupations such as this that the Pierleoni family first accumulated its fortune, and that Rabbi Jehiel had the training which enabled him to become financial administrator for Pope Alexander III. The physician-poet, Benjamin Anau, in a satire written in the early part of the thirteenth century, significantly castigates the luxurious living, the pride and the intolerance of the wealthy families who were at the head of the Roman community in his day. But as yet it is an anachronism to think of the "Jewish moneylender" in Italy. A few individuals who sometimes engaged in this occupation may be traced here and there, but they are exceptional, and St. Thomas Aquinas (who died in 1274) absolved the Italian Jews of any stigma on this account. The characteristic usurers, other than the local merchants and patricians, were rather the Paduans, whom Dante condemns so scathingly in his Inferno; or, more universally, the Tuscans from Sienna, Florence and Lucca. In the thirteenth century, companies of usurers from this region were to be found in economically backward areas all over Italy. Hence they extended their operations beyond the Alps, especially to England and France, where the activities of these "Lombards," as they were generically called, became notorious. These foreign operations, which were extremely lucrative and on an enormous scale, proved a powerful counter-attraction to the Italian usurers, who tended to abandon their petty activity in decadent Italian cities and flock across the Alps, either on their own account or on that of great firms like the Bardi of Florence, whose trade in cloth proved a convenient cover for the unorthodoxy of their finance. Thus, from about the middle of the thirteenth century, the lesser field was left open for the much maligned infidel.

Wealthy Jews now began to push out from Rome into the surrounding territory to fill the economic gap. Cities throughout central and northern Italy, finding that the Canon Law had made conditions desperate for the poor, and that the secret usurers were developing into an intolerable burden, entered one after the other into negotiations with groups of Jews and invited them to come and open their loan-banks — we would today call them "pawnbroking establishments." A civic Jewish loan-banker became nearly as universal a figure in many regions as the civic physician or schoolteacher, and enjoyed very much the same status. Very careful conditions, known as the *condotta*, or "conduct," would be laid down, as in the analogous cases, in a document solemnly ratified by both sides. And in one place after the other the settlement of these financiers and the formulation of their *condotta* proved to be the origin of a new Jewish settlement and the kernel of a new Jewish community, which in subsequent days sometimes attained great fame. It was to this process that Jewish history in northern Italy, beyond Rome, owed its regeneration after the eclipse that had come about in the Dark Ages.

The *condotta* regulated the affairs and activities of the loan-bankers in minute detail. The precise arrangements differed considerably from place to place, but the general lines were on the whole much the same. It was invariably for a term of years — usually three, five, seven or ten, but exceptionally as many as twelve or even twenty. On its conclusion it was generally renewed with such modifications as experience had shown to be desirable; though sometimes the monopoly would be ended and a competitive element introduced by granting a second concession to another loan-banker. In case the original concessionaire died or transferred himself elsewhere, a representative of the commune would be commissioned to visit various centers of Jewish population and find someone to fill the vacancy. In return for the concession, the loan-banker would pay a considerable amount outright or a fixed charge year by year, or else would agree to lend the city or the local potentate a certain sum free of interest when called upon, the latter becoming in effect a sleeping partner. The Jews were, indeed, supposed to be exempt from all other taxes, but this was not always scrupulously obeyed, such exploitation obviously helping to keep up the rate of interest. The amount of the capital to be put into the business was frequently specified — e. g., 3,000 ducats when the bank was opened in Fano in 1439, or 5,000 at Urbino in 1464. It was regarded as an institution for the public utility; hence, so long as funds were available and adequate security forthcoming, all requests for loans had to be met. The objects taken in pledge were to be kept for a stipulated period — generally a year or eighteen months. After this, they were to be disposed of by public auction. Any surplus over the amount due had to be returned to the borrower; but if, on the other hand, there was a deficit, the banker had to bear the loss, so that it was very much to his interest to be conservative in his estimate, however much his clients reviled him for it.

A register had to be kept containing full details of all transactions. A number of these, replete with interesting economic details, have been preserved to our own day — some in Hebrew, some in Italian, as in the end became obligatory. It was plainly necessary for the financiers to be expert universal valuers, for all manner of objects might be brought to them from time to time — from the household utensils of the penurious housewife to the rich clothing of the patrician, from the precious codices of the embarrassed humanist to the jewelled collar of the merchant who needed capital for a special enterprise. Objects used in Catholic worship were not supposed to be accepted, but an extravagant ecclesiastic might forget this restriction on occasion.

It was part of the banker's obligation to take reasonable precautions so as to keep the objects deposited in good condition — especially the clothing, which had to be shaken and dusted at least twice a year. Sometimes he even contracted to have a cat to keep the mice in check. Persons of standing might borrow also — generally, on less favorable terms — on their note-of-hand, though some centers of finance, such as Florence, cannily forbade this.

The rate of interest was naturally one of the principal problems dealt with in the *condotta*. It varied greatly, being affected by local conditions, physical security, economic circumstances, former experience, and the extent of competition. Generally, it varied between 15 per cent and 25 per cent, or exceptionally as much as 37½ per cent, per annum, which in view of the circumstances is hardly to be considered unconscionable. (In the fourteenth century, the Patriarch of Aquilaea had tried to limit the rate of interest chargeable by Christian usurers to 65 per cent, and in France some of the Florentine financiers charged as much as 266⅔ per cent.*) The rate on small pledges — paid, that is, by the most needy class — was usually higher than it was on larger loans, in view of the greater amount of trouble entailed by the temporary deposit of household goods; but sometimes the reverse was the case, the popular character of the institution being thus maintained. As it was intended for the benefit of the locality, strangers usually had to pay half as much again as natives. The interest was calculated by the month, and in no circumstances could accumulate so as to exceed the value of the pledge. It sometimes happened — though this was irregular — that the Jews acted as straw men for clandestine Christian usurers, who

---

* It may be mentioned, for the sake of comparison, that in some parts of the United States today the legal interest on pledges can rise to as much as 12 per cent monthly, or 144 per cent per annum, while in England that on the smallest loan for the shortest (three-day) period is at the rate of 260 per cent per annum.

advanced them money to carry on their operations. The banks might be in shops or houses, often with their distinctive signs (as "The Lily" at Modena, "The Cow" at Florence, and so on) or else would be set up under an awning at fairs or in the marketplace. Breaches of the regulations on the part of the Jews were punished by imprisonment or fine, sometimes disproportionately, or providentially, large.

On the whole, transactions were on a small scale, and cannot by any stretch of the imagination be designated as "high finance." This was left to the great non-Jewish banking houses which, lending to governments or financing great commercial and industrial enterprises, were saved from coming into direct contact with the human misery for which they were responsible, were rewarded by aristocratic alliances or noble titles, and sometimes in the end joined the ranks of the ruling princes. The nature as well as the scale of the Jews' financial business must be borne constantly in mind. The *banchi* which they controlled were not "banks" in the modern sense of the term. Deposit-banking, in the modern sense, was unknown among them, if only because they lacked in a conspicuous degree the physical security which is the primary requisite of that institution. When the foundations of modern capitalism were laid in the thirteenth century in northern Italy — as when about 1250 paper money was introduced for the first time at Como, or a little later the first modern banking house was established at Genoa — no or virtually no Jews were so far as is known living there and able to participate, whatever romancers may allege. Even letters of exchange, we are informed by a sixteenth-century economist, were unknown among Italian Jews of his day. If a few of them were wealthy, they were not to be mentioned in the same breath as some of their Gentile contemporaries. The Da Pisa family, one of the most affluent of all — of which more will be said later on — is estimated to have commanded in the fifteenth century a combined capital of 100,000 florins all told; Lorenzo de' Medici and his brother left some 250,000 each, while the Roman banker Chigi bequeathed 800,000 to his heirs.

The *condotta* guaranteed the loan-bankers physical protection and the free exercise of their religious rites — for example, the slaughter of animals for food in accordance with Jewish humanitarian requirements. Where necessary, they were authorized to maintain their synagogue and burial-ground. They were not to be compelled to transact business on the Jewish Sabbath and festivals, just as they were not allowed to do so on Christian feast-days. Sometimes, they received a formal grant of citizenship in the place where they took up their residence, though this did not generally signify very much. As moneylending was not a full-time occupation, the financier was often formally empowered to engage in trade. Those who received the concession did not always exercise it. Arrangements were often made with a wealthy financier or group of financiers already operating in some other center or centers — sometimes women as well as men. They would not come in person, but would send a representative to open the new establishment. Later on, when it had proved a success or when it was found that local conditions were favorable, one of the principals might follow. There were thus a few important firms with branches in a large number of places, those at their head being veritable magnates in their day. Thus at the beginning of the fifteenth century a Roman Jew named Angelo (Mordecai) maintained loan-banks, sometimes in partnership with other persons, in at least twelve places in Tuscany and central Italy; while the illustrious family of Da Pisa, with its headquarters in that city and Florence, had banks also in at least six other cities in the Florentine territory. That they filled a function of real importance was generally recognized. "The people are obliged to borrow money daily from the Jews in order to discharge their continuous needs," stated the government of Bologna in an official communication; while that of Florence in an application to the Pope, maintained that a great city such as theirs could not get along without Jews.

The number of persons involved in such activities, directly or indirectly, was considerable. With the principal, or manager, there might come some of his relatives and friends to assist him, all perhaps with their children, as well as a tutor to supervise the education of the latter and probably a ritual slaughterer to prepare meat in accordance with the Jewish prescription and perform other religious functions. Hence, even when one family held the monopoly, there might be the nucleus of an organized community, sometimes solid enough to maintain a proper synagogue and to purchase a burial-place. We know of one fifteenth-century instance when a banker's household comprised thirty-three persons. A large city, indeed, gave scope to a relatively large number of establishments — perhaps a dozen or more. In such cases the granting of a concession to the loan-bankers was tantamount to authorizing a synagogue.

But this was only the beginning. Hitherto, the Jew had, as a rule, been excluded from, or at least not welcomed in, most of the places in question on purely religious grounds. There are traces of settlements here and there, but they must have been small and precarious, and in any case left no permanent mark. But, once the objection was waived in the case of the loan-bankers, it was illogical to maintain it in the case of others. Nothing can show more clearly that the former policy of exclusion, however much justified by religious argument, was in fact motivated by a narrow economic jealousy. Hence the loan-bankers, as it were, opened the flood-gate for a Jewish settlement in which the widest variety of callings were represented. There were of course merchants, dealing above all with commodities such as furs, skins, or paper, from other lands — Germany, Spain, Africa, the Levant; indeed, the loan-bankers' *condotta* sometimes specifically permitted them to buy and sell whatever they pleased and to import merchandise free of toll. It is unlikely that Fermo, in the Marches of Ancona, was the only city where the Jews participated in the August fairs, as they were expressly permitted to do in 1331, or where, as was specified in 1310, Jewish merchants were allowed to come without any formality for business for periods of ten days at the time; while Parma was certainly not alone in stipulating that it was permissible for the Jews to follow any liberal craft on the payment of an annual tax. Above all, the Jews dealt in cloth, sometimes of their own manufacture. It is significant that in 1442 a Roman landlord arranged with his Jewish tenant to pay the rent in Cremona weave, and a hundred years later the Jewish and Christian manufacturers here came to an amicable arrangement regarding the weaving of Romanesque cloth. Opposition continued in some quarters against the activities of the Jewish merchants, sometimes successfully; but it was in practice found impossible to prevent them from doing business at least in second-hand commodities, which meant at that time a great deal more than it does in these days of mass production. Objection was raised even to this in some places, but it was ineffective, and in certain cities there were guilds of Jewish old-clothes men as early as the fifteenth century. Peddling too, both in the towns and in the countryside, was common; thus at Casalmaggiore in Lombardy, and the vicinity, the Jewish women were accustomed to go about the fairs and markets to dispose of their wares without an escort, greatly to the distress of some moralists. Dealing in precious stones — a useful subsidiary of pawnbroking — was a traditional Jewish occupation, and gem merchants were numerous, some of them going as far afield as Egypt and Palestine for purposes of trade. The outstanding liberal profession was of course medicine. There is hardly any Italian city that has not a long and honorable record of Jewish practitioners, many of whom received official appointments under a *condotta* of their own as communal physicians. At Rome, in the course of the fifteenth century, at least fifteen are recorded as being in the papal service; in Florence, between 1440 and 1490, there were nearly twenty; and the roll is by no means complete.

Of the handicrafts, the most general was tailoring, sometimes combined with the reconditioning of second-hand clothes. This had always been common in Rome, where a Jewish tailors' guild existed probably from the fifteenth century. A professional census which was taken here in 1527 — unfortunately, unique of its kind — shows that 44 Jewish householders out of the 104 whose callings are indicated were engaged in various branches of the clothing industry. Goldsmiths and silversmiths were also found universally. Scattered documents and references indicate in addition the most varied pursuits — paper-makers, booksellers (even of Latin theological works), manufacturers of gunpowder, makers of playing-cards, printers, tavern-keepers, and even musicians and dancing-masters. The loan-bankers dominate the political scene, so far as the Jews were concerned; below them there begins to emerge a throbbing, eager, and kaleidoscopically varied Jewish proletariat.

In consequence, the economic distress which necessitated the invitation to Jewish loan-bankers to open a money-lending establishment finally resulted, in place after place in central and northern Italy, in the establishment of Jewish communities, with a far wider economic basis, which sometimes attained considerable numerical strength and great importance in the Jewish world. For some time, indeed, the financiers remained the principal figures, with their great wealth, their contacts with the ruling classes, their numerous dependents, their widespread connections, their leisure for study, and the lavish patronage of letters which resulted from this. The code which specified the rights and the duties of the Jewish communities as such sometimes went long afterwards by the name "Regulations for the Jewish Bankers," this being the most affluent and important section; and in some places the management of the communal affairs was vested entirely in their hands, other elements existing only on sufferance, or else enjoying only limited rights. From the middle of the sixteenth century, with the change in political as well as economic circumstances, this class lost its prominence. Nevertheless, here and there the maintenance of loan-banks for the benefit of the poor — now no more than mere pawnbroking establishments — remained a general obligation of the Jewish community and a condition of its toleration.

The process was assisted by the curious political mosaic in North Italy at this period, city republics, oligarchies and absolute states jostling one another in a bewildering fashion, and not infrequently changing complexion from year to year. By and large, it is possible to say that the republics tended to look upon the Jews with disfavor, and if economic circumstances compelled their admission it was usually not for long. The absolute rulers, less swayed by religious fanaticism and more objective in their political outlook, were more tolerant, and the ubiquitous, versatile, experienced Jewish banker was often a welcome figure for his own sake at their courts. Hence the curious phenomenon that the Jewish communities flourished least where the old city-republics retained their vitality, and that an absolutist revolution might be followed by the establishment of a Jewish community, while a democratic one would be succeeded sometimes by its destruction. It must, however, be added that "democracy" at this period is only relative, and that the ordinary city-state, at its most liberal, was generally governed by an oligarchic mercantile clique — a fact which partially explains its policy.

At the outset, the new communities which were thus set up were of no great numerical importance. In the fourteenth century it is doubtful whether any of them exceeded two or three hundred souls. Smaller cities probably had difficulty in assembling the quorum of ten adult males for public prayer; while in many places the single family which operated the loan-bank had recourse for religious requirements to one of the neighboring towns, business being suspended during the holy day season for as long as two or three weeks on end. Later on, with the widening of economic opportunity and the immigration which followed expulsions elsewhere, the Jewish population increased; but the Italian communities at no time reached figures even remotely comparable with the great agglomerations of other lands and ages, even Rome having, in 1527, only 285 families, or some 1,500 souls — a small figure whether relatively or absolutely.

It is in the last quarter of the thirteenth century — coinciding, significantly enough, with the great assault made on Christian usury at the Church Council held at Lyons in 1274 — that the new communities began to make their appearance in central and northern Italy, those in the south being somewhat later. The earliest *condotta* preserved relates to Matelica, in Umbria, where two Roman Jews opened a loan-bank in 1287, thus replacing the Florentine usurers who had previously worked there. In 1292, a similar contract was entered into at Todi, not far off. From now on almost every city of any consequence in this region acquired its Jewish settlement. At the same time, the process started in the Marches of Ancona, where in the course of the fourteenth century upwards of twenty-seven places made arrangements with Jewish loan-bankers. Thence they spread into the adjacent areas, some going southwards into the kingdom of Naples to revive or reinforce the old artisan communities. The names of these places now begin to figure in literary history as the homes of rabbis and poets and copyists, to whom we owe large numbers of precious Hebrew codices.

Meanwhile, a second tide of migration had begun. Across the Alps, above all in Germany and the Rhineland, the economic forces that had driven the Jews into moneylending had made themselves felt somewhat earlier, and were stimulated by the almost continuous persecutions which made it desirable for them to have their property in an easily portable form. These tragic happenings moreover sent wave after wave of refugees across the Alps into Italy in search of peace and quiet, bringing with them sometimes their accumulated capital and an aptitude gained by experience. These performed in the northern cities the same functions that the wealthy Jews of Rome did in those of the central regions. We find them at Cremona in 1278, at Udine in 1287, at Treviso in 1294, at Cividale in 1296. The massacres at the time of the Black Death intensified the emigration, so that in the course of the fourteenth century their colonies spread throughout Lombardy, Venetia, Istria and so on. By the end of the century this region began to reach the saturation-point, and they now pressed southwards, intermingling in the Po valley with the native stream originating in Rome, which had founded colonies at Padua in 1369, at Montagnana in 1383, and at Este six years later. From about the year 1400, loan-bankers of German origin figure in the first-named city by the side of their indigenous coreligionists, and before long they all but dominate the settlement.

Italian Jewry was now beginning to assume, from the geographical point of view, its modern physiognomy.

xvii

THE NEW COMMUNITIES

The foregoing pages have described, in general lines, the process which introduced the Jews to Upper Italy and was responsible for the origin of a majority of the communities (the one outstanding exception being Rome) with which Italian Jewish history was subsequently to be most intimately associated. It may be said that during this period there was hardly a place of importance in the northern half of the peninsula which did not thus receive a Jewish settlement, though not all retained them. To a limited extent, the same was true even of the kingdom of Naples, which now began to recover from the blow of the forced conversion of 1290. Having given the general picture in its broad outline, it is now desirable — even at the cost of a certain amount of repetition — to fill in the details, so far as some of the most important centers are concerned.

One of the most flourishing cities in central Italy was the seaport of Ancona, on the Adriatic coast. In this neighborhood, as has been mentioned above, Jews had been settled on the land in the tenth century. The earliest actual document referring to the Jews of the city, however, dates from 1279, being a hymn composed for recital in the local synagogue on the occasion of the destructive earthquake of that year; apparently therefore a community existed even earlier. From the beginning of the fourteenth century the names of numerous Jewish savants are associated with the city and the community became the second in importance of the entire region, being surpassed only by that of Rome. In 1348, the native element is said to have been reinforced by a number of refugees from the terrible persecutions that raged in Germany at the time of the Black Death. Though not much is known about the activities of the local Jewish financiers until somewhat later, there is little doubt that they constituted the backbone of the community; and, indeed, Ancona is to be reckoned together with Rome as the center from which the loan-bankers expanded throughout the vicinity.

The entire coastal strip around this port, known as the Marches of Ancona, also became the seat of flourishing communities, some of which played a significant part in subsequent Italian Jewish history. Among the oldest was the seaport of Fano, where Jews lived at least as early as 1214 and where, by 1332, the loan-bankers were so solidly established and so prosperous that they could lend the lord of the city, Galeotto Malatesta, 1,000 ducats to help in the acquisition of the fortress of S. Sepolcro. When heretics were expelled by the zealous townsfolk in 1367, the Jews were expressly exempted; and the town continues to be mentioned frequently in Jewish literature. In Senigallia Jews settled not later than the first half of the fifteenth century, attracted not only by its port but also by its famous fair which gave lucrative opportunities to money-changers. The settlement at Urbino, among the hills some distance inland, dates back to much the same period, a certain scholar known as Master Daniel coming there from Viterbo early in the fourteenth century to trade and to open a loan-bank; at the same time another savant, Solomon d'Urbino, was on cordial terms with Count Frederick. For many years to come, the family of the former dominated the community, and new arrivals who infringed their monopoly had to make a payment to them by way of compensation. During the fifteenth century, nevertheless, other firms established themselves, the number rising ultimately to eight. They found lucrative openings in the luxurious atmosphere of the ducal court; and there was also a sprinkling of physicians and petty traders. To the south of Ancona, the settlement at Recanati, a seat of learning even in the thirteenth century, soon attained some importance in intellectual life. Of the twenty or thirty other places in the Marches where Jewish loan-banks were set up in the course of the fourteenth century, the seaport of Pesaro, also a Jewish center not long after 1200 and destined to be of great importance later on, deserves special mention. Fermo was memorable in the early years of the fourteenth century as a scene of the activity of the poet Immanuel of Rome* who in his old age found hospitality in the house of a wealthy local magnate.

---

* Below, page 143 ff. He had previously apparently been in the service of the Ancona community.

On the other side of the Apennines, to the west, lies the lovely hill-country of Umbria, also nominally under the control of the Church. In city after city of this region, loan-bankers had been summoned from Rome as early as the thirteenth century. The most important center probably was Perugia. The Podestà* had been enjoined in 1279 to expel all Jews from this city — there had therefore been an older settlement — but the sentiment of exclusiveness was modified before long. In 1310, there were five Jewish householders, assessed at 3,000 lire in taxation, and officially considered to be "useful and necessary to the City..., especially when occasion arises to borrow money from them for war or for other purposes"— as indeed happened in the following year, when they had to lend 1,200 florins to the commune. Immanuel of Rome tells an amusing story of a Jewish bookdealer from Toledo whose packages were opened at Perugia, during his absence, by some eager students who copied the precious contents for their own use. In 1381, the number of householders had risen to thirty-three, who were given the rights of citizenship for themselves and their descendants after them.

In Orvieto, famous for its wine and notorious for its feuds, a *condotta* was issued in 1297 for a four-year period, to be renewed for seven in 1301. Two years later, in recognition of their assistance in raising money to relieve the city from the burden of a papal interdict, the Jewish loan-bankers were given citizenship rights, together with new powers to exact their debts, and the privilege of bearing arms. The feelings of gratitude were short-lived, and it was only as a result of the intervention of the lord of the city that these privileges were confirmed in 1351. Nevertheless, later in the fourteenth century, the Orvieto statutes made provision to encourage Jewish as well as other immigrants, exempting them from all taxation for a period of

* = City Governor.

years if they introduced a new industry or practiced a useful calling such as medicine. In 1334 a Jew was sent by the city as ambassador to a sister-state; and several worked for its finances in the fourteenth century. Orvieto attracted, in 1396, a group of immigrants from the nearby city of Viterbo, where there must have been a relatively early settlement, as it was by a financier from this place that the Urbino community had been established half a century before. At Terni we find six households in 1430, paying as a price of their toleration fifteen florins for acquiring a piece of cloth on the occasion of the Easter Monday fair — presumably to serve as a banner, this being a not unusual Jewish obligation. Jews from Spoleto are recorded in 1412, from Assisi in 1441, and from Foligno at about the same period. Although the secular records regarding Norcia, the original home of the prolific and distinguished Norsa family, date only to this time, we know of a Hebrew poet living there a hundred years earlier, presumably not in solitude. At the papal city of Anagni, which produced four Pontiffs in the course of a single century, the Jews had a high prestige, for one of the terms of the Capitulation with Boniface IX in 1399 was that they should continue to enjoy the privileges and dignities of the city as other citizens did.

Thus the Jewish settlements in the States of the Church increased in number, or, to put it in another way, the ancient settlement at Rome expanded until it had planted prosperous offshoots throughout the region. In the sixteenth century, there were in the papal territories (by this time, indeed, somewhat enlarged) upwards of eighty places at which synagogues and established Jewish communities were to be found.

To the north of the Marches of Ancona stretches the region known as the Romagna, where the streams originating from Rome and Germany respectively began to intermingle. The ancient seaport of Rimini, where the Malatestas held magnificent sway, must have received an early settlement, as local financiers were exceptionally active in establishing loan-banks in various places in northern Italy from 1369 onwards. (As we have seen above, Jews were not unknown there in the twelfth century.) At the important inland center of Forlì, a home of Hebrew scholarship from the thirteenth century, the civic statutes of 1359 show the Jews solidly established and engaging in the usual activities; and it became a notable center of Jewish financiers and finance, as was also the case with Cesena, between the two cities last mentioned. Probably the oldest settlement of the neighborhood was Ravenna, where it is possible that the community that had existed in the Dark Ages had never been uprooted. Here, it is recorded, the Emperor Frederick intervened to save a Jew from an unjust exaction as early as 1226 — nearly a quarter of a century before the city was annexed to the papal dominions. It is certain that, under the new rule, the loan-bankers became solidly established in the quarter near the Church of S. Pietro Maggiore; and when in 1441 the city passed under the domination of the republic of Venice, the treaty of surrender provided that, in the general interest of the inhabitants, the Jews should be permitted to remain, lending money at the rate of five denarii for each lira to natives and six to strangers. San Marino, which has maintained its independence among its hills to our own days, knew a Jewish loan-banker from Rimini as early as 1369, and there seems to have been a well established community by 1442 — including a certain woman financier named Anna, who lent money to the republic on her own account. At one point during the fifteenth century a Jew named Saul was accused of organizing a conspiracy against the republic, the information emanating from the Podestà of Montefeltro; the details are unfortunately lacking.

Venice, Queen of the Adriatic, was for a long time particularly intolerant of the Jews, whom she considered dangerous rivals in trade, even excluding them from her ships.

For such a policy to be maintained perpetually was obviously impossible in a mercantile city, and in the eleventh century Jewish traders, whether from the Levant or from Germany, began to make their appearance there for short periods. So far as is known they did not form an organized community. But Venice was not able to escape the economic influences which were making themselves felt elsewhere in Italy. By 1298, the rate of interest charged by the local Christian usurers had grown so crushing that a commission was appointed to inquire into the abuse. The only solution that offered itself was that adopted in other places. At the beginning, traditional prejudice was so strong that the Jews had to carry on their operations from Mestre, the nearest point on the *terra ferma*. The inconveniences were enormous, and in the end the republic was constrained to invite them to set up their loan-banks, three in number, in the city itself, in consideration of an annual payment which ultimately rose to 4,000 ducats. The *condotta* was periodically renewed up to the end of the fourteenth century, when a resurgence of anti-Jewish feeling led to its cancellation. A minor economic crisis automatically followed, no help being available to the poor in case of emergency. Accordingly, a fresh arrangement was hastily concluded with the exiles. In order to save appearances they were not allowed to return to the city itself, but again had to make their headquarters at Mestre, whence they were allowed to come over to Venice for periods not exceeding a fortnight at a time. Meanwhile, Jewish merchants from Venice's newly-acquired possessions in the Levant had also obtained a temporary footing in the city. Thus the Jew was by no means a stranger there, while in her territories both on the mainland and overseas there were flourishing communities. Nevertheless, it was not until the beginning of the sixteenth century, and in consequence of external circumstances, that a permanent settlement among the lagoons was at last legally authorized.

Beyond Venice, the community of Trieste dates its origin to the beginning of the fourteenth century, though there is a spurious document of 949 and an isolated mention of a financial operation by a Jew in 1236. The regulations contained in the civic statutes of 1350 and 1375 were very liberal, the Jews being placed in a position of virtual equality with the other inhabitants; and so much less exacting were they than the Florentines whose place they took that on one occasion, when the debts owed to the latter were reduced by law by one-half and a moratorium on them granted for two years, the Jews were unaffected. Their importance was amply attested by the fact that the official city banker was allotted quarters in the Town Hall. After the city came under the rule of the archdukes of Austria, in 1382, there was a new influx from the north, persons from Strasbourg, Nuremberg, Marburg, Constance, and so on, being mentioned; some Jews thus belonged henceforth to the archduke and some to the city. In the Istrian peninsula, Jews arrived from Germany about 1380 and began to displace the Tuscans from the monopoly they had enjoyed here too for the past century; before long they are found all over the region — at Capodistria (1386), Isola (1420), Pola (1427), Pirano (1483), and elsewhere. At Gorizia, Jews are first mentioned in 1349. In Cividale, a rabbinic court is recorded as having assembled in 1239, but it was thirty-four years later that a community was formed under the protection of the dominant family, the first agreement with loan-bankers dating from 1321; while from 1296 Jews are found in Udine, where, however, the earliest *condotta* preserved is of 1348. At Treviso, where Jews had been present in the Dark Ages and the first traces of a new settlement date to 1294, there were five loan-banks by 1398, when, contrary to the terms of the agreement, an annual tax was imposed by the government on them and those of the neighboring township of Ceneda (later renamed Vittorio Veneto). Trent, a sovereign bishopric throughout this period, received a settlement in the first half of the fourteenth century, governed by special episcopal ordinances and employed by the bishop for his personal affairs.

At Padua, as at so many other places in northern Italy, Jewish history begins in the second half of the thirteenth century, Jewish scholars now making their first appearance. In the fourteenth century, under the rule of the house of Carrara, the settlement increased, merchants, money-changers, jewellers and second-hand dealers being attracted by the opportunities offered by the brilliant court and the development of the great university. Moneylending here too had formerly been a monopoly in the hands of the Tuscans. But in 1369 the first Jewish loan-banks, which also engaged in commercial operations, were opened by two firms from central Italy, to be followed shortly after by a third and fourth. At the beginning of the fifteenth century competitors of German origin began to make their appearance, this being the first city in the valley of the Po reached by this element. With the fall of the Carrara and the beginning of Venetian rule in 1405, their position deteriorated and they lost the right of citizenship. But the central government (*La Serenissima*) was unwilling to forego the 850 ducats which they paid yearly as the price of their toleration, and safeguarded their fundamental rights, so that their prosperity was not greatly affected. Ten years later, when the Jews closed their loan-banks as a protest against the reduction of the legal rate of interest — the first of a series of shut-down strikes — the students led the protest; it was indeed officially held that "the city is unable to exist without moneylenders, especially because of the university." Padua naturally offered lucrative opportunities also to persons who followed other callings, and as early as 1448 there was in the city an organized guild of Jewish ragmen and secondhand dealers (*strazzaiuoli*) — the earliest such association of which we know. After their establishment in the city, we find the Jews beginning to open up establishments in the surrounding countryside, as, for instance, at Montagnana (1383), and Este (1389).

The date of the re-establishment of the community of Bologna, after the expulsion of 1171, is unknown. From the beginning of the fourteenth century it seems to have prospered. It is related that in 1308 a learned monk named Aymerich received from it as a "gift" a very ancient copy of the Pentateuch, the origin of which went back to Ezra; and several Hebrew manuscripts written there at this period are known.* In 1394, two brothers from Rome, belonging to the ancient De' Fanciulli family, acquired a synagogue and cemetery for the community. It is probable that they were loan-bankers; for henceforth persons following this calling play the dominant role in the history of Bologna Jewry. In return for the right of maintaining their establishment in the city and its territory, the Jews paid the commune each month four pence on every lira of their profits, this tax being made over in 1412 by the Pope to the Bentivoglio family, who had recently established their ascendancy. They took a natural interest in civic life. The text of the prayer recited in the synagogue during the siege of 1403 is still extant, while at a similar juncture forty years later they assisted in constructing the fortifications. Hence the local authorities were determined that they alone should be allowed to exploit the Jews, whose rights were championed vis-à-vis all other persons, however eminent. The recurrent attempts of the Popes to mulct them were consistently opposed, on the grounds that any additional imposition would harm the entire city, and in 1463 a diplomatic crisis arose, as the result of the illegal imprisonment of a Jew by the bishop, which was settled only through the intervention of the Duke of Milan. Among the recognized

---

* In the Spanish College, there was formerly a fresco depicting the expulsion of the Jews from the city by Cardinal Albornoz, who acquired it for the Holy See in 1360. But their absence must have been brief.

financial burdens was one of an unusual nature at the time, though afterwards a commonplace: at least as early as 1401, it was obligatory on the Jews to contribute 24 lire every year to the students of the university for a special banquet. It must be added that though Bologna followed the example of the other North Italian communities, it retained something of its former economic characterization. As late as the beginning of the sixteenth century, there was a Jewish silk-weavers' guild ("the brothers engaged in the manufacture of silk"), who supported Hebrew scholarship in their corporate capacity. This was the only place in the Papal States, other than Rome, where no formal agreement was made with the loan-bankers, free competition being unimpeded; and in the fifteenth and sixteenth centuries it was probably second in importance only to Rome in Italian Jewish life.

In Lombardy, German immigrants had the field to themselves. Milan, the chief city, seems to have harbored a Jewish settlement in the thirteenth century, but in 1320, at the time of a general assault on heresy, the Podestà was obliged to promise to expel all Jews. Thereafter no permanent community established itself, for any length of time, until the period of the French Revolution. In 1387, however, Giangaleazzo Visconti made an agreement with a group of Jews from Germany to set up their loan-banks in the duchy. They started their operations, not in the capital, but in Pavia, which had been a seat of Jewish settlement in the past. It was now outdone in importance by Cremona, where regulations for the bankers are known as early as 1278. Thereafter, indeed, we hear little about them for some time; but there must have been a considerable immigration if, at the beginning of the fifteenth century, they were said to occupy four streets and the citizens petitioned Bianca Maria Sforza to admit no more, "the city being filled with these unbelievers." This was not only the most important community of the duchy, but also for a long period one of the most famous seats of Jewish learning in Italy, the immigrants introducing the taste for talmudic scholarship which they had developed in their former home on the Rhineland. At the lakeside town of Como they were settled at least as early as 1406 and a loan-bank was set up shortly after. Another important community was that of Lodi, where the Jews are first mentioned in 1420. Also tributary to the dukes of Milan throughout most of this period was the city of Alessandria (*Della Paglia*, or "of the straw," as it was called, after one of its staple products). Here, there was certainly a Jewish colony before the unfriendly regulations of 1457 which forbade the slaughter of animals for food according to the Jewish rite, in a manner anticipatory of modern antisemitism; the record of loan-banking does not, however, begin until the last decade of the century. The revenue derived from the Jews of the duchy was, as is to be imagined, considerable and constantly increasing. Standing at no more than 3,000 lire in 1463, it doubled before long, and in the end was assessed at no less than 20,000.

In Ferrara, the Jewish settlement legendarily goes back to the eleventh century, and eminent scholars lived there in the thirteenth. The earliest reliable information relates to 1275, when a decree was issued guaranteeing protection on the ground of the Jews' utility to the city. The first mention of a loan-bank here is a good deal later, but it is hardly to be doubted that the city knew the institution at a relatively early date. The community soon began to attract attention, for about 1300–1310 several Ferrara Jews, including a physician named Bonaventura, were penalized by the Inquisition, and in 1376 antisemitic verses were written by the court poet Francesco di Vannozzo. In the course of the fifteenth century, the community increased apace, becoming one of the most important and active in all Italy. At Lugo, not far off, and subsequently seat of a highly cultured settlement, a tombstone inscription of 1285 provides us with our earliest evidence, while Cento was apparently, about this time, the home of successive generations of the famous family of scholars and translators who go by the Hebrew name of Meati.* The situation in this area was mainly dependent on the benevolence of the enlightened rulers of the house of Este, who, having purchased a papal authorization to tolerate the Jews, imposed their will on the cities subject to them, the local authorities being able only to regulate the details. Also under their rule at this time were the cities of Modena, where loan-banks were first set up in 1373 by Jews from Fermo, Perugia and Rimini; and Reggio (not to be confused with the city of the same name on the Calabrian coast in the extreme south) now known as Reggio Emilia, where they were summoned in 1413 in order to bridle the "biting usury" exacted by the Christians. Twenty years before, a Jew had been sent thither by the duke of Milan to collect his dues. This was the seat of the activity, in the fifteenth century, of one of the most important financial magnates in Italy — the quarrelsome, capable, tenacious, Jonathan ben Moses Finzi (Zinatan di Moiseto) with his repeated loans to the city government and business interests extending to Parma, Montecchio, Modena, Ferrara and Bologna; the documents regarding him are so numerous that it has been possible to reconstruct his life, vicissitudes and household in elaborate detail.

Rovigo with some neighboring places received a Jewish settlement in 1391, when, with the authorization of the marquis of Este, Jewish financiers were called in to begin their activities, at the same time, it seems, farming the taxes. When in 1484 the Polesine district was acquired by Venice, conditions were unchanged. For a long time, the bank at Rovigo was in the hands of the Consiglio family, with whom the republic renewed its agreement every five years, and around whom the whole community was grouped. As early as the fifteenth century, Jewish capital financed

* See for them page 148 n. Hebrew *Meah* = Latin *Cento* = 100.

the flourishing local woolen industry. Verona, as we have seen, had been the seat of a community as early as the tenth century, and was associated with eminent scholars in the thirteenth. The brilliant court of Cangrande della Scala, at the beginning of the fourteenth century, is described by the poet Immanuel of Rome, who must have been familiar with it; and he indicates that he was not the only Jew there. There was an interlude during which none was to be found in the city itself, though they were not unknown in the outlying villages. Then, in 1408, shortly after the acquisition of the city by Venice, bankers from Germany were invited to begin operations, in order to reduce the extortionate rate of interest charged by the Christian usurers. Other persons, with wider interests, followed at their heels; but in vain, as they were forbidden in 1443 to engage in any other calling than moneylending. In 1498-9 they were banished from the entire province, the Christian usurers entering once again into their own; but the latter proved so rapacious that before long the Jews were invited back. Not far away, Bassano — where a Jewish petty landowner is encountered in 1264 — summoned loan-bankers of German origin, at the beginning of the fourteenth century, to take the place of the Tuscans, who had abused the monopoly which they had formerly enjoyed. Brescia seems to have known Jewish loan-banks from about the time of its acquisition by Venice in 1426.

If there was a Jewish community at Mantua at the time of Abraham ibn Ezra's visit in the twelfth century, it has left no record; but the settlement continued into the fourteenth century, if it is true that on the outbreak of the Black Death in 1348 the Jews were held responsible by the populace, who set about them in bloody riot. However that may be, the numbers involved cannot have been very significant, for no references to them have been found in the civic muniments. At this time, recourse was had for loans, when necessary, to the local patricians, who lent money at ostensible rates varying between 20 and 30 per cent. A sequence of war, plague and famine in the second half of the fourteenth century increased the public need. About 1369, therefore, an agreement was entered into with a company composed of two Jews, one from Forlì and one from Padua, for opening a loan-bank; shortly after, another was established, provided with capital from Rimini, Bologna, Padua, and Forlì, and managed by the partner who hailed from the last-named place. Later on, German financiers also joined in the operations. By 1428, there were in Mantua seven loan-banks operated by eleven families, six of them being of Italian origin, four German, and one French. The earliest mention of a synagogue and cemetery — and therefore an established Jewish community — is in 1420. Later, merchants and so on — especially traders in textiles — took advantage of the new opening in such numbers that in 1477 the consuls of the merchant guild protested to the reigning marquess. Notwithstanding this, in 1482, he gave a fifty-year concession to a number of Jewish merchants, divided into four groups, to traffic in his dominions. This element now steadily increased in importance. Henceforth there existed in Mantua two parallel organizations — the Corporation of Jewish Bankers, on the one hand, and the Generality (*università*) of the Jews, on the other; the former, however, contributing as they did the majority of the revenue, continued to claim exclusive control of Jewish affairs.

The date of the origin of the Parma community is unknown. Jews were settled there early in the fourteenth century, for here too it is said that there were riots on the outbreak of the Black Death in 1348. When, in 1449, a general assembly agreed to surrender the city to Francesco Sforza, duke of Milan, one of the conditions was that the existing privileges of the Jews should be maintained and extended to those who should join them later. They were on the whole well treated, and a quarter of a century later were exempted by the duke from the obligation of wearing the Jewish badge. Besides the businessmen, several physicians of note resided here in the fifteenth century, including Master Elias, the duke's personal attendant, who is said to have taught formerly in the medical school of Pavia.

Tuscany, too, was affected by the new economic conditions and fashions. It does not seem as though the trading community which Benjamin of Tudela had found at Pisa had been seriously disturbed in the intervening period. In the thirteenth century, the Jews are mentioned intermittently in the civic legislation as being prohibited to give evidence against Christians, confined to a special quarter, and compelled from as early as 1221 to wear the distinguishing Jewish badge. On the other hand, in 1317, some of them are referred to as having long been Pisan citizens. By this time loan-bankers begin to make their appearance, and we find not only references to their contracts but also various regulations for their activities. From 1317, there is a blank for a number of years, and possibly in the meantime the Jews were expelled. The great plague of 1348, however, left the city impoverished and largely depopulated; and it seems to have been in consequence of this that in 1354 an invitation was issued to the Jews to come and settle in it, under a guarantee of protection and of immunity from all personal obligations. By the end of the century, it is certain that a *condotta* had been granted to a group of Jewish loan-bankers — we know that their houses were sacked with those of other usurers during a riot in 1393. In the fifteenth century, the community reached the pinnacle of prosperity. In 1406, Jehiel, or Vitale, ben Mattathias of San Miniato, a scion of the Roman family De Sinagoga, or Min ha-Keneset, founded a loan-bank in the city with the approval of the newly installed Florentine government. His descendants, famous as the Da Pisa family, were henceforth prominent throughout Italy for their wealth, their learning and their public spirit.

Lucca, formerly so flourishing, was now in decadence,

and the original community had in all probability died out; but early in the fifteenth century a loan-banker from Forlì opened his establishment here. When the penurious Emperor Sigismund passed through the city in 1422, he forced the Jews to disburse 1,000 ducats to him, as heir to the Roman emperors who had subjugated their fathers. This and similar experiences made them disinclined to remain, with the result that, in 1432, their *condotta* was made more attractive, authorizing as much as 33⅓ per cent interest — a rate which nevertheless compared favorably with the 40 per cent which the most moderate of the Christian moneylenders had hitherto charged at their *casane* in the marketplace. The civic conscience was appeased by a Bull of Pope Nicholas V, of 1452, permitting the admission of Jewish usurers, and by an opinion of the great Savonarola to the effect that, while it was not proper for them to invite Jews in order to lend money, Jews who happened to be moneylenders might be admitted without any twinge of remorse. Sienna — the one Italian city which treated the problem of finance with complete frankness, permitting the practice of usury to any person of good repute, provided he was duly licensed — had its Jewish financiers in the thirteenth century, and its synagogue, still standing, is said to go back to the fourteenth. The successive *condotte* entered into here at this time between the Signoria and Jewish loan-bankers, preserved in the state archives, fill a massive volume.

The record of Florence has some particularly interesting features. At the time when the citizens were acquiring notoriety throughout Europe for their rapacity as moneylenders, Jewish financiers and others were piously excluded from within its walls. An occasional traveller or emissary or itinerant physician served to prove the rule here, as in every other place in which exclusion was officially in force; but there was clearly no place for infidel moneylenders in the city which was the center of European finance. In the places subject to Florence, on the other hand, the exclusion was less rigorous, and already in the fourteenth century various communes, such as S. Miniato and S. Gimignano, began to conclude agreements with Jewish financiers with the approval of the central government. Later on, the example was followed by Pescia (1402), Arezzo, Prato (1406), Volterra, Castiglion Fiorentino, Montepulciano, Pistoia, Empoli (1407), and so on. Thus, nearly thirty places in the *contado* had their loan-banks in the end. But in the city, opposition remained strong, and an attempt made in 1393 to introduce Jewish moneylenders met with failure owing to the popular aversion. In 1406, indeed, all moneylending in any part of the Florentine dominion was prohibited under stringent penalties. This turned out to be little more than blackmail. Not only the Jews, but also the communes, protested; and when a liberal gift was offered as an additional persuasion, the embargo was lifted. Before long, a different atmosphere began to prevail in Florence too. For internal purposes, the canonical restrictions in matters of finance had gradually made headway; from the beginning of the fourteenth century, the practice of usury by natives was regulated and finally, at the beginning of the fifteenth, it was forbidden. The invariable problem now presented itself, of how the poor were to raise money in time of stress; and it was solved in the invariable way. The permission of Pope Eugenius IV was solicited and obtained, and on October 17, 1437, an agreement was concluded with a group of Jewish financiers, from San Miniato, Ferrara, Padua, and Bologna, to open a loan-bank in the city; this group being followed before long by others. It is noteworthy that the personal rule of the Medici had just begun; for the change of policy was evidence not only of their personal enlightenment, but also of their policy of gaining the sympathy of the populace, the *popolo minuto*, whatever the moneyed classes might think.

The community rapidly attained an outstanding reputation, reaching the heyday of prosperity under Lorenzo the

Magnificent. It was affected, as we shall see, by the spirit of the Renaissance in its intellectual interests, its extravagant tastes, and its polished way of life. The Jews were unpopular, indeed, with certain elements of the population, who envied their prosperity; but, on the other hand, the aristocracy, following the example of the ruling family, treated them with conspicuous favor. We shall see later how the fortunes of the Florentine Jews waxed and waned according to the prevailing political tendency, until in the sixteenth century their settlement was secured on a durable basis with the final triumph of the house of Medici.

Genoa "the Proud," another great center of international finance and cradle of modern banking, piously maintained its policy of complete exclusion; for the Jews were barely known in Liguria until the sixteenth century.* In turbulent Piedmont, with its confusing medley of petty independent states, constantly at war among themselves, the counts (subsequently dukes) of Savoy were now becoming supreme. In their French-speaking possessions, the Jews had certainly been known in the thirteenth century, and the settlement elsewhere was probably little if at all younger. The Jews of Nizza [Marittima], the present Nice, are mentioned as early as 1357, and owned a cemetery by 1408, by which date they had a special officer or *bailo*, to supervise their affairs. On the Italian side of the Alps, there were old-established communities at Asti, Fossano and Moncalvo, where exiles from France introduced their ancestral rite of prayer — different in many details from the native Italian tradition — which they continued to follow in certain respects, with memorable consistency, for centuries. Since the expulsions from France took place in 1306 and 1394,

---

* This fact makes even less probable the highly romantic, but wholly legendary story of Zaccarias Guizolfi, a Genoese Jew, who is said to have risen to eminence in the colony in the Crimea in the fifteenth century and to have become ultimately the independent ruler of the Taman Peninsula.

it is virtually certain that these communities date back to the fourteenth century; and the same is presumably true of some others in the region, though a reference at Biella, in 1251, is probably apocryphal. In 1430, Duke Amedeo VIII of Savoy issued drastic regulations for the control of the Jewish communities under his rule, in terms which make it certain that they were solidly established. Ten years later, his successor formally empowered the Jews to practice usury, and thereafter an agreement was concluded every ten years authorizing them to live in the duchy in return for an annual tribute of 700 florins. Though they were subjected with exceptional severity to the usual canonical restrictions, they were protected from injustice, and in 1447 certain officials accused of extortion were dismissed. In 1454, an edict of expulsion was issued, but was apparently cancelled before it could be put into execution.

The most important community in the duchy was, as might be expected, that of Turin. Here the Jews were first formally permitted to settle in 1424, the pioneer being a German known as Elias Alamanni (Alamandi), formerly physician to the duke of Burgundy. The origins of the settlement at Vercelli date to 1446, when the city council licensed a Jewish family to open a loan-bank on condition that, when required, they loaned the city the sum of 100 florins, on which no interest was to be charged for the first six months. The earliest settlers apparently hailed from the south, following the Roman ritual, but some generations later the German element became dominant. The Jews were established in Novara before 1448, in Cuneo before 1452 and in Savigliano, seat of an important school of talmudic scholarship at this period, before 1455, when certain Jewish privileges were restored. In the marquisate (subsequently duchy) of Monferrat, with its capital at Casale, there are similarly traces of a Jewish settlement from the close of the fifteenth century, and the same is true of that of Saluzzo, where, it is stated, there was an expulsion from the little township of Piasco at about this time.

Thus the Jews were solidly implanted throughout Italy from the Sicilian waters to the foothills of the Alps, and from the French frontier to the semi-Slavonic at the head of the Adriatic sea.

xviii

Light and Shade

This period of expansion was from some points of view the golden age of Italian Jewish history. In the south, the ruined Jewries were being nursed back into life; in the north, there was steady growth, general prosperity and a ferment of intellectual activity. A flow of immigrants arrived from abroad, new centers were established in almost unbroken succession, the older ones constantly expanded. In their new homes, especially in the little cities of Umbria and the Romagna, the Jews lived in close touch with the people and the countryside, owning and tending their olive-orchards and vineyards, enjoying a high status in the cities, busily engaged in studying Hebrew literature and copying Hebrew works. In France, there was at this time a succession of onslaught followed by expulsion; in Germany, an almost unbroken record of violence, reaching a crescendo at the time of the Black Death; even in Spain, intermittent attacks and steady deterioration culminated with the wave of massacre in 1391. Only in Italy did the Jews enjoy general well-being. A few setbacks are chronicled, but they are isolated and exceptional. If, during civic disturbances, the Jews may sometimes have suffered more than their neighbors, this did not betoken a persecutory spirit among the people. It is perhaps significant that almost the earliest inkling we have of any sort of corporate action among the Italian Jewish communities relates to a conference held at Foligno, at the beginning of the fourteenth century, in order to concert measures for the assistance of the Jews of Germany at a time of persecution. That they enjoyed the status of citizens seems to have been generally recognized, and was sometimes specifically stated; and it not infrequently happened, as we have seen, that their rights were mentioned and guaranteed in negotiations between governments.

Yet no event in the Jewish world or in Italy as a whole could fail to leave its impression. When, as the result of happenings in France, the Talmud was condemned by the Pope in 1239–42, it appears from covert allusions in dirges by the poets of the Anau family that many copies were seized and destroyed in Rome, if not elsewhere in the land. Contemporaries obscurely hint that the Jews again suffered in the course of the disorders later in the thirteenth century, when the city was abandoned to factions. So, too, when a wave of hysterical religiosity spread throughout Italy at the heels of the Flagellants, first attracting notice at Perugia in 1260, it can hardly be doubted that there was fresh reason to tremble. In 1270, the mob desecrated the cemetery in Rome. Clement IV's Bull of 1267, *Turbato corde*, expressing his anxiety over the conversion of Christians to Judaism and ordering the newly appointed inquisitors to take steps against all who were implicated, was not occasioned by conditions in Italy, but nevertheless added a fresh complication to Jewish life there. Nicholas III, in the hopes of weakening their religious allegiance, instituted in 1279 the forced sermons which the Jews had to hear — not, indeed, at this time the utterly intolerable abuse they were afterwards to become. In Lombardy, the task was specifically assigned to the Dominicans — testimony to the growth of Jewish settlements in this area and to the anxiety with which they were regarded by over-nervous ecclesiastics.

Nearly twenty years later, in 1298, during the pontificate of Boniface VIII — the first Pope who is recorded to have poured obloquy on the heads of the Jewish deputation who came to congratulate him at the beginning of his pontificate — Rabbi Elijah de' Pomi was put to death by the Holy Office in Rome on a secret charge. This procedure opened up unlimited possibilities of blackmail, and a Bull was procured excepting the Jews, despite their wealth, from the category of those "powerful persons" who could be denounced anonymously to the inquisitors. It was in consequence of this tragic episode that the ancient De' Pomi family left Rome and settled at Spoleto in Umbria, where it continued to produce eminent scions for many generations.

The most unhappy innovation of the thirteenth century, from many points of view, had been the badge, prescribed by the Lateran Council of 1215, which placed the Jew on the same level as a leper, and his womenfolk on that of prostitutes. It was enforced at the beginning only sporadically and in general terms — in Sicily and Naples for example, as well as Pisa, in 1221. So far as the Papal States were concerned, the obligation was first specifically imposed, so far as is known, in a Bull issued by Pope Alexander IV in 1257. (There is extant a moving penitential hymn written on this occasion by Benjamin Anau, expressing the passionate indignation of the Roman Jews at this humiliation.) For men, it was supposed to take the form of a circular yellow patch, a hand-span in diameter, to be worn in a prominent place on the outer garment; for women, two blue stripes on the veil. Before long, this fell into neglect. But the Council of Ravenna repeated the injunction in 1311, and in 1360 the city statutes of Rome ordered male Jews, except the physicians, to wear a red tabard, and the women a red petticoat. Officials were designated to supervise this; and the populace, too, were enlisted as accomplices, those who denounced offenders being granted one-half of the stipulated fine of eleven soldi. This led to such abuses that, in 1402, fresh regulations were issued making unauthorized interference more difficult, and absolving Jews from the degrading obligation in their own quarter. In Venice and its possessions, the badge was prescribed, in the form of a yellow O, from 1394, to be altered, from 1496, to a yellow hat, which could less easily be concealed. Amedeo VIII introduced it into Savoy in the form of a round patch of red material sewn in front of the outer garment, and another behind the left shoulder. Similar regulations were sporadically issued elsewhere in Italy; and the Jew was often to be recognized, not only by his features and his calling, but also by the unsightly disfigurement of his clothing. Nevertheless, it was not until long after this that the enforcement became general and consistent.

At this period we first hear of another abuse. Every year there took place in Rome, and perhaps other cities — something of the same sort is known to have been customary in Sicily — two mock tournaments: one among the populace in the Circo Agonale (Piazza Navona), the other among the soldiers at the Monte Testaccio, in the course of the bellicose games before Lent. In this horseplay, Jews were originally used as mounts, and the utmost brutality was practiced. In 1312, accordingly, the community agreed to make an annual payment, originally fixed at ten gold florins, to be relieved from this degradation. This, afterwards known as the Tribute of Agone and Testaccio, was the earliest specific levy imposed on the Roman Jews other than the tithe, and the precedent for what afterwards became an utterly intolerable burden. The Jews of the capital, regarding it as a normal tax, attempted to distribute part of the burden among the other communities of the Papal States. It did not prove an easy matter; that of Ancona, one of the wealthiest of all, pleaded poverty, and was threatened with exclusion from the advantages of privileges secured by common action; and we still have the mellifluous letter written on its behalf by the poet Immanuel of Rome begging for a period of grace. The disputes on the subject continued. In the end, in 1421, the Roman community was formally authorized by the Pope to share the burden, now become very considerable, with the communities of the Campagna, Romagna, Lazio, Tuscany, Spoleto and the Marches — all areas which now had flourishing Jewish settlements.

Over a good part of this period, Rome was no longer the papal city. From 1305 to 1378, the Popes avoided the disorders which threatened them in Italy by removing their official residence to Avignon in France, where, too, a very ancient Jewish community lived on under their aegis. The city was thus left deserted, a prey to warring factions; and even after the end of what was termed the "Babylonian Captivity" a schism in the Papacy continued for nearly half a century, until 1417, Rome being the seat of only one of two or more claimants to the Throne of St. Peter. The remoteness of control during the intervening period and the growing local autonomy favored the formation of new communities under semi-independent lords or communes. On the whole, it does not seem that the Jews suffered to any great extent during the interlude. We have, on the other hand, only sporadic glimpses of their life — being granted a protective privilege by "the Roman people in the Parliament of the City" in 1310; sending a deputation with the customary Scroll of the Law to greet the Emperor Henry VII, on the occasion of his state entry in 1312 (a pictorial representation of the scene is extant); doing the same in honor of Lewis the Bavarian in 1328, and contributing 10,000 gold florins to the levy of 30,000 imposed by him on the city — evidence of their reputed wealth; being assigned, in 1354, the task of disposing of the body of the romantic demagogue Cola di Rienzi, their neighbor, whom apparently they had favored. Some while earlier, political conditions had compelled them to send a deputation to Avignon to intercede with Pope John XII and King Robert of Naples, Senator of Rome, on the occasion of some danger that threatened — possibly the papal decree of September 4, 1320, again ordering the burning of the Talmud, with which was to be coupled, according to Jewish legend, a general expulsion from the Papal States. This at least (a scheme of Queen Sancia, misrepresented in the ancient chronicle as being the Pope's sister) was avoided, thanks to enormous gifts of money. But the condemnation of the Jewish sacred writings was unaffected; and on the feast of Pentecost, in 1322, pyres were once more lighted in Rome, and probably elsewhere, for the destruction of copies of the Talmud and the allied literature. In the disorders which accompanied this, the father-in-law of the poet Immanuel of Rome apparently lost his life. It was about this time (1320) that the Jews were expelled from Milan; and though Italy was on the whole unaffected by the universal wave of anti-Jewish violence at the time of the Black Death in 1348–9, the outbreaks against the newly-established communities of Mantua and Parma were perhaps not isolated. The same spirit manifested itself in an episode of 1336 in Cividale, where the Jews were accused of walling up images of the Madonna and crosses — perhaps the debris of some abandoned church — among the building-rubble used in the construction of their new synagogue in the Zugaita, as their street was called. (Is it possible to see in these episodes in the north of the country the baneful Germanic influence?) It is recorded, too, that, when the Ghibellines captured Fermo in 1396, the Jewish dwellings were sacked. But there is little else to recount, other than the steady but monotonous expansion of the area of settlement, the periodical conclusion of new agreements for loan-banks, and the genesis of new communities. Perhaps history may overlook or minimize untoward episodes here and there, and the life of the Italian Jews in this period may not be so carefree as our sources would lead us to believe. But it is obvious that there was until the fifteenth century nothing in the nature of a general reaction.

XIX

The New Literary School

The period with which we have been dealing in the foregoing pages witnessed the emergence in Italy of the new school of poetry — the "sweet new style" — the greatest figures in which were Dante and Petrarch. Jews cannot, of course, be immune from the intellectual currents of their environment, and there was inevitably a parallel movement among them. To some extent, it was occasioned by the process that has just been described — the breaking up of the old centers, with the distribution of their population into smaller fractions in which serious study was in some ways less easy, the influence of the environment more palpable, and potential patrons both more numerous and more approachable; to some extent, it was the result of the somewhat tardy advent to Italy of the new tastes that had developed, under Moslem influence, among the Jews of Spain, very different from the rugged but forceful Italo-German tradition of former days.

The foremost figure to be taken into account — the most gifted, perhaps, in the entire course of Italian Jewish literary history — is Immanuel of Rome, whose career and interests reflect to perfection the spirit of the new era. He was an almost exact contemporary of Dante and a Roman by birth. But he spent a good part of his life in the new settlements in central Italy, probably as teacher or perhaps employee in some business house — among other places at Ancona, where he acted as the literary mouthpiece of the community; at Gubbio in Umbria, with which place he was so closely associated that non-Jews knew him as Manuel da Gubbio; and at Fermo in the Marches. Here he lived for a long while in the household of a wealthy patron of learning — probably one of the new loan-bankers — whom, after the fashion of the time, he extolled as his "Prince." He had a facile pen and wide interests, writing philosophical commentaries on various books of the Bible, a work on the symbolism of the Hebrew alphabet, another on scriptural hermeneutics. But he was essentially a poet, showing a mastery of Hebrew equalled by very few others in the Middle Ages. From the writers of the Spanish school he adopted the rigid meter and the elaborate technique which they had taken over from Arabic; to Italy he owed such details as the sonnet structure which he introduced for the first time, with remarkable success, into Hebrew literature. But the influence of the environment over him was by no means restricted to form. He fell under the spell of its spirit too, showing in his verses not merely a flippant, but a licentious outlook hitherto unknown in Jewish literature, and writing, in addition to hymns, a number of poems of a distinctly erotic tendency. To employ the figure of the greatest of Jewish historians, he dressed up the sober and dignified Hebrew muse in the skirts of a ballet-dancer. His poems of all types — from the devotional down to semi-indecent narrative — are collected together in a work entitled the Compositions of Immanuel (*Mahberot Immanuel*) which has a rough narrative framework after the style popular in the Arabic-speaking world, which was shortly after to attain its highest pitch of perfection at the hands of Boccaccio. The last section, entitled *Tophet and Eden*, is an account of an imaginary visit to Heaven and Hell. Though lacking its elaboration, its polish, its profundity, and its splendor, this is closely modelled on Dante's *Divina Commedia* from the beginning ("When three-score years had slipped my mortal span . . . ") to the end (" . . . with those who aid men's merit, like the stars"). Yet there are some points — as for example its tolerant spirit and the place of honor reserved in Paradise for righteous non-Jews — in which this parergon compares favorably with that greatest of poems.

That Immanuel was acquainted with the *Commedia* is indubitable — was it for this reason that he called his guide through the after-world by the name of Daniel? He shows, indeed, in general a close familiarity with the vernacular literature of the time, the conceptions and sometimes the forms of which he imitates on occasion. He is remembered also as an Italian poet of not insignificant caliber — the father and prototype of the distinguished series of Jews who contributed so valiantly to Italian literature down to our own day. He exchanged sonnets with litterateurs, such as his fellow-townsman Bosone da Gubbio and even the delicate poet and great jurist Cino da Pistoia, who themselves wrote commemorative verses on the occasion of his death. Among his Italian works is also the curious onomatopoeic poem, *Il Bisbidis*, which vividly conveys in a series of word-pictures the feverish atmosphere of the court of Cangrande della Scala, Lord of Verona, where the poet apparently spent some time. It was long maintained that Immanuel was a friend of Dante's, and the phraseology of the sonnets which have been mentioned suggests that they had at least some degree of personal acquaintance. In Italian Jewish literature, Immanuel's is indubitably one of the greatest names. But time was revenged on him for his coarseness. The rabbis frowned upon his poetical work; when it was printed, some of them forbade it to be read; its circulation remained restricted; and it is only in the course of the past generation or so that he has come into his own.

Immanuel's ability and range were such as to overshadow the contemporary poetical school, who were lacking neither in number nor in merit. The most eminent was the physician Benjamin Anau of Rome, who wrote a considerable mass of liturgical poetry, including penitential hymns occasioned by certain outstanding events of his time, which form a precious historical record, and a satirical composition in rhymed prose castigating the wealthy, *Massa Gei Hizzayon* ("The Burden of the Valley of Vision").* The Anau family pro-

---

* Isaiah 22.1.

duced at this period, in addition, a whole school of liturgical poets, all of some ability — Moses, Zedekiah and especially Jehiel, author of an ethical work, *Ma'alot ha-Middot*, which became a popular classic. The *Mahberet ha-Teneh* ("Composition of the Basket"), by Ahitub ben Isaac of Palermo, embodies another vision of the future life which may also be inspired by Dante and sometimes reaches a high imaginative level. Judah Siciliano was also a poet of outstanding genius, if we are to judge from the admiration of his contemporaries, but none of his poems has come down to us. The small cities of central Italy all shared in the productivity — as witness the names of Daniel of Montalcino, the Bible commentator Benjamin of Bozecco, Mattathias of Larippa and Norcia and his son Joseph (author of a hymn in dialogue form between the living and the dead, obviously modelled on *laude* of the school of Fra Jacopone da Todi), Moses of Viterbo, Solomon of Perugia, and Mattathias of Lucignano, all of the 14th century — eloquent testimony to the extension of the Jewish communities and to the intellectual vitality of those who composed them. "Master Callo," or Kalonymus ben Kalonymus, who had been imported from the Provence to carry out translations for King Robert of Naples, lived in Italy for many years as a member of the Roman Jewish poetical and literary circle. It was in their spirit that he composed his talmudic parody entitled *Masechet Purim* ("The Purim Tractate"), complete with elaborate rabbinic arguments, fictitious sages with preposterous names, exaggerated directions for the toping that the festival requires, and sly allusions to current events and personalities. In this no less than in some of Immanuel's verses there is to be seen the spirit of contemporary Italy, unable to take anything seriously for long, parodying innovations almost as soon as they became known, and alternating jeers and prayers with a perplexing rapidity.

Immanuel of Rome's tradition as a vernacular poet did not end with his death. We know of another fourteenth-century Italian Jew, Salamone *ebreo* of Ferrara, whose love-poems were greatly admired at the time, though none of them have come down to us; and thereafter there is a fairly constant succession of writers in prose and verse, though for some while none of outstanding merit. The earliest translations of the prayer book and of the Bible into Italian for the use of the women and the ignorant — as yet written always in Hebrew characters — go back to about the same period; while there is preserved an elegy for synagogal use in Judaeo-Italian, in the dialect of the Marches, which cannot be much after, and may be before, the year 1200, and is of considerable importance to students of Italian literature. The secular influence on this, as well as on some of the compositions mentioned above, is obvious; and it is not difficult to imagine Jews joining the circles which thronged around the wandering ballad-singers in the market place and imitating what they heard for their own religious and domestic purposes.

It was not only in its poetical tastes, but also in its philosophical bent, that Italian Jewry showed its spiritual kinship to the Spanish school. The outstanding figure in the period with which we are dealing was the physician Hillel ben Samuel, a grandson of the great talmudist Eleazar of Verona and therefore misleadingly called Hillel of Verona. A physician who had studied at the great medical school of Montpellier, as well as at the feet of some of the eminent rabbinical authorities in Spain, and was in personal relations with the professors of the University of Bologna, he lived successively in Rome, Capua, Ferrara and Forlì, not only healing the sick but also lecturing on the philosophy of his beloved Maimonides. His principal work, *Tagmule ha-Nefesh* ("The Soul's Rewards"), reviewed the opinions on this subject of the classical, the Arabic and the Jewish writers; and he showed his versatility by translating various scientific works from Latin into Hebrew. Among those of his contemporaries who shared his interests, the most prominent was Isaac ben Mordecai, known as Maestro Gaio, who was in medical attendance on Pope Nicholas IV or Boniface VIII — the first of the long and distinguished series of papal physicians produced by Italian Jewry. An expert no less in Arabic than in European medical methods, he too had various translations of scientific classics executed for his use and had keen philosophical interests as well.* More profound than either of these, if not so prominent at the time, was Immanuel of Rome's cousin, Judah ben Moses ben Daniel, generally known in his day as Leone de Ser Daniel and at the present time as Judah Romano, who, as has been mentioned, taught Hebrew and Bible to King Robert of Naples, and was the first scholar to compare the tongue of Isaiah with that of Cicero. Thoroughly at home in Latin and steeped in the writings of the scholastic philosophers of the day, he naturalized many works which were current among the Christian thinkers by translating them into Hebrew — including even the compositions of paladins of the Church such as Thomas Aquinas and Albertus Magnus. His independent writings, though by no means insignificant, are of minor importance when compared with this courageous and not wholly abortive attempt to create a new philosophical synthesis. Another member of the Roman philosophical circle was the Spaniard Zerahiah ben Shealtiel (surnamed Ḥen), also a physician, who translated various Arabic works into Hebrew and elucidated the Bible on the one hand, and the *Guide to the Perplexed* — the Bible of

---

* Maestro Gaio employed for this purpose Nathan ha-Meati, (i. e., "of Cento"), whose son and grandson after him did a good deal of work of the same nature. Another person who worked along these lines in northern Italy at this period was Master Jacob Bonacosa, who translated Aristotle's *Colliget* from Arabic into Latin in 1255 at Padua — important testimony, incidentally, to the intellectual tradition of that subsequently famous university town. But the translations made for their own use by the Jews in central and northern Italy — largely from Latin into Hebrew — had nothing like the importance of those carried out at the Neapolitan court.

the rationalists — on the other. So interested were the Jews of Rome in Maimonides' writings that they commissioned one of their number, who went to Spain, to search out for them a full copy of the Hebrew version of his *Commentary on the Mishnah*, as yet inaccessible in Italy — a task which occupied two years. It was a tribute no less to the worth of the book than to the intellectual vitality of the community.

In 1289, there arrived in Italy from the Levant a French fanatic named Solomon Petit, who was endeavoring to stir up opposition — if necessary with Gentile support — against Maimonides' philosophical writings and to have them condemned and destroyed, as had already happened in France. The news reached Hillel at Forlì in his old age. Deeply shocked, he threw himself into the fray with commendable but disconcerting vigor. He naively endeavored to summon a rabbinical conference to consider the crisis. He sent out a torrent of communications, impetuous but, to the good fortune of posterity, highly informative, to his old friend and fellow-student Maestro Gaio, imploring him to attempt political action in Rome; but the latter, as befitted his position, was circumspect and non-committal. Two of his sympathizers, however, took energetic steps, obtaining the ear of some person prominent in the Papal Curia — according to the exaggerated report which spread abroad, Pope Nicholas IV himself — who consented to lend the weight of his authority. A proclamation was thereupon read in the Roman synagogues testifying to the fact that Maimonides' great work contained nothing that could be considered prejudicial to faith, and threatening any person who traduced it with a heavy fine.

Scholars such as those who have just been mentioned, who came into contact with non-Jewish savants, were inevitably compelled from time to time to enter into discussion on religious questions or to defend their faith against attack. Such polemics are reflected in the writings of Solomon de' Rossi — the earliest member of that erudite and famous family to achieve prominence — who composed a primer of religious disputation. He disapproved indeed of the practice, for whatever the outcome it was dangerous and, in his view, invariably resulted in harm. Yet, if Jews were forced to engage in such discussions, it was necessary for them to be properly equipped, and for that reason he strongly recommended a knowledge of the Latin language and theological literature; though he warned disputants to remain on the defensive and to refrain from attacking Christian dogma. The work is not, unfortunately, preserved in its entirety, but such fragments as survive throw a welcome light on a side of Italian Jewish intellectual life of which we would otherwise know nothing.

The new philosophical school overshadowed but did not overwhelm the mystical interests which had been so solidly established in Italy in a former day. The outstanding exponent now was Menahem of Recanati, whose mystical commentary on the Pentateuch, strongly tinged with the coloring of the German school, subsequently exercised a very potent influence in non-Jewish as well as in Jewish circles, though it was less esteemed by contemporaries. The most important figure in Italian Jewish mysticism in the period was, however, a foreigner, Abraham Abulafia of Saragossa, one of the most memorable characters in the history of Cabalism. It was in 1274, at the age of thirty-four, that he left his native land to spend the rest of his life wandering from place to place, especially in Italy, expounding his strange, esoteric doctrines and writing his strange, esoteric books. At Capua, he had at one time a promising circle of disciples, who nevertheless disappointed him in the end. In 1280, we find him in the Papal States, proposing to present himself before Pope Nicholas III, in his summer residence at Suriano, and to demand the release of the Jews from their captivity. The news of his plan became known, and instructions were given that he should be burned when he arrived. The stake was prepared just outside the walls:

but undeterred, the mystic passed on. When he entered the city gate, he learned that the Pope had succumbed to an apoplectic stroke during the previous night. After being detained in the Franciscan college for twenty-eight days, he was released. He is next heard of in Sicily, where he apparently proclaimed himself Messiah, causing such scandal that he was driven out. On the desolate rock of Comino, between Malta and Gozzo, where he was forced to dwell "against his will, for many days," he composed his apocalyptic *Book of the Sign*, filled with hardly-veiled invective against the inhabitants of the island; and not long after, in 1291, he disappears from view.

Meanwhile, rabbinical studies of the traditional type were still flourishing. In the first half of the thirteenth century, Rabbi Samuel of Verona had been in correspondence with Isaiah of Trani, one of the most eminent rabbinical authorities of his day, who emigrated to North Italy — he discussed the permissibility of travelling in a Venetian gondola on the Sabbath — and was thus a connecting link between the traditions of Apulia and of the Rhineland. He wrote extensively on various tractates of the Talmud, bringing the decisions up to date in accordance with the most recent opinions. (One of the earliest known references to the *fazzoletto*, or handkerchief, is to be found in this work of his; though some scholars hold that it is a later marginal gloss.) His grandson, Isaiah of Trani the younger, who lived into the fourteenth century, followed his path in an important talmudic compendium, still to be consulted with profit. Among the grandfather's pupils was the Roman Zedekiah ben Abraham Anau, brother of the poet Benjamin, who composed there in the thirteenth century his *Shibbole ha-Leket* ("Forgotten Sheaves"), a rich collection of material from many sources, some of which are no longer extant, on religious usages, throwing a great deal of incidental light on social conditions of the time.

The names that have been mentioned are those of only

some of the outstanding personalities. What was more remarkable was the degree of the diffusion of Jewish culture. Many were the places that could boast their expert scribes, their gifted rhymesters, their students of philosophy, their learned rabbis. A very large proportion of Hebrew manuscripts of the later Middle Ages now preserved were copied, and many of them composed, in little and little-known places in central and northern Italy at this time — sometimes, indeed, the earliest evidence that Jews lived there. By this means, rabbinic experts in remote lands were made familiar with the names at least of obscure centers of population of which their most erudite neighbors had never heard.

CHAPTER V

The Renaissance

xx

Councils, Pontiffs and Friars

THE remarkable geographical and economic expansion of Italian Jewry in the course of the fourteenth century entailed danger as well as prosperity. Zealous ecclesiastics saw with dismay the presence of infidels, in close touch with the population, in many areas where they were not to be found hitherto, synagogues in places that had once known only churches, Jewish savants in little towns where the Christians were perhaps served only by ignorant parish priests. Their nervousness may have been exaggerated, but that they were nervous was natural. It happened, moreover, that this was the period of the growth of the Hussite movement in Central Europe, which the Jews were wrongly believed to have inspired. As a result of this, the Church was impelled to set itself a new and stricter standard, as evinced in the attempts at reform made by two successive General Councils. All such readjustments involved the enforcing of the old ecclesiastical disciplines, including those against the Jews. And there was a more urgent consideration so far as they were concerned. Their new economic interests had brought the Jews squarely into the pathway of the body of men who were probably actuated by a purer religious idealism than any other in the Catholic Church in that age of turmoil. About 1370, the "Observantine" reform had started in the Franciscan Order, on the basis of reverting to the "poor and scanty use" of the world's goods preached by St. Francis himself. Thus they came once more into intimate touch with the poor, to whose spiritual needs the Order had been supposed to minister from the beginning. Formerly, it had been the Dominican Order of "preaching" friars, the Church's watchdogs against heresy, who had been the arch-enemies of the Jews and the leaders in so many persecutions. Now, for a space, the Observantine Franciscans took the primacy. Moving as they did among the destitute, they heard complaints on all sides against the ubiquitous Jewish moneylender or pawnbroker, whose presence was so much appreciated when a loan was required but so resented when payment was due. The opposition thus aroused, originally economic, extended more and more, until in the end the godly followers of the gentle Friar of Assisi seemed to become filled with a veritable frenzy and attacked the Jews everywhere, at all times and on all grounds, in the most unmeasured language and with little regard for probability or truth. From every pulpit, in season and out — but especially at Eastertide, when memories of the Passion of Jesus were renewed — wandering preachers now inveighed against the familiarity between Jews and Christians in the new settlements and pressed for the enforcement of the old canonical restrictions intended to cut them off from any sort of intercourse with the faithful. Above all, they demanded their segregation in a special area of the cities where they lived, the wearing of the prescribed Jewish badge to make them always recognizable, the prohibition of the employment by them of Christians even for the performance of essential domestic services, and, above all, a ban upon the practice of usury. Another point at issue was the possession of real estate, on which the Jews objected to paying tithes as the Church demanded. With the expansion of their area of settlement and the acquisition of urban and rural holdings, whether by normal purchase or in the course of their business, the problem became more obvious and another demand was put forward

— that the Jews should not be allowed to own landed property, and presumably to lend money on such security, thereby cutting off the most lucrative part of their business. Sometimes, the friars added to all this more extreme demands, or allegations of abhorrent crime which could be atoned or prevented only by the most drastic measures.

It seems paradoxical that this obscurantist agitation should have coincided with that marvellous surge of artistic and intellectual revival known as the Renaissance. Yet to survey this movement only from the aesthetic and intellectual aspects is misleading to a degree. It was symbolic of the period that, beneath the widespread scepticism and the cultural eclecticism, there flowed an undercurrent of sincere and sometimes fanatical religiosity. The Renaissance spirit, for all its occasional license, was accompanied by a no less characteristic mood of piety, which expressed itself in curious extravagances. If the one aspect constantly benefited the Jews and welcomed their participation, as will be described later on, the other which hovered in the background was a constant menace. The balance was so delicate that their status moved between the two extremes with a rapidity which is always extraordinary and sometimes confusing. The Popes were obliged to maintain ostensibly the bigoted code imposed by Canon Law, but, enlightened and broadminded as they generally were, were inclined to set a milder standard except when driven to action by special circumstances or at times of crisis for the Church. Locally, a a temporizing policy was generally followed; but it was strongly influenced by their example. The upper classes, with exceptions based on personal zeal, tended to be consistently friendly; the bourgeoisie considered their economic interests to be threatened by Jewish competition, and were correspondingly stern; while the populace swayed uncertainly between the two extremes in accordance with the prevailing mood. From time to time — especially during Lent, or in consequence of a visit from some famous Franciscan preacher — religious passions worked on economic greed, and smoldering prejudice burst out into violent flame. This, however, never blazed for long nor did it extend over a large area, Italy thus maintaining its record as the only European country which, until our own day, never knew a general persecution of the Jews.

For it must be remembered that the Italian's temperament is no less volatile than versatile. As recent years have demonstrated, he can easily be stirred up to a frenzy by an orator who plays on his sentiment. But these moments of passion cannot last for long, and when they are passed he reverts to his easygoing, indolent, friendly self. Sometimes, a bloody riot might be caused by the inflammatory flow of rhetoric from the pulpit. But after the wave of feeling had ebbed, and the series of sermons was ended, and the friar had moved on to another city, the frenzy would die down as suddenly as it had risen. The Jew repaired his broken windows, and the needy plebeian again began to bring along his valuables in the hope of raising money, and there would be laughter and singing and perhaps drinking in the streets, and somber ecclesiastics would once again begin to mutter at the excessive cordiality, and it would again be true that in no part of the world did such a feeling of friendliness prevail as in Italy between the people and the Jews.

However this may be, the early decades of the fifteenth century witnessed a momentary triumph of reaction. Pope Boniface IX, who tried to restore papal authority in the long-neglected Italian possessions of the Holy See, had been exceptionally tolerant, highly favored a succession of Jewish physicians, and in 1402 granted a charter of protection to the Roman community in which their rights as citizens were specifically recognized. But twelve years later, in 1414, an Oecumenical Council met at Constance to discuss the all-important questions of the restoration of unity to the Church, and the extirpation of the heretical movement which was spreading in central Europe. Shortly after it opened, the Spanish anti-Pope Benedict XIII, whose concern with the Jews was in the nature of a monomania, issued a series of regulations of fantastic severity in the hope of driving into the Church those of the area which admitted his authority, and thereby securing a much-needed personal triumph. Realizing their danger from all this, the communities of northern Italy summoned a conference, which met at Bologna in 1416 and was attended by representatives from Rome, the Papal States, Tuscany, Ferrara and Padua. Except that a Vigilance Committee of twelve was set up to watch over the interests of Italian Jewry for the next ten years, its outcome is unknown.

The Council at Constance achieved its greatest and indeed only outstanding triumph in 1417, when the schism in the Church was at last ended by the deposition of three rival candidates to the Papacy and the election of Cardinal Colonna to the dignity as Martin V. Henceforth, only one person could seriously claim to be Vicar of God on earth; and Rome again became the unquestioned center of the Catholic Church, as it had been until the previous century. During the following spring, the Jewish Vigilance Committee assembled at Forlì, in the Romagna, to consider the situation. It determined to send a delegation to wait upon the new Pope on his return to Italy and to ask for his protection and the confirmation of the rights enjoyed in the past. At the same time, the Committee decided on a number of regulations to suppress various abuses in Italian Jewry — above all, anything that might ostensibly encourage anti-semitic agitators; for the prosperity of the loan-bankers had obviously resulted in a highly undesirable display of luxurious living. Especially in places where there was a convent of the friars, restrictions were placed accordingly on personal costume and public display, on card playing and gambling, on the wearing of rich materials and expensive jewelry, on entertainments on the occasion of domestic celebrations and on gathering in the streets in unnecessarily large groups, on the number of persons who might ride out to greet a bride or might be invited to a circumcision feast. In order to secure funds for the expenses and gifts which would obviously be needed by the delegation, the Committee imposed a combined property and capitation tax on all families belonging to the constituent communities, except those supported by charity.

The Jewish representatives duly appeared before the Pope at Mantua on his way to Rome, and in 1419 he issued a Bull in the time-honored phraseology, taking under his protection the Jews of the northern and central provinces — excluding those of Bologna and Ancona, who had apparently broken away from the general body and approached him for themselves. His subsequent actions showed that this expression of benevolence was intended seriously. He authorized the Roman community to distribute part of its burden of special taxation among the others of the Papal States. When informed that a priest had baptized a Jewish infant at Montagnana near Padua without the parents' permission — an abuse which was becoming widespread — he categorically forbade such action henceforth in the case of children under twelve. His personal physician was Elijah ben Sabbatai, who, as Elias Sabot, had gone to England some time previously to attend on the ailing King Henry IV; and he not only confirmed the privileges of several other Jewish physicians living in the Papal States, and tried to restore peace in the Roman community by appointing one of them as its president, but also abolished the general prohibition against the treatment of Christian patients by Jews.

But even the Pope was not able to resist indefinitely and consistently the pressure of the Observantine reactionaries. Their deadly urge was now personified in the somber figure of "the scourge of the Jews," Giovanni da Capistrano (later canonized), whose name is more fraught with tragedy than almost any other in the whole course of Italian Jewish history. Though he had adopted a religious life only at a relatively advanced age, he had rapidly made his name known as a champion of uncompromising orthodoxy. Wherever he went, from the Straits of Bizerta almost to the shore of the Baltic, he brought disaster to heretics and unbelievers. He first came into prominence in this connection in 1417, when he was commissioned to act as special inquisitor in Mantua. From now on, his propaganda against the Jews was incessant, and their position became more and more serious. In 1422, they succeeded in obtaining from the Pope a further edict of protection, in which their former safeguards were renewed and the friars were warned not to continue to incite the populace against them. Capistrano was appalled, and induced Martin to withdraw the brief barely a year later, on the grounds that it had been obtained fraudulently. This was almost a summons to an antisemitic crusade. The Vigilance Committee of the communities hastily reassembled — this time at Perugia — and decided to impose another levy for the important work in hand; but payment was dilatory, and conditions continued critical. The center of agitation now moved south. In 1427, Capistrano persuaded the queen of Naples to issue an edict cancelling the privileges conferred on the Jews by her predecessors and enforcing all the traditional restrictions demanded by the friars. It was perhaps his greatest triumph, but it was shortlived; for there were protests on the part of Christians as well as of Jews, the Pope himself being impelled to intervene, and within a few months the edict was repealed.*

The Franciscans were neither discouraged nor deterred by this setback; and a report which arrived in Italy from the Holy Land in the following year gave them a colorable pretext. The Turkish officials in Jerusalem had seized a chapel belonging to the Franciscan convent on Mount Zion,

* See below, pages 274–5.

and the blame for this, vastly exaggerated, was put on the Jews. In retaliation for what had occurred, the Pope forbade the seafaring republics of Venice and Ancona, under pain of excommunication, to permit Jews to be conveyed to Palestine on their vessels (March 9, 1427); and some sea-captains, in excess of zeal, went so far as to fling their Jewish passengers into the sea. This interdict remained in force for over half a century, compelling pilgrims to embark in Sicily, after a long overland voyage. In the kingdom of Naples, Queen Joanna, by way of recompense for her recent tergiversation, not only promulgated the Bull, but in addition imposed a poll-tax of a third of a ducat on every Jew in order to indemnify the Franciscans for their loss. Benjamin da Corinaldo, the treasurer of the Vigilance Committee, did what he could to cope with the dangerous situation that had developed; but the funds at his disposal were insufficient, and in the end it was found necessary to assemble a third plenary conference of the Italian Jewish communities (where and when the second had taken place is unknown). This met on neutral ground, at Florence, where no community yet existed, in the autumn or early winter of 1428. Here, besides various disciplinary regulations — one of them being directed against the exaction of interest from needy fellow Jews — new fiscal measures were taken, more satisfactory than on the last occasion. The result was seen in a new Bull issued by the Pope in February 1429, in which the friars were categorically forbidden to preach against the Jews, to attempt to interrupt their normal relations with their neighbors, to infringe upon their religious rights, or to exclude them from normal activities (including attendance at universities, which their enemies had apparently managed to impede). Seldom in the history of the Holy See had so sweeping a measure of protection been known.

To be sure, the papal example was not universally followed, and up and down the country reaction triumphed locally. In 1417, for example, S. Niccolò Albergati, on his appointment as bishop of Bologna, had put into execution in his diocese the friars' program, including the wearing of the Jewish badge and segregation in a separate quarter of the city. During the agitation regarding the treatment of the Franciscans in Jerusalem, the eloquent preaching of Fra Jacopo da Monteprandone (S. Giacomo della Marca, as he is called) resulted in similar measures at Ancona, and at the same time they were enforced at certain places in Umbria. In practice, the street to which the Jews were confined was generally contiguous to that set aside for those other social pariahs, the prostitutes, moralists complaining bitterly at this degrading and dangerous juxtaposition. The city of Padua applied, in 1419, for permission to expel the Jews outright. Though this was not granted, the Venetian government prohibited them in 1423 to own land or real estate, which had to be disposed of within two years; and this was henceforth the rule in all the wide territories subject to the *Serenissima* (since 1394, no Jews were to be found in Venice itself). In 1439, the badge was introduced even into Sienna, though not, preposterous though this was, for the loan-bankers, who were in fact exempted not infrequently from the consequences of the reaction of which they were the principal cause! In Piedmont, Amedeo V (subsequently to retire into a hermitage and then to become anti-Pope) gave a foretaste of his piety in 1430 in a series of regulations for the Jewish communities in which the friars' persecutory program was embodied in full — confining them in a special quarter, compelling them to wear a distinguishing badge, forbidding the erection of new synagogues, threatening the severest penalties for any offense against the Christian religion, interrupting their social relations with non-Jews whether as associates, employees, or servants, and above all suppressing the practice of usury. After his abdication, his successor, Ludovico, cancelled this last restriction, so disastrous to the interests of the ducal treasury. But the remainder of the code continued in force uninterruptedly from that time on, and in 1448 the duke sent a sharp reminder to local officials ordering them to enforce his father's regulations. From this year, segregation and the wearing of the badge were enforced in Vercelli and Novara, not far off. In 1426, there was, moreover, a general onslaught on Jewish literature in Savoy, where pious owners buried their books to save them from confiscation, and some while later another in the duchy of Milan as the result of the agitation of an apostate named Vicenzo. Little is heard of more violent manifestations, but there was an outbreak against the Jews of Pesaro in 1431 which was not perhaps isolated.

Pope Eugenius IV, who succeeded Martin V in this year, followed his example at the beginning of his pontificate. He, too, had his Jewish physician. He renewed the guarantee of Jewish privileges, first generally and then for the communities of Lombardy, the Marches and Sardinia, which were now acting in conjunction; and he again warned the friars against disturbing the Jews or preventing Christians from entering their employment and performing domestic services for them. But the influence and activity of Capistrano and his associates were unchecked. His own zeal was rivalled, if not outdone, by that of his former master, Bernardino of Sienna, the ascetic head of the Observantines. The latter's saintly qualities were wholly submerged when Jews were concerned, they and personal cleanliness being among his greatest abhorrences. It was a mortal sin, in his opinion, to eat or drink with a Jew; and he seriously considered the problem whether Christian love should embrace them also — general love, he opined, yes; particular love, decidedly no! To his horror, he found that in Padua, Vicenza and Verona they were not compelled to wear the Jewish badge, and he questioned the right of the Pope himself to exempt them. Travelling barefoot throughout Italy with his perpetual summons to repentance, and filling the cathedral squares with vast crowds eager to hear his flamboyant oratory, he was in his day one of the most influential figures in the country. In 1408, he had heard Vincent Ferrer, the Spanish arch-antisemite, preaching in Alessandria, and from that moment was filled with an identical urge and identical prejudices. In 1427 we find him inveighing against the Jews in Umbria, at Viterbo and Orvieto, with the results that we have seen, and at Sienna, where he secured the enactment of some galling restrictions against them and the moneylenders. Thereafter, he extended his agitation as far north as Brescia, scandalized by a report that the City Fathers had requested the Pope's license to summon loan-bankers, and as far south as the kingdom of Naples. Here, in 1438, he preached a series of twelve anti-Jewish sermons at Aquila, King René being among the vast audience who heard him on one occasion; and it was only to be expected that the Church could subsequently boast a number of converts.

Pope Eugenius thus never lacked incitement to action against the Jews; and the General Council which opened at Basel just after his accession, to consort measures against the Hussites and heresy in general, impelled him to pose as a champion of stern and unbending orthodoxy. The anti-Jewish legislation enacted at the instigation of the Castillian delegates at its nineteenth session (September 7, 1434) was therefore echoed perforce in a Bull of unusual severity, directed in the first instance against the Jews of Spain, but afterwards it seems extended to those of Italy. They were forbidden normal intercourse with Christians, to attend on them in the capacity of physicians, to employ them for domestic service or as nurses, to dwell in the same houses, to build new synagogues, to engage in handicrafts, to settle without express permission in fresh places, to be admitted to any sort of public office, to lend money at interest, and even — the most distressing provision of all — to study the Talmud and the allied literature. The news was greeted with consternation. A further representative conference met at Tivoli, being subsequently adjourned, perhaps for political reasons, to Ravenna; and this time, it proved easier to raise money from the terrified communities. Even the Sicilian Jews sent a delegation to Rome to take action. Negotiations were entered into with the marquess of Mantua to induce him to extend his favor to the refugees from the Papal States, the result being the benevolent regulations issued on June 28, 1443, empowering the Jews to settle in his dominions with the right to observe their religion publicly, to settle internal disputes in accordance with talmudic law and to engage in all legitimate occupations without interference. Meanwhile conversations were continuing between the Apostolic court and the representatives of the communities of all parts of Italy, north and south, who were empowered to disburse large sums of money to secure their object. Ultimately the Pope, by no means unkindly by nature, and hardly desirous of losing his lucrative Jewish subjects, was induced to realize that his recent regulations were economically inadvisable, and after long and costly negotiations they were withdrawn. Once the immediate danger was over, the Jewish communities fell out among themselves on the question of finance, leaving that of Rome to shoulder the entire burden. We are afforded a glimpse of how its rabbi, the poet-physician Moses da Rieti, tried to arouse his coreligionists to a sense of their responsibilities, but there is no indication whether he was successful or no.

With Eugenius' successor, Nicholas V, who aimed at making Rome the center of Italian cultural life, the magnificent tradition of the Renaissance Papacy began to reach fruition; and his policy towards the Jews might have been expected to reflect this. At the outset of his pontificate, in 1447, he confirmed, indeed, their right to enjoy those privileges accorded them by Canon Law — no more! — and issued briefs safeguarding the position of those of Ferrara and the other territories subject to the house of Este, where the inquisitors had joined the friars in attacking them. But over against the Pope, and in some respects more influential than the Pope, loomed the menacing figure of Capistrano, who had foretold his illustrious career and whose influence on him remained profound. As a result, he was induced within a few months of his accession to renew, with special reference to Italy, his predecessor's persecutory Bull of five years previous, with one difference: whereas Eugenius had given thirty days for it to be put into execution, Nicholas would allow only fifteen. Capistrano himself, their archenemy, was commissioned to see that the measure was carried into effect. The results were tragic and immediate. In Rome, the Jews had to barricade themselves in their houses to save themselves from violence, and the disorders spread thence throughout the Papal States and beyond. The community of Recanati found conditions so serious that it tried to organize another conference in order to discuss measures of protection. If this took place, it was entirely ineffective. Capistrano and his disciples continued active up and down Italy without restraint. In the Jubilee Year 1450, he staged a religious disputation in Rome; and his opponent was so intimidated that he had to confess defeat and accept baptism, together with some forty others. The friar ultimately felt so confident of success in his attempt to purge the Eternal City of the taint of unbelief that he offered the Pope a ship in which the remnant of the community could be transported overseas.

Though he was disappointed in this and though the provisions of the Bull remained unobserved in many places — the Pope himself, indeed, authorized moneylending and the consequent personal intercourse in some regions — the repercussions were felt throughout Italy. In 1452, Franciscan agitators secured the expulsion of the Jews from Cuneo, but the blunder was immediately realized and, after a single month, they were recalled. Two years later a similar measure, similarly shortlived, was enacted for the whole of Piedmont. At Reggio, owing to the propaganda of Fra Giovanni da

Prato, there was physical violence. At Padua, the preachers darkly threatened divine vengeance unless conditions altered, with the result that in 1453 the city at last obtained permission from the authorities at Venice to expel the loan-bankers on the expiration of their *condotta* two years later. They were, however, able to continue operations in the surrounding villages — thus being legally entitled to charge a higher rate of interest — and before long were readmitted to the city for three days a week. There must have been similar agitation in Lombardy, though in 1452 its Jewish communities obtained through their duke, in consideration of the inevitable payment, a Bull safeguarding them against further clerical onslaughts.

On the accession to the papal throne in 1455 of Capistrano's Spanish disciple, Calixtus III, a riot took place against the Roman Jews, whose gift of a richly decorated Scroll of the Law aroused the mob's greed on this occasion. Later on, he, too, annulled the privileges granted by his predecessors and confirmed the adverse legislation of Eugenius IV and Nicholas V, though the property confiscated as a result of this was not to be used, as hitherto, for the construction of cathedrals, but for the projected crusade against the Turk, who had so recently captured Constantinople. By now, Capistrano had passed north, to work for the Catholic Church in Bohemia and the adjacent lands, Jewish blood continuing to stain his path. Italian Jewry breathed somewhat more easily; but he left impassioned disciples and followers to carry on his work.

xxi

THE MONTI DI PIETÀ

The preaching of the Franciscans against the Jews became the more effective when the policy they championed ceased to be purely negative. It was indubitable that the moneylenders against whom they inveighed filled an indispensable economic function, especially as regards the poor — Popes, crowned heads, nobles and town councils agreed upon this point. Hence the agitation, directed as much against usury as against the Jews, failed to have any durable effect, even though it might temporarily arouse anti-Jewish passions. Towards the middle of the fifteenth century, however, a new idea began to be put forward. If loan-banks were, indeed, necessary for the common people, then the obvious solution to the religious problem was to set up public institutions, maintained at the public expense and without any idea of making profit — "Funds of Piety," or *Monti di Pietà*, as they were termed. Then, and then alone, it might be possible to get rid of the Jews, once for all.

In the end, it turned out that the problem was not quite so simple. Either the *Monte di Pietà* charged interest, or else it did not. If it did not, then obviously it could not pay its way, and the little capital which was forthcoming from public funds and private benevolence was soon exhausted. If it did, however small the rate might be, this was strictly speaking a breach of Canon Law, all the more heinous since it was under public and religious auspices. Those responsible were therefore constrained to allow the *Monte di Pietà* to charge sufficient interest to cover expenses. Even this was objected to by the stricter elements: in such circumstances, what was the use of inveighing against the Jews? A long and tedious controversy on the lawfulness of usury now began, which may be followed in large numbers of the ponderous theological works of the period. It was ended only when, at the beginning of the sixteenth century, Pope Leo X declared that the *Monte* was a proper and useful institution even if it charged interest, and threatened with excommunication anyone who questioned its legality in Canon Law.

The theological problem was not of course the only one. In order to succeed, such an establishment, however altruistic its object, must have a competent staff, with its interests at heart, and qualified to value the pledges that were offered. In default of this, it was doomed to failure and insolvency. This, indeed, was not obvious at the outset, when the new idea was first put forward with infectious zeal by the Franciscans — all the more eager on this point as their Dominican rivals refused on principle to admit any compromise on the problem of usury. Thus, from the middle of the fifteenth century, a campaign began to be conducted up and down Italy by the Franciscans on behalf of the *Monti di Pietà* and, with renewed violence, against the Jews, who were rendered superfluous and could be expelled once the new organization was introduced.

The father of the idea was Fra Michele da Milano who, in a series of sermons delivered at Perugia in 1462, declared that the city had fallen into excommunication by reason of its arrangement with the loan-bankers, and urged that a public institution should be set up to take their place.* They were compelled to advance a loan of 1,200 gold florins towards the initial capital, and next year the *Monte di Pietà* was opened and their services could be dispensed with; though they were not immediately expelled, as happened in many other places. Next year, a similar establishment was opened at Gubbio; and next, one at Orvieto — the first which was really successful. Before long, the institution had become very widely spread especially in central Italy, where the Franciscans now regarded it as one of their main objects. By the end of the century, at least thirty public pawnshops on the new charitable basis had been set up in the Marches and Umbria alone; and other regions did not lag far behind. Restricting oneself to places where there was a fairly vigorous Jewish settlement, whose livelihood must have been deeply affected by this innovation,

* There had been an earlier experiment eight years before at Ancona under the name of the *Monte dei Prestiti*.

the *Monte di Pietà* now came into existence at Foligno (1465), Monte S. Sepolcro (1466), Assisi, Recanati, Pesaro and Urbino (all in 1468), San Severino and Osimo (1470), Fano and Viterbo (1471), Sienna (1472), Bologna and Pistoia (1473), Genoa (1483), Mantua and Ascoli (1485), Vicenza (1486), Lucca (1487), Parma (1488), Brescia (1489), Piacenza, Verona and Ancona (1490), Modena and Padua (1491), Ravenna (1492), Pavia (1493), Reggio (1494), Treviso, Udine, Pisa and Florence (1496), and so on. In several of these instances, it was considered to be a natural corollary that the Jews were now superfluous and might be expelled without compunction. On the other hand, sometimes they remained, either to supplement the *Monte* when its capital was exhausted, which often took place very soon, or for operations on a larger scale for which it was not intended, or for other economic functions if they could find them. It occasionally happened that the new institution was unsuccessful and they were summoned back after a few years to supply by their ability what it had proved impossible to replace by mere enthusiasm. This was, for example, the case at Sienna, which was empowered in 1489 to conclude a fresh agreement with Jewish loan-bankers to supplement the *Monte* established such a short while previously.

It is noteworthy that in some cases the loan-bankers, realizing that a charitable pawnbroking establishment institution was necessary for the poor, supported the *Monte* with legacies and spontaneous as well as forced donations. Sometimes, moreover, they found it useful for their own purposes, depositing in it the pledges left with them and thus raising capital for further operations — a courtesy which the officials of the *Monte* reciprocated, on occasion, though with wasteful results in view of the difference in the rate of interest. The ultimate outcome was sometimes the reverse of what the founders intended; for finding existence impossible in the larger places where they had formerly lived, the moneylenders transferred themselves to smaller centers where no *Monte* was likely to be set up, thus widening instead of contracting the area of Jewish residence. This is what happened in the neighborhood of Parma and Piacenza in 1488, and of Modena in 1494, where a score of little places thus acquired Jewish settlements. In such cases, their urban clients had to go out to seek them and, as strangers, could be made to pay a higher rate of interest.

From the point of view of the relations between the Jews and their neighbors, the results of the movement were deplorable. The populace was made to think that the loan-banker, with whom they had lived in amity for years, symbolized the very power of darkness. He began to appear in their eyes, not as their succor in distress, but as its cause; and there was a tragic revulsion of feeling, often resulting in bloody riot. The friars on their side were naively induced by their prejudice to believe in and to communicate the most atrocious anti-Jewish libels, from ritual murder downwards, thereby adding fuel to the flames. To be sure, when the city authorities wished it, they were able to put an end to the agitation without difficulty. At Florence, for example, when a certain Observantine friar, named Visconti, preaching in Santa Croce during Lent in 1458, turned his invective against the Jews and incited the populace to pillage their houses, the archbishop himself (a Dominican, as it happened) ordered him to stop, and the *Signoria* had him escorted summarily from the city.

The movement received a great impetus when Capistrano's diminutive admirer and disciple, Fra Bernardino da Feltre, one of the most remarkable orators and preachers of his day, began his activity. In place after place, from the kingdom of Naples to the borders of Germany, he delivered his inflammatory sermons in favor of the *Monte di Pietà* and against the Jews. In place after place the new charitable institution was set up, though it did not always prove successful. But in place after place, too, there were excesses against the Jews, sometimes with the most tragic consequences.

Fra Bernardino entered into Jewish history in 1475, when, now aged thirty-seven and at the height of his powers, he delivered the Lenten sermons at Trent, on the German border north of Venice. Here Jews had been resident from the beginning of the century, had proved useful to the bishop and lived on friendly terms with their neighbors. But their eloquent, fanatical visitor changed this. He informed his hearers of the alleged Jewish practice of ritual murder, and warned them to look after their children on the approach of Passover. Normally, Italian kindliness and scepticism would not entertain charges of this sort, which never found a receptive soil in the country. But here, so near to Germany, things were somewhat different. As it happens, on Maundy Thursday, a boy of twenty-eight months, named Simon, actually disappeared. The houses of the Jews were searched, but no trace was found. On Easter Monday, some of them, naturally anxious, saw a body floating in the river. They hastened to inform the authorities, but this heightened the suspicion against them. A dubious apostate, then in jail, saw the opportunity to shorten the term of his imprisonment by asserting, as the friar had done, that the Jews used the blood of Christians for their Passover celebrations. The proceedings now followed the usual course. The whole of the Jewish community was arrested and put to the torture, until some sort of confession had been extracted. The principal members, including Master Tobias the Physician, were then dragged to the font, forcibly baptized, and afterwards executed, the survivors being expelled. The superstitious people now began to regard the child as a martyr, and to speak of miracles performed by his remains. A papal commissioner, sent to inquire into the case, reported that it was based on sheer fantasy, his personal suspicion being directed against a non-Jew of infamous character; and the Pope issued an encyclical in which he prohibited the faithful to pay religious honors to the "victim" any longer. Yet ultimately popular pressure proved too strong and, in due course, the dead infant was beatified.* The Blessed Simon of Trent entered into the official calendar of the Catholic Church — one of the very few cases in which the atrocious blood libel has retrospectively received its official sanction. In the cathedral of the little town near the Italian border, his remains are still venerated; and there are preserved in the treasury some of the Passover utensils which are alleged to have been used in the martyrdom.

The repercussions of this tragedy were felt all over northern Italy. Broadsheets recounting the new martyr's history and the miracles performed at his shrine were hawked about the streets. His picture was painted and publicly displayed everywhere. Sermons on the recent events were delivered in every church, and in many places it became dangerous for a Jew to show himself in the streets. The authorities, indeed, would not tolerate disorder. The Venetian government ordered protection to be given to the Jews throughout their territories, and prohibited sermons based on the gruesome episode. The duke of Ferrara did the same, vehemently refuting the charges. In the following year, Fra Bernardino repeated at Reggio the procedure that had been so successful elsewhere, warning the populace to take special care of their children in view of the approach of Passover, while another Franciscan seconded his efforts at Modena, where a person suspected of complicity in the Trent affair was manhandled; but thanks to the ducal protection both preachers were silenced. In the Venetian territories, Fra Bernardino meanwhile carried on his agitation in place after place, notwithstanding the disapproval of the authorities. At Bassano, he succeeded in stirring up feeling to such a

* That the process, begun in 1479, was completed only in 1582, is itself significant.

degree that the *Serenissima* was asked for permission to expel the Jews — though within a short while there was such a revulsion of feeling that the bishop excommunicated a number of the townspeople for attending a Jewish wedding! At Brescia, the government had to intervene to check an outbreak of violence, and again two years later to muzzle a visiting preacher. In 1478, accusations of ritual murder were brought up, though without serious outcome, at Reggio and Mantua. In the following year there was a general wave of accusations all over the duchy of Milan — particularly at Arena, where judicial procedures were opened and confessions extracted by torture. The houses of the Jews in Pavia were sacked; and the local communities, in alarm, petitioned the duke and duchess for protection. This was forthcoming in the most ample terms; yet in the following spring the authorities found it necessary to cut short the friar's inflammatory Lenten addresses at Pavia. That same year, a number of householders living at Portobuffolè, near Treviso, were barbarously executed on a charge of kidnapping a Christian child in order to use his blood for the Passover celebration, the survivors being imprisoned and then banished (six lawyers from the university of Padua, who had agreed to defend the accused, were compelled to surrender their fee to the Church of S. Antonio, the patron saint of the city). At Verona, too, the charge was brought up that year, with fatal consequences. In 1485, it was repeated at Viadana near Mantua, the drowned body of the missing child being discovered only just in time to save the Jewish community; and at Vicenza, where the episode served to prepare the ground for the establishment of a *Monte di Pietà* the next year. At Fano, however, the municipal council intervened on behalf of the Jews when the abomination raised its head there in 1492.

Fired by his successes, Fra Bernardino came again to Mantua in 1484. Here the community had grown apace under the somewhat fickle benevolence of the house of Gonzaga, who already in 1462 had demonstrated its sympathy with the idea of the *Monte di Pietà* by forbidding all moneylending, though the suspension lasted for only four years. In an impassioned series of sermons delivered before enormous crowds in the cathedral square, the friar pleaded fervidly on behalf of his cherished idea and assailed the ruling house for the favor shown to the Jews and their "perfidy." A *Monte di Pietà* was in consequence set up during the following year, with the approval of the Pope. The Jewish loan-bankers were not displaced, but their position was greatly weakened. Not long after, a certain Daniel Norsa, member of one of the most affluent banking families of the city, bought a new house which had an image of the Madonna painted on the wall. On application to the bishop, he received permission to have it removed. But what was good enough for the bishop was not good enough for the mob, who demonstrated their objections so vigorously that Norsa had to sue for protection. Just at this time Duke Francesco Gonzaga returned from the "victory" over the French at Fornovo, on July 6, 1495, where he owed his life, as he thought, to a vow made to the Madonna on the field. The Jew's appeal suggested a manner of fulfilling his promise at no personal cost. The house where the sacrilege had been committed was torn down and a splendid church erected on the site. This was dedicated to the Madonna of Victory (*Madonna della Vittoria*); and over the high altar was placed a painting by the great Mantegna, executed at Norsa's expense, showing the Virgin Mary with her mantle spread over the Gonzaga family in sign of protection.*

---

* This is now in the Louvre in Paris. Another painting was executed for the church by one of Mantegna's pupils, showing the enthroned Virgin being presented with a model of the building. Below, there can be seen Daniel Norsa and the members of his family, the men wearing the Jewish badge; and above may be read the legend "The Temerity of the Jews subdued."

The Last Page of the First
Printed Hebrew Book
(Rashi, Reggio di Calabria, 1475)

Daniel Norsa and his Household
An Italian Jewish Family of the Fifteenth Century

An Italian Jewish Wedding
(Renaissance Period)

Fra Bernardino had meanwhile transferred his agitation to central Italy. In 1485, his preaching brought about the temporary expulsion of the Jews from Perugia, and in the following year from Gubbio. In 1488, flushed with his triumphs, he delivered the Lenten sermons in Florence, arousing tremendous enthusiasm and beseeching his hearers to implore Christ daily that he should inspire the *Signoria* to expel the Jews and set up a *Monte di Pietà*. The result was that a mob of two or three thousand young hooligans delivered an attack on the loan-bank of the humanist financier Manuel da Camerino, and massacre once more seemed imminent, as had been the case in 1458 and again in 1471. Thanks apparently to the intervention of Lorenzo de' Medici himself (of course, it was alleged that he was bribed) soldiers were called out to suppress the disorders and the preacher summarily escorted out of the city. Next year we find him, nothing daunted, preaching against the Jews in Aquila, Chieti, Lucca, and Sienna, and the next in Bologna and Padua, where, notwithstanding the demands made by the civic authorities for their expulsion, the loan-bankers had been permitted to re-establish themselves since 1482. Here, he had the satisfaction of hoisting the banner over the long-discussed *Monte di Pietà*. To his chagrin, however, the Jews were allowed to continue their activities, mainly for the benefit of the university students, and from some points of view the following two decades were their period of greatest prosperity. That same year, there was a riot at Forlì, where the loan-banks were plundered and the Jews forced to flee. At Ravenna, in 1491, he succeeded, not only in securing the establishment of a public loan-institution, but also the destruction of the beautiful synagogue, and nearly of the Jewish community as well. In 1492, he stirred up trouble in Venice, Castelfranco, Bassano, Genoa, and Crema — where, to his horror, Christians had not scrupled to attend Jewish wedding festivities! — and managed to get the tiny community expelled from Campo S.

Pietro. Next year he visited Florence (though under pledge of good behavior), Rimini and Ferrara; but here he was speedily silenced, notwithstanding the protection of the duchess, less enlightened than her husband. A couple of his colleagues then called supernatural forces to their assistance, foretelling an outbreak of plague in the Este dominions within eight months if no *Monte di Pietà* were set up. This ingenuous experiment, though ineffective in the vicinity of the ducal court, met with some success in Reggio and Modena, where advantage was taken of the situation to arrest two leading loan-bankers on the charge of professional malpractices; yet, after the initial enthusiasm had waned, the new institution lapsed into complete inactivity. Fra Bernardino had meanwhile continued his agitation at Monselice and Asti. His last triumph was at Brescia, where in 1494, in spite of the opposition of the Venetian government, he at last managed to secure the partial expulsion of the Jews, which had been under discussion for several years.

That same year he died; and with the passing of their arch-enemy and the waning of the first impetus of zeal that had brought the *Monti di Pietà* into being, the life of the Italian Jews became more tranquil. The following decades witnessed the heyday of some of the greatest Jewish capitalists of Renaissance Italy, such as Asher Meshullam (Anselmo) del Banco of Padua, reckoned the wealthiest of all, the overbearing Immanuel Norsa of Ferrara, the Da Pisa family in Tuscany, or Salamone di Bonaventura of Ancona. It was true that occasionally the friar found imitators, and that from time to time religious zeal and economic jealousy again combined, with tragic results. But it had by now been discovered that the *Monte* was not a final solution to the economic problem of the poor, that it did not necessarily improve their lot, and that its coexistence with a Jewish settlement was not in fact preposterous. For rather more than half a century, the communities of central Italy enjoyed a reprieve.

xxii
The Communities in the Sixteenth Century

In 1471, the worldly, free-living Francesco Rovere was elected Pope as Sixtus IV, and the secularization of the Papacy reached its climax. Rome was not so much henceforth, in the eyes of the world, the center of Christian spiritual life as the seat of one of the most luxurious, cultured, and in some ways corrupt courts in Europe. Gone were the days when the Popes connived at — much less incited — the persecution of the Jews; now, they set the example of toleration. Fanatical friars and their prejudices could no longer obtain authorization for their propaganda from the Vatican; instead, it systematically kept them in check. Nowhere in Europe was the network of anti-Jewish regulations, elaborated by the Lateran Councils and enunciated in successive papal Bulls, less carefully studied or more systematically neglected: nowhere was the Jewish community more free in body and in mind. From Rome, the new spirit radiated throughout Italy — except the South, where foreign influences fostered a different outlook. The sun of the Renaissance was shining in its fullest splendor, and the Jews enjoyed its fecund warmth as never before.

It was a byword throughout Christendom that anything could be obtained at Rome for money; and it was a growing realization of the pecuniary potentialities of the Jews, as well as altruistic benevolence, that caused the Popes to modify the stern intolerance which had prevailed in the middle of the century. For the purpose of his projected crusade against the Turk, Calixtus III had attempted to exact from the Jews a levy comprising a twentieth (*vigesima*), or five per cent, of their income; though indeed, he had great difficulty in collecting it even in places like Bologna where papal influence was strong. Pius II, his successor, that strange figure of humanist turned crusader, though kindly enough to forbid the baptism of Jews below the age of twelve, increased the assessment to five per cent of their capital and insistently pressed the various Italian states to see that it was exacted; though the duke of Milan replied that his Jews were already taxed to the limit of their capacity to pay, and the government of Venice shrewdly consented to collaborate only if there were an international guarantee that the proposed expedition was really to take place. In the event, of course, it did not and the crusaders waiting at Ancona ultimately sold their arms to the Jews to pay for their journey home. The succeeding Popes realized that, notwithstanding the difficulties and the objections raised when their rapacity became too obvious, the *vigesima* on the Jews on the pretext of a Holy War (never again indeed levied on capital, though on one occasion raised to 12½%) was a very useful source of income. For them to be protected, and their business affairs to be allowed to flourish, thus became a matter of some importance to the papal treasury. Their example inspired more than one of the enlightened princelings who were now so numerous in the Peninsula, with their miniature courts and their resplendent entourages and their somewhat sceptical attitude towards Christian dogma. In these territories, too, feelings of tolerance became more marked, and Jews began to play a more prominent role. In such circumstances, the loan-bankers were now sometimes able to extend the scope of their activities, developing from moneylenders who catered for the lower classes to financiers interested in larger-scale operations, court-purveyors, and even financial agents of some of the petty princes. Ferrara, Sassuolo, Mirandola, Scandiano, and other places, all knew such figures, who enjoyed some prominence for a while.

It was at this time that the crowning tragedy of the Jewish Middle Ages was enacted, with the expulsion of the Jews from Spain and Sicily* in 1492. Italy was the only

*Below, pages 254–61.

land in Christian Europe open to the refugees, and some 9,000 in all made their way thither — especially to the kingdom of Naples, where members of the Abrabanel family henceforth took a leading part in communal life.* The noble-hearted Isaac da Pisa, now head of the famous Tuscan banking-house, spared neither exertion nor expense to succor the sufferers, and there were many others who showed similar zeal; but the problem was far too great for private charity to solve. Even contemporaries were shocked by the spectacle which presented itself at Genoa, where ardent friars wandered among the famished groups on the quay-side, a crucifix in one arm and loaves of bread in the other, offering food in return for conversion. "You would have thought that they wore masks," wrote a Christian eyewitness. "They were bony, pallid, their eyes sunk in the sockets; and had they not made slight movements it would have been imagined that they were dead." Only a few were permitted to remain in the city, but before long the animosity of Fra Bernardino da Feltre and the jealousy of the local merchants were aroused, and they were given the choice of embracing Christianity or being sold into slavery; twenty-one families, more fortunate than the rest, received permission from the enlightened duke of Ferrara to settle in his dominions, where they brought a rich stimulus to intellectual as well as economic life. A chronicler of the next generation reports that certain Roman Jews, fearing that the influx would bring with it an outburst of antisemitism, requested the notorious Borgia Pope, Alexander VI, to exclude the refugees, supporting their petition with a gift of 1,000 ducats. The Supreme Pontiff, true to the highest tradition of his office, refused what was asked of him, but demanded another 2,000 to permit the petitioners themselves to remain. Whatever the truth of this, there were in Rome henceforth, in addition to the half-dozen old-established Italian congrega-

*Below, page 189.

tions, and those maintained at that time by immigrants from France and Germany, synagogues following the Castilian, the Catalan, the Aragonese and the Sicilian rites as well. Later on, further fugitives were to arrive from Portugal (1497), the Provence (1498), Naples (1510, 1541) and even Tripoli (1511). Families of foreign origin — the Lattes and Sarfatti from France, the Ascarelli, Ambron, Corcos and others from Spain — henceforth play a leading role in Roman communal life. A parallel process was taking place in the cities of the north, where, in addition to a sprinkling of Spanish refugees, there was a continuous immigration over the Alps, from Germany and central Europe; while in 1499 a party of refugees, driven from Rhodes by the Grand Master, was admitted to Nice.

This heterogeneous agglomeration resulted in a long-drawn and sometimes bitter dispute in Rome and elsewhere between the Italians on the one hand and the foreigners, generically but not quite accurately known as *Transmontani* or Transalpines, on the other; the former, as the original inhabitants, desiring to perpetuate their control of the community, the latter wishing to obtain in it a share at least proportionate to their wealth and numbers. This was complicated by the jealousy between the banking oligarchy and the other, less affluent, economic interests. At length, in 1524, recourse was had for a settlement to the friendly offices of Daniel da Pisa, a member of the famous Tuscan family, who maintained an establishment in Rome as well. He elaborated a new, carefully-balanced constitution, whereby the administration was made over to a *congrega* of sixty persons chosen equally from the three classes into which the medieval Jewish community was conventionally divided — the upper class (here identified with the bankers and those belonging to the same circle), the merely well-to-do, and the poor, excluding, however, those who paid only an insignificant amount in taxation. This body was to elect the various executive officers in equal proportions from the native and foreign elements, the former preponderating when exact distribution was impossible. It was by this constitution, with slight modifications, that the Roman community continued to be governed for hundreds of years, though the distinction between the Italians and foreigners, bankers and others, lapsed in the end. The problems that arose in Rome were reflected in every other major Italian community of the time, with the disparity of national elements and economic interests. Thus at Mantua the group of bankers, who had obtained the original concession and contributed some three-quarters of the common revenue, was reluctant to surrender its autonomy except on terms which would leave it supreme; and there was no satisfactory outcome to the attempt to coalesce the two communities on the basis of allowing it a half or a third of the total representation. It was only a generation later that the final fusion took place, under the stress of external happenings. On the other hand, the clash between the Italian and German elements was settled here at the close of the sixteenth century by allotting the former a representation of two-thirds, and the latter of one-third, on all communal boards.

The general well-being of Italian Jewry during the heyday of the Renaissance did not imply unbroken tranquility. Indeed, the fact that the Jews were patronized by the courts might involve attack by the resentful populace; while favor by one civic faction sometimes resulted in banishment when its rivals came into power. Moreover, the agitation of the friars against the Jews and in favor of a *Monte di Pietà* did not end with the death of Fra Bernardino, the most impassioned advocate of the idea. Indeed, his influence survived him in a suggestive fashion. When, in 1527, there was an outbreak of plague at Pavia, the people appealed for protection to the saint, who had been so uncompromising an enemy of the Jews while he lived, promising that if the pestilence were averted they would expel the unbelievers from their midst as he had desired them to do. This vow they punctually carried out — though a generation later they petitioned the Pope to absolve them from it. The period was thus punctuated by minor disorders — always, however, of short duration, and always strictly localized.

Popular excitement on great occasions frequently manifested itself in attacks upon the Jewish quarters — for example, at Modena, on the election of Clement VIII to the Papacy in 1523; at Bologna (where the community had faced a preposterous charge of arson a quarter of a century before) on the coronation of Charles V in 1520; or at Mantua, (where the dowager duchess celebrated her son's marriage in 1550 by presenting the Jewish cemetery to an adjacent monastery) on the birth of an heir to the ducal house in 1562. When the duchy of Urbino passed, in 1508, into the hands of Francesco Maria della Rovere, nephew of the reigning Pope, a reactionary period began at least in theory, the new duke thinking it his duty to cancel all concessions to the Jewish loan-bankers, to prohibit landowning, to insist on the Jewish badge, and even to introduce minor vexations, such as a prohibition to buy food in the public markets until the evening. There is no evidence, on the other hand, that these provisions were ever put into effect, and, though moneylending was again forbidden forty years later, Jewish life in the duchy was apparently undisturbed. From time to time, a *Monte di Pietà* would be established and the Jews either expelled, as was the case at Piacenza in 1504, or driven out of business, as at Ancona in 1547. Occasionally, the friars would again attempt to organize a boycott, as they did about this time at Empoli in Tuscany; though on this occasion the Jews appealed for help to the Pope, who intervened on their behalf. Conditions were probably worst in regions where German influence was strongest. For example, at Udine, north of Venice, the butchers were instructed to mark the meat for Jewish consumption with a yellow pennant, horses owned by Jews were not admitted to the races, and in 1543 the handful of Jews was segregated in two houses, which proved convenient to sack, not long after, on the pretext that a recently-arrived family had introduced the plague. The ritual murder libel, sedulously fanned by ignorant preachers, was brought up more than once, though without serious result — at Novi in 1509, at Modena in 1530, at Asti in 1553, and at Rome, where the Pope and the Cardinal Farnese intervened to suppress it, in 1555.

At Genoa, the changes of policy were almost bewildering. Though the refugees from Spain were so brutally received in 1492, a small number of Jews were permitted to establish themselves there at the beginning of the sixteenth century. In 1516, they were chased out by Ottaviano Fregoso, but were readmitted under strict limitations in the following year by his opponents of the Adorni family. (The outstanding member of the community now was Joseph ha-Cohen, the physician, whose *Valley of Tears* is one of the most vivid sources of Jewish history at this time.) In 1550, owing to the jealousy of the medical faculty, the ostentatious conduct of some Jews and the preaching of the Dominican, Fra Bonifazio da Casale, they were expelled from the city, and in 1568 from the territory; but in 1570 some were permitted to return and open shops and loan-banks. The new settlement lasted for little longer than the former one, but before the close of the century the Jews were once more expelled. The volatility in this case was perhaps extreme, but it was not unique. In periods of general disorder, the Jews continued to suffer exceptionally. Thus, in the autumn of 1536, the Jewish quarter at Casale in Monferrat was twice pillaged: once by the French soldiers when they seized the city, again by the imperial troops when they recaptured it. At Asolo, in the Venetian territories, where a little Jewish settlement had existed since 1508, there was an onslaught by a band of brigands in 1547 and many persons were killed or wounded, the community never being re-established.

Above all, the Jews were an object of attack during the

foreign invasions that became so frequent after Charles VIII's descent into Italy in 1494 — all the more so since many of those who did the fighting were Germans and Spaniards, arch-enemies of the Jews in the one case, ardent supporters of the Catholic faith in the other. It will be told later* how the disorders which accompanied the French invasions ruined Neapolitan Jewry. At the other extremity of the Peninsula, there was a similar onslaught at the time of the invasion of the Venetian territories by the Emperor Maximilian in 1509 in the name of the piratical League of Cambrai, when the Jews proved to be the first object of attack by the invaders, of suspicion on the part of the defenders, and of revenge of whomever remained in possession. On the approach of the enemy, the houses and loan-banks of the Jews at Treviso and Verona were sacked, and they were expelled shortly after, though not, indeed, for long. At Bassano, the authorities intervened to protect them, but nevertheless they were driven out after the war. The Cividale community was accused of plotting to hand over the city to the enemy. Asolo, Castelfranco and Cittadella were the scenes of similar disturbances. Moreover, all over the Venetian territories the Jews, dreading the cruelties for which the *Lanzknechts* were notorious, left all they had on the approach of the armies and fled for safety. At Padua, the community was mulcted mercilessly by the invaders, blamed by the government for paying, and sacked by the rabble when the town was reoccupied, even though some stalwart young Jews marched with the relieving force.

These events, in many ways disastrous, had one favorable outcome. It has been seen how the Venetian republic, more from commercial jealousy than religious zeal, had done everything to keep the Jews at a distance. There had been an interruption in this policy only for a few years, after 1366, when loan-bankers had been invited to the city

---

* Below, pages 279 ff.

in order to satisfy the requirements of the poor; but after 1394 their *condotta* had not been renewed. They had to retire in consequence to Mestre, the nearest point on the mainland, no individual being allowed in Venice, however pressing his business, for more than a fortnight all told each year. Now, Mestre lay a heap of smoking ruins, plainly visible across the lagoon. Its inhabitants, Jews and non-Jews, together with refugees from all other parts of the Venetian territories, had sought refuge in the capital, where they continued to carry on their activities as loan-bankers or second-hand dealers; and in such circumstances it was obviously impossible to exclude them. When order was in some measure restored, an attempt was made to send them back. But their homes lay in ruins; and, moreover, the contributions which were squeezed out of them for financing the war could not easily be dispensed with. In the event, notwithstanding the general prejudice and constant complications, they were grudgingly allowed to remain, though ostensibly only for an emergency period of three years — largely owing to the adroit leadership of Anselmo del Banco, who had taken refuge in the city from Padua and is to be reckoned the founder of the community. When the time-limit had elapsed, a new *condotta* was issued for a similar span, ultimately to be prolonged to five years and in the end to ten, which was repeatedly extended. Thus, down to the period of the downfall of the Venetian republic at the end of the eighteenth century, its Jewish community was tolerated, not outright, but for a ten-yearly period — always indeed renewed, but conditional on the maintenance (ultimately, at a serious loss) of loan-banks for the benefit of the poor. Later on, Levantine and other merchants, formerly admitted only for brief periods, were also permitted to settle permanently in the city. This was the origin of the great Venetian Jewish community, for some generations one of the most famous in the world.

The anti-Jewish prejudice did not of course disappear,

and many citizens regarded this new development with frenzied disapproval. Continuously, the preachers demanded from their pulpits that the city should be restored to its pristine purity of faith. A strong antisemitic faction was to be found in the administration, and on more than one occasion the community narrowly escaped expulsion. Meanwhile, there was a perpetual clamor for the enforcement of the canonical restrictions and the prohibition of any sort of social intercourse with the Christian inhabitants. In the end, notwithstanding a tenacious resistance on their part, it was determined to make them take up their residence in the area known as the New Foundry, or *Ghetto Nuovo*. This was to be shut off from the rest of the city from sundown to sunrise and provided with Christian watchmen to see that the denizens did not venture outside during prohibited hours. The transference took place, after various delays, in the spring of 1516. Some time later, the Levantine merchants, who had hitherto received preferential treatment, were ordered to be concentrated similarly in the adjacent Old Foundry, or *Ghetto Vecchio*. Frequently before, the Jews had been restricted to a special street or quarter of the towns in which they lived — generally known as the *giudecca, giuderia, via* or *contrada degli ebrei*, and so on. This, however, was the first time that they had known such strict segregation, which suppressed all possibility of normal intercourse with their neighbors and reduced them almost to the status of permanent prisoners; and it was only half a century later that the example was generally followed. From Venice, the name "Ghetto" ultimately spread throughout Italy, and figuratively throughout the world, as the designation of the Jewish quarter.

The influx to Italy of Jewish refugees from Spain and Portugal was meanwhile changing its character. The original fugitives were succeeded by a stream of Marranos, who had been compelled to conform outwardly to Christian observances and now fled to escape the Inquisition and worship

God after their own way without molestation. Many of them came to Italy, relying not only on local unfamiliarity with their antecedents, but also on the relative insouciance of the Italians in matters of faith. Towards the end of the fifteenth century, they began to make their appearance singly or in groups throughout the Peninsula. A number found their way to Rome, with the result that the king and queen of Spain registered a solemn protest with the Pope. Occasionally the latter would think it proper to take action, enriching his treasury in the process — for example in 1493, when a large body was intercepted outside the gates of the city, or ten years later, when a single raid resulted in eighty arrests; but there was seldom any tragic sequel. From Venice, the Marranos were expelled by decree of the Senate in 1497, and again in 1550. In 1540, there were wholesale arrests in the duchy of Milan (then under Spanish rule) of fugitives on their way to the Levant. But all this made little impression, and it was officially reported at this period that there was no place in the whole country where refugees from the Inquisitions of Spain and Portugal were not to be found. In the second quarter of the sixteenth century, two cities above all contained important communities formed of ex-Marranos now professing Judaism openly: Ancona, under the control of the Pope himself, and Ferrara.

The Jewish colony here had become, under the enlightened rule of the dukes of the house of Este, one of the most important in Italy. The reigning dynasty controlled also Modena and Reggio, both with important Jewish groups, as well as in due course a number of smaller places such as Carpi, Cento, Pieve, Lugo, Finale, Correggio, and so on. To foster the immigration of useful elements, irrespective of origin or prejudice, was part of their general policy and resulted in a period of exceptional prosperity for their subjects. The first duke, Borso I, had obtained from the Pope an absolution for Jews to live in his dominions, to maintain their religious institutions there, and to lend money at a moderate interest. His successor, Ercole I, continued this policy and, on the grounds that he did not desire to deprive his people of the services of the Jewish loan-bankers, exempted them in 1473 from the excessive contributions demanded by the ecclesiastical authorities and promised restitution of what had been unjustly taken in the past. The community prospered and increased. There was immigration of German Jews from the north, and of Italian Jews from the south. Though at the outset they were not supposed to construct any public synagogue and were severely punished by the Inquisition in 1458 for daring to do so, the duke intimated eight years later that he would henceforth raise no objection; and the *scuola* established in 1481 by "Ser" Samuel Melli of Rome, and bequeathed by him to the community five years later, is still in use as the official place of worship. Recurrent attempts of the friars to make trouble were put down, even Fra Bernardino of Feltre being summarily silenced in 1493. During a passing phase of religiosity three years later, when public penitence was performed in order to avoid the war and famine announced by a Lazarist preacher, there was, indeed, one of those brief interludes of reaction so characteristic of the age. The Jews, hitherto immune from any such degradation, were ordered to wear a distinctive badge of shame in the form of a yellow circle on the breast — though this did not, indeed, apply to those valuable subjects, the bankers and physicians, nor even the students. Moreover, after the duke and his court had solemnly attended church for several days in succession and heard the exhortations of the preacher, the Jews were compelled to do the same. But the moment of enthusiasm passed, and the duke speedily reverted to his normal easygoing tolerance.

Duke Ercole was quick to realize the benefits that might accrue to his dominions through the refugees from Spain. A group of twenty-one families — merchants, craftsmen, physicians — was welcomed to the city after being turned out of Genoa in 1492, and were given autonomous rights which were thereafter confirmed time after time. Henceforth, there was in the city a self-contained "Sephardi" community, constantly reinforced by fresh immigration, which ultimately outdid the older-established elements in importance, if not in number. On the accession of Duke Alfonso I, in 1505, when the rights of the Jews were again confirmed, the outlying communities were subordinated for financial purposes to those of the capital. Though a *Monte di Pietà* was established here two years later, the loan-bankers were neither expelled nor molested nor even supplanted. Ercole II, on his accession, confirmed the rights of the Jews in the most generous terms, and gave a cordial welcome to new immigrants from Germany and Central Europe, who in 1532 founded a fresh synagogue according to the "Ashkenazi" rite. In 1509, a visiting preacher at Modena inveighed continuously for twenty-two days in favor of the languishing *Monte di Pietà* and against the Jews, but without result. When the Jews were banished from Naples in 1541, the noble Abrabanel family, refusing to avail themselves of special permission to remain, petitioned the duke of Ferrara to be allowed to settle in his dominions. This was immediately and cordially granted, and the city became the headquarters for some time to come of the business, literary and charitable activity of that family — headed, after the death of Don Samuel in 1547, by his wife and cousin Doña Bienvenida, who played in Jewish life a part not unlike that of the great noblewomen of the age in secular affairs. About the same time the settlement of the Marranos in Ferrara began, refugees from the onslaught of 1540 in the duchy of Milan and elsewhere being encouraged to take up their residence. On February 12, 1550, comprehensive letters of protection were issued for persons of this class, who were guaranteed immunity from any sort of persecution on religious grounds and granted privileges such as to arouse the envy of the native Jewish population. For a generation, the city was the greatest center of the organized religious life of the unhappy refugees from the Inquisition — the seat of the first printing press which served their needs, the scene of activity of their poets and litterateurs, the temporary refuge on the way from Flanders to Constantinople of outstanding figures such as Joseph Nasi, later Duke of Naxos.

Totally different, but as yet of minor importance, was the development of Jewish life in Florence. Girolamo Savonarola was successful here where Bernardino da Feltre had failed. When, in 1494, the great Dominican drove out the Medici and set Florence up as what might be termed a theocratic democracy, he reverted to the other's ideals, all the more readily as the Jews had been protected by the former ruling family and shared its unpopularity. On December 26, 1495, a provision was passed which set up a public pawnbroking establishment at last — the matter had been under discussion for upwards of twenty years. The Jews were now given twelve months to settle their affairs and leave, the official pretext for this being the preposterous allegation that they had accumulated no less than 50,000,000 florins in profit during the past sixty years — a mathematical, and probably a metallurgical, impossibility. It took some little while longer before the expulsion was actually carried into effect. Thereafter, their position in the city was a sort of barometer of its political state; when the Medici returned in 1512, they came too, and when the Medici were driven out in 1527 they accompanied them, as always after a little delay. It was only when the ruling house was at last securely established, from 1530 onwards, that the interruptions end and the continuous history of Florentine Jewry begins.

So far as the Roman community was concerned, the sun of prosperity set on that tragic day in the early summer of 1527 — it happened to be the first day of the feast of Pentecost — when the city was stormed by the German and

Spanish troops and given over to sack. When aged humanists and eminent ecclesiastics were butchered or despoiled of every shred of property, Jews could not expect to be spared. Many of them took refuge in the palace of the Cardinal della Valle, not far from their quarter, where in return for a lavish bribe an officer of the imperial army promised them protection. But many were put to the sword or — like the grammarian Elias Levita, who had been so highly esteemed by Christian scholars and Church dignitaries — lost all they possessed and were driven out destitute into the world. Neither Rome nor Roman Jewry ever completely recovered from this blow.

Such cataclysms, coupled with their own recent tribulations, made the Jewish world look forward with redoubled eagerness to the promised messianic deliverance. In 1502, a certain Asher Lemlein made his appearance in the Istrian peninsula beyond Venice and announced the imminent coming of the Redeemer. Some pious souls believed in him so implicitly that they destroyed their Passover ovens, confident that they would never be needed again. The prophet disappeared as suddenly as he had arisen, but the messianic ferment remained. In 1524, there arrived in Italy from the East a plausible, tawny-skinned adventurer of mysterious origin, named David, who claimed that he had been sent by his brother, king of the independent Tribe of Reuben, to obtain military assistance from the potentates of Europe in his struggle against the Turk. The Jews of Venice were so impressed by his astonishing tale that they smoothed his path to Rome, where he was entertained by Cardinal Egidio da Viterbo, the Hebrew-loving humanist, and rode on a white horse to the Vatican. Here, he was received in audience by Pope Clement VII, who later gave him letters of introduction to the various potentates of Europe. Thereafter, all the wealth and culture of Italian Jewry lay at his feet. He was lavishly supplied with money. He never appeared in the streets without an escort of ten young Jews and a crowd of inquisitive Christians. Doña Bienvenida Abrabanel sent him a silken banner embroidered with the ten commandments. Daniel da Pisa, hard-headed banker though he was, gave him the hospitality of his house and subscribed liberally towards his expenses. He made an almost royal progress through Bologna, Mantua, and Ferrara, giving it to be understood that the hour was near for the regathering of the Diaspora under the auspices of his nonexistent royal brother. His departure for Portugal, on the next stage of his mission, was watched with eager expectation. Here, after a promising beginning, he found his prospects undermined by reason of the excessive expectations that he aroused among the Marranos, and before long we find him back again in Venice, where the Senate had his tale investigated, without very satisfactory results, by Giovambattista Ramusio, the noted traveller and linguist.

Among the crypto-Jews whom he had encountered in Lisbon was a promising young official named Diego Pires, whose enthusiasm had been raised to such a pitch that he had circumcised himself, left the country, studied Judaism, and was now known by the Jewish name of Solomon Molcho. After immersing himself in the Cabala in Salonica and Safed, he too had come to Italy, where he aroused enthusiasm in the synagogues of Ancona by his eloquent preaching, sat at the gates of Rome among the beggars and the maimed in order to fulfill in his own person a rabbinical legend regarding the Messiah, and gained the ear and favor of the Pope, to whom he is said to have foretold a flood of the Tiber. Some Jews, such as the philosopher-physician Jacob Mantino and the poet-rabbi Azriel Diena, saw danger in his activities. Partly through the former's intrigues, he was arrested and condemned by the Inquisition; but, it is said, the Pope secured his escape by sending a convicted criminal to suffer in his place. Ultimately he fell in with Reubeni again in northern Italy, and the two approached Charles V at Ratisbon to persuade him to arm the Jews of Europe against the Turk. The Emperor, bigoted as he was unimaginative, had them thrown into chains and dragged at his heels to Mantua, where Molcho was condemned on a clear charge by an extemporized inquisitional tribunal and burned alive as an apostate from Christianity. Reubeni suffered similarly in Spain a few years later. The messianic hopes of Italian Jewry, which had burned so bright for a little time, were dimmed. There was perhaps some measure of solace, for the upper and more cultured class at least, in the tolerant intellectual atmosphere of the Renaissance world.

xxiii

The Jews and the Renaissance

Italy was now at the height of that ferment of artistic activity, intellectual curiosity, philosophical discussion and literary research, with a background of alternating religious enthusiasm and moral laxity, which is generally designated the "Rebirth," or Renaissance. The Italian Jews, always particularly susceptible to prevailing currents, were inevitably influenced by this. There were some aspects of the revival in which they took a significant share; there was none the fringes, at least, of which they did not touch. They introduced the new conceptions into their own intellectual and social life. Above all, their personalities and characters reflected the spirit of the new age, Italian Jewry thus displaying during these years all the warmth, the color and the human interest which give Renaissance Italy its perennial fascination and delight.

The two scenes, greater and less, were by no means lacking in affinity. Just as the great merchant-princes and enlightened tyrants in the Italian city-states regarded it a point of honor to patronize artists and to support learning so the affluent loan-bankers who constituted the Jewish aristocracy considered it their duty to maintain scholars and to subsidize literature of the sort which interested them more specifically. Their profession, moreover, though remunerative, was far from exacting, and afforded them a degree of leisure for intellectual pursuits comparable to that enjoyed by the Christian patrician whose wealth was based on commerce, and they used it in much the same way. They immersed themselves in literary studies, searched Italy to find the best tutors for their children, saw to it that philosophy and prosody were included in the curriculum as well as Bible and Talmud, avidly continued their own studies down to their last days, prided themselves on their literary style, threw their houses open to erudite visitors or learned refugees from other lands, sometimes presided over or else subsidized regular courses of instruction for all who cared to come, and in certain instances carved themselves out a niche in the annals of Hebrew literature. Like non-Jewish humanists, they insisted for their libraries on the finest materials and clearest calligraphy, rich decorations and elegant bindings, with the result that the noblest Hebrew manuscripts that have survived from that more ample age are of Italian provenance, many of them bearing the names of owners famous in the world of affairs. The assistants in their business establishments devoted some of their leisure to copying rare codices for their employers, whose qualities they dutifully celebrated in verse and prose; and affluent householders, not necessarily of Socratic or Solomonic intellect, found their family chronicle commemorated by their dependents in floods of complimentary verses, which were of course suitably rewarded.

In other directions, too, they extended a patronage reminiscent of the Christian merchant-princes of the time, to whom so much of the artistic patrimony of the Renaissance was due. One of the wealthy Paduan bankers, whose house was sacked at the time of the disturbances in 1509, had a

THE JEWS AND THE RENAISSANCE

domestic synagogue of unusual beauty and richness, with brocades for the Ark and the Scroll of the Law said to be worth 500 ducats, ostentatiously adorned with his crest. If Jews were not available to do such work, though indeed there were some able artificers among them, recourse was had to Christian artists of the utmost eminence. (The synagogue of Rome, for example, has silver appurtenances ascribed to no less a person than Benvenuto Cellini.) Occasionally this might have curious results, motifs being introduced into the illumination of Hebrew works which from the rabbinical point of view were, to say the least, unusual.* The great Gentile craftsmen of the day were patronized, too, for household and domestic purposes. We are informed how the Florentine Jews appreciated the achievements of the great metal-worker, Niccola Grosso (known as *Il Caparra*), though he surlily refused to work for them. When the artist Ducena was in Bologna in 1539, he was befriended by the Jewish banker Joab (Dattero) da Rieti, a fellow Florentine, who was always seen about in his company. In the Jewish quarter at Sienna there was a fountain over which stood a statue of Moses executed by, and perhaps commissioned from, the sculptor Antonio Federighi. When Michelangelo was at work on his wonderful figure of the same hero of Hebrew antiquity for the tomb of Pope Julius II in the Church of S. Pietro in Vincoli, the Roman Jews suppressed their traditional inhibitions and went on pilgrimage on Saturday afternoons to gaze upon their Lawgiver's marble features. Some of the wealthier Jews had portraits modelled by the finest medallionists of the time, such as Pastorino; and it is to be imagined that their likenesses were painted also, though no specimens earlier than the seventeenth century are known.

* Apart from such minor incongruities as scenes of Jews performing their religious rites bareheaded, one finds, for example, *amorini*, figures of classical mythology, and even representations of the Almighty.

A knowledge of music and dancing was considered an integral part of the education of any Jewish child, boy or girl. Hence the teaching of these subjects became a characteristic Jewish occupation in Renaissance Italy, notwithstanding the vehement disapproval expressed in clerical and official circles. In 1443, the authorities at Venice ordered that schools of music, singing and similar accomplishments kept by the Jews should be closed forthwith, and that they should be stopped from teaching these subjects under pain of imprisonment and fine. Nevertheless, this provision had to be re-enacted frequently. Among the complaints voiced by Fra Bernardino da Feltre at Parma was that some of the noble ladies took lessons in dancing from Jewish women, whom he succeeded in getting expelled from the city for the glory of God and of Holy Church. A foremost exponent of the art in Italy at the close of the fifteenth century was the Jew Guglielmo (Benjamin) da Pesaro, who settled in Bologna and then in Florence under the auspices of Lorenzo de' Medici and there composed his *Trattato sull' arte del ballo* — almost the earliest modern treatise on the subject — which was honored by a complimentary sonnet from the pen of Mario Filelfo, son of the illustrious humanist. Even when intimate relationships between the adherents of the different faiths had been effectively interrupted, and a dourer spirit prevailed in the synagogue, dancing continued to be included in the educational curriculum of the Italian Jew, and Jewish dancing-masters with a Christian clientele still occasionally attracted the attention of religious zealots.

Interest in music was naturally more widely spread, and a number of gifted Jewish instrumentalists and composers emerge from the general anonymity. At the court of Lorenzo de' Medici, together with Guglielmo da Pesaro, was Giuseppe Ebreo, who set one of the other's dances to music. Another member of the same brilliant circle was the flautist-composer, Giovanni Maria, a somewhat disreputable convert, subsequently in the service first of the doge of Venice and then of Pope Leo X, who enfeoffed him with the Castle of Verocchio; he is said to have served as the model for Sebastiano del Piombo's famous painting, *The Violinist*. Another papal protégé of the period was Jacopo di Sansecondo, equally famous for his personal beauty and his exquisite ability as a violinist, who played at the wedding of Lucrezia Borgia in 1502 and sat to Raphael as the Apollo on Parnassus. Elia Vannini, who wrote music for the Carmelites, is also said to have been of Jewish birth. Later on, the center of Jewish musical activity in Italy moved to Mantua, where, at the end of the sixteenth century and the beginning of the seventeenth, we find working for the Gonzaga instrumentalists such as Abramo dell' Arpa and Isacchino Massarano, vocalists such as the member of the De' Rossi family known as "Madame Europa," composers such as David Civita, Allegro Porto, and Anselmo de' Rossi, and above all the court musician Salamone de' Rossi who collaborated with Monteverdi, imitated Palestrina, and, besides publishing a great many original compositions which he dedicated to various Italian and foreign potentates, made a brilliant though unsuccessful attempt to introduce the new aesthetic standard into synagogal music. In Venice, too, there was a Jewish singer, Rachel, who often performed in the salons of the nobility.

In the development of the theater, Italian Jewry played a part of real importance. Their popular drama dealing with the story of Esther, associated with the Purim festival, provided them with elementary training, and we know that it was followed with great interest by their neighbors, who flocked to witness it so long as they could do so with impunity — for Authority frowned even on this. In the middle of the sixteenth century, the Marrano poet Solomon Usque composed a formal play for this occasion, which was more than once presented in Venice before a mixed public. A few other pastoral comedies by Jewish authors, in the spirit of the age, were subsequently produced. But the great center of theatrical interest and proficiency at this time was Mantua. The Jewish actors here were famous; and their reputation was by no means confined to their own quarter. Throughout the sixteenth century, whenever it was desired to have a comedy presented on the stage for the delectation of the duke or in honor of distinguished visitors, recourse was had as often as not to the services of the Jewish community. Indeed, on feast-days the spectacle had to be curtailed or postponed, and on Fridays to begin early, so that it could be finished in time for the Sabbath. The Jewish participation was not confined to acting. Leone da Sommi Portaleone, known otherwise as a Hebrew poet and founder of a synagogue, was not only a distinguished playwright but also the first scientific theatrical producer of modern times. He was a prolific versifier in Italian and wrote both pastoral plays and dialect comedies, on specifically non-Hebraic themes, in which no trace of Jewish sentiment is to be discerned. He supervised the stage management at the court theater with rare insight, even the poet Manfredi relying on his judgment. But he is especially memorable as author of a volume of *Dialogues on the Representative Art* — the first work of its sort — in which he displays an intuition of the minutiae of theater-craft so detailed and so advanced as to have received the compliment of publication in an English translation three and a half centuries after it was first written.

In the visual arts, most closely associated with the Renaissance in the popular mind, Jewish participation was relatively small, for they afforded slender opportunities for persons who could not or would not work for the Church. But this does not imply that interest was lacking. An apostate Jewish artist and bookbinder was implicated in the ritual murder charge at Trent in 1475; and we know of the artist-engravers Moses da Castellazzo in Venice and David da Lodi in Cremona, and of two Jewish members of the painters' guild at Perugia, though little or nothing of their output is traceable. In metal-working — not so intimately ecclesiastical, and closely connected with the traditional goldsmith's craft — a more important part was played. Master Isaac of Bologna was goldsmith to the Neapolitan court in 1484, and Benvenuto Cellini numbered among his masters one Graziadio of the same city. A figure of all but first importance was Salamone da Sessa (subsequently converted, as Ercole de' Fedeli), who worked at the courts of Mantua and Ferrara as well as for that most discriminating patron, Cesare Borgia, for whom he made the masterpiece now at the Louvre which has been termed the "Queen of Swords." Jewish majolica workers, who produced some objects for Jewish use, are found at Padua, Faenza, Urbino and elsewhere in the neighborhood. The metal-workers Joseph Levi and Angelo de' Rossi, of Verona (probably but not certainly Jews), whose productions are still sought after by collectors, belong to a later generation. More than one Italian court made use of the services of Jewish art-purveyors.

In scientific inquiry and achievement, too, Jews collaborated. At the beginning of the fifteenth century, a Jewish hydraulic engineer named Salomone, subsequently in the service of the Este family at Ferrara, was consulted by order of the Venetian Senate about the possibility of diverting the waters of the river Brenta for sanitary purposes. Half a century later, admitting for once that where the public utility was involved no difference of race or creed should be taken into account, a certain Christian mechanic was authorized by the same body to seek Jewish collaboration in developing a machine he had devised. In 1587, the Pope gave a monopoly to one Meir Magino to introduce an improved method of silk-manufacture into Rome; later on, he received a patent for a vegetable oil, which produced remarkable results in polishing mirrors and cut glass. Much interest was aroused in 1515 by a report that some Jews had discovered an improved method of manufacturing saltpeter, the main ingredient of gunpowder, and the Cardinal de' Medici advised his cousin Lorenzino to secure their services for Florence. Interest in astronomy and the allied subjects was particularly keen, the Jews traditionally having a great reputation in this connection. Angelo (Mordecai) Finzi, a prosperous Mantuan loan-banker and the first member of that family to achieve prominence, was a mathematician and astronomer, who wrote extensively on both subjects besides translating works from other languages and composing a set of astronomical tables which were printed in part after his death. Though the majority of his work was in Hebrew, he is known to have been in relations with contemporary non-Jewish scientists, and a reciprocal influence can hardly be doubted. In Rome, the papal physician Bonet de Lattes, who came to Rome with the Provençal exiles in 1498, invented an instrument for calculating the altitude of the sun at any hour of the day, which he described in a Latin monograph dedicated to the Pope. The physician Raphael Mirami, of Ferrara, wrote an ingenious work in Italian on the refraction of light, which was published in 1583. It is not easy to assess whether his contemporary, Abraham Colorni, who vaunted his ability as an inventor, prestidigitator and military engineer,* was, in fact, a thwarted scientist or a mere charlatan; but he enjoyed a very high reputation among contemporaries. Nor should one fail to mention Isaac of Noyon, the engineer, known as Maestro Achino, who in 1437 offered his services to the duke of Milan for constructing a bridge over the Po.

Investigations less useful, but perhaps more characteristic of the time and place, also figured in profusion. A converted Venetian Jew, named Mark Raphael — who at the time of the divorce of Henry VIII of England was consulted, with many others, regarding the interpretation of certain

* Below, page 210.

relevant biblical passages — invented an invisible ink for use in the secret diplomacy of the *Serenissima*. We know of several Jews who dabbled in alchemy, astrology, and the search for the philosopher's stone. There was a famous beauty-expert in Rome at the beginning of the sixteenth century, Anna the Hebrew, who was consulted by members of the ruling classes such as Catherine Sforza, countess of Imola; and later on Bianca Capello, the ill-fated grand duchess of Tuscany, is said to have received unguents and preservatives from Jewish women and to have saved the Florentine community from expulsion as a token of her gratitude. Nor were there lacking more important contributions to personal hygiene. A French visitor to Ferrara calls attention to what he considered the disgusting habit of one of the local rabbis, who carried a piece of cloth about with him and used it as a handkerchief, instead of expectorating on the floor like a decent Christian.

An exceptionally important part in intellectual life was played by the many Jewish physicians, whose tradition went back for centuries. Canon Law, reinforced by the decisions of more than one Church Council and the fulminations of more than one Pope, disapproved of the practice of medicine by Jews except among their coreligionists, lest they should acquire an improper physical and moral influence over their patients. Yet the honoring of this rule more in the breach than in the observance began in Rome itself. From the thirteenth century at least, Pope after Pope had a Jew in his employment as his personal medical attendant, and almost every prince in Italy followed his example. The roll of illustrious Italian Jewish practitioners in the Renaissance period is so long that it is impossible here to do more than mention some of the most important names. There was Elijah ben Sabbatai (Elias Sabot), the first of the Jewish physicians knighted in recognition of their skill, who was in the service of Pope Eugenius IV and his successor as well as of the court of Ferrara, and was in practice all over Italy; Angelo (Mordecai) son of Manuel of Trastevere, citizen of Rome, appointed by Boniface IX as his physician in 1392 and (with his two sons) as surgeon to the Roman militia some ten years after; Moses da Rieta, philosopher and poet as well as physician to the commune of Fabriano from 1458 to 1460, and personal attendant on Pius II; Lazzaro da Pavia, who was driven from Faenza by Fra Bernardino da Feltre because he was so popular with the townsfolk and was summoned to the deathbed of Lorenzo de' Medici too late to save his life; Samuel Sarfatti, or Gallo ("The Frenchman"), reputed to have been the most able physician in Italy in the early years of the sixteenth century, who was in the service of the Medici in Florence and of several successive Popes in Rome; Marco Modena, so esteemed by the anti-Jewish Emperor Charles V that he was created a Knight of the Golden Spur. Another great contemporary name is that of the ex-Marrano Amatus Lusitanus, also at one time a papal physician, who lectured at Ferrara and from whom Giovanni Battista Canano received the first impetus for his discovery of the importance of valves in connection with the circulation of the blood. His *Centuriae curationum*, comprising the history of some of his outstanding cases, was a classic in its day and is one of the most valuable sources of our knowledge of medical practice in the sixteenth century.

In some families, medicine was practiced with distinction over many generations. Typical was that of Portaleone, which derived its name from the quarter adjacent to the main Jewish settlement in Rome. Guglielmo, or Benjamin, Portaleone, who flourished in the second half of the fifteenth century, was successively in the service of Ferdinand I of Naples, by whom he was knighted, Galeazzo Sforza of Milan, and finally the Gonzaga in Mantua, with which city his family was henceforth associated. His elder son, Abraham, was physician to the duke of Urbino, and attended Giovanni delle Bande Nere, ancestor of the grand dukes of Tuscany, on his deathbed; the younger, Lazzaro, practiced at the court of Mantua, as did his descendants after him. The reputation of the family culminated in Abraham Portaleone, great-grandson of the founder of the family, who was greatly esteemed by Christian as well as Jewish contemporaries and composed, at the request of Duke Guglielmo Gonzaga, the first work ever written on otology (the science of the diseases of the ear) and another on the medicinal use of gold. The family continued to provide the Mantuan court with its physicians down to the sixth generation, in the second half of the seventeenth century. Nor were the subsidiary subjects neglected; two Jewish dentists "famous for their art," were at this period in the employment of the dukes of Milan. The reputation of the Italian Jewish physicians spread far outside the boundaries of Italy, Elias Sabot not being the only one who was in attendance on a foreign potentate. We know, for example, of a certain physician named Leone, or Judah (possibly identical with the rabbi-philosopher Judah Messer Leon) who was summoned in 1490 to the court of the grand duke of Muscovy, but was executed when he did not succeed in healing the heir-apparent. Later on, many Italian or Italian-trained Jews received employment at the Sublime Porte in Constantinople. Vesalius, the greatest of anatomists, tells us of two Jews (one, Lazzaro de Frigiis, whom he calls his intimate friend) who helped him in his great work at Padua. In the renewal of medical study in Italy, the Jewish share was of solid importance.

Naturally, it was in the intellectual sphere that their influences were most strongly felt. The revival in the study of the classics, which was one of the motive forces of the Italian Renaissance, inevitably implied a revival among the learned of interest in Hebrew — not generally motivated, as elsewhere, by theological considerations, but in the main considered rather as a branch of the humanities. The passion for the languages of antiquity and everything written in them had thus been followed by the recognition of the importance of the Holy Tongue, coupled with a certain vogue for those who knew it and could teach it. The Florentine scholar-statesman Giannozzo Manetti set the fashion, characteristically teaching philosophy to the loan-banker Manuel da San Miniato in return for his lessons. He attained considerable proficiency, later on keeping a converted Jew in his house as his tutor and speaking to him only in Hebrew. When Pope Nicholas V offered a prize of 5,000 ducats for the discovery of the "original" Hebrew text of the Gospel according to St. Matthew, he began to bring together the corpus of Hebrew manuscripts which constitutes the nucleus of the marvellous collection — one of the greatest in the world — now in the Vatican library. Pope Sixtus IV not only added to these by purchase, but also employed copyists for Hebrew as he did for the other tongues of antiquity, and had cabalistical works translated into Latin. Hebrew manuscripts were widely collected by others also, and in some libraries, like that of the dukes of Urbino, special attention was directed to them. In 1464, a Chair of Hebrew was established at the university of Bologna, and in 1514 one at the Sapienza in Rome. The court of Mantua ardently searched out Hebrew books which interested it, and the vogue for the Holy Tongue was considered by some as the characteristic feature of that city's intellectual life, its study being so popular that some humanists preferred it even to Greek.

We have already seen how in the south of Italy, at the courts of the Emperor Frederick and his successors, Jewish savants had been engaged to carry out a series of translations into Latin of various works composed or, more commonly, preserved in Arabic or Hebrew, especially those of Aristotle and his medieval commentators. The capture of Constantinople in 1453 and the events leading up to it had brought to Italy a flood of scholars and of manuscripts, resulting in a sudden surge of interest in everything Greek — but above all in writings and the philosophy of Plato. Yet there was much of which the Greek original was still to be discovered, but which was available in the medieval Hebrew versions; while those to whom this great store was open were regarded as the authoritative exponents of the Aristotelian system, as the Greeks were of the Platonic. Hence, all over Italy, Jewish scholars made their appearance, in the gatherings of the humanists and in the courts of the humanistic rulers, discussing, teaching, copying, translating. The rich tapestry of Renaissance thought was shot with Hebraic threads, not an obvious part of the pattern, yet essential to its full appreciation.

The climax of the Hebraic revival was reached when Pico della Mirandola, the knight-errant of humanism, purchased by chance a copy of the *Zohar* and became convinced that in it, and in the Jewish cabala in general, he had found the key to the verities of existence, and even confirmation of the Christian faith. He now threw himself with infectious enthusiasm and under the most distinguished guidance into Hebrew and rabbinic studies, stimulating the German humanist Johannes Reuchlin, when they met in Florence in 1491, to follow his example, and thus influencing indirectly the development of the Reformation in Germany. During the two years the latter subsequently spent in Rome as ambassador of the Elector Palatine (1498–1500), he became associated with several Jews — above all the physician Obadiah Sforno, at one time head of the community, who is still remembered for his Hebrew commentary on the Pentateuch, though the Latin polemic against Aristotle which he addressed to Henry II of France has been forgotten. It was upon his instruction in particular that the German humanist's profound knowledge of Jewish literature was based. Back in his native land, Reuchlin took up arms in defense of the Talmud and of Jewish learning, which had been condemned by the Dominicans as the result of the libels of the notorious ex-butcher Pfefferkorn. A great Battle of Books ensued. When, in 1513, the Ecclesiastical Court at Mayence proscribed Reuchlin's defense of the Talmud, he appealed to Pope Leo X and not being sure of his standing in Rome, he, the Christian, wrote a Hebrew letter to the papal physician Bonet de Lattes asking for his support — not only as a Jew, but as a scholar and a person of authority. In the event, Reuchlin was reacquitted; and though in 1520 this decision was reversed, that same year the Pope permitted the printing of the Talmud, so that in fact the obscurantists had only an empty victory to enjoy.

The person to whom Pico della Mirandola owed his introduction to Jewish studies, Elijah del Medigo, perhaps typified the spirit of the age to a fuller extent than any of his Jewish contemporaries. A native of the island of Crete, which with its ancient and cultured Jewish communities had for some time been under Venetian rule, it was natural for him to find his way to Venice. With his simultaneous and exceptional access to the Hebraic, the Hellenic and the Latin heritages, he found himself courted by scholars (such as Domenico Grimani, later Cardinal of S. Marco, and his inseparable friend Antonio Puzzamano) to an extent greater than his attainments perhaps warranted. A philosophical treatise on the *Efficiency of the World*, composed in Venice in 1490, earned him such a reputation as an exponent of the Aristotelian system of philosophy that he was summoned to Padua to act as umpire in a dispute which had arisen in academic circles. Subsequently, he was invited to lecture at the university, though not apparently in an official capacity. It was here that he made the acquaintance of Pico who commissioned him to translate into Latin for his use various philosophical treatises extant only in Hebrew, and afterwards invited him to Florence. Here, during 1484 and 1485, he continued his literary work, studied various metaphysical subjects with his patron, and even, it appears, gave public lectures in philosophy before an eager audience. In Pico's company, he encountered other members of the famous Florentine circle of scholars and humanists, such as Marsilio Ficino. There is reason to believe that he is the bearded Jew who figures in the train of the Magi, together with Pico himself, in Gozzoli's famous fresco in the former Medici palace.

There can be little doubt that Elijah del Medigo was sometimes to be met among that brilliant company which assembled to discuss philosophical problems in the Orti Oricellai. But he was not the only Jew. Another member of the circle, probably more gifted though less famous, was Johanan Alamanno, an expert in the Greek and Arabic philosophies who had been brought up in the cultured home of the business magnate Vitale (Jehiel) da Pisa. At Pico's suggestion, he composed a Hebrew commentary on the Song of Songs — not exclusively for Jewish use, as is obvious — in the tradition of contemporary Tuscan philosophical thought. In the preface to this work, there is a pen-picture of Lorenzo the Magnificent and his circle, and a penetrating analysis of the Florentine character, with its highly developed intellectuality, its keen love of liberty, and its strong civic sense. In a letter to Domenico Benivieni, Marsilio Ficino spoke of the occasions when they had been present at the learned discussions in Pico's palace between the peripatetic Jewish physicians, Elias and Abraham on the one hand, and the learned Sicilian convert, Guglielmo Moncada, on the other — feasts of learning which were long remembered.

Elsewhere in Italy, there was similar contact between Jewish scholars and the leaders of contemporary thought. A deservedly great reputation in many spheres was enjoyed by the Spanish physician Jacob Mantino, who after being in attendance at Venice on some of the most aristocratic families as well as half of the diplomatic corps — who used their influence to have him excused from wearing the Jewish badge — came to Rome as personal physician to Pope Paul III. In 1539, he was officially nominated lecturer in medicine at the Sapienza — one of the very few authenticated instances of the holding of a university appointment by a Jew before the nineteenth century. Philosopher as well as physician, he translated a number of works from Hebrew into Latin, dedicating his version of Averroes' commentary on Plato's *Republic* to the Pope; and he was familiar with many of the best-known Christian scholars of the day — among them the warrior-humanist Guido Rangoni, whom he taught Hebrew, and the German polymath Johann Albrecht Widmanstadt, who had studied it with Rabbi David ibn Iacchia in the house of Don Samuel Abrabanel in Naples. There were in Rome several other exceptionally cultured Jews who were in touch with the foremost intellectual circles. Mention has already been made of the physicians Bonet de Lattes and Obadiah Sforno, both of whom enjoyed a great reputation in their day. Here too lived the Jew whose real identity is obscured by the sobriquet Flavius Mithridates, who corresponded with Marsilio Ficino, was Pico della Mirandola's teacher in the Oriental tongues, and translated various cabalistical works out of Hebrew into Latin; and Joseph Sarfatti, subsequently to acquire a baleful reputation by his activities as an apostate, who was associated with the first awakening of interest in Syriac scholarship in Europe. Leone Ebreo (Judah Abrabanel), author of the *Dialogues on Love*, frequented the most cultured society whether in Naples, Rome or elsewhere, composed a treatise on the *Harmony of the Heavens* for Pico della Mirandola (whether uncle or nephew is uncertain), and was on the most intimate terms with the humanist Mario Lenzi. Cardinal Egidio da Viterbo, the cultured General of the Augustinians, had parts of the *Zohar* translated into Latin for him by Baruch of Benevento, and patronized Hebrew learning as zealously as any Jewish enthusiast. He long gave hospitality in his palace to the German scholar-grammarian Elias Levita (Elijah ha-Levi), who linked together the medieval Jewish philologists and the Christian Hebraists of the age of the Reformation, and was responsible for the dissemination of what was then the sensational theory that the Hebrew vowel-points were relatively modern; later, he worked in Venice, where also he had fruitful contacts in Christian circles. Here, moreover, Cardinal Grimani, patron in former days of Elijah del Medigo, had in his service the distinguished Abraham de Balmes, a refugee from the kingdom of Naples, who not only wrote standard works on Hebrew grammar but also made Latin versions of Averroes' writings which were still used as textbooks at Padua a hundred years later. At Spoleto, in Umbria, lived the physician Moses Alatino, subsequently of Ferrara, who translated Galen from Hebrew into Latin, and spent five years on a rendering of Aristotle's *De Coelo* from a Hebrew manuscript in his library. The part that Jews were playing in the humanistic ferment was not fundamental, but it was widespread and had a durable influence.

The distinguishing feature of the age was a universal intellectual curiosity; and as a result of this Jews made their appearance in the most unexpected places, expounding the rabbinic point of view or explaining the Jewish standpoint in matters of belief, as well as for more mundane purposes. They were familiar in the petty courts, in the households of princes of the Church, in patrician palaces, even in the Vatican. We have a glimpse of the versatile Sicilian scholar, Aaron Abulrabbi, appearing before a Pope — perhaps Eugenius IV — and the assembled Cardinals to demonstrate the reconcilability of the cherubim in the Sanctuary with the stern prohibition of images contained in the Ten Commandments. In Rimini, a group of Jews was called upon to explain the basis of Judaism at the court of Sigismondo Malatesta, in answer to certain strictures made by Giannozzo Manetti. Johanan Alamanno was received by the Gonzaga in Mantua as well as the Medici in Florence. Moses Alatino took the waters at Padua together with one of the sons of the duke of Camerino. The poet Solomon

Usque was in correspondence with Ottavio Farnese, and the critic Azariah de' Rossi with the abbot of Monte Cassino. Abraham Farrisol, a versatile synagogal functionary and skillful copyist — who in his pioneering geographical work, *The Paths of the World*, mentions how he saw in Florence the giraffe sent to Lorenzo the Magnificent by the sultan of Egypt — had an amicable religious disputation at Ferrara, in 1503, with two eminent Christian clerics, in the presence of the duke and all his court.

In other capacities, too, Jews came into prominence, and a motley group gathered round some of the petty Italian potentates. Jews were prominent at the court of Urbino from the fourteenth century, while that of Mantua knew them from the fifteenth. Don Isaac Abrabanel, after having been in the service of the king of Naples, as he had formerly been in that of the Spanish sovereigns, exerted himself in his old age to negotiate the spice-treaty between Venice, where he lived, and Portugal, where he had been born; while his philosopher-son Leone offered to go on a mission to Turkey on behalf of the *Serenissima*. A little later, the ex-Marrano, Daniel Rodrigues, creator of the commercial port of Spalato and its prosperity, negotiated the release of the captives held by the piratical Uscocchi on the Dalmatian island of Lissa. Mention has already been made of the protean Abraham Colorni, long in the service of Alfonso II d'Este of Ferrara — engineer, inventor, and perhaps something of a charlatan, who delighted the assembled lords and ladies with his card tricks, supervised the construction of the fortifications of the city, purveyed ancient works of art, invented the earliest machine gun, described some ingenious new musical instruments which could be used as weapons in case of need, was an expert dueller, devised the first recorded taximeter, and wrote books on physiognomy, mensuration, and secret writing. He also made a fleeting appearance at the courts of Mantua and of Savoy, and later on even at Stuttgart and Prague. At Ferrara, too, lived Abraham Bondi, who settled the details of the investiture of Modena and Reggio for Alfonso d'Este. Most important — though little is known of him — was Joseph (Ippolito) da Fano, intimate of the dukes of Mantua and of Modena at the close of the sixteenth century, who was used for various delicate diplomatic missions and was created a marquess — the earliest Italian Jewish noble.

We have seen something of the impact of the Renaissance spirit on those Jews who became prominent in general life. But it was not confined to them; and, indeed, the influence could hardly have been more universal or more far-reaching. There was no other time, and no other place, in which amorous offenses make their appearance in Jewish life to the extent that they do in fifteenth-century Florence, where, out of eighty-eight cases tried before the civic magistrates at this time, seventeen were for gambling and thirty-four for moral misdemeanors! There was no other time, and no other place, in which the establishment of a disorderly house in the Jewish quarter could even have been discussed. There was no other time, and no other place, in which rabbis could have invoked "chaste Diana" in their sermons. There was no other time, and no other place, when erotic poetry in Hebrew could have presented a problem to moralists. There was no other place where a talmudist of unflinching orthodoxy would have discussed, in a commentary to the Book of Proverbs, whether or no Petrarch's Laura was a real person; where a rabbi's literary achievements could have included a translation from Ariosto's *Orlando Furioso*; or where a delicate ode to a Gentile lady of rank would have been penned on the flyleaves of a Hebrew prayer book.

Local patriotism among the Jews was typically intense. We find one at Rimini, in 1392, making a bequest for the improvement of the harbor and the repair of the walls of Rome. Occasionally, they would leave spontaneous legacies for the *Monte di Pietà* for the benefit of the local poor, dangerous though its competition was. They were often recognized as full citizens of their places of residence, for example, at Rome in 1310 and 1402, or had the citizenship specifically granted to them, as was the case with a series of physicians there in the early fifteenth century. Their rights were occasionally guaranteed in treaties between one town government and the other. They celebrated petty local triumphs and vicissitudes in patriotic verses — not necessarily in Hebrew; assisted when it was needful, as at Bologna in 1443, on the fortifications, and marched on occasion with the citizen forces, as when Venice reoccupied Padua in 1508. Indeed, though those of Sicily admitted their lack of warlike propensities, the Italian Jews were, according to David Reubeni, intrepid and powerfully built, better material for fighting men than those of any other land. Later on, David de' Pomi was to write a work demonstrating the divine origin of the republic of Venice, and to show how the victory of Lepanto was predicted in the Bible. Conversely, the cities often exerted themselves strenuously on behalf of their Jewish inhabitants, as when Bologna championed Elias, owner of the loan-bank at Castel S. Pietro, against the captains of so redoubtable a leader as Cesare Borgia and procured his release. At Cividale, the Jews patriotically celebrated, in 1568, a fictitious millenary of the earliest mention of their community, like true sons of the Renaissance. The banker Laudadio da Rieti — eager rabbinic scholar though he was — frankly confessed that he preferred his beloved Sienna to a hypothetical home in Jerusalem.

The Jews' pastimes were much like those of their neighbors. They played cards — sometimes excessively. The conference held at Forlì in 1418 endeavored to restrict the vice, and numerous individual communities followed suit, but the reiteration shows that the prohibition was not effective. It was an occupation that might be wasteful of money as well as of time. Even rabbis are known to have been reduced to the verge of ruin as the result of it. The case is on record of a Jew who lost 3,000 ducats at a single sitting, in 1479, while playing with the duke of Ferrara; a circumstance which helps us to understand why in the same city an unlucky gambler of the period registered a vow against gambling on the flyleaf of his prayer book. We know of Jewish card manufacturers in Italy at this time, including a couple who carried on clandestine activity in Florence when, in a puritan interlude, the government had set its face against it. The most detailed description extant of the game of rackets, as it was played in the period of the Renaissance, is to be found in a responsum of a Mantuan rabbi, who was asked whether it was permitted to indulge in the pastime on the Sabbath and saw no valid objection, provided it was not played for money or during synagogue service. When the Jews retired in the heat of the summer to their villas in the country, like other urban patricians, some occupied their time in hunting; and there is still extant the letter sent by one of the Da Pisa family to Lorenzo de' Medici to accompany a gift of game.

Intellectual life and training were profoundly Italianized. Jewish young men were admitted to study in the universities — mainly, but not exclusively, with the object of embracing a medical career — as was specifically authorized, after a brief interval, by the papal Bull of 1429. Jewish students are recorded at this period at Perugia, Sienna, Ferrara, Naples, and especially Padua; though, indeed, there was some restriction of the usual ceremonial when they took their degree. Not even the most deeply conservative rabbis voiced any objection to this, though it was discussed whether they should wear the academic robes, and if so whether these should be provided at the corners with the ritual fringes prescribed by the Mosaic law. Here and there they received appointments as university lecturers — Jacob Mantino in Rome and in the Archiginnasio at Bologna, Leone Abrabanel in Naples, Master Elias at Pavia — though only, as it seems, in the faculty of medicine, in which they excelled.

In 1564, David Provenzale of Mantua launched a scheme for setting up a Jewish academy which should teach Jewish and secular subjects simultaneously — including Latin and Italian composition, logic, mathematics, oratory, astronomy and, of course, medicine — enabling its alumni to pass their university examinations in the shortest possible period and without being submitted to an excessive assimilatory influence. It is not known whether anything resulted, but what is certain is that the secular authorities at least would have raised no objection. When, in 1556, a more conventional plan had been mooted at Ferrara by a certain Solomon Riva, who asked for permission to set up a Jewish *studio* at which Rabbi Jacob Reiner was to have taught, the duke exempted those inscribed in it from all tolls, observing that "this can only prove to be to the honor and advantage of our city, for the advantage to be derived from it by many Jewish and non-Jewish students, both natives and foreigners." There could have been no more eloquent testimony to the completeness of the emancipation of Jewish studies.*

In view of the prominence of women in the Italian Renaissance, it was natural for the normal tendencies to domesticity to be somewhat modified. Some Jewish matriarchs were capable financiers, carrying on business when their husbands were dead or ailing, and concluding *condotte* with identical acumen. In the north of the country as well as in Sicily we encounter women physicians, licensed to practice among their own sex. There were a few notable bluestockings: the Paola Anau who copied many Hebrew manuscripts at Rome in a beautiful hand in the thirteenth century, or, in the sixteenth, Pomona da Modena, ancestress of a number of litterateurs of high reputation, who could boast profound rabbinical scholarship. Sometimes, they patronized

* This surprising document (Balletti, *Gli ebrei e gli estensi*, 2nd edition, pp. 96–97) clearly refers to the Rabbi Jacob Reiner (Reicher) of Ferrara, mentioned in the responsa of David Darshan, p. 8, and in Ms. Montefiore 464.

learning, their names figuring in the dedications of the works
which they helped to sponsor. A few attained proficiency
in writing Italian verse, such as Deborah Ascarelli of Rome,
some of whose work was published at the end of the sixteenth
century, or Sarah Coppio Sullam, of Venice, famous among
non-Jews as well as among Jews for her beauty, her salon,
and her poetry.* A few outstanding Jewesses played a part
in public life comparable to that of the *grandes dames* of
the age. The most notable was Doña Bienvenida Abrabanel,
daughter of Don Jacob and wife of Don Samuel**— deeply
pious, deeply charitable, a keen woman of affairs and withal
a munificent patroness of learning. In Naples, she had
assisted in the education of Leonora, daughter of the Spanish
Viceroy, Pedro de Toledo, who subsequently became grand
duchess of Tuscany. The friendship between her and the
younger woman, who called her "mother," was never interrupted, and proved useful for the Abrabanel family and
for the Jews at large. She is described by a contemporary
chronicler as "one of the most noble and high-spirited
matrons who have existed in Israel since the time of our
dispersion ... a pattern of chastity, of piety, of prudence
and of worth." In Ferrara, too, there lived for a time Doña
Beatrice de Luna, or, to use her Jewish name, Gracia Mendes,
aunt and mother-in-law to the Duke of Naxos, who first
reverted there to the practice of Judaism — the most adored
Jewish woman of that or any other age, as notable for her
religious enthusiasm as for her public spirit and her knowledge of affairs. The Italian Jewish communities were thus
a microcosm of Italian life, in which the two civilizations
were blended consistently and, on the whole, not inharmoniously — a phenomenon which was not to be witnessed
again until the nineteenth century.

* It may perhaps be mentioned that Guistina Levi-Perotti, who is said
to have exchanged sonnets with Petrarch, is a figment.
** Below, pages 285 f.

xxiv

Books and Authors

The spirit of the Renaissance could not fail to influence the inner cultural life of Italian Jewry, but the extent to which it did so is none the less remarkable. In the same way as the humanistic scholars modelled their prose style on Cicero and Livy, abandoning the barbarous traditions of medieval Church Latin, so their Jewish contemporaries went back to the Bible. The grammatical and lexicographical works of Elias Levita, Solomon d'Urbino, Abraham de Balmes, and David de' Pomi — most of them incidentally bilingual, and thus available also to the outside world — assisted in laying the foundations of linguistic purity. The Italian Jews became famous in the Jewish world for their flawless style and composition, in striking contrast to the studied inelegance of their northern European contemporaries. Special attention was paid to these subjects in the scheme of education; correspondence was carried on as far as possible in the diction as well as the language of Scripture; stylists could count on supplementing their incomes as letter-writers; and model collections of the epistolary art were compiled, and even published, for general admiration and the imitation which was its most obvious expression.

Literature and study soon felt the impact; and there was a miniature literary renaissance in the Jewish quarters. Though other places, such as Ferrara, ran it close, the main center was Mantua, where the scheme for a Jewish para-university had been launched and where Hebrew education was so highly developed that down to a late date all congregational regulations were issued in that tongue, which was obviously intelligible to all. Most of those who took the lead in the revival lived in or were associated with this city. Here, for example, the Hebrew Scriptures were for the first time edited in accordance with the methods and standards of the new scholarship, though with exceptional industry and acumen, by Solomon Jedidiah Norsa, the scientific text which he produced being the basis of those of our own day. Special emphasis was laid on homiletics, gifted orators such as Judah Moscato, Azariah Picho, and Judah del Bene (stringently criticized for the incongruous pagan allusions which he let slip in the pulpit) opening a new chapter in the history of Jewish preaching. Abraham Portaleone, the eminent physician, wrote in addition to his medical works a massive Hebrew treatise on the antiquities of the Bible and Talmud. The first book by a living Hebrew author ever to be published was a work on rhetoric, *Nofet Zufim* (c. 1478), by the versatile Judah Messer Leon, known in the secular records as "Leo the Jew, Doctor of Arts and Medicine, and Knight, as well as Doctor of the Hebrew Law" — a description which testifies to the high status of the Jewish scholar in Renaissance Italy. The work was intended to demonstrate to the non-Jewish world that the Jews were not hostile to secular culture; and the author shows the influence of the environment not only in his choice of subject but also in his lavish use of classical writers such as Cicero and Quintillian in addition to the standard Jewish authorities. There was not, indeed, universal agreement on such matters, and a quarrel ensued between the author and his hyper-orthodox fellow-townsman Joseph Colon,* the profoundest rabbinic scholar of the age, which the marquess of Mantua summarily but conclusively settled by expelling them both from his dominions.

The Renaissance brought about a quickening of the historical sense, which was no less reflected in Jewish life. It was in the spirit of the new age that Jewish scholars inspected and studied ancient Palestinian coins that had been brought to Italy, and for the first time turned to the investigation of the Samaritan alphabet. This renewal of interest in the

* Below, page 220.

past in conjunction with the new literary fashions opened a new chapter in Jewish historiography, as exemplified in the artificial but moving *Valley of Tears* of the physician Joseph ha-Cohen of Genoa, or his *Chronicle of the Kings of France and Turkey*, or the unnecessarily imaginative *Chain of Tradition* of Gedaliah ibn Iacchia of Imola (whose name is indicative of his Spanish extraction), or a number of local records of less fame but in some cases more merit. Geographical literature included *The Paths of the World* by Abraham Farrisol, which has already been mentioned. Italian Jews specialized, moreover, in accounts of travel — especially to Palestine; and some of them, like a certain Abraham of Perugia, made a point of collecting documents regarding the state of the Jews throughout the world, if only in the hope of being able to trace the Lost Ten Tribes. In the field of economics, the banking magnate Vitale, or Jehiel Nissim da Pisa — author of an informed if unadventurous examination of the relative validity of philosophy and revelation, entitled *Minhat Kanaut* ("The Offering of Zeal") — composed in 1559 a treatise upon the laws of usury, in which he described with notable acumen the mechanism of financial operations and discussed how and how far they were reconcilable with Mosaic law. It is to be noted, incidentally, that he specifically states that the use of the letter of exchange was hardly known among his Jewish contemporaries — a useful corrective to the current notion that they controlled the money market. In 1571, a series of earthquake shocks at Ferrara drove into the country for refuge a certain Jewish scholar — native of Mantua, but formerly resident at Bologna — named Bonaiuto (Azariah) de' Rossi, who thus came into contact with a Christian savant who plied him with questions regarding various problems of Jewish antiquity. This was the genesis of his famous work *Meor 'Enayim* ("The Enlightenment of the Eyes"), in which Hebrew literature and history were considered in the light of those sources extant only in Greek, and the critical principles of the Renaissance were applied for the first time to Jewish records. The work would be a noteworthy one if only for its range of knowledge, references to the Bible being supported from the Greek and Roman classics, the medieval talmudists jostling incongruously with the Church Fathers, and contemporary humanists figuring side by side with the Jewish writers of every land and age. The experiment was made too late, as the spirit of reaction (imposed as we shall see from outside) had by now begun to make itself felt in Jewish life. The book aroused a storm of opposition for its unrestricted critical spirit, and a sharp polemic followed in which scholars from all northern Italy took part. In the end, its perusal was restricted to persons over the age of twenty-five, or those who had received a special license; and it is more important as a mirror of the intellectual outlook of an enlightened Jew of the age than for its actual influence on life and thought.

The cult of poetry was carried to the verge of exaggeration. The Italian school continued to make use of the flawless medium that had been evolved in the golden age in Spain. Every style and subject was known — hymns, elegies, love-poems, but, above all, occasional verses in an unending flow. As in the Christian world, it became customary to greet every momentous event, whether in the life of the individual or in that of the community, with floods of verses, as a rule highly artificial. It was typical of the country and age that there were several of those interchanges of poems championing or condemning the female sex, so beloved of Renaissance litterateurs — some of them in Hebrew and Italian intermixed. None of Immanuel of Rome's successors equalled him, indeed, either in genius or in license. The outstanding figure of the fifteenth century was the papal physician Moses da Rieti, who composed a vision of Paradise modelled on the *Divina Commedia* entitled *Mikdash Me'at* (the "Lesser Sanctuary"), written throughout in flawless though languid *terza rima* — "as pure, as melodious, as forceful and profound — and therefore as difficult to understand — as Dante's own work." A somewhat more virile tradition was established a little later by Moses ben Joab of Florence, who wrote not only religious compositions but also verses on contemporary events, such as the siege of Florence of 1529–30; and Samuel Anau, of Bologna, noteworthy for the quality as well as for the mass of his occasional poetry. Giuseppe Gallo (Sarfatti), son of the papal physician Samuel Sarfatti, introduced the drama into Hebrew by an adaptation of the famous Spanish comedy *Celestina* — probably unaware that the author, Fernando de Rojas, was a Marrano; while the Mantuan scenic producer, Leone de' Sommi, has attributed to him a most un-Hebraic pastoral play, in the artificial style of the age, written in the purest Hebrew. To be sure, the tradition of religious poetry was by no means dead, and collections of hymns were composed at this period which attained very wide currency throughout Italy and beyond.

The traditional Jewish disciplines, centering in the Talmud, were not neglected by reason of the intense interest in other aspects of scholarship. They flourished above all in upper Italy, where as early as the thirteenth century Transalpine immigrants had introduced their characteristically intensive methods of study to Verona, Treviso and Ferrara. The outstanding figure of the fifteenth century was Joseph Colon, or Colombo. Born at Chambéry in France, he was active in a succession of north Italian cities and was regarded down to his death in 1480 as the outstanding rabbinical authority of the day, the inquiries addressed to him faithfully reflecting every facet of Italian Jewish life in this time of change and turmoil. Among his notable decisions was one which became generally accepted — that it was permissible to impose a special levy on one community in order to save another in time of persecution. Schools of talmudic learning were now to be found all over Lombardy and the Venetian territories. That of Padua, the leading figure in which was Judah Minz,* acquired a particularly great reputation, enlisting students, not only from other parts of the Peninsula, but even from Germany and the Levant; while among the other academies there was one presided over by an exile from France who discussed matters of common interest with his Teutonic colleagues in Hebrew. On Judah Minz's death in 1509, the leadership was taken over by his son Abraham, and then from 1541 to 1565 by the latter's son-in-law Meir Katzenellenbogen, known as Meir of Padua, one of the greatest talmudists of the day and likewise author of important and informative responsa on problems of Jewish law. Contemporaneously with the latter, Joseph Ottolenghi, an immigrant from across the Alps, with exceptionally strict scientific standards, made Cremona for a time a great center of talmudic studies.

But the humanistic currents of Italian Jewry tended to assimilate these stern Transalpine interests. Even Rabbi Judah Minz was reported — apocryphally indeed, but there must be some kernel of truth in the story — to have taught in the University of Padua and to have had a statue erected to him in the Great Hall. Jacob ben Judah Landau, an immigrant from Germany who settled first at Pavia (1480) and then in Naples (1487), composed his famous but not very original compendium of Jewish law, known as the *Agur* ("Bundle"), for the benefit of a native pupil whose time was so taken up with the study of natural science and philosophy that he had no leisure for the Talmud. It is perhaps symbolic that the outstanding talmudist produced by Italy at this period, Obadiah da Bertinoro (a small place not far from Imola), composed his famous commentary on the Mishnah, not in his native country, but in Jerusalem, where he arrived in 1488 after a long and eventful journey of which he has left an absorbing account.**

*I. e., of Mainz, the family name was later transformed into Levi-Minzi.
**See pages 243–5.

That rabbinical and literary life was influenced by economic factors and reflected the communal dichotomy was inevitable. The accomplished and enlightened scholars who flourished under the patronage of the loan-bankers, often living in their houses as private tutors, were sometimes at loggerheads with the official rabbis employed by the larger but poorer non-banking community, whose interests and outlook tended to be somewhat more narrow. The latter, on their side, resented outside intervention, and by dint of communal and intercommunal ordinances endeavored to prevent the interference of others in the internal affairs and legal disputes of the wider body. Prolonged paper battles frequently raged between the two parties — sometimes originating in rival claims to a loan-bank concession, or the right to exercise rabbinical functions — which would involve half the talmudists of Italy, result in the launching of wholesale though harmless excommunications, and perhaps end in a protracted schism in one community or another; for the Italian Jew was nothing if not litigious.

It is clear from what has been said before that the upper classes at least of the Jewish communities were thoroughly Italianized, linguistically and culturally. So far, indeed, was this the case that they began to call their learned gatherings by the name "Academy," though they ingeniously tried to find a Hebraic derivation for the term. Immigrants from other lands might retain relics of their former tongues for a generation, but they were soon assimilated to their native-born coreligionists who, though they might retain archaic forms or Hebraic terms for domestic purposes, could use the purest Tuscan when necessary in their outside relations. Frequently, indeed, they wrote their Italian in Hebrew characters, whether for convenience, for secrecy, or from ignorance; and a small literature in this Judaeo-Italian form is preserved in manuscript and print, including various translations of the prayer book produced for the benefit of the womenfolk. In the sixteenth century, Jewish writers occasionally collaborated with Christians in volumes of complimentary verses; and the Spanish playwright, Solomon Usque, besides translating Petrarch's sonnets into his native language, published an Italian poem on the Creation, which he dedicated to Cardinal Borromeo. Leone Abrabanel's *Dialoghi di Amore*, first published, if not written, in Italian, and one of the most famous philosophical compositions of the age, was well known among his coreligionists, being soon translated into Hebrew and parts being incorporated in a rabbinical commentary on the Song of Songs. Besides Usque, a number of other Marrano immigrants made themselves known in literary circles, perhaps the most gifted being the physician Diego Pires or Didaco Pyrrho Lusitano, later of Ragusa, one of the foremost neo-Latin poets of the time, who lived at Ferrara under the protection of the ducal house and was familiar with the great Tasso.

Italy was not the pioneer of the new art of printing, but one of its earliest homes and the land where it reached its highest degree of perfection. The same was true of printing in Hebrew. It now appears possible that this was established in Spain before reaching Italy, but it was here that the great majority of early Hebrew printed books were produced. Italian printing itself began about the year 1464. In 1475, the first two dated Hebrew books were passing through the press at opposite ends of the country: at Piove di Sacco — not far from Padua, where a little group of Jews had been established for the past century — under the direction of the physician Meshullam Cusi; and at Reggio di Calabria, on the Straits of Messina, where a certain Abraham ben Garton had set up his press and was at work on an edition of the classical commentary of Rashi on the Pentateuch. It was this that was finished first and enjoys the honor of being the earliest dated Hebrew book now extant. In the next couple of decades, Jewish presses — most of them owned and conducted by wandering craftsmen in search of patronage — were set up in place after place in Italy, at least two-thirds of the one hundred and fifty traceable Hebrew incunables being of Italian origin. One of the first was that of Rome, though some of its earliest productions were undated. At Mantua, the physician Abraham Conat and his learned wife, Estellina, set up their press in 1476. Abraham the Dyer, of Pesaro, followed their example next year at Ferrara, later transferring himself to Bologna, where a German master-printer had made his appearance also in 1477. A Roman and a German working in partnership, in conjunction with some enthusiastic bankers who provided the capital, brought the new art in 1485 to Naples. Here, later on, three presses flourished simultaneously and in the next nine years more Hebrew books were published than in any other single place in Italy — and it goes without saying, in Europe — at this period; they include the first complete edition of the Hebrew Bible (1491–3), and the five-volume *Canon* of Avicenna for the use of physicians — the most ambitious production of early Jewish typography.

The most important record in the early annals of Hebrew printing is that of a family which, a century before, had won legendary reputation in Germany for its opposition to the persecution of Fra Giovanni da Capistrano, and later settled in the little town of Soncino in Lombardy, from which it took its name. Here Israel Nathan Soncino the physician (the constant recurrence of the profession in this connection is noteworthy) set up his press in 1483, his work being carried on by his son, Joshua Solomon, and his grandson, Gershom ben Moses. During its half-century or more of activity in Italy the press moved about considerably; it can be traced successively at Casalmaggiore (where the prayer book according to the Roman rite was first printed in 1486), Soncino for the second time, Naples, Brescia, Barco, Fano, Pesaro, Ortona, and Rimini; subsequently, members of the family are encountered, still following the same profession, in Salonica and Constantinople. Of the known

Italian Hebrew incunables, nearly one-half were produced by this gifted clan, who showed their taste no less in their choice of literature than in the fine type they used, their beautiful decorations and their artistic arrangements. The most active of the family, Gershom, known to his Christian contemporaries as Geronimo, did a great deal of work also in Latin and Italian, including the statutes of certain municipalities, and is a memorable figure in the history of printing. True to the scholarly Jewish tradition, he went to particularly great pains to search out manuscripts so as to establish the correct text of the works which he produced, his edition of Petrarch being especially noteworthy. Moreover, he contests with the great Aldo the credit of first realizing the potentialities of the so-called italic type.

Gershom Soncino ascribed the decline of his fortunes, with some acerbity, to new competition at Venice, henceforth the great haven of Jewish publishing. Here there arrived at the beginning of the century a wealthy Antwerp burgher named Daniel Bomberg, strongly pro-Jewish in feeling, who indeed assisted many Marranos to escape into Turkey. In his new home, he came into contact with an apostate Jew named Felice da Prato, who called his attention to the importance and potentialities of a new Hebrew press, which no Jew, however, might establish owing to the exclusive legislation of the republic. Bomberg accordingly obtained the necessary privileges and, in November 1516, produced a Pentateuch with the prophetical lessons for synagogal use. This is the first work in the noble tradition of Venetian Hebrew printing, which was to continue for three hundred years. For some thirty years, books continued to pour out from Bomberg's press in an almost incessant stream. It is difficult to say whether they are most noteworthy for the fineness of the paper, the beauty of the type, or the excellence of the matter. Time after time, the Bomberg Press produced pioneer editions — for example, that of the uniform Talmud (1519–23) or the Rabbinic

Bible, with all standard commentaries (1517–8) — which even today remain authoritative. All told, he brought out, in the course of the three decades of his activity, about two hundred works, some of them being commissioned by remote Jewish communities of other lands; indeed, the Jewish book-export trade must for a long time have been a source of considerable income to the republic. When, in 1525, his privilege expired, there was some difficulty in having it renewed, as the obscurantist party in the Senate raised objections against the publication of works which were "against the faith;" but at the price of a hundred ducats he was at length licensed to carry on as before for another ten years. Even when the general standard of printing had so fallen in Venice that the works published there were excluded from Rome in the interests of scholarship, the productions of the Bomberg Press knew no decline from the high level which it had originally set itself. There is no person in the whole annals of Hebrew typography whose record can compare with that of this Christian enthusiast.

In his old age, Bomberg returned to Antwerp, and in 1548 his press closed its doors. But by this time there were others engaged in Hebrew printing in Venice, Jews and non-Jews, the most important being a patrician named Giustiniani; and for one or two generations more the city continued to enjoy its typographical primacy. Meanwhile, presses were set up in other Italian cities: at Ferrara, where Abraham Usque and his associates produced, not only many books in Hebrew and a number of liturgies and the like in Spanish translation, but also a few works of general interest in that language and in Portuguese, such as the first edition of the Portuguese bucolic classic *Menina e Moça*; at Riva di Trento, where yet another physician, Jacob Marcaria, worked from 1558 to 1562 under the protection of Cardinal Cristoforo Madruzio (whose arms surmounted by a Cardinal's Hat figure on the title page of some of the works), producing in addition at least one of the official publications of the Council of Trent; at Sabbionneta under the patronage of Vespasiano Gonzaga, one of the most enlightened of all Renaissance princes; as well as at Cremona, Mantua, and other places. It is superfluous to give a full account here of this activity. Enough has been said to show the importance of book production in the life of Italian Jewry in the Renaissance period. It was not until the middle of the following century that the country lost its primacy; and, for that, external circumstances were mainly responsible.

CHAPTER VI

The Islands and the South

XXV

Sicilian Jewry

WHEN the pride of the Jewish communities of southern Italy had been broken by the persecutions at the close of the thirteenth century, those of Sicily, at that time under a different rule, had been unaffected. The island continued to be the greatest center of population of Italian Jewry, with settlements in the more important cities which were hardly exceeded numerically even by that of Rome. In the main, Sicilian Jewish history continued on its own path, local color differentiating the background in some important respects from that of the country as a whole. Its antecedents were not the same, for it continued to reflect the island's long period of Saracen rule and influence. This was, of course, intensified by its nearness to Africa and the Moslem world, so that to the end Sicilian Jewry had many of the characteristics of a Moresque community. Moreover, it happened that, for reasons partly political and partly genealogical, Sicily was ruled from the close of the thirteenth century by sovereigns of the house of Aragon, frequently — and with disastrous consequences in the end — kings of that country as well. Hence Sicilian Jewish history had in certain respects closer affinities with Spain than Italy. All this had far-reaching effects politically, culturally, and even economically. It may be added that, at a period when our information regarding the greater part of Italy has to be pieced together from a wide variety of scattered and scanty sources, the preservation of the Sicilian records and the enthusiasm of Sicilian scholars makes it possible to reconstruct the life of the Jews on the island, from the fourteenth century onwards, in minute and sometimes fascinating detail.

Sicilian Jewry was on the whole unaffected by the new currents described in the preceding chapter, its backbone being to the end a hardworking proletariat of manual laborers. The Emperor Frederick had, indeed, legalized moneylending early in the thirteenth century for the Jews of his Italian dominions; but those of Sicily, at least, did not take to it, and in 1398 successfully petitioned the government to prohibit usury between Jew and Christian in the same way as it was prohibited between Jew and Jew. Though subsequently the prohibition fell into desuetude, and usury was legalized retroactively in 1451, the moneylender remained a rare figure in the island communities. They included a sprinkling of merchants, supply-brokers and physicians. But the vast majority were artisans — weavers, dyers, cobblers, silverworkers, blacksmiths, joiners, saddlers, and so on, down to porters, stevedores and dockers. Itinerant peddlers and linen-drapers might be met throughout the island, and in the capital at least the poorer women helped to support their families by their weaving. Some of the master craftsmen were of outstanding ability. In 1486, the *jurati* of Messina, while acidly observing that it was prejudicial for the Jewish population to increase any further, conferred citizenship rights on a Jewish silk-weaver from Catanzaro who had taken up his residence there; while at Palermo there was a guild of Jewish master carpenters, to the wardenship of which Joseph Caschisi was appointed by the king in 1451 in consideration of his skillful work in the construction of the royal palace.

By the fifteenth century, the total Sicilian Jewish population was probably about 20,000. This is far fewer than older writers suggested, but even so there were perhaps as many Jews in the island as in the whole of northern Italy. They were distributed in upwards of sixty communities. The greatest and most influential by far was that of Palermo, which claimed authority to speak on behalf of the Jews of the entire realm and was organized in a *università* parallel and, in its limited sphere, equal in authority to the Christian municipality. Here, the Jews were reckoned at as many as 5,000 souls, being approximately one-third of the total population. It would appear that this community was in the fifteenth century rather more than twice as large as the next in importance, that of Trapani. This was followed by Sciacca and Messina, where the number of Jews increased from about 200 in 1170 to 180 families or some 900 souls in 1453.* Catania, which was reckoned fifth in numerical order, had two Jewish quarters, the upper and the lower (*giudecca di susu, giudecca di giusu*), each with its own synagogue. Other relatively important centers were Castroreale, Nicosia, Mazzara, Girgenti and Marsala, where they comprised 9% of the population. But the majority of the communities were small, such as S. Marco (300 souls), Castronuovo (120 souls) or Salemi (six families). The size of the Jewish colonies on the outlying islands — Malta, Gozzo, even Pantelleria — was unexpectedly large, that of the latter place being, from the fiscal point of view, on a level with some of the most important in the kingdom.

The communities were exceptionally well organized and closely knit. They enjoyed local autonomy, held occasional representative assemblies to deliberate on matters of common interest, levied their own taxation, and enforced decisions, whether in financial or administrative matters, by the ban of excommunication, their employment of which was recognized, approved and even implemented by the

---

* These data are based on the revenue figures, which are not likely to favor the Jews; they therefore represent a maximum rather than a minimum. Trapani had risen greatly in importance at the end of this period.

state. The executive officers at the head of each community, known as "syndics" (*sindachi*), were chosen in rotation for three-monthly or longer periods among the members of the deliberative council of *proti* (Greek πρῶτοι: the corresponding Hebrew term was apparently *zaken* or "elder"), generally twelve in number. This body appointed, too, the *percettori* who levied taxation, the *limosnieri* who administered charity, and the *auditori di conti* who reviewed the accounts and prevented financial irregularities. In 1397, the system of election to the council was reorganized by the Crown so as to ensure that the three conventionally recognized classes of the community — the rich, the well-to-do, and the self-dependent poor — were all represented on it in identical number; the proportions were clearly unequal, but this made for something more nearly approximating to a democratic system. Later on, in the first quarter of the fifteenth century, an attempt was made to convert the governing body from an elective to a nominative one, the members holding office henceforth at the king's pleasure or for life; while in 1484 it lost its last democratic vestige, and became self-perpetuating, the outgoing representatives henceforth designating their successors. Dissent was out of the question, since already in 1398 the communities had petitioned and the Crown agreed that no meetings should be permitted among the Jews without the consent of superior authority "for this is the beginning of unrest and dispute." Occasionally, the constitutional forms might be suspended, the king cancelling the elections or nominating a Christian official as "governor" of the Jewish community, like a city manager or government commissary of later times. However much an individual might disapprove of the manner in which public affairs were conducted, it was impossible for him to disinterest himself, attendance at meetings of the community being enforced by law. These would be held in some public building in the town — for example, the hospital — if there was no room in the synagogue.

The salaried officials included, besides the rabbi (known as *giudice spirituale* or spiritual judge,* the most important of his functions being the settlement of disputes in accordance with talmudic law) a number of minor functionaries — the notary or scribe to draw up legal documents,** the *manigliore* or sacristan, and the *scannatore* or *shohet* (ritual slaughterer). Communities of any size had, by the side of the synagogue, the usual subsidiary institutions, religious and secular, such as the public baths of which there are still some architectural traces here and there; the hospital founded at Nicosia by a childless Jew before going to end his days in Jerusalem;*** the school endowed by a generous benefactor at Girgenti but not allowed to remain in Jewish possession; and the wine-shops, one of which (there were three in all) we know to have been in disturbing proximity to the synagogue at Palermo.

The influence of successive French, German and Spanish rulers forced upon the Sicilian Jews a status of political inferiority unknown in northern Italy — that of "serfs of the Royal Chamber," as they were very often styled. This inevitably resulted in a particularly close governmental control, which manifested itself sometimes in the most unexpected ways. When, in 1421, the communities of the realm desired to suppress the practice of bigamy, not yet forbidden according to Jewish law among those who lived under Moslem influence, they applied to the Crown for confirmation; though as a matter of fact childless husbands occasionally obtained the royal license even now to take a second

---

* This obviously corresponds to the Hebrew *dayyan*, the title rabbi being presumably conferred on any person learned in the Law, whether he occupied an official position or no. It is perhaps significant that the earliest known Sicilian Jewish scholar, Mazliah ibn al-Bazak (above, page 57), is so designated.

** Older historians discovered a picturesque equivalent, *idubi*; but this is based on a misreading.

*** Possibly the Gothic building in the Via della Giudecca at Trapani, still known as Lo Spedaletto.

wife. In 1419 — not for the first time — the jovial Jews of Trapani were forbidden, under extravagant penalties, to waste their substance by playing the game of chance, called *zara*, of which the communal authorities disapproved. On the other hand, when towards the close of the century, the puritans in the community of Sciacca used the threat of excommunication to stop mixed dancing, the civil authority quashed the ordinance. New regulations for the general guidance, which were decided on by the delegates of the Jewries of the realm and sometimes those enacted by the individual communities, governing matters such as the exaction of taxes, the election of officials, and even sumptuary laws, were given additional force by being submitted, like legislative acts, to the king or his representative for confirmation. The general assemblies of delegates which met at intervals to vote money, discuss matters of common interest, and decide on new regulations to be submitted for royal approval, may fairly be described as Jewish parliaments.

As was invariably the case in the medieval community, the Sicilian Jews were taxed as an entity, not being included in the general financial scheme; though it was understood that the amount levied from them in each town should normally bear an approximate relationship to their proportion in the population. The principal impost was a poll-tax known by the Arab name of *gisia*; another bore the title, of uncertain origin, *augustale*. There were other levies: on animals slaughtered in the Jewish fashion, on wine and cheese prepared for Jewish use, on cloth of Jewish manufacture, and so on, as well as a "beam tax" on the sale of houses. Frequently, the communities made a freewill offering to the Crown in recognition of some concession made to them or for the abolition of a galling restriction; while from time to time they would pay heavily for a "general pardon," whether the misdeeds in question were real or hypothetical. There were minor imposts galore, more galling than burdensome, though in the aggregate they must have represented a considerable load. On the great Church festivals the Jews of Malta had to give a present to all the officials of the island, and those who had formerly held office did their best to have themselves included. Those of Syracuse had to contribute a golden "ounce"* daily to the expense of the royal table when the king visited that city. At Palermo at least, there was up to 1393 a special tax known as the *jocularia*, or *jugalia*, on every marriage, the amount varying in proportion to the number of cornet-players in attendance, in accordance with Saracenic practice; and on every birth, though naturally at a lower rate for a girl than for a boy. In time of war or of emergency, obligations increased. For the royal service, though officially for no other purpose, beasts of burden might be temporarily requisitioned. In 1397, the Jews of Girgenti had to equip a force of 200 foot for one of the king's military expeditions. Those of Malta furnished oil for the loggia where the guard assembled; while those of Gozzo maintained the expense of a man-at-arms at time of emergency or of special danger. The Palermo community was expected to provide the civic officers with beds and other furniture for their lodgings. There was an ancient and general obligation — abolished however in 1421 — to furnish the banners for the royal castles and ships of war (presumably an outcome of the Jewish association with the silk-weaving and dyeing industry). The wine-tax was sometimes converted into a congregational monopoly. In such circumstances abstention became an anti-social act, and we find the Palermo community on one occasion raising a loan from the Jewish tavern-keepers and wine-merchants to defray its share in a gift to the king, and on another compelling wealthy Jews to advance the money on a certain amount annually for the next four years. As in the south

---

* The *oncia* or "ounce" was the standard unit of currency in Sicily; in modern values perhaps $60. It was equivalent to eight ducats, each ducat being divided into five *tari* and 20 *grani*.

of Italy, jurisdiction over the Jews and the consequent financial profit had passed during the Norman period to the bishops and archbishops, but had been reclaimed for the Crown under the Emperor Frederick. During the confusion that followed his death, the Apostolic Vicar again asserted the ancient ecclesiastical claims, which were generally recognized during the Angevin period. The rulers of the house of Aragon proved less complacent in this matter than in many others and insisted on their rights — except at Palermo, where the Church's claim to jurisdiction over the Jews was too well established. Yet even so some relics of the ecclesiastical pretensions survived. Thus the Jews of Mazzara were obliged to present the bishop from 2½ to 5 pounds of pepper (then an extremely valuable commodity) every year: while at Messina, up to 1482, the archbishop claimed a death-duty of 25 per cent on all legacies.

Perhaps because the Jews of Sicily were so poor, perhaps because a strong Byzantine tradition continued in the island, they were compelled to perform many burdensome and unpleasant labor-services and so on (*angherie*), thus supplementing the unending financial exploitation. As serfs of the Royal Chamber, they were expected one and all, except for a few privileged persons, to clean and sweep the royal castles and palaces, to dig ditches, and to haul the king's ships to the beach. Whenever necessary, they had to act as executioners for capital sentences, these being carried out in their burial ground for the sake of additional odium — a function that cannot have enhanced their popularity. Those of Messina could hardly complain at having to mount guard on the walls of the city near their quarter, but their coreligionists in Sciacca had to patrol the entire fortifications, securing exemption only in return for a payment. Down to the eve of the expulsion, the Palermo community had not only to clean out the castle each Friday, but also to toll the bells, scrape the fountains, clear the mud from the streets, sweep the courtyards of the public buildings, and carry the benches of the city officers from one place to another. It is true that in some places, such as Girgenti, the Jews were supposed to be exempt from all personal service, except what was required on the occasion of a royal visit; but the local authorities, both ecclesiastical and secular, nevertheless did their utmost to assert their claims. Various petty annoyances, sometimes accompanied by violence, also had the sanction of custom, and eventually of law. Many places maintained the ancient abuse common in South Europe, of stoning the houses of the Jewish quarter on Good Friday; and it is easy to see how this might degenerate into a riot. At Marsala, the Jews had to attend the church services on Christmas and on St. Stephen's day, being subsequently escorted home with stones by the vengeful mob; and even after this barbarous custom was abolished they were still expected to be present at Mass on the latter occasion. Here, too, as was the custom at Rome at carnival-time, they were used as mounts for the mock tournament on St. John's day. On Christian feast days, they had to keep within their houses, with the doors and windows closed, and were forbidden to do any work that could be seen from the street. So onerous did these occasions of enforced repose become, in view of the multiplicity of minor church celebrations, that in 1420 the community of Catania secured from the viceroy a limitation of the number to be observed.

Even religious institutions were kept under royal control in so highly centralized a system. As early as the thirteenth century, the king exercised the prerogative of nominating the rabbi of Palermo — the case of Master David the Physician, appointed in 1283, was presumably not the first. Even the sacristans, readers, and ritual slaughterers sometimes owed their appointment to the Crown, though occasionally the bishop claimed the right. It was, however, in the fourteenth century that the royal control over the intimate affairs of Sicilian Jewry reached its climax. In 1396, King Martin appointed his physician, the Catalan Joseph Abenafia, who had possibly accompanied him from Spain, as Chief Judge (in Hebrew, *Dienchelele*, or *Dayyan Kelali*) over all the Jewish communities of his realm, with full authority in civil and criminal matters. The diploma suggests that the appointment was made at the request of the Jewish communities, but the statement is clearly disingenuous, as considerable opposition developed among them. So great indeed was the resentment aroused at Palermo that the municipality itself urged the king to exempt their Jewish fellow-citizens from his control. It is not easy to describe the office in modern terms. Inasmuch as the *Dienchelele* was officially supreme judge of the Jewish communities of the realm in matters concerned with Jewish law, it is not wholly inaccurate to describe him as Chief Rabbi.* But his functions were in the main secular. He was on the one hand the royal agent in matters concerned with the administration of the Jewish communities, probably including questions of taxation, and, on the other, the mouthpiece of the Jewish communities when they wished to approach the king. We find him soliciting revised regulations for internal government, travelling after the court to secure new privileges or the withdrawal of obnoxious ordinances, organizing the redemption of Jewish captives, and so on. But there must have been much that was far less palatable, to justify and explain the loathing with which the office was obviously regarded. The emoluments, at the outset, were 36 ounces annually — by no means a burdensome sum. The effective exercise of authority throughout the kingdom by the same person was impossible, and the *Dienchelele* later appointed substitutes to represent him in various localities, to interpret Jewish law and enjoy all the privileges appertaining to his office.

At the beginning of 1408, Joseph Abenafia died, the Jewish communities being enjoined to pay the arrears of his salary

---

* If the local religious leaders were known as *dayyanim* (see page 232), the *Dayyan Kelali* would correspond almost exactly to this term.

to his widow. His successor, appointed after consultation with the representatives of the principal Jewries, as promised ten years earlier, was a certain Rais of Ragusa, whose style was, however, somewhat less ambitious; and his successor, in turn, was Isaac of Marseilles, another physician, who succeeded in 1414. The office reached its culmination with the appointment, in 1420, of Moses, son of Bonavoglia of Messina, usually known as Moses Bonavoglia (in Hebrew, "Hefetz"). He was a royal favorite, who from his youth had been laden with privileges by the Crown, so that when he went to study medicine at the university of Padua, in 1413, he received a cordial letter of recommendation to the rector. Young and inexperienced, his nomination aroused a storm of protest, even the municipalities of Palermo and Messina claiming that it was an infringement of their privileges. After a few months, accordingly, it was revoked, but by the autumn of the following year Master Moses managed to enlist sufficient support from his coreligionists for it to be renewed. His regime continued to be unpopular, and in 1431 the communities of the realm offered the government a large sum of money in return for abolishing the office, the secular functions of which were now entrusted to the High Treasurer. Eight years later, Master Moses returned into favor, and was formally reinvested with authority by proxy, on March 9, 1439, in the synagogue of Palermo, while he was in attendance upon the king at Naples. Notwithstanding the automatic protests of the municipality of Palermo, he managed to retain his office to his death in 1446. He was now at the height of his reputation, and enjoyed a great prestige at court; so much so that we find numerous customs-grants for his benefit, and even a generous gift from the king on the occasion of the marriage of one of his daughters. His successor was Joshua Bonartino, similarly one of the royal physicians. The term of office started auspiciously, with the quashing of some inquisitorial proceedings against him. But the opposition which developed among the Jewish communities was this time irresistible, and on May 9, 1447, in consideration of a gift of 600 ounces offered by their delegates, the king definitely abolished the unpopular office. It was understood that this was to be succeeded by a democratic regime, the rights formerly vested in the *Dienchelele* belonging henceforth to the communities as a whole, and fresh elections were accordingly held for all offices that had been filled by nomination in recent years. Thus, after a duration of a little more than half a century, the episode was liquidated.

Bonavoglia was not the only individual to enjoy the royal favor. Two centuries before him, the Emperor Frederick employed a Jew named Gaudio, or Isaac, in the financial administration. In the Aragonese period, Sicilian Jews, like their coreligionists in Spain, sometimes served in public office, or were chosen for their linguistic ability to represent the interests of the sovereign abroad. Thus, in 1409, Samuel Sala of Trapani went to Africa to negotiate peace between King Martin and the ruler of Tunis, his family receiving certain privileges by way of reward; and it is improbable that this was the only case of the sort. As late as 1492, when Sicilian Jewry lay under the shadow of the final tragedy, Master David the Physician, agent of the Jewish community of Palermo, was in the royal service.

A profession widely followed in Sicily, as throughout the Jewish world, was that of medicine, notwithstanding the stringent canonical prohibition. Legally, indeed, a Jewish physician who attended on a Christian was liable to imprisonment on bread and water for a whole year and the forfeiture of his fee, the patient, on the other hand, being imprisoned, if he recovered, for as long as three months. The restriction was not an unqualified misfortune, for it did not give an opening to accusations of plotting the death of Christian patients, such as brought about the execution at Palermo in 1430 of the Majorcan Moses Rimos (who left behind an exquisite ethical testament, which is one of the gems of medieval Jewish literature). But Jewish physicians, who did not restrict their attentions to coreligionists, were numerous nevertheless. They considered themselves a privileged class, and like their non-Jewish confreres claimed — though not with complete success — to be exempted from taxation. The case is on record also of a Jewish barber-surgeon of Malta who was excused from filling communal offices in view of his importance to the island gentry. A list of upwards of one hundred and fifty Jews who practiced in the island between 1363 and 1492 has been compiled; but even this high figure is manifestly incomplete. Several of them (Master Busach of Palermo, 1237;* his son David, 1282; Master Aaron of Messina, 1367; Gaudio, or Isaac, of Messina, 1376; and at least two of the *Diencheleli*) were in attendance at court; while the cities of the island sometimes employed Jews as official physicians. The profession was followed by women also; thus, in 1376, Virdimura, wife of the physician Pasquale of Catania, was empowered to practice medicine throughout the realm. Generally speaking, it was necessary for the Jew to obtain such a license, presumably after what was considered to be adequate private study, before he was allowed to follow this calling; and in 1403 the *Dienchelele*, Joseph Abenafia, is referred to as the official "examiner of the Jews promoted to the exercise of the physical art." This arrangement was not ideal; and the Sicilian universities, unlike some of those on the mainland, were apparently unwilling to regularize matters by admitting Jews. Among the privileges secured in 1451, in return for a gift of 10,000 florins, the practice of medicine among all classes, without religious distinction, was thrown open to all. It seems that there was now an influx to the profession. The communities of the island determined therefore, in 1466, upon an amazing new venture — none other

---

* Possibly he belonged to the family of the tenth-century scholar Mazliah ibn al-Bazak, of Palermo.

than to establish their own Jewish university in order to facilitate the studies of young Jews who were thirsting for knowledge. They presented their petition through their representative, Benjamin Romano of Syracuse, and were formally authorized by King John to set up a university, or *studium generale*, in any city they might choose, to engage and discharge doctors, jurists and others, "and in the said university to arrange instruction in all the approved sciences for those who seem proper thereto and others." Moreover, the king took under his protection "all the doctors, jurists, masters, students, and others who shall frequent the said *studium generale* . . . as well as the said *studium* itself." The precise object of the new foundation is not clearly stated. It is, however, obvious that it must have been intended in the main for the study of medicine and the conferring of academic degrees in that subject. From the repeated mention of jurists, it is probable that civil law — in which Jewish experts were obviously needed — was to be another subject. That the humanities were envisaged, except incidentally, is hardly probable, and Jewish studies would plainly have been out of place. The scheme, as a matter of fact, proved too ambitious, and whether the Jewish university functioned for a short time or no we hear nothing more of it.*

The intellectual interests of the Sicilian Jewries were of the traditional type. We know of schools founded by generous benefactors in various places; and a curious document of 1472 shows us an eager student in Syracuse contracting with a certain scholar to teach him the entire Talmud and the Jewish laws in the extremely brief period of two years. Yet persons so laboriously engaged could not have much leisure for study, and Hebrew scholarship cannot be said to have flourished in Sicily at any time. During the centuries of Christian rule, a few names only stand out: the rabbi-

---

* In the sixteenth century, a somewhat similar idea was broached by certain Jewish scholars in Northern Italy; see above, page 216.

physician of the end of the thirteenth century, Ahitub ben Isaac of Palermo, who furnished posterity with a description of his voyage to Paradise in his *Sepher ha-Teneh* ("Book of the Basket"); Judah Siciliano, friend and correspondent of Immanuel of Rome, who settled in that city and enjoyed a great reputation as a poet; Aaron Abulrabbi of Catania who travelled widely, studied at Treviso in North Italy, compiled a defense of Judaism, now lost, and an acute super-commentary on Rashi's biblical expositions, and explained before the Pope, probably Martin V (1417-1431), the reconcilability of the Cherubim with the Second Commandment.* Sicilian, too, by birth was the Jacob Sikilli, who lived in Damascus and Aden in the fourteenth century and compiled, rather than composed, a homiletic commentary on the Pentateuch, *Midrash Talmud Torah*. It is hardly an impressive record over so long a period, but much of the Sicilian Jewish literary production may have been lost. One notable, if not very likeable, figure of Jewish birth was the apostate Raimondo da Moncada, of Girgenti, one of the most distinguished European orientalists of the fifteenth century, who lived for years at the expense of his former coreligionists, translated the Koran and other works from the Arabic for the duke of Urbino, taught theology in the world-famous Sapienza of Rome, and enjoyed the patronage of successive Popes and princes of the Renaissance.

The immemorial urge of the Jew to his former land seems to have been particularly strong in Sicily. There is frequent mention of transference to Jerusalem, and in 1455 there took place what can only be best described as an anticipation of the modern Zionist movement. (It is possible that it is to be brought into relation with a messianic excitement in Catania at an unspecified date towards the close of the Middle Ages, curious details of which are given in a recently

---

* For Siciliano and Abulrabbi see above, pages 146 and 209.

discovered Hebrew document.*) A band of Jews from various parts of the island determined to set out together for the Holy Land. The party comprised representatives of all the greater communities — Palermo, Messina, Termini, Syracuse and Catania, which provided a contingent of no fewer than twenty-four enthusiasts. The leader of the expedition was apparently Master Azcaruni of Palermo, a physician. All arrangements were made, and a Spanish ship chartered to bring them to their destination. Yet, however much the presence of Jews was disliked, their departure was resented. When the news became known, the archbishop of Palermo, as president of the kingdom in the king's absence, gave orders for the fugitives to be arrested, as they had forfeited both freedom and property through their attempted flight. The communities of the realm, headed on this occasion by that of Syracuse, took up their case. Early in the following year, they reached a settlement with the viceroy on this and other points, paying 1,000 ounces by way of showing their gratitude. The prisoners were released and allowed to continue their journey, provided that they exported no precious metal and took with them nothing but what was necessary for their sustenance. Future emigration on a large scale was forbidden, no parties of more than eight persons being allowed henceforth to leave the kingdom at one time.**

On his way to Palestine in 1487, the distinguished North Italian scholar, Obadiah da Bertinoro, unable to take ship nearer home owing to the embargo on Jewish travellers

---

* J. Mann, *Texts and Studies in Jewish History*, I, 34–44.

** Just thirty years later, we are informed of the migration to Palestine of a party from Palermo, who were thrown into gaol, on arrival at Messina, on the pretext that they had not received an emigration-license. When the ship's captain produced the necessary papers, their release was ordered, and the official responsible arrested in turn by the municipal authorities, to be released on the receipt of an angry letter from the president of the kingdom.

which was still in force,* spent some time in Sicily, and gives a graphic account of Jewish life in the island in a letter to his father in Città di Castello. In Palermo, he found about 850 Jewish families, living together in their own quarter, mainly coppersmiths, iron-workers, laborers and porters, and much despised by the Christians by reason of their ragged clothing. As a distinguishing mark, they had to wear a piece of red cloth, about the size of a ducat, over their hearts. The synagogue here was the most beautiful he had ever seen. There was an outer court supported by stone pillars, surrounded by enormous vines; then an inner courtyard, with a fountain; and then the synagogue itself, with five cantors, who chanted the prayers more sweetly than he had ever heard before. Around the place of worship there were numerous subsidiary buildings, such as the hospital, hospice, and courtroom.** He was favorably impressed by the communal autonomy, though not by the way in which it was exercised, or by many local usages, some of which bordered on superstition. He found himself venerated, for example, almost in the manner of a Catholic holy man, so that the common people competed for fragments of his clothing as a remembrance! At Messina, there was a community of about 400, living under much the same conditions as at Palermo. He was greatly interested in the festivities he witnessed here at a Jewish wedding. After the religious service, the bride was mounted on horseback and led through the town. Before her the bridegroom went on foot, surrounded by the elders of the community, while boys and girls carrying torches filled the air with wild shouts. Thus they made the circuit of the Jewish quarter and of the principal streets, the Christian inhabitants joining in the jubilation. From the secular sources, however, we are informed

---

*See above, page 160; for Obadiah da Bertinoro, page 221.
**The arrangement had apparently remained customary here for 1,000 years; see above, page 45 and also page 232.

that at Palermo the civic authorities tried to blackmail the community into paying for the privilege of having the traditional torchlight procession on these occasions, the royal protection being repeatedly solicited. Another local custom confirmed by the royal authority was that of having Christian mimics to add to the hilarity on the occasion of weddings and other festive occasions, while, when a Jew died, Christian professional keeners, known as *reputatrici*, were engaged to lead the mourning. It was customary at such times for the Jewish women to scratch their faces until the blood came, contrary to Mosaic law; and the royal authority was enlisted in 1398 to stop this practice. Generally speaking, one has the impression of a highly individual social life among the Sicilian Jews, characteristically Sicilian as well as characteristically Jewish, yet by no means lacking in African influence and coloring.

xxvi
Reaction and Expulsion

The Norman rulers who reconquered Sicily for Christianity realized the need to conciliate and combine all the heterogeneous elements in the population — Moslems, Italians, Byzantines and Frenchmen, as well as Jews. Hence the last-named element were allowed to continue in the possession of their former privileges. The work of the Jewish savants in the brilliant courts of Palermo and Naples, of which an account has been given in a previous chapter, symbolizes the tolerant synthesis which the sovereigns endeavored to achieve. It was characteristic that, in 1071, Hebrew legal instruments were officially recognized as having the same validity as those drawn up in Latin, Arabic or Greek; and that when, in 1129, Roger II granted a general privilege to the city of Messina, he specified that its provisions should extend no less to the Jewish than to the Christian inhabitants. The Emperor Frederick followed the same policy when he became king of Sicily. Although he fixed the communal fine payable when a Jew was found killed at only half the rate in the case of a Christian, he forbade open discrimination against them, and his regulations of 1231 for the administration of justice insisted that their rights should be respected, while he employed a certain Gaudio (or Isaac) as his mint-master at Messina. On the other hand, as has been mentioned, he found it desirable to vindicate his highly questionable orthodoxy by obeying canon law meticulously in matters which did not closely concern his interests. As early as 1221 we find him, for example, ordering the Jews to wear a distinguishing mark in obedience to the canons of the recent Lateran Council — henceforth generally enforced in Sicily.

The advent of the house of Aragon, after the Sicilian Vespers of 1282, when King Pedro was welcomed by a deputation of the Jews of Messina bearing a Torah scroll, introduced a new spirit to the island. In some ways, it was the freest country in Europe; yet from Frederick II (1296–1337) the intolerance which was beginning to infect Spain made itself felt here as well. In 1310, in a series of "constitutions" published at Messina, the king renewed the conventional canonical restrictions against Jews and Saracens: that they should not own Christian slaves, or hold any sort of judicial office, or give evidence against Christians in courts of law, or practice medicine except among their coreligionists, or live on familiar terms with Christians, and so on. A famous preacher, St. Albert of Trapani, emphasized all this and more in his sermons; and as a result the Jews were ordered to isolate themselves in special areas, generally outside the city walls — the earliest instance in Europe of such segregation enforced by law. Although the outcome was not quite what was anticipated — at Palermo, for example, their former quarter was left deserted and measures had to be taken to induce Christians to settle there; while in 1375 the community of Syracuse obtained a special exemption in their own case — this policy remained nominally in force for upwards of a hundred years. Later Aragonese rulers followed this lead. In 1347, several Jews were put to death at Messina on a charge of ritual murder, commemorated by an inscription part of which may still be seen outside the cathedral. In 1373, the Holy Office was installed and a fresh offensive was begun against synagogues newly constructed in defiance of the canonical regulations. Though the authority of the inquisitors was subsequently limited — on one occasion, one of them was made to refund fines extorted from certain Jews for amorous adventures with Christian women— they remained intermittently active and potentially dangerous. The wearing of the Jewish badge, again enjoined by Frederick II in 1310, was never allowed to fall into desuetude. In order to ensure punctilious obedience to the ordinances regarding it and the synagogues, the external decoration of which was now rigorously forbidden, Fra Nicholas of Palermo was appointed in 1366 to the office of "Curator" or "Revisor" of the Jewish badge (*Custos*, subsequently *Revisor, Rotellae*), which continued to exist so long as Jews remained in the island. It was henceforth supposed to take the form of a scarlet circle or O, not smaller than the largest royal seal, to be worn on the right side of the outer garment over the breast, a palmsbreadth below the chin; the Jews of Palermo were, however, permitted a smaller diameter, as Obadiah da Bertinoro was to notice. Any irregularity was punished by a fortnight's imprisonment. Not only the Jews had to be thus distinguished, but also their butchers' shops, lest a Christian should commit the grave sin of eating Jewish meat!

Such seed inevitably produced a bitter crop. On June 6, 1391, a wave of massacre broke out at Seville which in the end spread throughout the Iberian peninsula and shattered the pride of Spanish Jewry. The episode showed — as does all history — that the example of violence is infectious. Not only did the massacres spread from Castile into Aragon, but they extended thence to the possessions of the Crown of Aragon overseas. Not long after the outbreak, Martin, the brother and successor-to-be of the Aragonese ruler, arrived in Sicily as king consort; and it is obvious that the virus of intolerance came in his train. On the following Easter, the classical season for religious epidemics, conditions were so menacing that special measures had to be taken to safeguard the Jewish quarter of Palermo. But they were insufficient, and before long the disorders swept the entire country; a distinguishing feature, as in Spain, being the number of insincere converts who remained when the tumult had died down. It was in June, 1392, that the beginning was made, at Monte S. Giuliano, where the whole community was compelled at the sword's point to receive baptism, those who refused being brutally murdered. When the news reached the capital, the king issued stern orders forbidding such attacks, actuated, as he said, more by greed than by zeal. But this was to little effect — all the less when the ecclesiastical authorities obtained permission to proceed against backsliding neophytes notwithstanding the circumstances of their conversion. Before long, attacks had taken place also in Palermo, Catania, Trapani, Syracuse and elsewhere. Every Sunday, when the faithful left church, the Jews trembled for fear of another émeute. It was only due to Martin's incessant efforts, in letters of warning addressed to one city after the other, that the outbreak was restricted to a relatively modest scale.

From this time onwards, the condition of the Sicilian Jews deteriorated. In the Lent of 1403, there was an attack on the Jews of Marsala, and in 1413, on the night of Good Friday, another at Polizzi. In 1415, the queen expelled them from her town of Vizini, at the request of the inhabitants. The next year, the Jews of Mineo were thrown into prison for venturing to go about on the royal business and attend service in their *moscheta* at Easter, when they should have remained cooped up in their houses. The agitation of the Franciscans against the loan-bankers of Upper Italy extended across the Straits, although conditions were so fundamentally different, and similar demands were put forward. In 1426, the citizens of Girgenti petitioned the Crown, though unsuccessfully, for permission to enforce a new anti-Jewish code of regulations. Two years later, in obedience to an old papal bull that had taken on a new urgency, the Jews of the realm, together with the Saracens, were ordered to attend conversionist sermons to be given by the fiery Fra Matteo di Girgenti, who had received an official appointment to the new office of *Lettore degli Ebrei*, or "Reader to the Jews." At the same time, there was a renewed attempt, as in the north, to enforce the confinement of the Jews in separate quarters, out of all contact with Christians, as had been legally obligatory for the last hundred years. In consternation, the *Dienchelele* Moses Bonavoglia went after the king to Spain on behalf of the communities of the realm. In consequence of his representations — or rather, of the gifts he bore — the new legislation regarding conversionist sermons was revoked, and the Jews were formally empowered to live wherever they pleased as in the old days (January 5, 1430-1). Having had difficulty in obtaining reimbursement of his expenses, Bonavoglia refused to act the next time, in 1443, when the news of the persecutory Bull of Pope Eugenius IV reached Sicily.* With the approval of the viceroy, the united communities now sent a delegation to the mainland, consisting of Isaac di Guglielmo (i.e., ben Benjamin) and Haninu (Hayyim?) Balbo, to implore the king and the Pope for mercy. The Bull was, in fact, withdrawn, as we have seen; but the respite was only temporary. Shortly after, Fra Giovanni da Capistrano extended his anti-Jewish activity to Sicily in the capacity of inquisitor,

* See above, pages 163-4.

and his inflammatory sermons disturbed the peace here as elsewhere. As a result of his complaints, the Jews were forbidden in 1447 to hold real estate, and a certain Giacomo Xarch was appointed, two years later, as special papal and royal commissioner to investigate various charges against them of practicing usury and other breaches of canon law. Nothing incriminating was discovered, but it cost the communities 3,000 ducats to secure the confirmation of their privileges and the withdrawal of Xarch's commission. In 1451, the Holy Office fraudulently acquired new powers by producing an elaborate privilege said to have been granted by the Emperor Frederick in 1224, but in reality a forgery; and henceforth the Jews and other infidels had to supply the inquisitors each year with all they required for their official journeys. Although the office of "Reader to the Jews" no longer existed, a renewed attempt was made to compel them to listen to conversionist sermons, to the accompaniment of the inevitable annoyances and disorder. In 1453, the king was again persuaded to prohibit this abuse, simultaneously confirming the privileges granted by former rulers and Popes. Nevertheless, only fourteen years later, authority was given to the Dominican Giovanni da Pistoia to compel the Jews to come to hear him, so as to wean them from their disbelief. At Messina a determined attempt was made in the middle of the century to oust them from the profession of brokerage. Notwithstanding the reiterated confirmation of Jewish rights and expressions of royal benevolence, the physical onslaught continued, petty local annoyances alternating with major outbreaks. Every Easter, orders had to be issued protecting the Jews, now of one place and now of another. Thus, in 1453, shortly before Holy Week, the community of Marsala was taken under protection, though too late to prevent a bloody assault. At Polizzi, the Easter riots became an annual affair. In 1456, the Dominicans of the beautiful hill-town of Taormina complained to the Pope that the Jewish synagogue and cemetery were inconveniently near their conventual church, and orders were issued for their transference to a more convenient site. But this, too, proved unsatisfactory in the eyes of the friars, and before the year was out the new place of worship also had to be abandoned. On St. Stephen's day in the same year, when the Jews of Marsala had been driven to church to attend service, fire was set to their houses, and that night they were attacked by brigands. In 1470, the synagogue at Savoca had to be transferred to a less prominent site. The Trapani community suffered from a venomous official onslaught in 1473 for the offense of receiving into Judaism the daughter of a Jewish mother and Christian father, the leaders of the community being thrown into prison and a general pardon being obtained only at tremendous cost.

The next year (1474) the attack became general. The immediate occasion was a charge brought against the Jews of Palermo of perpetrating atrocious blasphemies against the Christian faith in word and deed. The kernel of the accusation was apparently the alleged composition of some anti-Christian work, perhaps a muddled reference to the Talmud. A number of them were arrested, tortured until they made some sort of confession, and then burned at the stake. Ultimately, the remaining prisoners were released in consideration of a gift of the great sum of 5,000 florins. But, meanwhile, the onslaught had spread. The Jews of Termini were somehow implicated in the statements that had been extorted, and a royal commissary was sent there to search for anti-Christian writings. At Sciacca, too, the community was accused of *lèse majesté* and blasphemy. Popular passions were keyed up everywhere to fever-pitch. In August the Feast of the Assumption of the Virgin was celebrated at Modica by a mob-attack on the Jewish quarter, to cries of *Viva Maria, e periscono gli ebrei* ("Long live the Virgin, and death to the Jews!"). There followed the most appalling massacre in the whole of Sicilian, and perhaps of

Italian, Jewish history. According to the official figure, there were 360 victims — men, women and children — some of whom were tortured to death by the local officials on the demand of the rioters. Although the viceroy went in person to restore order and had the ringleaders hanged, the example spread like wildfire to Noto, Monte S. Giuliano and Sciacca, and protection was needed also at Palermo, Naro, Castrogiovanni and Messina, where it was purchased at a particularly heavy price; while in 1476, when new outrages are recorded at Caltagirone and Agosta, the endowments of the Jewish school recently established at Girgenti were confiscated, on the pretext that it would have been a center of anti-Christian teaching. In 1480, it was the turn of Mineo, and in 1483 of Marsala, where some unpleasant horseplay took place on St. John's day. In 1486-7, in consequence of the frenzied Lenten sermons of Fra Giovanni da Pistoia and other preachers, who were endeavoring to imitate the achievements of Bernardino da Feltre in the north of the country, there were serious disorders in Syracuse, Caltagirone, Sciacca, Malta and elsewhere, notwithstanding the steps taken to restrain them. During the following Eastertide, the stoning of the Jewish quarter at Taormina, in accordance with the barbaric old tradition, resulted in a riot; while the same year the synagogue at Corleone was desecrated. 1490 witnessed fresh onslaughts at Castroreale and Santa Lucia. It is to be noted that these outbreaks were for the most part connected with the religious anniversaries of the Christian year; in the case of the poverty-stricken Sicilian Jews, economic motives were barely present.

On November 30, 1469, the citizens of Palermo staged elaborate festivities in honor of the marriage of the Infant Ferdinand, son and future successor of the king of Sicily and Aragon, with Isabella, heiress to the thrones of Castile and Leon. Among the other notable spectacles, there was a procession of four hundred richly dressed young Jews, who performed dances in the streets for the diversion of the spectators. Little can they have imagined that the wedding which they were celebrating so lightheartedly was destined to spell the destruction of Sicilian Jewry after over fifteen hundred years of continuous history.

Fifteen years later, the bride of 1469 ascended the throne of Castile, and five years thereafter her husband became king of Aragon, the two thus uniting the greater part of the Peninsula under their joint rule. Among the problems with which they had to deal was that of the Marranos, or crypto-Jews, who had been left by the successive waves of persecution that had devastated the Spanish communities from the end of the fourteenth century onwards — Christians in name, for that was the only manner in which they could save their lives, but Jews at heart, though in many cases less so than they were generally reputed to be. To allow them to revert to Judaism openly was, at that time, unthinkable; to permit them to continue their double lives seemed a sacrilege. It was in order to deal with this problem that the Spanish Inquisition was established in 1479. But it proved ineffective; for it was impossible to suppress Judaizing while Jews remained undisturbed, and illogical to burn a person baptized by force for the sin of performing in secret a single item of the elaborate Jewish code, when his unbaptized coreligionists were performing all of it openly with complete impunity. Moreover, Queen Isabella's genuine piety, Ferdinand's greed, and the mounting tide of militant religious nationalism all pointed in the same direction. With the capture of Moorish Granada, for which object the Sicilian communities had been compelled, like those of Spain, to contribute lavishly, this reached its climax. On March 31, 1492, the Spanish sovereigns signed an edict by which all Jews were to leave Spain within four months, the reason given being that they had encouraged their former coreligionists to be unfaithful to the sacrament of baptism.

This state of affairs did not apply in Sicily. The anti-

Jewish agitation in and after 1392 had not been allowed to make much headway, and in consequence there had been no great wave of forcible conversion; moreover, the Sicilian Jews were made of sterner stuff than their coreligionists in Spain, and had not lost their morale during the previous period of reaction. Hence, although there was in the island a number of recent converts whose sincerity was suspect (an inquisition on the Spanish model had been set up in 1487 to deal with them) the problem which served as the pretext for the expulsion of the Jews from Spain did not exist there on any scale. Nevertheless, the fatal edict extended, not only to the Spanish mainland, but also to the insular dependencies of Aragon — above all, Sardinia and Sicily, with its great Jewish population. Later generations invented, indeed, a feeble justification. It was alleged that during the week of prayer preceding Christmas, 1491, while a crucifix was being carried in procession through the streets of Castiglione, in the diocese of Messina, one of the arms was broken by a stone thrown by the "Rabbi" Biton through an open window. The mob, led by two brothers named Andrea and Bartolomeo Crisi, immediately rushed into the house with drawn swords and put the delinquent to death. The murderers then fled to Spain for protection. Here, it is said, they found favor with King Ferdinand, who praised their action and asked them what reward they desired; to which they replied by soliciting the expulsion of the Jews from their native land. There is a good deal of incoherence in the story, and in any case this pretext was unnecessary. Sicily was a dominion of the Crown of Aragon; and nothing more was needed to seal the fate of its Jewish inhabitants.

On May 31, 1492, after the precautionary measure of taking the Jews under royal protection and cancelling all licenses to bear arms, the royal order was secretly communicated by the viceroy to the local authorities throughout the island. Ten days later, the Jews were ominously warned not to attempt to emigrate or conceal their property or sell any of their possessions without license. When all preparations were complete, the edict of banishment was solemnly proclaimed on June 18, to the blare of trumpets, in every town in which Jews were to be found. Three months only were allowed for the preparations to be made and for the settlement of their debts, whether to private individuals or to the municipalities. By September 18 — four days before the Jewish New Year — all were to have gone, any who remained on the island after that date incurring the death penalty. It was decided that by way of emigration tax, they were to compensate the Crown before leaving for the revenue which would be lost to it by reason of their absence. To ensure this, all their property was sequestered forthwith — including even the synagogues with their sacred contents — being sealed with sheets of paper bearing the royal arms; 6,300 of these had been providently ordered from the printer, Andreas of Bruges, ten days before. As a final precaution against evasion, Christians were forbidden to enter the Jewish quarters or houses on whatever pretext. On the whole, the secret had been maintained; though at Messina a number of persons made an unsuccessful attempt to smuggle their belongings over the straits. Among the sequestered goods were the tools of the craftsmen who formed the majority of the Jewish population. Unable to work, they were now faced with starvation; while owing to the freezing of their assets it was for a long while impossible to send a delegation to the king to ask for mercy, or even to offer up prayers to a more approachable Sovereign in the occupied *moschete*.

One regulation after the other issued in the following days filled out the details of the infamy. The Jews were enjoined not to conceal their property, or to transport it to other houses. Their creditors were instructed to present all claims within a fortnight. In view of the vast number of distraints on Jews as well as Christians which were necessitated by the forced liquidation, it was ordered that only one-third of the normal dues should be exacted by the bailiffs. When the inventories were completed, the Jews were authorized to re-enter into enjoyment of their communal property and to resume public worship until the time of their departure; though the moveable synagogue appurtenances were of course kept back. Repeated orders were issued for their protection from maltreatment — obviously, it was sorely needed. It was ordered that any person who became baptized should have his property respected and be treated like any other Christian. Petitions from various communities soliciting minor concessions, to facilitate the winding up of their affairs, were coldly considered.

The news of what was intended was greeted with general consternation. The Jewish communities, after an emergency conference, determined to send a delegation to the king of Spain to implore him to withdraw his edict, and they were in the end empowered by the viceroy to arrange for a letter of exchange in Rome to cover the expenses. If the envoys arrived, and if they managed to secure an audience, they had no more success than their coreligionists in Spain. But the high officials of the kingdom were no less convinced that the expulsion of the Jews would be detrimental to its best interests. On June 20, the members of the Privy Council — including the justices of the High Court, the principal financial authorities, and other officials — met together at Messina under the presidency of the Grand Justiciar to consider the situation. In a memorandum drawn up for submission to the king, they emphasized what harm would be done to the country if his intention were carried out. They pointed out that the Jews spent approximately a million florins each year in Sicily, so that their departure would give its economic stability a serious blow. Important industries would languish — above all iron manufacture, in which the Jewish craftsmen had a virtual monopoly. In case of war, or of a Turkish onslaught, the defenses of the island would be weakened by the lack of armaments as well as the absence of so many stalwart persons from the fortifications; while the strategic islands of Malta, Gozzo and Pantelleria would be dangerously depopulated. The loss to the treasury was obvious, and would be irreparable. The Council was not deaf, moreover, to the call of humanity. The vast majority of the Sicilian Jews were wretchedly poor; and, ejected in this manner, with no possible means of support, large numbers would perish miserably of hunger. In consideration of all this, the councillors humbly petitioned the king to reconsider his decision, or at least to give a longer time for it to be carried into effect. The municipality of Palermo, in a petition presented on July 11, pointed out in addition how the proposed step was a breach of the city's privileges. The pretext, that the Jews were endangering the orthodoxy of their neighbors, was utterly false according to them, an inquisitor having recently testified to the fact; while it was universally recognized that, so far as the practice of usury was concerned, Sicilian Jewry presented no problem whatsoever. They implored the viceroy and his associates to join in their intercession, and asked for time to send a delegation to Spain to submit their protest, so that the city and the kingdom should not be utterly destroyed.

In spite of all, the administrative machine grounded its way inexorably onward, the only concession being that, in return for a bribe of 5,000 florins, the time limit was extended from September 18 — first for two months, then for forty days, and then, owing to the difficulty in collecting the appallingly heavy levies, and finally to the bad weather, for two lesser periods, bringing the final date down to January 12. Meanwhile, negotiations had been in progress regarding the composition to be paid to the king to make good the direct loss of 4,000 florins annually which he would suffer by expelling his Jewish subjects. The legal interest rate in Sicily at this time was ten per cent. Hence it would have been natural for this preposterous levy to be capitalized at ten years' purchase. But what was proper for the Jewish miscreant was out of the question when Christian interests were concerned, and the sum actually demanded was 100,000 florins, or twenty-five years' purchase, at a capitalization rate of four per cent! In addition, the Jews were compelled to promise the viceroy, as a token of gratitude for his services, a "freewill" gift of 5,000 florins. These amounts, divided up on a proportionate basis among the forty-five communities then in the island, were exacted from the sequestered property. On its payment, the Jews were to be free to depart. What remained was not, however, returned to them to do with as they pleased, as nothing of value was to be taken overseas. Everything had to be realized and the proceeds exported in the form of letters of exchange, which in the circumstances could obviously be obtained only at ruinous rates.

The Holy Inquisition loyally warned the faithful not to help the unbelievers to evade the recent dispositions, though it was a pious duty to wean them away from their disbelief, thus saving their souls from eternal agony as well as their bodies from transitory discomfort. Regulations had already been issued regarding the exodus of the poorer members of the Jewish communities. They were allowed to have with them the clothes they were wearing (but not their best finery), a blanket of wool or serge, a secondhand mattress of scant value and a used pair of sheets, some provisions, and the magnificent sum of three *tari* for the expenses of the voyage. The wealthier were permitted to take twice this amount, but still only a single modest dress. The communities appealed pathetically to be allowed, in addition, sufficient ready money to pay their passage to their destinations. Later, they submitted a petition requesting some further concessions, heartbreakingly trivial. They asked leave to have two shirts each, and two cloths for each household. They desired that they might convey with them their precious Scrolls of the Law, and the tools which might enable the craftsmen to earn a living again. They desired that those who had elected to become baptized should be compelled to grant a divorce to their wives if the latter had remained faithful to Judaism, thus enabling them to take up the threads of married life again if they wished to. They asked for their synagogue trappings, which would be valueless in Sicily henceforth, to be disposed of on behalf of the Crown to Jewish communities overseas, who would care for them reverently. Two clauses of the petition are especially worthy of note, illustrating the relative attitudes. True to the last to their traditional humanity, the Jews asked that those of their former slaves whom they had freed in happier days should retain their liberty. This was granted. They asked also permission to take with them the symbolic drapings (*tallith*) used in prayer. This was refused.

There was much unnecessary suffering in many places. One of the feudal barons, the lord of Ciminna, threw the Jews living on his lands into prison, refusing them access to their houses; and the viceroy's protection came too late to save many of them from dying of famine. The baron of Cammarata did worse, the Jews of that place being closed up in their *moscheta* without food for six days, in a manner which even contemporaries considered to be thoroughly inhuman. At Girgenti, where the communal leaders had been arrested and imprisoned without any cause, the peculation of the treasurer was on such a scale that he was arrested. Protection came in such cases only when the worst was over. One ray of humanity only is discernible in the vast mass of official documents relating to these tragic days. There had recently arrived at Palermo a number of poor Jews expelled from the Provence. They were permitted to depart freely, without any further financial obligation, as it was admitted to be inequitable that they should undergo the agony of spoliation twice in a single year.

The tragic date was now very near. Already, the poorer Jews from the inland towns had been permitted to assemble in the seaports where they were to embark, the wealthy remaining behind as a guarantee that all financial obligations imposed on them would be settled. Those of Castronuovo, Piazza, S. Marco, Castroreale and Caltagirone made their way to Messina, to join their coreligionists of that place; those of Ragusa and Lentini collected at Catania; those of Camarata and other places in the west of the island at Palermo. To prevent the evasion of the stringent restrictions on the export of their property — strikingly similar to what we have known in our own day — all the exiles were searched before leaving. The perquisition did not extend only to the miserable chattels left to them — including their mattresses, which were slit open to rummage for hidden articles — but even to the cavities of their bodies, in which it was thought that they might have secreted precious stones. The community of Taormina obtained permission to take with them some stones of no value and a nail-studded door — presumably the tombstones from their old cemetery and the entrance to the former synagogue, of which they had been deprived thirty-seven years before.

Thus, destitute and desperate, but still trusting to the eternal mercy of the God of Israel, the Sicilian Jews left their native land. Following the line of least resistance, the greatest body of the exiles transferred themselves to the adjacent mainland — those of Sciacca and elsewhere to Naples, those of Syracuse to Reggio, and so on — there to encounter fresh tribulation in the end. But not all arrived at their destination; a whole shipload were murdered by the sailors on a vessel belonging to Gallipoli (on the Gulf of Taranto) on its way to that place. Many others joined the main current of emigration from the Spanish dominions and sailed eastwards, to the Turkish empire, where the enlightened policy of the sultans ensured them a humane welcome. A few must have found refuge in North Africa. For many years after, Sicilian congregations — noteworthy apparently for the attention they paid to synagogal music

— continued to exist in many places in the Levant, including Constantinople and Aleppo. The *Scuola Siciliana* remained in existence at Rome almost to within living memory; and down to our own day the descendants of the exiles in Salonica maintained their congregational individuality, although their synagogal tradition was long since submerged.*

Elsewhere, expulsion sometimes marked an interruption in Jewish life rather than a final and irrevocable disaster — but not in Sicily. Some cravens lingered behind, as nominal Christians, to be reinforced from time to time by fugitive Marranos from Spain. It was against the latter category that the Holy Office of the Inquisition was most zealous, its activities reaching their height in the sixteenth century and thereafter dwindling away. Occasionally, Jewish travellers or refugees from the mainland visited the island for short periods; and an anaemic attempt was made in the first half of the eighteenth century to form a community again, but without success. When, after the consummation of Italian unity, the old intolerance disappeared, a handful of Jews settled in the island, and a small congregation was established in our own day in Palermo. But it could hardly be said to have renewed the old historic connection; and so far as we are at present in a position to tell, that January day in 1493 ended Sicilian Jewish history for all time.

As the ships bearing the exiles sailed out of the harbor of Palermo, it is recorded, the inhabitants stood on their housetops to wave farewell so long as they might to their old neighbors who had dwelled in their midst, harmlessly and laboriously, for so many eventful centuries.

* There is reason to believe that the Saragossan synagogue at Salonica was founded by immigrants from Syracuse — "Saragozza" in the Italian records of the time — whose descendants still observe annually the "Purim Saragossa," celebrating an escape from persecution in romantic circumstances in the Middle Ages. The ritual customary among a section of Sicilian Jewry which hailed from northern Africa, printed in Constantinople about 1572 and containing many otherwise unknown early hymns, has recently been rediscovered.

xxvii

Sardinia

Another dominion of the house of Aragon, since the beginning of the previous century, was the island of Sardinia — before that period a Pisan, and earlier still a Byzantine dependency. Local Jewish history started early: it will be recalled how at the beginning of the Christian era the Emperor Tiberius had deported thither two thousand youths from Rome, and how at the end of the sixth century Pope Gregory the Great had protected one of its synagogues from molestation. There does not seem to have been any interruption in the history of the colony during the troubled centuries that succeeded; but, notwithstanding the ingenious attempt of a nineteenth-century forger to fill the gap, evidence is almost completely absent. It is only with the beginning of the Spanish domination in the fourteenth century that a consistent picture can be put together. When the Infante Alfonso invaded the island in 1323, two Spanish Jewish physicians were in his train, as well as a somewhat disreputable Jewish factor; and it may be that some of his nobles were similarly escorted. The principal communities found by the newcomers were at Sassari and Cagliari, where, when it had been fortified by the Pisans in 1258, a site had been assigned in the Citadel for the Jewish quarter. There were other settlements in the district of Logudoro and the diocese of Sorres. Under the Aragonese rulers immigrants arrived from Spain, the Provence, the Balearic Islands, and even from Germany. The maximum level of the Jewish population in the Middle Ages has been estimated at 5,000 — a figure which is probably higher rather than lower than the facts warrant.

The upper stratum of the community was engaged in wholesale trade, their transactions carrying them as far afield as Sicily and Spain. There were, of course, a few physicians, such as Hayyim of Cyprus, author of a work on the medicinal plants of the island, and Solomon Avronques, who made his name known as a skillful surgeon. Other Jews were in the financial administration or engaged in tax-farming — in particular, in the fifteenth century, the brothers Nino and Moses Carcassonna, who once advanced the government large sums for the equipment and commissariat of a military expedition. Less commonplace was their interest in mining, which was extensive. In 1327, orders were issued for the Jews to be excluded from the city of Iglesias and the silver-mines, owing to suspected malpractices. The ban did not last for long. In the early years of the fifteenth century, the community of Alghero paid a large sum for the exclusive right of prospecting, excavating and mining in this region, the local authorities being enjoined to give them every possible assistance. Later on, two Jews, Isaac Isbili (i.e., of Seville) and Brona Cap, were licensed to prospect for precious metal here, on condition that onehalf of what they found went to the government. But the vast majority of the Jewish population belonged, as in Sicily, to the proletariat, eking out a laborious livelihood by peddling and handicraft. Jewish packmen penetrated all over the island, sometimes travelling as long as fourteen hours to effect a single sale: and the Jewish quarters, with their blacksmiths, coppersmiths and tinkers, could be recognized by the constant din of hammering on metal which resounded from them.

From the administrative point of view, there was little to distinguish the island Jewries from others elsewhere, except perhaps for the exceptional authority enjoyed by their lay representatives — probably a consequence of the relatively low level of rabbinical culture. Every year, three administrators or "secretaries" were elected, who had judicial power in all disputes between Jews, and even in those between Jews and Christians where sums not exceeding five lire were involved. In 1387, an edict was issued guaranteeing the inhabitants of the island, Jews as well as Christians, that they would not be put under any special judicature or inquisition; every citizen, whatever his faith, was to be judged by his ordinary magistrates. The community of Cagliari was regarded as the principal one in the island; in 1335 it was accorded all the privileges enjoyed by that of Barcelona, and the right to levy a contribution from all Jews from other places who resided in the city for more than thirty days. At the same time, the Town Council was ordered to withdraw some anti-Jewish regulations which it had recently issued, and sternly warned not to repeat the experiment; obviously, the Jews were considered by the Crown to be a useful asset.

The Aragonese rulers set about developing the seaport of Alghero, in the northwestern corner of the island, which they occupied in 1354 (the Catalan spoken by the new settlers whom they introduced still lingers here). The Jews collaborated in the enterprise, solidly though not perhaps spontaneously, one of the city towers bearing an inscription to the effect that it had been constructed at the expense of the community of Cagliari. Hence Jewish settlers who could help to develop the town found themselves exceptionally favored. They were exempted from the payment of customs dues, and the local authorities were urged to protect their business interests. New immigrants arrived, not only from other parts of the island, but even from Spain. In 1381, the construction of a synagogue in the road leading to the citadel was authorized; and, when it was enlarged half a century later, permission was given for the interior walls to be adorned with the royal arms. On the other hand, members of the community repeatedly gave money for the restoration of the fortifications, and in 1370 ran heavily into debt in order to supply King Pedro with money and provisions for his armies — a token of fidelity which he rewarded by giving them a moratorium for two years. This position of privilege continued well into the next century. In 1448, the councillors of the city and the secretaries of the Jewish quarter, acting almost as equals, petitioned for a general amnesty, which was granted, except for serious crimes. Three years later, the Jews of this region were exempted from the obligation, now general elsewhere, of wearing the Jewish badge and being compelled to attend Christian ceremonies and hear conversionist sermons, and were authorized to retain slaves for twelve months even after they had embraced Christianity; and the secretaries were given authority to enforce these regulations.

Only one personality stands out in the entire course of Jewish history in the island. This was Judah ben David the physician, known as Bonjudes ben Davin (Bonjudes Bondavin), who settled in Alghero about 1390 after practicing medicine at Marseilles. He had formerly been in the service of Queen Marie of the Provence, and now attended on King Martin II, being admitted to court among the other dignitaries on the occasion of the latter's visits to Sardinia. In addition to his medical skill, Bonjudes had a considerable knowledge of talmudic literature. In consequence, the Jewish community of Cagliari recognized him as rabbi. This appointment was confirmed by the king, who extended his jurisdiction over all the Jews of the island. The sole specimen of his rabbinical correspondence that has been preserved throws a rare gleam of light on the daily life of Sardinian Jewry (unique except for the record of a curious episode of 1425, when the community of Alghero was divided into two warring groups on account of the rival claims of two young men for a maiden's hand; the quarrel became so acute that it reached the ears of the king, who ordered it to be settled by recourse to a great rabbinical authority abroad!). We see Rabbi Bonjudes, during the Christmas festival in the winter of 1408, standing among the notables at court, and watching them play at dice; the king recognizing a notoriously adept Jew among the bystanders, and ordering him to take a hand; the latter excusing himself, on the grounds that there was a communal regulation against gambling which he would not willingly offend; and the curious complications from the point of view of Jewish law which ultimately ensued. It is a lively picture of a Jewry largely assimilated, refreshingly free, and completely untrammelled.

Yet as time went on, Jewish life in Sardinia came to be subjected to the same annoyances as elsewhere in the Aragonese dominions, increasing in severity with the passage of years; and the reaction brought about by the propaganda of the Observantine Franciscans spread speedily over the narrow dividing stretch of sea. In 1410, the bishop of Sorres admonished the Christians of his diocese not to enter into relations with the unbelievers, whether for business or otherwise. From 1430 onwards their position rapidly became worse, the commonplaces of the current anti-Jewish codes — the conversionist sermons, Jewish badge, and so on — being put into force in all their rigor. In the following year, the local communities associated themselves with those of the rest of Italy in procuring a protective Bull from Pope Eugenius IV, but its effect did not last for long. For the moment, the central authority kept local extravagance under control; when, for example in 1451, the archbishop of Sassari attempted to confine the local Jewish inhabitants into a segregated quarter of their own, the rabbi of Alghero successfully appealed to the Crown on their behalf for protection. But all moderation disappeared after the accession of Ferdinand the Catholic to the throne of Aragon. In 1481, the penalty for employing Christian servants or workmen was increased to 200 stripes and a fine of 200 ducats, instead of the former 20; and it was ordered that any Jew guilty of offenses against Christianity, or what were considered such, should have his hands cut off. Four years later, in 1485, by a new proviso communicated solemnly by the viceroy to the leaders of the community of Cagliari, the Jews were declared to be the king's property, and as such were placed under the jurisdiction of the royal representatives. Henceforth therefore it was forbidden for them to leave the island except to go to other parts of the Aragonese dominions, and even so only with the permission of the procurator and on giving warranty that they would return within the prescribed time-limit. When, about this time, two brothers from Cagliari obtained a safe-conduct from the king in Barcelona, it was conditional on their furnishing proof that they would not end up in Constantinople under the protection of the Grand Turk, as so many of their coreligionists did at this time. Naturally, they were forbidden, too, to export any of their property.

In 1488, the climax was reached with the enactment of an entire anti-Jewish code, of almost unexampled ferocity and pettiness. The Jews were to be allowed no contact whatsoever with Christians, having to live henceforth isolated in their own quarter. They were to wear special headgear by which they might be recognized in the streets, as well as the distinguishing badge of shame on their clothing. They were to have special stalls in the market for their meat, the residue of which should not be sold to Christians. They were again forbidden to have Christian slaves or servants in their employment. During Christian feast days they were not to display merchandise for sale or to carry on any occupation, such as metal-working, the noise of which could be heard in the street. The rabbi of the Cagliari synagogue was to inform the archbishop immediately of the arrival of any Jews from overseas, so that the necessary steps could be taken for safeguarding the faithful from contamination — the penalty was death. If carnal intercourse took place between adherents of the two faiths, the Jew was to lose his life and the Christian his property as well as the right to stay in the island. No Jew of either sex might wear any golden ornament or precious stone or silken garment, or shoes of any color other than black. An exception was made in favor of a bride, who was graciously permitted to adorn her person with her betrothal gifts; yet even so she would have to be constantly on guard, for if a Christian kissed the hand of a Jewish maiden, or of a venerated rabbi to whom he wished to show respect, he was to be flogged publicly, and the person so honored had to pay a fine of 200 ducats.

As the record of the Jews in Spain and in Sicily moved towards its tragic climax, so did that of their coreligionists in Sardinia, who, from 1492, saw the Inquisition installed and, later that year, through the same accident of politics, found themselves included in the edict of expulsion from the Spanish dominions. A few wealthy families, such as that of Carcassonna, whose ancestors had played so important a role in a previous generation, apostasized and were allowed to remain; the rest chose the path of exile. According to the oldest Sardinian chronicler, who wrote at the beginning of the sixteenth century, all the Jews of the island assembled at Cagliari, whence they set sail for Africa on July 31, 1492, bearing with them their sacred books; later on, he says, a great part of them went on to Constantinople. A Hebrew record informs us vaguely that many were killed on their journey. Here, the record ends except for a few sudden glimpses, such as that of two shiploads of Jews from Cagliari which put in at Gaeta, and one which disembarked at Naples, in the following autumn. No further trace of the exiles is discernible, their descendants merging completely with the residue of their storm-tossed brethren.*

Within the island, the Inquisition continued sporadic activities — mainly as it seems against refugee Marranos from Spain — for some time to come; and certain modern historians have fancied that Jewish practices are still discernible among the inhabitants. But the Jewish connection was irrevocably broken; and down to our own day it has never been renewed.

---

* The surname *Sardaigna* is still, however, to be found in Turkey; and the more common *Sardi* may also denote Sardinian origin.

xxviii

The Kingdom of Naples

A number of the exiles from Sardinia, to be followed by shipload after shipload of those from Sicily, sought refuge on the other side of the Straits, in the kingdom of Naples, as yet under independent rule. Here, new tribulation was in store.

It has already been seen how the Jewish settlement in Apulia was among the oldest in Italy, how great a role it had played in the dissemination of Jewish culture in the Dark Ages, and how at the end of the thirteenth century its pride and strength had been broken by the forced conversions during the reign of Charles II, of the house of Anjou. The region never thereafter recovered the importance that it had once had in Jewish life. Nevertheless, once the original impetus of fanaticism waned, the southern communities began to emerge again to the light of history. King Robert, Charles' son and successor, was more tolerant than his father, and his keen interest in Hebrew scholars and scholarship would not have been compatible with a continued persecution of the Jews. In several cities, now, the former synagogues were restored to their original use, as at Gerace in 1311, or Rossano and Cotrone in 1324; while at Amalfi an organized Jewish community is mentioned again as early as 1306, and at other places not long after. There is, however, a curious duplication for some time. By the side of the open and declared Jews we find constant references to the newly-baptized "neophytes" (*neofiti*) and their descendants, who maintained their individuality and were suspected, obviously not without reason, of adhering in secret to their fathers' creed and practices. Their most important center was Trani; those of Nola, Sessa, Lecce, Bari, Salerno and Lucera also figure very frequently in the records. It was, indeed, only their religion that they had ostensibly changed. They continued to follow their former occupations, as a result of which the terms "merchants" and "neophytes" were sometimes used almost as synonyms; while at places like Salerno they still enjoyed a monopoly of the dyeing industry. Socially, their cohesion was unimpaired, for they were organized, at least in some places, in officially recognized corporations, and sometimes had permission to worship as Christians in the synagogues that they had built as Jews. In the circumstances, it was not a matter for surprise that they still remained liable to the same suspicions and accusations as their former coreligionists — as, for example, that they engaged in usury — and to some of the same financial exactions, especially on the part of the Church, always reluctant to surrender its jurisdiction and its revenues. Occasionally, moreover, they were the objects even of similar popular attacks, due to identical religious and economic causes. It is not, indeed, always easy to tell whether the reference in documents and chronicles of the period is to the declared Jews or to their apostate kinsmen.

A lengthy series of edicts and regulations shows how serious was the problem which they presented in the eyes of the Church and State. In 1311, Fra Matteo da Ponsacco, inquisitor of the kingdom of Sicily, persuaded the king to order the newly-converted Jews to live dispersed among the Christians, so that they should not be tempted back into Judaism, and threatening those who relapsed with drastic punishment. This proved so little effective that in 1343 the reverse policy was tried, the neophytes being enjoined to live together, so as to be kept more easily under surveillance; while the next year the papal legate was instructed to open proceedings against any who were found backsliding. In Trani, where the number of households involved is reported to have risen to 870, and where they were exempted from the archbishop's jurisdiction in 1385, an attempt was now made at full emancipation by reserving two out of the sixteen seats on the municipal council for their representatives. The experiment was not much of a success, for in 1422 the archbishop managed to reassert his authority. Well into the fifteenth century, friction persisted. A quarrel between one of the neophytes and a sailor at Taranto, in 1411, led to a general onslaught on persons of Jewish stock, in the course of which the city captain was killed as he attempted to restore order. Under Pope Eugenius IV an attempt was made to solve the problem in a new fashion by relieving the *neofiti* of all disabilities in return for a written undertaking to abandon Jewish practices. The spontaneous results were so disappointing that in 1454 Fra Pietro da Mistretta was sent into Apulia to enforce obedience — the formal abjuration now signed by the *neofiti* of Lucera is still extant. The new attempt at settlement was no more successful than the former had been. As late as 1463, there were excesses against the "New Christians" of Bari and Lecce who, reinforced by later converts, continued to present a problem even after the last professing Jews had left the kingdom.

As far as these were concerned, the later rulers of the house of Anjou reverted to a policy of strict enforcement of the canonical restrictions, counterbalanced by insistence on their legal rights and their protection against physical attack — as at Gerace in 1310, when in accordance with the almost universal tradition their houses were stoned during Holy Week, or at Brindisi in 1325, when the citizens first tried to force them into baptism, and when they fled for safety wished to bring them back on the grounds that the city could not afford to lose them. There were various minor vexations, too, from which they had to be safeguarded: attempts of the customs officials to exact double tolls on their silks, the levying of a duty on corpses on the road, molestation on the public highways, the claim of the royal representatives to be provided with furniture for their lodgings, the recurrent endeavor of the ecclesiastical authorities to exact from them the same dues as before notwithstanding the fact that they had reverted to the royal jurisdiction. In all such cases the Jews expected, and generally received, protection. For the first time, the amount of their annual taxation was fixed, and their duly elected *proti*, as they were termed here as well, were formally recognized as competent representatives for the discussion of fiscal and other matters. So effective was King Robert's attempt to nurse the communities back into a healthy state that, at a critical moment in 1328, he was able to justify the imposition of a new poll tax, of 15 *tari* a head on all persons above the age of fifteen, on the grounds that the Jews in his realm were less oppressed than in any other part of the world.

The new community was in many ways different from the old. It lacked the former intellectual distinction. A few south Italian scholars of the period are known, but they were for the most part immigrants, and they did not compare either in number or in eminence with those who were now carrying on such fruitful activity in the north of the Peninsula. Their occupations, too, were in some ways different. There remained among them, indeed, goldsmiths, artisans, tanners, weavers, leather-workers and so on. At Catanzaro, in 1417, the king confirmed the right of the Jewish as of the Christian citizens to continue to work iron, steel, ploughs and mattocks as they had formerly done. The dyeing industry was still very prominent, though an attempt was made in Calabria to prevent the Jews from drying cloths out of doors during Holy Week, while at Fondi, from the fourteenth century, they were prohibited from using public places for the purpose at any time. A great deal is heard of merchants and petty traders, who sold their wares, especially textiles, all over the country. At the opening of the great fairs, they marched in procession together with the civic dignitaries, the guilds and the representatives of the corporations of foreign merchants, often too providing the banner which was carried at the head of the parade; in 1476, they obtained permission to absent themselves from such functions when they were held on the Sabbath. Among other commodities they dealt in luxury cloths acquired from the Venetian, Florentine and Milanese importers, which they sold on credit, on a primitive installment system.

The changing economic circumstances and the diminishing prosperity of the south resulted in the emergence by the side of this element of an increasing number of professional loan-bankers, as was now the case in northern Italy. The legal rate of interest on advances, fixed in 1231 at 10%, had risen steeply as a natural result of the economic backwardness of the kingdom and of royal rapacity, being higher than anywhere else in the Peninsula. Yet the system of open usury was less burdensome than that hitherto practiced by the Venetian and Florentine merchants, who when approached for a loan would insist on making it partly in the form of merchandise, which they would buy back at panic rates when the borrower was again in need of ready cash. Hence the arrival of Jewish moneylenders was considered a boon; the city of Brindisi, for example, though not conspicuously pro-Semitic, expressed profound gratitude to the king when the local Jews were empowered to lend money at interest, declaring that otherwise they would have been forced to dispose of everything they possessed at a derisory price in order to raise money.

This development was to take place in the main under Robert of Anjou's successors — a complicated genealogical tangle — who continued his policy on much the same plane throughout the fourteenth century. The best disposed was Ladislas, who on July 27, 1400, issued a liberal charter of privileges, obviously intended to attract loan-bankers from central Italy. They were given the right to live where they pleased, to own houses and land, and to maintain their synagogues and cemeteries; they were guaranteed freedom of movement, equality of taxation and immunity from unwarranted arrest; and they were absolved from the obligation to wear the humiliating badge of shame, the *tau*. The legal rate of interest was now raised to 40% — a significantly high figure. As an additional attraction, the special tax, probably on wine, known as the *morthafa*, was henceforth abolished in many places. The Jewish colony in the south now began to resume something of its former importance. Under Queen Joanna II — the most sensuous woman of a sensuous age, with whom the rule of the house of Anjou in Naples drew to its close — the stream of immigration continued, patents of protection being given to affluent financiers who settled in Aquila, Sulmona, Cotrone, Venafro and other places, whose Jewish communities were thus renewed or reinforced. When Catanzaro was captured after a period of unrest, the Jewish inhabitants shared equally with the Christians in the privileges guaranteed by its new charter, were exempted together with their neighbors from special taxation, and were accorded communal autonomy. That the archbishop of Trani was permitted to reassert his jurisdiction on the Jews and neophytes of the town, or that the bishop of Gerace was ordered by the Pope to take proceedings against those Jews who transgressed any church regulations, did not affect the general tranquillity.

A brief interlude of feminine inconsistency followed. At the outset of his anti-Jewish crusade, Joanna fell for a time under the influence of Fra Giovanni da Capistrano,[*] who persuaded her to embark on a campaign of persecution in accordance with the program of the Observantine Franciscans. In May, 1427, she suddenly issued an edict ordering the communities of her dominions to surrender to him for cancellation all the letters and privileges granted to them by former monarchs, and empowering him to coerce them, under such penalties as he should think fit, to abandon usury and to conform to the other canonical restrictions. He himself took up his residence at Lanciano, where as a beginning

[*] See above, page 159.

he shut up the Jews in a single street, made them wear the sign, restricted their economic life and chased away as suspected usurers those who were engaged in trade, as though their profession, too, were contrary to Canon Law. The news of his appointment was received with consternation, not only by the victims. Many cities sent petitions to court, protesting against his innovations. At Naples, a certain citizen, named Cristino, dared the friars and placed himself at the head of the opposition. The Jews on their side despatched a deputation to Rome, consisting of Solomon of Anagni the physician and Vitale of Aquila. The arguments of golden florins were perhaps more effective than those of silver tongues, and the Pope himself counselled moderation. In the following August, the queen withdrew her edict and restored the Jews to their former position, declaring how greatly her people as well as her treasury benefited from their presence. As if to emphasize the point, a few days later the officially licensed rate of interest was raised to the unprecedented figure of 45%. The imposition, in 1429, of a levy of one-third of a ducat on every Jew, in order to compensate the Franciscan convent in Jerusalem for its alleged sufferings at Jewish hands,* was presumably intended as a solace to the friars after this disappointment.

On Queen Joanna's death, there was a long dispute for the Neapolitan throne, ending in 1442 in the triumph of Alfonso I of Sicily. A man of great personal charm and very popular with his subjects, he, like his Hohenstaufen and Angevin predecessors, made his court a center of culture and learning. Though in Sicily he did not particularly favor the Jews, local circumstances in Naples made him continue his predecessors' policy, and his example was followed on his death by his illegitimate son, the licentious, tyrannical Ferrante I, who succeeded him on the Neapolitan throne. Supremely avaricious, he did not overlook the benefits which

* See above, pages 159–60.

could accrue to his treasury through the industry of the Jews. He conceded them full liberty of residence and circulation in the kingdom on the payment of an annual tribute, permitted them to construct new synagogues, and in return for a handsome gratuity absolved them again from the obligation of wearing the distinguishing marks on their clothing. To this was added, in a remarkable charter of March 13, 1468 — unique perhaps in medieval Jewish history — a concession of full rights of citizenship in the towns where they took up their domicile. As a safeguard both of the royal rights and of their own security against ecclesiastical and baronial claims, a central tribunal was set up with full jurisdiction over all the communities of the realm, except Reggio, where special circumstances prevailed.

The attempt to strengthen the Jewish settlement was very successful. Approximately fifty centers in the kingdom of Naples are known in which Jewish loan-banks existed in the second half of the fifteenth century. In all, there were between 150 and 200 places where Jews are recorded as having lived at this time, though not all were perhaps the seats of organized communities. In Calabria, in 1481, there were 3,750 taxpaying households comprising, in addition to the paupers and those who were exempt, a total of 12,187 souls. Taxes were levied on the assumption that the total Jewish population of the kingdom was approximately 50,000 — perhaps something of an exaggeration, but a figure which gives some idea of the numbers involved. Their importance to the treasury was inestimable. General conferences of the Jewish communities were held in the various provinces to allocate the financial burden among themselves, and when the royal control was reasserted in South Italy after the civil wars, the cities vainly demanded the participation of the Jews in ordinary treasury contributions, on the ground that the present method created two communities side by side in the same city. A royal order of 1469 promised that all foreign Jews who desired to come and traffic should enjoy the same privileges as their native coreligionists; and immediately afterwards there was an influx of wealthy Hebrews from Rome, Ascoli, Fano, Bologna, and other places in the north of the country. From the middle of the century, an eddy of the migration from Germany is to be discerned, as well as the arrival of a few families from the Provence. The activity of the Hebrew printing press in Naples in the last decade of the century* testifies to the varied origin, the number, the munificence and the intellectual alertness of the community.

Unqualified tranquillity was naturally not to be expected. During the great rising of the baronage and peasants in Calabria between 1458 and 1463, the Jews were made to pay the price for the royal favors. At Acri, the *giudecca* was attacked and set on fire; when Lecce revolted, the Jews were chased away; much the same happened at Bari; and in many places the Church took the opportunity to reassert its old claims. To be sure, when the king recaptured any city, he saw to it that these valuable subjects of his were readmitted if they had been expelled and that their position was specifically guaranteed; and later on, in recognition of their loyalty and support, he enforced their rights in one municipality after the other on the same basis as those of other citizens, paying no attention to the protests of places (such as Bari) which still tried to discriminate against them. On the other hand, as a sop to their enemies, though in direct contravention of their own privileges, he subsequently proclaimed a moratorium on all sums owing to them. This was a particularly serious blow to those who sold goods on credit, as the North Italian mercers expected to be paid for the cloth taken from them for sale on credit, demanding interest on arrears and throwing defaulters into jail and behaving "as though they wished to be paid in blood rather than in goods." The royal intervention imposed

---

* See above, page 224.

a certain degree of moderation on them, and almost immediately afterwards, in 1476, the communities of the realm succeeded in obtaining a charter of privileges according them full pardon for any misdemeanors of which they might have been guilty — and Jews in the fifteenth century had difficulty in not falling into some unwitting transgression of the many restrictions placed on them. The preaching of the friars in northern Italy continued to have its echoes in the south, but without any serious consequence. A *Monte di Pietà* had been established at Aquila in 1466 through the energy of Fra Giacomo della Marca — one of the relatively few in this part of the country — but the Jews continued their activities without interruption. When, in 1488, Fra Bernardino da Feltre attempted to "create a bestial and unjustified tumult against the Jews" in his sermons, he was rapidly and effectively silenced; and the anti-Jewish preaching of the Dominican Fra Gaspar in the Abruzzi in 1491 was not allowed to lead to untoward results.

With the expulsion of the Jews from the Spanish dominions in 1492, large contingents of the exiles arrived in the kingdom of Naples — one of the few areas of western Europe which was open to them and where they were actually welcomed. Entire Sicilian communities transferred themselves in a body to any place to which they were admitted, sometimes forming new communities with their own officers by the side of the long established native ones. To Reggio, the nearest point on the mainland, where Syracuse Jewry came with all its institutions, they brought the art of indigo-dyeing, afterwards so important and lucrative; while those who disembarked at Naples were so numerous that a special arrangement was made regarding the payment of customs-dues on what they had managed to salvage from the disaster. On August 10, 1492, a large party from Spain, thousands strong, arrived in this port, where they were joined later by a contingent from Sardinia, the main body of whom, however, put in at Gaeta. Thus the Jewish population in southern Italy was momentarily brought up to what was probably a record level. One of the very few conditions imposed on the immigrants was that they should be inspected to make sure that they were free from infectious disease. Notwithstanding this, pestilence stalked at their heels, though its dimensions, and their responsibility, were nothing like so great as was subsequently alleged. The populace (encouraged by a Spanish friar, who, according to the story told by the novelist Bandello, faked a miracle in the name of S. Cataldo in order to influence the king) did not look upon the strangers with a kindly eye, but for the moment their resentment simmered under the surface.

Of the Spanish immigrants, the most noteworthy family was that of Abrabanel, which for a short time played a dominant role in local affairs. At its head was the famous Don Isaac, financier, scholar, philosopher and exegete, who had formerly been in the service of the Spanish sovereigns and had worked in vain to secure the withdrawal of the edict of expulsion. He now became associated with the Neapolitan treasury, continuing at the same time his literary work. His sons, Joseph and Judah (the philosopher known to posterity as Leone Ebreo), both skilled physicians, and Samuel, an able man of affairs, accompanied him, as did also his brother, Don Jacob.

King Ferrante died in January 1494, to be succeeded by his son Alfonso II, of whom it was said that "never was any prince more bloody, wicked, inhuman, lascivious or gluttonous than he." The change of ruler led to the epoch-making descent of Charles VIII of France, who had some sort of dynastic claim on the throne of Naples. For the next half century, Italy became a campaigning ground for foreign armies, and the international rivalries that now began left an imprint on European history the consequences of which can be discerned even today. The Jews now paid the price of the favor that they had received during the past half-century. From the moment of the accession of the new king, and above all on the approach of the French, there took place throughout the kingdom outbreaks of disorder, accompanied by savage attacks on the Jewish quarters. No Jews being allowed to live in France at this time, the French soldiery were all the more prone to indulge in anti-Jewish excesses on their own account. Everywhere there were scenes of murder, pillage and destruction. An onslaught on the Jews at Naples before the French entry, which the king was unable to suppress, was followed at Lecce, Acquaviva, Catanzaro, Bitonto, and elsewhere all over Apulia. At Bari, their losses were estimated at 10,000 ducats. In many places, the debts owing to them were cancelled, and they were forced to restore the pledges in their hands; while at Brindisi, they tried to safeguard themselves by "spontaneously" forgiving their creditors, though they thought better of it once the immediate danger had passed. Don Isaac Abrabanel lost his precious library for the second time during the disorders. After following his royal master to Sicily, where as a professing Jew he was unable to remain, he sought refuge at Monopoli, then under Venetian rule, and ultimately in Venice. At Cosenza, the majority of the community embraced Christianity, and the emigration through the port was on an impressive scale. Twenty-two families fled from the country from a single small town, Monteleone. Almost the only places unaffected by the disorders were Tropea, which accorded the Jews the rights of citizenship in recognition of their good conduct during the siege, and Gallipoli, which generously welcomed the fugitives from the neighboring centers and even exempted them from taxation. Later on, when the place surrendered to the Spaniards, the security of its Jewish population was specifically safeguarded in the terms of capitulation — a unique display of consideration. The general ruin was completed by a war levy pitilessly exacted by the French, and by the legalization of acts of rapine by conferring property on royal favorites. Even though, in the summer of 1495, the legitimate sovereign reoccupied his capital, the situation barely improved. In the following year, after chasing out the Marranos newly arrived from Spain, the popular representatives obtained a royal edict expelling the Jews, too, from the city and the region (October 26, 1496). The history of the Jews in the kingdom of Naples was to drag on for another half-century; but only a broken remnant was henceforth in question.

Possibly, former conditions might have been restored had the old royal family managed to re-establish itself permanently. Indeed, the new king, Federigo, reverted as far as he was able to the pro-Jewish policy traditional in his house — so much so, that a party of refugees who arrived from Portugal in the spring of 1497 were almost exuberantly welcomed. He did what he could to restore conditions of tranquillity for those Jews left under his rule, ordered that they should be protected by all officials, confirmed their old privileges, and authorized the resumption of their normal activities and the collection of their debts, notwithstanding an ordinance of the previous years, though at the price of sharing the proceeds. He even refused to countenance a renewal of the old obligation to wear the Jewish badge, on the somewhat shaky ground that this had never been the practice in his realm. But this respite lasted for only a short while. The treaty of Granada, signed in November, 1500, divided the kingdom of Naples between Louis XII of France and Ferdinand the Catholic of Spain. Before long, the latter foxed his fellow-brigand out of his share of the booty and, after helping to dispossess the unfortunate king of his domains in the summer of 1501, conquered them for himself in the course of the following year. Thus the kingdom of Naples passed under the same intolerant rule as Aragon, Sardinia, and Sicily, with the same tragic results for the battered remnant of its Jewish communities.

Ferdinand and Isabella, like the antisemites of more recent days, regarded the "Jewish problem" from an international point of view. It was in their opinion useless to attempt to stamp out Judaism in one country while others were willing to receive the fugitives; a concerted onslaught was needed in all countries at the same time. Hence the Jews had been expelled, not from Spain alone, but from all lands under Spanish rule; hence their banishment from the adjacent countries was subsequently worked for and secured; hence an attempt by diplomatic means to obtain the ejection of the refugees in other lands — even England; hence, therefore, the immediate peril in which the communities of the newly acquired possessions on the Italian mainland now stood. It happened that the military leader responsible for the conquest was Gonzalo da Cordova, the "Great Captain" who had taken up arms to defend the Marranos of his native city during an attack in 1473, employed Judah Abrabanel as his body-physician, and possibly had Jewish blood in his own veins. He did what he could to defend the Neapolitan Jews from the onslaught. Hardly was the conquest completed when he received instructions to rid the newly acquired territories of the taint of disbelief. He ventured to expostulate, basing his opposition on the grounds that there were too few persons involved to constitute any sort of problem, and that the real difficulty to be confronted was that of those who pretended to be Christians. For the moment, therefore, the onslaught was diverted from the declared Jews to the still unsolved problem of the *neofiti* and the immigrant Marranos. Ferdinand needed no encouragement to introduce the Inquisition on the Spanish model, one of the attractions of which was that it brought in vast profits to the Crown. Local opposition was so fierce that he had been compelled at the time of the conquest to promise that the dreaded tribunal would not be set up. He had, indeed, a convenient theory, which he communicated to Da Cordova, that no Catholic was required to observe obligations in derogation of the Faith; and down to the end of his reign he continued without intermission to work and to intrigue for the object so dear to his heart. Although popular antagonism remained too strong for him, this did not safeguard persons of Jewish origin, for the bishops and local officials occasionally took action with devastating result. Meanwhile, local prejudice resulted in the expulsion of the Jews from Nola in 1506 and in a similar attempt against those of Capua.

By now the "Great Captain's" protection was lacking, and when Ferdinand confused the issue regarding the Inquisition by switching his attack back to the Jews, they had no one to plead their cause. On November 19, 1510, the new viceroy, Raimondo de Cardona, invited the representatives of the city of Naples to his palace to hear a communication just received from the king banishing from Apulia and Calabria all Jews and persons of Jewish stock, including fugitives from Spain. Thus, he explained, no one of suspected orthodoxy would be left, and the introduction of the Inquisition would be unnecessary. The news was received at first with general rejoicing, and some quarters of the town were illuminated. But later, suspicions began to arise, not unjustifiably, and the heralds were not allowed to proclaim the edict of banishment until further guarantees were given. For the moment, measures were taken only against the declared Jews, who were ordered to leave the realm by March 1 of the following year, taking with them all their property except gold and silver, the export of which was forbidden. Two hundred families only were to remain, on the payment of an annual tribute of 3,000 ducats. A reprieve of a few months was apparently obtained, as it was only on July 25, 1511, that the Jews of Reggio crossed the Straits. The synagogue at Castrovillari was disposed of to the municipality; that of Lecce became a church. But the handful of families which stayed behind were enough to perpetuate the Jewish associations of the realm for a few years longer; and indeed there is reason to believe that the edict of banishment was not in fact meticulously obeyed.

Nothing at all seems to have been done regarding the Christians of Jewish stock, as Ferdinand gruffly reminded the viceroy in the summer of 1513, and that autumn their number was swollen by the arrival at Naples of four hundred fugitives from Sicily who were trying to escape from the rigor of the Holy Office. The local representative of the less formidable Papal Inquisition applied to the king in December begging him to take action; for in Calabria and Apulia, he said, the New Christians were living as Jews and maintaining semi-public synagogues. In the winter of the following year, an order was issued for the expulsion of the *neofiti*. This was carried into execution in April and May, 1515, but incompletely; for not only were some of the native New Christians left unmolested, but, in addition, the new regulations were construed as though they did not apply to newly arrived immigrants.

The handful of declared Jewish families who had been permitted to remain — headed by Don Jacob Abrabanel, a brother of the statesman — had the grim satisfaction of witnessing how much harm was done to the economic structure of the country by the departure of their coreligionists. Trade and manufacture were languishing, and the rate of interest on pledges with Christian usurers rose precipitately until it touched 240 per cent. The population began to regret what had happened. Some cities obtained permission to harbor Jews again during the annual fairs; refugees expelled in 1515 from Ragusa, on the Dalmatian coast, were permitted to establish themselves in various Adriatic seaports; and in 1520 the citizens of Naples petitioned the viceroy to give greater facilities to the handful of Jews then in the city and to invite others from abroad to restore the economic situation. (It looks very much as though the Abrabanel family, with a sense of publicity in advance of their day, organized the pro-Jewish expressions of opinion which now became so frequent.) The King-Emperor Charles V, determined antisemite though he was, received the application benevolently in view of the "abominable" usury which was now practiced by Christians in secret. On November 23, 1520, an edict was issued from Madrid giving the Jews permission to carry on financial and trading activities without restriction for five years, reducing their tribute by half, and permitting a further forty or fifty wealthy families to set up their establishments. Communities now seem to have been revived in some of the greater cities: Lecce, Taranto, Otranto, Brindisi, Sulmona, Castrovillari, Ostuni and Nardò, with isolated families at least in Bari, Gallipoli and Copertino. There was a relatively numerous settlement also at Capua, where in 1526 an attempt was made to control their business activity and in 1531 to restrict their rights and shut them up in a special quarter. Of conditions at Naples, with its handful of wealthy patrician families mainly from Spain and Portugal, we are informed in the querulous autobiographical notes of the Portuguese exile, David ibn Iacchia, who had what he considered to be the misfortune of serving as rabbi there for a few years.

For a short while, the terms of the agreement were observed; though the next year a fanatical friar was able to stir up sufficient ill feeling to secure an order imposing the yellow badge. There was a turn for the worse with the arrival from Spain of Don Pedro de Toledo as viceroy. He was personally on friendly terms with Samuel Abrabanel, now head of the community; and his daughter Leonora (later grand duchess of Tuscany) had her education partially directed by Doña Bienvenida, the other's gifted wife. He brought with him, nevertheless, instructions to make an end of what was now the only Jewish settlement remaining in the Spanish dominions. On January 5, 1533, in flagrant infringement of the contract of thirteen years before, which guaranteed notice of a year and a half before terminating the agreement, he published an edict for the Jews to leave the realm or else apostatize within six months. The news threw Naples into an uproar, the citizens pointing out how, since 1520, the Jews had always behaved in an exemplary fashion and helped the people in their necessities. In consequence, the expulsion was first postponed and then cancelled, a fresh agreement, more liberal in some ways than the old, being made at the close of 1535 through the medium of Samuel Abrabanel, in return for an advance payment of 10,000 ducats. This turned out to be only a reprieve. On November 10, 1539, it was once more intimated that the Jews were to be expelled. The Neapolitans summoned a popular "Parliament," which demanded that they should be left undisturbed at least until 1550, on the ground that their departure would entail widespread ruin. This time, their expostulations had no effect, and after long discussions on the financial terms — for it was not considered necessary to observe the royal pledge meticulously in such a case — the edict of banishment was at last published, in May, 1541. No reason was given, not even the hackneyed one that the victims had practiced usury; in view of the attitude of the people, this would have sounded ironical. A Roman Jew, named Solomon, was sent to Ratisbon to intercede with the emperor; but the latter was adamant. By the following November, all declared Jews had left the realm — some, headed by the Abrabanels, for Ferrara; some for Rome and the Papal States, en route in certain cases for Palestine; some to be intercepted by Ragusan pirates and taken as prisoners to Marseilles, where, but for the humane intervention of the French king, they would have been sold as slaves.

But, long before this, the historic communities of South Italy were scattered far and wide. Apulian and Calabrian congregations, distinguishable by certain peculiarities of Hebrew pronunciation* as well as by their rite of prayer, long

---

* According to Azariah de' Rossi, who personally knew some of the survivors of Apulian Jewry, they did not differentiate between the Hebrew sounds *ch* and *h*.

preserved their individuality along the Dalmatian coast (at Arta and Lepanto, for instance, there were both Neapolitan and Sicilian settlements), in Constantinople and in other important centers of the Turkish empire. The exiles from Otranto alone were numerous enough to maintain a special synagogue at Salonica, where no section of the Diaspora was unrepresented. To Corfu, the Apulians brought their own dialect of Italian, which continued to be spoken among the Jews of the island down to our own day, and their own folk songs, embodying some of the oldest fragments of the vernacular literature of southern Italy now extant. At several places in the region, there are streets with names such as the *Via Sinagoga, Strada della Giudea* and *Via Scolanova* (Trani), or *Via Iudecca* (Brindisi), which bear testimony to the existence of the Jewish colony uprooted four centuries ago; while here and there (for example, the present-day churches of S. Anna and S. Maria dei Martiri at Trani) the ancient synagogue buildings may be seen. Family names, such as Pugliese or Di Capua, common among Italian Jews, still bear witness to southern origin. But the physical connection, uninterrupted since the classical period, was now at an end.

Economically, the tragic events of these years left a profound trace. A contemporary chronicler recorded that on the expulsion of the Jews "who had lived in the country for many years to the great advantage of the poor," the latter lost those conveniences that they had formerly enjoyed, with the result that "the Christians began to do worse than the Jews." According to one recent writer, the retrograde state of the province of Calabria in our own day is due to the blow that it suffered by their banishment, since when its economic life has stagnated.

Long after the edict of expulsion, the persecution of the remaining *neofiti* of Jewish origin continued. Noble families hesitated to intermarry with them, notwithstanding the advice of broadminded scholars like Galatino. Even in the seventeenth century, several were burned alive in Rome for fidelity to the faith of their fathers, just as was the case with the Iberian Marranos, a few of whom also found their way to Naples in the Spanish period. Some managed to migrate overseas, to Salonica and so on, and declared their Judaism in public. To the present day, it is said, vague traces of Jewish beliefs and practices are to be discerned among their remote descendants who can still be traced in southern Italy. As for declared Jews, the kingdom of the Two Sicilies henceforth knew nothing of them, except for occasional furtive visitors. In the last decade of the seventeenth century, indeed, in order to restore the languishing economy of the region, an attempt was made to entice a few families back hither as well, under harsh conditions, but it proved a failure.* It was only in the nineteenth century that a community, never of great importance, was re-established in Naples, and this was the only one in the south of the country. The scene on which the epic history of the Jews in Italy was enacted is now definitely changed. The southern centers are henceforth deserted; but the blight of intolerance which had ended their existence was soon to infect those parts of the Peninsula which had as yet remained immune.

---

* See below, page 351.

CHAPTER VII

The Catholic Reaction

xxix
Prelude

WHEN Martin Luther nailed up his famous Theses on the cathedral door at Wittenberg, thereby setting the machinery of the Reformation in motion, the fate of the eager Jewries of Renaissance Italy was sealed. Threatened by this dangerous movement of secession, the Catholic Church began to set its house in order, more systematically and more comprehensively than ever before, in the process known as the Counter-Reformation. No longer were the Popes to be pre-eminently enlightened patrons of literature, science and the arts, with worldly inclinations and interests. Henceforth they were chosen among those in whose eyes the requirements of the Church, spiritual and temporal, were paramount; who looked for inspiration to the most narrow pronouncements of the Church Fathers and enactments of the Church Councils; who considered Canon Law in all its severity to be the standard of Christian practice, whatever inconvenience might be caused to groups or individuals; who, like some of their eminent predecessors, regarded the Jews as a leaven of disbelief which positively endangered Christianity and Christendom — at least, unless they were segregated from intercourse with other men, as the Lateran Councils had prescribed three and a half centuries before. This was the point of view above all of the somber Cardinal Caraffa, member of a noble Neapolitan family, who threw himself with burning zeal into the work of securing an inner reform of the Church and, notwithstanding their worldly characters and interests, attained great authority at the Vatican under Pope Paul III, founder of the Jesuit Order, and his successor, the elegant Julius III.

The first indication of the new spirit, so far as the Jews were concerned, was the establishment in Rome in 1542, on Cardinal Caraffa's advice, of a Supreme Tribunal of the Holy Office organized on the same lines as the redoubtable court instituted by Ferdinand and Isabella in Spain sixty years earlier. Six cardinals with power to appoint delegates were nominated as inquisitors for either side of the Alps. Although their authority officially extended over "heretics" and not "unbelievers," the latter too came within their purview if they were suspected of deliberately undermining Christian faith; and the implications to Jewish life were soon apparent. The next year, at the instigation of Ignatius Loyola, there was set up in Rome a Home for Converted Jews (*Casa dei Catecumeni*) later to witness some tragic scenes within its walls. On the ingenious pretext that their burden was diminished when the poorer among them apostatized, a good part of the upkeep of this institution was imposed before long on the Jews themselves, each synagogue in the Papal States having to pay ten ducats yearly for the purpose — clearly a moral as well as economic burden, and one bitterly resented.

On September 4, 1553, a Franciscan friar, named Cornelio da Montalcino, who had embraced Judaism as a result of his studies, was burned alive on the Campo de' Fiori. The episode must have been welcome to the reactionaries, provided thus with evidence which appeared to confirm their theories regarding the dangerous influence of Judaism. Already, attention had been directed to this through another medium. As it happens, a dispute broke out at Venice at this time regarding their rival productions between two Christian printers of Hebrew books, Marcantonio Giustiniani and Alvise Bragadini. The former spitefully denounced the other to Rome for producing works which contained matter offensive to the Holy Catholic Faith. It was easy enough for him to find a few apostates who were prepared to support this view and to seek out passages which, by dint of some dialectical effort, the suppression of the context or the neglect of the historical setting, might be distorted into an objectionable significance. Bragadini was not long in following suit, denouncing on similar grounds and through similar means the works published by his competitor. (It is impossible to overlook the phenomenon of the extraordinary outburst of anti-Jewish activity at this period on the part of a group of apostates — persons sometimes of considerable learning and belonging to eminent families — who set themselves systematically to malign Judaism and everything connected with it in the hope of forcing the Jews into Christianity. Their religious beliefs sapped by the spirit of the Renaissance, and seeing no hope for the future of Judaism and the Jews after the recent catastrophes, they were impelled by self-interest, apart from conviction, to change their faith. Henceforth, they felt a constant urge to justify their conduct, not only, or not so much, by theological argument as by calumny, even though this may have reacted in retrospect upon themselves. Moreover, they obviously hoped to justify an action of which they were subconsciously ashamed by securing general imitation of their example.) Soon there were two rival sets of renegades in Rome working on behalf of the one printer or the other and systematically maligning, partly through interest and partly through spite, some of the noblest products of the Jewish intellect — especially the Talmud, republished by Giustiniani a few years before. Noteworthy among them were Joseph Sarfatti (Andrea del Monte) and Hananel da Foligno, who found suitable allies in two grandsons of Elias Levita, the famous humanist of the previous generation, Vittorio Eliano (formerly Elijah) and Giovanni Battista (Solomon Romano), who had become converted and taken Holy Orders. This coterie now renewed the worst medieval libels against rabbinic writings, hopelessly exaggerating isolated statements and incidental allusions, and asserting that it was full of insults to Christianity and to its founder. At Rome, where the censorship of heretical publications had recently begun under the auspices of the Inquisition, the atmosphere was increasingly propitious for all this, and from a private dispute between two printers the affair developed into an onslaught upon Hebrew literature as a whole. On August 12, 1553, after a commission of cardinals had solemnly reported in an adverse sense, the Pope issued a decree stigmatizing the Talmud and its kindred works as blasphemous — notwithstanding the fact that its printing had been specifically authorized by Pope Leo X — and condemning it to be burned.

A month later, on the Jewish New Year's day (September 9, 1553), an auto-da-fé was held on the Campo de' Fiori, at which Hebrew books in enormous number, seized almost haphazardly from the Jewish houses, were committed to the flames. Immediately after, an edict was issued by the Inquisition describing what had happened and summoning all rulers, bishops and inquisitors throughout Italy to take similar steps. The order was of course obeyed implicitly in the Papal States, especially in Bologna and Ravenna. The dukes of Ferrara and Mantua, of Urbino and Florence, false to their normal enlightenment, followed suit. Especially drastic was the action taken in Venice, the center of Hebrew printing, where the accumulated stocks presented special opportunities for destruction. On October 21, the Council of Ten issued a decree ordering the surrender, not merely of the Talmud itself, but also of all "compendia, summaries and other works dependent thereon." The phraseology was so comprehensive as to embrace almost all Jewish books. Even copies of the Bible were sometimes added to the pyre, while the books in the possession of eminent Christian scholars, such as Andrea Masi, who compared the cardinals' verdict on the Talmud to the opinions of the blind concerning color, were not immune. Only the duchies of Milan and Monferrat, at this time under Spanish and French control respectively, escaped for the moment the obscurantist orgy.

The Jewish communities could not look on idly while this was happening. The rabbis of Rome made counter-representations to the Pope and found support from at least one enlightened member of the College of Cardinals, Cardinal Sacristo. They were not wholly unsuccessful, for on May 29, 1554, a Bull was issued which specified that only the Talmud and such works as contained blasphemies against Christianity were to be destroyed; others, including the compendia essential for decisions on points of Jewish law, were now to be submitted to censorship, their possession and study being thereafter permitted. A month later, representatives of the Italian rabbinate met together in Ferrara to consider the new situation, which implied disaster if anything appeared that could be interpreted in an anti-Christian sense. They coped with the problem by instituting a pre-censorship of their own, ordering that no book should be printed henceforth without the license of three duly ordained rabbis and the lay leaders of the nearest large community. At the same time, they tried to discipline Jewish life, and thus minimize Gentile interference, by restricting jurisdiction to the local rabbis in disputes between one Jew and another, prohibiting recourse to secular courts, stopping competition for houses owned by a non-Jewish landlord or for licenses to open loan-banks, and forbidding, in normal circumstances, application to the Pope for permission to take a second wife, as was still sometimes done in the Italian communities. Henceforth, some of the most eminent Italian savants meticulously revised the standard texts before publication, to make sure that nothing was included which might possibly give offense to even the most sensitive theologian. The censorship system, instituted to prevent the publication of what was considered objectionable by the Church, came to be used in the end as a means of suppressing what one scholar or another happened to consider contrary to the doctrine of the Synagogue. Later on, the ban against the Talmud, after the excision of certain passages, was temporarily lifted. Nevertheless, raids on Jewish libraries, the mutilation of Jewish books, pyres for the destruction of what Christian zealots considered pernicious, remained a commonplace for generations, especially in those cities which were under the rule of the Church. The offensive against Hebrew literature was henceforth an endemic feature of Italian Jewish life.

xxx

Cum Nimis Absurdum

On May 23, 1555, Cardinal Caraffa, inspirer of the Catholic Reaction and deadly enemy of the Jews, was elected to the Papacy, taking the name of Paul IV. On July 12, he issued his famous Bull, beginning with the words *Cum nimis absurdum:*

> Forasmuch as it is highly absurd and improper that the Jews, condemned by God to eternal slavery because of their guilt, should, on the pretext that they are cherished by Christian love and permitted to dwell in our midst, show such ingratitude to Christians as to insult them for their mercy and presume to mastery instead of the subjection that beseems them; and forasmuch as we have been informed that in Rome and elsewhere their shamelessness is such that they presume to dwell among Christians in the neighborhood of churches without distinction of dress, and even to rent houses in the more elegant streets and squares of the cities, villages and places in which they live, to purchase and possess real property, to hire Christian maidservants and wetnurses and other salaried attendants, and to perpetrate divers other misdeeds to the shame and contumely of the Christian name; and considering that the Roman Church tolerates the Jews in witness of the true Christian faith ... we do therefore order the following measures, which are to be perpetually valid. ...

This is one of the landmarks in the history of human persecution and of Jewish martyrdom. Successive clauses, one more galling than the other, reiterated down to the last bitter detail all the oppressive medieval legislation regarding the Jews, the enforcement of which zealots had so long been urging, together with some further elaborations. They were henceforth to live segregated from all other persons in a special street or, if they were too many for this, in a special quarter, which was to be cut off from the rest of the town and to have only one single entry and egress. They were to be allowed no more than a single synagogue in each city, all others having to be destroyed and no new ones tolerated henceforth. They were no longer to possess real estate, which must be sold to Christians forthwith. They were to wear the distinguishing badge of shame to mark them off for contumely from others — a yellow hat in the case of the men, some other prominent token (in practice, a veil or kerchief) for women. They were not to have Christian wetnurses or servants of either sex in their employment, to work in public on Christian holidays, to associate with Christians on familiar terms, or to be addressed by any title of respect, such as *signor*. Their livelihood was restricted on all sides. Jewish physicians were no longer to be allowed to attend on Christian patients, notwithstanding the example of so many recent pontiffs down to a few years before. The conduct of their loan-banks — the prosperity of which in Rome had been affected by the foundation of a public *Monte di Pietà* in 1539 — was subjected to various regulations: the account-books were henceforth to be kept in the Italian language and writing (not in Hebrew letters as hitherto), unredeemed pledges to be retained for a year and a half before they could be sold, interest to be reckoned by the day when the month was unfinished and never to accumulate in excess of the original sum. They were not to deal in corn or any necessity of life. The only "art" by which they were to be allowed to earn their living henceforth was dealing in old clothes and second-hand goods (*sola arte strazzariae seu cenciariae, ut vulgo dicitur*, as the Latin inelegantly phrased it). All personal or local privileges which in any way conflicted with this ill-conceived and imperfectly digested measure were declared to be null and void.

This code embodied all the demands put forward so persistently by the friars during the past hundred and fifty years and, though more systematic, was not essentially different from those issued during some earlier interludes of reaction, as, for example, in the thirteenth or fifteenth centuries. But there was one outstanding difference. Those expressed, as it were, a vague ideal, this was vigorously and consistently enforced; those were temporary, this was in effect permanent; those were enforced only locally, this was ultimately accepted over almost all Italy, and a good part of Catholic Europe as well. Hitherto, the Papacy had generally figured in history as the protector of the Jews against excess. Henceforth, though still it never tolerated violence, it exemplified as well as instigated the severest repression. This policy survived, moreover, into the liberal age which was about to dawn in northern Europe. Thus Italy and the Papacy, from being synonymous in Jewish history with an easygoing tolerance, became associated for three centuries with the darkest reaction, creating an impression which subsequently proved very difficult to dispel.

At the outset, the new code applied only to the Papal States. These, comprising the Campania, Romagna, Marches of Ancona and good part of Umbria, straddled across central Italy from sea to sea. The area covered was thus greater than that of any other single state except the kingdom of the Two Sicilies, already free of Jews, and with its scores of organized centers probably comprised at this time a greater Jewish population than all the rest of Italy together. The community of Rome offered 40,000 scudi for the withdrawal of the regulations, but in vain — this was no attempt at blackmail, such as they had been familiar with in the past. A certain David d'Ascoli, who naively imagined that he could assist by publishing a defense of his people, was clapped into jail for his effrontery. The code was put into effect with unprecedented speed. On Saturday, July 23, the Jewish badge had to be worn in the stipulated form for the first time. Some persons tried to circumvent the regulations by dressing entirely in yellow, but such pleasantries were dangerous — a Jew who had suggested that this provision was an adroit business project of the Pope's was publicly scourged. Three days later those who did not live there already were driven from their old homes into the area on the left bank of the Tiber assigned for the Jewish quarter, the construction of the wall of enclosure beginning forthwith. Within two months it was finished, its cost being exacted from the luckless victims. Before long, the area came to be called by the name "Ghetto," after the Jewish quarter in Venice;* and thereafter this name spread throughout Italy as the designation of the areas assigned to the Jews as their residence, and provided with gates and, if necessary, walls which shut them off from the outside world. This as we have seen was not a new idea; it had first been officially prescribed, in a somewhat less extreme form, by the Third Lateran Council of 1179, which, for the sake of the purity of faith, forbade Christians and Jews to live together, and was part of the program for which the friars had been pressing with occasional success since the beginning of the fifteenth century. Henceforth, it was to become the rule in Italy. The justification for it varied perplexingly. Originally, the idea was that such segregation was necessary in order to prevent the contamination of the purity of faith by contact with the infidel. Later, other pretexts were found: that the Jews

---

* See above, page 186. The other suggested derivations (e. g., from the Hebrew *get*, or divorce) are unsound, and for the most part fanciful.

practiced magical arts, that it was necessary to immure them so as to prevent amorous adventures between adherents of the two faiths, or that this was the only way to minimize the risk of the unthinkable horror, that the Blessed Sacrament might sometimes be borne before the unbelievers' scoffing eyes.

From Rome, the plague spread. In the following spring (May 8, 1556), the Ghetto was instituted at Bologna, the second community of the Papal States, with its eleven synagogues and its Jewish silk-weavers' guild in addition to the numerous loan-bankers. At about the same time a beginning was made in other cities. Within six months, moreover, all real estate in the possession of the Jews in the Papal States, where besides their houses in the towns many possessed vineyards and olive-orchards in the country, had to be sold at a ruinous loss: 100,000 scudi was realized, but this was less than one-fifth of the estimated value. For the moment, it proved difficult to enforce the somewhat confusing economic restrictions, and it was decided that the Jews might continue to deal in any sort of merchandise, except wine, grain and foodstuffs, and follow any liberal art other than medicine; but later on these concessions were withdrawn, and the original provisions of Paul IV's terrible Bull were outdone.

The enforcement of the new regulations was unnecessarily harsh. The Jews found themselves accused of having manipulated fictitious sales of their property while retaining effective ownership. Commissaries were appointed to conduct an inquiry into this and the conduct of the loan-bankers, whose account books for years past were removed for examination; and to ensure the fulfillment of any penalty that might be decided, all their property was sequestered forthwith. The chronicler Gedaliah ibn Iacchia, who had his business at this time in Imola, calculated his personal losses at 10,000 scudi. All over the Papal States, the Jewish communities now found themselves delivered into the hands of petty tyrants, the most notorious being a certain Bernardino Campello in Umbria and Cesare della Nava in the Marches. At Spoleto and Viterbo at least the leading Jews were thrown into prison; illustrious families, like that of the physician David de' Pomi at Todi, hitherto prosperous landowners, were reduced to poverty. In many places, proceedings were conducted so brutally and the impoverishment was so general that large numbers of persons sought refuge in Christianity, one of the most deplorable instances being Benevento, at this time an enclave in the kingdom of Naples, where there were two synagogues; while at Moro di Valle, a tiny place in the Marches of Ancona, seventeen persons were converted and the rest of the community fled. There was no city in the entire papal territories, it was said, where no secessions took place at this time; and those able to transfer themselves and their property intact overseas or to the dominions of more tolerant rulers, such as the dukes of Urbino or of Ferrara, were considered singularly fortunate. In some places, the Jews were now forbidden access to the markets to buy food until the Christians had been served. When, in the course of the following year, the French armies marched into the Papal States, the Pope forced the Jews to labor on the fortifications of Rome, announcing that he would not tolerate them henceforth unless they proved themselves advantageous to the public.

Conditions at Ancona were such as to make the reaction take a particularly grim form. Here, a group of Marranos from Portugal had settled at the time of Pope Clement VII, twenty or thirty years before, attracted by the flourishing trade with Turkey and the Levant. Safe, as they thought, from the Inquisition, they discarded their enforced and highly transparent disguise of Christianity and reverted to the Judaism in which they had secretly been trained. Their number steadily increased, as the persecution in the Peninsula drove fresh waves of refugees to seek shelter abroad. In 1547, they were accorded by Pope Paul III a safe-conduct, promising that in case of prosecution for apostasy they would be subjected to the papal jurisdiction exclusively. The local authorities also guaranteed them immunity for five years, with the additional safeguard that any of them against whom proceedings were meditated would be allowed time to leave. These articles were confirmed in 1552 by Pope Julius III. In such circumstances, the settlement felt itself secure. It numbered something over one hundred households. They took a preponderant share in the maritime traffic of the port, a good deal of the overseas commerce of the entire Papal States passing through their hands. Many important mercantile houses of the Levant employed them as agents. A synagogue was established, by the side of the original one of the Italian rite, at which worship was conducted according to the Spanish and Portuguese tradition. Among the outstanding members of the community were Amatus Lusitanus, one of the most eminent physicians of the day, and Didaco Pyrrho (Lusitano), who had made his name widely known as a writer of Latin verse.

Upon this prosperous community, disaster suddenly fell, in one of the most gruesome tragedies in the whole course of Jewish history. On April 30, 1556, Paul IV suddenly withdrew the letters of protection issued by his predecessors, and ordered immediate proceedings to be taken by the Holy Office. The unhappy victims endeavored to raise 50,000 ducats to secure a respite, but were unable to bring the amount together in time. It was useless for them to deny the fact of their baptism, as it was notorious that for the past sixty years no declared Jews had been allowed to live in Portugal. Twenty-four men and one woman, who remained proudly steadfast to the end, were burned alive in successive "Acts of Faith" in the spring and early summer — down to our own day, elegies in their memory were recited year by year by the local communities during the service on the fast of the Ninth of Ab (commemorating the fall of Jerusalem). At least one committed suicide. Twenty-seven professed penitence and were reconciled, being sent as punishment to Malta to row in the galleys; but they succeeded in regaining their freedom before they arrived there. Thirty had escaped from prison before trial, as the result of a heavy bribe to the papal commissary, who managed to enrich himself indecently out of this human misery and subsequently escaped with his loot. The Sultan — on this occasion a paladin of humanity, as compared with the Pope — protested vigorously and insisted on the release of those prisoners who could lay claim to Turkish nationality, and his plea was supported by the city of Ancona, nervous for its overseas trade. The few persons who were left unscathed fled, mainly to the neighboring seaport of Pesaro, where, on the instructions of the duke of Urbino — not unmindful of the commercial advantage that they might bring — they were hospitably received.

The Jews had only one weapon by which they could retaliate for this outbreak of savagery — the economic one. Doña Gracia Mendes, the Marrano *grande dame* and business magnate, formerly resident at Ferrara and now a great figure in Constantinople, was among the first to recognize this clearly. Under her inspiration, an attempt was made to bring about a complete boycott of the port of Ancona and the Papal States as a whole on the part of the Jewish merchants who controlled the maritime trade of the Turkish empire, their agencies being transferred to the more congenial atmosphere of Pesaro. The plan was enthusiastically espoused by the communities of Constantinople, Salonica and Adrianople. That of Brusa, on the other hand, demurred, with regrettable results. Moreover, the native Jews of Ancona appealed pathetically for reconsideration of this policy, which, they urged, would bring reprisals as well as ruin upon their own heads. The final result was complete though honorable failure. What was worse, the duke of Urbino, disappointed in the hope of transferring the trade of Ancona to his own ports, expelled the Marranos from his dominions shortly afterwards (March, 1558).

Meanwhile, local persecutions continued. In virtue of a license from the Pope, two apostates, Sixtus of Sienna and Fra Filippo, went from place to place in the Romagna forcing their way into the synagogues, setting up a crucifix in front of the Ark and delivering opprobrious sermons to win the Jews over to Christianity. On the Day of Atonement of 1558 the latter attempted this at Recanati, where the Jews were already in serious trouble because the synagogue had not been transferred to the Jewish quarter, as stipulated by the recent regulations. Goaded now beyond endurance, some hotheads threw themselves on the apostate and ejected him by force, of course being savagely punished. The next year, several of the leading Jews of Civitanova were thrown into jail on a charge of attempting to convert a Franciscan friar, named Ambrosio, and smuggle him to Palestine — a capital offense. That winter, a corrupt official, emboldened by the general spirit of reaction, had attempted to exact from the communities of the Marches with the utmost brutality, for his own benefit, the alleged arrears of a levy imposed long before. All the other restrictions on the Jews were stringently enforced meanwhile, and when, in May, 1557, a single unauthorized book (it was an innocuous medieval biblical commentary) was discovered in the German synagogue in Rome, the entire community was heavily fined and the building closed for nine months.

The reaction had spread by now beyond the limits of the Papal States. Even the liberal-minded Duke Alfonso d'Este was unable to prevent the establishment of the new Holy Office in his dominions, to the terror of the Marranos settled there. At Ferrara, as the result of the publication of an elegy on the martyrs of Ancona, not only were proceedings taken against the poet, but Hebrew printing was suspended; and Isaac Abrabanel, one of the leading members of that noble family, was thrown into prison, though released when two Christian scholars testified to his character. At Reggio, the eminent jurist Gherardo Mazzoli secured, in 1555, an enactment forbidding the Jews to own real estate without special license; while in 1570 the wearing of the Jewish badge was re-enjoined in the duchy. The duchy of Milan had hitherto refused to enforce the papal regulations regarding the suppression of Jewish literature — not so much from feelings of tolerance, for it was under Spanish rule, as from political antagonism to the Pope. Indeed, when the offensive was at its height, and printing was suspended even in Venice, the city of Cremona became for a decade (1556–1567) one of the most active centers of Hebrew publishing in Italy. In 1557 the Inquisition had attempted to secure the application of the papal Bulls against Hebrew literature, but for the moment without result. Shortly after, there was a dispute between a certain Joshua de' Cantori and Rabbi Joseph Ottolenghi, the eminent but quarrelsome scholar who had made the school of Cremona famous. As a result, the latter was denounced to the Holy Office, whose attention was thus again called to the question, and, egged on by the apostate Vittorio Eliano, it ordered the Jews of the duchy to surrender their books. On the governor's intervention, a commission was appointed to examine the confiscated works and decide which of them were included in the proscribed category of talmudical literature. Its decision was, of course, unfavorable — nothing else could be expected after the recent events at Rome — and the governor now gave his assent perforce to the burning, the Spanish troops quartered in the duchy being ordered to give their cooperation. Under the zealous leadership of Fra Sixtus of Sienna, who had now taken the lead here, they burst into the houses of the Jews and the local printing shop and seized everything they could find — including even the freshly printed edition of the *Zohar* edited by Vittorio Eliano himself. This, however, had to be restored, as Sixtus imagined that its mystical pages confirmed in some way the dogmas of Christianity. In the spring of 1559, more than 10,000 volumes were committed to the flames in Cremona alone. Without the essential literature, it was impossible for intellectual life to flourish; and henceforth the fame of this city as a center of study was ended. Meanwhile, there were frequent attempts to stir up popular feeling against the Jews here and elsewhere in the duchy — especially at Pavia — in the hope of securing their elimination.

Paul IV had been highly unpopular. As he lay dying, in the hot summer of 1559, the mob began to destroy his escutcheons in the streets and squares of Rome, while his statue on the Capitoline Hill was dislodged from its pedestal and dragged about the city, the head being crowned with a Jew's yellow hat and used as a football by the street-urchins. Meanwhile the prisons were broken open, including that of the Holy Office, where several Jews awaiting trial were released. The impetus of persecution now waned for the moment. The new Pope, Pius IV, whose very election was a compromise, combined sympathy with the objectives of the Counter-Reformation with a taste for luxurious living and an intense detestation of the rigors of his predecessor, whose nephews were executed before long on somewhat dubious charges. In the circumstances, it is not remarkable that in a Bull issued on February 27, 1562, he mitigated the more galling of the regulations of the previous pontificate. The Jews were empowered to lay aside the yellow badge when travelling, to enlarge the Ghetto and to acquire shops outside it, to own real estate up to the value of 1,500 ducats, to deal in any commodity, and to lend money at a rate of interest not exceeding 18 per cent. The account books and communal records confiscated by Paul IV's commissaries were restored, and pardon promised for all infringements of his decrees, except crimes involving major offenses such as murder. It was stipulated, moreover, that rents in the Ghetto should not be unreasonably increased,

A Corner of the Roman Ghetto

Scene at a Conversionist Sermon

thus checking an abuse that had already become manifest. But it was not so much the legislation as the atmosphere that was changed. The brutal repression of the previous reign was suspended. For the next six years, the Jews could breath again.

At the beginning of 1562, the great Church Council which was to set the affairs of the Catholic Church in order reopened at Trent. One of the matters that it took into consideration was the censorship of literature. The Jewish communities despatched a deputation to watch developments on its behalf, headed by a certain Jacob di Bonaventura. They managed to have the final decision referred to Rome, where further representations were made, amply supported, and with partial success. When the *Index Librorum Prohibitorum*, as authorized by the Council, was published in March, 1564, it was found that, although the stricture against "the Talmud, its glosses, annotations, interpretations and expositions" had been retained, it had been modified by the qualification that "if published without the title 'Talmud' and without calumnies and insults to the Christian religion, they shall be tolerated." Though the Talmud itself was never again published in Italy, Hebrew printing, reduced to a mere trickle during the past decade, could now be resumed at Venice above all, provided that sufficient precautions were taken, much as before.

After a pontificate of just six years, Pius IV died. He was succeeded by Pius V, who as Cardinal Ghislieri and head of the Inquisition had led the assault on Jewish literature during the past decade and whose devotion to the cause of the Counter-Reformation was signalized by his subsequent canonization. With his election, in 1566, the former atmosphere of repression returned. The regulations of 1555 were renewed, the concessions made by his predecessor revoked, and within a short time orders issued for the real estate purchased in the Papal States during the past few years in pursuance of them to be alienated forthwith.

Two decrees of October 11, 1567, and October 16, 1568, completely prohibited the lending of money at interest, under the most severe penalties, thus undermining the economic basis of the Jews of the Papal States — a far-reaching blow, the effects of which were all the more serious in view of the tragic occupational restriction that had already been imposed. With such official encouragement, Jew-baiters now became active again. In Bologna, long one of the most prosperous Italian communities, an apostate named Alessandro repeated the old libels, including those against the Talmud. Notwithstanding the fact that the charge had been made and probed so frequently and so recently, a commission of inquiry was set up to investigate them. How it would decide was obvious from the outset. Despite a prohibition to leave the city while it was in progress, some of the more notable members of the community bribed the gatekeepers and fled (long after, Azariah de' Rossi remembered his escape with thanksgiving); others were thrown into prison and tortured to make them confess what was desired of them. Almost all did so — with the honorable exception of the rabbi, Ishmael Hananiah di Valmontone — and had to pay the penalty.

One of the Pope's ambitions was to purify his dominions religiously. In pursuance of this, he attempted at the beginning of his pontificate to eject the prostitutes from Rome. Their number with their dependents was so large that after three weeks he had to repeal this order. The Jews could not hope for similar mercy. On February 26, 1569, the climax was reached, with the Bull *Hebraeorum Gens* which, in punishment for various alleged malpractices, religious seduction and soothsaying, expelled them from the whole of the Papal States, with the exception of Rome and Ancona where it was desirable that they should remain because of their importance for trade with the Levant. It was a terrible blow — decided, it is said, in the teeth of the opposition of the College of Cardinals. In something like four score places, where prosperous congregations had existed for many generations past, the Jews were banished, the places of worship were closed and the cemeteries were destroyed: from Bologna, where the "House of Life" was made over to the sisters of a neighboring nunnery and the bodies removed for reburial at Pieve di Cento in the Este dominions, to tiny rural places in the hill-country of Umbria and the Campania. Among the communities which now came to an end were those of Benevento, with a continuous history dating back to the legendary days of Ahimaaz and the Lombard rule, Camerino, Fano, Orvieto, Spoleto, Ravenna, Terracina, Perugia, Viterbo and many more. The majority of the exiles had no choice but to crowd together in the already-congested Roman Ghetto, adding to the difficulties of life and to the general unsanitary conditions. To the present day, the typical Roman Jewish surnames, deriving from little provincial centers of the region — Tagliacozzo, (di) Tivoli, (di) Nola, Spizzichino, (di) Segni, Foligno, etc. — besides some of those mentioned above — testify to this fact. As though to add insult to injury, and injury to insult, the two surviving Jewish settlements in Rome and Ancona had henceforth to pay to the *Casa dei Catecumeni*, or Home for Converted Jews, the levy of ten scudi yearly for each of the one hundred and fifteen synagogues that were now closed down.

The refugees found themselves pursued mercilessly from place to place. A number of them found a temporary haven in the duchy of Urbino. The Pope, however, put pressure on the duke, so that two years later instructions were issued for all recent arrivals to leave. Meanwhile, hundreds of refugees from all parts — far more than local charity could cope with, as sister-communities were tearfully informed — congregated destitute at the ports of Senigallia and Pesaro, to await shipping to take them to Turkey or Palestine.

"The Hosts of the Lord," a contemporary chronicler recorded, "departed from the Romagna and were scattered at Ferrara, Mantua, Urbino, and in all the cities of Tuscany and the Milanese. They abandoned their houses; their fields and vineyards passed to strangers, and they sold their property at a low price, as it stood, for less than half of its value. And Israel was greatly reduced at that time."

The most influential Jew in Europe at this period was Joseph Nasi, nephew and son-in-law of Doña Gracia Mendes, who had been created Duke of Naxos by the Sultan and enjoyed great influence at the Sublime Porte. With a practical sense of humanitarianism centuries in advance of his time, he set himself to the task of succoring his distressed brethren in faith by constructive measures. His most remarkable enterprise was the establishment of a Jewish center at Tiberias in Palestine, almost in the spirit of later Zionism. This was specifically intended in large measure for the succor of the communities of central Italy, now in their hour of greatest trial. Letters were distributed far and wide announcing that all the persecuted and distressed who were willing to labor, whether as peasants or as artisans, could find a home in this colony; and arrangements were made for any of those of the Papal States who so desired to be transported on the duke's own ships from the growing miseries of their daily existence. The community of Cori in the Campania — 200 souls in all — determined to emigrate *en bloc*, and sent emissaries to their better-situated coreligionists elsewhere to solicit assistance in carrying their project into effect. One party who set sail from Pesaro fell into the hands of the Knights of Malta, who regarded all Jews and unbelievers as fair prey. The Tiberias experiment achieved only a very qualified success. Nevertheless, the Turkish empire managed to absorb a good number of the refugees who left Italy in this period, synagogues which followed the historic Roman rite existing henceforth in some of the important centers of population, especially of course Salonica and Constantinople, and the Italian element in the "Four Holy Cities" of Palestine being of notable importance.

xxxi

THE EXTENSION

From the States of the Church the reaction spread throughout Italy — in part as a result of the expansion of papal rule, in part from conventional orthodoxy, in part through political pressure. It was some while before the process was complete, but by the beginning of the seventeenth century triumph was assured.

Pius V had insisted that his anti-Jewish legislation was incumbent on all Catholics, and it was natural for him to write to the various Italian rulers enjoining them to follow his example. In the duchy of Milan, owing to the fervid support of Cardinal Borromeo, the Jewish badge was obediently imposed and usury prohibited (though not for long) as early as September, 1566 — an earnest of the more extreme measures that were in store — and in the same year isolation was enforced at Alessandria. Genoa had already expelled its Jews in 1550; now, in 1567, the central government issued orders for all the other cities of the territory to do the same within a period of three months. In 1570, segregation was introduced into his dominions by the pliable Guidubaldo della Rovere, Duke of Urbino. That same year, through the zeal of the bishop, they were displaced from Parma and Piacenza, though before long they were summoned back to the minor centers of the duchy; while the handful who had found a home in Lucca were ejected in 1572. In the region under German rule, or near the

German frontier, much the same took place: the community of Udine having been expelled in 1556 (the order was to be repeated in 1622), the Jews forbidden to live in Gorizia and Friuli in 1561–5, and an abortive attempt made against the Jews of Trieste on the pretext of atrocious crime in 1583.

The course of events in the greater Italian states was, of course, more significant. Cosimo I, Duke of Florence, had hitherto followed the liberal tradition of the house of Medici as far as the Jews were concerned, as well as in other respects. He was on cordial terms with his wife's old tutor, Doña Bienvenida Abrabanel, and long since had empowered her — and later on the Da Pisa family — to open loan-banks in several places in the Florentine territory. Alarmed moreover by the declining prosperity of his dominions, he issued an elaborate concession in 1551 through a certain Servadio (Obadiah) of Damascus, in the hope of attracting a settlement of Levantine Jews, so useful for the Turkish trade, who were granted exceptional privileges. He was, however, anxious to assume the higher style and title of Grand Duke of Tuscany, which would raise him above the run of petty territorial nobles; and since the emperor was unwilling to accord him this promotion, he could only hope to obtain it from the Pope. He thus became, when it seemed necessary, obsequiously orthodox; and the unfortunate Jews of his dominions, now including the former territory of Sienna, came to be a pawn in his involved diplomatic game. As an earnest of his good intentions, he imposed, in 1567, the obligation to wear the Jewish badge, in the form of a yellow O on the hat. When the Jews were driven out of the smaller cities of the Papal States two years later, he refused to grant them asylum, and a group which arrived at Volterra was summarily expelled. In 1570, on the pretext that the Da Pisa family had been guilty of a breach of its agreement, he cancelled all the banking-licenses issued for his dominions — not only theirs — thus achieving under the cloak of injured rectitude the same result that the Pope had obtained by his recent downright prohibition. Finally, by a decree of October 3, 1570, he ordered all the Jews of the twenty-one centers of the Florentine *contado* to be concentrated henceforth in Florence, where a Ghetto was to be formed for their reception; while fourteen months later, on December 19, 1571, a similar edict assembled all those of the territory of Sienna in that city. It was on the last day of July of that year (once again it happened — surely not by coincidence — to be the Ninth of Ab) that the Ghetto of Florence was inaugurated in a district in the center of the town formerly known as *Il Frascato* ("The Arbor"), the adaptation being carried out under the direction of the eminent architect Bernardo Buontalenti; the former Via dei Giudei had been beyond the Arno, almost in the shadow of the Palazzo Pitti. Cosimo had already been paid his fee when, in March, 1570, the Pope had solemnly crowned him in Rome as Grand Duke of Tuscany.

Venice, on the other side of the Peninsula, had rigorously enforced segregation and the accompanying humiliations ever since the Jews had been reluctantly admitted into the city during the War of the League of Cambrai. Accordingly, there was grave danger that here the reaction might assume an extreme form. When the news of the great victory of the combined Christian fleets over the Turks at Lepanto reached the city, in the autumn of 1571, it was determined to express the general gratitude in a fitting manner, by ejecting all Jews of whatever grade or condition from the city on the expiration of their *condotta* two years later. For a year and a half, the Venetian community — now one of the most important in Europe — lay under the sentence. Many had already departed — some for the cities of the *terra ferma*, others for the Moslem lands of the Mediterranean littoral — when, on July 7, 1573, the Senate suddenly revoked its previous decision. According to some contemporary reports, the explanation was to be found in a lavish expenditure of money on the part of the Jews, who promised, moreover, to reduce to the nominal figure of 5 per cent the rate of interest at the loan-banks which they had to maintain as a price of their toleration. There was indeed another reason. During the interval which had elapsed since the edict of banishment, friendly relations had been re-established with the Ottoman Empire and a treaty of amity concluded. When he arrived at Venice, the high dignitary who brought home the news is said to have passed in the harbor a shipload of refugees about to sail. He made it his business to point out to the doge how such a display of bigotry was ill calculated to inaugurate the new era of understanding, and that the exiles would not only strengthen the power of the Turkish empire but also embitter their coreligionists there, who were influential in the state. The warning was not perhaps unwelcome, for the flush of religious enthusiasm that had succeeded the Battle of Lepanto had by now waned, while no fresh arrangements had been made to replace the Jewish loan-banks. No doubt, all these reasons contributed to the change of attitude. A year later, almost to the day, the wheel turned full circle, when a Jew arrived in Venice as ambassador of the Sublime Porte — Solomon Ashkenazi, of Udine, who had studied at Padua and was now body-physician to the grand vizier and a powerful influence in Turkish politics.

In Piedmont (the duchy of Savoy) the Jews had been compelled to live in separate quarters, apart from Christians, from as early as 1430, this injunction being periodically repeated. The institution of a formal Ghetto was thus hardly necessary, but a worse fate loomed from time to time. Duke Emanuele Filiberto, known as Iron Head, who re-established the independence of the duchy after a lengthy French occupation, had shrewd ideas of turning orthodoxy to personal profit; and in July, 1560, although he had confirmed their privileges very recently, he issued instructions for the Jews to leave his dominions within two months. They managed to secure the favor of the Duchess Margherita — whose death some time after was to be mourned by Azariah de' Rossi in verses in four languages — and thanks to her intercession the order was revoked. But in the following years they were accused of violating the terms of their agreement, and the edict of expulsion was renewed, being cancelled this time on the payment of the sum of 20,000 florins — only half, indeed, of what was originally demanded. New charters, obtained in 1565 and 1572, improved their condition in certain respects but already obscurantism was firmly established.

In the duchy of Monferrat at present united dynastically with that of Mantua, with its handful of communities centering about that of Casale, the reaction penetrated as early as 1560, when the new ten-yearly *tolleranza* proved to be less cordial than had hitherto been the case and various conventional restrictions were introduced. The change of atmosphere was manifested in an outbreak of disorder two years later at Acqui, the second city of the duchy. The next *tolleranza*, of 1570, prescribed the size and fashion of the badge that had to be worn by the Jews — up to ten years before they had been expressly exempted from this degradation — prohibited them to enter into close relations with Christians and forbade them the possession of real estate. Shortly after, a commission was appointed to see that the regulations were obeyed. One Sabbath in 1575, its instigator, a certain Ullio, raided the Casale synagogue and arrested all the worshippers for no other purpose than to determine whether they were wearing the badge in the prescribed form; while the following Monday the books of the loan-bankers were sequestered, those who ventured to protest being thrown into jail. This was the prelude to a new comprehensive code, issued in 1577, intended to break off entirely all intercourse between the ordinary population and the Jews, who were forbidden to maintain familiar relations with Christians, to enter their houses "to sing, play and dance," to act as marriage-brokers, to work openly on Christian feast-days, to be seen in public when the sacrament was borne through the streets, or to live in houses which abutted on those of Christians or overlooked churches or cemeteries. In 1600, a further perquisition similar to that of fifteen years previously took place, a Jew finding himself in serious trouble for having given food to the Christian midwife who had assisted his spouse. Though no formal Ghetto in the new sense was introduced, the Jews of Casale were confined, from 1612, in two streets which were assigned as their residence. Thus, the reaction was firmly installed here as well, and there was to be no looking back.

Meanwhile, the assault on the Marranos in Italy had continued. Since the merciless destruction of the colony at Ancona in 1556, their greatest center had been Ferrara, which became known as the principal station for the readmission of New Christians to Judaism, and where, for a short while, there was a flourishing literary life and a printing press where liturgical books in Spanish and Portuguese for Marrano use were first produced. Scandalized Catholics or renegades, returning to Spain and Portugal after a voyage abroad, were filled with horror at what they had seen here; and in 1578 the inquisitor general at Lisbon drew up for submission to the Pope a list of refugees who were Judaizing in the dominions of the house of Este and elsewhere in Italy. Duke Alfonso was unable to resist the pressure that was now brought to bear on him. In 1581, vigorous steps were taken. Many members of the Portuguese community at Ferrara were thrown into prison, compelled to profess repentance and revert publicly to Christianity. Three, worse offenders than the rest, were sent to Rome, where they were burned on the Campo di Fiori on February 19, 1583. The memory of one of them in particular, Joseph Saralbo, alias Gabriel Henriques, who prided himself that he had brought no less than eight hundred Marranos back to Judaism, was long cherished by his coreligionists as that of a martyr. The Marrano colony of Ferrara was thus broken up; the main stream of emigration, as far as Italy was concerned, was directed for the next generation to Venice, always willing to compromise with her orthodoxy when material advantage was involved. Moreover, the quarrel with the Papacy over the authority of the Inquisition associated with the name of Fra Paolo Sarpi, which was about to blaze up, helped to secure the position of persons who might otherwise have been proceeded against as renegades. Here there was henceforth an additional "Ponentine" (or Western) community of Spanish and Portuguese origin, mainly engaged in wholesale trade, which speedily became the most important and wealthy, though not the most numerous, element in the Jewish population.

By now, further humiliations had been added to the lot of Italian Jewry by Pope Gregory XIII, the reformer of the calendar, who had succeeded Pius V in 1572. Kindly of nature, and in his younger days hardly of blameless life, his pontificate was in some ways reminiscent of a milder age. He protected the Roman Ghetto from assault by the mercenary troops during the Easter after his accession, and did something to ameliorate the economic condition of the community, even legitimizing moneylending as in the past. But he was normally weak and ineffective, and sometimes, under the influence of the more reactionary members of the College of Cardinals, painfully obscurantist. Hence, while the Papal States drifted to the verge of ruin through sheer misgovernment, he was induced to add fresh elaborations to the anti-Jewish code. Since the thirteenth century, conversionist sermons had been known, the Jews being expected either to attend them or to give the hospitality of their synagogues for the purpose; but they had been delivered only sporadically, and there was as a rule nothing to enforce attendance. The element of compulsion was introduced by a Bull of Gregory's of September 1, 1577, ordering the Jews of Rome and the Papal States to send a certain quota of their number to church on specified occasions to hear an address which was to open their eyes to the true faith. The example penetrated before long to other parts of Italy, the sermons delivered to the Jews in the Church of S. ta Croce in Florence by the apostate Vitale de' Medici (Jehiel of Pesaro) as early as 1583 having been published. Precisely seven years after the first enactment, on September 1, 1584, the conditions were finally elaborated in the light of recent experience. Henceforth a certain number of Jews and Jewesses had to be present in church each week to be preached at (generally by an apostate, whom they regarded with aversion) and if possible — a remarkable though perhaps undeserved tribute to their standard of education — in Hebrew. All the expenses, including the preacher's fee, devolved upon the Jewish community. The path had been prepared for these unwelcome mentors by Fra Andrea del Monte, formerly Joseph Sarfatti — one of whose addresses was heard by Montaigne when he was in Rome in 1581 — who used such unmeasured violence of language that the Jews appealed for protection to Cardinal Sirletto. Thus, one more horror was added to the life of the Jews in those parts of Italy which were under papal influence.

Another problem to which Gregory was induced to turn his mind was the practice of medicine by Jews. In a Bull of March 30, 1581, he confirmed all the previous legislation on the subject, forbidding Christians to summon the aid of Jewish physicians and Jews to answer any such summons if they received it. Three years later, this pronouncement was printed and circulated in order to put an end to the abuse, once for all. A doughty defense was offered by David de' Pomi, of Venice, a noteworthy writer and medical practitioner, in a dignified *De medico hebraeo enarratio apologetica* ("Apology for the Jewish Physician"), dedicated to the duke of Urbino, furnished with a preface by the printer Aldo Manuzio, and presented to the doge and Senate. But it was of little use. Individual Jewish physicians are encountered henceforth, but the golden age of

Jewish medicine in Italy was at an end. Gregory was also responsible for extending the jurisdiction of the Inquisition over the Jews in cases of alleged blasphemy, the employment of Christian servants, the possession of forbidden works, or the protection of heretics (those who harbored fugitive Marranos were obviously envisaged). One of the first results was a fresh raid on Jewish libraries, the Jews of Rome being ordered to surrender within ten days, and those of other parts of Italy within three months, all copies of the Talmud and other suspected literature.

There was an unexpected respite for the Jews of the Papal States when, on his death, in 1585, Gregory was succeeded by Sixtus V. Though deeply pious, he was personally tolerant, having a former Marrano in his employment as administrator of his finances and showing himself benevolently disposed to individuals who solicited his favor. The deplorable condition in which his predecessor had left the Papal States called, moreover, for prompt measures — no less for the re-establishment of the public finances than for the restoration of order. In view of this, he hardly had any alternative but to reverse the ruinous anti-Jewish policy of the past thirty years — incidentally helping to replenish his treasury, for every concession was paid for. His Bull of October 22, 1586, fittingly headed *Christiana Pietas* ("Christian Piety") permitted the Jews to return to the States of the Church on the payment of a poll tax, to dwell again where they pleased, to employ Christian servants and enter into familiar relations with the general population where it was necessary, and even to exercise the profession of medicine among them as in former days. As in the case of his other pronouncements, the document was issued in Italian instead of the conventional Latin, so that there should be no excuse for ignorance of its contents. It happened, moreover, that Sixtus reverted to the stringent medieval attitude as regards usury, the practice of which by Christians he condemned as "detestable to God and man." In order to cope with the widespread economic distress, he was thus driven to renew the older expedient and to make use of the services of the Jews. Not content with permitting the practice of moneylending, he virtually organized it, providing for the establishment for the benefit of the poor of a system of Jewish loan-banks throughout the area under his rule — fifty-five in Rome alone. From 1587 onwards, "absolutions" began to be issued by the Apostolic Chamber for Jews to open such institutions in various places in the Papal States and northern Italy at a rate of interest which was not to exceed 18 per cent. In the circumstances, the atmosphere that had prevailed during the spacious noontide of the Renaissance was temporarily restored. Jewish life in central Italy experienced a revival, some refugees even returning from the Levant to Rome and elsewhere. In several places, from Bologna to Cori, communities were re-established and synagogues reopened. In Ancona, the population rose again so steeply after a considerable decline, that in 1588 it was found necessary to enlarge the Ghetto; while in 1590 an alley was designated for the accommodation of the handful who returned to Perugia. It was inevitable that the new spirit which manifested itself in these years at the center of Christendom was reflected in the other Italian states, where orthodoxy was to a great extent a question of imitation or obedience. Moreover, a conference of the Italian communities was held at Padua in 1585, with the energetic Bezaleel Massarani of Mantua at its head, to consider a new approach to the Pope on the question of printing the Talmud. (It was now available only in a censored and emasculated edition which had appeared some little time previously in Basel under the title *Six Orders*, thus avoiding the hateful name.) The application, supported by 2,000 scudi, proved successful, although certain textual modifications were specified. In order to forward the scheme, half a dozen of the major communities undertook to dispose of seven hundred copies among their members. The appeal of the elders of the Roman community to their fellow Jews for their collaboration is eloquent of the profundity of their feelings: "If you do so much to prevent a threat of expulsion," they wrote, "how much more should you do to preserve the sacred writings which are 'thy life, and the length of thy days'?"

The interlude lasted for only a brief while. The three short-lived Popes who followed Sixtus V in 1590 had no opportunity to formulate their policy; but with Clement VIII the tide of the Catholic Reaction was resumed, and Rome once again set Italy an example of repression. The old legislation was once more enforced by the Bull beginning with the significant phrase *Caeca et obdurata* ("Blind and obdurate") of February 25, 1593, which again drove the Jews out of the minor cities of the Papal States — other, that is, than Rome and, at the express request of the inhabitants, Ancona — in which they had re-established themselves during the past few years. The literary offensive was renewed in its fullest stringency, the projected reprint of the Talmud never in fact appearing; its expurgation, the Inquisition had decided, was a ridiculous and pointless task. Notwithstanding this tragic retrogression, the essential wisdom of Pope Sixtus' policy was tacitly recognized in the fact that for nearly a hundred years the Jewish loan-banks were left undisturbed; indeed, the number in Rome was raised from 55 to 64 and licenses were issued for establishments even in cities, such as Bologna or Perugia, where no other Jews were allowed to live. Over a thousand such "absolutions" were registered in all during this period for places in the Papal States and northern Italy: and it is significant of the economic function they filled that no attacks on the concessionaires are recorded. Except for this, the regime of Paul IV and Pius V was restored down to the last detail; and, this time, the reaction was to be in effect final, lasting down to the nineteenth century.

It was particularly unfortunate that the formulation of

the anti-Jewish policy of the Popes was followed by a great expansion in the area of the papal dominions. In spite of some isolated episodes, the house of Este at Ferrara had succeeded on the whole in withstanding the pressure brought to bear upon them from Rome, and their dominions remained a bulwark of relative tolerance. During the famine of 1590–3, the Jews had actually been included in the free distribution of food to the starving population. But in 1597, Alfonso II died leaving no direct heir, and Pope Clement took advantage of the technical overlordship of the Church to annex the duchy, though a collateral branch of the house was allowed to establish itself in Modena and Reggio. Henceforth, the city and its dependencies formed part of the States of the Church, being governed by a papal legate, generally a cardinal. Forthwith, the Lateran policy began to be imposed. In the following year, the wearing of the badge of shame was enforced, it was forbidden for Jews to own real estate, the censorship of Hebrew books was instituted, and moneylending was prohibited, though after a while the right was restored for at first two and then four loan-banks at Ferrara and two elsewhere. At the same time, most of the eleven synagogues were closed down, only one being allowed to remain for each rite — the Italian, the German and the Spanish. The antisemitic element in the population had hoped that, with the change of rule, the city would be rid of the presence of Jews. Though they were disappointed in this, and warned not to take advantage of the wearing of the yellow badge to stir up disorder, further anti-Jewish measures were not long delayed. In 1624, orders were issued for a Ghetto to be installed in spite of the remonstrances made at Rome by a deputation headed by the physician Bonaiuto (Azriel) Alatino, who had courageously upheld the Jewish cause not long before in a public disputation forced on him by a Jesuit. Three years later, notwithstanding continued opposition, it was inaugurated, the cardinal legate issuing detailed regulations about the translocation and everything connected with it — the level of rents, the relations between the tenants and their Christian landlords, the paving of the streets, public sanitation, the creation of new thoroughfares and a piazza, and so on. Ferrara, too, now ceased to be a great center of Jewish life. Emigration set in on a large scale, many Jews electing to follow Duke Cesare d'Este to Modena. Within four years of the change of rule, the Jewish population had fallen by one-quarter, from 2,000 to 1,500. Many houses in the Ghetto stood empty and application was made repeatedly, though in vain, for the area to be reduced so as to lessen the community's financial responsibility. On the other hand, the Jews now received the same rights of trade throughout the Papal States as were enjoyed by the privileged Levantine colony of Ancona, the economic standard of the community remaining relatively high. In 1639 the Pope ordered the Jewish population of the former duchy to be confined henceforth to three places only, where they could be kept under close surveillance, on the model of what had already happened in central Italy. There were designated for the purpose, besides the capital, the small cities of Lugo and Cento. Here therefore the Jews of the surrounding area — for example, Bagnacavallo and Massa — were now concentrated, Ghettos being set up to accommodate the swollen population.

Much the same happened in the duchy of Urbino, which passed into papal hands in 1631 in consequence of the abdication of Francesco Maria della Rovere, the last duke. There were living here at the time some 1,500 Jews, the largest community being now in the seaport of Pesaro, with 19 Jewish loan-bankers, as against only eight in Urbino itself; there were a few more scattered about between Senigallia, Fossombrone, Monte Barroccio, and some lesser places. Other economic interests were, however, amply represented. Before long reaction followed here as well, restrictions in accordance with the papal policy being introduced at once, the Ghetto founded in 1634, and no Jews being allowed henceforth to live outside the three major centers.

Paradoxically, the Jews had meanwhile been undisturbed in the duchy of Milan, though since 1535 it had been under the direct rule of the king of Spain, who tolerated them nowhere else in his dominions. They now totalled rather fewer than 900. None lived in the capital, where they were not allowed to stay for more than three days at the time; but there were communities in Pavia, Alessandria, Lodi, Casalmaggiore and especially Cremona (which contained rather more than one half of the total), governed by the somewhat severe restrictions embodied in the Milanese Statutes of 1573. The annual tribute that they paid as the price of toleration came at this period to 20,000 imperial lire. At intervals, indeed, they had narrow escapes in times of popular excitement, but the protection of the governor and the Senate never faltered. The king had issued an order of expulsion from Madrid in 1550, and again in 1566, but it was not carried out. In 1582, however, the murderer of a Jew at Cremona was taken out of sanctuary to be punished, and popular feelings became so excited that the municipalities of that city and Pavia, which had already given more than one indication of their feelings in this matter, demanded that the duchy should be purged of the unbelievers once for all. The king consented; but the governor granted first a reprieve, and then an indefinite suspension, on the ground that in a time of famine like the present the presence of the Jewish loan-banks was a positive necessity to the common people. On the death of Sixtus V, when the forces of reaction began to sweep everything before them, the application for drastic action was renewed, with the support of the king's confessor. After a further thwarted attempt in 1591, Philip again ordered the expulsion of the Jews from the duchy. The governor, Juan Fernandez de Velasco, was instructed to permit no further delay; but he was a man of humanitarian feelings rare when the Jews were concerned, and not only allowed them two months to settle their affairs but also gave them a military escort to the frontier and distributed 5,000 ducats among the poor to defray their expenses. Two families only were permitted to remain in Cremona, Lodi and Alessandria, to collect outstanding credits and to settle an old dispute about taxation. Thus, the Jewish settlement of the Milanese territory succumbed before the same blight of intolerance which half a century earlier had ended the existence of those of southern Italy.

By now, the reaction had spread also to the Venetian possessions of the *terra ferma*. At Verona, where Italian immigrants had reinforced the original German elements, the Jewish population had by now risen to nearly 500, living in all parts of the city, and since the decline of the academy at Cremona it was considered a major center of Jewish scholarship. At the beginning of 1585, the central government in Venice determined that a Ghetto should be established for them, and the local authorities began to look for a suitable locality. The discussions dragged on for a long time, the Jews meanwhile facing more than once the danger of expulsion. The records of the community give us an intimate insight into the anxieties and perplexities of this period, and the steps taken to ensure that ambitious individuals did not intrigue so as to install themselves in the best locations to the detriment of the rest. No agreement could be reached regarding the area that was to be taken over until in the spring of 1599, when, as the result of the intervention of the cardinal archbishop, a decision was at last made, the area chosen being a convenient one in the center of the town formerly known as *sotto i tetti*. All preparations on the Jewish side were entrusted to a commission of eighteen, which allocated the houses and appointed three *conservatori* to carry the statutes into execution and see to the sanitary arrangements. It was regarded as an outstanding triumph that they managed to secure the custody of the guard-room keys, converting the Ghetto, as it were, from a prison to a stronghold; and shortly after, as an additional safeguard, a sort of Ghetto "militia" — perhaps it would be better to term it an armed police-force — was set up. So unpleasant had some of their recent history been, and so many difficulties had to be overcome before the translocation was completed, that the community regarded the process as anything but an unmitigated disaster, and for two centuries the anniversary of the dedication of the new synagogue, in 1601, was commemorated each year by a festive celebration.

At Padua, the Jews had been ordered to live in their own quarter of the town, apart from the rest of the population, as early as the first half of the sixteenth century; though this was not cut off in the style of the later Ghetto, and some of the wealthier had their houses among the Christians in the most elegant streets. From time to time, complete segregation was demanded, and in 1581–4 it was agreed in principle to introduce the Ghetto on the Roman or Venetian pattern. No suitable site could be found, and all that happened for the moment was that they were confined more strictly to the area already assigned to them. Ultimately, in 1601, owing to the insistence of the bishop, the Town Council decided, by 62 votes to 6, to carry the policy into execution forthwith, the district specified centering around the little square in which the synagogue was already situated. The expenses of the translocation and adaptation were to be borne by the Jewish community, the municipality advancing 3,000 ducats for six years as a loan for this purpose. Four deputies were appointed by the Jewish community to supervise the new arrangements, their first obligation being the characteristic one that, before anything else, they should "for the honor of the Blessed God choose a place for the study of Jewish learning;" only then were they to allocate the shops and houses. Thus at last, in the spring of 1603, the quarter was inaugurated. Elsewhere in the

Venetian possessions, the Ghetto was decided on at Rovigo in 1612 and established three years after, at Conegliano in 1637, and at Este in 1666.

Particularly tragic in some respects was the reaction at Mantua, where the Gonzaga had shown themselves with certain exceptions to be among the most enlightened rulers of the age, and where, as we have seen, the Jews had played a part of exceptional importance in general cultural life. In 1591 there were here 1,844 Jews, comprising between four and five hundred households. The outstanding family among them was that of Torazzo (a branch of the Norsa clan) at this time considered to be the wealthiest in Italy; while Joseph da Fano was highly favored at court. From the outset, the ducal house had not shown themselves altogether loath to follow the new papal policy of persecution, as was seen in 1577 in the new regulations which cancelled various Jewish privileges, forbade the owning of real estate, and regulated the wearing of the Jewish badge, or in 1590 in the expulsion of "foreign" Jews. Nevertheless, "for the convenience of their subjects," as the dukes frankly admitted, they refused to go further than this, and even used Jews in the financial administration.

With the turn of the century, a new spirit became manifest. On April 22, 1600, an old Jewess of seventy-seven, named Judith Franchetti, was burned alive in the public square of Mantua on a charge of sorcery, the principal accusation against her being that she had bewitched a certain nun recently converted from Judaism. An alleged pupil and accomplice, named Jacob Fano, suffered with her, and two others who had fled were also implicated. This episode served to prepare the ground. There was going about North Italy at this time, preaching repentance in the old style, an unbalanced but superbly eloquent Franciscan friar named Bartolommeo Cambi, who seized every opportunity to attack the Jews. In 1602, his sermons at Mirandola proved so effective that the Jews were shut up in an alley with a tiny piazza and compelled to wear the Jewish badge. Thence he went on to Modena, where in a sermon of July 28 he castigated the local negligence in these matters. The duke obediently enforced the wearing of the badge, but nothing more was done. The propaganda was renewed, however, in the Advent sermons of 1618, with greater prospect of success, as the Town Council and the guilds offered to assume part of the cost; but it was ultimately decided that the problem of finding accommodation for the forty-three families resident outside the proposed Jewish quarter was too difficult to cope with, and in the event there was a reprieve for twenty years.

Going on thence to Mantua, Fra Bartolommeo preached in the square before the cathedral, before a crowd estimated at no fewer than 30,000, a ferociously anti-Jewish sermon calling attention to the recent happenings and to the favor enjoyed by the Jews. The audience was profoundly stirred; and the duke, who was present, had to promise to consider the matter. Not long after, a little band of irresponsible youths was surprised in a courtyard, where one of them was executing a parody of the friar's sermon in what may be considered, if the story is true, an eminently Italian fashion. The friar, furious as well as scandalized, now demanded a general expulsion from the city. The duke was unwilling to concede this, but had seven culprits barbarously executed and banished their families from his dominions in perpetuity. It was in vain that the regular clergy of the city protested against this arbitrary action, even going so far as to menace the duke with excommunication and to take proceedings against the friar, who had by now almost lost his reason and was raving against the duke, the bishop, and anyone else who seemed to stand in his way. Even when he was summoned to answer for his conduct before the Pope, he persisted in continuing his agitation in place after place on his journey. After being silenced at Ferrara by the cardinal legate, he went on to Venice in the teeth of the government's prohibition, the Jews trembling at the thought of what might now happen to them. Here, however, he was promptly arrested and sent in irons to Rome, where after a lengthy inquiry it was determined to take the sting out of him and his pretended miracles by ridicule.

In Mantua, meanwhile, energetic steps had been taken to protect the Jews, and the duke showed clearly that in his opinion matters had gone far enough. The Pope, of course, thought differently, and continuously pressed for the execution of the plan so dear to his heart. He was outspoken in a conversation with the duke's agent in September, 1602: "We are waiting to hear that His Highness has begun to put restrictions on the Jews and to bridle this *canaglia* as it deserves and as is proper, and are sure that His Highness will not fail in his promise." He had his own ways of exerting further pressure, as the case of Fra Bartolommeo was still undecided. Two months later (November, 1602), the Mantuan Jews were at last ordered to be confined to a Ghetto. As a result of their protests and arguments and demonstration of the harm that this would bring to the city as a whole, the execution of the edict was postponed; but at the beginning of 1610 it was confirmed. Meanwhile, it had been forbidden for Jewish physicians to treat Christian patients without special permission — this in the city where the Portaleoni had been for so many generations in attendance on the ducal court! — or for Jews to teach singing, music and dancing — this in the city where they had played so outstanding a part in the development of the theater! — and it was ordered that all real estate belonging to them should be disposed of within a year. The separation was signalized by the creation of a new official, called the Commissioner for the Jews (*Commissario degli Ebrei*), whose office continued in being almost to the end of the Ghetto period. It was in February, 1612 — a date thereafter commemorated here too by a special service in the synagogues — that the work of adaptation was ended and the Mantuan

Jews, or rather those of them who as yet lived elsewhere, took up their residence in their new quarter.

Thus, by the end of the first quarter of the seventeenth century, the Ghetto and all the accompanying degradation had been introduced into nearly all the cities of those parts of Italy where Jews were now allowed to live — complete segregation, the red or yellow badge, exclusion from honorable callings, the forced sermon, the censorship of literature, the House of Catechumens, and all the rest. It implied also in many areas the exclusion of the Jews from the small townships in which the establishment of a formal Ghetto would have been absurd or impossible, thus assisting to divorce them even more completely from the countryside. Only one or two places lagged behind. The Ghetto was introduced to Modena only in 1638; to Reggio, though it was under the same rule, through the personal influence of the duchess in 1669–71; to Gorizia in 1648; to Trieste in 1693–5. Since in Piedmont the segregation of the Jews in single streets or districts was already the rule long before, it was possible to postpone the creation of a formal Ghetto at Turin to 1679, though it was proposed already in 1621, and at Vercelli to 1724, while it was universally imposed in this region only in 1728–9. In the district of Monferrat similarly it was not applied until the eighteenth century, some little while after its annexation by Piedmont. Finale, in the duchy of Modena, only knew it in 1736, while Correggio, under the same rule, as well as one or two other places where special circumstances obtained, for some reason escaped down to the end, notwithstanding an agitation to introduce the institution as late as 1736 and 1779. These instances were, however, exceptional. By and large, the last years of the sixteenth century and the first of the seventeenth witnessed everywhere in Italy the triumph of the policy of the Catholic Reaction and the establishment of the Ghetto, with all the miseries — and at the same time all the warmth — that term implied.

CHAPTER VIII

The Age of the Ghetto

xxxii

THE ITALIAN GHETTOS

A PREVIOUS chapter gave a general picture of the Italian Jewish communities as they were seen by a traveller of the twelfth century. It is desirable to pause at this stage and re-evoke the scene that would have presented itself five hundred years after, in the heyday of the Ghetto period, to a Jewish visitor of similar tastes and interests.

One fundamental difference, to which attention has already been drawn, must be borne constantly in mind. In Benjamin of Tudela's day, all the communities of major significance were situated from Rome southwards, those of Upper Italy being so far as is known few and unimportant. Now, as a result of the expulsions of 1492 and 1542, there were none at all south of Rome, all those in existence being situated from that city northwards. It is on these, with their relatively brief record, that the reputation of Italian Jewry to a large extent depends.

Something like a quarter or a third of the Italian Jews in the age of the Ghetto were to be found in the Papal States, this being the largest group under a single rule. Half of them were concentrated in Rome. Nowhere in the entire country — nowhere perhaps in all Europe — did the Jews live under worse conditions. The Ghetto was situated in the fetid, low-lying quarter on the left bank of the Tiber, frequently inundated by the overflowing of the river and heavily visited at time of plague, such as that of 1656–7, when at least 800 persons perished out of a total of 4,127. Segregation here was particularly rigorous. Though from 1644 to 1669, under Popes Innocent X, Alexander VII and Clement IX, the repressive code was enforced somewhat less severely, the difference was only relative, and from the beginning of the seventeenth century there was no real intermission. After 1605, so as to prevent any possibility of neglect, the Holy Office of the Inquisition was given authority in the Ghetto conjointly with the Apostolic Chamber, and the communal autonomy, which had probably been unbroken since the classical age, was progressively whittled down henceforth. By the middle of the century, the hold of the Popes over the internal affairs of the community was absolute. The attempts to relieve the desperate economic condition of the Roman Jews, by such expedients as temporarily allowing them at the close of the seventeenth century to open shops outside the Ghetto, could obviously be no real palliative.

On the whole, the same system applied elsewhere in the Papal States. In the now decadent seaport of Ancona, the reaction under Clement VIII had at first been put into force as grimly as in the capital. But in a city that lived by overseas commerce this proved dangerous, and the commercial crisis that ensued showed that it was necessary to introduce certain modifications, enabling the Jews to continue to engage as before in trade with Turkey and the Levant. This was the basis of the community's economic life. Jewish families from those parts settled in the city in consequence, and there was a richly decorated Levantine synagogue, in addition to the ancient place of worship according to the Roman rite reconstructed in the Ghetto in 1595-7 at the expense of the Catholic Confraternity of SS. Rocco and Sebastiano, who had been permitted to expropriate the old building. Two-thirds of the trade of the port, according to the rough-and-ready official estimate, was in the hands of the Jewish merchants, and only one-third in that of the Christians, the taxation being divided in the same proportion. But notwithstanding their economic importance, the position of the former was by no means secure. In 1659, Pope Alexander VII decreed that they should not be allowed to have shops or warehouses outside the Ghetto, or to carry on any sort of business or transactions there even though they had been licensed to do so by the bishop, or to confer there whether with Christians or Jews, or to pass the night for whatever purpose outside the precincts, or to leave them between nightfall and daybreak under pain of a fine of 50 scudi or public flogging. The magistracy protested that these regulations would be ruinous to the city, and certain clauses were modified, but the rest of the code remained in force. As in Rome, conditions became worse and worse during the following century, though not touching quite the same depth of degradation.

Sixteen miles to the north lay the little port of Senigallia, which had passed under papal rule in 1631 with the duchy of Urbino. At this time, the Jewish community consisted of some thirty-nine families, comprising perhaps a couple of hundred souls. During the course of the following century and a half, the total rose to nearly three times that number. It was swollen still further at the time of the great annual fair, when the synagogue was too small to accommodate all the worshippers and an emergency chapel-of-ease had to be opened. The income of the community was partly derived from a share in the tolls paid by Jewish merchants on this occasion. The public spirit and charitableness shown at times of general distress seem to have been particularly noteworthy. A memorable example was in 1649, when a prominent share was taken in ransoming Polish Jewish captives sold into slavery at the time of the Cossack Wars. Pesaro, twenty miles further to the north, had also been part of the duchy of Urbino. Its community was perhaps older than that of Ancona, and under the dukes it had known a brief period of outstanding prosperity. It still had a synagogue according to the Hispano-Levantine rite as well as one for the native Italian element, this being of exceptional beauty. But the advent of papal rule had ruined its prosperity. In 1628, its Jewish inhabitants numbered 631; in 1656, they barely touched 500; a century later, there were less than 450 — an index of the general decay.

The magnificence of Urbino itself, formerly the capital of the duchy, now belonged to the past. At the time of its annexation to the Papal States, though already beyond its prime, it comprised 64 families or 369 souls. A century later, the number was diminished by half, the majority being now old women and children. Many houses in the Ghetto were empty, the synagogue itself was partly owned by Catholics, and the community had great difficulty in levying the essential taxation. In 1718, they petitioned the Pope to exempt them from the dues payable by the Roman Jews, reminding him that but for previous assistance they would already have been obliged to abandon the city. If the application was successful, it could only have been at the expense of their overtaxed Roman coreligionists.

There was another group of communities under papal rule in the dominions of the house of Este, which had been annexed to the Holy See in 1598. The most important was that of Ferrara itself, one of the great centers of Jewish life in the Peninsula, its communal activities still centered in the synagogue presented to the original "Italian" community by Ser Samuel Melli in 1481. There were also places of worship according to the German and Spanish rites, though it was no longer a safe haven for Marrano refugees as it had been in the past. The populace, once friendly, had been influenced for the worse by the change in the attitude of the government, and when in 1648 a Jew was sentenced to death for murder — a very rare happening — the opportunity was taken to deliver an assault on the Ghetto. The Jewish population continued to be diminished by emigration to places where treatment was milder, the community thus becoming progressively impoverished and finding difficulty in paying the high rents for the empty houses for which it was held responsible. In one point only did its treatment compare favorably with that elsewhere in the Papal States. Notwithstanding the attempts of the cardinal legate, jurisdiction in mixed disputes between Jews and Christians was reserved for the ordinary magistracy, the *giudice de' savi*, while down to 1708 Jewish autonomy was retained in civil cases, a dignified courtroom being constructed for the purpose. This perhaps was one reason for the outstanding vigor of the intellectual life of the community, Ferrara being considered the greatest center in Italy for the study of talmudic law.

There had formerly been a number of communities in the territory around Ferrara, but the Jews had now been expelled from all except Lugo and Cento, where Ghettos also existed. The influx to the former place was so great that in the middle of the seventeenth century the community was swollen to some 600 souls — a high proportion of the total population of the little city. But there was no economic justification for such a number, and a hundred years later there were less than 250. In point of scholarship, however, this small group was reckoned among the most distinguished in the country. The outstanding family was that of Del Vecchio, which for generation after generation provided the community with its rabbis. The settlement at Cento is said to have owed its origin to a horrible crime at the neighboring township of Pieve di Cento, which led to wholesale transference to the new center. Among the local families, it may be mentioned, was one (probably of Levantine origin) called Israeli, whose descendants prefixed a "D" to the name and included a prime minister of England.

The most important community of North Italy was that of Venice. Its legal existence still depended on a *condotta* issued every ten years. One of the conditions of this was that three loan-banks should be maintained for the purpose of lending money to the poor, at the utterly uneconomic rate of 5 per cent, this making the establishment of a public *Monte di Pietà* unnecessary. Accordingly, there was a constant stream of needy Gentiles to the three subsidized pawnbroking establishments in the Ghetto, known chromatically as the Red, the Green and the Yellow bank. Though the Ghetto system was strictly enforced here, life was somewhat more ample than elsewhere because of the important part which the Jews played in wholesale commerce, this being the only occupation other than pawnbroking and second-hand dealing that they were legally supposed to follow. The once vigorous mercantile classes of Venice had by now degenerated into a languid aristocracy, and what was left of the former overseas trade — westwards with Spain and Portugal, eastwards with the Turkish dominions — was to a large extent in the hands of the Jews. Immigrants from these parts were hence encouraged to make their homes in the city, and there were in the Ghetto three "Nations" — the old-established Germans with the Italians, the original settlers and still by far the most numerous group; the Ponentines or Westerners, mainly ex-Marranos from Portugal, the wealthiest element of the three, maintaining a vigorous Iberian culture on the alien soil and to a large extent controlling communal ife; and the Levantines from Turkey, who dressed at the beginning in the Oriental style and dutifully prayed for the welfare of the Grand Turk. Of the eleven lovely places of worship the majority followed the German rite, two the Italian, one the Spanish and one the Levantine, constituting thus a veritable liturgical mosaic. The Venetian Ghetto covered a relatively considerable extent, the Newest Ghetto (*Ghetto Nuovissimo*) having been added in 1633 to the former *Ghetto Nuovo* and *Ghetto Vecchio*. During the course of the seventeenth century the Jewish population increased rapidly. From little more than 1,000 at the turn of the century it rose by 1632 to 2,414 and in

1655 is believed to have touched the record level of 4,870, in a total population of 158,722. If this figure is correct (but there is some reason for doubting it) this was probably the largest Jewish community in Italy, and one of the largest in Europe, at that time. In any case, with the general decadence of the city and its trade, thereafter the figure rapidly fell.

This is not the place to speak of the Jewish settlements in the Venetian possessions overseas, in the so-called *stato del mar* — for example Spalato, where the port was the creation of the enterprising Marrano, Daniel Rodrigues; Crete, up to the Turkish conquest in the seventeenth century; Zante, and especially Corfu, last stronghold of the ancient Byzantine Jewries on the one hand and of the exiled Apulian communities on the other.* The mainland possessions of the republic, or *terra ferma*, comprised, on the other hand, one or two communities of considerable reputation. Especially important — not so much for its numbers of little more than 700 souls as for its intellectual life — was that of Padua. For greatest among the glories of that city was its ancient university, to which students streamed from every part of Italy and beyond, and which, before the age of Emancipation, was virtually the only one in Europe which opened its doors to the Jews in any numbers (though a few graduated also at Sienna, Perugia and elsewhere). From the middle of the sixteenth century to the middle of the eighteenth, Padua was thus the recognized center of study for aspirant Jewish physicians. They came not only from various parts of Italy, but even from the *Judengassen* of Germany and of Poland, in some cases achieving remarkable success in subsequent life. In addition, four youths were admitted to the university each year to study law and conveyancing, though only for the purpose of practice among

---

* For a general account of these extremely interesting Jewish settlements, see my *History of the Jews in Venice* (Philadelphia, 1930), chapter IX.

their coreligionists. The Jewish students were permitted to wear a black headdress like others. On the other hand, they were excluded from the political fraternities or "nations" into which the student body was divided, though in some cases expected to pay the dues, had to provide the others with sweetmeats in expensive profusion on the occasion of their graduation, and were admitted to degrees only with a modified ceremonial. They generally took advantage of the opportunity to study at the talmudical seminary of the city, often qualifying as rabbis and physicians simultaneously. The life of the Jewish community as such was also affected by the presence of the university. They came into close business contact with the student body, notoriously extravagant when it was not penurious. At the same time, they were the victims of its high spirits, were compelled to pay it certain special dues as a ransom from petty persecution, and were submitted to recurrent annoyance over the question of providing cadavers for the dissecting rooms, this occasionally leading to the disturbance of Jewish funerals, and sometimes even to bloodshed. Dependent on the Paduan community for fiscal purposes were Este and Monselice, each with its diminutive Ghetto and handful of Jews.

North of Venice, too, there was a group of little Jewish settlements, of which the principal were Conegliano, where in the beginning of the seventeenth century the Venetian community attempted to set up a talmudic academy to provide free education for Jewish youths prevented from studying in other parts of Italy; and Ceneda (now known as Vittorio Veneto), where the congregation consisted almost exclusively of the descendants of a certain Israel da Conegliano, who had been summoned by the bishop to open a loan-bank there in 1597. In Friuli, there were little settlements at Gonars, Spilimbergo and San Daniele. These were in close relationship with the community of Trieste, since 1382 under Austrian rule but not yet of much importance.

In the middle of the seventeenth century, its Jews numbered only about 60, in a total population of 3,000, though thereafter the increase was considerable. Here, Italian and Teutonic influences intermingled. The reactionary triumph at the imperial court, which led to the expulsion of the Jews from Vienna in 1670, inevitably had its repercussions. In 1684–7, the local antisemites demanded drastic action as in the capital; and to content them, after the induction of a new archbishop in 1693, the Ghetto was ordered, together with the Jewish badge and the conventional bar upon the employment of Christian servants or journeymen. The community put up a spirited resistance; there was a prolonged dispute about the site, which ultimately had to be carried to Vienna for adjudication, the Jews considering it too miserable and their enemies too elegant; it was found useful to stage an accusation of ritual crime in 1695 in order to stimulate the requisite degree of popular ill-feeling, though without success; and it was only in 1697 that the Jews at last had to give up their houses and take up residence in the Ghetto that had been chosen for them. In 1728, the city was created a free port, and thereafter the increase of population was very rapid, the Jewish colony rising by the end of the eighteenth century to some 1,500 and thus becoming one of the most important in the north of Italy.

Also under Austrian rule was the community of Gorizia, in the Dolomites, some thirty miles to the north, with a few lesser centers such as Gradisca d'Isonzo. In 1624, in consideration of the manner in which they and their forebears had lavished their bodies, goods and blood on his behalf in the recent wars, the Holy Roman Emperor accorded the families of Pincherle of Gorizia, Morpurgo of Gradisca and Parente of Trieste the rank of Court Jews, with the special privileges attached to that category in Germany. The Gorizia Ghetto dates back to 1648; at Gradisca the group was so small that none was ever established.

Between Padua and Ferrara lay Rovigo, also under the

rule of Venice. Here seventeen Jewish families entered the Ghetto when it was set up in 1615 — not including the loan-bankers who collaborated with the *Monte di Pietà* by accepting from it, at a higher rate of interest, the pledges received from the poor. The Jewish community was dominated by the Consiglio family, which had originally held the contract for the loan-bank and with which the republic still renewed its agreement periodically. It retained its supremacy communally as well as economically, and the office of warden of certain congregational institutions was hereditary in it. The Jews took a notable part in the development of the woolen industry in this region, and in the middle of the eighteenth century five Jewish firms at Rovigo were engaged in this, notwithstanding the protests of their competitors. The majority of the community were, however, miserably poor, as was always the case. Verona too retained its importance. In the course of the seventeenth century a number of Jewish immigrants of Spanish and Portuguese origin, many of them ex-Marranos, were permitted to settle here for the purpose of trade, necessitating an addition to the Ghetto and constituting a "Ponentine" community by the side of, and at times at loggerheads with, the existing official body which followed the German rite.

The greatest Jewish center in Lombardy was Mantua. The affairs of the community here were regulated by a General Privilege (*Tolleranza Generale*) renewed every eight years, with any necessary modifications, in return for a heavy payment; and since the establishment of the Ghetto an official called the *Commissario degli ebrei* had been in control of Jewish affairs. During the dynastic dispute which followed the extinction of the male line of the house of Gonzaga, in 1627, the Jews showed themselves conspicuously loyal to Charles de Rethel, the nearest kinsman of the last duke, notwithstanding the traditional anti-Jewish riot which followed his state entry. During the subsequent siege by the imperial *Lanzknechts*, they prayed for him in their synagogues, provided his troops with necessaries, and labored on the fortifications with the assent of their rabbis even on the Sabbath. They suffered, too, on his behalf with their fellow townsmen as a result of the operations, the Great Synagogue being struck by a shell during the bombardment and many persons losing their lives through plague. In the summer of 1629, after an heroic resistance, the city fell. The Jews now paid the penalty for their loyalty. In midsummer, under the burning sun, they were driven out of the city by the brutal German military command — men, women and children, except for some of the wealthier who were held to ransom. With them, they were allowed to take property not exceeding the total value of three ducats each, all the rest being seized; and much even of this was extorted from them by blackmail. They were assaulted on the way by bandits, were overcharged indecently by the peasants for the bare necessities of life, succumbed by the score to accident, disease and hunger. As the long procession wound down the dusty roads into exile, friars went among them persuading them to change their faith and thus remain; not one, it is said, yielded to the temptation. The prince of the petty state of Mirandola and the duke of Bozzolo had the humanity to give them refuge, but at a tremendous price. For weeks, their only support was the alms sent by their ever-charitable coreligionists. It was one of the saddest episodes in Italian Jewish history until our own day. But the action of the military command was unauthorized. On appeal to the emperor, he gave instructions that the Jews should be reinstated. It was, nevertheless, winter before the exiles came back to their ruined homes, and full reparation proved impossible. Only one in three of those who had been driven out were in the emaciated parties that returned to reopen the synagogues and renew the tradition of Jewish life; most of their property was untraceable; and petty oppression and spoliation on the part of the German commanders continued. Ultimately, the ducal dynasty was restored, and the remnant of the community was slowly nursed back to something approaching its normal life; but it never perhaps recovered its former importance and prosperity. One minor result of the period of tribulation was that it appeared absurd to renew the old dual organization of privileged "bankers" on the one hand, and the *università degli ebrei* on the other, the former now losing their separate identity and treatment and being merged in the general body. At the beginning of the following century, the duchy passed under Austrian rule (1708), but this brought about no noteworthy change in its general condition, and the Jewish colony continued to have all the characteristics of an Italian community. In the neighborhood of Mantua there were a number of little settlements, including Pomponesco, Rivarolo, Sermide, Revere, Ostiglia, Viadana, Ostiano, Bozzolo (formerly capital of an independent duchy) and Sabbionneta (also at one time independent, and seat of an important printing press in the sixteenth century) — all with beautiful synagogues and a flourishing communal life, but of slender numerical importance.

The rule of the house of Este was now restricted to Modena and Reggio, with the surrounding territory, including little communities in Correggio, Novellara, Brescello, Scandiano, Carpi and — somewhat larger than the rest — Finale. Here, the Jews were tolerated on the basis of a ten-yearly agreement (*capitoli*) in return for which they paid, in addition to other taxation, 1,200 doubloons outright and 500 gold scudi annually. The government was among the more enlightened in Italy. Though a Ghetto was established in Modena in 1638, it was only in 1681 that it was introduced into Reggio, as the result of the application made by the citizens, and it was not until the eighteenth century that it was known in Finale. In 1652, the duke of Modena, envious of the profitable results of the immigration of Marrano merchants to other parts of Italy, issued an invitation to merchants of the "Ponentine Nation" to settle in his dominions on attractive terms — at the outset, they were not even compelled to live in the Ghetto — with the result that synagogues following the Sephardi rite were established in the two principal cities. The principality of Mirandola was added to Modena in 1710: but the diminutive Jewish community, confined in a Ghetto after 1602, had been extinct since the middle of the seventeenth century, following upon the destruction of the synagogue by order of the Holy Office.

In 1578, Duke Ottavio Farnese had given permission for loan-banks to be set up in eight places in the territory of Parma and Piacenza — not however including the two principal cities — as against twice that number before the expulsion of eight years earlier. The concession was constantly renewed for twelve-yearly periods up to the suspension of banking by the Popes in the seventeenth century, after which an annual tribute of 15,000 lire still secured the right of residence and liberty to follow certain callings. The most important of the communities in the duchy was that of Busseto; there were others of inconsiderable size at Cortemaggiore, Soragna, Colorno, Borgo S. Donnino, Monticelli and Fiorenzuola d'Arda, as well as in the microscopic duchy of Guastalla, annexed to Parma after 1749.

In point of area, the principality of Piedmont was one of the largest political divisions of the Peninsula, and contained perhaps one-fifth of the Italian Jews — approximately the same as the Venetian territories — divided into a large number of small communities. Half priestly, half military, it was, except for the Two Sicilies, the least progressive of the Italian states, the Jews therefore filling in it much the same role of traders and loan-bankers as they had done in the Middle Ages. From 1551, they were under the jurisdiction of an officer of state called the *Conservatore degli ebrei* — the title reflects French influence, a similar official having existed in the northern provinces of the house of Savoy — the first incumbent being the bishop of Aosta.

After 1572, the office was decentralized, separate *conservatori*, of senatorial rank, being appointed for Savoy, Nice and Piedmont. In the minor centers, vice-conservators with similar judicial functions were appointed as their deputies. In 1603, Duke Carlo Emanuele I promulgated, in return for a gift of 60,000 scudi, a new and relatively liberal code for the Jews of his dominions on this side of the mountains, guaranteeing them juridical autonomy, protection from violence, the right of studying and practicing medicine and certain economic privileges. Twice every year, representatives of the communities of the duchy were to come together to elect deputies, distribute the burden of taxation, and deliberate on matters of common interest, preserving thus a degree of autonomy which now became increasingly rare in the Jewish world. The charter remained valid for twelve years, after which it was regularly renewed on similar terms.

The most important Jewish settlement in the region was, of course, that of Turin, numbering in the eighteenth century about 1,500 souls, which arrogated to itself the imposing title: "The Community of the Jews of the Estates of His Royal Highness." Other communities, in order of importance, were to be found at Vercelli, Asti, Cuneo (where some refugees from Avignon had been allowed to settle in 1570), Fossano, Ivrea, Mondovì, Chieri, Savigliano, Cherasco, Biella and Trino. Saluzzo, capital of an independent marquisate down to the sixteenth century, and famous for its gastronomical contributions to Jewish life, was under a separate administration, the privileges enjoyed by the other Piedmontese communities being extended to it, and the dependent centers such as Carmagnola, after 1610, in return for a handsome payment. Almost all of these places had their own petty chronicle, reflecting to a large extent the political and military vicissitudes of the country. Thus, for example, Cuneo is said to have owed its deliverance during the siege of 1691 by the French to the courage of a young Jew named Abraham Lattes, who slipped through the enemy lines bearing an important message, and the patriotic sentiment of the banker Moses Foà, who provided the city with funds and supplies; and according to report it was in reward for this that the market day was altered from Saturday to Friday to permit the Jews to participate.

In Alessandria — at that time in the duchy of Milan — a little Jewish nucleus had been allowed to remain after the expulsion of 1591. It was headed by Samuel Cohen Vitale, who had gone as envoy of the Milanese communities to King Philip of Spain and had played a prominent role in public life, being used, for example, to negotiate the settlement of foreign merchants in Piedmont in 1572. Around his household and descendants a relatively important community grew up in the course of time, most of them bearing, most perplexingly, the same surname. Only this family, however, and that of Levi enjoyed special privileges, in fact, unusually ample; the rest were almost rightless. Nevertheless, it was to the loyalty of a Jew that the city owed its safety when it was besieged in 1657. This place, too, was added to Piedmont in 1706, the history of its Jewish community being henceforth indistinguishable from that of any other place under the same rule.

The duchy of Monferrat, with Jewish communities at Acqui, Nizza (Monferrato), Moncalvo and especially Casale (where the walls of the sixteenth-century synagogue were covered with inscriptions recording providential escapes during the succession of sieges for which the city is famous), was united with the duchy of Mantua from 1566 to 1703. Up to this date, the Jewish communities had lived under relatively favorable conditions, in accordance with the terms of their twelve-yearly *tolleranza*: though they suffered considerably during the wars at the beginning of the seventeenth century, seventeen out of the twenty-nine loan-banks in the duchy being ruined for good, and the Acqui community in particular being plundered and impoverished.

When, however, at the beginning of the eighteenth century, the duchy was annexed to Piedmont, conditions altered for the worse, and it was only after this change that the formal Ghetto was introduced. The present-day Nice (Nizza Marittima), at that time still a purely Italian town, contained a miscellaneous colony, among whom immigrants from the papal possessions in France played their part by the side of the loan-bankers of Italian origin. From 1618 to 1622, it was subordinated to the Turin community, but thereafter recovered its independence by combination of a bribe with a threat of emigration *en masse*. On paper, the Jews here enjoyed preferential treatment in some ways; for at the beginning of the seventeenth century, in the hope of developing its trade, the dukes established a free port in its environs, at what is now called Villefranche, specifically inviting Jews and Marranos to settle there. As a result, there was a trickle of immigrants from many parts — the old Provençal communities of Avignon and Carpentras, the various cities of northern Italy, and even North Africa after the Spanish capture of Oran in 1668. But the experiment was not outstandingly successful, the concessions were whittled down in practice, and the Jewish community, though varied and colorful, was of no great importance.*

A similar attempt was made about the same time at Genoa, where merchants of all nations were invited to settle on very much the same terms in 1648. A small number of Jews, as usual largely ex-Marranos, took advantage of the summons. They were nevertheless submitted to severe restrictions, and no more than a handful lived in the Ghetto set up for them; while from the rest of Liguria they were entirely absent. Lucca, famous from the Dark Ages, did not have a settled Jewish community after the fifteenth century.

* There is a *rue du Ghetto* at La Turbie, in the hills above Nice. But there is no evidence that Jews ever lived here, the name being probably derived from *guet* (watch).

The grand duchy of Tuscany, on the other hand, had an important settlement. In Florence, the capital, the Jews had been undisturbed since the final return of the Medici in 1530. The Ghetto to which they were confined a generation later was situated in the center of the town, near the Mercato Vecchio, in an area of notorious character from which it was redeemed by its laborious, despised Jewish inhabitants. In the second half of the sixteenth century, a further "Levantine" group from Turkey had been established on the express invitation of the grand duke, anxious to develop the languishing commerce of the city, especially the textile export trade, formerly so important. There was great dissension as usual between the two elements, the one privileged and the other not, settled at length in 1688, when they were fused into a single community, the synagogues alone henceforth remaining under separate administration. In accordance with the terms of the regulations issued when the Ghetto was established, a tax of two gold scudi was paid annually by every Jew from the age of fifteen. There were other communities in the grand duchy — in lovely Sienna, with its already ancient synagogue (restored in 1786) immediately behind the towering Palazzo Pubblico, its feuds and disputes being depicted for all time in the memoirs of a quarrelsome Ghetto huckster; in a few lesser places to which they drifted back in inconsiderable number in the course of time, such as Monte S. Savino, Lippiano, Arezzo, and Borgo S. Sepolcro, none being of sufficient importance to have a Ghetto; in Pitigliano, on the borders of the Papal States, where a number of refugees from the rigors of Jewish life in Rome settled, creating a community out of all proportion to the natural importance of the town; in the ancient seaport of Pisa; and above all in Livorno (Leghorn, as the English sailors called it). The history of the Jews in this place stands in a category of its own.

At the close of the sixteenth century, in order to foster the prosperity of his dominions, Ferdinand I, Grand Duke of Tuscany, decided to erect this little harbor into a free port, together with the ancient and at that time far more important city of Pisa not far off. This he implemented by his famous Charter of July 10, 1593, subsequently known by the affectionate diminutive, *La Livornina*, addressed to "men of the East and West, Spaniards and Portuguese, Greeks, Germans, Italians, Hebrews, Turks, Moors, Armenians, Persians and others." The third clause was particularly significant:

We moreover desire that ... none shall be able to make any inquisition, inquiry, examination or accusal against you or your families, although living in the past outside our Dominion in the guise of Christians.

This was little less than an explicit invitation to the Marranos of Spain and Portugal, who had hitherto found a welcome at and added to the prosperity of Ancona, Ferrara, and now Venice, to come and settle in the new trading center. (Traces of a previous Jewish settlement are, indeed, to be found there, but it was of no importance as yet.) There was nothing really novel about this. Duke Ercole d'Este had issued a similar charter specifically guaranteeing the security of the Marranos in 1550; Ferdinand's own father had summoned infidels from the Levant in strikingly similar phraseology in 1551; the duke of Savoy casually invited them to Piedmont in 1572. But the results on this occasion were no less than sensational. The plan of a free port, exempt from all fiscal restrictions and outside the customs frontier of the state, proved an extraordinary success, and New Christian merchants from Spain and Portugal were especially drawn to it. At the beginning, indeed, the new community was in every sense secondary to that of Pisa, by which it was controlled. But, owing to the silting up of the Arno and the consequent decay of the latter port, it speedily outdistanced its foster-mother, which was henceforth to a large extent dependent on it. Within a generation, it had become one of the entrepôts of

Mediterranean trade and one of the greatest Jewish communities of the world, second in the Marrano Diaspora only to that of Amsterdam. Poets, soldiers, physicians, aristocrats, and even priests from Spain and Portugal found refuge there under the shelter of the God of Israel. The Sephardi rite of prayers of course prevailed, the Italian rite followed at Pisa from time immemorial being now overwhelmed. Down to the nineteenth century, communal business was transacted in Portuguese, the *lingua franca* of Mediterranean commerce. Spanish remained a semi-sacred tongue, used for public instruction and similar purposes, as well as in the literary academies which were organized in pallid imitation of fashionable life at Madrid. The same languages were employed on the tombstones — frequently splendid marble monuments, surmounted by elaborate hidalgo coats-of-arms. Not that the community was exclusively Marrano in origin. Native Italians from the inland cities, Berberiscos from North Africa, Levantines from the Near East, even immigrants from Germany and Poland, figured in not inconsiderable number. But the backbone of the community remained Spanish and Portuguese; and so high was their cultural standard, and so strong their assimilatory capacity, that they succeeded in absorbing the later immigrants — even the Italians, the natives of the country, who — as in the case of the Montefiore family, to cite one of the best known — embraced their ritual, made use of their language, and adopted their customs. It was only in 1715, by which time the original elements had established a cultural hegemony which it was impossible to shake, that the others were so much as given a voice in the management of the community.

The organization of this body was no less distinctive. In its final form, as elaborated in the constitutions of 1693 and 1715, the supreme authority rested in a council of sixty members designated by the grand duke, whose seats were to descend for three generations from father to son by inheritance (this hereditary principle was abandoned at the close of the eighteenth century). Twenty members sat in rotation each year, the whole council being convoked only for purposes of special importance. Three "censors," nominated biennially, supervised expenditure; while five *massari*, assisted in matters of particular moment by a Commission of Twelve, exercised general control over communal affairs. There were also a number of special "deputations" which supervised education, the cemeteries, and so on, in addition to a rabbinical commission for purely religious matters. No new immigrants were allowed to enjoy the right of residence without the approval of a two-thirds majority of the council, this securing them *ipso facto* the status of naturalized subjects of the grand duke. There was complete internal autonomy in both civil and criminal cases, the secular authorities being enjoined to enforce the sentences of the Jewish courts, and appeal being allowed only to His Highness himself. There was an elaborate system of taxation, the proceeds of which covered all communal expenditure — political, religious, charitable and social. The community was recognized, moreover, as the legal heir of the property of those of its members who died intestate.

Leghorn was thus, with Pisa, virtually the only place in Italy where the repressive policy of the Catholic Reaction made no headway. The Ghetto, with all the degradation which it implied, was never introduced; there was barely any restriction on economic life; the Jewish badge was unknown. By a special concession, householders were legally permitted to carry arms, though the communal authorities did not always approve. At a period in which it was regarded as a serious crime in the Papal States for a Jew to be seen riding in a carriage, no fewer than sixteen Jewish families in Leghorn owned their coach and pair. The monumental synagogue, begun in 1602 and superbly enlarged in 1789, was considered one of the sights of the town, and was often inspected by visiting royalty. Cynics sneered that it was safer here to strike the grand duke than one of the Jewish "Nation." The public spirit of the community was made manifest on many occasions, as for example in 1767, when they erected a naval asylum at their sole expense.

The foundation of Leghorn's prosperity continued to be the free port, the communal magnates being for the most part great wholesale merchants, with contacts in every port of the Mediterranean as well as in the trading centers of northern Europe, with which they corresponded in Spanish and Portuguese. Of about one hundred and fifty commercial houses at Leghorn in the middle of the eighteenth century, fifty were Jewish, the trade with Turkey, Egypt and North Africa especially lying in their hands. In addition, they set up a number of minor industries — soap-making, silk-weaving, paper-manufacture and so on, as well as the import of drugs. One branch of activity in particular, introduced by the Spanish refugees, was of the utmost significance for the prosperity of the city. In the course of the seventeenth century, the coral industry — at that time of the greatest importance for the satisfaction of female vanity — received a tremendous impetus, Leghorn being its principal center. Apart from the local market, the finished commodity was shipped to Russia, China, and especially India, where there was a tremendous demand for it, the returns being taken largely in diamonds which were handled by the international Jewish gem-dealers who were everywhere so prominent. The story of the rise and fall of the Leghorn community is measurable in part in terms of the popularity of this substance. So great was the importance of Leghorn in Mediterranean trade that in Tunis the Livornese, or "Gorni," Jewish colony maintained its own community, with its rabbi and its synagogue, which was the most important in the city. There was also a tiny offshoot of the Leghorn Jewry on the island of Elba, under the rule of the princes of Piombino.

The outstanding success of the economic experiment at Leghorn invited imitation. In succeeding years other Italian rulers also tried to attract Spanish and Portuguese merchants. As has been mentioned, in 1648 the duke of Savoy tried to set up a rival free port at Villefranche, while the Genoese government made a similar attempt for that city, Marrano settlers being specifically invited on each occasion. But there was very little success in any of these cases, and the supremacy of Leghorn was unquestioned. From the general picture of the suffering of miserable, repressed Italian Jewry of the seventeenth and eighteenth centuries, this group must constantly be excepted.

The area of settlement remained virtually unaltered throughout the Ghetto period. Though Sardinia passed, in 1720, from the Spanish sphere of influence after four centuries and came under the rule of the dukes of Savoy (henceforth the title of the state was the kingdom of Sardinia), there is no record that it attracted any Jewish settlers. General Paoli tried to tempt some from Leghorn to Corsica during its brief period of independence in the middle of the eighteenth century, promising them naturalization and autonomy; but few if any accepted his invitation, though they supported the patriotic regime financially and economically. In spite of a half-hearted attempt to secure the resettlement of the Jews in the Milanese in 1638, it was not until the duchy passed under Austrian rule that a handful found their way there, subject to the same regulations as their coreligionists in Mantua, and without setting up a synagogue or community until the close of the eighteenth century. Malta, from the seventeenth, presented the unique phenomenon of a community of slaves, composed of the Jews captured in forays by land and sea by the Knights of St. John and held to ransom, their charitable coreligionists of Venice and Leghorn maintaining the synagogue and burial-ground for their use. A few merchants sometimes came there spontaneously to traffic, but in very small number.

In the kingdom of Sicily, an experiment was made in 1695 to encourage visits from Jewish traders, in view of the deplorable economic situation. This having little result, the safe-conduct was amplified in 1728, and permission was given for the establishment of a synagogue in Messina under severe restrictions. This, too, was not a success, and in 1702 a handful of Jews who had settled on the mainland were expelled after only a fortnight's notice. After the reunion of Sicily and Naples under Charles IV of Bourbon, a more determined attempt was made. On February 3, 1740, he issued an invitation to the Jews to come and settle in the kingdom of the Two Sicilies, in accordance with a code of thirty-seven articles, hedged about by numerous restrictions in a bigoted medieval spirit. The number of places at which residence was authorized was limited to twelve — eight on the mainland, four in Sicily proper. The populace, primed by the clergy, proved highly unfriendly; and on the feast of San Gennaro the *lazzaroni* of Naples made themselves ready to attack the infidels if the saint's blood failed to liquefy at the appointed time. A Capuchin friar warned the king that his impious action had deprived him of the hope of male posterity. The initial twenty families, from England, Holland and Leghorn, were speedily reduced to three, who were hardly worth retaining. In consequence, on September 18, 1746, after the experiment had lasted for little more than six years, the charter was cancelled, and the few remaining settlers were expelled.

Although Italian Jewry attracted a great deal of attention — almost as it were as a "museum piece" — and although it played a relatively great role in history, it must be remembered that its scale was never large. It is only in the course of the past century that vast Jewish communities have come into being in the world's most important centers; such were unknown before the French Revolution, when a nucleus of 10,000 souls would have been considered of exceptional importance. But even on this scale the Italian communities were not very significant, notwithstanding the unnatural expansion caused by the expulsion from smaller places and concentration in the Ghettos. Numerically, the most important community was, in general, that of Rome, but, though some visitors and even officials estimated the figures at more than double this, it is unlikely that the total ever exceeded 5,000 at any time in the Ghetto period. The community of Venice was in its heyday perhaps about the same size, if the maximum estimate of 4,870 is accepted, but this is somewhat doubtful. Leghorn, with little more than 1,000 Jewish inhabitants in the middle of the seventeenth century, climbed up rapidly in its subsequent golden age, partly at the expense of other places in Italy, so that by the close of the eighteenth there were about 4,500. The Mantuan community may have reached as many as 2,500; while those of Ancona, Ferrara, Turin, Modena and (towards the end of the period) Trieste had at their peak between 1,000 and 2,000. We have fairly exact figures for Verona, where the Jewish population climbed up steadily from about 400 in 1600 to 933 (2 per cent of the total) in 1751. It is unlikely that any other Italian Ghetto had as many as 1,000 inhabitants. Reggio, for example, had about 1700 some 900, or one-fifteenth of the general civic population; Pisa in 1617 had about 500 (in a total of some 15,000). Many indeed, which enjoyed some reputation in the Jewish world, did not probably exceed a couple of hundred. On the other hand, there were some tiny places, such as Cento or Lugo, which we would not today consider as much more than large villages, where a community of this size constituted a considerable element of the total population and created a misleading impression of number. Some of these small colonies mainly consisted to the end of the descendants of the household or households who had settled there in the first place, such as the Conegliano family at Ceneda or the De' Benedetti, Bedarrida and Foà who constituted the entirety of the community of Nizza Monferrato.

All told, the total Italian Jewish population in the Ghetto period was probably between 25,000 and 30,000, or perhaps one quarter of one per cent of the total population. Excluded, however, as they were from the Italian islands and from the southern part of the Peninsula, as well as from the Milanese and Liguria, they constituted in the areas in which they were tolerated rather more than one half of one per cent — still an extremely low proportion. The importance of Italian Jewry, throughout its two millennia of history, has been qualitative rather than quantitative.

xxxiii

LIFE IN THE GHETTO*

Italy of the seventeenth and eighteenth centuries, center of pilgrimage for all who loved antiquity, music and art, was noteworthy for an institution no less characteristic of the country and age than the rococo shrines and splendid ecclesiastical pageants — the Ghetto. The traveller's eye might first be caught, as in Rome, by a contemptuous biblical citation outside a church, referring to a "stubborn and wayward people." Facing it, a sonorous Latin inscription over a low doorway related how the abominable race of the Jews had been segregated here, at the close of the sixteenth

* The picture that follows is necessarily a composite one. The general structure is borrowed from the chapters dealing with the subject in my *History of the Jews in Venice* and *Short History of the Jewish People*, but the material is in great part entirely fresh.

or beginning of the seventeenth century, for the glory of God and conservation of the Catholic faith. Beneath there hurried a stream of swarthy, voluble, red- or yellow-hatted humanity, fearful of insult but intent on their livelihood. As the curious tourist passed within — there were many such, whose impressions are recorded in various volumes of memoirs — one of the Gentile doorkeepers might have looked out and warned him to make haste; for after nightfall the gates were closed, and it was as much a crime for a Christian to be found within the Ghetto as for a Jew to be found outside without a special pass, valid only for a few hours. This was the case also during the greater solemnities of the Christian year, especially from Holy Thursday to the following Saturday, when it was forbidden even to look out of the windows. Although the Bull *Cum nimis absurdum* had prescribed that there should be no more than one entrance and egress, this was found to be impracticable, and sometimes there would be as many as five or even, as at Rome itself, seven. It should not be imagined that what lay between them was necessarily a mere *via dei giudei* — a single street barred off from the rest of the town. To be sure, in some small places the whole consisted of no more than a single fetid courtyard — a real *Hazzer* or court, as the Ghetto was termed in Hebrew by the Italian Jews. In larger places, however, a whole labyrinth of streets and alleys was to be found — a township within the town. Thus, in Rome, the main entrance was on the Piazza Giudea, half of which lay inside the Jewish quarter and half outside. Hence the principal Ghetto street, the Via Rua, twisted its way through the entire Ghetto, while a dank passage gave access to the Piazza delle Scuole, with its comforting fountain of clear water from the Alban hills, where the five synagogues were situated under a single roof. This was connected in turn by a warren of miserable courtyards and alleys, all teeming with poverty-stricken humanity, with the Piazza del Macello and its shambles. The low-lying Via Fiumara near the Tiber, dripping with damp, was the first part of Rome to be under water when the river overflowed its banks, the walls of the houses up to a certain level being perpetually of a dirty yellow color. In the same way, at Venice, the narrow Ghetto Vecchio, with half a dozen alleys behind it, after broadening out into the Campiello delle Scuole where there were situated the Spanish and Levantine places of worship, led into the ample square of the Ghetto Nuovo, this in turn giving access to the Ghetto Nuovissimo and the connected area. The street nomenclature within these districts long gave testimony to the nature of the life that pulsated within them: in Rome, besides those mentioned above, the Piazza delle Azimelle, where the unleavened bread for Passover was baked; in Florence, the Cortile de' Bagni, with its public bath; in Verona, the Vicolo Sagatino where the slaughterhouse stood, or the Piazza Spagnuola, where the Marrano immigrants congregated and worshipped. Sometimes, as in the case of the Calle Mocato in Venice, they took their name from the principal residents. Here, too — but this perhaps was unique — one patrician mansion had a garden attached. Almost every sizeable Ghetto had its piazza, where the market and the annual Purim fair were held. At Cento, on the other hand, the houses were so interconnected that it was possible to traverse the area from end to end without once going out into the street. It may perhaps be accentuated that in most places the Ghetto was established in a district already largely Jewish in population; the adaptation would consist in concentrating all the Jews in it, excluding the Christians, and providing walls and gates.

One immediate difference would strike the visitor as he entered — the great height of the buildings. The extent of the Jewish quarter was rarely increased, and the only expedient to accommodate the growth of population, due more to solicitude for children's welfare than to the legendary prolificness, was that adopted centuries later in the New

World. Instead of the lateral expansion forbidden them, the Jews had recourse to vertical extension by the addition of story upon story to the already rickety buildings. From a distance, indeed, it sometimes seemed as though the Jewish quarter, towering above the city, was actually built on rising ground. But the constructions were more audacious than solid; and it not infrequently happened that they collapsed under some unusual strain, converting the celebration of a betrothal or a marriage into an occasion for general mourning. The most tragic of these episodes took place at Mantua on May 31, 1776, when sixty-five persons (including a bride) met their death, besides many who were injured — innocent martyrs of the Ghetto system. A similar catastrophe in Rome in 1693 involved a number of Christian visitors, including some priests. Another constant dread of Ghetto life was fire; for buildings were so high and so inflammable, and the isolation from the outside world so complete, that enormous damage might be done before succor could arrive. In larger places at least, the Jews maintained their own apparatus for fighting the flames, but it was not always effective. There were particularly destructive outbursts, with considerable loss of life, in Venice on the night of April 14, 1752, and in Verona on October 30, 1786, to cite only two instances out of many. Natural disasters, too, proved particularly formidable in such circumstances, such as the earthquake which destroyed half of the Ghetto of Modena in 1671, or that of 1690 long commemorated by an annual celebration at Ancona.

The sanitary arrangements were necessarily primitive, though the Ghetto had to defray the expense of some sort of street-cleaning, or else employed its own scavenger. Hence outbreaks of plague were sometimes responsible for terrible mortality — for example, that of 1630–1, which lived in Italian history as that of 1665 does in England, when the Ghetto of Verona is said to have been infected by a bundle of clothing deliberately thrown in from outside, and 421 of the 721 Jews in Padua died; or that which raged for nine months in 1656–7 in Rome, when a special pesthouse was set up for the Jews, the synagogues were closed, and the preacher addressed the people from the windows of his house. In Rome the destructive floods of the Tiber also added to the general misery from time to time. The onslaught of disease was made worse by the incredible overcrowding. Some of the houses in the Ghetto had formerly been mansions of the nobility, whose armorial bearings were perhaps still to be seen over the doors. Thus, the malodorous Vicolo dei Cenci at Rome, the center of the ragpicking fraternity, took its name not from the rags but from the notorious patrician clan whose home it skirted; while at Chieri in Piedmont the palace where Charles VIII of France had once lodged was included in the Ghetto precincts, part being used as the synagogue. Now, the spacious chambers and halls were turned into warrens of miserable humanity. Most households did not have more than a single room, and some, in Rome above all, only a share in it, the solitary bed being used in rotation by different families.

The overcrowding in the Ghetto had curious consequences in law. The Jew, legally forbidden to hold real estate, was unable to purchase his house from the Christian owner. With the growth of population and the consequent increase in the demand for accommodation, there was no check upon the rapacity of the landlord, and no security for the tenant if a higher rental were offered by someone else. The solution of the difficulty was found in the adaptation of the ancient Jewish law of *Hazakah*, or proprietary right. This established, under the most severe social and religious sanctions, a sort of tenant-proprietorship which secured the occupant against overbidding by his neighbor and thereby against exploitation by the landlord. Pope Pius IV in 1562, followed by Clement VIII in 1604, gave the system legal sanction by prohibiting the increase of rents in the Ghetto and the ejection of the present occupants. The tenancy-right over the property thus became almost absolute. It could be disposed of by gift or purchase; it devolved by inheritance from father to son; it was included in the dowry of a daughter — but, so long as the rent was paid, occupation was secure. Ultimately, the *jus gazaga*, as it was called, with a curious admixture of Latin and Hebrew, received the recognition of the civil authorities throughout Italy, being introduced for example to Florence under Cosimo I at the outset of the Ghetto period, and to Piedmont when that of Turin was set up in 1679. There was, indeed, another side to the arrangement. If the population fell, many houses necessarily stood empty, as Gentiles were not allowed to live in the Ghetto, and the proprietors stood to lose heavily. Hence, as part of the system, the community as such was made responsible for paying all rents, whether the houses were occupied or no. In the end, with the depreciation of the currency, the general rise in prices and the dilapidation of the buildings, the fixed rentals became inadequate to compensate the owners even for the cost of the most necessary repairs, which were increasingly neglected; and this was one of the causes of the structural disasters that have been mentioned.

Perhaps it was its density of population which gave the Jewish quarter its reputation for noisiness, *fare un ghetto* becoming synonymous with making an uproar; and perhaps this in turn was the cause of the high-pitched voices which became characteristic. The language spoken was, of course, Italian; for the ancient settlers, fortified by the superior culture of the country, easily assimilated any foreign strain, except at Leghorn and for a time at Venice. True, the Jews tended to preserve, as in some other countries, an early stage in the development of the language, based in this case on the medieval Roman dialect, and affected to only a minor extent by the Tuscan which had become fashionable. Moreover, the admixture of tongues which was inevitable among them resulted in borrowing

Marriage

Circumcision

Scenes in the Venetian Ghetto

Funeral

Interment

Scenes in the Venetian Ghetto

from one language or another — especially from Hebrew — words in common parlance, which were occasionally given Italian inflections. To these features were added, as a natural consequence of close inbreeding, certain peculiarities of pronunciation and expression. The result was the creation of a distinctive Judaeo-Italian dialect, similar in nature to Yiddish (Judaeo-German) and Ladino (Judaeo-Spanish). Like its brothers, it was frequently written and sometimes even printed in Hebrew characters. Down to the twentieth century, the old type Italian Jew could be distinguished from his Christian compatriots by turns of language and pronunciation, and in Rome at least Judaeo-Italian still survives to some extent among the lower classes. While social life among the Jews and their neighbors was much the same, there were some inevitable divergencies. Certain Ghetto delicacies — for example, artichokes *alla giudea* in Rome — were famous; certain vegetables, such as the beet and eggplant, were little eaten except among the Jews; and their fondness for goose, especially in Piedmont, was proverbial.

The nomenclature of the Jews reflected their history. Italian Jewish surnames went back to a remote period, and were general from the sixteenth century; there was no question of their being artificially formed and governmentally imposed, as happened in more northern climes at the period of the French Revolution. There was a small group of very early family names (De' Rossi, De' Vecchi, and so on) which linked up, according to legend, with the oldest settlers in the country, at the time of the fall of Jerusalem. Many others were derived from places, mainly in central and northern Italy, though the Jewish settlement in them was sometimes only a memory — Bassano, Pavia, Orvieto, Camerino, Viterbo, Perugia, Fano, Cividale, Foligno, Rieti, Recanati, Montefiore, Sonnino, and so on. Ultimate foreign provenance was demonstrated by Grego (the Greek), Polacco (the Pole), Tedesco (the German),

Gallico (the Frenchman). Foreign place-names were sometimes elegantly Italianized in the course of time, as in the well-known cases of Luzzatti or Luzzatto (from Lausitz), Morpurgo (from Marburg), and Ottolenghi (from Ettlingen). A group of Spanish and Portuguese names (Athias, Cardoso, etc.) derived from Marrano settlers of the seventeenth century; while there were some conventional Italianizations of Hebrew names — Pacifici for Solomon, Sacerdote for Cohen, Buonaventura for Mazol-tob — and a few which remained in the original (Jarè, Ravà, Bemporad), or, especially at Leghorn, were taken over from other tongues, such as Arabic. Personal names were often Italianized even at an early period in a very modern fashion: not only in such conventional instances as the invariable replacement of Leone for Judah, or Marco (sometimes Angelo) for Mordecai, but — more surprisingly — in the substitution of approximate homophones with a vaguely reminiscent sound, such as Guglielmo for Benjamin, or Cesare for Hezekiah.

The inhabitants of the Ghetto would not have seemed, to the foreign eye, easily distinguishable from the rest of the population. Unlike the Jews of other parts of Europe, there was nothing of the alien about those of Italy, who had been settled in the country since before the Christian era. So, except perhaps for features more Oriental and more mobile, eyes sharper and more expressive and, according to some, somewhat larger lips and mouths, there was little to differentiate them from the Italian of the same class. Their dress too was much the same, and, to the astonishment of hirsute rabbis from other lands, the majority shaved their beards. In consequence of this outward resemblance, the institution of the Ghetto was not considered sufficient to prevent the contamination of the faithful by the leaven of disbelief. Hence the distinctive Jewish garb was now rigorously enforced, from the age of thirteen or fourteen upwards. It was at this time generally in the form of a hat, or in the case of women a kerchief, of a distinctive color —

yellow in the States of the Church, red in other places such as Florence and Venice, where a French traveller described it in 1680 as a hat covered with crimson cloth, lined and edged with black, the poorer classes using instead a waxed material. In certain areas the distinguishing mark was somewhat less conspicuous: in Piedmont a strip of yellow stuff sewn on the right shoulder; in the duchy of Modena, a red band of a finger's breadth, covering an eighth part of the hat. Heavy penalties were inflicted on those who dared to stir from the Ghetto without the *Simman*, or *Sciamanno*, as the Jews called it. Periodically, inquiries were made into the neglect of the regulations and steps were taken to enforce them; anyone who saw a Jew whose headdress was not of the proper color or style could snatch it from his head and take it to the police, being rewarded if a conviction ensued; and in the Papal States it was ultimately made obligatory for it to be worn even inside the Ghetto. Some privileged persons were exempted from the obligations, such as physicians, university students, protégés of foreign powers or (in more enlightened parts of the Peninsula) those who had deserved well of the government; while when travelling outside the city, and thereby exposed to attack, Jews were generally licensed, though not in the more orthodox areas, to wear the same headgear as ordinary men.

The center of Ghetto life was the *scuola* (literally, school) or synagogue, which was in some places one of the sights of the town, and frequently visited by curious Christians. Unpretentious from the exterior, as it had to be for fear of exciting Gentile cupidity, the interior sometimes presented fine proportions and design; while even in the smallest place, there was exquisite rococo detail such as could be found in no other country. The ritual followed and melodies used would reflect the provenance of the worshippers' forebears. Throughout central Italy, the original "Roman" or "Italian" rite was followed; in many places in the north, the "German" or *Ashkenazi*, though with various local peculiarities and its own musical tradition; in the seaports of Leghorn and Pisa, and in part Ancona and Venice (with various inland places which stood in close relation to them) the "Spanish" or *Sephardi*. In Piedmont, there was a little group of communities — Asti, Fossano and Moncalvo, known to scholars by their initial letters AFaM — where the ancient French rite, practiced in France before the expulsions of the fourteenth century, was preserved down to our day, at least on certain occasions of the year. In many towns, places of worship according to different traditions existed side by side: for example, Venice and Ferrara, with the German, Italian and Spanish (and in the former case also Levantine) synagogues; or Rome where, since only one synagogal building was allowed, a single edifice housed conventicles according to the Castilian, Catalan, Sicilian and Roman rites (there being two of the latter) — the famous "Five Schools," or *Cinque Scuole*. It may be mentioned that what was elsewhere regarded as one of the main differentiations between the various traditions did not exist, as all used the same pronunciation of Hebrew — the Italian variant of the *Sephardi*. Sometimes the synagogues were maintained by, or for, a single family, which with the passage of time might develop into a sturdy congregation — for example, the *Scuola Cases* at Mantua, numbering by the middle of the eighteenth century no fewer than 300 individuals. In the same way as the immigrants from other lands brought their liturgical tradition into Italy, so emigrants from the Peninsula brought to other strands the Italian rite, which was known in Constantinople, Salonica and elsewhere in the Turkish empire, and at one time in Amsterdam and perhaps other places in northern Europe.

Over and above the major liturgical differences, every city of Italy developed in the course of the ages its own synagogal tradition: its special fasts in commemoration of some local misadventure, or its special feasts to record deliverance from some more recent Haman. More than one of the ancient synagogues bears on its walls an inscription recording a providential escape from an otherwise forgotten disaster. At Padua, they celebrated until the twentieth century an annual feast day, the *Purim del Fuoco*, in thankfulness for their deliverance from a conflagration of 1795; at Casale a *Purim degli Spagnuoli* commemorated their good fortune during the siege by the Spaniards in 1630; at Leghorn, they fasted on the anniversary of the earthquake of 1742; and at more than one place a so-called *Purim della Bomba* recorded the escape of the synagogue or Jewish quarter from disaster during a bombardment in time of war.

By the side of the synagogue — before it, almost, in the consideration in which it was held — came the school. This was always given pride of place in the Jewish scheme of things, and the Jews of Italy did not fall in this respect behind their coreligionists. A typical arrangement for the eighteenth century, in a community of less than 1,000 souls, set up a free school for boys and girls alike, attendance at which was universal. (At Ferrara instruction was obligatory up to the age of thirteen if children were educated privately, and up to sixteen if they attended the communal free school.) All expenses were defrayed from voluntary contributions, nothing being accepted from the parents. The elements of the vernacular were taught as well as of Hebrew. There would be at least three teachers, with as many assistants, the size of the classes being thus restricted to twenty or thereabouts. The poorer pupils actually received free meals, and every year in midwinter, during the Hanukkah festival, collections of footwear and clothing were made for their benefit. On leaving school, the boys were expected to continue to study until they were eighteen, and their employers were compelled to allow them time for this purpose. Private teachers would give lessons also in vernacular literature, versification, music and dancing. Adult education was a commonplace, and every householder considered it a matter of course to study or to attend public lectures in his spare time. In Rome a special Talmud Torah for girls was opened in 1745. Elementary teaching was mainly — this was characteristic of Italian Jewry — in the care of "Dames' Schools" conducted by women. In consequence of all this, at a period when illiteracy was generally rampant, in the Ghetto it was exceptional, if not absolutely unknown. In the eighteenth century, it was observed that while the general population in the great seaport of Leghorn maintained only a single free school, with one master, there were many supported by the Jewish community, in which not a single child remained without education.

Besides education, almost every phase of life was cared for by one of the many pious confraternities — in Rome, for example, upwards of thirty; at Leghorn in its heyday upwards of sixty — which flourished in the Ghetto; for the Jewish conception of religion was broad enough to embrace almost every sphere of activity. There were numerous associations with purely spiritual objects — for fasting and confession and midnight prayer, in order to avert the divine wrath and hasten the coming of the Redeemer. Alongside these, there were others for study — in the Jewish scheme of things, an alternative or supplementary form of worship. Others again looked to the provision of clothing, food and shelter for the poor, or assisted them in the performance of religious duties. There was an association to help women in childbed, and an association to admit male babies into the covenant of Abraham. Brides were dowered by one confraternity, and prisoners solaced by another. At every stage of want or necessity, the unfortunate could confidently expect succor from his neighbors, in one capacity or another. When a man fell ill, the confraternity for visiting the sick came to comfort him and bring him medicaments and food; when he died, one fraternity looked after the mourners, another saw to his burial, and yet others cared for the widow and orphans. Every Ghetto had, moreover, its *Hekdesh* — half hospital, half hospice, for the destitute or foreign poor, though for the well-to-do there was generally an inn. Special bodies in Venice and Leghorn, supported by a tax on imports and exports, organized the ransoming of Jewish travellers captured and sold into slavery by the Knights of Malta or Barbary corsairs, equally pitiless where Jews were concerned. There were also, apart from the religious and charitable associations, a few professional organizations, for example, the Jewish Merchants' Guild which existed at Ferrara in 1693. It is to be imagined too that such organizations as the Tailors' Guild in Rome, or the Ragmen's Guild in Padua, which we know to have existed somewhat earlier, survived into the Ghetto period. At Modena, the Merchants' and Ragmen's Guild were combined at the close of the seventeenth century into a single body.*

The community, or *università degli ebrei*, represented the Ghetto in its collective capacity, its duly appointed officials being authorized to act for their coreligionists juridically and politically. The system of government can hardly be termed democratic. It varied in details from place to place, but a single general pattern emerges. The wardens (*massari, gastaldi, fattori*, etc.), generally serving in pairs for two months at a time in rotation, were chosen by lot out of a small responsible council over which they presided. There was another, somewhat larger and meeting relatively seldom, for the decision of matters of greater importance. These two bodies were elected by a General Congregation (*Congregazione* [*di pagatori*]) comprising all the major contributors to the communal taxation. As time went on the prescribed tax minimum increased, and this body tended to become more and more restricted: in

* It should be recalled that mutual-aid societies, linked up with occasional religious activities and associated with places of worship, were common, if not as common, in general Italian life; some reciprocal influence is certain.

Ferrara, for example, at the close of the eighteenth century it had no more than thirty members out of a total of at least ten times as many householders; while at Padua in the course of the seventeenth century the number of electors dwindled from some forty to fourteen, greatly to the distress of the democratically-inclined rabbi, Isaac Vita Cantarini. The proletariat was thus deprived of all voice in the conduct of affairs, this reflecting the increasingly oligarchic tendency in general life. Besides the political *massari*, there were in larger places other similarly-named functionaries: *massari del ghetto* for internal discipline, *massari della polizia* for matters of sanitation, *massari alla carità* for charitable affairs, who looked after various aspects of administration. The executive officers were usually selected by lot, so as to ensure that all served in due course, refusal being impossible.

Upon the *università degli ebrei* as thus organized devolved the duty of raising the heavy taxation which was exacted by the government year by year as the price of toleration. Added to this were the internal expenses of the community: the maintenance of the synagogue, the relief of the poor, the upkeep of the burial-ground, and the payment of the communal officials. Among these were reckoned, not merely those most intimately connected with religious life, such as the rabbi or the beadle, but also such officials as the *sagatino*, or ritual slaughterer, the secretary and the scavenger. There was also in larger places a postman, whose functions were sufficiently lucrative for him to pay for his monopoly. In addition, there had to be found the salary of the gate-keepers of the Ghetto, in whose appointment the Jews had no voice and with whose services they would in most cases gladly have dispensed. The sums necessary to defray all these expenses were raised by a graduated tax on income or capital. In a narrow circle, in which each man was not only the other's neighbor but also his business competitor, a strict inquiry into means was not easy; and it was left largely to the individual conscience to assess contributions. In Venice, Padua, and other cities, the assessments were made by a secret commission of *tansadori*, whose identity was kept concealed from the mass of contributors. From the close of the seventeenth century, a new system was widely introduced, known as the *cassella*, after the "box" in which amounts were collected at the stipulated times. In some places, money-boxes were to be found also in certain buildings in the Ghetto, where the prescribed percentage on brokerage could be deposited immediately. The conditions governing the system, which differed greatly from city to city, were usually printed at intervals for the guidance of the contributors. In Mantua, where apparently the standard of education was particularly high, these texts were always circulated in Hebrew; elsewhere, in Italian. A special sermon, stressing the needs of the community and the obloquy of evasion, was in some places delivered in the synagogue as an additional encouragement; and a generic obsecration was promulgated against those who should knowingly be remiss — a spiritual penalty which, however, was more dreaded than any merely physical punishment. Nevertheless, it was sometimes found impossible to raise the full sums demanded; the communities ran into debt in order to be able to meet their obligations; and in the course of the eighteenth century more than one was reduced to bankruptcy.

The system at Rome was perhaps exceptionally complicated. Benjamin of Tudela had remarked in the twelfth century that the community did not have to pay any special taxation. Now, in addition to extraordinary impositions from time to time, regular levies comprised one for the upkeep of the *Casa dei Catecumeni*, which included the contributions formerly paid by the communities uprooted in 1569; another for the expenses of the carnival; another nominally for the discontinued annual games at Monte Testaccio and Piazza Navona; yet another on account of a pension to a certain apostate, which was made permanent after his death. The basis of the financial system here was a tax not on income but on property of all descriptions, first officially authorized in 1577, and fixed at 5 per cent in the following century; in addition, there was a hearth-tax and a meat-tax — one of the most lucrative sources of income. Elsewhere in the Papal States, too, the tax on capital continued to be imposed though at a far lower rate — 3 per cent at Ferrara, 1 per cent (later to be raised 1¼) at Ancona. The problem of assessing taxation on visitors was a delicate one — all the more so since they were not admitted to residential rights without much difficulty. This led to protracted controversies between various cities, as, for example, in the eighteenth century between Verona and Mantua. Sometimes, on the other hand, two communities, such as the latter and Modena, would conclude reciprocity pacts, giving one another's members the same rights as natives.

Besides the direct taxation, the Jewish communities often had to make loans to their respective governments which were in effect little different. Thus, those of the Venetian territories had to advance upwards of half a million ducats, at only 4 per cent interest, between 1669 and 1691. In the end, the local Jewries maintained a fixed capital of 1,500,000 ducats on perpetual loan to the treasury, at a variable interest which was never high.

The community was paternal not only in the extent, but also in the intimacy, of its control. It possessed (at least in theory) the right of veto over new settlers; though Jewish warmheartedness on the one hand, and governmental greed on the other, tended to override this. Although in some places, especially in the Papal States (as at Rome from 1692 and Ferrara from 1708) the authority of the Jewish courts was in the end restricted to religious matters, judicial autonomy continued elsewhere — for example, in Leghorn, Modena and Mantua, where new regulations for legal procedure were agreed upon by the Jewish representatives, and sanctioned by the duke, in 1671.* Generally speaking, however, jurisdiction tended to pass — as happened in Venice — from the hands of the rabbis to those of the lay leaders of the community, who, to the sorrow of the learned, enforced a system of arbitration rather than the elaborate talmudic jurisprudence. When a Jew appeared in the ordinary law courts, he had to take an oath in a specially elaborate form, administered to him by the rabbi, over the phylacteries (*tephillin*) worn in prayer; the grotesque formalities insisted on elsewhere do not seem to have been maintained here.

In order to curb ostentation and extravagance — doubly dangerous in view of Gentile hostility — almost every community had its code of sumptuary laws, generally known under the name of *Pragmatica*, which was periodically revised and published. The community of Mantua, for example, issued periodically from 1598 onwards Hebrew broadsides, which were affixed to the walls of the synagogues and other public places, and gave the housewife detailed instructions as to what she might or might not wear or provide at table even on very special occasions during the forthcoming seven years. Other communities (Rome, Ancona, Reggio, Modena, etc.) published their regulations in Italian, in pamphlet form. In Venice the sumptuary laws of 1696–7 forbade any person to wear brocade or lace or more than two rings at a time, or to spend more than twelve ducats for a periwig, or four for a fan, or five for a muff. No more than two ducats should be squandered on flowers on the occasion of any domestic celebration, nor might more than twenty guests be invited. In Ferrara in 1748 it was forbidden to hold masquerades — which sometimes might lead to unfortunate results even

---

* This subject is now treated exhaustively in an important new monograph by V. Colorni: *Legge ebraica e leggi locali*, Milan, 1945.

in the Ghetto — on the occasion of a wedding or a circumcision. The *Pragmatica* of Ancona, of 1766, specified the number of torches which might accompany the bridegroom when he went to visit his bride, the amount of money that could be spent on the bouquet he presented or on the illumination of the marriage contract, and forbade flowers or sweets to be thrown down on the bridal cortège. The number of guests and of dishes that might figure on the occasion of a wedding feast and the like was also minutely regulated, though by a characteristic touch it was added that there was no limitation on the number of the poor who could be entertained. Some codes prohibited gambling and card playing except on special occasions — another preoccupation of the communal authorities, which led on one occasion at least to a spirited protest on the part of a learned but obstreperous rabbi, with a weakness for the card table, who painstakingly demonstrated that the measure was *ultra vires*.

The economic life of the Italian Jews was now almost intolerably restricted. As has been seen, in 1589, Pope Sixtus V had reorganized loan-banking in the Papal States, and his action had repercussions throughout the country. The calling was no longer a source of almost boundless prosperity as in the past, the hundred petty establishments in Rome boasting a combined capital of no more than 150,000 scudi all told. In the seventeenth century, when the legal rate of interest here was lowered from 18 per cent to 12 per cent, it was reckoned that after allowing for expenses only 4½ per cent was actually earned on the capital invested. In 1682, the old complete prohibition of usury was renewed by Pope Innocent XI, and this chapter ended. Loan-banks, now reduced to pawnbroking establishments of the most sordid description, continued to exist in some parts of Upper Italy, the Jewish *condotta* being conditional in Venice, for example, on the maintenance of the three subsidized pawnshops in the Ghetto, conducted at a dead loss. This could no longer, however, be considered a characteristic occupation of Italian Jews except in some backward areas, such as Piedmont where there were in all 55 loan-bankers, authorized to advance money at a rate of interest not exceeding 18 per cent, and each paying on an average 4,800 florins yearly for his concession. Here, indeed, it was notorious that many were no more than strawmen for clandestine Christian usurers, who received a proportion of the profit.

While their old source of livelihood was restricted, no new ones were opened. Generally speaking, Jews were not allowed to have shops outside the Ghetto, or to engage in retail trade except among their coreligionists, or to practice any organized handicraft, or to follow any liberal profession, or to enter any branch of manufacture, or to employ Christian labor. So rigorously was this enforced that Hebrew printing had to be conducted at Venice, still the main center during the greater part of this period, in the name of a patrician family, the Bragadini and Vendramini graciously, though not gratuitously, lending their cooperation for the purpose. Moreover, whenever the Jews made the slightest attempt to extend their range of activity, their Gentile competitors appealed to the government for action. Thus, for example, when in the seventeenth century some Paduan Jews attempted to maintain themselves as turners and carpenters, the Christian guild indignantly and successfully protested, forcing the *Serenissima* to intervene. From the textile industry only, in which the tradition of Jewish participation at every stage from manufacture to sale was so constant, it proved impossible to uproot them entirely. Nevertheless, the attempt was periodically made everywhere, except perhaps in the duchies of Mantua and Modena, so that the position of the Jews was never secure. Thus at Rovigo, where they had financed the industry as far back as the fifteenth century, introduced silk-weaving in 1614, and revived the languishing woolen industry later on, there was a protracted and ultimately successful attempt to eject them from it. In Padua, much the same happened, the silk industry having been introduced by the Jew Moses Mantica in the fifteenth century and a single firm being said, a hundred years later, to give occasional employment to 6,000 persons; here too there was a constant struggle against them, perquisitions for "illegally" manufactured cloth being periodically made in the Ghetto (the most drastic in 1683) and the Jewish manufacturers being driven out of business at last in the eighteenth century. In Florence, similarly, the Christian drapers protested continuously against the part played by the Jews, it being the turn in 1620 of the silk weavers and in 1678 of the woolen manufacturers, who now scored a complete success. A ducal order of 1649 forbade the Jews to deal in any new textiles or other commodities, which had to remain a monopoly of the Christian guilds, restricting them thus to secondhand dealing and the export trade. Nevertheless, at Sienna in the eighteenth century the woolen trade was wholly, and the textile industry partly in Jewish hands. In Piedmont, the charter of 1603 legally permitted the Jews to engage in commerce and to practice handicrafts; but this privilege was only nominal, for it remained necessary to obtain the permission not only of the *Conservatore degli Ebrei* but also of the corporations or trade-guilds, which made difficulties about admitting non-Catholics. Here, nevertheless, they were ultimately able to obtain a footing in the industry, so that in the eighteenth century there were silk and cotton mills owned by Jews in Alessandria, Casale, Acqui, Cherasco, Moncalvo, Fossano and Busca, and a fair proportion of the cloth imports from abroad passed through their hands. So great, indeed, was their interest that when they were shut up in their Ghetto at Turin in 1679, it seemed to jaundiced observers as though the textile trade deserted the rest of the town. These developments were, however, localized, and at the best could affect only a minority. By and large, the economic history of Italian Jewry in the age of the Ghetto is a record of fruitless endeavors to extend the range of activity, alternating with bursts of savage repression.

At the top of the scale therefore during this period there was a small aristocracy of wholesale importers and precarious textile magnates, the former class being particularly strong among the Spanish and Portuguese element. The Turkish trade, for example, lay very largely in the hands of the firms of Bonfil and Vivante at Venice, Gentilomo at Pesaro, and Morpurgo at Ancona, which were among the most important in Italy. The proletariat, on the other hand — a vast majority — were in the main itinerant hawkers, ragpickers and secondhand dealers. The laborious, ubiquitous Jewish old-clothes man with his raucous voice and his insalubrious burden was a feature of every town, and the Ghetto was noisome with the heaps of filthy rags which were picked over and if possible reconditioned. It is hardly a matter of surprise that sometimes the provisions were evaded, new clothing being deliberately torn and then repaired and sold as new. In Rome indeed there was a considerable tailoring industry which was officially permitted by the *Ruota* from the seventeenth century, on the grounds that it was impossible for all the Jews to earn a living from ragpicking. On a summer day, men and women might be seen gathered in front of the doors in every Ghetto street, plying their needles; and they had such a reputation for finer work that they were often employed for this by non-Jewish tailors. In Florence, button-making too was in Jewish hands. Ragpicking led naturally to another even less healthy occupation — wool-carding and the reconditioning of mattresses, which was invariably carried out by Jews who gave notice of their approach by striking sticks together. Another occupation which could not easily be suppressed and which therefore figured largely among the Jewish proletariat was peddling, which has been very common in Italian Jewry from classical times down to the present day. Jews could be forbidden to open shops for selling merchandise, but (though as a matter of fact Cosimo III of Tuscany made the attempt) it was not easy to prevent them to shoulder their wares and bring them to potential customers. They were thus familiar everywhere in the fairs and the streets and the villages, their packs filled with easily-portable trivialities — trinkets, lace, silks, buttons, sometimes even lengths of cloth; or they might combine the purchase of secondhand goods with the sale or exchange of frippery of this sort. However, they were not allowed to frequent the fairs and markets without a special license, or to peddle at the gates of the monasteries — much less, of course, to penetrate beyond them.

Ramazzini, the father of the study of occupational disease, described the Italian Jews of his day and the ailments which affected them in moving terms in his famous book, *De morbis artificum* (1700):

> Almost all Jews, especially of the lower class (who are the majority), follow sedentary and stationary occupations. They are mainly engaged in needlework and the mending of old clothes, especially the women, young and old, who earn their living by the needle. In this, they are so practiced and expert that they mend clothing of wool, silk and other materials so skillfully, that no trace of it appears; this is termed in Rome *rinacchiare*. Such work compels them to apply their eyes closely. All the Jewish women, moreover, keep at their sewing throughout the day and far into the night, using a small lamp and thin wick. Hence they incur all the ailments consequent upon a sedentary life and in addition suffer in the end from serious shortsightedness; and by the time they are forty are blind in one eye or else very weak of vision. Moreover, in most cities the Jews live in conditions of misery, shut up in narrow alleys, while their women do their work at all seasons of the year, standing by open windows to catch the light. This results in various affectations of the head, such as headache, earache, toothache, colds, sore throats and sore eyes. Many of them, especially of the poorer classes, are hard of hearing and blear-eyed. As for the men, they sit all day long in their booths stitching clothes, or stand looking for customers to whom they can sell old rags. Hence they are mostly cathetic, melancholy and

surly, and there are few even of the more wealthy who do not suffer from the itch....

Besides their tailoring it is customary, at least in Italy, for the Jews to remake mattresses the wool in which has become caked by years of use on beds.... They lay the wool on basket-work, beat it with sticks and shake it out, thus making the mattresses softer and more comfortable to lie on. By this work they earn some little profit about the houses. But the old wool has been wetted through time after time and soiled in other manners. In shaking and combing this they inhale a great deal of foul dust. This causes serious ailments, a racking cough, difficulty in breathing and stomach trouble.... It is the custom among us after a death and funeral to call in a Jew to shake and cleanse the wool mattresses in a sunny place. Thus the Jews cannot help inhaling deadly matter, and at the same time they contract affectations of the lung.

It was thus that the typical Jew of the Ghetto period appeared in the eyes of a careful observer.

On the other hand, it was not always possible to keep down ingenuity and determination, and a handful of persons managed in spite of all restrictions to find a profitable outlet for their ability. Even at Rome, not only was a foothold retained in the manufacture of silk (introduced by Meir Magino under Sixtus V) but there was also a small Jewish manufactory of colored glass in the seventeenth century. Here, moreover, in order to alleviate the desperate economic condition of the Ghetto, the Jewish community as such enjoyed, after 1698, the nominal monopoly of providing beds and bedding for the papal soldiers, this being one of its regular sources of revenue. (There had been an experiment in this direction half a century earlier which turned out unsuccessfully, as the stipulated price was not paid and the concession was surrendered before long.) The spice trade was introduced to Rome in the seventeenth century by a Jewish family from Ancona, though in 1750 Jews were excluded from it. Jewish workers in Venice and elsewhere long manufactured by a secret process the chemical ingredients used in artists' colors. A Jew named Lazzaro Levi revived the majolica industry in Mantua in 1626, though he was forced to close his workshop as a result of the tragic events three years later. Goldsmiths, silversmiths and jewellers were familiar almost everywhere; though in Piedmont, owing to the protests of the Goldsmiths' Guild, they were temporarily excluded from the craft after 1623. In the Mantuan Jewish quarter, indeed, there was a street of Jewish *orefici*, while the Formiggini family, who had their private synagogue at Modena, were court jewellers to the Este dukes, generation after generation, for two centuries.

In the little principalities of the north especially, some Jews exercised the government monopolies — for the manufacture of paper or distilled water, the sale of tobacco, and so on. At Correggio and in the duchy of Modena, Jews managed the mint in the seventeenth century, sometimes being even commissioned to execute coinage for the Levant. Even the antisemitic Cosimo III, grand duke of Tuscany, was compelled after various failures to farm out the tobacco monopoly to the Jew, Salamone Vita Levi. Some ill-feeling was aroused at Mantua in 1755 when it was alleged that all of the newly appointed tax contractors belonged to the Jewish community. Yet there was nothing approaching a monopoly in this respect; for not long before, in 1749, they had been completely outbid by a non-Jewish firm, who had, moreover, promised a considerable amount in ready money.

Another widespread and occasionally lucrative profession was that of *sensale* or commission-agent, whose function was bringing together buyer and seller, or searching for some urgently needed object or commodity on a commission basis. This was commonly followed among the Jews of the seaports and distributing centers, though even in Piedmont its legitimacy was by no means unquestioned and those who were so engaged sometimes suffered disturbance. In Rome and Venice, the furnishing of palaces, rented temporarily by wealthy foreigners who came to make the Grand Tour, was a source of considerable profit.

The old cultural interests were not entirely forgotten: here and there teachers of dancing and singing are still to be encountered, while at Mantua at the close of the eighteenth century there were in the Ghetto fifteen professional musicians, and Verona was the birthplace of the Giacomo Basevi Cervetto who introduced the cello to England in the time of George II. Some of the proletariat could eke out a living in the most lowly and strenuous occupations: again at Mantua, for example, there were at this time as many as thirty-six porters, in a Ghetto population of 2,200.

In 1645, the Roman Inquisition had pronounced that no Jew should henceforth be licensed to practice medicine among Christians. During the past couple of generations, since the Bull of Gregory XIII, exceptions had been increasingly rare; from now on, they were almost unknown. Nevertheless, a few practitioners of eminence emerged outside the Papal States, such as Benjamin (Guglielmo), the last of the physicians of the Portaleone family, authorized to practice at the court of Mantua, as the result of an urgent appeal of the duke in 1655; or Mario Morpurgo, whom an eighteenth century doge of Venice called his walking library because of his amazing erudition; or Solomon Conegliano, who conducted preparatory courses in medicine for aspirant Jewish physicians in his house in Venice; or — perhaps the most remarkable of all — his brother Israel Conegliano, who after being physician to the Venetian ambassador at Constantinople gradually came to be entrusted with diplomatic business and was in fact, though not in name, the principal Venetian delegate to the peace conference held at Carlowitz in 1698. Besides those who have been mentioned, a high proportion of the official rabbis of the Ghetto period were at the same time physicians: it is enough to call attention to Jacob Zahalon, subsequently of Ferrara, who in his book of popular medicine, *The Treasury of Life*, gives a moving account of the plague in Rome in 1656–7; and Isaac Vita Cantarini, chronicler of the vicissitudes of the Jews in his native Padua, who is said to have been consulted widely by his Christian colleagues. There were, too, in North Italy a number of ex-Marrano physicians of high eminence, such as Elijah Montalto of Venice, a doughty polemist, subsequently summoned to the court of France by Marie de' Medici; or the prolific but religiously unstable medical writer Ezekiel (Pedro) de Castro, for a time official physician to the community of Verona; or Isaac Cardoso, an eminent apologist of Judaism, who in his *Philosophia Libera* (Venice, 1673) made a stupendous attempt to erect a complete and up-to-date edifice covering the entire field of natural science and philosophy. Between the Jewish physicians of the Ghetto and those of a happier age there was, indeed, one outstanding difference: the latter had owed their reputation, at least in part, to their access to Hebrew and Hebraeo-Arabic tradition; the former were simply European doctors, who had overcome the manifold difficulties in their way and had managed to qualify and to achieve distinction.

Perhaps the most terrible of the abuses that developed during the Ghetto period was that of forced baptism. Pope after Pope, from the early Middle Ages onwards, had issued Bulls in which he explicitly condemned any attempt to secure conversion to Christianity by other than peaceful means. But it was not always easy to assess the nature or degree of compulsion, especially in the case of children; and it was left to those in control of the *Casa dei Catecumeni*, founded in Rome by Paul III and speedily imitated elsewhere, to investigate the matter — not always objectively. In 1635 it was decided that the baptism of the head of the household could entail, if he expressed the desire, that of all his family who were under age or dependent upon him, and this was subsequently extended to cover more remote cases. It now became customary that any Jews over whom the Church had the slightest claim for some reason or other might be carried off, on the pretext of "exploring" their wishes, to the *Casa dei Catecumeni*, or, where this existed, its feminine counterpart, the *Monastero delle Convertite*, where every endeavor was made to bring them to appreciate the spiritual pre-eminence of the Christian faith. To attempt to dissuade them was punishable by scourging, and the severest penalties were imposed on any Jew who so much as approached the building, lest he should attempt to contaminate the halting faith of the neophytes, who as an additional precaution were forbidden to look out of the windows. As late as 1794, three Jewish old-clothes men were denounced, in enlightened Venice, for crying their wares along the *fondamenta* outside! There had, moreover, grown up a popular superstition that any person who secured the baptism of an unbeliever was assured of Paradise; and it often happened that a sin-stained ruffian or superstitious servant-girl would pounce on a Jewish child in the street, perform the mere parody of a baptismal ceremony with ditch-water, and declare him to be a Christian. In the middle of the eighteenth century, Benedict XIV decided that once baptized, even against the prescriptions of Canon Law, a child was to be considered a Christian and brought up under Christian influence. Henceforth, the outrages, though ostensibly condemned and forbidden in frequent proclamations, had to all intents and purposes official license. An ill-timed jest, or a foolish prank, or the reputed wish of an apostate relative, was sufficient for children to be torn from their parents' arms to be brought up henceforth, remote from their care, as Christians, and for some who were no longer children to be dragged to the font almost by brute force.

It is today hardly possible to credit the extent and the callousness of some of these outrages. In 1602, an unfortunate Roman Jew was seized by a priest and handed over to a person who kept him under restraint while endeavoring to persuade him to be baptized. Three days later, in desperation, he attempted to commit suicide by throwing himself out of a window, but escaped with his life. Transferred to another instructor, he managed to find his way back to the

Ghetto, but was dragged out. After another fortnight of persuasion, Faith was triumphant, and he consented to receive baptism. Two years later, Rabbi Joshua Ascarelli with his wife and four children were brought to the House of Catechumens on some pretext. The parents stood fast and were released after a long period of detention; the children resisted for a time with fortitude remarkable for their age but were at last converted. One day, in 1639, a Roman Jew bandying small talk with a Dominican friar offered to have one of his children baptized if the Pope acted as godfather. This pleasantry cost him not one child but two, the younger being seized out of the cradle. This was more than even the downtrodden Roman Jew could bear, and brought about a veritable insurrection in the Ghetto, savagely repressed. In other cases an apostate father, whose wife refused to follow him into baptism, "claimed" his unborn child, which therefore had to be brought into the world in a Christian environment and was immediately taken out of the mother's arms to be baptized. Similar outrages, sometimes no less appalling, took place in other Italian cities. Even in Venice, where the government professed to object strongly to forced baptism, the Jewish community was on one occasion fined heavily for refusing to disclose the hiding-place of the wife and children of an apostate husband. Alfonso III, the duke of Modena, who after a few months' reign abdicated and became a Capuchin friar under the name of Giambattista d'Este, proved a particularly zealous conversionist, both before and after his metamorphosis, and had many outstanding achievements to his credit. At Reggio, during the plague of 1630, a barber summarily christened after his own style seventeen or eighteen Jewish children in the extemporized pest-house that had been set up, shaving their heads so as to be able to recognize them afterwards. Only two survived — to be seized subsequently and brought up as Christians. As late as 1785, an attempt was made to secure for the Faith a young married woman at Ferrara, then pregnant, in consequence of a prank played upon her by a playmate aged six some twenty-five years before. It was largely by such means that between 1634 and 1790 fully 2,430 Jews were converted in Rome alone — Benedict III personally baptized no fewer than 26 — and 68 in Ferrara in the single decade 1691–1700. This became one of the greatest horrors of Jewish life in Italy — particularly in the area under papal rule — and was responsible for a good deal of emigration to places where there was a prospect of greater security. The baptisms were celebrated with great *éclat*, with processions, fireworks, public festivities and jubilant poetical publications, and sometimes provoked hostile demonstrations in the Jewish quarter. If the person seized refused to embrace Christianity, further annoyance was in store for the community, which was actually expected (could meanness go further?) to defray the cost of his maintenance in the Home of Converts during the experimental period!

Bound up with this was the institution of conversionist sermons, now a regular feature in many parts of Italy. Reorganized by Pope Gregory XIII, limited to a very few occasions of the year (and perhaps suspended entirely) by Sixtus V, they were reintroduced by Clement VIII and were henceforth an established institution. It was a popular diversion for the rabble to lie in wait for the Jews as they passed on their way to church and pelt them with anything that came to hand. Obedience was ensured, in the Papal States at least, by fixing a regular quota for attendance — in Rome, for example, 150 each week — for whose presence the *fattori* were held responsible. Beadles armed with rods prevented the obvious expedient of slumber; while the ears of the audience were submitted to preliminary examination to ensure that they had not made themselves deaf physically as well as intellectually. At Ferrara, in order to avoid the insults to which the Jews were subjected on the way, a special entrance was made from the Ghetto into the Church of S. Crispino, where the sermons were delivered. Compulsory attendance was never enforced in Venice, and was abolished in the duchy of Mantua in 1699, but over great areas, especially the Papal States, it continued to be the rule. The unpleasantness of the institution was enhanced by the fact that the preachers — whose fee of course had to be paid by the Jews! — were frequently apostates.

Another recurrent pretext for molestation was the censorship imposed on Hebrew literature. From time to time raids would be made on the houses and public buildings in the Ghetto and every book discovered would be removed for inspection. Copies of the Talmud or similar prohibited literature were burned in public, their owners being severely punished. Other works could be retained only if they contained a license from the non-Jewish authorities or else bore the signature of an ecclesiastical censor testifying that they now contained nothing prejudicial to Christianity. The latter was, of course, paid by the Jewish communities — yet a further tax upon them, resented all the more since he was almost invariably a renegade. Equivocal passages or words were carefully obliterated, or erased, or even cut out, the censor appending his signature at the close of the book, sometimes in Hebrew, to certify that it had been duly "expurgated." (One such professional vandal of the late sixteenth century claimed to have dealt with over 29,000 volumes.) This, however, would not save it from being re-inspected on some future occasion by another censor, perhaps more severe, certainly no less mercenary. There was drawn up at this period a semi-official handbook for the censors of Jewish literature with detailed instructions regarding their work. Sometimes the results were ludicrous, as when the very word "Talmud," even in its literal sense of "study," was removed, or every reference, however innocuous, to "Gentiles" or "peoples." In addition, the censorship benevolently protected the Jews — sometimes displaying a curious unimaginativeness — from what it was pleased to consider superstitions or puerilities in the traditional literature. The severity of the censorship varied from place to place — from the incredibly harsh standard which prevailed in Rome, where little but the Bible and liturgical works were permitted, to the relative liberalism of Venice. At Leghorn, as promised in the charter of 1593, there were no restrictions at all. Apart from the deadening intellectual effect, the activity gave constant opportunities for blackmail. In order to put an end to the disturbances, the duke of Savoy promised in 1603 that permitted literature, once inspected, should not be subject to further censorship, and this example was followed in some other parts of the country. Nevertheless, in 1630, on the instigation of a recently converted Jew, a raid was made on the Ghetto at Reggio and every scrap of written or printed paper that could be found — including account-books! — was removed for investigation, the bishop naively imagining that he had discovered magical materials of the highest import. After the middle of the seventeenth century, there was a temporary alleviation, the old books having by now been repeatedly purged and repurged and new publications being submitted to rigorous censorship. Nevertheless, later on there was a general recrudescence.

Minor annoyances — most oppressive in Rome and the States of the Church, least so in Leghorn and Pisa — were innumerable. Occasionally, as happened at Mirandola in 1637, new synagogues which had been built without license were destroyed by order of the Inquisition. Jews were not supposed to have Christians in their employment, even for such trivial yet (to them) essential purposes as the lighting of fires on the Sabbath day; and though governments like that of Venice were inclined to be lenient on this point, great severity was shown in the Papal States, where a special permit, valid for only a limited period, was necessary for the purpose even when the regulations were somewhat relaxed. Similarly, it was illegal for a Jew to employ a Christian wet-nurse for his children. In cases where this was unavoidable, not only was it necessary to procure a special license, but a register was even kept, so that the names of all those involved whether actively or passively should be permanently on record. Even the employment of Christian midwives was rigorously forbidden. In the Papal States, moreover, with exceptional pettiness, the Jews were prohibited from escorting the dead to the cemetery with lighted tapers in the traditional fashion and to chant psalms as they went; while after 1625 they were not even allowed to erect tombstones over the graves, except by special license from the Holy Office, which was very difficult to obtain. From time to time, an inquiry would be made regarding breaches of this regulation and gravestones set up in contravention of it were destroyed or removed to the houses of children or kinsfolk, where they remained a macabre memorial, until the Ghetto was destroyed.

In many parts of the country, the *fattori* and rabbis were held personally responsible for crimes alleged to have been committed by Jews, and would be haled off to prison if a suspect was not available for arrest, or even if a stolen object believed to have been brought to the Ghetto could not be traced; while in Piedmont at least they could be arrested if the creditors so desired on account of any Jew's debts. In Tuscany, at the close of the seventeenth century, the priest-ridden Cosimo III vied with the Popes in enforcing the sternest anti-Jewish measures. He rigorously forbade Jews to employ Christian women as wet-nurses except by special license and under their own roofs. Time after time, he issued proclamations prohibiting intercourse between Jews and Christian women, under savage penalties. In 1680, he warned Jews and Christians not to dwell under the same roof or even to have a window, terrace or well in common, and threatened with a heavy fine any person who should give food, lodging or employment to a Jew. Even at Leghorn, the employment of Christian servants was forbidden, Jews were prohibited under stern penalties from proselytizing their

Moslem slaves, and conversionist sermons were delivered, though in accordance with the undertaking in the privileges of 1597 attendance at these could not be enforced.

In towns where there were universities, it was a student prerogative to bombard the Jews with snowballs on the occasion of the first fall of the year — a right which was compounded at Turin by an annual payment of twenty-five ducats and at Mantua by a heavy ransom of confectionary and writing-paper. At Padua, besides paying a tribute of confetti on this occasion, the Jews had to give a number of fat capons, or the equivalent, on St. Martin's day, so as to inaugurate the academic year in proper style. At Pisa, it was customary for the undergraduates to weigh the fattest Jew they could find each year on St. Catherine's day, the official beginning of the winter, and exact his weight in sweetmeats from the community. At Rome, there were additional petty impositions — such as a toll on Jewish corpses — during a papal interregnum. The community of Mantua, which after 1619 managed to enforce a contribution for the purpose on those of the Monferrat, had to contribute to the maintenance of the duke's archers.

In most places, their burdens included the provision of tapestries, hangings and other decorations for the public buildings or special pavilions on various special celebrations. On occasions of public rejoicing, it was often incumbent on them to build a triumphal arch, decorated with laudatory inscriptions and verses, or to stage a public spectacle, or to provide prizes for the horse races, or, as was usual at Leghorn, to erect a so-called *cuccagna*, a treacherously elaborate structure surmounted with good things to eat and drink, for the delectation of the populace and the amusement of spectators. Of course, gifts had to be presented on important occasions to the ruling families, who would not demean themselves to accept trivialities; the bride of the heir apparent of the duchy of Modena, for example, would be content with nothing less than a diamond necklace from the community of Reggio on her marriage in 1608. Public officials, too, such as the *Capitano Grande* or Police Chief at Venice, expected to receive the customary gifts from time to time — for example, when they assumed office or on the New Year.

Among the other sources of petty persecution were the anti-Jewish songs chanted by the rabble, notwithstanding the periodical expressions of disapproval on the part of the government, which sometimes formed the prelude to outbreaks of violence. At the beginning of the eighteenth century, for example, a scurrilous poem by one Antonio Viccei, *Il pasto degli ebrei* ("The Jews' Repast"), caused a great deal of annoyance and expenditure — by no means the worst instance of the sort, as will be seen. In pontifical Rome, where a better sense of values might have been expected, plays known as *giudate*, mocking Jewish life and customs, were an essential part of the traditional popular drama acted on ox-carts around the streets during the carnival; while the Fishermen's Guild also specialized at this season in burlesques of Jewish ceremonial, such as the mock-funeral of a rabbi which was the *pièce de resistance* of the masquerades in 1709 and was repeated before his palace at the special request of Prince Alexander Sobieski of Poland. (It was only in 1768 that this abuse was forbidden.) Even at Leghorn, the Jews had to ask, in 1737, for the suppression of an antisemitic comedy which was creating an unpleasant atmosphere. All these things were perhaps trifles in themselves, but they were susceptible sometimes of distressing consequences.

Over a good part of the Ghetto period, there was one particular indignity to which the Roman Jews were subjected. Pope Paul II had added variety to the Roman carnival in 1466 by introducing a series of footraces, a piece of cloth (*palio*) serving both as goal and prize; on one day it was run by boys, on another by old men, on another by buffalos, and on another by Jews — originally, under twenty years of age. At the outset they were fairly innocuous. There is extant a description of the proceedings in 1511, when twelve Jews raced from the Piazza S. Pietro to the Castle of S. Angelo under the direction of the Pope's physician, "Messer Rabi" (perhaps Samuel Sarfatti), who had an escort of a hundred armed Jews riding before him and fifty more at his side bearing olive branches and banners with the escutcheons of the Pope and the city of Rome. When the proceedings were over, it was related, he entertained the winners in his house. But as time passed and the general atmosphere deteriorated, the races developed into an intolerable abuse. The participants, naked except for a loin-cloth, had to make their way through jeering crowds, with mounted soldiers galloping behind them to urge them on. Often the race had to be repeated, on the pretext that there had been some slight irregularity. The limitation on age was removed, old men being found more amusing than young, and they were forced to stuff themselves with food before starting, so as to make their performance more ridiculous. On one occasion at least, one of the participants collapsed and died. This procedure continued year by year until 1668. Then, for the sake of public order, not humanity, it was abolished, together with the obligation for the representatives of the Jewish community to appear in the senator's festive procession before the jeering public at the opening of the carnival; yet there were substituted a new tax and a humiliating ceremony of homage before the *conservatori* of the city, in grotesque garb, with short breeches and floating capes.

It still remained necessary even after this for the Jewish representatives to greet each new Pope on his first solemn entry, or *Possesso*, as their fathers had done from time immemorial. The ceremony had to take place near the Arch of Titus, symbol of their national disaster, which they were compelled to decorate on such occasions; they refused, indeed, to go beneath it themselves for whatever reason, paying a fee to pass through an adjacent house if their way lay in that direction. With them, they bore the scroll of the Pentateuch, which the Vicar of God returned to them with opprobrious remarks. Pope Urban VIII, in the seventeenth century, added a new and hardly credible humiliation to the ceremonial; henceforth, at such audiences, the Jews might no longer kiss the foot of the Pope, but only the spot where it had stood.

But even now, when Jewish misery had touched its depths, Italy was still Italy, and Italians were still Italians, with all the native kindliness of their people. The tribulations of daily life were extreme. Yet outbursts of violence were few and far between, and hardly any were on a large scale or such as to entail loss of life. There were occasional echoes of the ritual murder libel — at Verona in 1603, Casale in 1611, 1628 and 1700, Venice in 1705, Viterbo in the same year, Ancona in 1711, Senigallia in 1721. But, though riots ensued in some of these cases, and judicial action was sometimes begun, they never received official sanction or led consequently to a really serious outcome. Indeed, even at the worst period of reaction the Popes never countenanced this abuse; and one of the noblest documents in the struggle against it is a memorial drawn up by Cardinal Ganganelli, subsequently Pope Clement XIV, at the time of the wave of accusations in Poland in the middle of the eighteenth century, when the communities of that country sent a delegation to seek redress from the Holy See.

From time to time, there were anti-Jewish outbreaks, sometimes artificially stimulated; but they were almost invariably suppressed without bloodshed, the communities of one place or another establishing new annual celebrations to commemorate their escape. The worst of these occasions was in 1684, at the time of the siege of Buda, when the Turkish defenders were alleged to be assisted by mythical hordes of Jews. There was now a good deal of ill-feeling throughout Italy. In Rome sentiment ran so high that it was dangerous for Jews to venture into the streets unescorted, and the Ghetto was saved from assault only by the solidity of the gates. In various parts of the Venetian territories, conditions were no better. At Padua especially, where some ill-feeling had been engendered among the citizens by a recent decision empowering the Jews to participate in the textile trade, riots took place for six days in succession, and the Ghetto was in imminent danger. External happenings, too, occasionally caused disorder, the shops at Turin being sacked, for example, when the city was captured during the civil war in 1639; while at Pisa the high spirits of the student body led to some unpleasant moments in the Jewish district when a new vice-rector was elected in 1718. But even on the worst of these occasions, everything passed without actual bloodshed. Though it was a period of constant humiliation, though Jewish life was made a perpetual misery, though everything was done to stir up popular aversion, though it was always unpleasant and sometimes dangerous for a Jew to venture into the street, there was throughout the Ghetto period nothing in the nature of the pogroms which have disgraced the twentieth century. In part, this was due to the fact that the Ghetto, however much it may have been a symbol of humiliation, made it easier for the Jews to be defended and to defend themselves. In the end, indeed, some rabbis, impressed by this and by the fact that it was at least superficially a powerful preservative of communal solidarity and of traditional culture, came to consider the institution a boon, and the annual feast on the inauguration of the new Ghetto synagogue was converted, at Verona and Mantua at least, into a service of thanksgiving for the Ghetto itself. It was perhaps the most tragic feature of all that the prisoners should have so lost the conception of freedom that they thanked God for their prison.

As though to console themselves for the miseries of their present, the Jews of the Ghetto elaborated marvellous tales and legends, which were transmitted from father to son, fictitiously exalting their state or elaborating the marvels of their past: Tales of the exiles from Spain and their sufferings and their achievements in Italy. Tales of mystics who saved menaced Ghettos by affixing cabalistic charms to the gates. Tales of the steadfastness of persons inveigled into the dread *Casa dei Catecumeni*. The tale of the neophyte who, on the eve of being raised to the purple, was suddenly persuaded that the bells were ringing to announce the coming of the Messiah. The tale of the miraculous escape of the Jewish community, penned up by an angry mob in their synagogue when the city was beleaguered, and saved only by the miraculous explosion of a shell between them and the assailants. The tale of the grand duke and his appreciation of Ghetto delicacies. The tale of the rabbi whose wisdom saved the hapless youth chosen by lot on Holy Week to be surrendered for torture. The tale, above all, of the stolen Jewish boy who became bishop, or cardinal, or even Pope. The folklore of the Italian Ghetto has never been collected, and now it is unhappily too late.

The artistic spirit of Italy penetrated the Ghetto to a marked degree. The synagogues were constructed sometimes by the most eminent architects of the day — men like the great Longhena, for example, at Venice — and no pains or expense were spared to make them places of aesthetic inspiration. In that of Pesaro, two gilded lions, brought as relics from Ascoli when that community was dissolved, long guarded the approach to the Ark, without arousing criticism even from the hyper-orthodox. Objects of ceremonial use were elaborately chased, not always by Jewish craftsmen; the women would strain their eyes during the long winter nights over the most intricate embroideries; the betrothal rings were sometimes masterpieces of the goldsmiths' craft; brides carried prayer books in exquisite silver bindings with them to synagogue; and there was in general no part of the Jewish world where religious life was given so aesthetic a form. Not only the scroll of Esther, read upon the hilarious feast of Purim, but also such documents as the marriage contract or even rabbinical diplomas were frequently illuminated, with perhaps an excess of ornament; the Italian liturgical melodies were set to music almost two centuries before such a thing was known elsewhere; the use of the organ to accompany them was permitted by some authorities; and in the early seventeenth century, the Mantuan court musician, Salamone de' Rossi, assisted by the Venetian Rabbi Leone da Modena, made a courageous though premature attempt to reorganize synagogal music in a modern sense, in accordance with the new conceptions. The Ghetto aristocrats, and even some of the rabbis, did not disdain to have their portraits painted, the second commandment notwithstanding, and in Florence elegant Ghetto houses contained frescos of some merit representing Old Testament scenes. We know of a Jewish painter in the style of Salvatore Rosa who lived in this city in the seventeenth century, named Jonah Ostiglia; an artist and art-dealer named Jacob da Carpi who emigrated in the eighteenth from Verona to Amsterdam, where he built up a flourishing clientele: and a seal-engraver from Germany named Aaron Wolf who worked at Leghorn about the same period. It may be added that the active Venetian church-painter Francesco Ruschi, and the Pietro Liberi who became court artist at Vienna, both belonged to Jewish families.

It was not only in such things that the Ghetto reflected the life of the outside world. The fashions and social habits of the rest of the Italian people found ready imitation among the Jews. The young men often carried arms, notwithstanding the disapproval of both civic and communal government, and did not hesitate to use them on occasion. Crimes of violence were rare, but by no means unknown; though indeed it is a matter of record that settlement by the Jews sometimes redeemed a densely populated quarter from a reputation for lawlessness, to which it reverted when they departed. Though in Rome they would run the risk of being flogged by the public executioner if discovered — notwithstanding the fact that so large a proportion of the expenses were defrayed by the community — the Jews mingled at carnival-tide in the riotous celebrations of their fellow citizens, their identity concealed by mask and domino, which they wore regardless of a possible forbidden admixture of materials. Indeed, the sermons at synagogue were sometimes suspended at this season, in order to permit the faithful to go about their pleasure betimes.

The Ghetto by no means lacked its diversions. At Venice in 1629, refugees from music-loving Mantua assisted in establishing a Jewish orchestral society, going by the nostalgic name *When we remembered Zion*, which through the rabbi who directed its activities exchanged courtesies and compositions with analogous non-Jewish bodies. On the night of the feast of the Rejoicing of the Law, the Ghetto ladies, coquettishly masked, visited the men's synagogues, and there must have been a good deal of harmless flirting. On Purim, in larger places, there would be a Ghetto fair, and mumming, and jollity, and the young people again went about in masks (though some pietists speculated whether this was reconcilable with the rigors of biblical iconoclasm); while at least down to the end of the sixteenth century it was customary to elect a burlesque "Purim King" to impose his will on the Jewish quarter. This, too, was the season for amateur Ghetto theatricals, with representations of the stories of Mordecai and Esther, or of Joseph and his brethren; and even now, Christian enthusiasts attended when they were permitted. Similar performances took place on other feasts, such as Passover, and occasionally the schoolchildren presented moral dialogues in dramatic form for the edification of their elders. The climax was reached when, in seventeenth-century Venice, to the distress of some pietists of the day, a theater was actually instituted in the Ghetto, men and women of every class thronging enthusiastically to the performances. Histrionic interests did not end with the seventeenth century: even in Rome, towards the end of the eighteenth, the Jews were graciously allowed to present comedies in the Ghetto, provided that no Christians were present; while in Sienna, permission was accorded in 1793 for a *tragedia sacra* to be performed on the coming Passover, though men and women were seated separately, and it was planned to have a special performance for the tender sex.

The Ghetto was insufficient to interrupt entirely the friendly relations between Jews and Christians even at this period. They drank together, experimented together, gambled together, travelled together, sometimes even flirted together. Sternly punished though it was (as late as the seventeenth century, the mistress of a Roman noble was burned alive when it was discovered that she was a Jewess) amorous intrigues between Jews and Gentiles were not unknown; and pious rabbis bewailed the neglect of the ceremonial laws as Jewish fops learned to shave their beards, forego the wearing of phylacteries, and have their toilet attended to even on the Sabbath day! Christians often visited the synagogues, and listened appreciatively to the sermons, notwithstanding the frenzied disapproval of the ecclesiastical authority; and rabbis occasionally returned the compliment in the churches. It is said that in some places, where the civic government would not permit Christians to go into the Jewish houses to attend to the fires on the Sabbath, the Ghetto gatekeepers themselves sometimes performed that kindly office; and that when a perquisition for forbidden literature was planned, the Jews were often forewarned by Christian friends. The Venetians, according to a Jewish writer of the seventeenth century, were "more pleasing and kindly with the Jews than any other in the world," while, notwithstanding the prejudices of some patricians and zealots, the common folk were "friendly and sociable, liking them greatly." When there was no external interference, the same might have been said of other cities.

The frequency of edicts, even in Rome, denouncing amicable intercourse between Jews and Christians is ample evidence of its regularity and spontaneity. It could hardly be otherwise; for the Ghetto was a segment no less of the Italian than of the Jewish world; and no degree of regimentation could eradicate the common humanity of the two sections of the same people.

xxxiv

THE HOUSES OF STUDY

The institution of the Ghetto, the censorship of Hebrew books and the protracted offensive against the Talmud and the allied literature, could not fail to have a corrosive effect on Jewish intellectual life in Italy. The daring speculations, the untrammelled intercourse, the penetrating influences of the Renaissance period were now remote memories. The environment was unfavorable for uninhibited poetry like that of Immanuel of Rome or acute criticism like that of Azariah de' Rossi, whose works were, indeed, banned by the neo-orthodox; the fructifying influences of an Elijah del Medigo or a Leone Ebreo would actually have been impeded by law. Literary activity hence moved perforce in a narrower orbit. It is probably true to say that, whereas before the Renaissance the general intellectual standard of the Jews was higher than that of their neighbors, now it lagged behind, the outstanding minds receiving general recognition despite, and not as hitherto by virtue of, their Jewish background. It was in its way symptomatic that the two most eminent Italian Hebraists of the period in a modern sense were Catholic priests — Giulio Bartolocci, in the seventeenth century, whose gigantic *Magna Bibliotheca Rabbinica* is a landmark in the history of Hebrew bibliography; and Giovanni Bernardo de' Rossi, in the eighteenth, one of the most remarkable bibliophiles of all time, whose superb collection of Hebrew manuscripts is the glory of what was once the Ducal Library at Parma.

Yet, thanks to its high literary tradition and the survival of a humanistic scheme of education, still very comprehensive, Italian Jewry was exceptionally (and in some ways misleadingly) articulate. In chronicles, letters, poems, addresses, elegies, personal memoranda — for the most part in the purest Hebrew, and sometimes of high literary quality — a record was left in each community, however small, of every event which was in any way out of the ordinary, and of any personality who attained the slightest degree of distinction. We know in absorbing detail of petty triumphs, momentary annoyances, messianic dreams, mystical coteries, communal quarrels and escapes, personal grievances, trivial achievements and disappointments. The amount of material is out of all proportion to the numbers involved and the importance of the subject; and personalities of slender significance left a mass of writings which endow them with an unjustified prominence in the eyes of posterity. The accessibility of the printing presses of Venice, Leghorn, and for a time Mantua and elsewhere, gave durability to much ephemeral material which otherwise would soon have been forgotten, so that the mere number of writers, whether in prose or verse, is almost overwhelming. It is not easy sometimes to assign the proper importance to those whose productivity was perhaps incommensurate with their genius, or to choose among an array of fecund and at one time celebrated authors, in a manner that can command universal agreement, the few who were indubitably above second rank.

Though the intellectual life of the Ghetto was increasingly petty, and the writings that emanated from it increasingly trivial, certain characteristics could not be submerged: a wide intellectual curiosity, a considerable competence in the vernacular, a familiarity with general literature, and conspicuous ability in the manipulation of a pure and effective Hebrew. The typical figure of the age is the famous Leone da Modena, of Venice, the most characteristic and most paradoxical child of the Italian Ghetto: infant prodigy and hoary prodigal; jack of twenty-six trades (which he carefully enumerates) though master of none; polemist against his own convictions and practicer against his own precept; a fortune hunter, addicted to alchemy, who lost a small competence at gambling, repeatedly condemned the vice, but was never able to tear himself away from it; leading spirit of the Ghetto musical academy and director of its performances; the innovator of the macaronic poems which made equal sense, whether much or little, whether read as Hebrew or as Italian; withal a scholar of unusual breadth though little depth, a prolific writer both in the vernacular and in the sacred tongue, and an eloquent preacher who attracted Christian clerics and even princes of the blood to hear his sermons. He was responsible for a score of volumes — sermons, responsa, letters, poems, a grammar, an autobiography, a dictionary, even a treatise on Jewish ceremonies written in Italian for presentation to King James I of England. All or nearly all are interesting, but none is really important. On the other hand, few Jewish scholars of any age, including our own, have enjoyed so great a reputation in non-Jewish circles; and his contacts with Christian savants, Italian and foreign — men like John Selden in England, the Bishop of Lodève in France — though superficial, were of some consequence. Modena's colleague in the Venetian rabbinate, Simone (Simha) Luzzatto, was apparently a man of greater originality and penetration, though not much of his writing has survived except two Italian works: one, *Socrate* (Venice, 1651), intended to demonstrate the impotence of Reason unless assisted by Revelation; and another, his *Discorso circa il stato degli ebrei* ("Discourse on the State of the Jews," 1639), examining the social and political situation of the Jews in a non-Jewish community, with special reference to Venice, which remains to the present day one of the most memorable contributions to Jewish apologetic literature and anticipated or inspired most subsequent publications of the sort. These two were survivors, on the one hand, of the inquiring Renaissance spirit, anticipators, on the other, of the nineteenth-century learned publicist. They had in this respect no successors who carried on their tradition in full measure. On the other hand, there were in the next century a few others of this type — such as Raphael Rabeni, secretary of the community of Padua, who polemized with Christian scholars about the nature of biblical poetry; or Jacob Saraval, of Mantua, who challenged anti-Jewish propagandists on their own ground. Others, moreover, wrote in Spanish or Portuguese on both Jewish and non-Jewish subjects: such as the physician Isaac Cardoso, whose works include a classical monograph in defense of Judaism and the Jews; and Roderigo (Jacob) Mendes da Silva, formerly historiographer to the court of Madrid.

The organization of talmudic study in Italy at this time was highly characteristic. It was grouped about the *Yeshibah* that existed in every major center — not, as elsewhere in the Jewish world, a place of instruction for the adolescent, but a sort of academy (by which title indeed it was known in Italian) for mature students, who came together morning and evening for study and discussion. The three foremost scholars in the group, who generally included the official rabbi, acted as the *Bet Din,* or Court, for the decision of disputes in matters of religious and, where it was allowed, civil law. It was before the *Yeshibah* that questions of importance were discussed and settled, and by its authorization that scholars would be given their rabbinical diplomas. Outstanding among those of the Ghetto period were the *Yeshibot* of Mantua, Venice, Modena, Padua, Leghorn, Ferrara, and Lugo — Rome, of course, could not figure, its intellectual life having been stricken a mortal blow by the persecution of Jewish literature; and the same applied, though not quite so fully, to Ancona. Promising students would be admitted to attend the meetings and listen to the discussions, but did not become full members until they had given proof of their ability. Some communities set aside special apartments, impressively furnished, for the purpose of these assemblies. Besides the "General Academy," or *ha-Yeshibah ha-Kelalit*, there were in most places analogous bodies, sometimes under private auspices, for specific or perhaps less advanced branches of study, so that in the age of the Ghetto every Italian Jew had access to some adult scholastic institution fitted for his abilities and tastes.

Profound rabbinic scholarship was now, to be sure, difficult to attain, in view of the fact that over so great a part of the country the mere possession of the Talmud and much of the allied literature was a penal offense. In many places only the emasculated legal compendia were accessible, so that some of the greatest savants of the age had to study, to write, and even to teach without the aid of the essential material, unless they owned it furtively or were endowed with prodigious memories. The level of achievement was in the circumstances far higher than might have been anticipated. There was a succession of talmudists who enjoyed a high reputation in their somewhat restricted circles, their published writings (largely casuistic responsa) being a treasure-house of information regarding the life of Jewish Italy: in the seventeenth century, men like Samuel Aboab, the Sephardi rabbi of Venice, the merchant-physician Samson Morpurgo of Ancona, and the lovable bibliophile Abraham Graziani of Modena; or in the eighteenth, Isaiah Bassani of Reggio, Daniel Terni of Florence, or Ishmael Cohen (Laudadio Sacerdote) of Modena, besides others who are mentioned elsewhere in these pages in a different connection. Above all, Isaac Lampronti, physician and rabbi at Ferrara, compiled a superb epitome of this activity in his gigantic rabbinic encyclopaedia, *Pahad Yitzhak*, comprising under subject-headings thousands of opinions and responsa, largely by Italian rabbis of this age. It may be described as the swan-song as well as the greatest monument of talmudic study in Italy, and is to this day an inexhaustible source of material for the legal, religious, social and literary historian.

The only place in Italy where Jewish intellectual life was completely untrammelled was Leghorn. Here, in accordance with the terms of the charter of 1597, there was no interference with Hebrew literature; and in consequence the city became a great center of learning, ultimately outstripping the older seats of culture in the Mediterranean. A printing press was established, which for a time served all the communities of North Africa and the Levant and continued to flourish down to our own day. Nowhere were scholars treated with greater respect or their voices listened to with greater deference; nowhere was there a greater number of amply-endowed academies for rabbinic learning; and from some points of view the honorific title, "the Little Jerusalem," was justly applied. Of its native scholars (it is impossible to take into account the large number of immigrants from other lands), the most distinguished was probably Malachi Cohen, author of a famous work on talmudic methodology; but there were many others whose fame fell little short of his. The seal was set on Leghorn's reputation when at the close of the eighteenth century, after many visits, the famous Palestinian cabalist, bibliophile and globe-trotter, Hayim Joseph David Azulai, whose reputation still lives among the Jewish masses of the Mediterranean, chose the city as the seat of his activity and residence of his last years.

One branch of literature only could be said to flourish universally in this age, and this was poetry, which had a tremendous vogue. To write verse was considered part of polite education and an essential qualification of a self-respecting rabbi. Every Ghetto had its poetasters, who greeted with a flood of polished rhyme any event in the life of the community and of outstanding individuals; births, marriages, deaths, betrothals, anniversaries, graduations, and so on, at first imitating and in the end outdoing the general Italian fashion in this respect. Liturgical compositions too were popular, few writers failing to try their hand at them — sometimes with considerable success. Generally speaking, the perfection of form and choiceness of diction — unique at that time in the Jewish world — was equalled only by the almost invariable vacuity of thought. In the eighteenth century, the enigmas fashionable in the outside world became common, and societies were actually established for no more fruitful purpose than their composition and solution. Vast numbers of such productions, in broadside and manuscript and miscellaneous compilations, have been preserved. But very little of it rises above, and a great deal does not even attain, mediocrity. Only a very few names can be considered really worthy of commemoration: such as, at the outset of this period, Samuel Archevolti, contemporary and friend of Leone da Modena, whose writings on Hebrew prosody had a widespread influence among Christians as well as Jews; or the anti-cabalistic brothers Frances, Jacob and Immanuel (also author of a well-known work on the same subject), whose rationalistic tendencies made it necessary for them to leave their native Mantua and settle in Florence and Leghorn respectively; or Moses Zacuto, the cabalist (born indeed in Holland, of Spanish descent), the universally respected rabbi of Mantua, whose mystical hymns attained a wide popularity and who wrote in addition one of the few Hebrew dramas of the period, depicting the fiery youth of Abraham, and a vision of the after-life in a vaguely Dantesque tradition (this was to be supplemented after his death by Jacob Daniel Olmo, of Ferrara, who added a vision of Heaven to the original one of Hell); or Samson Cohen Modon, of Mantua, renewer of the Hebrew sonnet, who won golden opinions when he was sent on a congratulatory mission to the Emperor Charles VI; or, on the threshold of the new era, the wandering Samuel

Leone da Modena

Samson Morpurgo

Romanelli, playwright as well as poet, who in addition compiled an account of his wanderings in a highly artificial style; or the brothers Isaac and Ephraim Luzzatto, the latter carrying the new fashion to London when he settled there in the middle of the eighteenth century as physician of the Spanish and Portuguese community. A mere roll of the poetasters of minor ability would occupy pages.

One figure stands head and shoulders above all the rest — Moses Hayyim Luzzatto, a kinsman of the two last-named, and son of a wealthy Paduan silk-merchant, who is one of the most important names in Jewish literature and links the poetical tradition of the Middle Ages with that of today. A cabalist, whose dreams embroiled him tragically with the authorities, he was at the same time an unusually sensitive poet, with a force of imagination and depth of thought that his contemporaries generally lacked. In his delicate hands, the mechanical Hebrew prosody so popular in Italy was revitalized and fecundated by the new tendencies that had emerged in general literature. He wrote, besides an ethical treatise, *Mesillat Yesharim*, which became enormously popular throughout the Jewish world, very many occasional poems, a book of Psalms in imitation of the Bible, and two allegorical dramas on the model of those of Guarini, which subsequent generations considered epoch-making. Enforced wanderings spread these achievements abroad, so that they had a profound influence upon the new age in Jewish literature that was beginning to gather strength independently in Germany and was to spread thereafter to Russia. He is thus regarded — though not quite fairly, in view of the long Italian tradition which he inherited — as father of modern Hebrew poetry, founder of the school which was to culminate in our day in Tchernichovsky and Bialik.

The narrowing of intellectual horizons inevitably warped the former sense of proportion in Jewish life. Trivialities now attained an importance which the intellectual giants of a previous age would have found ridiculous. Many were the petty points of talmudic law which engaged the attention of the entire Italian rabbinate, who exchanged reams of mellifluous prose and occasionally launched excommunications against the recalcitrant. In the early years of the eighteenth century, the intervention of the cardinal legate was requested in order to settle a violent dispute which had arisen in the synagogue of Ferrara over the manner of chanting the traditional priestly benediction; while in Rome, at the last stage of the Ghetto period, the whole community was divided into two warring camps for an entire generation because of a difference of opinion regarding the pronunciation of half-vowels in Hebrew, the police having to intervene to restore order. The popularity of sermons was characteristic of an age in which the employment of leisure presented so great a problem; and several eloquent preachers — Azariah Picho of Venice was one of the most prolific — set on record in the conventional Hebrew the addresses they delivered in the vernacular, lasting sometimes for as long as three hours. (The earliest sermon published in Italian, at the beginning of the eighteenth century, must have taken quite this time to read.) Characteristic, too, was the polemical literature which, though for obvious reasons never published, continued to be written in some quantity, especially after the intensification of the literary onslaught on Judaism at the beginning of the eighteenth century — defensive in Italian, by scholars such as Leon Briel of Mantua, replying to the attacks of Father Pinamonte and others, offensive in Hebrew by his pupils, Jonah Rappa and Joshua Segrè, in biting satires which passed from hand to hand in manuscript.

The fact that over a great part of the country the possession of the Talmud was now a penal offense inevitably helped to divert interest to that part of Jewish literature, still generally available, on which the Catholic Church had once looked with a certain degree of positive favor. In the sixteenth century, a new school of mystical study, based upon the idea that the individual could by his spiritual exercises, properly directed, hasten the coming of the Redeemer, had been established at Safed in Palestine by Isaac Luria and his pupil and prophet, Hayyim Vital Calabrese (whose parents had hailed from the kingdom of Naples). This soon obtained a tremendously strong hold in Italy — pre-eminently at Modena and Mantua. The passionate attention formerly devoted to philosophy on the one hand and rabbinic law on the other was henceforth turned in an increasing degree, notwithstanding the distress of some stalwart rationalists, to the study of the *Zohar*, the search for mystical elements in the Bible and the liturgy, and the repetition, sometimes quite mechanical, of esoteric texts. All the minutiae of religious observance, every letter of the liturgy, every action of daily life, became infused with a new latent significance — frequently bordering upon superstition, but often beautiful and sometimes profound. Mystical study-circles, such as had recently originated in Palestine, now spread like wildfire through the country, not even the smallest community lacking them. Prayer groups were formed for the practice of religious extravagances and austerities. Special fast days, with specially-composed liturgies, multiplied. To oppose the mystical tendencies became inadvisable, and almost dangerous. When the school of Safed began to decline, its tradition was maintained to a great extent by Italian rabbis, such as Aaron Berachiah da Modena, composer of some of the standard mystical liturgies; Menahem Azariah da Fano and Moses Zacuto of Mantua, or Benjamin Cohen Vitale of Reggio, whose names are of first importance in the history of Jewish mysticism in its later developments. All, it may be added, were at the same time prolific poets with a subtle mastery of Hebrew, writing epithalamia as well as hymns, in a manner characteristic of Italy alone.

The diversion of interest from the mental discipline of the Talmud to the speculations of the cabala, coupled with the state of misery which now sharpened their eager expectation of Deliverance, made the Italian Jews peculiarly susceptible to any wave of visionary fervor; men who rose at midnight to pray for the speedy coming of the Redeemer could not fail to be stirred when there were signs that Redemption was imminent. Hence, when Sabbatai Zevi, the messiah of Smyrna, began his meteoric career in the Levant in the middle of the seventeenth century, the Italian Ghettos were swept by a wave of expectancy. Everywhere, the news of his achievements was recounted, exaggerated, and broadcast to the furthest ends of the Jewish world in dithyrambic letters and reports. Sober merchants made ready their imminent departure for the Holy Land. The Italian courts were primed with information by their half-credulous agents in the Levant. At Leghorn, whither the impostor sent for his bride, the entire congregation was carried off its feet in a frenzy of expectation. In Venice, the venerated poet-cabalist, Moses Zacuto, took the lead, and the rabbinate sent an official missive to Constantinople asking for full details. Mahalalel Civitanova, rabbi of Ancona composed a hymn in the pretender's honor, apparently for recital in synagogue. As the poet-brothers Frances experienced, rationalists (as well as counter-claimants) were in danger of their lives.

Even when the impostor, brought before the sultan, decided that apostasy was preferable to death, being imitated by thousands of his adherents, the spell was not entirely broken. It was easier to find justification than to confess error. In many parts, some men continued to profess belief in the pusillanimous messiah, claiming that this degradation was part of his destined fate. The rabbinate, indeed, had by now come to its senses; and when Nathan of Gaza, Sabbatai's prophet and propagandist, came to Venice with the intention of conducting a missionary tour throughout the country, he was forced to sign an abjuration which was circulated everywhere before he arrived and finally discredited him — though not before he had endeavored to bring about a destructive flood at Rome by cabalistic means. At Leghorn, Sabbataism lingered on, under the auspices of visionaries like the Marrano physician Miguel Cardoso, once the darling of the ladies of Madrid; and for some time there was a Sabbatian conventicle here under his leadership, until he was driven to emigrate. Still, echoes of the craze persisted, and propagandists of the curious belief in the messiah who had apostatized — such as the wandering Palestinian, Nehemiah Hayyun, who set Ghetto after Ghetto in turmoil, even when the eighteenth century was well advanced — found a ready audience among the Italian mystics. Some eminent rabbis, like Benjamin Cohen Vitale, are believed to have remained long afterwards secret votaries of this strange vagary. Nevertheless, no drastic revulsion of feeling followed the disappointment. Thus the saintly preacher of repentance, Mordecai Eisenstadt, who in the end came to consider himself the true messiah whose way Sabbatai Zevi had been sent to prepare, found a fervid initial welcome in Modena and Reggio; though later his opponents denounced him to the Inquisition, and he thought it safer to flee. There was a further echo of the movement in 1702, when the wealthy and pious Abraham Rovigo, one of the outstanding members of the community of Modena, evaded the difficulties which had delayed his departure and, expressing messianic yearnings in the most practical fashion, led a party of like-minded mystics by way of Leghorn to settle in Palestine.

The Italian rabbinate was determined not to permit a recurrence. Moses Hayyim Luzzatto, the most gifted Hebrew poet of the age, was at the same time a votary of mystical lore, his powerful imagination carrying him to excess. About 1727 he and some of his admirers established in Padua a secret circle for the perpetual study of the *Zohar*, in the hope of hastening the Redemption. Their hopes were centered in their leader, who believed himself to be in intimate communication with Heaven, wrote new esoteric compositions for which he claimed the authority of revelation, and actually seems to have considered himself the Messiah. As the result of the indiscretion of one of the group, a Polish enthusiast who had come to Padua to study medicine, the secret came to the knowledge of those who were now endeavoring to extirpate the dangerous remnants of Sabbataism. The Venetian rabbinate now began a veritable heresy hunt, with a pertinacity which overcame the somewhat lukewarm sympathies of its colleagues in other places. Luzzatto was compelled to surrender his cabalistical treatises, and to foreswear writing in future any which purported to come from a supernatural source. But this was not enough. He was suspected of perjury, found himself pursued by suspicion and misunderstanding when he emigrated to Holland, had his writings past and future solemnly put under the ban, and died in Palestine, a young man, still suspected by the rationalists though venerated by the mystics. It was perhaps symbolic of the Italian Jewry that the writer with whom the record of modern Hebrew literature conventionally begins was in himself essentially a child of the Middle Ages, intellectually far less advanced than his predecessors of the time of the Renaissance.

XXXV

De Profundis

By the middle of the eighteenth century, the breath of Emancipation could already be felt in northern Europe. In England and Holland, not to speak of America, Jews were by now living on terms of virtual equality with their neighbors, save for certain political disabilities. Even in Germany, some elements in the Jewish population were socially emancipated. But Italy, once in the forefront of progress, was a stagnant backwater, pre-eminent only in her monuments and her music; while the Popes, formerly the most enlightened of European sovereigns, now nursed the delusion that reaction was the bulwark of religion. Their influence was potent throughout the Peninsula. There had once been no part of the world where the Jews were better treated. The rest of the world had by now begun to entertain more tolerant ideals; and there were few parts of it where at present they were treated worse.

Economically, the country was by now at its lowest level, the fabulous prosperity of the Renaissance period being a mere memory. In the Jewish communities, the distress was accentuated by the paralyzing restrictions on every activity. The growing miseries of daily life resulted in a steady emigration from the Italian Ghettos — directed above all to Leghorn and to the new centers of northern Europe, where from the seventeenth century Italian Jewish settlers were common. (So far as England is concerned, it is enough to mention the names of Montefiore and Disraeli to demonstrate the importance of the colony.) In addition, there was an uninterrupted stream of secession to Christianity, which took away, in addition to many of the feeble-minded and destitute, a number of the wealthiest and most cultured families. In some places, the decline of population was catastrophic. At Venice, it went down from nearly 5,000 in the middle of the seventeenth century (if the figures are correct) to little more than 1,500 a hundred years later; at Lugo, from 606 souls in 1629 to 242 in 1703. These figures were perhaps exceptional, but a similar shrinkage was discernible elsewhere, aggravating the economic straits of those who remained. For, while emigration increased and prosperity diminished, the financial burden on the communities, originally fixed at a time of swollen population and economic ease, remained unchanged, or by reason of the spread of pauperism even increased. In many places the decay of the textile industry in the course of the eighteenth century hastened the disaster. It was in vain that attempts were made by the rabbis and *gastaldi* to enforce the payment of taxation by emigrants or to extract a lump sum from them previous to their departure, on the grounds that they could not renounce responsibility for the general indebtedness of the community to which they and their fathers had belonged; this resulted in long-protracted squabbles and arguments, but little more.

To meet the most pressing demands, annuities were arranged or money borrowed even from Christians — sometimes from religious bodies — at high rates of interest. This could only bring a temporary alleviation, and in the long run increased the burden of debt. The governments refused to take the obvious and humane step of reducing the weight of taxation to reasonable proportions, calculated with reference to present conditions rather than past memories. In the end, the only possible recourse was that followed by individuals or firms in the same position — bankruptcy. The Roman community for example owed by 1668 over 250,000 scudi — 166,000 being funded in the form of a debt to the *Monte di Pietà*, and some thousands more on commercial paper to individual creditors, for the most part non-Jews. The prohibition of loan-banking in the Papal States in 1682 proved a serious blow to the general stability, and the results soon became apparent. In 1698, after successive Congregations of Cardinals had made investigations and various palliatives had been attempted — including the reduction of the Ghetto rents by 12 per cent, payable henceforth instead by way of taxation — the community was forbidden to contract any further debts except by special license, the first step towards legal bankruptcy, which ensued when in 1755 the Jewish community was included in the list of those who could not be expected to satisfy their creditors. Similarly, in 1735 the community of Venice was declared bankrupt, in 1761 that of Padua, and about the same time that of Rovigo, the financial systems being reorganized so that whatever means the Jews still possessed should be exploited to the public advantage. The pathetic spectacle was now presented of the ancient Venetian Jewry raising a quasi-charitable loan from coreligionists in northern Europe, yet being unable in the end to repay. The extremity of the crisis can be realized from the fact that this community and several others, including Finale and even Ferrara, petitioned the government at this time to exclude poor strangers, as they were unable to face the prospect of any addition to the eleemosynary burden.

In these years, moreover, as though to celebrate its ruler's assumption of the royal title, the Ghetto system was at length universally enforced in Piedmont, the new "Constitutions" of 1729 ordering a special quarter to be set up for the Jews in all those cities where they were tolerated, and those living elsewhere to transfer themselves thither within twelve months. The usual agonies of compulsory translocation followed, several little communities being broken up now; the members of that of Cuorgnè, for example, transferred themselves in a body to Turin, where henceforth there was a new little synagogue which perpetuated their traditional *Ashkenazi* rite. A short while after, the system was introduced into the newly-acquired provinces of the Monferrat, where annexation to Piedmont at the beginning of the eighteenth century made a distinct change for the worse; here we know how the handful of Jews at S. Salvatore had to crowd, in 1737, into the Casale Ghetto, and those of Monastero into that of Acqui.

The assault on Judaism was meanwhile intensified, the protagonist now being the apostate Paolo Medici, a Livornese Jew who had embraced Christianity at the age of sixteen (not by any means the only apostate who took the name of a ruling house and whose descendants may today boast an august ancestry) and henceforth venomously attacked his former coreligionists. His first sermons, delivered at Borgo S. Sepolcro in Tuscany for two years in succession, were so violent as to make it necessary for the tiny group established there to appeal to the grand duke for protection. In 1697 he published a brochure in which he unblushingly renewed the charge of ritual murder. Despite protests at Florence and at Rome, he was not silenced. For some forty years or more he continued to go about Italy, preaching, writing and working in the same sense — by no means fruitlessly, his greatest triumph being the conversion, after long endeavors, of an authentic Ferrara rabbi, one of Moses Hayyim Luzzatto's most able followers, with all his family. Numerous other apostates of the period, pre-eminent among whom was one Niccolò Stratta, seconded his efforts. Tranquillo Vita Corcos, at first physician to the Roman community and from 1702 to 1730 its rabbi, was as capable a figure as Italian Jewry had ever known; but he had to devote a great part of his energy to the thankless and sometimes dangerous task of protecting his flock from calumny. In the second half of the century, with the spread of rationalism, the old religious prejudices began to be presented in a new form, in such works as the *Dissertation upon the Religion and Oath of the Jews,* attributed to the lawyer G. B. Benedetti of Ferrara, and courageously answered by Rabbi Jacob Saraval; or *The Influence of the Ghetto in the State* by the eminent Mantuan political economist, Giambattista Gherardo d'Arco, which provoked a reasoned reply by the young Jewish physician, Benedetto Frizzi (who was later on to found the first Italian medical periodical), throwing a great deal of light on the economic conditions of Italian Jewry in his day.

All the old abuses and excesses meanwhile continued unabated or even intensified. Their neighbors, not realizing the degree of penury that prevailed in the Ghetto, considered that the general economic distress was due to their competition, and in the narrowest mercantilistic spirit imagined that the remedy lay in extruding them even more strictly from ordinary activities. In the States of the Church especially, under Popes Benedict XIII (1724-30) and Clement XIII (1730-1739), a renewed severity began to be shown. During the latter's pontificate, in 1733, Cardinal Petra drew up, after detailed study, a new anti-Jewish code of regulations in elaborate detail. Not only were the old restrictions renewed or codified, but various novelties were introduced — for example, that the Jewish badge was to be worn even when travelling and that rabbis were not to be allowed any distinguishing dress, like ordinary clergy. It was henceforth difficult for Jews even to have their linen washed by Christians — in any case, only if it were taken to their houses by specially licensed porters, the purity of whose faith was above question. In 1746, under Benedict XIV, this code was renewed. One day during Passover in 1755, the Inquisition of Ferrara demanded the keys of the burial-ground and had all the tombstones broken to fragments, sternly forbidding others to be set up in future. In 1766, the Roman rabbis were imprisoned because they were unable to help in discovering the whereabouts of a Jew who was wanted by the police, while eight years later the *fattori* were actually tortured on a similar occasion.

The persecution of Hebrew literature continued unabated, being given renewed ardor in the middle of the century through the zeal of Giovanni Antonio Costanzi, copyist in the Vatican library. New edicts were frequently issued relating to this, and from 1731 onwards wholesale confiscations succeeded one another. One night in 1753, after the gates of the Roman Ghetto were closed, a house-to-house examination was made by the police accompanied by notaries, and thirty-eight carloads of "forbidden" volumes — including books of psalms and liturgies for synagogal use — were seized and removed, many being subsequently destroyed. Another perquisition took place in the following year, and the work was completed in 1755 by an edict entirely prohibiting Hebrew books, with certain exceptions.

The same policy was, of course, followed in the lesser cities under the rule of the Holy See, as well as in some other parts of Italy. At Mantua, the eminent Rabbi Solomon Basilea, an encyclopaedic scholar with an amazing range of secular knowledge, who had defended Judaism against the assaults of the conversionist Benetelli in a work circulated in manuscript, was arrested on a charge of having in his possession some Hebrew books in which the expurgated passages had been restored. After being kept in prison for many months, he was released owing to ill health, but later on was confined first to his house and then to the Ghetto for three more years. When a Roman Jew of exceptional intellectual range, named Sabato Ambron, published in 1710 a criticism of current astronomical theory, without any immediate theological application, it was confiscated and suppressed by the Holy Office; and the same happened in 1758 to one of the fashionable collections of poems produced in Ancona in celebration of a Jewish marriage.

The middle years of the eighteenth century witnessed an extraordinary series of disturbances all over Italy, caused in an eminently Italian fashion by a popular ballad. In 1752, a scurrilous song was published under the title *Gnora* Luna*, describing with a wealth of grotesque detail a mishap which was alleged to have attended a recent Jewish wedding. The author, according to one account, was a blind Florentine nicknamed "Dirty Mug," or *becco sudicio*; according to another, a spiteful apostate, or else a young debtor desirous of avenging himself on a Jew who had thrown him into jail. Set to a catchy tune, "The Minuet of the King of Sardinia" (afterwards elaborated on by Paganini), it became amazingly popular. It was to be heard in every street and alley, was chanted by an attendant rabble at the heels of any red- or yellow-hatted Jew who passed, was bawled in chorus at the entrances to the Ghetto or under the windows of

---

* = Signora.

the Jewish houses, and in place after place led in the end to serious commotions. At Mantua, in July, 1754, the arrest of one of a crowd of apprentices who were besetting the Ghetto to the familiar strains resulted in such an outbreak of violence that it was found necessary to call out the military. In the following September, when the authorities at Ferrara tried to suppress similar disorders, veritable riots followed and the cardinal legate himself was menaced. In Alessandria, the governor treated the matter over-seriously, posting pickets at the first sign of trouble and forbidding the ballad to be sung under severe penalties — with no result, however, except to bring himself into ridicule, and ultimately into trouble. In many other places, similar scenes took place; and the song, which proved to be the forerunner of an entire cycle on the same scabrous topic, continued to cause minor unpleasantness well on into the nineteenth century. But it was not the only occasion for disturbance. Even at Leghorn the populace was less friendly than it had formerly been, and there was a dangerous outburst of feeling in 1751, on the pretext, completely unfounded, that a Jew had discharged a musket at a house in which two women were being instructed in the rudiments of Christianity, and another in 1765. Similarly, there were disturbances at Verona in 1745 (we know no details) and in 1753, when the community was plunged in grief on the occasion of the funeral of a much-loved rabbi. In Rome, the artificially stimulated feeling against the Jews reached such a pitch that it was sometimes physically dangerous for them to venture unaccompanied into remote quarters of the town, as more than one mutilated or blinded Ghetto mendicant knew only too well.

Pope Clement XIV (1769–1774), who had been responsible as Cardinal Ganganelli for the famous report condemning the ritual murder libel, was deeply impressed by the misery into which the Jewish communities of the Papal States had fallen, and wished to do something to improve their economic position. Among other reforms he accorded them a certain degree of liberty of occupation and freed them from the immediate jurisdiction of the Inquisition; while he showed marked favor to the Roman Jewish leader, Alessandro Ambron. But this proved only a very brief interlude. In 1775 Pius VI became Pope. Faced with the gravest of problems all over Europe, he seems to have felt that liberalism in the observance and interpretation of the laws against the Jews was the most pressing of all. Within a few months of his accession, he issued a systematic *Editto sopra gli ebrei* summarizing in forty-four clauses, one more degrading than the other, all the persecutory measures of his predecessors. It was forbidden for Jews to pass the night outside the Ghetto under pain of death. They were not to possess, buy, copy, translate, sell, or otherwise dispose of any codex or book on the Talmud, or any volume containing statements against the mysteries of the Christian faith. They were not to utter forecasts or to teach anything regarding the occult. Christian silversmiths were forbidden to make them amulets or charms, or to fashion them seven-branched candelabra for religious use. On the occasion of a funeral, they might light candles and practice the traditional rites in synagogue, but no public cortège was to be allowed. The distinguishing yellow badge was to be worn by men and women alike, both inside the Ghetto and outside. They were not to sell or distribute meat, bread or milk to Christians. They were not to have shops or lodging houses outside the Ghetto, whether in their own name or otherwise. Jews might not invite Christians into their synagogues, nor Christians enter them. They might not avail themselves of the services of their neighbors as servants, nurses or midwives, or even to light their fires on the Sabbath. They were not to enter into familiar relations with them, whether in private houses or public resorts. They were not to drive in a carriage in Rome or its environs, nor to wear any sort of clerical garb. The rabbis were to be responsible for the attendance of their flock at the periodical conversionist sermons. No Jew — not even the old-clothes dealers — might enter a church or monastery, or approach within thirty ells of the House of Catechumens. In this appalling code, which has been termed one of the most inhuman acts in the history of man, the whole of the old abominable system was given fresh life, serving as an inspiration to reactionaries everywhere.

The ten-yearly *condotta* of the Jews of the Venetian territories was about to expire. For many years past, its renewal had been little more than a formality. Now, fresh restrictions were proposed, inspired partly by narrow economic theories and partly by theological obscurantism, and were embodied without exception in the *ricondotta* of 1777. The Jews throughout the territories of the *Serenissima* were forbidden to engage in any sort of manufacture, to employ Christian hands, or to deal in grain or foodstuffs. They were no longer to hold any agencies, to act as brokers, to hold any government agency, or to occupy any post whatsoever in connection with the administration of finance, including state monopolies. Save for the handful of wholesalers engaged in foreign trade, they were to be restricted henceforth to dealing in rags and second-hand goods. Manufacture of any sort would be permitted only by special license. Long-neglected ecclesiastical regulations were reiterated. No Jews were to be allowed to live in any place which did not have a Ghetto for their accommodation. The status of the communities of the region was thrown back by generations. The proposals were greeted with general consternation. In more than one place, the municipal councils protested; some leaders of opinion at Venice actually maintained that the amendments, besides being inadvisable, were unconstitutional. The Jews decreed public fasts, and implored the rabbis of the Holy Land to pray on their behalf at the Temple site. But all opposition was overcome in the end, after an interlude of uncertainty during which the reactionaries threatened to set fire to the Ghetto if they were thwarted. The new code was immediately put into force, with tragic results. In Padua, for example, though they continued to offer stout resistance and to avail themselves of every loophole for evasion, the Jews were driven out of the silk-industry, for the introduction and development of which they had been responsible. At Verona, the prosperity of the community was affected to such an extent that in the following year barely one-sixth of the offerings necessary for the upkeep of the synagogue were forthcoming. Meanwhile instructions were issued, "in the name of order and good governance," for the Jews to be driven out of the places without a Ghetto, this being carried into effect forthwith in little places all over the Venetian dominions — Montagnana, Conselve, and Cittadella in the Paduan region, Spilimbergo and S. Daniele in Friuli — where communities had long existed. A number of refugees from the latter area were permitted to establish themselves under Austrian rule in Trieste and Gorizia, where the Jewish settlement thus received a considerable impetus. The next Venetian *condotta*, of 1788, proved to be somewhat milder than that of 1777, but the damage done during the past decade was never remedied.

In other parts of Upper Italy, the atmosphere was now similar. Thus, as late as 1737, the Jews were expelled from Genoa, though not indeed for long. In the duchy of Modena, where the *capitoli* governing the Jewish communities were renewed in 1750 for fifty years, instead of ten as hitherto, the Jewish loan-banks were suppressed in 1767, on the foundation of a *Monte di Pietà*; and a Ghetto was at last established at Finale in 1736. That same year, an attempt had been made also to introduce the institution to Correggio, which was repeated in 1770; this, too, proving unsuccessful, the civic authorities consoled themselves by forbidding the Jews to carry walking-sticks and canes, though in the end they had to withdraw this ridiculous order. The twenty-three clauses devoted to the Jews in the new code of laws issued for the duchy in 1771, though somewhat more liberal in economic matters, repeated almost without exception all the old obligations regarding the Ghetto, the Ghetto system and the Jewish badge; and it was regarded as a great concession that after 1780 the notaries were permitted to style Jewish merchants in official documents as "signor." Nine years later, fresh restrictions were imposed here on the acquisition of real estate. In 1758, the Jews of Busseto and the other little communities of the duchy of Parma were menaced with expulsion by the new Bourbon duke (who had characteristically begun his reign in 1749 by forbidding them access to his capital for more than twenty-four hours at a time) unless they trebled their former tribute or produced 600,000 ducats. In the kingdom of Sardinia (Piedmont), the collection of special legislation relating to the Jews published in 1744 filled a substantial folio volume; and the new *Laws and Constitutions* for the kingdom issued in 1770 renewed the obligation to live in Ghettos and to observe all the rest of the repressive network of regulations, not overlooking the old prohibition to enlarge synagogues. So rigorously was the code applied that even under the threat of emigration some of the wealthiest merchants of Turin were unable to obtain permission to set up house immediately outside the Ghetto area. In 1780, the Nice community was deprived of its cemetery on the demand of a monastery in the immediate vicinity which wished to enlarge its accommodation. At Acqui, as late as 1789, the Jews were forbidden to appear in public on Christian feast days, on the somewhat disingenuous pretext that their debtors, here considered to be exceptionally numerous, might thereby be discouraged from attending church.

As far as the Papal States were concerned, the code of 1775 was brutally enforced, in every detail, in a fashion which would have shocked the Pontiffs of the Middle Ages and Renaissance. The economic distress increased from day to day, some of the business houses who had long been the mainstay of their coreligionists now being reduced to ruin. In 1785, the inquisitor general of Ancona, in a characteristic pronouncement, forbade Jews, "by virtue of his habitual clemency," to take dancing or music lessons from Gentiles or to employ Christian servants. Forced baptisms and similar abuses continued, some of the worst instances dating from this period. The climax was reached one night in 1783, when the authorities demanded the immediate surrender of two orphan children living with their grandmother in the Roman Ghetto, at the request of a very distant relative of part-Jewish blood, so that they might be brought up as Christians. While the leaders of the community expostulated against this unprecedented abuse, the opportunity was taken to smuggle the children into hiding. The *sbirri* now began to seize as hostages all the infants they could lay their hands on, and it seemed as though scores would be sacrificed for the sake of two. Nothing was left but to give the unfortunate orphans up to their fate, but the next day an armed force entered the Ghetto and arrested sixty of the ringleaders of the night before, who were dragged off to prison. This episode could not be allowed to pass without protest. In view of the great number of conversions in Rome during the past few generations, however induced, there was hardly a person in the Ghetto who did not have some relative who professed Christianity, and if this precedent were followed no man could consider his children safe. A lengthy petition was presented to the Pope imploring for some measure of restraint and regularity in this matter henceforth, and at the same time pointing out the intolerable condition of the Jews in other respects — the insanitary and exiguous area allotted to them, the deadly prohibition to engage in any liberal calling, the crushing weight of taxation, their material and moral degradation. Although a commission of inquiry was appointed and a courageous memorandum presented to it by twelve friendly Christian advocates, nothing ensued, and the leaders of the community frenziedly canvassed the prospects of organizing wholesale emigration to England or some other less bigoted land.

By now, the process of impoverishment and pauperization had made terrible strides all over Italy. In Rome, before the degradation had touched its depths, it was reckoned that no more than 200 persons out of some 4,500 were even well-to-do, while only five could be described as wealthy. The annual proceeds of the property tax fell, between 1696 and 1720, from 11,000 to 6,000 scudi, and by the end of the century hardly exceeded 2,000. In Mantua the number of synagogues was reduced from nine to six. At Venice, out of a total Ghetto population of about 1,500, there were only 457 males of productive age, between 14 and 60. In Verona, the number of indigent households increased between 1700 and 1768 from 24 to 81. In Pesaro, where the Jewish population was now reduced to 73 families, one person in ten was wholly dependent on charity, and nearly one-third of the communal income was spent on poor relief. In Ancona, which because of the trade with the Levant was considered relatively prosperous, nearly one-half of the community received public support in one form or another. It has been computed that in the country as a whole the ratio of Jews had declined in the course of the century from 0.263 per cent to 0.177 per cent.

Many of the Italian Ghettos were now places of sheer misery. Typical was the description by a compassionate Catholic priest of conditions at Urbino in 1717:

There was a time when the Jews of Urbino derived their sustenance from banking-business and commerce. Now, they are in a calamitous condition. Just as it is said of this people that they are dispersed throughout the world without priesthood, without temple, without sacrifices and without monarchy, so it may be justly added of those of Urbino that they are without bread, so great is the penury and the beggary in which they live.

The picture painted of affairs at Rovigo in 1752 by the Podestà of the city, in an official report to the central government at Venice, was little less depressing:

The shopkeepers among those of this nation number fourteen. There are only two general shops, badly provided. All the rest are reduced to dealing in miserable rags, with the exception of two which sell food, but of little or no significance. The rest of this people have to live by the most restricted occupations, which provide (though badly) for only a few of them, so that the rest are reduced to being a burden on the community, which supports them by alms.

Similar conditions prevailed in other Italian cities, with a very few exceptions, the most important being Leghorn. It was obvious that such a state of affairs could not continue indefinitely.

In other respects, too, the influence of the Ghetto on Italian Jewry had become apparent. One tends to judge it too much from its formative period, when the tradition of an ampler and freer life was still strong, and before the policy of exclusion had become absolutely effective. In its later stages Ghetto life was more restricted, more monotonous and more dreary. The circle of human interests was intolerably confined. Life became indescribably petty, as Ghetto memoirs of the period exemplify this only too plainly. There was a superlative degree of inbreeding — physical, social and mental. The results were tragically obvious. Physically, the type of the Jew had degenerated. He had lost inches off his stature; he had acquired a perpetual stoop; he had become timorous, and in some cases neurotic. Degrading occupations had become second nature, hard to throw off. Pauperization had increased beyond all bounds, and the systematic blocking of opportunity made recovery almost impossible. Emigration had reached a disastrous level, those who were least able to fight the battle of existence being left behind as a burden on their coreligionists. Superstitions were on the increase, having in many cases acquired a semi-religious sanction. After two centuries of Ghetto life, the repression of Italian Jewry — intellectual and physical, but not moral — was far advanced.

CHAPTER IX

The Breaking of the Bonds

xxxvi

Revolution and Napoleon

NOTWITHSTANDING the general gloom, there could be discerned here and there in Italy, in the second half of the eighteenth century, faint signs of the new era that had already dawned beyond the Alps. In 1752, intolerant Genoa readmitted the Jews, this time without imposing the Ghetto system, in the hope that they might relieve the economic stagnation into which she had fallen since the rise of Leghorn; though no more than a handful took advantage of the invitation. In Piedmont, textile manufacturers were empowered to open their establishments, though not to reside, outside the Ghettos. In the Venetian dominions, the Jewish badge had fallen into desuetude, though some preposterous individuals continued to wear it out of sheer conservatism. In Nice, the obligation was formally abolished in 1750, with a few other restrictions, in return for a douceur of 7,500 lire; and elsewhere, too, persons who could afford to pay were exempted from it with increasing frequency. Here and there in the duchies — especially in that of Parma — Jews had timidly begun to acquire land and interest themselves in farming. In some places, gifted individuals had established something of a position at court or in the world of affairs. At Reggio, for example, Moses Benjamin Foà, one of the great booksellers of his age — whose Hebrew manuscripts were subsequently added to the famous collection at Parma — was exceptionally favored by the duke and made tyrant of the Jewish community. Moses Vita Coen, a wholesale merchant of Ferrara, saved the Papal States from famine in 1764 at a grave financial loss by large-scale importation of corn, and had his services amply recognized by the cardinal legate, who went so far as to address him in his letter of thanks, in contravention of all the regulations, as "illustrious sir." In intellectual life, there were belated echoes of the friendly intercourse interrupted two hundred years earlier. Joseph Athias, of Leghorn, inheriting the enlightened Spanish as well as the older Italian tradition, was in correspondence with the bibliophile Magliabecchi, the scientist Vico and the historian Muratori; and his rich library, in the palace in the center of the city which still goes by his name, was the meeting-place of the local savants and distinguished visitors. Here, too, was the home of Abraham Isaac Castello, preacher and cantor in the local synagogue, who conversed on equal terms with Lessing and was considered by the duke of Brunswick to be a purer metaphysician than Mendelssohn. The tradition of composition in the vernacular never died out among the Italian Jews, but the fame of no previous writer equalled that of the draper-poet Salamone Fiorentino, of Monte San Savino near Sienna, whose admirers actually compared him, *mirabile dictu*, with Petrarch, and who was appointed Court Poet by the Grand Duke Ferdinand III. Contemporaneously with him, Lorenzo da Ponte (who had been baptized, indeed, in childhood) was associated as Mozart's librettist with some of the most exquisite imaginative productions of the age.

In 1781, the Emperor Joseph II of Austria, greatest of the enlightened despots, issued his famous *Toleranzpatent*, laying down the principle that the Jews should be encouraged to share in the life of their neighbors and that with this object in view the restrictions on them should gradually be abolished. The results, north of the Alps, were by no means as great as had been anticipated in the first moments of enthusiasm — in part because it was suspected that the emperor desired to break down religious as well as social separatism. But considerable areas of Italy, too, were now under Austrian rule — Trieste with its hinterland (including Gorizia and the tiny center of Gradisca d'Isonzo) and since 1708 the duchy of Mantua with its ring of minor communities. Here, too, the new imperial laws applied. Indeed, during the previous seventeen years, since the emperor had been associated in the government with his mother as co-regent, minor reforms had been introduced one after the other, so that the duchy had been in a way a testing-place for the later comprehensive measure. Thus in 1765, the office of *comissario degli ebrei*, which kept the Jews under a separate regime, was abolished; after 1772, they were empowered for the first time to borrow money at the public *Monte di Pietà*; while by a new code issued in 1779, which abolished the authority of the Inquisition, they were permitted to acquire real estate, to engage in arts and manufactures even outside the Ghetto, to deal in foodstuffs, to practice as physicians, and to frequent the public academies for training. At the same time, the responsibility of the Jewish community for the delinquencies of individuals belonging to it was abolished.

In Trieste, which was by now a center of some importance, conditions improved similarly. After 1738, the wearing of the Jewish badge began to be neglected; from 1753, some of the wealthier members of the community were allowed to live outside the Ghetto; and when Venetian obscurantism drove the Jews out of the smaller centers of Friuli in 1778, Austrian tolerance admitted them. Thus the *Toleranzpatent*, with its patronizingly benevolent spirit and its elaborate minor concessions — the abolition of ecclesiastical restrictions, encouragement to take up handicraft and agriculture and to engage in commerce on a larger scale, admission to educational institutions — did little more than codify and regularize the position that already prevailed in the Austrian possessions in Italy. It was none the less welcome for this reason to the Jews, and no more so to their enemies. If in Gorizia the Prince Archbishop would not allow the parish priests to read it to their congregants until he was compelled to, in Gradisca it was greeted dithyrambically in a public address by Elia Morpurgo, the head of the community, in which he extolled the liberality of the house of Austria and expatiated on the intellectual progress lately made by the Jews. Five years later there was a further advance, even more remarkable for those days, a fresh imperial edict ordering that two Jews should always be included among the members of the commercial tribunal. In Italy there did not seem to be anything objectionable in the much-criticized attempt made in Germany, under the auspices of Moses Mendelssohn and Naphtali Hart Wessely, to establish a reformed educational system in accordance with occidental conceptions, though indeed this was hardly a novelty there. There was accordingly no land in which the latter's proposals received so cordial a reception; and the new school, opened almost immediately afterwards at Trieste, did something to put his ideas into practice. In 1785, the gates of the Ghetto here were destroyed, though some of the more conservative and more timorous among the former population raised objections; however, the city and its Jewish community were so rapidly increasing in importance that the retention of such a relic of barbarism was now against public policy. A deputation of the Jews of Mantua which waited after his accession in 1790 upon the Emperor Leopold, Joseph's brother and successor, succeeded in having their "General Tolerance" made permanent — previously it had to be periodically renewed, the community having thus no real security of tenure. It was his intention, the monarch declared on this occasion, to place the Jews on a footing of equality with his other subjects, so far as was compatible with the general welfare.

The Austrian influence was strong also in Tuscany, which Leopold ruled as grand duke from 1765 to 1790. Here also, therefore, the spirit of the new enlightened despotism made itself felt. The beginnings were trivial; in 1767, for example, the Jews were graciously permitted to keep their shops open on Catholic feast days, while in Florence the grand duke succeeded, though not without difficulty, in procuring their admission to the fashionable literary society, the *Academia dei Faticanti*. The first really important reform came in 1778, when Jews were authorized to become members of the newly established municipal councils, an official representative of the community being included in that of Leghorn — the first time that any such privilege had been enjoyed in Italy since the downfall of the Roman Empire. In the duchy of Parma and Piacenza, the Jews were allowed after 1783 to own real estate and were exempted from special taxation; in Modena, the regulations of 1780, among the maze of intolerant restrictions, permitted them to frequent the public schools for medical instruction and to engage in any occupation they pleased. Towards the end of the century, proposals were made to introduce similar reforms into Piedmont, in the interests of the population as a whole; and in 1790 a civil servant named Bissati prepared an enlightened memorandum on the subject, though without any practical result. In the Papal States and in some other areas of Italy, the darkness was unrelieved; elsewhere, an expert eye could have seen signs of approaching dawn.

Yet the mild reforms attempted were too much for public opinion, in some parts at least; and when the news of the French Revolution and its excesses arrived, the hands of the reactionaries were strengthened. After the Grand Duke Leopold went to Austria in 1790 to succeed his brother as emperor, Tuscany was ruled for a time by a Council of Regency. It proved so weak and so incompetent that, before long, riots broke out in place after place, ostensibly caused by the former ruler's attempt to curb the influence and wealth of the clergy, but with a pronounced anti-Jewish tendency. At Leghorn, a Jew had imprudently purchased some material from one of the sequestered churches, and its marbles were reported to have been used in decorating the synagogue. Hence the "Insurrection of Santa Giulia," which began on the feast day of the patron saint of the town, at the end of May, developed into an incipient pogrom. The Jewish quarter was assailed by a crowd of dock-laborers and longshoremen, the synagogue stoned, and one hundred and fifty coaches crowded with refugees left the town. It was not until after three days of rioting, a little bloodshed, and considerable expenditure of money that order was restored. When the news reached Florence, the example was followed, and a massacre was averted only by the courage of the Archbishop Antonio Martini, who threw himself in the pathway of the rioters and said that they would enter the Ghetto only over his dead body. In the States of the Church, no similar pretext for disorder was available. Nevertheless, after the assassination of the representative of the French Republic in Rome in January 1793, the mob demonstrated its anti-revolutionary fervor by assailing the Ghetto. Although the military were called out to restore order, logs were piled around one of the gates with the intention of burning it down and so forcing an entrance. A providential downpour damped both the fire and the enthusiasm, but nevertheless acute danger continued for the next eight days. To calm popular feeling the authorities promised to restore strictly all the old anti-Jewish regulations. The *Editto sopra gli ebrei* of 1775 was again put into force — not only here, but in the diocese of Ancona as well; and, while armies were massing and thrones trembling throughout Europe, the papal government devoted its attention to arrangements for sealing the Ghetto windows which looked outwards (of course at the expense of the victims, those who argued being arrested) and the delicate task of choosing between half a dozen samples in order to decide the exact shade of the badge of shame. Later on, the rabbi and *fattori*, with other prominent members of the community, were arrested because of a rumor that a tricolor cockade had been found in the possession of a Jewish dealer, and there were renewed disorders when the news of the execution of Louis XVI reached the city.

But popular violence and reactionary legislation were insufficient to stem the onsweeping tide of Revolution. In September 1791, the Rights of Man had been somewhat tardily extended, as logic demanded, to the Jews of France, and they were now in every respect equal before the law to their fellow citizens. Five years later, the French forces invaded Italy, bringing with them revolutionary ideas more explosive than gunpowder and more deadly as weapons than their inadequate cannon. Human equality was the principal among them — no longer a theory, but a dogma, held all the more passionately since it implied a blow at ecclesiastical omnipotence. Hence, in every place entered by the invading armies, one of their first actions was to abolish religious disabilities, to destroy the Ghetto gates and to summon the Jews out into the open air to enjoy the rights of free men. It was thus inevitable that the latter, on their side, enthusiastically embraced republican doctrines, called themselves by the title of "citizen" instead of the contemptuous "Jew," eagerly entered the new Civic Guards which were established, and sought election to the new Municipal Councils; and it was inevitable no less that, suspect as they were, they suffered at the hands of the reactionaries and the ever-volatile mob when the French were expected or were temporarily forced to withdraw. As a matter of fact, the matter was not quite as simple from their point of view as their enemies thought. The more pious deeply distrusted, at least at the beginning, the anti-religious tendencies of the Revolution, no less than the Catholic priesthood did; and the wealthy had reason to dread as much as any other men their novel methods of supporting war by levies on the country, as a result of which the Jewish communities were mulcted relentlessly by their deliverers. Indeed, some of the Italian revolutionary leaders, such as the Piedmontese

"Citizen Ranza" and the Jacobin journalist Giuseppe Latanzi, suggested that the war should be financed by taxes on the nobility, clergy and Jews, thus placing the last in the same category as their inveterate enemies.

It was in 1792 that the armies of the French Republic entered Nice, the first Italian town to be occupied, and in a contemporary's phrase "the walls of the Ghetto began to dance." It was a strange liberty that the Jews were summoned to enjoy, for the town was incorporated outright into France, and later on the laws establishing the cult of the Goddess of Reason, and forbidding public religious manifestations, were enforced there. A number of Jews were in fact arraigned for erecting the traditional booths on the Feast of Tabernacles, as the commissaries of the police discovered on surveying the town from the clock-tower of an adjacent monastery. This sort of extravagance was not, however, indulged in elsewhere in Italy, into which a young general, named Bonaparte, led his troops in the spring of 1796. While a detachment was setting siege to the ancient fortress of Fossano — the seat of one of the three communities in Piedmont following the ancient "French Rite" of prayers — the reactionary elements sacked the Ghetto, the Jews cooped up in their synagogue being saved only by the providential bursting of a shell between them and their assailants; and almost on the same day those of Savigliano had a somewhat similar escape. The French victory was speedy and sweeping. After only a fortnight's campaign, the king of Sardinia was compelled to conclude a peace treaty which saved his possessions for a little while, though in a more democratic atmosphere of which the Jews were able to enjoy the benefits. Their experiences must have been enough to determine their attitude to the invaders, if it was ever in doubt. In Fossano, Abraham Senigallia became the foremost republican orator; while, when the French troops entered Acqui after the Battle of Montenotte, the young Abraham Azariah (Bonaiut) Ottolenghi (later rabbi of the place, and destined to witness a succession of kaleidoscopic political changes in his long life) threw himself into the revolutionary cause and delivered a public address on the significance of the Tree of Liberty, which was erected here as everywhere else as a symbol of the new era. In another city, a Catholic priest actually made his appearance in the synagogue and in a public speech congratulated the Jews on their deliverance.

Meanwhile, Napoleon pushed on against the Austrians, whose catastrophic defeat at the Bridge of Lodi sealed the fate of the princelings of northern Italy. In the summer, the Este duke was chased out of Modena, and a democratic regime set up; but it was not until the French occupation of the duchy in the autumn and its incorporation in the Cispadane (later Cisalpine) republic that Jewish disabilities were formally abolished, this being the first part of Italy in which emancipation became effective. A proclamation of the new government enunciated that "every man is born and remains free, and should fully enjoy all rights. The Jews are citizens, and must be recognized as such in society;" and they were invited to send their delegates to the constituent assembly that was about to be held. On their side, they feared (with justification, as events were to show) the possibility of repercussions, and proved timorous about entering into enjoyment of their new privileges. Though their special tribute was suspended, they preferred to waive the honor of serving in the new National Guard. For a while the Ghetto gates remained, at Reggio at least being closed as before every night, but at length some of the republican extremists took matters into their own hands and removed these symbols of slavery. On February 2, 1797, after the Austrian defeat at Rivoli, Mantua surrendered after a six-months' siege; and the Ghetto gates here, too, were torn down by the republican mob.

Napoleon now prepared to sweep upon Rome, and the Romagna was occupied before the terrified Pope had time to sue for peace. When, on June 23, General Robert marched into Ferrara, the Jewish delegation which waited on him was instructed to see that the Jews stopped wearing their badge of shame forthwith and that the gates of the Ghetto were kept open at night for the general convenience. Shortly after, on the evening of June 25, those of Cento formally discarded the *sciamanno*, amid the jubilation of their neighbors. At Lugo, the same happened, though the Jews had suffered considerably when the city was sacked by its captors. The changes were given legal sanction when, on September 2, Citizen Saliceti, commissary of the French Directorate with the Army of Italy, issued a decree to the effect that the Jews were to enjoy the same rights as all other citizens, and ordered the military authorities to see that this was carried into effect forthwith. When in November the Civic Guard was organized in Ferrara, Jews were included in it, and in the following month sent their delegates to the Constituent Assembly which organized the Cispadane republic; but it was only in the following spring that orders were issued for the removal of the Ghetto gates. Since the local authorities did not hurry themselves about this, a hundred soldiers of the Civic Guard marched fully armed to the Ghetto of Cento on the night of April 30, 1797, assured the terrified Jews who looked out of their windows that no harm was intended, removed the three gates and carried them off to the Piazza, where they were burned amid cheers for liberty. On receiving the report the general in command at Ferrara replied that he could only approve of what had been done, as no barriers should exist between citizens on account of their religious opinions. The pace of the changes was nevertheless over-rapid, the population not being prepared for such a complete reversal. More than one pamphlet was published attacking the Jews in the old style. When, in February, 1797, a service had been held in the Cathedral of Ferrara to celebrate the fall of Mantua, the presence of one or two Jews who omitted to uncover their heads led to such an explosion of feeling that it was found necessary to call out the military and post artillery for the protection of the Jewish quarter, and to exclude the Jews temporarily from the Civic Guard. But the episode was soon forgotten, the Guard including before long nine Jewish officers and the municipality four Jewish members.

In Ancona, there had been continuous friction since the beginning of 1793, when a plot had been discovered to set fire to the Ghetto on the pretext that a Jewish merchant had removed an image of the Madonna — with the permission of the ecclesiastical authorities, as a matter of fact — from the site of a new warehouse. A contemporary tells us plaintively of the quandary in which the Jews now found themselves when they went about the town on business: if they wore the Jewish badge they would be assaulted, and if they did not, they were liable to imprisonment. Early in 1797 the war approached the city, and their danger increased; for they were alleged to be engaged in a plot to supply the invaders with arms, and a house-to-house search was made in the Ghetto to find evidence, some suspects being arrested. When the French forces finally entered, on February 10, after bringing deliverance to the community of Pesaro, the Jewish quarter was actually being beleaguered by an angry mob. Among the first to arrive were, as it happens, a number of Jewish soldiers, who hastened to the help of their coreligionists. The mob melted away, and the Jews were saved. An eyewitness recounts how the French troops themselves led the march of liberation into the Ghetto, tearing the yellow badge from the heads of the Jews and replacing it by a tricolor cockade. Three Jews were appointed to the Municipal Council and one, Salvatore Morpurgo, was included in the delegation sent to secure Napoleon's approval for the proposed republican constitution. Their jubilation could not, however, fail to be modified by the fact that over one-half of the levy of 240,000 piasters imposed on the city by its captors had to be paid by the Jewish community.

So, too, in Rome, the moments of anxiety during the *Viva Maria* riots, when the French were expected, were ended by the entry of General Berthier on February 10, 1798, followed five days later by the proclamation of the Roman republic. That same evening, the Jews laid aside their badge of shame; and two days later, to the strains of music and with the entire district brilliantly illuminated, a Tree of Liberty was erected in the Ghetto. On February 21 — the day after Pope Pius left the city as a captive, never to return — the Jews assembled at Monte Cavallo, bearing republican banners and wearing tricolor cockades, to hear a proclamation in the name of the French general which abolished all special regulations concerning them and declared them full citizens, with the same rights as their neighbors. The silver-tongued Ezechia Morpurgo, who had been sent to Rome to plead for the maintenance of the titular independence of Ancona, was sent to sit in the Senate, by the side of Duke Cesarini and the Prince Borghese. The latter presented a horse to Major Isaac Barrafael, as a symbol of his sympathy, when after a little difficulty he and other Jews were admitted to the newly-established National Guard.

In northeastern Italy, Napoleon had meanwhile picked a quarrel with the Venetian republic and hostilities had commenced. On June 3, 1796, Verona was occupied, the gates of the Ghetto being torn down and burned in the public square hard by. On April 29 of the following year the revolutionary forces entered Padua, where they were enthusiastically received. A Jew, Dr. Michael Salom, who had been imprisoned on the suspicion of revolutionary sympathies some while before, was one of the twenty-two members of the new municipality, and here too the Jews entered freely into the various patriotic societies and associations, including, in spite of the usual initial opposition, the Civic Guard. On August 28, the Ghetto was abolished here and at Rovigo by the military authorities, the Jews being permitted to live where they pleased henceforth and its name being changed to *Via Libera* ("Free Street"). Later that year, orders were issued for the gates and walls to be levelled, so that no ostensible relic of the infamous system should remain. By now, the French forces had marched on Venice itself. As they approached there was a moment of acute danger, the Ghetto being occupied by Slavonic mercenaries to prevent treasonable correspondence with the enemy; but on May 16, the venerable oligarchic government was overthrown. By the new revolutionary constitution, all citizens were declared equal before the law. Notwithstanding some outcry, three of them — Moses Luzzatto, Vita Vivante and Isaac Grego — were elected members of the somewhat drab municipality which succeeded to the government by doge and grand council, and sat on one or the other of the various committees to which it delegated its powers. The new spirit in politics speedily penetrated the Ghetto, where a popularly elected regime was set up under a republican stalwart and with a more democratic appellation, official documents were headed with the magical words "Liberty, Equality," communal meetings closed with cheers for Fraternity, Democracy and the Italian Nation, and the religious head and communal factotum were henceforth called "Citizen Rabbi" and "Citizen Beadle" respectively. On Monday, July 7, a detachment of the newly enrolled Civic Guard, to which Jews had been admitted from the outset, paraded in the Jewish quarter, henceforth to be known as the *Contrada della Riunione* ("Street of Reunion") where a Tree of Liberty had been erected. The Ghetto gates were now torn off their hinges and dragged into the middle of the square, where they were hacked to pieces and burned, a delirious mob of Jews and Christians dancing the carmagnole with linked hands around the flames.

Before the end of the Italian campaigns, Napoleon, hoping to emulate Alexander, had been carried by his grandiose dreams to Egypt, and the coalition formed against the Revolution during his absence brushed the French momentarily out of the country. Everywhere the Jews suffered in this interlude — not so much perhaps for their sympathy with revolutionary principles as for the offense of having received elementary human rights from the revolutionary armies. From the Alps to the Tiber, there was a universal wave of assault, culminating in some places in appalling massacres — the nearest approach to a general physical persecution in the whole course of Italian Jewish history until the twentieth century. In September, 1798, Rome was captured by the Neapolitans, who at once laid a heavy levy on the Jewish community, as indeed the French had done, though in a different spirit. For weeks it was unsafe for a Jew to be seen outside the Ghetto, and even the verses affixed to the popular oracle "Pasquino" proved unexpectedly bitter. The reaction continued here with a nine-month interlude until the summer of 1800, the treatment of the Jews faithfully reflecting successive phases. Thereafter, a modified papal regime, under strict control, was reinstated. Fortunately, there was no serious disorder here. But, as the French retired from central Italy in the summer of 1798, they were followed by swarms of undisciplined peasants and guerrillas, who occupied the evacuated area in the name of the old regime and the Catholic religion, and vented their zeal above all and first of all on the unfortunate Jews. When, on June 7, the change of government took place at Pesaro, the two synagogues were sacked and the Jews reduced to terror, remaining for two months virtually blockaded in the Ghetto, until they paid an enormous fine as ransom. A week later, on the French withdrawal from Urbino, similar disorders began; but after a few houses had been sacked and some atrocities committed, the new civic government stationed a guard at the Ghetto gates which preserved order. Far worse took place in Senigallia, where the reactionary bands, who followed up the French retirement, attacked the Ghetto on June 18 and sacked it from end to end. No less than thirteen persons were killed and many more wounded. The rest, some 600 souls, fled utterly destitute under cover of night to Ancona, still in French occupation, where the community had passed through more than one moment of acute anxiety during the past two years — in the previous January, the Ghetto had actually been fired. General Monnier, when he surrendered this city in the following October, after a strenuous defense largely financed by levies on the Jews, specified that no persons whatever their religion were to be molested for actions on behalf of the Republic. Though there was a little unrest here too, the Jews being accused of summoning the foreigner and heavily mulcted yet again, this agreement was generally observed, owing to the Christian kindliness of Cardinal Onorati, bishop of the See. The exiles remained accordingly for two years, until a papal edict compelled them to re-establish their community and resume their former heavy financial burdens.

The disorders reached their height on the other side of the Apennines, where the grand duke of Tuscany had long maintained a precarious neutrality. From June 1796 to January 1797, Leghorn had been in French occupation, and General Bonaparte once honored the stately synagogue with a visit. During this period, the wealthy Jewish merchants unwillingly paid heavy levies to the army of occupation and were unreasonably blamed for it by the loyalists, but otherwise suffered no harm. In the spring of 1799, however, the grand duchy was drawn disastrously into the vortex of war. On March 25, the French occupied Florence and set up a democratic republic, the Jews being emancipated forthwith. Four days later, the same took place at Sienna. The republican commissary here went out of his way to show his sympathies. The Jews were invited to participate in the national feast that took place at the beginning of the next month, and it is said that each evening they solemnly went to water the Tree of Liberty planted on the Campo. At Leghorn one of these symbols of enfranchisement was set up in the Jewish quarter, Jewish members were elected to the new municipal council, two Jewish companies of 100 men enrolled in the militia, and some Jewish damsels went about somewhat ostentatiously in the company of French officers, safe now from ecclesiastical penalties at least; on the other hand, there was some dissidence in the community between the ruling plutocracy and those with democratic sympathies, led by a certain Solomon Michel, who agitated against the oligarchic constitution. Elsewhere in the duchy, the revolutionary principles were entirely triumphant until June, when the citizens of the dour and strenuously Catholic city of Arezzo rose and expelled the French garrison. Emboldened by this success the *sanfedisti* now marched to deliver the rest of the province from the yoke of the invader, under the banner of the miraculous Madonna S.ta Maria del Conforto, who had manifested her approval of the movement in the conventional fashion. One detachment entered Florence, where the Archbishop Antonio Martini, who had already saved the Jews during the disorders nine years earlier, again intervened to protect them. By a bribe to the revolutionary leader, a noble gift to the public hospital, and a contribution for the equipment of the counter-revolutionary troops, they escaped serious consequences. At Leghorn, where revolutionary sympathies were less decided, the community had time to take precautions. Hence, although there was a little rioting — repeated in the following July, when a number of houses were searched for the weapons alleged to be kept in readiness for the return of the French — it was on a restricted scale. The handful of residents at Monte San Savino (among them the poet Salamone Fiorentino, who had vainly solicited precautionary measures from his patron, the grand duke) were crudely warned of the impending attack and anticipated it by taking refuge in Sienna and elsewhere, leaving their houses to be sacked; and the community was never reconstituted. Much the same occurred at Arezzo itself and at Lippiano. In Pitigliano, after cutting down the Tree of Liberty, the mob assaulted the Ghetto as a matter of course, but the better elements in the population intervened and, though many persons were arrested and narrowly escaped butchery in prison, only one was killed. But when a fortnight later, the Aretines entered Sienna and forced the French garrison to capitulate (June 28), there took place here an episode of stark horror, which has few parallels in the long story of Italian Jewry. The Ghetto was assaulted, the houses pillaged, and thirteen persons, including some of the refugees from Monte San Savino, were pitilessly done to death to incongruous cries of "Viva Maria." Many of the victims met their fate in the synagogue, where the doors of the Ark still bear the marks of the axes used to force the lock. (The Siennese still tell how that day the Madonna herself came down from heaven to save the Bible from destruction.) In the Campo, the Tree of Liberty was cut down and burned, the bodies of the dead and even the dying being flung upon the flames. To crown all, an Austrian officer who arrived that night to take charge in the city imposed a heavy fine on the Jewish community, threatening to burn the Ghetto to the ground and deport the inhabitants unless the sum were produced forthwith. His action was endorsed by the Tuscan Senate, which, searching every avenue for money to support the Austrian army of occupation, imposed a tremendous contribution on the Jews, by way of punishment for their alleged Francophile sympathies. The grand duke, however, first suspended and then cancelled this imposition, and in the end even reimbursed what had been extorted — a unique happening perhaps in Jewish history.

Much the same was meanwhile taking place further to the north. During the spring, an Austrian army under

General Klenau had blockaded Ferrara, aided by a swarm of rudely armed peasants from the surrounding countryside. When, on May 22, the French troops retired into the citadel, they had great difficulty in restraining the delighted populace from sacking the former Ghetto, as attractive a bait under its new name as it had ever been under the old. The Austrians despatched a picket of cavalry to protect it immediately they entered, but at the same time reimposed the old oppressive regulations and levied a contribution of 50,000 scudi on the Jews, who did not dare to be seen about the town for several days. At Lugo, the Ghetto was sacked for the third time in three years and a similar levy was exacted, as happened also at Cento. In Reggio and Modena, the communities were subjected to enormous fines on the charge of having purchased Church property. The former Venetian territories had been tossed as a sop to Austria at the beginning of 1798 by the infamous treaty of Campoformio; and both at Padua and Verona, and to a minor degree at Venice, there were anti-Jewish demonstrations on the entrance of the Austrian troops, repeated in Verona in the summer of the following year when conditions were so critical elsewhere. Though the Ghetto system was not revived in this region, the Jews lost their newly acquired civil rights and some of the old restrictions came into force again. Piedmont, reoccupied by the French at the end of 1798, had now become a seat of hostilities and was overrun by peasant bands, giving chase to the invaders and those who favored them — especially the Jews, considered one and all to be Jacobins. Already in the previous July there had been rioting in Chieri when it rose against the Revolution, the Ghetto being sacked. In place after place, there were riots or narrow escapes. In Alessandria, wholesale arrests were carried out among the Jewish community; at Acqui, the Ottolenghi family in particular suffered for their devotion to the revolutionary cause. At Fossano, Abraham Senigallia, who had made himself prominent during the republican interlude, was seized by the mob with the intention of burning him alive on the spot where he had formerly harangued his fellow citizens; but his life was saved by a wit who threw his wig into the flames, saying that this was sufficient sacrifice.

After the initial excesses, the reaction against the Jews assumed a more urbane form. The anti-Jewish song, *Gnora Luna*, which had caused so much trouble half a century before, again became fashionable. A disgruntled priest had the idea of converting it into a play, *Il matrimonio ebraico* ("The Jewish Marriage"), which was taken up by the company of the comedienne Marta Colleoni. It was first produced at Ferrara in 1798, notwithstanding the disapproval of the police, and proved a triumphant success, leading, however, to such an uproar that troops had to be called out to restore order. In 1799, it was staged in Modena on the eve of the arrival of Pope Pius VI on his way into exile, and similar scenes resulted, the authorities having to intervene here as well. There was similar trouble elsewhere, especially in Milan and Bologna; and the scurrilous strains of *Gnora Luna* could once again be heard in the mouth of every street-urchin. Anti-Jewish publications, such as Benedetti's posthumous *Gli ebrei smascherati* ("The Jews Unmasked," Ferrara, 1799), once more began to appear. In the territories subject to the house of Austria, the Jews, rightless once again, were now subjected to suspicion and discrimination, and many were deported on charges of disloyalty or subversive activity — among them Zachariah Carpi, of Revere near Mantua, an ardent revolutionary, who has left an account of his long and eventful imprisonment in elegant Hebrew. Solomon Finzi, rabbi of the diminutive group in Elba, was imprisoned at this time on the charge of attacking the Catholic priesthood in a poem on the coming of the Messiah, *Il Messia verrà*.

But the reaction did not last long. In May, 1800, General Bonaparte, now First Consul, and soon to be Emperor, once more led his armies into Italy. In June, he won his great victory over the Austrians at Marengo; and for the next fourteen years French influence was supreme in the Italian mainland, whatever the constitutional figment — whether fully incorporated into France, as was the case with Piedmont, and later on with Parma, Tuscany and the greater part of the former Papal States; or joined with it under the same crown, as was the case with the titular kingdom of Italy in the northwest of the Peninsula, including the former Venetian and Mantuan territories; or as a client state, as was Naples. In fact, all were part of the French empire; and the essential unity of the country and of its Jewish community was restored for the first time since Rome fell. In that stern and sometimes harsh military regime, the equality of the Jews before the law was solidly established once more. Everywhere, they took advantage of the opportunities which opened up before them in this exciting new world. They expressed hyperpatriotic devotion to the emperor in prose and verse, both Hebrew and Italian. They were enrolled in the army, and laid down their lives in every campaign. The legend survives of how on the retreat from Moscow the Italian Jewish soldiers sang the Hebrew psalms round the campfire to the tune of the *Marseillaise*. They joined the National Guard, many becoming officers. For the first time, they were admitted to take a part in civic life. Everywhere they figured among the municipal councillors — in Nice, there were at one time as many as five. Moses Formiggini, who in 1796 had been elected one of the representatives of the people of Milan and was a member of the governing body of the Cisalpine republic in the following year and of the Lyons *consulta* which constituted the Republic of Italy in 1802, later collaborated in drawing up the Commerical Code of the Italian Kingdom. Gabriel Trieste was a member of the Electoral College and President of the Chamber of Commerce in Padua; Felice Coen, one of the two Jewish municipal councillors at

Mantua, was a councillor too of the Department of the Mincio; David Levi was deputy mayor of Chieri; and Israel Coen became a judge of the commercial tribunal at Verona. Even rabbis began to take a part in communal life, in a manner which could hardly have been possible in a normal age: thus Abraham Cologna, of Mantua, who was perhaps more politically than spiritually inclined, was a member of the Legislative Assembly of the Cisalpine republic and delegate at the *consulta* of Lyons, and Joshua Benzion Segrè a municipal councillor at Vercelli. Alessandro Sacerdote was sent by the Cisalpine Republic as consul to Leghorn — the only place in Italy, perhaps, where the Jews had some reason to deplore the change, for the privileged status of the community was now suspended. Giuseppe Treves de' Bonfili, president of the Chamber of Commerce at Venice and the official orator when a statue of the emperor was unveiled in front of the doge's palace, was created a baron — the first Italian Jew to be ennobled in modern times. All discriminatory legislation of course lapsed.

Jews could henceforth own land, and, especially in Piedmont, eagerly availed themselves of the opportunity, thus renewing their connection with agriculture and the countryside. For the first time they were admitted to the professions, and it was Gioacchino Basevi, of Mantua, who defended the Tyrolese patriot, Andreas Hofer, when he was put on trial. They snatched at the chance of sending their children to the public schools, now opened to them for the first time; though here and there (for example, in Acqui, antisemitic as always) they were excluded by local prejudice. Sometimes, indeed, it was found convenient to have their own educational institutions, but these too were imbued by the new spirit: thus the Jewish "Gymnasium" established at Reggio in 1802 combined a classical and modern education in a manner definitely in advance of its day. Ecclesiastical inhibitions were now swept away, and in 1802 the first normal

Italian translations of the prayer book, impossible hitherto except in Hebrew characters, were produced. If anti-Jewish manifestations took place, new methods of defense could now be used; for example, when an objectionable play was staged at Lucca in 1806, the Leghorn magnates secured its withdrawal by threatening a commercial boycott. When lawlessness or reaction momentarily gained the upper hand, the Jewish quarters — no longer Ghettos — might still be attacked or menaced, as happened in 1801 at Ivrea, in 1803 at Asti, and above all in 1809, in consequence of an agrarian revolt, in Sermide, Ferrara and Rovigo, where the assailants were turned back by a valiant priest; but all were sternly suppressed by the authorities. When in the summer of 1809 the cannon of S. Angelo announced the annexation of Rome to the French empire, Jewish equality was re-established here too, after a not over-drastic reaction which, combined with the magnet of better conditions elsewhere, had reduced the community during the past decade by nearly a third, to little more than 3,000 souls.

In 1806, Napoleon had convoked in Paris an Assembly of Jewish Notables — the prelude to his grandiose "Sanhedrin" — ostensibly the culmination of Jewish Emancipation, in fact empowered only to strike certain prescribed patriotic gestures. The Jewish communities of the kingdom of Italy, not including as yet Tuscany and the Papal States, were requested to send sixteen representatives, in addition to thirteen from Piedmont, considered an integral part of France, making in all twenty-nine out of a total of one hundred and eleven. A quarter of the number were rabbis; they included young Jacob Israel Carmi of Reggio, whose reports are one of our most valuable sources of information about the proceedings; the physician Graziadio (Hananel) Neppi, of Ferrara, a worthy heir to the learned traditions of that city and author of a famous biographical dictionary of Italian Jewish scholars; Isaac Raphael Finzi, of Padua, considered to be one of the most forceful preachers of the age; Abraham Cologna, of Mantua, who was to take a leading role in the proceedings and to remain in France as the first *Grand Rabbin* under the new dispensation; the unassuming Jacob Cracovia, of Venice; and Joshua Benzion Segrè, member of the municipal council of Vercelli. (The three last-named were appointed to the Commission of Nine which was entrusted with the very arduous preparatory work.) Emilio Vitta of Casale was one of the secretaries, and Isaac Samuel Avigdor, of Nice, acted as Italian interpreter and made a speech in which the Catholic Church was flattered perhaps over-effusively. A leading part in the proceedings was taken also by the arrogant Moses Formiggini, considered to be the outstanding Italian Jewish layman, who submitted a memorandum proposing among other things a uniform liturgy, combining all the divergent traditional rites, and a revised system of education. The Jews of Trieste, still under Austrian rule, but notoriously Francophile and republican, followed the proceedings with such interest as to attract police attention. The Italian representatives, nominated tardily, arrived for the most part only when the proceedings of the Assembly were well advanced, and they were gravely embarrassed by the fact that many of the communities, whether from indifference or from penury, failed to send them the funds they needed for their living expenses. Nevertheless, they took a prominent share in the work of the Assembly, which in February 1807 gave place to the Sanhedrin which was to endorse its decisions. Thirteen of the forty-five rabbis and six of the twenty-five laymen appointed to this body were Italians — one of the latter, Israel Coen, receiving more votes than any other individual; and Rabbis Cologna and Segrè were appointed first and second vice-presidents respectively. The members faithfully registered all that was required of them, including the melodramatic gesture of rising to their feet and replying "To the death!" when asked whether it was the Jew's duty to fight for his country. Other pronouncements included a condemnation of the practice of usury, which would have been even more sweeping but for the protests of the Piedmontese delegates, and a formal recognition of the incumbency on the Jew of the matrimonial laws of the state. It was all highly impressive, and from the point of view of Authority not unsatisfactory; but the letters of Rabbi Carmi reflect the perplexities and distress of those who were not fully persuaded that the interests of the emperor were an essential detail of the service of God.

The decisions of the Sanhedrin, and the readjustment of Jewish life that followed in 1808, applied in full measure to those parts of Italy under direct French rule. "Consistories" covering groups of communities were now set up at Turin for the Departments of the Po and Stura and at Casale for those of Marengo and Monferrat, and later on, as the boundaries of the empire extended, also at Leghorn, Florence and finally Rome, the last being pompously inaugurated in 1811 by the vice prefect. The same decree which introduced these innovations embodied also various restrictions on the Jews — intended in fact only against those of Alsace — which excluded them in effect from trade and forbade internal migration. Those of Leghorn were almost immediately exempted, for this would have implied the suspension of a good part of the commercial activity of that port; and they were soon followed by the remainder of those of the kingdom of Italy. Those of Piedmont, in some consternation, summoned a representative conference and submitted a petition which was accompanied by eulogistic testimonials from the local authorities testifying to the civic progress they had made since the gates of opportunity had been opened to them; and their exemption, too, soon followed. The consistories did little but supervise conscription, inculcate patriotism, issue an appeal in 1812 for the establishment of religious schools and suggest a few trivial ameliorations in matters of organization. One enthusiast, indeed, the old revolutionary Aaron Fernando of

Leghorn, who had fought against the Austrians and been deported, imagined that the era of universal brotherhood had now dawned, and published in 1814 a work in which he advocated the abrogation of most of the Jewish ceremonial laws and the reduction of the basic precepts of the Jewish religion to sixty (*Progetto filosofico di una completa riforma del culto e dell' educazione politico-morale del popolo ebreo*, "Tiberias," 1814); but the publication was denounced to the authorities as being prejudicial to religion and all traceable copies were bought up by the congregation and burned.

Napoleonic absolutism was liberal to a degree by comparison with what succeeded it. In 1814, the empire collapsed — not to be revived, so far as Italy was concerned, during the Hundred Days — and Napoleon's Jewish subjects were restricted henceforth to the half-dozen families in his temporary island-kingdom of Elba, his relations with whom are unrecorded.

xxxvii

The Recoil

With the fall of the Colossus, the states of the Italian Peninsula were reconstituted much as they had existed before the Revolution, but under the aegis and domination of the house of Austria. The only important territorial changes were the annexation of Genoa and the rest of Liguria to the kingdom of Sardinia and, more significant from the point of view of the Jews, that of the former Venetian territories to Austria. For the rest, the Papal States, the grand duchy of Tuscany, the duchies of Modena and Parma, and the kingdom of the Two Sicilies were reconstituted as before. But in the background there constantly loomed henceforth the gloomy shadow of the

Austrian chancellor, Count Metternich, who had been driven by the experiences of the past twenty-five years to believe in Absolutism almost as a religion, and would not tolerate any trifling with the dangerous principles of democracy and constitutional government. Hence it was not only the old rulers who returned, but also old institutions, the old ideas, the old prejudices, and so far as the Jews were concerned the old laws and the old discriminations. They were worn, perhaps, with a difference. It is not quite true to say, as is generally done, that conditions of slavery were renewed. The Jews had lived with their neighbors, mixed with their neighbors, fought by the side of their neighbors, laid down their lives with their neighbors in a series of campaigns. They had enjoyed emancipation, and shown themselves not unworthy of it; they had been admitted to public offices, and filled them with as much credit as others did. The old condition of pariahdom could not be restored by a stroke of the pen. Notwithstanding the statute book, there was an atmosphere now that had formerly been unknown, while there were opportunities in the heyday of the Industrial Revolution, even in backward Italy, that had not offered themselves hitherto. Yet, after a generation that had seen what freedom meant, conditions of the deepest degradation were re-established over the greater part of the Peninsula. Everywhere, the Jews lost, not only the political rights which they had enjoyed together with their neighbors under Napoleonic rule, but also the social rights they had achieved and the civil rights conferred on them, and not unworthily exercised, since the French invasion.

In the Austrian territories of the Lombardo-Venetian kingdom and the Küstenland (including Trieste) — the most efficiently administered part of the country, notwithstanding the arbitrary method of government and the hated alien control — their treatment was relatively enlightened, and their disabilities, though not trivial, could not be considered oppressive. In effect they were similar to those which prevailed elsewhere in the Austro-Hungarian empire — exclusion from public office, inability to follow certain callings such as that of apothecary (a curious medieval survival), and a prohibition to hold real estate except in special circumstances. Nominally, too, there was a restriction on immigration and on the number of marriages, as was practiced elsewhere in the empire in order to limit the Jewish population; but this was not put into effect and, on the other hand, the Jews were still enrolled in the armed forces. The spirit of the administration was far from unkindly, and in 1820 the emperor declared it to be his intention to associate the interests of the Jews with those of the State, so that all should participate alike in forwarding the general welfare of society. In two other political fractions of the Peninsula conditions were very similar to those in the Austrian territories. In Tuscany, the restoration of the *status quo ante* implied that reforms introduced by the government before the French Revolution remained in force. Hence, though the Jews lost the political rights that they had enjoyed during the past quarter of a century, they continued to enjoy their civil rights; special taxation was not reintroduced, they were still admitted to the universities, and the Ghetto system was not renewed. On the other hand, they were excluded, as elsewhere in Italy, from all public employment, military and civil, and had to submit to various minor restrictions; and, later on, when conscription was introduced, they were excluded from the honor of bearing arms, in lieu of which they had to pay a new levy. Leghorn Jewry retained, indeed, its privileged status, and in the course of the following generation was to maintain its highest level of numbers and prosperity. A Jewish magnate continued to represent it on the municipal council, Jews still figured in the chamber of commerce, and a foreigner admitted to the community still became naturalized automatically.

It was, of course, natural that the consistorial system introduced by Napoleon was now abolished, the Tuscan Jewish communities being reorganized on an absolutist basis as befitted the age, under councillors nominated for life by the grand duke, until a more democratic regime was introduced in 1849. In the duchy of Parma similarly, where under Napoleon's former wife the French code remained in force, the Jews retained the civil rights they had enjoyed under it, theoretically including admission to public as well as municipal office and to the armed forces. Moreover, they were henceforth allowed to live in the chief city, their condition thus being distinctly better than before the Revolution; but their tribute was reimposed, together with various minor annoyances.

These states covered only a relatively small area of Italy. Elsewhere, reaction now triumphed completely. In the kingdom of Sardinia, where the Jesuits were welcomed as never before and the old brutal penal laws were again enforced, the religious toleration of the past generation was formally withdrawn — the result it is said of a momentary hesitation on the part of the communities to pay the million lire demanded by the royal house on its restoration. By a royal edict of April 21, 1814, the whole of the former anti-Jewish code was once again enforced — more strictly in some ways than hitherto, for there was no more of the tolerant inefficiency or philosophic liberalism that had characterized the eighteenth century. Piedmont now became notorious as one of the most reactionary and unenlightened areas of Europe. The Jews were now once more confined to Ghettos, from which they were not to be absent after nine o'clock at night without special reason. Even in Nice, where the Prussian consul was a Jew and raised difficulties, an attempt was made to enforce this. Students were expelled from all educational institutions, from the elementary and trade schools to the universities — a particularly deplorable retrogression, as their admittance to seats of higher learning had been nominally legitimized by the concessions of 1580 and 1603 — those who had not completed their studies having to choose between idleness and exile. Once again, they were forbidden to build new synagogues or to enlarge the old ones or to employ Christian servants or wetnurses. They were not allowed to become lawyers, notaries, apothecaries or physicians, except for practice among their coreligionists. Parents were forbidden to exclude their baptized children from their inheritance. Special taxes, including even the most degrading levies, were reintroduced. Property-owners, who had become numerous during the Napoleonic regime, were given five years to dispose of their holdings; and since the process did not make sufficiently rapid progress, they were ultimately warned that what remained in their possession after the beginning of 1824 would be confiscated. It was understandable that fictitious sales and feigned conversions were resorted to in order to evade such regulations. All offices — municipal, governmental, administrative and military — were closed to them as in the old days. Manufactures, once common enough, were closed down. They were again reduced to the most abject trades and occupations in order to earn a living. The only alleviation made was that in 1816 — though only after some hesitation — the regulations regarding the wearing of the Jewish badge were rescinded. It was regarded as a great advance that the Codice Albertino, promulgated by King Carlo Alberto in 1837, while making no other concessions, recognized non-Catholics as citizens, enjoying the essential civil rights.

Conditions were very much the same in the duchy of Modena, another stronghold of reaction, where the illiberal code of 1771 was again enforced in its entirety. Once more, the Jews had to pay an annual tribute as the price of their toleration, fixed somewhat higher than ever before; they were forced to dispose of their real estate; they were ejected from the liberal professions; they were forbidden to employ

Christians; they were excluded from all educational institutions, except for the purpose of medical study; and they were compelled to go back to live in the Ghetto as in the old days, except that the gates were not restored.

Worst of all, however — for no Jewish community was as yet to be found in the ultra-reactionary kingdom of Naples* — were the conditions in the Papal States, where Pope Pius VII returned from his long exile determined to re-establish the ecclesiastical regime of the eighteenth century down to the last detail. It was in vain that the Jewish merchants of his capital, ordered to vacate their shops on the Corso, offered him 100,000 scudi to confirm the privileges they had enjoyed until now. The time for this was gone. Once more, the Jews were herded into the former Ghettos, and the gates which had inadvertently been allowed to remain in Rome were closed as in the old days every night at dusk. The Inquisition regained its power, and the cardinal vicar his jurisdiction. Jewish students were dismissed from the Sapienza and Jewish pupils from the ordinary schools, while in Ancona the Jewish sick and wounded were even ejected from the public hospitals. The wearing of the Jewish badge, though nominally prescribed, does not seem to have been actually enforced; but attendance at the conversionist sermons was once more made compulsory. Even the annual ceremonial of homage on the Campidoglio was revived, with all its formalities, though the Jewish representative was now allowed to wear ordinary dress instead of the old grotesque apparel, and after 1830 the senator dismissed him by placing a foot on his neck instead of kicking him as hitherto.

Pope Pius was moderate as compared with his successor, Leo XII who, immediately he became Pope in 1823, renewed

---

* A few Jews gathered, however, around Karl Mayer von Rothschild, the fourth of the famous brothers, after he set up a branch of the well-known international banking-house here in 1821. It should perhaps be added that the newly founded duchy of Lucca also had no community.

The Great Synagogue at Leghorn

Interior of the Synagogue at Leghorn
(from an engraving)

The *Cuccagna* of the "Jewish Nation" at Leghorn
(see page 385)

the fiercest reactionary prejudices. In a circular of September 13, 1825, he ordered the bishops and archbishops of those places where communities existed to restore the Ghettos in the strictest sense and to compel the Jews to put back the gates as before the French occupation. At Ferrara, with an exceptional sense of dignity, the Jews refused to participate in executing the order, but this did not of course save them from being compelled to pay the cost. In Rome, where two streets were now added to the area to accommodate the increase, the shops which his predecessor had tolerated elsewhere for the general convenience had to be closed within twenty-four hours, regardless of the distress and widespread ruin that this caused. Next year the Pope once more put into force the provisions of the infamous *editto sopra gli ebrei* of 1775. The employment of Christians by Jews was now so rigorously forbidden that patrols were sent into the Ghetto on the Sabbath to interfere if anyone attempted to perform the kindly service of lighting the fires. In 1828, orders were issued for the sale of all real property within a maximum period of five years. Once again, forced baptisms, at the request of some apostate relative or on the information of a conscience-stricken servant girl, became familiar throughout the Papal States. In 1826, as the result of a deathbed confession of her former nurse, the daughter of one of the best known Jewish families of Ancona was seized on the eve of her marriage and carried off to the House of Catechumens, ultimately being baptized. It was now considered advisable for any father who had once had a Christian servant in his employment to obtain a sworn statement testifying that she had never performed any action which might give the Church a claim over her erstwhile charges. Pope Pius VIII (1829–1830) found time in the course of his brief pontificate to forbid Jews to enter into relations with Christians for any purpose whatsoever, except in the course of business; his successor, Gregory XVI (1831–1846) even reimposed the carnival impost, which had replaced the ancient abuse of the Jewish *palio* and still retained the old degrading associations, and in 1836 expelled the handful of Jews who had ventured to settle in Bologna during the period of French domination. The distress was heightened by the general economic conditions, which were increasingly unfavorable. At Ancona, for example, the decline in the Levant trade undermined the prosperity of the entire Jewish community, whose formerly preponderant share in the trade of the port was reduced after the revolutionary wars to a subordinate place. So sunken now was the condition of Roman Jewry, mother of Hebrew scholarship in Europe, that it no longer produced any native spiritual guides and during the time of the papal restoration was generally without a rabbi.

The repression was nowhere a matter of form, but was rigorously carried into effect. In Piedmont, the enforcement of the regulations concerning the Ghetto was ordered time and time again, though the increased population and the problems of translocation made it very difficult. In 1822, the government gave five years for the process to be completed, but this proved insufficient and seven years later serious measures were threatened unless there was immediate obedience. In 1835, orders were issued for all shops and residences elsewhere to be vacated within a short period. Notwithstanding an ominous disaster at Alessandria, where a house in the Jewish quarter collapsed during a wedding at the cost of many lives, a commission was appointed two years later to enforce immediate obedience; and it was only in Nice, already a great tourist resort, that the experiment was abandoned, though with the greatest reluctance. The other restrictions were put into execution with equal severity. Even at Parma, a father who requested school facilities for his son — it was the young Enrico Guastalla, who was to make a name for himself later on as a patriotic leader — was not merely refused but even menaced with imprisonment. Excluded from the universities in the greater part of Italy, the Jews went to study where they could, so that in 1835 there were no fewer than fifty Jewish undergraduates at Padua. Forced baptisms and the like were not confined to Rome, but were condoned elsewhere as well, the general misery increasing the temptations of apostasy. In the decade 1801–1810, only one Jew was converted to Christianity in the duchy of Modena; from 1831 to 1840, there were forty-eight! Minor degradations continued everywhere. In 1819, the Jews of the duchy of Parma were warned not to display any outward pomp or ceremony at their funerals; at Ferrara, the community was fined, eighteen years later, because lighted candles had been carried behind the bier of their departed rabbi; and even in Leghorn it was permitted to bury the dead only in the early morning or late at night.

At Nice in 1820, and at Casale twenty years later, the Jews were compelled at great expense to decorate the royal box at the theater, in accordance with alleged precedent. The Turin community had to make New Year gifts of coffee, sugar and candles to the bishop, the president of the Senate, and other officials, as well as to pay the old degrading levy to the university in order to secure freedom from assault on the occasion of the first snowfall. In relatively liberal Tuscany, too, the university students were permitted to revive the old practice of exacting a Jew's weight in confetti at the beginning of winter, though this had been officially abolished even before the Revolution. When a deposit bank was founded at Genoa in 1844, Jews were not allowed to have any share in its management or activities. Even outbreaks of violence in the old style were now renewed — for example, in Rome, in the worst medieval tradition, when Leo XIII died in 1829. The old ballad *Gnora Luna* continued to be chanted about the streets and to bring on occasional unpleasantness. There were ritual murder accusations — abortive, yet menacing — at Mantua in 1824 and at Badia (near Rovigo) in 1855 — both, it may be observed, in the Austrian sphere; and in the former city there was a fresh outbreak of anti-Jewish feeling, violently expressed, in 1842. When, in 1840, menaces were heard against the Jews in Piedmont, the rabbi of Turin was actually forbidden to voice his protest in the press. Emigration from certain parts of the Peninsula now rose to a disquieting level. The effects on some little communities of the Papal States especially, such as that of Lugo, were very serious; and an export tax was authorized on the property of emigrants for the benefit of their impoverished coreligionists. In France, a philanthropic society was instituted for the purpose of assisting the emigration of the oppressed Jews of Piedmont. It had been proposed that the Italian communities should make representations about their treatment to the Congress of Aix-la-Chapelle in 1818, but they lacked both the courage and the cohesion. But for the influence of the house of Rothschild — at this time a greater force than many of the petty Italian states, to more than one of which, including the Papacy, it made itself financially useful — conditions in some parts of the country might have been still worse.

But Italian Jewry had tasted liberty; and the taste of liberty, once known, is never forgotten. It is not surprising that they threw themselves heart and soul into the movement for the overthrow of the reactionary regimes, the ejection of the Austrians and the petty tyrants whose thrones were propped up by their bayonets, and the creation of a free, united Italy. In this movement, known as the *Risorgimento* or Reawakening, to which modern Italy owes its being, the Jews took a part and paid a price out of all proportion to their numbers. The rabbis supported the sacred cause with their eloquence, the aged with their encouragement, the youth with their arms. They were represented among the exiles in every capital of Europe, amid the excitements of Paris and the fogs of London, hungrily awaiting the call to return — writing, working, praying, scheming. They subscribed lavishly when money was needed. They enrolled in the secret societies. They enlisted in the patriotic forces. They joined every forlorn hope. They distributed literature. They wrote eager verses and pamphlets. They shed their blood lavishly. They wasted the best years of their lives in Austrian prisons. The communal schools which they had been compelled to set up in consequence of their exclusion from ordinary educational institutions — especially the once famous Collegio Foà of Vercelli — became nurseries of patriotic sentiment. From the moment of Napoleon's fall, they took a share in the activities of the so-called *Carboneria* which began to work, with mystical but irresponsible self-sacrifice, for Italian freedom. At Leghorn, for example, as early as 1817, a police memorandum lists no less than 44 Jewish *Carbonari*, many of whom were arrested and imprisoned or exiled. In Modena and the Romagna, they were similarly active. The secret printing press in Florence for patriotic material was operated by the brothers Paggi. Elsewhere, they were habitually used for the transmission of literature and messages from place to place, for it was found that their interurban and international connections, and their trade in secondhand goods, made them exceptionally useful as intermediaries. They were not backward in action; an Abraham Fortis, for example, took part in the rising at Faenza in 1820. They suffered, too; Israel Latis was one of the *Carbonari* conspirators condemned at Rubiera in 1822 by the duke of Modena, and Angelo Levi was killed in the fighting at Salerno in 1828.

In 1831, a fitful ray of hope lit up the Italian scene. Under the impact of the "July Revolution," which had overthrown the Bourbon monarchy in France in the previous year, there was a succession of abortive outbreaks in central and northern Italy, as there had been in Naples and Piedmont ten years previously. Hitherto-veiled sympathies now became open and the part taken by some Jews was outstanding. In Modena, for example, the diminutive Angelo Usiglio was with his brother Emilio among the most devoted and daring supporters of the martyred liberal leader,

Cesare Menotti; the movement was supported financially by the Jewish banking-houses of Conegliani, Levi and Nacmani; and in the suburb of Concordia the five brothers Crema enlisted forty volunteers out of a population of 900. So, too, in the Papal States, young Jews eagerly embraced the movement. Its leaders, remembering the revolutionary era of the previous generation, immediately showed their sympathy with Jewish sufferings. When provisional governments were formed simultaneously in Rome and Ferrara on February 10 — in the latter case, without bloodshed — one of the first orders they issued was for the destruction of the newly erected Ghetto gates and the reinstatement of the Jews in the full rights of citizens; and the same happened in due course elsewhere — for example, in Ancona. At Modena, too, the anti-Jewish laws were repealed, though for various reasons the prohibition to acquire houses outside the Ghetto was maintained. But in fact this was no more than a gesture. The Austrian troops speedily restored the old regimes and reimposed the disabilities everywhere. The duke of Modena moreover, who had grimly sent for the executioner as soon as the revolt was suppressed, punished his Jewish subjects for their participation by reimposing all the restrictions, without exception, from which they had suffered before the French Revolution, rigidly enforcing the Ghetto system in every detail, exacting a heavy fine in addition to the former tribute, and even threatening the reimposition of the Jewish badge. The Austrian commander, who regarded such extremes as anachronistic, secured a certain degree of moderation in practice, though not as regards the financial clauses; but the reality was grim enough. Nevertheless, in some places there was a slight amelioration henceforth. At Ferrara, the Ghetto gates, though replaced, were chained back, so that they remained only a potential menace; while at Lugo and Ancona they were not restored, even the ecclesiastical authorities apparently realizing that they offended civilized ideas.

The fiasco of 1831 was succeeded by the reorganization of the movement of liberation, the secret *Carboneria* being superseded by the *Giovine Italia*, or Young Italy movement, under the inspiring guidance of Giuseppe Mazzini. The younger generation of Italian Jewry threw themselves into it heart and soul; their leader's character, moreover, so like that of an Old Testament prophet, seemed to strike a kindred note in Jewish hearts, and both in Italy and abroad some of them were numbered among his most intimate friends. Above all, during his long exile in London — where he was accompanied by the ever-faithful Angelo Usiglio, and used the passport relinquished by the Leghorn rabbi, Sabato Morais, when he left for America — the circle where he found the most cordial welcome and most sincere appreciation was that of the Italian Jewish family Rosselli (a name which was to figure continuously in the annals of Italian patriotism to our own day) and their kinsman Nathan. The house of the latter family became the principal center of activity in England for the sacred cause of Italian independence; and long afterwards it was in the Pisa house of Pellegrino Rosselli, faithful to the end, that he died, an exile in his own land.

At the outset, the work of *Giovine Italia* was carried on most actively in Piedmont, where a group of Jews from Vercelli, led by a bookseller and a sausagemaker, were the most active agents for the distribution of its propaganda. At Leghorn, there was an allied society, "The True Italians" (*I Veri Italiani*), at the head of which were two Jews named Ottolenghi and Montefiore, who were arrested for their participation; while Mazzini's ill-starred raid from Switzerland into Savoy in 1833 was financed by one of the Todros of Turin. The bard of the movement was the poet-banker David Levi, a native of the little community of Chieri and an eager Jew, who on the tragic failure of the expedition of the brothers Bandiera to raise the South, in 1844, wrote an ode in their memory which became the battle-hymn of the

Irredentists. Jews collaborated in all the patriotic journals and reviews, such as the *Antologia* of Florence and the *Corriere Livornese* of Leghorn and Mazzini's own *Giovine Italia*; and when, in 1833, the first of these publications was suppressed under Austrian pressure, two Jews, Ludovico Mondolfi and Abramo Philippson, led the protests and were arrested in consequence by the police. Not that other methods were overlooked. On the occasion of the visit of the Emperor Ferdinand to Milan in 1842, the communities of the Lombardo-Venetian kingdom sent a deputation to appeal for the abolition of their disabilities. He promised that the question would be considered, but nothing more was heard about it.

The Italian constitutional leaders were by now increasingly conscious of the degrading results of the disabilities from which the Jews suffered. The establishment of full rights for all sections of the population without distinction of creed — and in those days no one, least of all in Italy, thought in terms of the absurdity of "race" — now became a cardinal principle of liberal policy. In 1830, a scathing article on the condition of the Jews by Gabriel Pepe had appeared in the *Antologia*. Six years later, Carlo Cattaneo, the republican philosopher, published his famous *Ricerche economiche sulle interdizioni imposte agli Israeliti* ("Economic Researches on the restrictions imposed upon the Jews": reprinted from the Milanese legal periodical *Annali di giurisprudenza pratica*) which, though mutilated by the Austrian censorship, had a wide influence in enlightened circles. The philosopher, Vicenzo Gioberti, advocated the cause in moving terms in his great work on the *Moral and Civil Primacy of the Italians* (1842) — one of the monuments of the *Risorgimento*. The Catholic leader, Niccolò Tommaseo, pleaded for it in Venice. Ugo Foscolo, Cesare Balbo, Angelo Brofferio — the greatest contemporary political philosophers and writers — all shared these views. But their pronouncements did no more than crystallize opinion on the subject; religious equality was already regarded by all of the fighters for freedom as one of the fundamental principles of the new Italy they envisaged.

As the middle of the century approached, a fresh wave of expectancy swept the Peninsula. When in 1846 a cardinal of advanced tendencies was elected to the Papal Throne as Pius IX, he was greeted with general enthusiasm as the hope of Italian liberalism. He appointed a commission to look into the condition of the Jews under his rule, and immediately rescinded some of the restrictions placed upon them; he permitted them, after more than two hundred years, to erect tombstones over their dead, the conversionist sermons were delivered for the last time, and the annual carnival tribute, with its degrading associations, was abolished. A little later on, instructions were given for the removal (at the community's expense, indeed) of the gates and walls of the Ghetto; and on Passover night, as the Roman Jews celebrated their ancient feast of freedom, an impatient throng under the leadership of the famous demagogue, Ciceruacchio, razed this three-hundred-year-old symbol of degradation to the ground, never to be restored. To celebrate the occasion, David Levi composed an ode in which he hailed the Pope as liberator and called on him to take the lead in securing the regeneration of the Italian Jews. Elsewhere in the Papal States the Ghetto gates, where they remained, were removed, though at Ferrara the pillars to which they were attached were left. One difference was perceptible between this and what had happened half a century before. Then, the demolitions had been carried out by French sappers; this time, by a spontaneous popular movement.

A similar change of atmosphere was perceptible elsewhere. In Tuscany, non-Catholics had been admitted to municipal office in 1845, on the same terms as other citizens; in 1847, Jewish university students were allowed to compete for bursaries; and that same year the grand duke permitted the establishment of a National Guard. In this, the Jews were allowed to enroll themselves, and services of thanksgiving, attended by many Catholics, were held in the synagogues of Florence and Leghorn. Here (in imitation of what had happened not long before in Rome, where a pacification had been arranged between the Jews and the populace of the Trastevere) a symbolic reconciliation was staged with the inhabitants of the Venezia quarter, formerly foremost in any disorder; and there was an interchange of banners between the two sides after a patriotic advocate, standing on the steps of the high altar of a church between a Jew and a Christian, had exhorted his audience to brotherly love for the sake of the country. The Tuscan constitution, reluctantly promulgated on February 17, granted full religious freedom. Even in the Papal States, non-Catholics were accorded civil, if not political, rights by the *statuto* of the following month.

This was the prelude to the excitements of the Year of Revolutions, 1848, when the collapse of the monarchy of France was followed by a spontaneous outbreak throughout Italy, as almost throughout Europe, everywhere bringing religious freedom and political emancipation. In the events of those wonderful months, the Jews took a leading part, inscribing their names in letters of blood upon the standard of Italian liberty for all time. The whole country was stirred by the famous Five Days of Milan, from March 18 to March 22, when a fifteen-year-old Jewish boy, Ciro Finzi, was one of the leaders of the street-fighting, while his namesake Giuseppe Finzi, one of Mazzini's closest associates, was entrusted with a military command and the scholar Tullo Massarani and the poet Giuseppe Revere assisted to maintain fervor at the highest pitch by their patriotic articles. In Modena, twelve out of the two hundred strangers who enrolled in the Free Corps were Jews. At Turin, the rabbi and council of the community fervidly encouraged young Jews to join the three volunteer battalions of sharpshooters formed to fight against the Austrians, the Jewish contingent leaving for the front amid thunderous applause on March 22. Later on, it was recruited by Jewish volunteers from other communities, and formed the Seventh Company of Bersaglieri which acquitted itself gallantly in the approaching campaigns and saved the colors of the Sixteenth Regiment in the Battle of Bicocca. At Ferrara, when the news of the Five Days of Milan arrived, the congregation, after leaving the thanksgiving service in the Cathedral, marched to the Ghetto by torchlight, and destroyed the pillars to which the gates of evil memory had been attached. Here, Jews had already been serving in the National Guard since the previous year, and one of them, Salvatore Anau, secretary of the National Circle and later its representative at Turin, was among the most active members of the Provisional Government. In Venice, the Republic proclaimed on March 23 was led by Daniel Manin, a half-Jew, one of the purest and noblest figures in the history of Italian liberalism. Here, too, Jews enlisted and fought bravely in the National Guard; three were elected to the first Representative Assembly, and seven to the second; and several took a leading part in the work of the Provisional Government: Leone Pincherle as Minister of Agriculture and Commerce; Isaac Pesaro Maurogonato as Minister of Finance; and the Rabbis Samuel Olper and Abraham Lattes as members of the Assembly and fiery workers in the cause of liberty, to mention only a few. Among the "Forty" who were exiled from the city with Manin for their share in the Revolution, there was a remarkably high proportion of members of the community to which he traced his origin. "I could not have believed that this republican scum would be so competent" exclaimed the Austrian military governor when he examined Maurogonato's impeccable financial records. Never perhaps have Jews been identified with any similar episode to quite the same extent.

When the patriotic movement had been suppressed in Lombardy by the Austrian white-coats, the center of resistance was transferred to Rome, where the Pope had been scared into reaction by the terrifying progress of the liberal cause and driven into flight. On February 9, 1849, a Republic was proclaimed under the guidance of Mazzini and the military leadership of Garibaldi. Jewish volunteers and patriots now streamed to the Eternal City from every part of Italy, eager to play their part. Three were elected to the National Assembly: Giuseppe Revere, who on the suppression of the revolt at Milan had first gone to Venice, whence he had been expelled by Manin for his extreme views, was now the editor of Mazzini's *Italia del Popolo*, and signed with him the famous appeal from the National Association to the French republic; Abraham Pesaro, a cousin of Isaac Pesaro Maurogonato; and Salvatore Anau of Ferrara, who was sent on a mission to Venice. Leone Carpi, eminent later as a political economist, also occupied some important positions. Three Jews were elected to the City Council, and two to the Committee for Defense. From the beginning, they had rushed to enroll in the Civic Guard, and figured in it conspicuously, a proposal to segregate them into special companies having been defeated. From abroad, too, Jews came to fight for Italian freedom — for instance, Charles Alexander Scott of London, who had previously fought at Venice. There were five Jews among the 172 members of the Lombard Legion, some of them, including Ciro Finzi and the promising young physician Giacomo Venezian of Trieste, dying in the defense of the city. And, when the Roman republic fell, before the onslaught of French Zouaves sent to aid the Pope, Jewish volunteers were among those who followed Garibaldi on his retreat to the north, and Jewish patriots prominent among those who suffered for their recent participation.

As was to be expected, Jewish emancipation had been one of the principles of the revolutions of these wonderful months, imbued with recollections of the Napoleonic age, and Jewish disappointment was among the bitter fruits of the general disaster. The provisional revolutionary government in Milan had forthwith decreed the abolition of all religious disabilities in Lombardy. In Venice, one of the first acts of the republican government, on March 22, was to the effect that henceforth "the citizens of the United Provinces of the Republic, whatever their religious faith, shall enjoy perfect equality of civil and political rights" — largely through the efforts of the great patriotic writer and ex-priest Niccolò Tommaseo. In the duchy of Modena, the same was effected by a decree of April 10. Similarly, at Rome, it was declared that the rights of suffrage and election to the national constitutional assembly were independent of creed. In Tuscany, the religious equality granted by the Constitution of 1848 was of course maintained in the short-lived Republic of the following year. Much the same took place in other regions; and in October, when the clouds were gathering fast, the Federal Congress held at Turin was asked by the Jewish spokesmen to take immediate steps to secure religious liberty throughout the country as a fundamental principle of Italian politics. But in the subsequent reaction all was swept away. It had been another dream like that of 1831, like the longer one of the Napoleonic age. Realization seemed as remote as ever; and meanwhile, the price of failure had to be paid.

xxxviii

Enfranchisement

There was one area of the Peninsula where reaction failed to penetrate. Carlo Alberto, king of Sardinia, had tardily, almost reluctantly, placed himself at the head of the liberal movement in Italy. During the course of the past few years, the enfranchisement of the Jews in his dominions had become a living issue. This was largely the result of the work of the Jewish communities of Turin, headed by the eloquent Rabbi Lelio Cantoni, and of Casale. Committees for the cause of Emancipation had been formed in every city; public meetings were held; statesmen were approached; and patriotic sacrifice on the part of the Jews, to demonstrate their fitness for Emancipation, was sedulously stimulated, with results that have already been seen. Moreover, organized publicity was taken in hand, authors being encouraged to take up their pens in the cause and their publications widely circulated. In 1847-8 these appeared in a steady stream and with almost overwhelming force of argument. Among them must be mentioned the widely circulated historical survey, *Origine delle interdizioni civili israelitiche* ... ("The Origin of the Civil Restrictions Placed on the Jews and their Harmful Results") by the jurist G. L. Maffoni; an Italian translation of a famous work on Jewish emancipation first published in Hungarian by Baron Joseph Eötvös, with an introduction by the Jewish journalist Giacomo Dina discussing local conditions; *La rigenerazione politica degli ebrei in Italia* ("The Political Regeneration of the Jews in Italy") by the Abbé Giuseppe Gatti of Casale — who thereby lost his chance of ecclesiastical preferment — demonstrating that Jewish emancipation was demanded no less by humanity than by true Christian principles; and moving articles by the jurist Giovanni Battista Giorgini in his paper, *L'Italia,* of Pisa, in which he denounced the present state of affairs as "a blot, a shame, an anachronism, in the constitution of a civilized people." Most influential of all was *Dell' emancipazione civile degli israeliti* ("On the Civil Emancipation of the Jews") directed to the Pope by the statesman-philosopher Massimo d'Azeglio, one of the purest and most prominent figures in Italian life at the time. In this, which remains classical, the conditions of the Jews in the various parts of the Peninsula were passed in review and their rehabilitation was demanded, in the name of justice as well as of political wisdom, as being bound up inextricably with that of the Italian people as a whole. This, published in Rome in 1847, had a tremendous effect in liberal circles, reappeared in Florence in the following year, and was to a great extent responsible for the favorable developments during the Year of Revolutions.

The practical side was not neglected, as has been seen. In 1845, an influential Piedmontese committee had been organized to draw the attention of the government and the public to the problem. Its president was Count Roberto d'Azeglio, Massimo's brother — it was perhaps at his instance that the latter had taken up his pen — and it had the support of men like Vincenzo Gioberti and even Camillo Cavour, who had championed the cause of Jewish emancipation from the beginning of his career. The liberal press took the matter up with more and more insistence, treating the question as a part of the general one for constitutional government in Piedmont. In 1847, the momentous meeting of the extremely influential Agrarian Association held at Casale, in which Lombard representatives and the king's own aide-de-camp took part, passed a resolution in favor of the emancipation of non-Catholics. That November, Roberto d'Azeglio addressed a circular letter to the bishops of the kingdom asking them for their support, and two days before Christmas submitted a petition to the same effect, among the signatories to which were four of the prelates and some of the most influential persons in public life. When the king at last was induced to adopt a liberal policy, it was impossible to fail to take this agitation into account. Originally, the benefits of the constitution which he granted on February 8, 1848 — one of the cornerstones of the Italian revival — were confined to Catholics. Ten days later, they were extended to the Waldenses — the only dissenting Christian body in the kingdom. In the following month war was declared on Austria, the symbol of foreign and reactionary control. A Jewish deputation headed by the poet David Levi, which waited on the king before he left Turin, pointed out how the victory to which all Italians looked forward so eagerly would be disastrous to the Jews of Lombardy and the Veneto, who would lose thereby those rights they possessed, being reduced to the same miserable status as their coreligionists in Piedmont. This unanswerable argument was supported by the minister of the interior, Vincenzo Ricci, in a memorandum submitted on March 22, in which he advocated the full emancipation of the Jews on the most dispassionate practical grounds, pointing out that thus only could their status be raised and their abilities and resources become more serviceable to the state. Unable to hold out any longer, Carlo Alberto signed a decree, on March 29, 1848, on the battlefield of Voghera, extending civil rights to the Jews and other non-Catholics of his dominions and abrogating all laws to the contrary. By a curious coincidence, it was the exact anniversary of the initiation of the system which it ended, that is, of the establishment of the first Ghetto in Venice three hundred and thirty-six years before. Everywhere the news was greeted with jubilation, among non-Jews as well as among Jews; for it was not an artificial act of naturalization, but a formal recognition of the ineluctable fact that the Italian Jews were children of the country in the fullest sense, no less than any of their neighbors. Antagonism was shown only in reactionary Acqui, where the populace demonstrated its sentiments during the coming Easter by a riot, in the old style and with the old pretext, which the obscurantist bishop pointedly failed to discourage.

A fortnight after the publication of the original Edict of Emancipation, which had also admitted Jews to the universities — one of the privileges they particularly coveted — the honor of military service was also extended to them (those who had served hitherto were all volunteers). Meanwhile, the newly elected Chamber of Deputies had been discussing the position of religious minorities under the Constitution. So as to clarify the position, a motion proposed by the Liberal leader, Riccardo Sineo, was adopted on June 7, stipulating, with noble and notable brevity, that "Religious differences do not affect the enjoyment of civil and political rights on the part of citizens who do not profess the Catholic faith, or their admission to civil and military office." This, endorsed by the Senate ten days later, was immediately given royal approval. Just after this, the Piedmontese were overwhelmingly defeated at the Battle of Custoza — the first of a series of disasters which during the next twelve months ruined the patriotic hopes and brought the greater part of the Peninsula back again under the heel of reaction. Carlo Alberto abdicated, brokenhearted, to be succeeded by his son Vittorio Emanuele II. From preference as well as policy he retained the Constitution which his father had granted, and in the end marched to victory in its name. Thus, as in the course of the subsequent generation the other Italian states were united one after the other with the kingdom of Sardinia to become the kingdom of Italy, the provisions of the Piedmontese Constitution were extended throughout the country, and with them the emancipation of the Jews.

The regeneration of Italian Jewry was thus bound up henceforth with Piedmont and with the devoted work of Camillo Cavour, Vittorio Emanuele's prime minister from 1851 onwards. At every turn, as was to be expected, Cavour found Jewish sympathy and help. It was from the Rothschilds of Paris that the Piedmontese treasury received its main support during this fateful period — at one crucial stage, when money was necessary for the impending war against Austria, under the cover of the need for the cutting of the Mont Cénis tunnel, as the house always refused to lend money for military purposes. He personally received unremitting loyalty, when he needed it most, from the Jewish electors of Turin. His confidential secretary and faithful lieutenant was Isaac Artom, one of the most significant figures in the history of the *Risorgimento*. His official organ, *Opinione*, was directed by Giacomo Dina, for many years his literary spokesman and advocate. It is impossible to devote here more than a brief mention to these men, whose role in the consolidation of Italian liberty was so memorable.

Outside Piedmont, the years of reaction which succeeded the Year of Revolution cast Jewish hopes in the abyss once again. Emancipation was of course withdrawn, and in some places, such as Modena and Mantua, special fines or forced loans were again imposed on the Jewish communities in punishment for the help they had extended to the patriot cause. Even in Tuscany, the liberal constitution was rescinded and religious equality cancelled; and it was in vain that the Jewish communities petitioned for some amelioration of their condition in the new code of laws issued in 1851. Everywhere, Jews were among the exiled and the proscribed: Isaac Pesaro Maurogonato and a number of others at Venice, Leone Carpi at Ferrara, and many more. Two Jews who had served in the defense of Bologna were surrendered to the Austrians as hostages. All the minor advances so painfully secured were automatically reversed, excepting only that the Ghetto gates were this time nowhere restored. In 1851, the police excluded the Jews from the *Casino*, or Club, at Ferrara, to which they had been admitted five years previously. Henceforth, moreover, it was necessary to obtain a permit from the Inquisition if a Jew wished to leave the city; until five years later, when the Pope visited the Legations, a Jewish deputation, which waited on him at Senigallia, persuaded him to withdraw this regulation. As late as 1864, the Ferrara Ghetto was occupied by a squadron of military to make sure that no Christians worked there. In such circumstances, it was natural that the Jews continued active in the underground movement throughout unredeemed Italy. Typical of them was the heroic Giuseppe

Finzi, one of the principal associates and fellow sufferers of the famous Martyrs of Belfiore in the ill-starred and savagely repressed patriotic movement at Mantua in 1852.

But no degree of brutality could now do more than retard the consummation which was already inevitable. In 1859, with French help, the Austrians were ejected from Milan and the greater part of Lombardy. This in turn gave the signal for popular risings in Parma, Modena, Tuscany and the Romagna (occupied since 1849 by the Austrian troops) where the old rulers were overthrown and representative assemblies voted for annexation to the kingdom of Sardinia. In Modena, Reggio, Bologna and Ferrara, Jews served in the interim administrations, and everywhere in the field. In Tuscany, Sansone d'Ancona, who had in vain urged the grand duke to send troops to fight under Vittorio Emanuele, was director of finance and public works in the Provisional Government. All this devotion was amply justified, the reward coming in many places even before union with the kingdom of Sardinia was formally achieved. In Tuscany the Provisional Government, the day after it was formed, revived the articles of the Constitution of 1848 abolishing religious disabilities (April 30th). The municipality of Modena decreed the civil equality of the Jews on June 13, as one of its first measures, this being confirmed by the newly appointed governor ten days later; and the last quota of the special Jewish tribute was actually returned. On July 4, the governor general of Lombardy issued a decree declaring all citizens, whatever their religious belief, equal in the sight of the law. In the Romagna, the same was effected by a decree of August 10. The next year, Garibaldi and his Thousand — eight of them were Jews, including a German student, Adolph Moses, who was afterwards to become a rabbi in America — overthrew the Bourbons in the Two Sicilies, and there were similar risings all over the Marches and what was left of the Papal States. The demolition of the Levantine synagogue by the papal commander during the siege did not save Ancona from the liberating armies; and on September 25, even before its annexation was proclaimed, religious equality was extended by decree to this area as well. On March 17, 1861, the kingdom of Italy, under the house of Savoy, was proclaimed by the Italian Parliament, with Vittorio Emanuele as king and a system of government based on the Piedmontese Constitution of 1848. The emancipation of the Jews was complete throughout the land save for Venice, Mantua and Trieste with their daughter-communities (including Padua, Verona, etc.), still under Austrian rule; and, above all, Rome.*

Here, the darkest reaction still prevailed. From the Jewish point of view, it was the black spot of Europe — the focus of obscurantism and inhuman treatment, as Russia was to be in the next generation and Germany in our own day. When Pius IX returned embittered after the suppression of the short-lived republic, bigotry became triumphant. The Jews were charged with responsibility for the duration of the revolutionary government and were thrown back into the Ghetto, though the gates and walls were not renewed. Their shops and houses were searched for objects alleged to have been seized from the churches during the popular interlude. The old prohibition against the employment of Christian servants was again enforced, even more strictly than in the period of the Counter-Reformation. A Jew of good standing was actually sent to prison for having an elderly Christian woman in his house to look after his linen. There were sporadic outbursts of violence, or official perquisitions in the Ghetto which were little different. Notwithstanding the general change of attitude in the world, the Jews continued to be excluded from all honorable walks of life. No professions and few callings were open to them. They were prohibited to engage in any form of manufacture

* Nice was, however, ceded to France as part of the general readjustment at this period, the Jewish community passing henceforth out of the Italian orbit and losing its former Italian character.

by machinery. Even trade in old clothes required a special license. In 1862, they were forbidden to visit the markets in the countryside about Velletri. Two years after, shops maintained outside the Ghetto in the names of or in association with Christians were closed down. Jewish visitors from abroad, however distinguished, were allowed in the city only for limited periods, and were kept under strict surveillance while they remained. In 1858, the police were sent to search the Ghetto at Passover time in order to find some missing children — ultimately traced in another part of the town — on a suspicion of ritual murder. The former tribute to the House of Catechumens was regularly exacted, and in the heyday of the Victorian era that institution resumed its ghoulish work, unmoved by any normal consideration of humanity.

In 1858, there took place the most notorious of the abuses associated with it. At Bologna, a servant girl revealed to her confessor that six years previously, when she was employed (against the law, indeed) by a Jewish family named Mortara, she had performed some sort of baptismal ceremony over a year-old baby, Edgardo, whom she imagined to be in danger of his life. She was instructed to inform the authorities, who sent a squad of police to the house to seize the child from the parents and send him to Rome to be brought up as a Christian. A wave of indignation swept through Europe. Humanitarians everywhere took up the parents' cause. Francis Joseph of Austria and Napoleon III of France advised the Pope to yield rather than antagonize the public opinion of the world. The Jewish communities of the kingdom of Sardinia invoked the assistance of their government; a mass meeting of protest was held at the Mansion House in London; and the English philanthropist, Sir Moses Montefiore (Livornese by birth) went in person to Rome to obtain redress. Perhaps because, rather than in spite of, the extent of the outcry among the liberals. "Pio Nono" remained adamant. The Anglo-Jewish

Garibaldian, Charles Alexander Scott, planned an expedition to Rome with some companions, disguised as monks, to recover the child, but nothing came of it. After a triumphant parade through the Ghetto, Edgardo Mortara was baptized and brought up in the dominant faith, being admitted ultimately to Holy Orders and attaining distinction as a Catholic missionary in the course of a particularly long and active life.

This was not the last case of the sort, though by far the most notorious. One day in 1864, a priest enticed a Roman Jewish boy to the House of Catechumens on the pretext of giving him a pair of shoes to take to his master for repair. Before long, the Catholic Church received a new adherent; the boy's sister died as a result of the shock; his mother became mad; his father had to leave Rome; while another Jew was thrown into prison because he had dared to glance at the neo-convert when he was looking out of the window. It was in vain that the Pope was petitioned in the following year by some distinguished Christians, whose compassion had been stirred, to abolish the tribute still paid by the Jews to the grim institution. Such was the distress in the Roman Ghetto that no fewer than 2,000 persons, out of a total population of only 5,000, were in receipt of charitable support from the community.

But the hour of liberation was now approaching. Already in 1859, the year after the Mortara kidnapping, Bologna had been freed, with the remainder of the Romagna and the Marches. In 1866, taking advantage of Austria's war with Prussia, Vittorio Emanuele opened hostilities again in order to liberate the territories still under her rule. Once more, the Italian Jews flocked to the colors and several of them fell in battle. Though successful in the field, the emperor had to make peace, ceding the greater part of his Italian dominions. The important Jewish communities of Padua, Rovigo, Venice, Verona and Mantua, with some smaller ones, lost forthwith such disabilities as they had previously suffered; for a decree of Prince Eugene of Savoy-Carignano, in his capacity as lieutenant of the king, declared all citizens equal in the sight of the law regardless of religious belief. Except for Trieste — to remain under Austrian rule for a generation more — only Rome now remained unliberated.

Garibaldi made another characteristic raid in the following year, in which, as always, Jewish blood was shed; but it was unsuccessful. At long last, during the Franco-Prussian War, the French troops, who had propped up the temporal power of the Popes during the past quarter of a century, were withdrawn. In September, the Eternal City was entered by the Italian troops, amid scenes of jubilation such as were not to be known again for another three-quarters of a century. The silver-tongued Samuel Alatri, for many agonizing years the lay representative of Roman Jewry in all its negotiations with the papal government, was a member of the deputation which communicated to the king the results of the plebiscite that followed. On October 2, Rome was annexed to United Italy, of which it was henceforth the capital; and a royal decree of eleven days later formally abolished all the religious disabilities that had hitherto prevailed. The liberation of Italy and of Italian Jewry were completed by the same stroke.

CHAPTER X

The Age of Emancipation

xxxix

ITALIAN JEWRY UNDER EMANCIPATION

TWENTY-TWO years had sufficed to bring the emancipation of the Jews in Italy to fruition. In 1848, there was no European country (except Spain from which they were entirely excluded) where the restrictions placed upon them were more galling and more humiliating. After 1870, there was no land in either hemisphere where conditions were or could be better. It was not only that disabilities were removed, as happened elsewhere too during these momentous years, but that the Jews were accepted freely, naturally and spontaneously as members of the Italian people, on a perfect footing of equality with their neighbors. The reason for this is easy to understand, and has already been stressed in these pages. There was in the Italian Jew no element of the foreigner. Established in the country already for two thousand years, he was as much a native as any other component of the Italian people. So far, indeed, had the original purity of Italian "blood" been modified in the course of the centuries that he perhaps represented the only ethnic component in the entire population that had remained constant since the beginning of the Christian era. Even the newest elements in the Synagogue — the descendants of the German immigrants of the fifteenth and sixteenth centuries, or of the Marrano refugees of the seventeenth — were by now thoroughly established and acclimatized. The "dislike of the unlike" was not therefore complicated, as was the case elsewhere, by an element of xenophobia. There was no essential difference of language or of culture or of tradition — only one of religion; and when in the Liberal era religious disabilities were removed, and religious differences were universally considered to be of minor significance, the Jews were accepted in the fullest sense as Italians. Hence not only the disabilities but also the animosities disappeared, with unbelievable rapidity and completeness. Some rearguards of the ultra-Catholic party, devoid of influence, automatically maintained a spluttering guerrilla warfare, but it created more amusement than friction. The new antisemitism, when it began to rear its ugly head north of the Alps towards the end of the century, had no repercussions in the country. Nor when persecution broke out in the Russian empire in the eighteen-eighties did any appreciable eddy of the fugitives who swept the English-speaking world reach this poor and imperfectly industrialized Latin land and thereby disturb the balance.

There was thus no part of the world where religious freedom was more real, or religious prejudice so small. It was not that the Italian Jews no longer suffered from any political disabilities, but that they no longer suffered to any serious degree even from prejudice. The profession of Judaism was regarded as an amiable eccentricity rather than a social mistake. There was in the vast mass of the people not even the *arrière pensée* of anti-Jewish feeling. Whether it was in parliamentary elections or university appointments, charitable organizations or social gatherings, army messes or fashionable clubs, the question of a man's being or not being a Jew barely came into consideration, except perhaps in those circles which objected no less to Lutherans and Freemasons. In the eyes of the majority, the Jew attended — or perhaps in this age of scepticism did not attend — his synagogue on Saturday; the Christian attended — or did not attend — his church on Sunday, and there the essential difference ended.

The final manifestations of emancipation followed one on another, in the course of the second half of the nineteenth century, easily and rapidly. The few inadvertent relics of the age of intolerance were swept away — for example, the special oath *more judaico* in Tuscany, and the Christological declaration which prevented Jews from acting as notaries public. In 1851, the statutes of the old Piedmontese noble order of S. Maurizio had been revised so as to permit non-Catholics to be members. Those subsequently established had from the beginning no sectarian restrictions or coloring, and soon Jews, like their neighbors, flaunted the title of *cavaliere* (knight) and so on in somewhat absurd profusion. The Treves de' Bonfili family of Venice, raised to the rank of baron by Napoleon, had the title confirmed by the Austrian emperor and set an example for the ennobling of one or two philanthropic Jews in Piedmont even before 1848; by the end of the century, a dozen families had been given hereditary titles.

In political life, there was perhaps one significant difference between the scene in Italy and in other lands, where the Jews were mainly or even — except perhaps in the English-speaking countries — overwhelmingly identified with the parties of the Left. Here, owing to the fact that the prejudice against which they had to contend by reason of their origin was so slight, and that they had first entered into prominence in public life in connection with the nationalist movement of the *Risorgimento*, they tended to be fairly impartially recruited from all political fractions, from the one wing to the other. In 1861, Giuseppe Finzi, conspirator and fighter over so many years, who was to be raised to the Senate a quarter of a century later, had been elected to the first Parliament of United Italy, together with two other Jews; in 1874, there were eleven Jewish deputies in the Chamber, and in 1894 fifteen — a figure which was never to be exceeded and which, high though it indubitably was, could not have implied anything even approaching a dominating influence in politics even had there been some degree of cohesion.

The most important Jew in Italian public life in the age of the *Risorgimento* and for some time after was Isaac Artom, a member of an acient family of Asti, and one of the important figures in the Italian revival. He was successively private secretary to the great Cavour, member of the staff of the Italian embassy in Paris, chief secretary in the Italian Foreign Office, plenipotentiary in the peace negotiations of 1866, and from 1870 to 1876 Under Secretary of State for Foreign Affairs. In 1876, he was appointed a senator of the realm, together with Tullo Massarani, the artist-author who had played so prominent a part in the patriotic movements of the previous generation — the first Jews to attain this distinction. Thus far, none had been a member of any Italian cabinet. When Marco Minghetti formed his second ministry in 1873, the appalling state of the national economy gave rise to the gravest concern. Isaac Pesaro Maurogonato, whose administration of the treasury of the short-lived Venetian republic under Manin had been such as to arouse the admiration even of the enemy, and had been the first deputy elected by his native city to the Parliament of United Italy (of which he subsequently became vice-president) was the obvious choice for the all-important portfolio of Finance. But religious prejudice was not as yet entirely dead, and a "liberal" deputy named Pasqualigo went so far as to appeal to the king not to permit a Jew to occupy a cabinet position. Though the latter took no notice, and personally pressed Maurogonato to accept office, he refused, ostensibly for family reasons. No voice was, however, raised in criticism when in 1891 the same office was filled by Luigi Luzzatti, the economist who "spiritualized the power of gold" by his work for the cooperative movement, devoting his whole life to the improvement of the economic status of the people. He had already filled a minor government post as early as 1869, before he was old enough to be elected to Parliament, where he sat without a break from 1870 to 1921. Though not an observant Jew, his Jewish sympathies were always strong, especially when his people were attacked; it was as a Jew as well as a Liberal that he protested against Roumania's antisemitic policy. When he became prime minister, in 1909, after having held the portfolio of Finance time after time, it may be said that the enfranchisement of the Jews in Europe reached its culmination.

Other Italian Jews who occupied high public position in political life included Leone Wollemborg, founder of the rural savings banks in Italy, who was minister of finance from 1900 to 1903; General Giuseppe Ottolenghi, a veteran of the campaigns of liberation, minister of war in 1902–3; Gabriel Pincherle, honorary president of the Council of State; and Ernesto Artom, distinguished no less as diplomat than as parliamentarian. Sidney Sonnino, a half-Jew, was prime minister for brief periods in 1906 and 1909–10, and served as foreign minister from 1915 to 1919 in such a manner as to command the respect of even the most fervid nationalists. A state which had abolished religious discrimination so completely in domestic matters could not countenance it in diplomacy; and when Isaac Artom went to Copenhagen as minister plenipotentiary in 1862, he established a precedent not for Italy alone, but for all of Europe. Important, too, in this sphere was the long activity of Artom's younger contemporary and fellow-Piedmontese, Giacomo Malvano, for several decades permanent secretary to the Ministry of Foreign Affairs, and Italian representative in important international negotiations. The number of Jews who achieved prominence in municipal politics was of course extremely great. There was a symbolic importance in the appointment as mayor of Rome in 1907 of the Anglo-Italian Ernesto Nathan, a militant Freemason and son of the family which had befriended Mazzini in exile, who for six years remained responsible for the administration of the city where his kindred had so long been treated as prisoners.

In the Senate, chosen from the most distinguished persons in every sphere of activity, the number of Jews had risen by 1901 to seven, and by 1920 to nineteen out of a total membership of some 350.

The constant support of the royal family in this period of consolidation was noteworthy, and could not fail to have a profound effect. From 1848 onwards, the house of Savoy, previously so bigoted, showed itself conspicuously free from any trace of religious prejudice, and in successive generations went out of the way more than once to express its sympathies. The jurist Vittorio Polacco, and the soldier Giuseppe Ottolenghi, who has just been mentioned, were tutors to the royal family, and more than one Jew was on intimate terms in that simple court. When at the time of the Italo-Turkish war of 1911, some newspapers of the Right, irritated by foreign press criticism which they ascribed to Jews, referred glibly to a Judaeo-Masonic plot against Christianity in favor of Islam, Vittorio Emanuele III received a Jewish deputation led by Luigi Luzzatti, and shortly afterwards demonstratively visited two synagogues in succession.

Released from the Ghetto, Jewish genius became apparent in every aspect of Italian life. The long generations of intellectual training, the frequent hours of absorption in talmudic studies, now bore a remarkable crop. It was unnecessary for the Italian Jews, as it was for some of their coreligionists beyond the Alps, to become assimilated to the ruling culture before they could contribute to it. Their *Italianità* was already so complete that the period of transition was reduced almost to nothing. There was thus no country of Europe where the Jewish contribution to cultural life was proportionately so great. It was like a tree-trunk, held artificially below the water and forcing its way irresistibly to the surface once the obstacles are broken. The scions of the Ghetto did not rise above their level, but after the lapse of centuries they at last found their level. One reason was, of course, the traditional Jewish passion for education, which continued to be intense although its central interest had by now changed. At the outset of the age of Emancipation, in 1861, there had been only 5.8 per cent of illiterates among the Italian Jewish population above the age of ten, and it is likely that the exceptions were for the most part able to read Hebrew; the figure among their compatriots was 54.5 per cent, to be reduced only by half during the next sixty-five years. This could not fail to have its results. Few were the Italian cities — at least in the north of the country — which did not have streets named after illustrious Jewish citizens, sometimes applied to the former Ghetto area where they had been born; and it was perhaps not entirely a coincidence that those parts of Italy which now lagged so conspicuously behind the rest in general progress were those from which the Jews had been excluded long before. It is absurd to question or to criticize the fact that they made contributions to Italian life out of all proportion to their number. There was no reason why they should not have done so; and to suppress such talents as they had for fear of arousing jealousy would have been considered little less than treasonable. A statistician of repute asserted, rather than calculated, that the proportion of persons of distinction in the Jewish community outnumbered those in the country as a whole by sixteen to one, holding a clear lead in every field except the hereditary nobility and the Church. Some 8 per cent of the university professors in 1930 were Jews; while in the standard Italian handbook of contemporary biography, 169 out of the 2,515 notables listed, or 6.72 per cent, belonged to Jewish families, though the proportion of the Jews in the country was only about one-tenth of one per cent. No envy, and little notice, was aroused by this disproportion; those who were aware of it regarded it, quite properly, as no more than an interesting phenomenon, based on historic circumstances over which no one — least of all the Jews — now had any control.

In this connection, it is difficult to steer a clear course between the Scylla of generalization and the Charybdis of a catalogue; but a very few outstanding personalities must be mentioned individually. Foremost in many ways — for he was one of the greatest figures in the history of the revival of scholarship in Italy in the nineteenth century — was Graziadio Isaiah Ascoli, easily the first of Italian philologists and glottologists (and incidentally the editor of the ancient Jewish inscriptions of Apulia), who first introduced the exacting standards of modern scientific treatment into the country and thereby had a profound influence on its academic life. Supreme in his own sphere, too, was Alessandro d'Ancona, one of the founders of the historical method in Italy, whose works on the origins of the Italian theater and on Italian popular poetry are never likely to be superseded. The school of literary history and criticism which he initiated included, moreover, many of the most important scholars of the following generation, among whom may be mentioned Salomone Morpurgo, the expert on medieval Italian literature and curator of the National Library in Florence. In the realm of history, Samuel Romanin, the greatest historian of Venice, is only one out of the many names of first importance. One of the most distinguished of the art-historians whom Italy has produced in such profusion was Senator I. B. Supino, the authority on medieval sculpture. The tradition of Jewish participation in Italian literature had never been interrupted, and the close of the Ghetto age produced a few writers of repute, such as the poet Salamone Fiorentino who has been mentioned above. In the course of the next century there were many figures of at least as high distinction in their day, including Tullo Massarani, Giuseppe Revere and Eugenio Camerini, incidentally one of the outstanding Dante scholars of the period, all fighters in the wars of the *Risorgimento*, whose verses are to be found in many standard anthologies. Later came, to mention only a few out of a long roll, Umberto

Saba, Ugo Ghiron and Angiolo Orvieto, who with his brother Adolfo founded the Florentine literary weekly, *Il Marzocco*. Novelists include Alberto Cantoni, who introduced the Anglo-Saxon conception of "humor" into Italian letters; Guido da Verona, whose romances enjoyed a tremendous though perhaps meretricious popularity; and Enrico Castelnuovo, who in one of his books, *I Moncalvo*, made a not over-successful and unfortunately almost isolated attempt to depict some aspects of contemporary Italian Jewish life. It may be added that Italo Svevo, the Italian Proust, was half-Jewish. Of dramatists, besides Revere, whose historical plays were at one time immensely popular, Sabatino Lopez achieved in the twentieth century an outstanding popularity and reputation. Publishing in Italy never grew to so large a scale as to become impersonalized, and Italian literature of the nineteenth and twentieth centuries owed a great deal to certain Jewish firms, such as that of Treves in Milan. Artists included Samuel Jesi, a distinguished though now forgotten nineteenth-century sculptor and engraver; Serafino da Tivoli, founder of Italian impressionism; and of course Amedeo Modigliani, who made himself a reputation in Paris as a futurist Botticelli. In music, Alberto Franchetti, Frederico Consolo and, among the younger school, Mario Castelnuovo-Tedesco were of international repute; and there was a host of gifted interpreters, the most famous of whom was Giuditta Pasta, the greatest singer of her time, for whom Bellini composed some of his best-known works. Ugo Piperno was one of Italy's outstanding actors.

In other branches of intellectual activity, eminent names are to be found in similar profusion. Tullio Levi-Civita, one of the most distinguished of all Italian mathematicians, developed the absolute calculus which made possible Einstein's theory of relativity. Other names of great importance in this sphere are those of Eugenio Levi, whose death in action in 1917 cut short a career of exceptional promise, Federigo Enriques, Vito Volterra and Luigi Cremona, the last-named having been responsible for the reform of mathematical instruction in the country. In applied science, a figure of first distinction was Alessandro Artom, raised to the nobility for his services to radiotelegraphy. In medicine, the tradition of Jewish participation, stretching far back into the Middle Ages, was perpetuated by Cesare Lombroso, founder of the scientific study of criminology, whose *Man of Genius* was one of the most influential books of the nineteenth century; Senator Pio Foà, founder of modern pathological anatomy, and a host of others, including some of the most brilliant practitioners of our day. In economics, mention has been made already of the illustrious and venerated figure of Luigi Luzzatti. Other econonists of great distinction include Achille Loria and Augusto Graziani. Emilio Morpurgo, rector of the University of Padua and under-secretary in the Ministry of Agriculture, was one of Italy's outstanding educational experts as well as historian and economist. Felice Finzi may be reckoned the founder of the study of Assyriology in Italy before his tragic death at the age of twenty-five. In the field of law, there was a galaxy of genius: such as Ludovico Mortara, president of the Italian Supreme Court, in effect the chief justice of Italy, and the great systematizer of Italian legal procedure, son of a learned Mantuan rabbi, who became also minister of justice and vice-president of the Cabinet; and Cesare Vivanti, author of Italy's commercial code who with three other Jews, Leone Bolaffi, David Supino and Angelo Sraffa, founded the new school of commercial law. Leone Levi, equally eminent as jurist and statistician, popularized the Chamber of Commerce in England, and was largely responsible for the codification of international commercial law. Perhaps the most distinguished of all was Vittorio Polacco, the greatest expert on Italian civil law and rector of the University of Padua, the pride of Italian Jewry in his day.

Another channel in which the Italian Jews attained distinction was the Army. They had fought loyally and bravely in the campaigns under Napoleon, and in every battle of the *Risorgimento*. In the war against Austria in 1859, twenty Jewish volunteers served from Padua alone, out of a total population of barely 800, though they would have risked being shot out of hand had they been captured; in 1866, 104 volunteers from Modena and Reggio enrolled in addition to the conscripts — no fewer than one in four of the male population; during the Wars of Liberation, ninety Jewish officers served, five of them being decorated in the Neapolitan campaign of 1860 alone. With a tradition so strongly established, the attractions of a military career were very strong. When Rome was captured in 1870, there were in the army 87 Jewish officers; forty years later, over 150, holding ranks from lieutenant general downwards — and this at a time when in Germany no professing Jew was admitted to a commission. Indeed, so numerous were the professional soldiers in some of the Piedmontese families that they might have been described as a military caste. The founder of the first Jewish periodical in Italy, Cesare Rovighi, was one of the king's aides-de-camp. General Giuseppe Ottolenghi, the minister of war, was an outstanding but not a unique, and still less incongruous, figure in the community.

Nor were they backward in less conventional careers. Among the most romantic Italian figures of the nineteenth century was Rubino Ventura, of Finale, who after serving in his 'teens under Napoleon wandered about the East as a soldier of fortune and ultimately rose to the command of the armies of the rajah of Lahore. Of the Italian explorers of the nineteenth and twentieth centuries a number were Jews — Angelo Castelbolognese, who explored the Sudan; Edoardo Foà who followed the Zambesi to its source; Baron Franchetti, who penetrated into darkest Africa; and Aldo Pontremoli, one of those who lost his life with Nobile in 1928, in his ill-fated aeronautical expedition to the North Pole. The part played by Jews in educational, philanthropic and humanitarian activities, throughout the country, was worthy of their past. One name only need be mentioned — that of Arthur Serena, son of one of Manin's companions and fellow-exiles, who devoted the whole of the fortune he amassed in England to fostering good relations between the country of his birth and that of his residence, establishing in England chairs of Italian and in Italy of English, as well as institutes for spreading an appreciation of English culture. (The time was to come, alas, when Jews were to be ejected even from these.) Typical of a great number of such benefactions all over the country was Baron Franchetti's bequest of the Ca d'Oro, loveliest perhaps of the palaces on the Grand Canal, to the city of Venice.

It is pointless to continue this survey. In other countries, there would have been some essential Jewish quality — occasionally at least — in the careers of those who attained similar distinction; they would perhaps have emerged from an exotic or even a foreign environment, some Hebraic characteristic might have conditioned their progress or they might have had to fight against an anti-Jewish prejudice which gives their careers a specific interest. In Italy, almost from the beginning, this was not the case. Except perhaps for certain inherent qualities of mind and an exceptionally intense devotion to learning, Jewishness did not enter one way or the other into the careers of the great majority of those whose names have been mentioned, whose Hebraic contacts were, indeed, in some cases of the slenderest. They were no more than Italians of the Jewish persuasion, or merely of Jewish extraction, and the fact of their origin was regarded as being of purely sentimental interest.

Meanwhile, with the opening of the gates of opportunity, the economic structure of the Jewish communities changed. The old callings, at one time considered characteristic, tended to be abandoned with astonishing rapidity, though in Rome peddling continued to be the mainstay of the Jewish proletariat, as had to some extent been the case ever since classical times. The tailoring industry and certain branches of the textile industry also remained fairly widespread. But except for this the change was far-reaching. The secondhand dealers of the Ghetto developed into antique dealers, including some of the most important in the country; the shopkeepers expanded into every branch of retail trade; a few important manufactures (though not to any great extent in heavy industry) were set up; the professions — medicine, law, teaching, engineering, journalism, and so on — exercised an ever more profound attraction on each succeeding generation. Yet, though the Italian Jews remained predominantly an urban group, the magnet of the countryside exerted a very strong influence on some of them. Even in the first half of the nineteenth century, Jews were responsible for introducing new methods of scientific agriculture in the former Venetian territories, now under Austrian rule; and after emancipation the same tendency became apparent in Emilia (around Bologna) and Piedmont, where many outstanding families now invested their wealth in land. Symbolic in its way was the fact that the International Institute of Agriculture, set up in Rome in 1905, owed its origin to the enthusiasm and self-devotion of the American Jewish idealist David Lubin and the ready understanding of the Italian Jewish statesman Luigi Luzzatti, who enlisted the interest of the king. It may be noted that in the economic field, in which they might have been expected to excel, the place of the Italian Jew in the Age of Emancipation was not superlatively important, except in the insurance business, which they may be said, indeed, to have established and developed (the great Assicurazioni Generali of Trieste was founded by the poet Giuseppe Lazzaro Morpurgo). There were a few private banks, but none was of more than local importance. Though the economic standing of the community rose beyond recognition — despite the continued existence of a large and poverty-stricken proletariat in Rome and one or two other cities — and a number of moderate and one or two great fortunes accumulated, there were very few really outstanding names, whether in industry or in finance; and hardly any of the handful of Italians who were known in international business circles were Jews. The release of their pent-up ability helped them to rise in many cases into the ranks of the bourgeoisie, or even the upper bourgeoisie; but only in very few cases, if any at all, into that of the so-called international plutocracy.

At the same time, such physical differences as had formerly existed speedily diminished also; for the opening of the Ghetto gates had an immediate external influence on the Jews. The Ghetto type, Ghetto speech, Ghetto language, Ghetto characteristics, all melted away with amazing rapidity, though here and there, especially in the larger cities, relics could be discerned among the lower classes and the aged veterans. Even the Jewish physique altered for the good. According to the official war-office figures, the medium height of Jews born in Rome after the papal government had come to an end was nine millimeters more than that of those born before; the former were on the average a millimeter and a half shorter than their fellow citizens, the latter five millimeters taller.

After 1870, only one step remained to be taken, to complete the unification of historic Italy. Trieste and the hinterland (including Gorizia) were still under Austrian rule; and the urban population was Italian, though the surrounding areas were largely Slav. From the outset, the Jewish community had been unmistakably part of the Italian nucleus in culture as well as in language. Irredentist sympathies were particularly marked. Many of them transferred themselves to Italy rather than live under what they considered alien rule. One of the exiles, Salvatore Barzillai, journalist, jurist and politician, was sometimes spoken of as the "Deputy for Trieste" in the Italian Parliament, until he was appointed to the Senate — the only person ever so honored for patriotic services. His was one of the most influential of the voices which caused Italy to abandon the Germano-Austrian alliance and associate herself in the end with England, France and their allies in the war of 1914–8. The part played by Jews in this, the last War of Italian Unification, was noteworthy. Sidney Sonnino was foreign minister throughout the period of crisis, and is spoken of as one of the architects of victory. Large numbers of the youth, who could ill be spared by that dwindling community, lost their lives on the field; of the three professors in Italian universities who fell, two were Jews and one a half-Jew. More than 1,000 were decorated for valor. Eleven Jewish generals commanded armies in the field; and the French forces which marched to the Piave to help to throw back the enemy in 1917 were as it happens commanded by another, Camille Lévy. In Trieste, the loyalties of the community were so notorious that "Jew" and "Italian" were popularly used almost as synonyms; and when the news of the disaster at Caporetto was received, a congregational fast was observed, in deepest secrecy. By the peace settlement there were added to United Italy (besides a small number of groups of recent Central European origin in Meran, Fiume, Abbazia) the ancient communities of Gorizia and Trieste (that of Gradisca, swept by the war, was now defunct). The latter indeed, with the loss of its hinterland, found its importance diminished. Nevertheless, with its 6,000 Jews of miscellaneous provenance — largely from Central Europe, the Balkans and Corfu — grouped about the original nucleus, it was henceforth one of the foremost Italian centers, ranking after only Rome and Milan. Thus, for the first time in history, all the Italian Jewries were united at last under one rule.

xl

The Impact of Emancipation

In its domestic life, Italian Jewry was adapting itself in the course of these years to the new circumstances created by the opening of the Ghetto gates, the recognition of the former prisoners as Italians of the Jewish persuasion, and their reorganization as an essentially religious body indissolubly connected with an ethnic group. There was a universal wave of optimism. If their neighbors were prepared to forget, the Jews were more than ready to forgive. At last they were sons of free Italy, and nothing more was required to usher in the halcyon age than the readjustment of their institutions to modern circumstances. The change of attitude was symbolized in certain significant alterations in vocabulary. The former designation *ebreo* or Hebrew, honored by centuries of martyrdom and suffering, was now widely discarded, by reason of its derogatory associations in the popular mind; *giudeo*, always considered contemptuous, was seldom used except in an insulting connotation. Instead, the Jews now styled themselves and were styled Israelites, which was considered to stress the religious differentiation only, as had become fashionable too in certain other countries.* No longer were their places of worship designated by their neighbors *sinagoga*, or among themselves by the more intimate term *scuola*; with a somewhat unfortunate retrogression of ideas they were now termed "Temples," or in more modest cases "oratories," incidentally obscuring the former educational and social functions now so tragically neglected.

* Luigi Luzzatti wittily illustrated the use of the three terms. When a man asked for a loan, he said, he addressed the lender, respectfully, as *israelita*; once he had obtained it, he considered him *ebreo*; when the time for it to be repaid, he called him *giudeo*.

The one-time Jewish quarters were, of course, abandoned so far as was possible, some of them reverting in consequence to the reputation for lawlessness from which the Jewish influx had redeemed them. In many cases, the old buildings were swept away in the course of civic rebuilding schemes; that of Florence, for example, disappeared when the medieval *mercato vecchio* quarter was pulled down, to the irreparable loss of the city, to constitute the garish Piazza Vittorio Emanuele. Of the more famous of the old Ghettos, perhaps only that of Venice retained its architectural setting almost unmodified, though its population lost its exclusively Jewish character; while it was only in Rome that, in spite of attempts to disperse it and a considerable amount of reconstruction, a Jewish quarter in the old sense could be said to exist after the beginning of the twentieth century.

Emancipated the earliest, and thus not only given liberty of expression but also feeling most strongly the need of self-explanation, Piedmontese Jewry occupied for a while, in the second half of the nineteenth century, the primacy in Jewish Italy. The intellectual energy and religious zeal displayed at this period in some little communities in this part of the country of less than a thousand inhabitants, such as Vercelli or Cuneo, would seem hardly credible today. For two generations Casale was the intellectual center of northern Italy — indeed, of Italy as a whole — from the Jewish point of view, except as regards rabbinic studies. On the other hand, the community of Rome — always the largest in the country, and now increasing in numerical importance — filled at this time an almost insignificant role. For a long while it produced very few outstanding personalities, whether in communal or public life, being outdone in this respect by many relatively insignificant nuclei. Even in the matter of religious organization, the community of the capital long remained in a preposterous state of chaos, and it was not until several decades had elapsed that it began to play the part to which its traditions, numbers and importance entitled it. The long, hopeless generations of oppression had done their work only too well.

Conversely, some new centers came into prominence. Milan, where no Jews lived up to about the time of the French Revolution, now developed very rapidly, attracting numerous foreign immigrants as well as natives and eventually becoming the second of all Italy in numerical importance. At Bologna, which notwithstanding the brutal expulsion in 1836 had harbored a few quasi-illegal settlers even before the close of the papal regime, a synagogue was organized in 1864, though not legally constituted until 1911; and this, too, expanded rapidly, becoming one of the principal in central Italy. Genoa too began to develop rapidly and to absorb many immigrants — especially from Leghorn, when it ceased to be a free port and its Jewish population dwindled in consequence. In Naples, Jewish religious services began to be held in 1831, but it was only after its liberation from the Bourbons and its union with the kingdom of Italy that, in 1863, a public synagogue was established, this community too attaining importance. Elsewhere in the kingdom of the Two Sicilies, the memory of past sorrows, or else present economic backwardness, discouraged Jews from settling in any number, though after the war of 1915–8 a small community was established at Palermo.*

With the advent of Emancipation, the intimate Ghetto synagogues, situated in what were now slums with few or no Jewish inhabitants, were considered inadequate to express the dignity of the Jewish religion. In many places they

* Some sort of Jewish religious organization also came into existence at this time in a few smaller places, such as the port of Spezia, the seaside resort of Viareggio, and the old centers of Udine and Perugia. The census of 1911 had shown an unexpectedly large number of Jews in South Italy, Sicily and Sardinia, but the numbers were not maintained, and it is possible that the returns were deliberately confused by some persons who objected to the denominational categorization, or proclaimed themselves Jews for romantic reasons.

were now replaced by flamboyant structures in the spirit of the new age. The community of Turin, in particular, determined to erect a new place of worship which should be a monument to the enfranchisement of Italian Jewry, and commissioned Alessandro Antonelli, the most eminent architect of the time, to execute it. His design was strikingly original but over-ambitious. The building, begun in 1864, was only half-finished in 1877, by which time the original estimated cost had already been quadrupled, far exceeding the economic potentialities of the community. In the end it was taken over and completed by the municipality as a museum of the *Risorgimento*, and still stands under the name *Mole Antonelliana*, with its fantastic spire — the tallest brick building, it is said, in the world. Its successor, though ample enough, was more modestly conceived. In Florence, private beneficence was responsible for an exquisitely proportioned "Temple" in the Moorish style in the fashionable outskirts of the city, one of the finest examples of synagogal architecture in Europe; while in Rome the clearing of the heart of the former Ghetto of bitter memory made possible the erection of a grandiose construction in a prominent position on the banks of the Tiber.

The movement for reform in Judaism had, on the other hand, only slight repercussions in Italy; perhaps because Italian orthodoxy was at no time as rigid as it was north of the Alps, perhaps because there was no need for any cultural readjustment, perhaps because a Catholic environment was less conducive to such changes than a Protestant one, perhaps because emancipation was so closely followed by a widespread religious indifference. At the time of the Mendelssohnian reforms in Germany at the close of the eighteenth century, the Jewish world was indeed perplexed by a rumor, which found its way into the newspapers, that the Italian rabbinate had sanctioned certain radical alterations in Jewish practice, but the report was indignantly denied; and when during the Napoleonic era a Livornese

Jew named Fernando independently put forward similar suggestions, his work was immediately suppressed, as has been mentioned.* The few proposals made in a similar sense in the post-Emancipation period had no better success. The idea was, indeed, championed by Rabbi Samuel Olper, who had publicly kissed a crucifix at a public meeting in the Piazza S. Marco at Venice during the Republican regime of 1848-9, as a token of good will, and afterwards had to leave the Austrian territories to become rabbi successively in Florence, Casale and Turin. Here in 1873 he put forward suggestions for abolishing the traditional duplication of the solemn festivals — as had indeed been unsuccessfully requested at Mantua just twenty years earlier — naively leaving the decision to popular ballot. This led to a general outcry of protest, and though the results of the referendum were favorable, the experiment was very soon abandoned, for the frequenters of the synagogue belonged to the conservative wing. In the same place, one of his successors received almost unanimous support from the members of the community when he protested against certain changes introduced by the Council in 1899 without consulting him. Such proposals at least demonstrated an active interest which was lacking ultimately, when the problem of irksome observances was solved by the great majority by the simple process of paying no attention to them. On the other hand, minor adjustments such as the introduction of the organ, countenanced by some Italian scholars even in the Ghetto period, became commonplaces all over the country. Indeed, an elaborate ceremonial, and prayer in a tongue no longer spoken, seemed to be natural and proper in Italy, and it was in part in consequence of this fact that the question of reform was never seriously considered.

* Benedetto Frizzi's *Usi ed abusi degli ebrei nei luoghi ... sacri* (Milan, 1809) had a similar though more moderate tendency. Cf. also Moses Formiggini's proposals, referred to above, page 443.

Emancipation automatically destroyed the special juridical position of the Jewish communities, together with the power, which they had presumably enjoyed ever since the Jews first settled in Italy in classical times, to levy taxation for communal purposes, without which they could not continue to exist or the synagogues to function. Some new legal basis obviously had to be found. In 1848, the energetic Rabbi Cantoni had elaborated a scheme for a consistorial organization on the French model for the Jews of Piedmont, such as they had already known under Napoleon, controlled by a Central Council and Rabbinate with their seat at Turin. This hierarchical system aroused great opposition from the minor communities, which alleged that the champion of the scheme desired to set himself up as the Jewish Pope; and though the details were somewhat modified in the parliamentary bill at length introduced in 1854, it had to be withdrawn. An inter-congregational conference held at Vercelli in 1856 prepared another plan, providing for a larger measure of authority for the smaller communities and a triennial representative congress to deliberate on matters of common interest. But this, too, proved unacceptable; and the measure ultimately introduced to Parliament in January 1857 by Urbano Rattazzi, minister of the interior, gave every community complete autonomy. There was still some opposition from Liberal enthusiasts, who considered that religious organization should now be a purely private matter. Nevertheless, the bill was carried and received the royal assent later in the same year. Supplementary regulations settled the details in connection with membership, elections and so on, which thus became uniform over the entire kingdom of Sardinia as it then existed. The Jewish communities were thus constituted into autonomous corporations, empowered to hold property and having as their object the performance of public worship and religious instruction. The administration was entrusted to councils elected triennially by all adult male members, able to read and write, who contributed twenty lire or more each year towards the expenditure. All Jews were legally obliged to pay the amounts assessed on them for the maintenance of essential religious services, unless they formally dissolved their connection and renounced thereby the benefits of organized Judaism. As the kingdom of Sardinia expanded in the following decade into United Italy, this organization was adopted in the main by the communities of the other parts of the Peninsula, though some (e. g., that of Mantua, and even that of Rome) preferred to reorganize themselves on a purely voluntary basis, while in Tuscany and the former Austrian provinces they enjoyed somewhat greater rights. In 1865 it was intended to extend the Rattazzi Law to the whole of Italy, but for some reason or other the bill was allowed to lapse. Though the idea of a consistorial organization was relinquished, a loose Union of Italian Jewish Communities was established by a Congress held at Ferrara in 1863, but after another general gathering at Florence four years later, at which twenty communities were represented and certain pious resolutions approved, it was dissolved in 1871. In 1911, it was renewed in a different form as the *Consorzio delle Comunità Israelitiche Italiane*, which received the royal approval by decree nine years later, but was not thereby galvanized into any appreciable animation.

By this time, the traditional scheme of Jewish studies which lay at the basis of the intensive cultural activity, described in a preceding section, was dead in Italy. The decay had culminated with surprising rapidity during the course of the Napoleonic era. When the French Revolution broke out, intellectual life in the Ghettos was still solidly organized on the same lines as a century or two centuries before; at the time of Waterloo, there were here and there some stalwart survivors of the former era, and at Leghorn a Levantine enclave stolidly continued the old life; but Italian rabbinism, with its academies and its rigors and its zest and its correspondence and its intense scheme of adult education, was now dying beyond recall — in part as the outcome of the long proscription of talmudic literature and freedom of thought, in part of the cloying influence of a mysticism that had become mechanical, in part of the decline of the former juridical autonomy. But a new crop grew out of the well-tilled soil. Circumstances compelled the communities of the provinces under Austrian rule to take the lead. As part of his policy of qualifying Jewish separatism, the Emperor Francis I issued, in 1820, an edict ordering that henceforth no rabbi should be appointed in his dominions who had not given evidence of philosophical knowledge and religious competence. Though in other provinces, for which it was really intended, this was greeted with consternation, it was cordially welcomed in the Lombardo-Venetian kingdom; for here the Jews realized that, in order to prove their fitness for the civil rights that they hoped to regain, it was desirable to replace the old-style rabbi by persons who had received a modern training, and were qualified to represent their flock in the eyes of the outside world, as had indeed been common in Italy from the period of the Renaissance. A conference of the communities of the region, held in Padua in 1821, determined therefore to set up a Collegio Rabbinico for the education of rabbis in a modern sense. This was opened in Padua in 1829 under government supervision — the first of all modern seminaries for the training of Jewish spiritual leaders. Notwithstanding its various vicissitudes, the majority of the Italian rabbis for the next hundred years came out of this institution — successively transferred first to Rome, then to Florence, then to Rome again — which on the whole has maintained a consistently high standard of achievement.

The Collegio Rabbinico of Padua was the center of Jewish studies in Italy in the following generation. Its commanding figure was Samuel David Luzzatto, born in Trieste of working-class parents who had been compelled to leave the Venetian territories as a result of the reactionary measures of 1777. A man of exceptional ability and attainments, though virtually self-taught, he was on the one hand the heir to the enlightened tradition of Italian Jewish scholarship, on the other in close touch — owing to the temporary accident of Austrian expansion — with the Jewish intellectual revival in northern Europe associated with the birth of the *Wissenschaft des Judentums*, or the "science" of Judaism. In his person, Italian Jewry was worthily and effectively associated with this movement. His fame would perhaps have been even greater had he concentrated his attention on a single subject; for his range of interest was dazzling. He collected and saved from oblivion large numbers of ancient manuscripts. He first edited the works of the greatest of medieval Hebrew poets, Jehudah ha-Levi, whose greatness he may be said to have rediscovered. He wrote the first Jewish biblical commentaries in a modern sense. He translated the Bible and prayer book afresh into Italian. He collaborated in every Jewish learned periodical of the time, whether published in Hebrew or in German or in French. He provided the great foreign savants with bibliographical information. He set the science of Hebrew philology and grammar on a new basis. He edited the traditional liturgy according to the native "Italian" (or "Roman") rite. At the same time, he continued the literary tradition of Italian Jewry by his prolific and polished, but not perhaps always inspired, poems, which made him a significant figure in the revival of Hebrew *belles-lettres*. He has been termed "the greatest Jew in an age so peculiarly rich in great Jews" — at least, an arguable evaluation.

Luzzatto's great reputation overshadows that of his contemporaries and collaborators, who were, however, of high caliber. He was closely associated with Isaac Samuel Reggio, the Italian Mendelssohn, unpaid rabbi of the community of Gorizia and originator of the idea of the Collegio Rabbinico, who also contributed prolifically to the learned periodicals, collected manuscripts, commented on the Pentateuch, polemized against the cabala, and in a work on the *Torah and Philosophy* demonstrated, like some of his medieval predecessors, the reconcilability of the two aspects of study. Lelio della Torre, professor of Talmud at the seminary, was also a notable figure and wrote considerably on theological and historical subjects. The tradition of Italian poetry was maintained not only by Luzzatto but also by his close friends, Giuseppe Almanzi and Abraham Salom of Padua and his cousin, Rachel Morpurgo of Trieste, heiress to the literary tradition of Deborah Ascarelli and Sarah Coppio Sullam two centuries before, whose verses attained perhaps a higher poetical level than his own. There were some outstanding bibliophiles, whose services to Jewish scholarship were memorable — for example, Giuseppe Almanzi, whose great library ultimately enriched that of the British Museum, or Leone Vita Saraval, whose collection went to the Theological Seminary of Breslau. Luzzatto's son, Filosseno, showed very great promise, cut short by an early death. Marco Mortara of Mantua, Benedetto Levi of Ferrara, Abraham Lattes of Venice, Eude Lolli of Padua, Vittorio Castiglione of Rome, were the most active scholars among the rabbis of the following generation; and among the laymen Salvatore de' Benedetti of Pisa, Leonello Modona of Bologna and the far from rabbinical David Castelli of Florence. The names of two non-professional enthusiasts should not be passed over in this connection — Donato Ottolenghi, the last outstanding member of the once-famous community of Acqui, with his somewhat exaggerated views of the Jewish influences in medieval thought, and Felice Momigliano, who wrote with prophetic passion on Hebraic universalism.

Another center of scholarship in a way rival to that of Padua was Leghorn, which represented a completely different tendency. Here, more than in any other place in Italy, something of the ancient atmosphere still survived. It was still an important center of Hebrew printing, as it remained down to our day, though now serving in particular the needs of Eastern communities. Under its remarkable rabbi, Elia Benamozegh, its traditions took on a new life, the old academies being consolidated into a secondary rabbinical seminary. Benamozegh perpetuated, though in a modernized guise, the esoteric lore of a former generation, as against the tendencies of his older contemporary Luzzatto, with whom he carried on a vigorous polemic. Among the votaries of religious mysticism of all creeds throughout Europe his reputation was very considerable; he was highly esteemed by men like Mazzini; and his *Israël et l'Humanité*, demonstrating the universal aspects of Judaism, is still among the most effective works on that subject. Of foreign Jewish savants who occupied themselves with matters Italian, and were in close touch with many of those who have been mentioned, special mention should certainly be made of Moritz Steinschneider, the founder of the science of Jewish bibliography, who chronicled in a series of studies the part played by the Jews in the cultural life of the country in the Middle Ages and after; Abraham Berliner, the first historian of the community of Rome; and David Kaufmann, who illustrated many aspects of Italian Jewish life from his precious collection of manuscripts acquired during repeated visits to the country. But the mass of material bearing on Italian Jewry was so large, and its contribution to Jewish learning spread over twenty centuries so extensive, that there were few of the eminent Hebraists of the last generation whose steps did not lead them at one time or another to the great Italian libraries — especially those of Parma and of the Vatican — and in whose writings there is not something bearing upon the political or intellectual life of the country in the past.

Part of the equipment of the emancipated Jewish community was the Jewish periodical. As early as 1845, a premature attempt had been made by Cesare Rovighi, later a colonel and aide-de-camp to the king, to produce one in

Parma, under the title *La Rivista Israelitica* ("The Jewish Review"), which lasted for only three years.* In 1853, however, the publication began at Vercelli of a new monthly, *L'Educatore Israelita* which, originally intended for children, enlarged its scope and became a force in Piedmontese Jewry, its efforts being largely responsible for the reorganization of the communities and the *Legge Rattazzi* four years after. It enlisted the collaboration of some of the finest spirits in the country, from S. D. Luzzatto downwards. Subsequently, its name was changed to *Il Vessillo Israelitico* ("The Jewish Standard"), under which title it continued to appear until 1922. Though in its last years it tended to be trivial, it contained a large number of historical and literary studies which give its files a great importance to the student. The *Educatore* was nine years old when a rival periodical, *Il Corriere Israelitico*, began to appear in Trieste in 1862, intended in the first instance for the considerable Jewish group still living in the Austrian possessions. When these dwindled, it continued to act as mouthpiece of Italian Jewry, but with the outbreak of war between Italy and the Central Powers in 1915 its public was cut off and publication was suspended. In the following year, its place was taken by a new periodical, *Israel*, published at Florence, strongly orthodox and strongly Zionist in sympathy, which sometimes attained an extremely high journalistic level. Of the numerous minor publications which made more or less fleeting appearances during these three-quarters of a century, sometimes ambitiously produced in out-of-the-way centers, it is unnecessary to give an account here.

As a natural result of the modification of its economic structure during this period, the distribution of Italian Jewry underwent a profound change which had in turn

* It may be observed that Isaac Lampronti had produced, at Ferrara as early as 1715, a quasi-periodical rabbinical bulletin, and that some periodical fascicles of a work for female instruction, nominally a *giornale*, appeared in Venice in 1821.

important consequences in religious life. Everywhere, the tendency of Jews in the course of the past century and a half has been towards concentration in the greater and, in the end, the greatest cities. Nowhere was this exemplified more clearly than in Italy. Before the sixteenth century its Jews had been fairly generally scattered all over the country. With the Counter-Reformation they were not allowed to live in places which did not have Ghettos, thus being forced into a limited number of urban centers. Few of them, however, were large, and some, especially in Piedmont and the duchies, very small. Hence in the seventeenth and eighteenth centuries the Jews were identified with a number of picturesque townships in central and northern Italy, some of which, though familiar enough to students of Hebrew literature, are not to be found on any but the largest-scale maps. At the period of the *Risorgimento*, Italian Jewry consisted of about 40,000 souls distributed among some 67 communities, of which at least one-third were of inconsiderable size, not exceeding a couple of hundred souls. In the first generation of emancipation many of these attained their acme of prosperity, modernizing their organization, constructing new synagogues, and playing a respected role in civic life. But such places gave little scope for ambition or for commercial expansion, and the younger and more vigorous left one by one to seek their fortunes elsewhere. For a time, the congregations continued to function, though less and less intensely as the older generation passed away and religious indifference spread. In the end, perhaps the solitary survivor would be a nostalgic graybeard who piously opened the synagogue once or twice a year and recited his prayers in solitude, or a couple of families who would import an officiant — and sometimes even a quorum — to conduct the service in the old style on the most solemn occasions. In the end, even this might cease; and all that was left to commemorate the ancient settlement in a score of places once distinguished in Jewish history would be an alley still perhaps named the Ghetto, a baroque synagogue filled with lovely appurtenances, and a cypress-clad cemetery outside the walls. This was the fate of the communities of Sermide, Pomponesco, Viadana, Savigliano, Busseto, Fiorenzuola d'Arda, Sabbionneta, Cento, and a score more. Whereas one-fifth of the Jewish population had lived in rural centers at the beginning of the nineteenth century, not more than one-fortieth did at the beginning of the twentieth; while in 1840 the communities of less than 500 souls comprised one-quarter of Italian Jewry, a hundred years later the proportion was reduced to one-tenth.

In due course the same tendency was felt in larger cities, at one time important centers of Jewish life but now decadent. Thus Casale, which had played so prominent a part in history at the time of the *Risorgimento*, saw its Jewish population, which had stood at 869 in 1839, brought down to 160 a hundred years later; Rovigo dwindled in the same period from its nineteenth-century maximum of 430 to a mere handful of 52; Reggio, from nearly 1,000 to under 100; Acqui, in the Napoleonic era an important center with some 700 souls, was reduced to 500 in 1870, 200 in 1900, and fewer than 50 a generation later; Pesaro, which had 600 Jews at the beginning of the Ghetto period and 400 at its end, came down in the course of the nineteenth century to a couple of score; even Mantua and Modena, once among the greatest Italian communities, were now reduced to fewer than 500 souls. Leghorn remained an important center, but with the rapid decline in the importance of the port its Jewish population went down from 5,000 to a bare 1,700. In 1830, there were 108 synagogues in Italy, distributed among some 65 communities, all probably open for service twice each day; a century later only 38 of these were still in use, half of them functioning only irregularly. Even the handful of large cities — Milan, Turin, Naples, Bologna, Florence, in addition to the capital — which benefited by the shift of population, enjoyed only a superficial well-being from this point of view. As was the case with the remainder of the bourgeois element to which in the main they belonged, celibacy among the Jews increased, late marriages became common, and the size of families dwindled. Everywhere, the number of deaths exceeded that of births, the population in the larger centers being maintained only by immigration from the small decadent communities. With the drying-up of this reservoir, the larger ones, too, seemed to be approaching a critical stage. They comprised an increasing number of the elderly and an insignificant proportion of youth; and by the second quarter of the twentieth century statisticians had begun to predict that, within a short while, a sudden and catastrophic diminution in their absolute numbers was likely to set in, which would result ultimately in the quasi-extinction of most of the historic Italian communities.

This decline was intensified by the continuous emigration from the Peninsula. In most of the principal ports and commercial centers of the Mediterranean — especially Tunis and Alexandria — there were relatively large Italian-speaking Jewish communities, among whom the Livornese element was especially noticeable; and most of the world's great cities had at least a sprinkling of them. Proportionately, indeed, the demographic curve had already begun to fall, for while in the early part of the nineteenth century the Jews had constituted some 0.25 per cent of the Italian population, a hundred years later they barely exceeded 0.1 per cent, or one in a thousand, the absolute figure having increased very little indeed notwithstanding the great expansion in the country as a whole. The numerical importance of Italian Jewry was therefore still trivial. There were a dozen cities in the United States which contained more Jews than the whole of Italy; and no Italian community would have been considered at all significant elsewhere, other than perhaps that of Rome. This, with its solid, good-natured proletariat, was the one city of the country to which these depressing generalizations did not apply. Here, Jewish social solidarity was still strong even though Jewish observances were on the wane, the old Judaeo-Italian dialect was still widely spoken and early marriages with large families were still the rule. The combined effects of this and of the stream of immigrants attracted by its growing administrative and commercial importance increased the relative significance of its Jewish population, which by 1931 rose to 12,000 — something like one-quarter of that of the entire country. It seemed likely that within another few generations, when the larger provincial centers had followed the way of the smaller ones and all but died out or been absorbed, the Roman community, mother of Italian Jewry, would still survive — its last representative, as two thousand years before it had been its forerunner.

The impact of emancipation upon the internal life of Italian Jewry was immediate; in most respects, it was deleterious. It had withstood, cramped but unshaken, the onslaught of the long generations of oppression; but, as elsewhere, it proved unable to resist the insidious blandishments of the new world of opportunity and equality. Within a generation of the great edict of Carlo Alberto, assimilation had made appalling progress. Synagogues that were formerly open for service twice a day now had difficulty in assembling the necessary quorum once a week; and most of those who attended were graybeards, whose sons considered such things to savor of separatism and superstition. In places which had formerly had a plurality of synagogues expressing variations of origin or tradition (such as Mantua or Venice, with nine each) one alone was now sufficient in most instances to supply all possible requirements, the picturesque local variations being to a large extent forgotten and the divergent rites merged — not so much out of zeal for unity as from sheer indifference. After the death of Samuel David Luzzatto in 1865, the Collegio Rabbinico was first closed, then transferred in 1887 in a state of suspended animation to Rome, where its existence was little more than nominal. Every community of any size still boasted its Chief Rabbi or *Rabbino Maggiore*, but most of them would have been sorely perplexed to find the lesser functionaries presupposed by that title. Many were the once-famed congregations where there was no rabbi at all, or the functions were filled by an imperfectly educated factotum.

The artistic and literary patrimony of the communities was lightheartedly wasted. The great synagogal libraries that had been assembled by the devotion and piety of past generations were neglected or dispersed, wandering bookdealers and bibliophiles battening on the ignorance of the custodians. An ill-natured jest was told that a Hebrew-speaking stranger found himself cold-shouldered when he visited a synagogue, in the belief that any person with this qualification must needs be a Christian missionary. Intermarriage, with its corollary of secession from Judaism at least on the part of the next generation, grew alarmingly, the average rising in the early twentieth century to as many as one person in three, or in some places, such as Trieste, even more. Jewish education was generally neglected, ignorance reaching such a pitch that a prayer book transliterated into Latin characters was published for the solemn festivals. It was pathetic to meet persons who bore names honored in Jewish literature for a dozen centuries, or immediately descended from rabbis of deep learning and piety, abysmally ignorant of anything Jewish. The old *Yeshibot* for adult studies, once the pride of Italian Jewry ceased to exist or survived only as institutions for benevolent purposes or mechanical ritual recitals. The multitudinous charitable fraternities dwindled and decayed, and in many communities were merged into a single colorless and impersonal body covering all eleemosynary purposes. Observance dwindled to a vanishing point. Down to the period of emancipation, barely a single Jewish shop or business-house throughout the length and breadth of Italy was open on the Jewish Sabbath; a couple of generations later, it was not easy to find one anywhere that was closed. Deprived of the spirit of instruction, Judaism became not unlike a semitized Catholicism, with rabbi instead of priest, synagogue instead of church, lamps burning in front of the ark instead of candles before the altar, the Aramaic *Kaddish* instead of masses for the dead, and an incomprehensible Hebrew corresponding for liturgical purposes to the current incomprehensible Latin. Of those persons whose remarkable contributions to Italian life have been mentioned in these pages, many — and as time went on perhaps most — were Jews only by virtue of descent. Italy became a byword in the Jewish world for the completeness of emancipation on the one hand, for its deadly corrosive potentialities on the other.

xli
The New Hope

In 1890, as this period of unrelieved decadence was reaching its climax, Samuel Hirsch Margulies, a German rabbi of Galician origin, was appointed to the rabbinate of Florence. By this forceful personality, inspiring orator and ripe scholar, something was done at last to stem the tide. Just as Florence was now the intellectual capital of Italy, so Florentine Jewry under his guidance took the lead in Italian Jewish spiritual life. The Collegio Rabbinico, after a lengthy period of semi-inactivity, was revived under his direction in 1899, and he brought from abroad to teach in it some of the most promising of the younger scholars of the day — H. P. Chajes, subsequently Chief Rabbi of Vienna, and Ismar Elbogen, later the guiding spirit of Jewish intellectual life in his native Germany. From the revived school, most of the Italian rabbis of the younger generation — men in some cases of highest ability and character — emerged in the course of the next generation, so that their master's influence irradiated through them throughout the country. In association with the seminary, there was established a scientific Jewish review, a new *Rivista Israelitica*, which took its place by the side of the similar publications appearing in other countries and contained a goodly amount of important material bearing upon Jewish studies. The foremost member of the circle was Umberto Cassuto, outstanding no less as an historian than as a biblical scholar, who has shed a luster on Italian Jewish intellectual life such as it has not known since the days of Luzzatto, and taken his place as one of the most distinguished savants of our age.

In 1907, the first of a new nexus of Jewish cultural societies which speedily spread to other towns, under the name *Pro Cultura*, was established by Margulies' disciples in Florence. Four years later, as a result of his untiring efforts, a Jewish Youth Congress was held there, at which the new synthesis was taken as a basis for action; it was succeeded by further gatherings in Turin and Rome, the outbreak of the European war then suspending this promising initiative. The establishment in 1911 of the new *Consorzio* of Italian Jewish communities, with cultural rather than administrative or political objects, was another outcome of this movement of intellectual revival.

More important, however, than his organizing power was Margulies' personal influence. He inspired not only rabbis but also laymen; and though assimilation continued to make tragic strides, he succeeded in rallying to Judaism some of the outstanding intelligences in the younger generation. Completely Italian, by virtue of descent perhaps for a hundred generations, they were at the same time intensely Jewish in every sense; and an "integral" Judaism, embracing Jewish observance, Jewish culture and Jewish national solidarity, came to be fairly widespread among the younger intelligentsia. They found their mouthpiece in the new periodical *Israel*, founded and directed by the Florentine lawyer Alfonso Pacifici, a fascinating personality in some ways reminiscent of the mystics of the Ghetto period, who like some of them was in the end drawn by his yearnings to settle in Palestine. He worked in close association with Dante Lattes, a scholar and writer with a genius-touched pen, who would have made an even greater reputation but for the restricted environment in and for which he labored. Numerically, the group was unimportant; qualitatively, it was very significant, and for that reason very influential. It was noteworthy that some members of the group had been brought up in a tradition of the most utter assimilation.

The results were an unmistakable Jewish revival in the country, beginning in Florence but afterwards spreading generally. The numbers involved were, as has been indicated, small, and regarded from this point of view the outcome was inconsiderable. But to attend synagogue and to be interested in Jewish matters was no longer regarded, as it had tended to be before, a prerogative of the aged, which youth would not share. Moreover, those whose Jewish enthusiasms revived were in many cases the most intelligent and capable in the younger generation. But the modest scale of the revival was highly dangerous. Its potential public, barely 40,000 souls in theory, was far smaller in fact, in view of the rapid progress already made by complete assimilation. The death or emigration of a single person associated with it — and there was in fact an unhappy series of fatalities in the course of these years — implied a tremendous blow, and the number of persons influenced, outside one or two of the greatest centers, was pathetically small. Nevertheless, at a period of general decadence in Jewish life in most countries, Italy had given evidence, on however limited a scale, of an unmistakable revival. Whether the results could be durable, only time could show. But, alas, the opportunity was not forthcoming.

CHAPTER XI

Downfall

xlii

THE TOTALITARIAN STATE

WHEN, at the beginning of 1919, a wordy, unscrupulous journalist who had formerly been prominent in the ranks of extreme radicals founded the Fascist Party, under the cloak of militant patriotism, he found some of his earliest supporters among the Jews, oblivious of the tragic implications of his doctrine. The new party was rabidly nationalist, and for a hundred years past the Jews had been counted among the most fervent supporters of Italian nationalism; it was anti-Socialist, and the Italian Jews were now pre-eminently members of the bourgeoisie. Mussolini for his part was eager for support from whatever quarter it might come. Like other Italians, he did not differentiate between the Jews and other sections of the Italian people; they had, moreover, shown their devotion to the conception of a Greater Italy in recent years in the Chamber, on the field, even in d'Annunzio's melodramatic raid on Fiume. Accordingly, the attitude of the Jews to the new movement at its inception was indistinguishable from that of the general population. If some of them, of liberal political tendencies, abhorred it, others were its dupes and were included among its earliest and most fervent supporters. Half a dozen of them collaborated in its foundation, at least three were among the "martyrs" who gave their lives on its behalf in its earliest period of struggle, and were subsequently interred in its grandiose shrines.

The Italian Jews, in their attitude to Fascism, were no worse, but alas little better, than their compatriots.

During Mussolini's first years of power, their position remained ostensibly much as it had been before, and their place in Italian life was hardly affected. Aldo Finzi, a redoubtable airman, was for a long time the Duce's right-hand man, suppressed an anti-Fascist rising in Milan and became assistant minister of the interior; and incongruously enough it was his wedding with a Catholic, at which a cardinal officiated, that gave the opportunity for the first demonstration of the rapprochement with the Vatican. Carlo Foà, Italy's outstanding physiologist, was editor of the Fascist review *Gerarchia*, in which capacity he did a good deal to mould the party's opinions and policy. Margherita Sarfatti was one of Mussolini's favorites, collaborated with him in his journalistic work, and later became his biographer. Of the fifteen jurists who drew up the Fascist constitution, three were Jews; and Guido Jung, who was of foreign Jewish extraction, was for some years finance minister. The more sensitive might indeed have discerned certain unfavorable symptoms. It was not perhaps quite so easy for Jews to be elected to honorific functions; occasionally, they found their association interrupted even with organizations with which their families had been closely connected for generations; Ludovico Mortara, president of the Supreme Court — the highest office in the judiciary — was somewhat abruptly dismissed. Since local officials were now imposed from above, popular Jews could no longer be elected to office by the suffrages of their fellow citizens. Fewer of them were appointed henceforth to the Senate, or to high position in the Army and Navy, though this may have been only coincidence. It was noteworthy, however, that when the Italian Academy was founded, no Jew was nominated to membership, though some were unquestionably among the leading figures in the country's intellectual life. In the attacks on the Socialist leaders Modigliani and Treves, sneers at their Jewish origin were occasionally heard. There was, moreover, a perceptible diminution in the importance of individual Jews, though in a country where political power was concentrated in the hands of a single person this did not seem a cause for apprehension.

The Concordat concluded with the Vatican in 1929, which restored Roman Catholicism to its place as the state religion, also had certain untoward implications, notwithstanding the fact that one of its authors was the Jewish jurist Federico Cammeo. Not only did it strengthen the hands of the clerical elements throughout the country, but it extended the totalitarian idea to the field of religion and put an end to the secularized educational system that had been the rule for generations. As the result of a great speech in the Senate by the eminent jurist, Vittorio Polacco, special provision was made under the scheme for the benefit of the Jews, who were empowered to withdraw their children from Catholic religious instruction and, if they wished, even to open their own schools, which were given government subsidies; and the fact that many of the communities were too small or too apathetic could not be considered the fault of the system.

On the other hand, there was something to be put to the credit side, so long as Jew-baiting was generally considered disreputable. Mussolini personally intervened to suppress manifestations of it on more than one occasion. He intermittently condemned antisemitism, received foreign Jewish representatives, and was readily accessible to Italian Jewish leaders, such as Angelo Sacerdote, the lion-hearted Chief Rabbi of Rome, whom he assured in 1924 that "antisemitism is a growth which cannot obtain a foothold in Italy."

The Concordat with the Vatican made it necessary to clarify the position of those who were not Catholics. For the past seventy-odd years, the majority of the Jewish communities had been administered in accordance with the terms of the *Legge Rattazzi*, enacted for the benefit of those of Piedmont in 1857; a few of the most important bodies, however, standing aloof, or else being organized on a similar basis but as purely voluntary associations with a charitable object. In 1930, a comprehensive Law on the Jewish Communities was put into force, setting up a new organization. They were henceforth given full juridical rights, including that of levying taxation on their members for religious and cultural purposes. The voluntary basis of association was abolished; membership was henceforth compulsory on all persons of Jewish birth, provided that they did not formally renounce Judaism or embrace another faith. Uniform regulations were laid down for organization and administration and the appointment of all officials, ecclesiastical and lay. At the same time, a Union of Italian Jewish Communities was set up, thus carrying into effect at last the plans that had been discussed and timidly tested at intervals since the middle of the last century. This new body was given a considerable influence in the general affairs of Italian Jewry, which it represented henceforth before the government and the public, the Chief Rabbi of Rome thus becoming in effect Chief Rabbi of Italy. The small decayed or decadent centers, now so numerous all over the north, which could no longer carry out their essential functions owing to the decline or disappearance of their Jewish population, were to be merged henceforth with the nearest effective body, which was to administer their revenues and in return to be responsible for preserving their historic, artistic and bibliographic heritage. Thus famous old communities such as Saluzzo, Cuneo, Lugo, Cento, Fossano, Pesaro, and many more lost their identity after so many centuries of not inglorious history. The measure was in part the result of the Fascist urge for regimentation in all matters, in part intended to make Italian Jewry a more efficient instrument for carrying out those purposes at home and abroad which the government considered desirable; none the less, it was on the whole beneficial.

In view of the centralizing policy of the Fascist government, it was inevitable that the official seat of the new Union was Rome. This city, at the height of its artificial expansion, now attracted the young and virile elements from the provinces more and more. Thus, in these years, it became the center of Italian Jewry intellectually as well as politically, as it had not been since the early Middle Ages or even classical times. As a consequence, the Collegio Rabbinico was removed hither from Florence: the reorganization took place none too soon, for the dearth of rabbis had reached an almost catastrophic stage. A Union of Italian Jewish Cultural Societies was also established with its headquarters here, and other Jewish organizations tended to gravitate to the same center; and Roman Jewry awakened at last from its long torpor.

This period of febrile though artificial industrial development witnessed, and in part caused, the culmination of the redistribution of the population that has already been noted. Especially noteworthy was the very rapid expansion of the community of Milan, now the second in importance in the country, the remarkable commercial and industrial development of this place attracting also many immigrants from Central Europe and the Levant, and being in turn to some extent stimulated by them. The Jewish revival that had started in Florence began to find its echoes in these years elsewhere. A nexus of local cultural societies (*Convegni di Studi Ebraici*) was set up, spreading gradually throughout the country. The monthly literary supplement of the weekly *Israel*, going by the title *La Rassegna Mensile di Israel*, attained a standard excelled by few Jewish periodicals in any land; and a publishing house, established in Florence for the production of books of Jewish interest, had an output which, although small, was of remarkably high quality. In 1924 and 1928, Youth Cultural Congresses were held in

Leghorn and Venice, the former being especially successful; and as one of the outcomes a Jewish Museum, enshrining some of the ancient treasures of that once-famous community, was opened there. Italian Jewry was indubitably affected by the eager optimism of the age.

While at home the Fascist attitude towards the Jews was one of somewhat stiff cordiality, it was actively, and even pugnaciously benevolent towards their coreligionists abroad. This was especially the case as regards those of the Mediterranean basin, who were considered useful agents for the diffusion of Italian influence, with a view to preparing the foundations of the pinchbeck Roman empire that was being planned. The Italian consuls at Salonica and elsewhere in the Levant were, for example, instructed to encourage the descendants of Jews who had emigrated from Italy generations before to apply for or to retain Italian nationality. The appointment of an Italian rabbi at Alexandria, where the occidentalized portion of the Jewish colony was Italian-speaking, now became almost a question of state policy. At the Hebrew University of Jerusalem, a readership in Italian was maintained. Above all, thousands of Jews from Hungary, Roumania, Poland and elsewhere, who found their higher education interrupted by the *numerus clausus* and academic antisemitism at home, were enabled to come to Italy to study, being assisted by reduced fares, the virtual cancellation of fees, and even monetary grants. Thus a whole generation of Jewish professional men and intellectuals was brought into being in Central and Eastern Europe, Italian-speaking and, it was hoped, imbued with a profound respect for Italian institutions and culture.

Rome was now the capital not only of a country but of an empire. In 1911, Italy had seized Tripoli and Cyrenaica from the Turks; here, there was an ancient Arabic-speaking Jewish community, untouched by any occidental influence, numbering some 25,000, mainly concentrated in the two chief cities of Tripoli and Benghazi. After the war, moreoever, the Dodecanese Islands off the coast of Asia Minor, largely Greek in population, had remained in Italian hands; and there were here some 5,000 Ladino-speaking Jews, almost all in the ancient city of Rhodes, where a community had existed from time immemorial. All these now looked to Rome as their administrative center. The Italian culture and language spread rapidly among them, the sons of some of the leading families were sent to Italy for education, and Fascist institutions became somewhat incongruously established in the Jewish communities. The central government appreciated the remarkable assimilatory capacity of the Jews, and imagined that by Italianizing this eager element they would have a ready-forged instrument for influencing the more stolid masses of the population. The treatment of the Jewish communities of the "Empire" therefore left nothing to be desired, the influence of the metropolitan Jewry being thus artificially enhanced and stimulated. These new Jewish subjects could, moreover, be utilized to forward remoter objects. When a benevolent Modenese Jew, perpetuating an ancient family tradition of munificence, desired to give the Collegio Rabbinico in Rome an endowment which would have relieved it of some of its most pressing financial worries, Mussolini personally induced him to divert it to a new and entirely superfluous rabbinical seminary in Rhodes. This, it was hoped, might serve not only as a center for training rabbis, but also indirectly for diffusing Italianophile influences among all the Jewish communities of the Near East.

When in 1935-6 Italy ignobly conquered Abyssinia, a fresh sphere of influence opened up. There was here no more than a handful of resident Jews in the occidental sense; but it was the home of the mysterious tribes of black Jews, the Falashas, conservatively estimated at some 30,000 in number, preserving, together with their historic Jewish memories, only an imperfect knowledge of traditional Judaism. In the Renaissance period, it had been largely through the medium of devoted Italian Jews that knowledge of this remnant of Israel had penetrated to the outside world; and more recently, owing to their country's interest in Ethiopia, Italians had taken the lead in the movement, with its center in the Italian colony of Eritrea, for bringing them into line with Jewish tradition. Here therefore, once again, the Fascist government saw the opportunity of simultaneously welding a new spearhead of influence in its reluctant colony and impressing the outside world with its high-mindedness. The Union of Italian Communities was encouraged to send a representative to Ethiopia to report, Jewish communal organizations were established here and there, sites were assigned in the capital and elsewhere for the construction of synagogues, grants of land were made to the Jewish tribesmen, and it was arranged to set up schools of agriculture and handicraft for their benefit. When the Falasha leaders took the oath of loyalty, the governor unctuously declared that they would be accorded the same cultural and religious freedom and the same respect as the other religious bodies.

Yet, notwithstanding this adroit window-dressing, a number of the Italian Jews, true to the best traditions of the *Risorgimento*, refused to bend the knee to the Fascist Moloch, even when it was universally courted and flattered. There were everywhere members of the Jewish intelligentsia who maintained their opposition — openly so long as it was possible, afterwards clandestinely; while a number of others took the hardly less dangerous step of holding aloof. Some of the finest spirits found conditions intolerable and emigrated — to Paris, to London, to Palestine. In Piedmont above all, the home of liberalism, Jews were among the leaders of the resistance movement, and in 1934 a group of young Turin hotheads was apprehended in consequence of an attempt to smuggle "subversive" literature into the country. Carlo Rosselli, for many years the soul of the resistance to Fascism, who organized the Garibaldi Battalion to fight for the Republic in Spain, founded the periodical *Giustizia e Libertà* to keep alive the liberal flame in exile, and was ultimately murdered with his brother by Fascist gangsters in France, was a member of that same Jewish family who had harbored and aided Giuseppe Mazzini in a similarly dark hour for Italian freedom.

xliii
The Betrayal

When the Nazi regime came into power in Germany, there was a moment of apprehension among the Jews of Italy, lest the attitude of the totalitarian state in the one country should be affected by the frantic antisemitism of its counterpart. But they were soon reassured. The Duce's jealousy of his Teutonic imitator, his nervous susceptibility to the opinion of the world, his anxiety to show himself politically respectable, his substratum of shrewdness, the inevitable conflict of opinion on the question of Austrian independence, all combined in their favor; and indeed of the foremost figures in international affairs he was at first perhaps the most outspoken in his condemnation of the German policy. He poured ridicule, in repeated statements, on the idea of racialism, especially as applied to a country such as Italy. And his sympathy was not purely verbal. At a time when the frontiers of the world were rigidly controlled, a relatively large number of refugees from the Nazi horror were permitted to settle in the country — especially in Milan and other industrial centers. The Jewish Relief Committee, on applying for permission to begin activities on behalf of these unfortunates, was informed that it was their duty. Representatives of Italian Jewry were officially authorized to attend conferences abroad — not only for the relief of the sufferers, but also for quasi-political action.

Indeed, the Duce gave it to be understood that it was through his personal intervention that the boycott of the Jews in Germany was broken short in the spring of 1933.

The first tokens of an alteration in policy were to be discerned at the period of the wanton attack on Abyssinia. The onslaught, besides revolting the conscience of the world, was an obvious danger to Great Britain, whose life line to the East through the Suez Canal was now threatened on either flank. She therefore encouraged the League of Nations to strike a pugnacious attitude, and at one time it seemed probable that she would go to war in a case where her honor and her interests were both clearly involved. Finding his buccaneering condemned by the "respectable" powers, whom he had hitherto courted so sedulously, Mussolini was driven into the arms of his real spiritual affinity across the Alps — antisemitic Germany. And, finding it vitally necessary to embarrass England as greatly and as immediately as possible, he championed the cause of the ultranationalist section of the indigenous population in Palestine and set up a preposterous pose as the Protector of Islam, against Great Britain and Zionism.

The first fruits of the new policy were the artificially inspired riots which broke out in Palestine in 1936, causing serious difficulties for England and staining the noble history of the land's renewal with innocent blood. At the same time, the Fascist extremists began to take umbrage at the interest of Italian Jews in Zionism. This was, it may be said, one of the oldest manifestations of Jewish life in the country. When we first hear of the Roman Jewish community, before the beginning of the Christian era, we are informed that they were in the habit of sending their yearly tribute to the Temple in Jerusalem. Later on, in imperial times and throughout the Dark Ages, they had collected their oblations for the Palestinian schools. Already at this period, collectors came regularly from Palestine to Italy, and pilgrims went up from Italy to Palestine, crude inscriptions left by some of them having been found on the Temple Mount in Jerusalem. Throughout the Middle Ages, and throughout the Ghetto period, the intercourse continued. We know more perhaps of Palestine pilgrims from Italy than from any other land; the most interesting Hebrew accounts of the Holy Land that are extant, some of them illustrated with rough drawings, are from the pens of pious Italian visitors; and there was, too, a relatively numerous Italian colony in the principal cities. Every Italian synagogue had its collecting-box for Palestine just inside the main doorway; in Casale, a fresco of the Holy City could be seen beside the ark on the eastern wall; and there were unfinished patches on some Ghetto houses "in memory of the destruction of the Temple." The eager welcome extended to visitors and rabbis from the Holy Land was not lessened by the fact that most of them came to collect money. Treasurers for Palestine formed part of the congregational hierarchy in some places, and special provision was made for the regular payments to the Holy Land even at times of the most acute crisis. Among the eminent Gentile precursors of Zionism in the nineteenth century there was more than one Italian — Alessandro Manzoni, the greatest Italian novelist, who in his mystical moments dreamed of the return of the Jews, regenerated, to their ancient homeland; or Benedetto Mussolino, a fighter under Garibaldi and later senator, who in a curiously prophetic manner urged on Lord Palmerston the reconstitution of the Jewish people as a political nationality in Palestine under the British aegis. Hence when Theodor Herzl launched his ambitious and, as seemed at the time, chimerical scheme at the close of the nineteenth century, there seemed nothing incongruous in his ideas in the eyes of the Italian Jews of the old school, their traditional eleemosynary activities merging insensibly into the new, more practical plan. In 1898, the first Italian Zionist society was established at Ancona — within a short while, there were nearly thirty of them — and in 1901 the first Italian Zionist Congress was held at Modena, the great seat of mystical yearnings for Palestine in the past. In 1903, the king received Rabbi Margulies of Florence in the interests of the movement, and in the following year Herzl himself had an audience, with highly encouraging results. Fourteen years later, in the midst of the European war, the Italian government readily endorsed the Balfour Declaration in favor of the establishment of a Jewish National Home in Palestine. An influential non-Jewish pro-Palestine committee was set up later on in Rome, presided over by Senator Francesco Ruffini. There was even an officially recognized Italian representative on the Zionist commission in Palestine, Angelo Levi-Bianchini, a naval officer with a fine record, whose murder by Arab terrorists in 1920 aroused general horror.

The Italian people generally, with vivid recollections of the *Risorgimento*, was highly sympathetic to the idea of the creation of a Jewish National Home in Palestine, which strongly appealed to its own romantic sense. Nor did the Fascists, at the beginning, see the matter in a different light. Mussolini himself more than once professed his interest in and support for the Zionist objectives, and never suggested that they were incompatible with the stern demands of Italian patriotism. It was true, indeed, that this interest was not altogether altruistic. Fascist Italy was by now thinking in terms of Mediterranean hegemony and a revived Roman empire; at one time, there were vague hopes of utilizing Zionist discontent with the British administration to secure the succession to the Palestine mandate, the Italian Zionists being asked to press for this. But it soon became clear that it was impossible, whether because of British reluctance to evacuate the country or the most understandable lack of enthusiasm on the part of responsible Jewish leaders. A change of attitude now became perceptible. A sympathy — highly incongruous in view of the Fascist record in Libya

— began to be demonstratively shown for the Arab population of the Holy Land; the "menace" to the Catholic holy places, hitherto believed only by some reactionary clerical journalists, was brought into high relief; and Zionism was criticized on the grounds of its irreconcilability with essential Italian interests. When the Abyssinian War loomed on the political horizon, abusive articles began to appear with ominous unanimity, expressing sympathy with the Arabs, attacking Zionism as an instrument of British imperialism, and calling upon Italian Jews to abjure it. Mussolini himself cryptically declared that Fascist Italy could tolerate no divided loyalty, and within the Jewish communities ultranationalist elements thought it best to dissociate themselves completely from the movement of regeneration. Here and there disputes resulted in the resignation of the community councils *en bloc* and, since the anti-Zionist element often lacked the competence or understanding to form another, the appointment of a government representative to carry on the administration. In the spring of 1936, even the members of the Executive of the Union of Jewish Communities submitted their resignation. Meanwhile, in Libya, the government pointedly demonstrated its pro-Arab sympathies. Already some time before, the Chief Rabbi, Gustavo Castelbolognesi, brought over from Italy, had been deported for refusing to decide a matter of religious law in the sense demanded by the Fascist authorities. Now, orders were issued for shops kept by Jews in that strongly conservative community to remain open on Saturday, so as to preserve the occidental character of the new city; and since when driven to comply they refused to attend on their customers, a couple of hundred were arrested and the leaders flogged — an outrage such as had never been known in the Age of the Ghetto.

More dangerous by far than the Zionist issue, which was purely opportunist, was the Italo-German rapprochement which ultimately resulted from the Abyssinian dispute.

The new tendency implied that not even those aspects of Nazi policy which had been most vigorously condemned in the past could henceforth be criticized or reported objectively. Everything perpetrated by the noble ally of Fascist Italy became *ipso facto* praiseworthy, or at any rate beyond comment; and Italian Jews began to be eyed askance by the more susceptible of their neighbors. Although the Fascist leaders insisted that the new orientation involved no antisemitism, there was henceforth a notable change of atmosphere. Rumors of an impending reaction were more and more insistent. The visits of Nazi leaders to Italy became ominously frequent. When Joseph Goebbels, the Reich minister of propaganda, conferred with his Italian counterpart, Dino Alfieri, at the International Film Exhibition at Venice in August 1936, a joint propaganda campaign was apparently decided against the mythical Judaeo-Bolshevik menace. Before long, therefore, the onslaught on Zionism developed into one upon the Jews generally. In September, 1936, Roberto Farinacci, formerly general secretary of the Fascist Party, published a ferocious attack on Jewish "subversive" and anti-Fascist influence in his paper, *Il Regime Fascista*. This henceforth became a sounding-board for antisemitic propaganda in which the Jews, Great Britain, the League of Nations, international finance and anti-Fascism were vituperatively associated. Soon, other ostensibly serious periodicals followed this lead, including even *Il Popolo d'Italia*, Mussolini's own organ, which published a savage onslaught on the Jews of France, and threw the blame for the revival of antisemitism on the Jews themselves. Another pillar of the agitation was the German-subsidized daily *Il Tevere* of Rome, edited by Telesio Interlandi, which invitingly published a list of surnames by which Italian Jews might be recognized. From 1937, the same editor produced also a weekly, *Il Giornalissimo*, and a magazine, *Il Quadrivio*, which imitated German antisemitic obscenities so closely as to show that it was subsidized by the Nazi propaganda network. Meanwhile, an old antisemitic sheet, *Vita Italiana*, edited by Giovanni Preziosi, never before taken seriously, became increasingly shrill and menacing. By 1938, there were in Italy at least five periodicals with a considerable aggregate circulation which could be classed as actively anti-Jewish. Books, too, appeared discussing the "Jewish Problem" which had been suddenly created out of nothing, and about the existence of which most persons were in complete ignorance — Alfredo Romanini's *Jews, Christians and Fascism*; Interlandi's *Contra Judaeos*; Giulio Evola's *Three Aspects of the Jewish Problem*; and various less substantial works. The preposterous *Protocols of the Learned Elders of Zion*, which Preziosi had already edited in 1921, were reprinted more than once. The minor publicists were overshadowed when, at the beginning of 1937, the Fascist rector of the university of Perugia, Paolo Orano — once, when it had been fashionable, an ardent supporter of Zionism — issued a substantial monograph on the Jews of Italy, bitterly antisemitic in substance, which stigmatized Jewish separatism as inimical to the interests of the state and called upon the Italian Jews to dissociate themselves from their coreligionists and their anti-Italian, anti-social activities. The propaganda clearly showed its origin by its stress on those new aspects of antisemitism which had been so unsparingly condemned by the Pope; indeed, a volume by Giulio Cogni on racialism, glorifying the views of the Nazi extremists in this matter, was speedily placed on the Index by the Church authorities. *Il Tevere* and its associated publications went so far as to agitate for the prohibition of marriages between Italians and those of other "races." In September, an Italian delegation participated in the antisemitic congress held at Erfurt under the auspices of the German government, the proceedings of which were reported in Italy without a syllable of adverse comment. From February, 1938, Jews were not allowed to broadcast from Italian wireless stations, lest listening ears in Germany should be offended. But, when rumors of the deterioration in the condition of Italian Jewry became too insistent, an official statement, albeit couched in cryptic and somewhat sinister terms, denied that the country was in any way anti-Jewish or that antisemitic measures were in contemplation.

The internal rift had by now reached such a stage that it was impossible for the Rabbinate to remain silent. In September, 1937, a manifesto was issued "from the rabbis of Italy to their brethren," signed by all the spiritual leaders of the country — the first document of its sort in Italian history. With a courage which under the circumstances was memorable, they condemned those Jewish elements in the country which, under the influence of a mistaken ideology, were seeking to interpret Judaism in their own fashion and to create an Italian Jewry divorced from their coreligionists throughout the world. "None," they concluded, "has the right to question our fidelity and our loyalty; none can prevent us from being sincere to ourselves." This precipitated a fresh crisis. The quandary before Italian Zionists was as a matter of fact more apparent than real. It was no question of divided loyalties in the vulgar sense, but of something that should have been manifest from the beginning — the incompatibility of any other idealism with the totalitarian state.

A further phase began after the interchange of visits between the tyrants of the two totalitarian countries, with the ostentatious affirmation of the Rome-Berlin Axis. It now became part of the official policy of the Italian government to align itself ideologically with Nazi Germany, even on matters on which there had previously been profound disagreement. The fate of the Jews was obviously settled in the conversations between the heads of the two states. Germany needed Italy's moral support in this matter, somewhat trivial in the political sense, perhaps to give an element of respectability to a policy hitherto condemned by the world. Hardly had Hitler returned home, after his visit to Italy in the month of May, 1938, than a delegation of German experts on "race," headed by the chief of the Office for Racial Policy himself, paid an official visit to Rome to give technical advice. On June 2, Roberto Farinacci, the arch Jew-baiter, was appointed minister of state. Minor instances of discrimination now began to multiply. Managers of theatrical companies were ordered to omit from their repertoires works by Jewish authors, which might make a painful impression on visitors from across the Alps; booksellers told not to exhibit works by foreign Jewish writers in their shop-windows; and publishers instructed not to issue books by Jews without special authorization.

Meanwhile, a group of university teachers and professors — none of great eminence, but all faithful Fascists — had been instructed to draw up a report on racial problems, which was issued under the auspices of the Ministry of Popular Culture on July 14.* This document re-enunciated almost in their entirety the German racial doctrines, except for the natural fact that it failed to take into account the Nazi assumptions of the inferiority of the Mediterranean to the Teutonic races. It affirmed that the Italian population and civilization were "Aryan," unchanged for 1,000 years. The Jews thus represented the only element included in it that had never been assimilated, being made up of non-European racial elements which differed absolutely from those which gave origin to the Italians. This, it was suggested, was in fact basic to all that Fascism had accomplished hitherto, and must now be openly proclaimed. As a matter of fact, the whole thing was exceptionally preposterous — more so even than in Germany. A dwindling population of one-tenth of one per cent could not by any

* Some of this group (only two or three of whom had professorial status, though not in anthropology or ethnology, the subjects concerned) later stated that they had not actually signed the manifesto, though they did not have the courage to disown it.

stretch of the imagination be described as a "peril" to any country. That the Italian Jews were unassimilable was palpably false — they had assimilated so completely that their numbers were hardly increased from what they had been in the Middle Ages and the classical period, their proportion in the total population had greatly diminished, and there was every token that the process was about to culminate in the disappearance of a great number of the residue. Indeed, the constant stream of conversions to Catholicism had mingled their blood inextricably with that of their neighbors, so that in the north of the country at least it was improbable that many city-dwellers had no trace of Jewish ancestry. Moreover, it was not for a people largely descended from Roman slaves, miscellaneous invaders and medieval pilgrims, to speak in such contemptuous terms with regard to the only element in the country that had remained constant for the past 2,000 years.

This fatuous declaration was nevertheless greeted in Germany with an effusion of gratification; in Italy, it gave the signal for a vehement, unremitting and obviously inspired press campaign. Shortly after, the government set up a special Bureau for Demography and Race Protection; and a new popular review, *La Difesa della Razza* ("The Defense of Race"), directed by Interlandi himself, began to appear. The unflinching condemnation of the racial absurdity by the old, tired Pope was replied to by the Duce in the stubborn phrase *tireremo diritto* ("We will steer straight ahead") which he had already used when he defied Europe over the Abyssinian question. Formerly so accessible, he now refused to receive a Jewish deputation which desired to intercede with him. As the atmosphere grew more and more tense, the leaders of the doomed community issued an appeal to their coreligionists, urging them not to lose courage and declaring that, come what might, Italian Jewry would remain loyal.

At the end of August, as though to accustom the hospitable

Italian people to the idea of discrimination, orders had been issued for the exclusion of foreign Jews and even their children from all universities and educational institutions — a preposterous reversal of the policy that had hitherto prevailed of encouraging them by every possible means to come to Italy to complete their studies. This proved to be only the beginning. Hitherto, Jewish immigration had generally been encouraged; there were therefore in the country now some 15,000 Jews of foreign birth, comprising about one-quarter of the total community, mainly of very recent arrival — perhaps 5,000 Germans, as many Levantines, and the rest Poles, Austrians and others. The most important center was Milan, the remarkable development of which city in recent years had proved a powerful magnet. As the result of the press campaign protesting against the Jewish "invasion," an investigation had been made which revealed that about 1,500 refugees had settled here, in a total population of something like 1,000,000, since the German occupation of Austria. On August 30, orders were issued for them to leave; two days later, this was supplemented by a decree prohibiting Jewish immigration henceforth and ordering all foreigners of Jewish birth to evacuate the country within six months — including even those naturalized during the past twenty years. Meanwhile, a general census of Italian Jews on a racial basis was ordered, in the expectation of sensational results. Although the entire number, including those of mixed parentage and those who had never had the slightest contact with Judaism, could be brought up only to 57,422, action was taken as though this constituted a serious menace to a people of some 45,000,000.

The first victims were the intelligentsia. On September 5, a decree was issued excluding persons of Jewish birth, from the start of the new academic year, from all educational and cultural institutions under government control, from the kindergarten to the university, whether as students, teachers, or the humblest administrative employees; nor were textbooks written by Jews to be used henceforth — no fewer than 114 authors fell under this ban. A preliminary list of nearly 100 dismissed university professors appeared soon after, comprising some of the most honored names in Italian scholarship — Alessandro della Seta, the eminent archaeologist; Tullio Levi-Civita, the greatest of Italian mathematicians; and many more. Some branches of study, such as physiology, in which a majority of the university chairs happened to be filled by Jews, seemed to be completely denuded. As a corollary of the law, all Jewish members were dismissed from the academies and learned societies which they had so long adorned. To compensate for the exclusion of Jewish pupils from the public schools, the communities were empowered to set up their own, but in the tiny settlements dotted about the Peninsula this provision was farcical, and generally made possible only an elementary education. The exclusion from cultural life was completed by what was in effect the prohibition of the publication of books by Jewish authors.

This was only a preliminary. The main body of the new legislation was embodied in a series of decrees adopted by the Fascist Grand Council on October 7. The new law reduced the position of the Italian Jews to that of pariahs, on a lower level in many respects than in the darkest days of the Ghetto period. In accordance with the new Teutonic racial doctrines, marriage between Jews and non-Jews was prohibited, regardless of the religion professed by either party. Jews were forbidden to enter military service, in which they had so greatly distinguished themselves during the past century, whether in peace or war; to own more than 50 hectares (about 130 acres) of land; or to own or manage enterprises employing more than 100 persons. Worst of all, though it sounded trivial, they were ejected from the Fascist Party; for since almost all employment was conditional on producing the membership card, this implied exclusion from almost every possibility of earning a livelihood in subordinate capacity. Subsequently, they were forbidden to have any interest, even as shareholders, in enterprises of importance to national defense—a description which in a totalitarian economy could be applied to almost any; they were excluded from all positions in the Stock Exchange, in joint-stock banks, and in insurance companies, a branch of activity which in Italy owed its existence to Jews; and they were forbidden to open new businesses, in which the dispossessed might have found an outlet. Only early Fascists, and the families of those with especially meritorious military records, were exempted from certain of these restrictions, but as they were none the less excluded from the Party, this did not necessarily help them. A Jew was now defined as a person both of whose parents were Jews by birth, or who was born of a Jewish father and a mother of foreign nationality, or although born of a mixed marriage hitherto professed the Jewish religion, as was the case with a tiny number of persons in this category. Thus many persons were victimized who hitherto had barely realized that they had any Jewish element in their ancestry; and the appalling phenomenon became known of children or grandchildren bringing evidence of a woman's infidelity long before in order to secure themselves exemption from the legal discrimination. The new corpus of legislation was summarized in a fresh decree of November 17, in obvious imitation of the German Nuremberg Laws of 1935 though in certain respects even more severe. Unlike its prototype however this did not deprive the Jews of their citizenship, but created a new, anomalous category of "Italian citizens of the Jewish Race." The laws applied not only to Italy itself, but also to the Italian possessions of Libya and the Aegean Islands. One of the most appalling features about the persecution was its suddenness. In Germany, in a soil prepared by generations of poisonous propaganda, it had taken four years to reduce the Jews to their present plight; in Italy, the same took place almost overnight.

The publication of the antisemitic code caused blank despair among the Jews, who down to the last moment had been unable to credit that the country for which they had sacrificed so much, and of which they had certainly deserved no worse than any other element of the population, could deal them this shameful blow, and who had hoped against hope that something would happen to save them. They had never anticipated anything so tragically far-reaching. Protest, however moderately voiced, was impossible in a state in which criticism was regarded as a form of treason. The "Directorate General for Demography and Race Protection," which was responsible for enforcing the new legislation, would neither receive the representatives of the Jewish communities nor even reply to their communications. Among those dismissed from their positions were no fewer than fifty high naval officials who could ill be spared, including General Pugliese, director of naval construction — who was, however, brought secretly out of retirement two years later to advise on the retrieving of the warships sunk at Taranto. In the Army, the process of elimination was no less drastic. Colonel Segrè paraded his regiment and blew out his brains in their presence as his gesture of farewell; General Ascoli did the same in private. Civilians, too, followed the same road to escape from their perplexities, including Angelo Fortunato Formiggini, the publisher who had deserved so well of Italian letters, who threw himself down from the cathedral tower of his native Modena, where his ancestors had lived for so many generations. (It was found that he had left all his property to the poor.) There were some ridiculous developments, as when a Jewish "volunteer," sent back on a special mission to report on the progress of the war in Spain, and treated *en route* with the deference demanded by his status, found himself cashiered as he landed; or when the heir apparent inadvertently picked out a Jew from the ranks of a regiment which he inspected on its return from the front and was photographed by his side. Some monographs by Jewish writers which were already in the press, or works which could not easily be replaced, were ingeniously issued under fictitious authorship. On the other hand, the corrupt and greedy Fascist bureaucracy found in the new laws a convenient instrument for illicit gain, a sufficiently large bribe being the recognized way to secure a certificate of exemption from the application of the racial code.

In the following months, further restrictions followed as quickly as official ingenuity or Nazi prompting could devise them. Though the measure of October 7 had specifically guaranteed religious freedom, the ritual of *Shehita*, or the slaughter of animals for food in accordance with Jewish humanitarian precepts, was forbidden as a "barbaric" practice. It was prohibited to employ non-Jewish domestic servants of either sex and any age. Jews were excluded from social and sporting clubs, including those which they themselves had founded. Newspapers were instructed not to accept publicity from Jewish firms, or even to announce the deaths of Jews in their advertising columns. An agitation began for the exclusion of Jews from the professions, and as a preliminary a law was issued forbidding them to attend on Christians in a professional capacity. In December, those of Libya were deprived of their citizenship. The property regulations being found too lenient, instructions were issued that no Jews should be allowed to own land yielding an income of more than 5,000 lire (about $300), or urban property worth more than 200,000 lire (about $12,000). Anything held in excess of this was compulsorily alienated, payment being made according to an artificial valuation in non-negotiable government bonds bearing 4% interest, instead of the market rate of 7%, the result being equivalent to expropriation at one-half of the real value. Almost the only category of Italian Jewry as yet unaffected was the proletariat of street-pedlars, still common in Rome; but in the end they too were menaced.

As in the age of the Ghetto, treatises and handbooks on the new "Jewry Law" began to be published; and later on the ancient University of Padua, where Vittorio Polacco had once been rector, was dishonored by the establishment of an Institute for the Study of the Jewish Problem, with branches in Florence and Trieste. Even the tiny republic of San Marino, an independent island surrounded on all sides by Fascist Italy, considered it necessary to apply the racial code to the dozen Jewish families who had drifted thither in the past few years. The new Chief Rabbi of Rome was menaced with violence and had to leave the country. The constant propaganda could not fail to influence the impressionable youth or to be exploited by the Fascist gunmen; and in Rome, Milan, Florence and elsewhere there were outbreaks of disorder, though on a restricted scale — the first the country had known for an entire century. Notices excluding the Jews began to make their appearance in cafés, restaurants, cinemas and other places of public resort. Private firms and corporations demonstrated their zeal in the cause of racial purity by indiscriminately dismissing the Jews in their employment, even without legal obligation. The titles of cultural and charitable foundations which commemorated Jewish munificence — and they were many — were ungratefully but inevitably Aryanized. The same happened, of course, to streets named after distinguished Jewish citizens; while elsewhere the old *Via dei Giudei* was ingenuously rechristened. In some places, Jewish shops had to be removed from the main streets; while in Trieste, vandals patriotically smashed the statue of the poet Italo Svevo. It was not surprising that dictionaries qualifying antisemites as "imperfectly civilized persons" were withdrawn from circulation. Persons who expressed sympathy with the victims of persecution were expelled from the Fascist Party, this in effect excluding them too from the normal channels of earning a livelihood.

There was one factor that made the position somewhat

more bearable than might have been expected. Notwithstanding the excesses and the bawlings of some time-servers and extremists, a great or perhaps the greater part of the Italian people — kindly, friendly, superficial as ever — was unaffected by the unceasing torrent of propaganda. It was impossible for them to consider the neighbors, with whom they had lived on terms of unfettered intimacy for so long, as having suddenly become enemies of the human race in general and of Italy in particular. It was out of the question for them to break off abruptly cordial relations maintained since youth. Disregarding the personal consequences, many persons in all parts of the country did whatever was possible to mitigate the blow, or went out of their way to perform kindly services. Dark menaces against those guilty of *pietismo* — compassion for the oppressed — were uttered every now and again by the Fascist leaders or announced in the press, but in vain. Above all, the Church did not relax its efforts. In the eyes of those who had been brought up on memories of the Ghetto, it was paradoxical that now the Papacy openly defended the Jews. But it was consistent with its historic attitude and policy. It had opposed Judaism, not persons of Jewish birth. Pius XI had refused to admit the criterion of racialism in Germany — it was impossible for the Vicar of Jesus Christ, the successor of St. Peter, to do so; he could not do otherwise, on the threshold of the Vatican. Time after time, he voiced his intense disapproval of what was happening — "Spiritually, we are all Semites," he said. It was noticed with interest how savants excluded from the Italian Academy had been admitted, almost ostentatiously, to the perhaps more distinguished papal counterpart; and a handful of scholars ejected from their posts, found employment as in the old days in the Vatican.

Yet the mass of Italian Jews could now see scant hope for the future except in emigration, and many joined the hopeless throngs now seeking a fresh home overseas. The communities of the country had long maintained an organization for the relief of foreign Jewish refugees; now, they had to create a new one for assisting the resettlement of their own people. Although the government had made their departure inevitable, nothing was done to facilitate it; for according to the treasury regulations no person could take with him out of the country more than 2,500 lire — sufficient to maintain him for a few weeks at the most. Moreover, similar wanderers were now thronging the highways of the world, and there was little attention or help for this barely-recognized group, whose sorrows were overwhelmed by the outbreak of the November pogroms in Germany and the mass emigration that followed. Nevertheless, new homes had to be found. Some five or six hundred, whose Zionist enthusiasms now proved amply justified, settled in Palestine, on the land and in the cities, while a distinguished group headed by Umberto Cassuto, now appointed professor of Bible at the Hebrew University of Jerusalem, played a significant role in the intellectual life of the country. Some of the universities of South America, too, where the cultural background facilitated absorption, welcomed outstanding exponents of the scholastic tradition of the older Latin country, and a few found posts also in the United States and elsewhere. There were Italian Jewish colonies, hungrily seeking the opportunity of readjustment, in London, New York, Paris, Buenos Aires and every other still-civilized capital. Within eighteen months, notwithstanding all difficulties, the total number of Jews who had left Italy had risen to 5,500 — over one-tenth of the entire Italian Jewish population.

A large number of Jews, not quite comprehending the racial basis of the new persecution, sought refuge in baptism. This at least gave their children the possibility of a good education in the schools maintained by the Church, and it was hoped that their lot would be better in the end. Moreover, some priests were not above granting antedated baptismal certificates, which relieved them from certain slight disabilities and opened the gates of some of the South American republics which would not admit professing Jews. Hence the present number of apostates — more than had gone over during the entire three centuries of unremitting pressure in the Ghetto period; though a few of them, disillusioned or disappointed, soon reverted to Judaism. The catastrophic dwindling of the Jewish population, which in a short while was reduced by one-fifth or one-quarter, coupled with the progressive impoverishment of those who remained and the appalling increase of charitable demands, reduced the communities to the verge of ruin.

As time went on, and the stranglehold on Italy grew stronger, and the world outside became more preoccupied with matters of more general moment, yet further extravagances were enacted. The children of a Jewish father and non-Jewish mother were authorized to adopt the latter's name, and non-Jews to relinquish appellations generally considered Jewish. The publication of Jewish periodicals or works of literary or scientific interest was prohibited. Jewish scholars were no longer permitted to work in the libraries and archives. A bequest in favor of the Roman community for educational and charitable objects, now sorely needed, was confiscated. With a great flourish, the Jews were expelled from occupied Albania as an "unwanted element" — fewer than 200 of them, comprising one in 5,000 of the total population!

On the outbreak of the European War in September, 1939, the Jewish position deteriorated further, in view of the alliance with antisemitic Germany and the probability that Italy would be involved in hostilities at her side before long. Firms dealing with the government were now forbidden to employ Jews or do business with them. They were excluded from acting as journalists or notaries public. Orders were issued for the compulsory "Aryanization" of Jewish firms employing more than a very small number of hands. Passports held by Jews were withdrawn, so that henceforth they could only leave the country, not return. An official spokesman intimated that it was the intention of the government to eliminate them entirely from national life within eleven years. In May, 1940, anti-Jewish excesses broke out at Trieste and even in Rome, where, however, they were suppressed by the police before there were any serious developments.

The once-proud Italian Jewry was now reduced to a lamentable state. They had given up their intense Jewish life for the sake of emancipation, and now that emancipation was withdrawn they had nothing left upon which to rely. Of those who were now being subjected to so ferocious a persecution, only a minority perhaps were fortified by any real Jewish knowledge or consciousness. They were abandoned by many of the younger, stronger and most virile. Not more than a dozen qualified spiritual leaders remained to guide the destinies of the broken communities — cut off by political circumstances from contact with the Jewish world, by the unreasoning Fascist frenzy from the hope implicit in Zionism, by the corrosive influence of the past hundred years from the inspiration of the Jewish past. Broken, impoverished, decimated, hopeless, there was one thing only that they retained in fullest measure — their integrity.

xliv

The Catastrophe

Italy's entry into the European war on June 10, 1940, as ally of her traditional German enemy, filled the cup of bitterness for her Jews to overflowing. It was obvious that their interests, their hopes, and their future were bound up with the Nazi defeat. Hence they were for the first time in opposition, in a moment of nationalistic excitement, to the declared interests of the people at large; though they were, indeed, more than justified by events, and the better elements in the population secretly sympathized with them. For all Fascist boasting, Italy now became nothing more than a German satellite. The swastika was to be seen everywhere in the country, German jackboots trod heavily through the lovely medieval streets, and German ideas and ideology penetrated every department of the administration.

As one of the first apparent results, the anti-Jewish campaign was now intensified. Mass arrests were carried out among the residue of the foreign born who lost their nationality through the introduction of the racial laws. Jews were expelled from the islands of Sicily and Sardinia, on the grounds that these were important military bases. Fortunately there were not many of them; but later on they were excluded also from mountain and seaside areas in the fortified zones. In September, widespread searches were conducted in the homes of Jews in the hope of finding evidence of espionage. It was considered wise to deprive them of the chance of hearing or spreading news from abroad, and in consequence all the radio sets in their possession were confiscated. Their names were omitted from the telephone directories, and later on some were even deprived of their instruments. One of the few categories whose livelihood had as yet remained unaffected was the nucleus of street-traders who constituted the basis of the Roman community, something like one-third of the total population there; and when in the late summer their licenses were withdrawn, it was a crushing blow to them — but also to many manufacturers, as a result of which they were temporarily renewed in the following winter, to enable the latter to get rid of merchandise on hand. In October, antique dealers, too, were deprived of their licenses. Other new restrictions excluded them from all commercial agencies, from acting as brokers, from any activity which might bring them into contact with the customs officials, from selling textbooks, and from participating in the scrap-iron business. Few other than the small shopkeepers were undisturbed, but their position too was undermined. By the close of 1941, it was estimated that three-quarters of the Jews of the country had lost their means of earning a livelihood.

As the war progressed, conditions deteriorated still further. The extremist press began to agitate for the immediate liquidation of the Italian Jewish population. To establish a yet closer control, their banking accounts were blocked. The anti-British demonstrations that broke out in Trieste, Milan and Genoa in the winter of 1940, when the news of the reverses in Libya began to arrive thick and fast, easily took on an anti-Jewish coloring, since defenseless Jews were available for attack and British were not. At Trieste, the offices of the community were raided and a number of prominent Jews taken into custody on a charge of spreading anti-Fascist propaganda. In some other places, conditions were particularly bad — for example, Fiume, where a bitter antisemite was Podestà and did his utmost to force anti-Jewish regulations upon the reluctant population. Falsified "Aryan" certificates, granted by corrupt Fascist bosses to enable Jews to evade the regulations, rose to improbable levels.

When the threat of invasion became imminent, in the spring of 1942, the mobilization of male Jews between the ages of 18 and 55 for forced labor was ordered, though this was carried out only in a casual fashion. That autumn, however, on the eve of the Jewish New Year festival, an assault in full medieval style was made by the Fascist mob on the synagogue of Ferrara, where the rabbi narrowly escaped with his life. Twice attempts were made to destroy that of Turin, while the ancient *Scuola Tedesca* at Padua was actually burned. Persons considered "dangerous" were

Synagogue of Rome

The Mole Antonelliana in Turin,
built for a Synagogue

Synagogue of Florence

Liberation Scene in Modern Rome

now sent to internment centers and concentration camps, the numbers varying in accordance with the venality or the compassion of the prefects to whom the selection was left.

Disciplinary measures were taken against members of the Fascist Party who maintained personal relations with Jews, or went for advice to Jewish lawyers. But all this proved insufficient for the purpose, as became manifest when the Fascist Podestà of Florence and Padua were dismissed, and several officials in Turin cashiered, for their lack of alacrity in carrying out the new measures. When the military debacle began, the native Jews in the Italian possessions in Africa found themselves maltreated, arrested and despoiled, even public worship and instruction being banned lest pro-Allied sympathies should be expressed to the Almighty. Fortunately, the British victories of 1942-3 were so sweeping and so speedy that deliverance came before irreparable harm was done, though, on the evening before Tripoli fell, a great number of Jews perished in a German onslaught on the Jewish quarter.

As compared with the happy condition of Italian Jewry up to a year or so before, it was a purgatory. Yet, paradoxically, as compared with conditions elsewhere in Europe at this time — with the solitary exceptions of neutral Switzerland and Sweden — it was paradise. This was the period when the Nazi government began its campaign for the comprehensive extermination of the Jews. Throughout the wide areas in German occupation, measures were being enacted against them such as had never disgraced any uncivilized people at the most barbaric age. They were once more shut up in physical Ghettos, forced to mark themselves again with a badge of shame, deliberately deprived of the necessities of life, and deported by the thousand and ten thousand and hundred thousand to reservations in Eastern Europe, where they were submitted to the most appalling barbarities culminating in scientific massacre. The number of those wantonly done to death was incalculably large. The Italian antisemitic press may have applauded these barbarities; but the Italian people abhorred them, and even the Fascist government would not imitate them. The ancient Ghettos were still recognizable in many places in Italy, but the Jews were not confined to them. The memory of the *sciamanno* was not quite dead among the descendants of those who had worn it, but this was the only part of Europe under Axis control where the Jewish badge was not made obligatory. When Jews were sent off to forced labor, there were sometimes demonstrations of sympathy at the railway stations. What was more, in some places the Italian authorities were able to impose moderation on others; it was reported, for example, that, when an attempt was made to enforce the wearing of the Jewish badge in some occupied areas in the south of France, they intervened and stated roundly that they would not countenance this revival of medieval barbarity. Notwithstanding the attempts to rid the country of foreign Jews, some — mainly the elderly — were still left. They were recruited to a very considerable extent when the Axis conquests extended to the Balkans, and Jews fled to the Italian zone to escape the unspeakable Nazi horrors, most being shipped over to Italy. Their lot, as compared with that of their coreligionists and brothers in distress elsewhere, was fortunate. The greater number, including almost all the men, were interned in a number of camps and detention areas set up throughout the country, the largest being that of Ferramonte near Cosenza in South Italy, where there were some 2,000 — Germans and Austrians, Poles and Czechs, Jugoslavs and Croats. Life under such conditions must be far from ideal. But they received food, were not maltreated, and were subjected to no barbarities, nor were there periodical jail-clearances to swell the columns on their way to annihilation in Eastern Europe. Fifteen years of Fascism, five years of German alliance, three years of racial indoctrination, were insufficient to destroy the native kindliness and decency of the Italian character.

At last the Italian people, dispirited by a succession of defeats such as had never been known while Jewish generals still served in the Army, and always uncomfortable in the German alliance, threw off the yoke of Fascism. On July 25, 1943, Mussolini was dismissed from office and the veteran Marshal Badoglio appointed prime minister. In the spontaneous wave of rejoicing throughout the country, the walls of the moral Ghetto that had been set up during the past five years were broken down, just as the walls of the physical Ghetto had been in the popular uprisings of the previous century. With a thrill of happiness and expectation, Jews now came out of retirement, and in some cases were swept back to their former posts by general consent. The new government cancelled the recent laws which barred them from office and appointed a couple to minor posts in the administration. (In Sicily, the Allied Military Control had abolished all discriminatory laws as early as July 12, but this had affected only the barest handful of individuals.) Internment camps were thrown open and prisoners released, while many Party officials, and others accused of embezzling "Aryanized" property, were arrested and sent to take their place. Even San Marino repealed its racial code on August 9. It seemed that day had at last broken after these tragic years of artificial night.

That would indeed have happened had not political and military calculations miscarried. After unhappily prolonged negotiations, Italy surrendered to the Allied powers on September 8. But the Germans, forewarned, forearmed and utterly ruthless, reacted with a promptitude and efficiency which could hardly fail to win the admiration even of their enemies. Within a few days, it had become obvious that the greater part of the country was in effect in German military occupation, and that her fair provinces and ancient monuments were doomed to be swept by the tide of battle.

For the unhappy Jews, history had a last tragic irony in store. As the foregoing pages have shown, Italian Jewish life during the past four and a half centuries had been restricted to the north of the country. South of Rome there was only a handful of Jews, with a community of a few hundred in Naples, and a nominal one of very recent establishment, already liberated, in Palermo. This part of the country was freed without great difficulty before 1943 was over, and while defending it the Germans were too fully occupied with military problems to be able to devote any attention to their racial obsession. Hence the foreign Jews in the concentration camps at Ferramonte and elsewhere were liberated after little further suffering. The community of Naples similarly underwent no great molestation before the city was freed. But the expected Allied landing in the Gulf of Genoa, which would have made a rapid German retirement inevitable, failed to take place. Hence the area of Jewish settlement from Rome northwards, including the capital, was for long and bitter months under the complete control of the brutal German military command and the irresponsible desperados who had adhered to Mussolini's hollow Republican Fascist Party. This accident of politics and strategy spelled the death-warrant not only for many individuals, whose emergence into the open at the time of the muddled revolution of July 25 proved disastrous, but also for more than one ancient community, and was catastrophic for Italian Jewry as a whole.

In the bleak months during which the Allied armies were painfully fighting their way across the Campania, through cities and townships whose former Jewish settlements were still commemorated by the surnames of the Roman Ghetto, the Germans were strengthening their grip on Rome. The Italian authorities assured the leaders of the Jewish community that no extra-legal measures would be taken against them, thus lulling them into a false sense of security. But in the early autumn of 1943, German S. S. detachments arrived in Italy and began to function forthwith as the principal instrument by which the Nazi stranglehold was maintained. The first sign of their presence was the butchery of a couple of score of Jews in September in the lovely summer resorts around Lago Maggiore — the first pogrom in Italy since the age of the Ghetto. At Ferrara, several Jews were among the persons shot at this time as a reprisal for an attack on a Fascist leader; and there were arrests and acts of violence also in various cities of Piedmont. Meanwhile, on September 26, 1943, the German authorities imposed a levy of fifty kilograms' weight of gold on the Roman community, to be paid within thirty-six hours, under pain of the immediate arrest and deportation of two hundred Jews. The blood money was raised, after a tremendous effort, and without aid; though some non-Jews generously offered their assistance, and the Vatican intimated that the Pope, horrified at the outrage, was prepared to provide a considerable proportion of the total in case of need — an unforgettable gesture of humanity. Yet this turned out to have been a piece of sheer fraudulence on the part of the oppressor, whose ferocity was unrelieved by a particle of honor; for it did not save a single person or a single life.

On the morning of Saturday, October 16, 1943 — the blackest day in the long history of Roman Jewry — a great raid took place on the Jewish homes, both in the former Ghetto area and in the more fashionable quarters of the city, in accordance with haphazardly prepared lists. Upwards of 1,000 persons — nearly one-tenth of the total population, including women in childbed and old men on the point of death — were brutally rounded up and driven off in lorries. Whole families were seized together, in one case including father, mother and ten children; two persons died as the result of the shock; one woman was seized with labor-pains as she was being removed. The victims were conveyed first to the buildings of the Military Academy, where two more women gave birth that same night. Thence, after two days, they were taken to the railway sidings and transferred into cattle-trucks. Shortly thereafter, the train with its cargo of human misery moved northwards. It is known to have passed through Orte, then Chiusi, then Florence, whence it went on in the direction of Bologna and of the German frontier. It was never heard of again; and we will perhaps never know at what death-camp in Eastern Europe these unhappy victims of man's inhumanity to man met their end.

In the following weeks, there were similar tragic scenes all over North Italy, a specially designated S. S. squad going from place to place for the purpose. In Florence, the fatal day was November 6, when about 100 Jews were rounded up; in Venice, November 9; in Ferrara, November 14; and so on. In Genoa, the sacristan was compelled to summon the leading members of the community to the synagogue by telephone, those who obeyed being forced into waiting lorries and driven off; in Fiume, the synagogue was raided during a service, and the worshippers seized. By now, however, a good many persons, forewarned by the horrible tragedy in Rome, had fled into the country or taken refuge in the houses of Christian friends, and were temporarily out of danger.

The proceedings were later put on a more systematic, ostensibly legal, basis. A decree of the puppet Republican Fascist government, now functioning under German auspices at Verona, proclaimed that as from December 1, 1943, the Italian Jews were to be deprived of their citizenship and regarded as subjects of an unfriendly state — that is, as public enemies. This was supplemented by a further decree of February 2, ordering the immediate arrest and internment of all Jews still at liberty and the sequestration of their property. Henceforth it was not merely dangerous, but fatal, for them to live openly. Another series of raids now began. In Rome, for example, a further 655 persons were arrested on one occasion and 244 on another; and in February a second train-load of misery rolled northwards from the capital. In Florence, some 150 prisoners (in addition to 34 non-Florentines, who had hoped for safety in a town where they were unknown) followed the hundred deported on the first occasion; while in Venice, on December 5, all the persons who could be traced were rounded up, 300 in all; though those who were not of full Jewish descent were subsequently released. This was typical of what happened in these terrible months throughout the country. Episodes which could hardly be credited in the twentieth century were reported from all over Italy. In Rome, at least seventy Jews, arrested during recent raids and housed in the notorious Regina Coeli prison, were among the hostages butchered in the Ardeatine Quarries on March 24, 1944, in retaliation for the ambush of some German troops. Everywhere, many persons were shot outright — eight, for example, at Florence alone. The authorities had given it to be understood that those over seventy years of age were to be exempted from arrest. In consequence, the homes for the aged had been regarded as secure places of refuge. In the end, however, they too were raided and their inmates sent off for extermination. The octogenarian Senator Elia Morpurgo, who had once played a prominent role in Italian politics, died while he was being deported. Even mental patients from the public asylums were added to the pathetic convoys. At Pisa, a number of persons had taken refuge in the home of the venerable president of the community, Giuseppe Pardo Roques, a man who had formerly taken a most honorable part in civic life. On August 1, 1944, the house was surrounded by Germans, and the whole group was exterminated by hand-grenades, those who survived being finished off by machine-gun fire. Most of the rabbis lived up to the noblest tradition of their predecessors, remaining at their posts to the very last and suffering with their flocks: the scholarly Riccardo Pacifici, of Genoa; the blind, devoted Adolfo Ottolenghi, of Venice: the rabbis of Modena, of Pisa, and more than one other. Nathan Cassuto, of Florence, was seized while administering charity to the poor.

Whether it was the outcome of collusion or of inefficiency (neither possibility is to be discarded), the announcement regarding the new regulations was made over the radio on the night of November 29, two days before it was to come into force, and appeared in the newspapers on the following morning. Hence the Jews — or those at least who had not already taken precautions — were to some extent forewarned, the opportunity being given for them to go into hiding. A considerable number, especially from the northern cities, managed to make their way over the mountain passes into Switzerland, where they were received with all possible kindness and hospitality; though not a few were intercepted, or succumbed, on the journey. The majority of Italian Jews, however, "went underground." They abandoned their houses, they removed in great numbers into country places where they were unknown, they constantly changed their lodgings, they slept in lofts and stables, they appeared in public as little as possible (some did not venture into the streets for months on end), they assumed fictitious names, they obtained false identity papers. The story most conveniently put forward was that they were refugees from the southern provinces, already occupied by the victorious allied forces, and that they had lost all their documents in an air raid. Thus, furtively and miserably, in constant fear for their lives, the most part managed to continue their existence from day to day.

These subterfuges, however ingenious, would have been impossible but for two factors: the sympathy of the mass of the Italian people and the active help of the Italian Church. Many were those who suspected, or knew positively, the identity of the strangers who had come to live among them or whom they passed in the streets; but the number of betrayals was relatively small. Many Jews owed their lives to the Christian neighbors who, at the risk of their own, gave them hospitality. There was a considerable degree of connivance even from officials; while banks and similar institutions assisted by suppressing or else delaying information about Jewish holdings. The Church on its side lived up to its noblest traditions, inspiring the people to play their part and earning a debt of enduring gratitude from the Italian Jews. It did everything possible to mitigate the blow, to assist the fugitives, and to help the sufferers. The shelter of the Vatican City was made available as far as possible for those of Rome. A large number were actually harbored in monasteries and convents, with the complete connivance of the inmates and the authorities; in some cases at least, they were even afforded special facilities for their religious observances during their stay. Thus, in the twentieth century, the great wrong of the Italian Ghetto was atoned for.

Meanwhile, the Republican Fascist S. S. had been organized on the German model, out of the dregs of the native population. Henceforth, there were possibilities of onslaught at any moment, and not as hitherto only occasionally; for these new paladins, recruited locally, could often recognize the Jews, and arrested indiscriminately those whom they happened to encounter in the streets. Rewards, ranging in some cases up to as much as 50,000 lire, were offered for the denunciation of Jews: and though to the credit of the Italian people they were claimed relatively seldom, many persons had their hiding-places betrayed, or were denounced when they appeared in the streets. In January, householders had been ordered to give information to the authorities about any Jews living with them, hospitality being henceforth dangerous. Moreover, the ration cards issued to Jews were withdrawn, so that those who could not procure false papers were starved out. This was not, however, publicly announced, so that persons who made inquiries at the food offices found themselves arrested. At Milan, indeed, there was some alleviation when the underground anti-Fascist movement raided the administrative offices and destroyed the Jewish files, thus disorganizing the mechanism of the persecution; but such alleviation was unique.

The fury extended to the monuments of Jewish cultural and religious life, which were no less monuments of Italian civilization as well. Republican Fascist hooligans systematically destroyed, in November 1944, the lovely baroque synagogues of Ferrara, which were among the artistic monuments of the city, and looted their contents, so that ancient Scrolls of the Law found their way to leather-workers for making handbags, and bundles of irreplaceable archives were recovered later from rag shops. The same had taken place in December at Alessandria and about the same time at Fiume. The archives and contents of the Turin synagogue, destroyed during an air raid, were looted. Irreparable damage was similarly done with dynamite charges to the synagogue in Florence, reputed to be the loveliest in Europe, and to others. Moreover, in most places where it was possible the Germans seized and removed the synagogal appurtenances and so on, if they seemed to have the slightest monetary value. In Rome, for example, the famous libraries of the community and of the Rabbinical Seminary, both rich in manuscripts and in early printed works — two railway-wagons' load — were confiscated and sent north towards Munich and were not heard of again. At Florence, the precious synagogal appurtenances had been put as was thought into safety; but they were discovered and sent away. The property left in the Jewish houses, unless made over ostensibly to "Aryan" friends or agents, was frequently transferred to central deposits — sometimes the disused synagogues were used for the purpose — under the pretext that it would be distributed to the poor; though little was left for them after the Fascist bosses had taken their choice.

There were some places, however, such as Casale, where matters did not reach this stage, Jewish houses being looted outright.

The Fascist authorities had intimated that those arrested would not be sent out of Italy. A number of concentration camps were therefore set up in the north, on the German model and under the control of the S. S., the most notorious being that of Fossoli, near Carpi. (There were others at Potenza, Vo di Este, Pozzuolo, Salsomaggiore and Castelnuovo di Garfagnana, the last being reserved for foreigners.) From time to time they were partially emptied to make room for new arrivals, the inmates being despatched, notwithstanding all promises, across the Alps; for this was the period when the Nazis' incredible campaign of extermination was at its height. Others arrested by the Germans were deported without this intermediate stage. As early as November 1943, a convoy of Italian Jews, perhaps including the first party of Roman deportees, was reported to have arrived in the notorious camp of Treblinka, in Poland; but shortly afterwards this was liquidated, and no more was heard of them or their fate. Later, more and more were sent in densely packed cattle-trucks, in which many died outright, towards the extermination-camps of Auschwitz (Oswiecim) in Poland, or Buchenwald and Bergen-Belsen in Germany, to find death under circumstances of agonizing cruelty with hundreds of thousands of their coreligionists. A handful only were liberated by the Allies' advance; the vast majority were never heard of again. In this tragic fashion, a high proportion of the most virile elements in Italian Jewry — ten times more perhaps than had succumbed to all the medieval and Ghetto-age persecutions in a thousand years of history — met their fate.

From the autumn of 1943, the corporate life of Italian Jewry was ostensibly suspended. In Rome, for example, the synagogues were closed and sealed at the beginning of the German occupation, so that for the first time perhaps since the reign of the Emperor Claudius, two thousand years before, no open religious services were held in the Eternal City. Henceforth, worship took place only clandestinely, in private houses or, for the moment, in the homes for the aged and similar institutions, until they as well were liquidated. Occasionally, there was the extraordinary spectacle, at which former ages would have stood aghast, of Jewish functions in monasteries and convents. Jewish funerals, even, were possible only through collusion. Yet the Jewish communities retained their cohesion underground. In particular with noble and sometimes heroic devotion, they continued their charitable organization on behalf of the needy, now tragically increased in number; it was indeed while distributing alms to their coreligionists that some leading personalities, who might have remained in safety, were now arrested. In this charitable work too the Church was associated. In Rome, the well-tried Organization for the Relief of Jewish Emigrants (*Delegazione Assistenza Ebrei Emigranti*: known as *Delasem*) maintained its activity on behalf of natives and foreigners alike, contact being continued between the various clandestine groups through a self-sacrificing Capuchin friar, Father Benedetto.

Meanwhile, Jews had been playing an active part once again in the liberation of Italy. Everywhere, they took their share in the partisan movement, providing some outstanding leaders. Numbers of these fell in the course of the fighting — no fewer than fifteen from the Turin community alone. One of the best remembered martyrs of the period was the young philosopher Eugenio Colorni, who had edited the clandestine newspaper *Avanti* and was killed in circumstances of exceptional brutality in the streets of Rome. Enzo Sereni, who had come back from Palestine to participate in the liberation of his native land and had been parachuted behind the enemy lines on a special mission, was captured, dying later on in a German concentration camp.

The self-sacrifice and agony were not in vain, though the

deliverance was disappointingly slow. On June 5, 1944, after nearly a year of anguish, Rome was delivered by the Allied troops, and the fugitives came out of their hiding-places. There were indescribable scenes of jubilation in the former Ghetto area that day, as Palestinian soldiers made their first appearance, and as the British military chaplain removed the seals from the gates of the Great Synagogue, which was opened for worship once again. But, of some 12,000 Jews who had been in Rome two years before, fewer than 10,000 ultimately returned to their homes. Over 100 were known to have been killed; over 2,000 had been deported (some, immediately before the evacuation of the city) including 1,067 men, 743 women and 281 children — the vast majority to their death. Meanwhile, the German armies retreated, still fighting with all the frenzy of desperation, through Tuscany and into the area where Jewish communities lay relatively thick, many of them now coming into the firing line. More than one lovely synagogue was destroyed, including that of Leghorn, considered a national monument; and wanton damage too was added to the wreckage of war. But slowly the strangle-hold established by barbarism was weakened. Leghorn was liberated in July, Florence in August; and in the following spring this was followed by the general debacle. In place after place, deliverance was brought to ancient communities by Palestinian Jewish soldiers who found their way to the Jewish institutions and reopened the synagogues; while Lugo, an ancient seat of Jewish life and learning near Ferrara (now, indeed, almost abandoned), was actually liberated by the recently-formed Jewish Brigade fighting under the British flag. Finally, on April 29, the unconditional surrender of the German armies in Italy was signed, Fascism and Nazism in Italy ending simultaneously. The nightmare was over.

Already in the previous year, as has been mentioned, the corpus of anti-Jewish laws had been repealed by the legitimate Italian government, and plans were already well advanced for righting the wrong that had been done, for restoring the confiscated or illegally acquired property, and for reinstating in their former positions those who had been dismissed. On paper, it was possible to reconstitute Italian Jewry as it had been in former days; and indeed in some places the recovery, backed by the enthusiasm of the survivors, was both remarkable and instantaneous. It was impossible, however, to bring the dead back to life, impossible to cancel the memory of the evil years, impossible to redress the broken spirits. The devastation of the antisemitic interlude had been vast. Out of some 42,000 native Jews who had lived in Italy before 1938, large numbers had abandoned the community, some 6,000 had emigrated, and between 4,000 and 5,000 — one-sixth of the survivors (in addition to approximately 4,000 foreign Jewish refugees) — had been deported. Of these, no more than a few score returned: the rest lay in unknown graves, in the death camps of Poland and of Germany. There was hardly a Jewish family in the whole of Italy that did not have to deplore appalling losses; many had disappeared entirely, so that it became difficult to keep an accurate record. In some places, one person in three was missing; in Rome, one person in five; in Trieste, a community which had once numbered 5,500 and was reduced by 1943 to 2,300 was now brought down to only 900. Enforced dispersal enhanced the problem. Some ancient communities, such as those of Verona or of Mantua, had received such mortal blows that it was doubtful whether they would ever be reconstituted; others, which retained a certain degree of vigor, were so greatly reduced that their future was endangered. Not only had the habit of Jewish life been interrupted, but in many places its setting had disappeared — the lovely old synagogues ruined, the artistic and literary treasures despoiled, the historic archives dispersed. Such a blow could not fail to leave a lasting impression.

Perhaps, around the hard-tried but still solid nucleus of

Roman Jewry, it may prove feasible to build up again in the future a new nexus of communities, so that the oldest Jewish center of the Western world will be able to make its contribution to humanity again in the momentous days to come. This will depend only on its own zeal and devotion. For the great lesson of the past generation must be mastered and appreciated. It is only by retaining to the full a sense of Hebraic values, and by the passionate pursuit of righteousness in the spirit of its sublime heritage, that Italian Jewry can justify its existence, whether to Italy or to itself.

INDEX

Aaron (Abu Aaron), of Bagdad, 50 f., 63
Aaron of Messina, 240
Abbazia, 488
Abdullah ibn Riyahin, 63
Abenafia, Joseph, 236–8, 240
Aboab, Samuel, 398
Abot de-R. Nathan, 60 f.
Abrabanel, Doña Bienvenida, 189, 192, 215, 285, 310; family, 179, 189, 215, 279, 284, 286; Don Isaac, 210, 279 f., 302–3; Don Jacob, 215, 279, 284; Joseph, 279; Judah, *see* Leone Ebreo; Don Samuel, 189, 208, 215, 279, 285 f.
Abraham, physician at Florence, 207
Abraham of Perugia, 218
Abraham the dyer, 224
Abraham Abulafia, 150 f.
Abraham ben Garton, 223
Abraham ben Jehoshaphat, 53
Abruzzi, 81, 88, 278
Abu'l Hayy, 58
Abulrabbi, Aaron, 209, 242
Abydos, 68
Abyssinian War, 515, 518, 521, 526
Academia dei Faticanti, Florence, 425
Acilius Glabrio, Roman consul, 18
Acquaviva, 280
Acqui, 313, 343, 372, 409, 417, 428–9, 438, 441, 466, 498, 502
Acri, 277
Actors, Jewish, 23, 197 f., 482
Adelaide, countess of Sicily, 89
Adorni family, 183
Adrianople, 301
Aegean Islands, 529
Africa, 4, 40, 56, 61, 87, 112, 268, 539
African influences, 245
Agone and Testaccio, Tribute of, 140
Agosta, 252
Agrarian Association, Piedmont, 465
Agricola, Christian martyr, 22
Agriculture, Jews in, 31, 47, 68, 105, 423, 441, 486
Agrigento; *see* Girgenti
Agrippa, 7, 12
Agur, by Jacob ben Judah Landau, 221
Ahimaaz, of Melfi, 79
Ahimaaz, of Oria, 50 f., 63, 64, 307
Ahisamekh, 79
Ahitub ben Isaac of Palermo, 146, 242
Aid to Health, by Avenzoar, 95
Aix-la-Chapelle, Congress of, 454
Akiba, Rabbi, 16
Alamanni (Alamandi), Elias, 136
Alamanno, Johanan, 207, 209
Alaric, 37

Alatino, Bonaiuto (Azriel), 320; **Moses, 209**
Alatri, Samuel, 473
Albania, expulsion from, 535
Albertus Magnus, 148
Albigensianism, 97
Albornoz, Cardinal, 126 n.
Alcuin, 69
Aleppo, 261
Alessandria, 128, 163, 309, 322–3, **343, 372**, 413, 438, 452, 548
Alessandro, apostate, 306
Alessandro del Nevo, 105
Alexander III, Pope, 78, 106
Alexander IV, Pope, 139
Alexander VI, Pope, 179
Alexander VII, Pope, 330 f.
Alexander Severus, 19 f.
Alexandria, 503, 514
Alfieri, Dino, 522
Alfonso I d'Este, 189
Alfonso II d'Este, 210 f., 302, **314, 320**
Alfonso III, duke of Modena, 380
Alfonso II of Naples, 279 ff.
Alfonso I of Sicily, 275
Alfonso, Infante, of Spain, **262**
Alghero, 263 ff.
Aljama, in Sicily, 81
Almanzi, Giuseppe, 498
al-Muiz, 53, 57
Alphabet of Ben-Sira, 61
Alsace, 444
Amalfi, 48, 54, 79, 85, 86, 269
Ambassadors, Jewish; *see* Diplomats
Ambron, Alessandro, 414; family, **180**; Sabato, 412
Ambrose, Bishop, 34, 39
Ambrosio, Franciscan friar, 302
Amedeo V, anti-Pope, 161
Amedeo VIII, duke of Savoy, 136, **140**
Amittai family of Oria, 50 ff., 54, 60, **63, 78**
Anacletus II, Pope, 73 f.
Anagni, 121, 275
Anan ben Marinus, 91
Anatoli, Jacob, 93 f.
Anau, Benjamin, 106, 139, 145, 151; family, 13, 90–1, 138, 145 f., 151, *see* Min ha-Anavim family; Jehiel, 146; Moses, 146; Paola, 214; Salvatore, 461 f.; Samuel, 220; Zedekiah ben Abraham, 146, 151
Ancona, 68, 70, 77, 86, 113, 116, 118 f., 121, 140, 141, 143, 147, 158, 160, 161, **162, 168**, 169, 176, 178, 182, 187, 192, 296, 299 ff., 306 f., 314, 318 f., 321, 330 f., 346, 352, 356, 362, 368 ff., 375, 388, 397–8, 404, 412, 418 f., 426, 431 f., **435, 450 ff., 456**, 469–70, 472, 519

555

Ancona, d', Alessandro, 418; Sansome, 469
Andreas (Elhanan), 74
Andreas of Bruges, printer, 255
Angelo (Mordecai), of Rome, 111, 202
Anjou, house of, 94 f., 98 f., 269, 271, 274
Anna, financier of San Marino, 122
Anna the Hebrew, of Rome, 201
Annunzio, d', Gabriele, 509
Anselmo del Banco, 185
Anti-Jewish legislation, 38 f., 49, 51, 97, 132, 154 f., 161 f., 163, 177, 246 ff., 249, 264, 266 f., 294 ff., 309, 315-7, 320, 337, 384, 411, 414-8, 426, 448 ff., 468, 470-1, 528 ff., 544
Anti-Jewish publications, 386, 410, 439, 522-3, 526; plays, 386; see *Gnora Luna*
Antiochus Epiphanes, 2
Antique dealers, 486, 537
Antisemitism, 23, 30, 69, 128, 157, 475, 511, 517, 522-50; see Anti-Jewish
Antologia, periodical, of Florence, 458
Antonelli, Alessandro, 492
Antoninus Pius, 18 f.
Aosta, Bishop of, 341
Apulia, 36, 63, 64, 71, 79, 90, 93, 98, 100, 151, 269, 271, 280, 283 f., 286 f., 335, 481
Aquila, 163, 175, 274 f., 278
Aquilaea, 21, 76; Patriarch of, 109
Aquinas, Thomas, 86, 106, 148
Arabs, 521
Aragon, house of, 98-9, 228, 235, 246 ff., 252 ff., 262, 264
Arca of Lebanon, 20 n.
Arcadius, emperor, 35, 36
Archevolti, Samuel, 400
Archisynagogus, 19, 25
Archontes, 25; see *Gabbaim*
Ardingus Judaeus, 70
Arena, a town in Milan, 173
Arezzo, 134, 345, 436 f.
Arianism, 38 f., 41
Aricia, 21
Ariosto's *Orlando Furioso*, 211
Aristobulus, 4, 6
Aristotle, 103, 148 n., 204 f., 206, 209
Art, historians, 481; Jewish ecclesiastical, 28, 390-1; patrons of, 195
Arta, 287
Artisans, 103, 229, 272, 308
Artists, Jewish, 23, 198-9, 391, 482
Artom, Alessandro, 483; Ernesto, 478; Isaac, 467-8, 477 f.
Arukh, The, 91
Ascarelli, Deborah, 215, 498; family, 180; Rabbi Joshua, 380
Ascoli, 80, 85, 89, 169, 277, 390
Ascoli, d', David, 297
Ascoli, General, 530; Graziadio Isaiah, 481
Ashkenazi, Solomon, 312
Asia, 5, 22
Asia Minor, 4, 34
Asolo, 183, 184
Assimilation, 5, 23, 26 f., 56, 213 ff., 221 f., 265-6, 268, 269, 340, 347, 436, 474, 479, 485, 504-6, 507 f., 515, 525-6, 536
Assisi, 121, 169
Asti, 70, 135 f., 176, 183, 342, 362, 442, 477

Astrology, 201, 414
Astronomy, 61, 94, 200 f., 412
Aterno, 72, 81
Athias, Joseph, 422; surname, 360
Attacks on Jews, 41, 54, 73, 99, 100 f., 183 f., 247-8, 250-2, 271, 386, 388-9, 532, 536, 538; see Pogroms
Augustinians, 208
Augustus Caesar, 7, 8, 9, 10, 27
Auschwitz (Oswiecim), Poland, 549
Austrian army of occupation, 437-8, 440
Austrian rule, 124, 336-7, 340, 350, 416, 422 ff., 429, 438 ff., 443, 445-7, 453 ff., 465-70, 472-3, 484, 486 f., 493, 495 f., 500
Austro-Hungarian empire, 447
Avanti, newspaper, 550
Avenzoar, 95
Averroes, 94, 96, 206, 209
Aversa, 101
Avicenna, *Canon* of, 224
Avigdor, Isaac Samuel, 443
Avignon, 141, 344
Avronques, Solomon, 263
Aymerich, monk, 126
Azcarini of Palermo, 243
Azeglio, d', Massimo, 464-5; Count Roberto, 465
Azulai, Hayim Joseph David, 399

BABYLONIAN SCHOOLS, 64, 91
Bacoli, 22
Badge, Jewish, 56, 97, 98, 131 f., 139 f., 154, 161 f., 162, 174 n., 182, 188, 207, 244, 246 f., 265 ff., 273-4, 275 f., 281, 285, 295, 297, 303 f., 309 f., 313, 320, 325 f., 328, 337, 348, 354, 360-1, 411, 414, 417, 421, 423, 426, 430 ff., 449 f., 456, 540
Badia, 453
Badoglio, Marshal Pietro, 541
Bagdad, 50, 57
Bagnacavallo, 321
Baia, 22
Balbo, Cesare, 458; Haninu (Hayyim?), 249
Bandello, novelist, 279
Bande Nere, Giovanni delle, 202-3
Bandiera brothers, 457-8
Bankers, Jewish, 23, 131, 180 f., 188, 450 n.; "Regulations for the Jewish Bankers," 114; see Loan-banks; Moneylenders
Banks, 486-7; see Loan-banks; Savings banks
Baptisms, forced, 39, 41, 51, 171, 248, 253, 271, 378-82, 418, 449, 451, 453, 471 f.; see Conversions to Christianity
Barbary corsairs, 365
Barco, 224
Bardi of Florence, 106 f.
Bari, 13, 22, 49, 52, 53, 54, 60, 61, 62, 63, 64, 80, 81, 88, 90, 91, 101, 269, 271, 277, 280, 285
Bar Kochba revolt, 18
Barrafael, Major Isaac, 432
Bartolocci, Giulio, 394
Bartolommeo da Capua, 100
Baruch of Benevento, 208
Barzillai, Salvatore, 488
Basevi, Gioacchino, 441

INDEX

Basil, emperor, 51
Basilea, Rabbi Solomon, 412
Bassani, Isaiah, 398
Bassano, 130, 172, 175, 184, 359
Baths, public, 232
Battista, Giovanni (Solomon Romano), 291–2
Beards, 98
Beauticians, 201
Bedarrida family, 353
Belisarius, 40
Belles-lettres, 28, 58–65, 114, 116, 137, 143–52, 190, 194–227, 279, 287, 303, 399–401, 405–6, 481–2, 497
Bellini, Vincenzo, 482
Bemporad, surname, 360
Benamozegh, Rabbi Elia, 499
Benedetti, G. B., 410, 439
Benedetto, Capuchin friar, 550
Benedict III, Pope, 381
Benedict XIII, Pope, 411
Benedict XIII, anti-Pope, 157
Benedict XIV, Pope, 379, 411
Benetelli, missionary, 412
Benevento, 48, 49, 52, 63, 72, 79, 87, 299, 307
Benghazi, 514
Benivieni, Domenico, 207
Benjamin of Bozecco, 146
Benjamin da Corinaldo, 160
Benjamin of Tudela, 74–83, 84, 85, 86, 87, 132, 329, 367
Bentivoglio family, 126
Bergen-Belsen, Germany, 549
Berliner, Abraham, 499
Bernardino da Feltre, 170–6, 179, 181, 188, 190, 196, 202, 252, 278
Bernardino of Sienna, 162 f.
Bernice, the Herodian, 14
Berthier, General L. A., 432
Bertinoro, Obadiah da, 221, 243–5, 247
Bible (O. T.), 28, 95, 104, 147, 194, 216 f., 219, 292, 383, 403, 437, 497; printing of, 224, 225–6; *see* Commentaries; Pentateuch; Vulgate
Bibliophiles, 498
Bibliography, science of, 499
Bicocca, Battle of, 461
Biella, 136, 342
Bigamy, practice of, 232–3, 293
Bisbidis, Il, poem by Immanuel of Rome, 145
Bisignano, 80, 85
Bissati, of Piedmont, 425
Biton, "Rabbi," of Castiglione, 254
Bitonto, 280
Black Death, 117, 118, 130, 131, 132, 137, 142; *see* Plagues
Blacksmiths, 229, 263
Blancard, Solomon, 75
Blasphemy accusations, 72, 430–1
Boccaccio, 144
Bodo, French archdeacon, 69
Bohemia, 166
Bolaffi, Leone, 483
Bologna, 21 f., 76, 111, 126 f., 129, 131, 134, 157, 158, 161, 169, 175, 177, 182, 192, 195,
196, 199, 212 f., 218, 220, 224, 277, 292, 298, 306 f., 318 f., 439, 452, 468 f., 471 f., 486, 491, 498, 502, 544; University of, 127, 147, 204
Bomberg, Daniel, 225–6; Press, 225–6
Bonartino, Joshua, 238–9
Bonaventura, physician of Ferrara, 128; Jacob di, 305; Salamone di, 176
Bonavoglia, Moses, 238 f., 249
Bondi, Abraham, 211
Bonfil and Vivanti, firm of, 373
Boniface VIII, Pope, 139, 148
Boniface IX, Pope, 121, 156, 202
Bonifazio da Casale, 183
Bonjudes ben Davin (Bonjudes Bondavin), 265
Book of the Apple, The, 94
Book of the Creation, commentary on, 61
Books, Battle of, 205–6; burning of, 100, 142, 292–4, 303–4, 382, 445; confiscation of, 162, 411–2, 548; publication forbidden, 525, 528, 531, 535; *see* Censorship
Booksellers, 114
Borghese, Prince Camillo, 432
Borgia, Cesare, 199, 212; Lucrezia, 197
Borgo S. Donnino, 341
Borgo S. Sepolcro, 345, 410
Borromeo, Cardinal, 223, 309
Borso I d'Este, 187
Bosone da Gubbio, 145
Bourbons, 417, 455, 469, 491
Bozecco, 146
Bozzolo, 339 f.
Bragadini, Alvise, printer, 290 ff.; family, 371
Brescello, 340
Brescia, 21, 130, 163, 169, 173, 176, 224
Briel, Leon, 402
Brindisi, 8, 49, 50, 80, 87, 271, 273, 280, 285, 287
Brofferio, Angelo, 458
Brundisium; *see* Brindisi
Brunswick, duke of, 422
Brusa, 301
Buchenwald, Germany, 549
Buda, siege of, 388
Bulls, papal, 133, 138, 139, 142, 158, 160, 163, 165, 166, 177, 213, 249, 266, 293, 294 ff., 303, 304, 306, 315 f., 317, 319, 354, 377 f.
Buonaventura, surname, 360; *see* Bonaventura
Buontalenti, Bernardo, 311
Burgundy, duke of, 136
Busacco family, 57
Busach of Palermo, 240
Busca, 372
Busseto, 341, 417, 502
Butchers, 23, 182, 247
Byzantines, 41 f., 43, 47, 48 ff., 66, 335; Byzantine influences, 92
Byzantium, 29; *see* Constantinople

CABALISM, 150 f., 192, 204, 205, 208, 390, 400 f., 402–6, 498; *see* Mysticism
Caecilius, rhetorician, 8, 23
Caesar, Julius, 5, 6, 9, 10, 31

INDEX

Cagliari, 45 f., 262, 264 ff.
Cairo, 58
Calabrese, Hayyim Vital, 403
Calabria, 22, 36, 71, 80, 272, 276 f., 283 f., 286 f.
Calacte, 8
Calcarenses (synagogue), 24
Calendar, 60, 315
Caligula, Gaius, 10, 12
Calixtus III, Pope, 166, 177, 250–1
Caltagirone, 252, 260
Camarata, 260
Cambi, Bartolommeo, 325–7
Cambrai, League of, 184, 311
Camerini, Eugenio, 481
Camerino, 77, 307, 359; duke of, 209
Cammarata, 259
Cammeo, Federico, 511
Campania, 141, 296, 307 f., 542
Campello, Bernardino, 299
Campoformio, treaty of, 438
Campo S. Pietro, 175 f.
Canano, Giovanni Battista, 202
Candela, 80, 81, 89
Cangrande della Scala, lord of Verona, 130, 145
Cantarini, Isaac Vita, 366, 377–8
Cantoni, Alberto, 482; Rabbi Lelio, 464, 494
Cap, Brona, 263
Capello, Bianca, grand duchess of Tuscany, 201
Capistrano, Giovanni da, 158 f., 162 f., 165 f., 170, 224, 249–50, 274–5
Capitalism, foundations of modern, 110
Capodistria, 124
Caporetto, 488
Captives of war, 4, 13, 14, 15, 23, 82, 86; ransom of Jewish, 5, 237, 331, 339, 350–1, 365, 434
Capua, 22, 48, 52, 54, 63, 78, 85, 87, 89, 95, 101, 147, 150, 283, 285
Caracalla, emperor, 19, 30
Carboneria, 455, 457
Carcassonna family, 268; Moses, 263; Nino, 263
Cardoso, Isaac, 378, 397; Miguel, 405; surname, 360
Carlo Alberto, king of Sardinia, 449, 463–7, 504
Carlo Emanuele I, duke, 342
Carlowitz, peace conference at, 377
Carmagnola, 342
Carmelites, 197
Carmi, Jacob Israel, 442, 444
Carnivals, 140, 236, 386–7, 392, 450, 451–2, 459
Carpenters, 229, 371
Carpentras, 344
Carpi, 187, 340, 549
Carpi, Leone, 462, 468; Zachariah, 439
Carrara, house of, 125
Casa dei Catecumeni, 290, 307, 328, 367, 378–9, 381, 390, 415, 451, 471 f.
Casale, 136, 183, 313–4, 343, 363, 372, 388, 409, 443 f., 453, 464 f., 490, 493, 502, 519, 549

Casalmaggiore, 113, 224, 322
Caschisi, Joseph, 229
Cassino (San Germano), 80
Cassuto, Nathan, 546; Umberto, 507, 534
Castelbolognese, Angelo, 484
Castelbolognesi, Gustavo, 521
Castelfranco, 175, 184
Castelli, David, 498
Castello, Abraham Isaac, 422
Castelnuovo di Garfagnana, 549
Castelnuovo, Enrico, 482
Castelnuovo-Tedesco, Mario, 482
Castel Porziano, 21
Castel S. Pietro, 212
Castiglion Fiorentino, 134
Castiglione, 254
Castiglione, Vittorio, 498
Castrogiovanni, 252
Castronuovo, 230, 260
Castroreale, 230, 252, 260
Castrovillari, 283, 285
Catacombs, 26 ff., 59 f.
Catania, 22, 49, 55, 82 f., 230, 236, 240, 242–3, 248, 260
Catanzaro, 81, 86, 229, 272, 274, 280
Catholic party, 475
Cattaneo, Carlo, 458
Cavour, Camillo, 465, 467, 477
Cellini, Benvenuto, 195, 199
Cemeteries, 21, 22, 26 f., 58, 111, 112, 126, 131, 135, 138, 182, 251, 273, 307, 348, 366, 384, 411, 417, 459, 501
Ceneda; *see* Vittorio Veneto
Censorship of Hebrew literature, 293–4, 304, 320, 328, 382–3, 394, 397–8, 411–2; *see* Books
Census, professional, 114
Cento, 128 f., 187, 321, 333, 352, 355, 430, 438, 502, 512
Central Italy, 33, 41 f., 107, 111, 114, 116, 117, 118 ff., 125, 143 ff., 156 ff., 168, 175 f., 273, 296, 308, 318, 321, 359, 361, 434, 455, 491, 501
Centuriae curationum, by Amatus Lusitanus, 202
Cervetto, Giacomo Basevi, 377
Cesare d'Este, 321
Cesarini, Duke, 432
Cesena, 77, 92, 122
Ceuta, North Africa, 74
Chain of Tradition, by Gedaliah ibn Iacchia, 218
Chajes, H. P., 506
Charity, 179, 331, 348, 363 ff., 419, 472, 485, 505, 532, 535, 546, 550
Charlemagne, 66, 68, 69
Charles I of Anjou, 94 f., 98 f., 100 n.
Charles II, emperor, 100 and n., 269
Charles IV of Bourbon, 351
Charles V, emperor, 182, 192 f., 202, 284–5, 286
Charles VI, emperor, 400
Charles VIII of France, 184, 279–80, 357
Cherasco, 342, 372
Chief Rabbi, 505, 511 f., 532; of France, 443; of Libya, 521; of Sicily, 236–9
Chieri, 342, 357, 438, 441, 457

INDEX

Chieti, 175
Chigi, Roman banker, 111
Chiusi, 21, 544
Chrestus, 11
Christians, in employ of Jews, 97, 154, 161 ff., 266 f., 294 f., 317, 337, 371, 383–4, 411, 414 f., 418, 449 ff., 468, 470 f.
Christians, persecution of, 29
Christianity, 2, 10, 19, 20, 30, 31 ff., 38, 39, 42 ff., 56, 81, 100, 150, 154, 162, 163, 177 f., 186, 193, 205, 245, 246, 251, 266 f., 270, 289–328, 378–82, 414, 417, 425, 479
Chronicle of the Kings of France and Turkey, by Joseph ha-Cohen, 218
Church, 19, 30, 31, 42, 44, 47, 88, 89 f., 94, 97 ff., 104, 105, 108, 120 f., 126 n., 153 ff., 184, 196, 198, 206, 209, 216, 235, 249–50, 270, 274, 277, 282, 284, 289–328, 330 ff., 341, 353–4, 378–82, 388, 402, 408, 411–2, 427 f., 434, 443, 451, 465, 471–3, 480, 510–1, 521, 523, 533 f., 546–7, 550; *see* Papacy; Vatican
Church Councils, 153, 201, 289; Basel, 163; Constance, 156 f.; Lyons, 116; Ravenna, 139; Trent, 227, 305
Church Fathers, 21, 31, 219, 289
Cicero, 5 f., 148, 217
Ciceruacchio, 459
Ciminna, lord of, 259
Cino da Pistoia, 145
Circumcision, 18 f., 60, 364, 369–70
Cisalpine republic, 429 f., 440 f.
Citizenship, 19, 30, 111, 120, 121, 125, 132, 138, 156, 212, 229, 276, 280, 427–45, 449, 456 ff., 529, 531, 544
Cittadella, 184, 416
Città di Castello, 244
Cividale, 9 n., 76, 117, 124, 142, 184, 212, 359
Civil rights, 56, 447 ff., 460 ff., 466, 469, 496
Civita, David, 197
Civitanova, 302
Civitanova, Mahalalel, 404
Claudia Aster (Esther?), 8
Claudius, 8, 10 f., 12, 21, 550
Clement IV, Pope, 98, 138
Clement VII, Pope, 191, 299
Clement VIII, Pope, 182, 319 f., 327, 330, 357, 381
Clement IX, Pope, 330
Clement XIII, Pope, 411
Clement XIV, Pope, 388, 413
Clothing industry, 114
Clusium Luna; *see* Chiusi
Cobblers, 24, 229
Coen, Felice, 440–1; Israel, 441, 443; Moses Vita, 422
Cogni, Giulio, 523
Cohen (priest), 26
Cohen, Ishmael (Laudadio Sacerdote), 398; Malachi, 399
Collatio legum Mosaicarum et Romanarum, 28
Collegio Foà, 455
Collegio Rabbinico, 496–8, 504–5, 506–7, 513, 515

Colleoni, Marta, 439
Cologna, Abraham, 441, 443
Colon (Colombo), Joseph, 217, 220
Colorni, Abraham, 200, 210; Eugenio, 550
Colorno, 341
Colosseum, 13
Comino, rock of, 151
Commentaries on the Bible, 92, 96, 144, 146, 148, 150, 205, 207, 211, 223, 242, 497; printing of, 223, 225; *see* Bible (O. T.); Pentateuch
Commentaries on the Mishnah, 149, 221
"Commentary of the Romans," on the Talmud, 90
Commerce, Jews in, 64, 67 f., 69, 75, 80, 84 f.
Community, Jewish, 5, 6, 7, 17, 21, 24 ff., 69, 81, 101, 107, 112, 114 f., 121, 131, 177, 180 f., 230–2, 244, 263, 265, 269, 318, 331, 338, 340, 347–8, 365–70, 416, 423, 427, 485 f., 490–1, 493–6, 501 ff., 512 ff., 521, 550 f.; Law on, 512
Community center, Jewish, 45; *see* Synagogue
Community council, Jewish, 25, 231, 347–8, 365, 493–5, 521
Community secretary, Jewish, 25, 366
Como, 110, 128
Conat, Abraham, 224; Estellina, 224
Concentration camps, 539 ff., 549
Concordia, 21
Condotte, 107 ff., 111 ff., 116, 120, 123, 124, 132, 133, 166, 185, 214, 311, 333–4, 370, 415 f.
Conegliano, 336
Conegliano banking-house, 456; family, 353; Israel, diplomat and physician, 377; Israel da, loan-banker, 336; Solomon, 377
Conselve, 416
Consiglio family, 129, 338
Consistories, 444, 448
Consolo, Frederico, 482
Constantine the Great, 29 ff., 36
Constantinople, 29, 35, 36, 48, 51, 54, 55, 82, 85, 166, 190, 203, 204 f., 224, 261 and n., 267 f., 287, 301, 309, 377, 404
Conversions to Christianity, 12, 30 f., 33 f., 39, 41, 45, 46 f., 47 f., 51 f., 53 f., 72, 73, 89, 99, 100 f., 118, 158, 165, 171, 177 f., 179, 248, 259, 268, 269–71, 280, 285, 290 f., 299, 314, 325, 378–82, 404, 407, 409 f., 413, 418, 449, 453, 471–2, 526, 534–5
Conversions to Judaism, 3, 17 ff., 28, 31, 34, 69, 138, 192, 290, 314
Copertino, 285
Coppersmiths, 244, 263
Coral industry, 349
Corcos family, 180; Tranquillo Vita, 410
Cordova, 54, 63
Corfu, 287, 335, 488
Cori, 308, 318
Corleone, 252
Correggio, 187, 328, 340, 376, 416
Corriere Israelitico, Il, 500
Corriere Livornese, periodical, of Leghorn, 458
Corsica, 83, 350

Cortemaggiore, 341
Cosenza, 80 f., 89, 280, 540
Cosimo I of Tuscany, 310-1, 358
Cosimo III of Tuscany, 374, 376, 384
Costanzi, Giovanni Antonio, 411
Cotrone, 69, 269, 274
Counter-Reformation, 289-328, 348, 470, 501; see Protestant Reformation
Courts, Jewish, 333, 348, 368-9; rabbinical, 76, 124, 397
Cracovia, Jacob, 443
Craftsmen, Jewish, 23 f., 71, 78, 86 ff., 103, 113, 188, 199, 229, 255 f., 258-9, 390
Crema, 175 f.
Crema brothers, 456
Cremona, 77, 117, 127 f., 198, 221, 227, 303 f., 322-3
Cremona, Luigi, 483
Crete, 96, 206, 335
Crisi, Andrea, 254; Bartolomeo, 254
Cristino, of Naples, 275
Crusades, 72 f., 80, 98, 166, 177 f.
Culture, English, in Italy, 485
Culture, general, among Jews, 5, 17, 58-65, 114, 116, 137, 143-52, 193-227, 325, 335, 347, 358, 363-4, 377, 422, 475, 479 ff., 499
Culture, Italian, 514-5
Culture, Jewish, 58-65, 98, 101, 268, 269, 333, 389, 507-8, 548; contemporary revival, 508, 513
Cuneo, 136, 342-3, 490, 512; expulsion from, 165
Cuorgnè, 409
Custoza, Battle of, 467
Cyrenaica, 514

DA CARPI, JACOB, 391
Da Castellazzo, Moses, 198
Da Cordova, Gonzalo, 282 f.
Da Fano, Joseph (Ippolito), 211, 325; Menahem Azariah, 403
Da Foligno, Hananel, 291-2
Da Lodi, David, 198
Da Mistretta, Pietro, 271
Da Montalcino, Cornelio, 290
Dancing, art of, 114, 196, 327, 377
Daniel, of Montalcino, 146
Daniel, Rabbi, of Rome, 78
Daniel, of Viterbo, 119
Dante, 96, 106, 143 ff., 219 f., 481
Da Pesaro, Guglielmo (Benjamin), 196
Da Pisa, Daniel, 180, 192; family, 110, 111, 132, 176, 213, 310; Isaac, 179; Vitale (Jehiel), 207, 218
Da Pistoia, Giovanni, 250, 252
Da Ponsacco, Matteo, 270
Da Ponte, Lorenzo, 422
Da Prato, Felice, 225
D'Arco, Giambattista Gherardo, 410
Da Rieti, Joab (Dattero), 195; Laudadio, 212; Moses, 164, 202, 219
Darshan, David, 214 n.
Da Sessa, Salamone, 199; see Ercole de' Fedeli
Da Silva, Roderigo (Jacob) Mendes, 397
David the physician, of Palermo, 236, 239

David, son of Busach of Palermo, 240
David ibn Iacchia, 208, 285
Day of Atonement, 302
Dayyan, 232 n., 237
De Balmes, Abraham, 209, 216
De' Benedetti family, 353; Salvatore, 498
De' Cantori, Joshua, 303
De Cardona, Raimondo, 283
De Castro, Ezekiel (Pedro), 378
Decius, emperor, 20
De' Fanciulli family, 126
De' Fedeli, Ercole, 199
De Frigiis, Lazzaro, 203
De Lattes, Bonet, 200, 206, 208
Del Banco, Asher Meshullam (Anselmo), 176
Della Nava, Cesare, 299
Dell' Arpa, Abramo, 197
Della Valle, Cardinal, 191
Delli Mansi family, 13, 91 n.; see Piattelli
De Luna, Doña Beatrice; see Gracia Mendes
Del Vecchio family, 333
Dentists, 203
De' Pomi, David, 212, 216, 299, 316; family, 13, 139, 299; Elijah, 139
"Deported" Jews, 543-5, 549, 552
De Rethel, Charles, 338-9
De Rojas, Fernando, 220
De' Rossi, Angelo, 199; Anselmo, 197; Azariah (Bonaiuto), 210, 218 f., 286 n., 306, 313, 394; "Madame Europa," 197; family, 13, 197, 359; Giovanni Bernardo, 394-5; Salamone, 197, 391; Solomon (13th century), 149-50
Dertona, 21; see Tortona
De Sinagoga, or Min ha-Keneset, family, 132
De' Sommi, Leone, 220
De' Vecchi family, 13, 359
De Velasco, Juan Fernandez, 322-3
Di Capua family, 287
Didaco Pyrrho (Lusitano), 300
Diena, Azriel, 192
Dienchelele; see Chief Rabbi
Dina, Giacomo, 464, 468
Di Nola, Jewish surname, 307
Diplomats, Jewish, 2 f., 121, 377, 461 f., 477-8, 483, 488, 509
Discorso circa il stato degli ebrei, by Simone Luzzatto, 396-7
Di Segni family, 307
Disraeli, Benjamin, 333; family, 407
Di Tivoli family, 307
Dodecanese Islands, 515
Dominicans, 99, 100, 138, 154, 168, 170, 183, 190, 205, 250, 278, 380
Domitian, 15 f., 18
Domitilla, 18
Donnolo (Sabbatai ben Abraham), 54, 61-2, 80
Dress, 213, 267-8, 294, 334, 336, 360-1, 369
Ducena, artist, 195
Dues, 84, 256, 336; customs, 264, 278; ecclesiastical, 271-2; to fraternities, 336; Jewish harbor, 77; market, 85; to Roman Jews, 332; see Taxes

INDEX

Dyeing industry, 68, 78, 80, 86 ff., 229, 234, 270, 272, 278

EASTER, DISTURBANCES, 45–6, 72, 154 ff., 170 ff., 236, 248, 250 ff., 271, 466; protection of Jews, 250, 271, 315; restrictions, 354
Eastern Roman Empire, 35 f., 40 ff., 48, 49 ff., 55, 63, 68, 86, 262
Ebreo, Giuseppe, 196
Economists, 477–8, 483
Edicts, 9, 12, 16, 19, 29 f., 32, 49, 51, 54, 274, 285 f., 292, 435, 448 f., 496, 451, 465 ff., 504; see Caligula; Caracalla; Carlo Alberto; Francis I; Milan
Education, Jewish, 17, 28, 112, 194, 348, 363–4, 367, 395, 424, 443, 479 ff., 495–9, 505
Education, secular, 194, 241, 395, 398, 423, 441, 448–9, 450, 455, 479 ff., 483, 485, 511, 527 f., 534
Educatore Israelita, L'; see *Vessillo Israelitico, Il*
Egidio da Viterbo, Cardinal, 191, 208
Egypt, 2, 4, 8, 10, 22, 53, 56, 57 f., 75, 113, 434
Einstein, Albert, 482
Eisenstadt, Mordecai, 405
Elaea, 23
Elba, island, 350, 439, 445
Elbogen, Ismar, 506
Eleazar, Rabbi, 16
Eleazar ben Jose, Rabbi, 17
Eleazar of Verona, 147
Eliano (Elijah), Vittorio, 291–2, 303
Elias, physician at Florence, 207
Elias, physician to duke of Milan, 132
Elias, lecturer at Pavia, 213
Elias, loan-banker, 212
Eliezer ben Joel ha-Levi, of Cologne, 77
Eliezer ben Samuel, 92
Elijah ben Sabbatai; see Elias Sabot
Elijah del Medigo, 206–7, 209, 394
Emancipation, 270–1, 335, 406, 427–45, 446, 463–73, 472–3, 474–508, 536; publications on, 464–5
Emanuele Filiberto (Iron Head), duke, 312
Emigration, 381, 407, 420, 426, 454, 503, 533–4, 546, 550, 552; from Papal States, 381; from Piedmont, 454; from Sardinia, 267; from Sicily, 243, 254–5; to England, 407, 516, 534; to France, 516, 534; to Holland, 362; to Palestine, 308, 516, 534; to South America, 534 f.; to the United States, 534; see Expulsions
Emilia, 486
Employment restrictions, 528, 531, 535, 537–8; see Anti-Jewish legislation
Empoli, 134, 182
Engineers, 199 f., 210, 486
England, 65, 106, 485, 488, 518 ff.; Chamber of Commerce, 483; expulsion, 282
Enriques, Federigo, 483
Eötvös, Baron Joseph, 464
Ercole I d'Este, 188
Ercole II d'Este, 189, 346
Erfurt, 523

Eritrea, 516
Este, dominions of, 117, 126, 176, 187 ff., 307, 314, 332, 336; duke of, 429; house of, 129, 164, 187, 199, 320, 340, 376; marquis of, 129
Ethiopia (Abyssinia), 515–6, 518, 521
Etruria, 21
Eugenius IV, Pope, 134, 162 ff., 166, 201, 209, 249, 266, 271
Eupolemos (Ephraim?) ben Johanan, 2
Evola, Giulio, 523
Explorers, 484–5
Expulsions, 3, 4, 9, 11, 68–9, 71, 72, 75, 76, 77, 116, 120, 126, 127, 130, 132, 136, 137, 142, 165, 169, 171, 173, 175 f., 178, 181 ff., 187, 189, 190, 201, 235, 254–61, 268, 277–88, 302, 306 f., 309–13, 322–3, 325, 329, 339, 343, 351 f., 416, 452, 491, 527, 537

FABRIANO, 202
Faenza, 199, 202, 455
Fairs, 113, 119, 121, 272, 284, 331, 374
Falashas, 515–6
Falerii, 21
Fano, 77, 108, 118 f., 169, 173, 224, 277, 307, 359
Fano, Jacob, 325
Faraj (Ferragut) ben Solomon of Girgenti, 93, 94 f.
Farinacci, Roberto, 522, 525
Farmers, 103, 421
Farnese, Cardinal, 183; Duke Ottavio, 210, 341
Farrisol, Abraham, 210, 218
Fascism, 509–41, 547–51; books under, 525, 528, 531, 535, 548
Federal Congress (1848), 463
Federighi, Antonio, 195
Federigo, king of Naples, 281
Ferdinand of Spain, 252 ff., 266 f., 281–4, 290
Ferdinand I, of Austria, 458
Ferdinand I, of Naples, 202
Ferdinand I, of Tuscany, 345–8
Ferdinand II, emperor, 337, 339
Ferdinand III, grand duke, 422
Fermo, 112 f., 119, 129, 142, 143
Fernando, Aaron, 444–5, 492–3
Ferramonte, 540, 542
Ferrante I, 275–9
Ferrara, 76, 92, 128 f., 134, 147, 157, 164, 172, 176, 178 f., 187 ff., 190, 192, 199 ff., 209 ff., 213 ff., 218, 220, 223 f., 225, 286, 292 f., 299, 301 f., 308, 314, 320 f., 326, 332–3, 337, 346, 352, 362 f., 365 f., 368 ff., 377, 380–1, 397 f., 400, 402, 409 ff., 413, 422, 430–1, 438 f., 442, 451, 453, 456, 459, 461 f., 468 f., 495, 498, 500 n., 538, 543 f., 548, 551; duke of, 172, 176, 179, 189, 210, 213 f., 292, 299
Ferrer, Vincent, 163
Ficino, Marsilio, 207 f.
Filelfo, Mario, 196
Filippo, Fra, 302
Finale, 187, 328, 340, 409, 416, 484
Finance, Jews in, 122, 415, 477–8, 487; see Loan-bankers; Moneylenders

Finance, ministers of, 477–8, 510
Fines, 434, 437 f., 456, 468; *see* Taxes
Finzi, Aldo, 510; Angelo (Mordecai), 200; Ciro, 460, 462; Felice, 483; Giuseppe, 460, 468–9, 476; Isaac Raphael, 442–3; Solomon, 439
Fiorentino, Salamone, 422, 436, 481
Fiorenzuola d'Arda, 341, 502
Fiscus Judaicus, 14, 15, 19, 29
Fiume, 488, 409, 538, 544, 548
Flaccus, L. Valerius, 5
Flagellants, 138
Flavius Clemens, 18
Florence, 21, 76, 106, 109 f., 111 f., 114, 132, 133 ff., 160, 169, 170, 175, 176, 190, 195, 196, 200 f., 204 f., 206 f., 209 ff., 213, 220, 273, 292, 310–1, 316, 345, 355, 358, 361, 372 f., 391, 398, 400, 410, 412, 425 f., 435 f., 444, 455, 458, 460, 465, 481 f., 490, 492 f., 495 f., 498, 500, 502–3, 506–8, 513, 520, 532, 539, 544 ff., 548, 551
Florentine financiers in France, 109; in Trieste, 124
Foà, Carlo, 510; Edoardo, 484; family, 353; Moses, 343; Moses Benjamin, 421–2; Senator Pio, 483
Foligno, 121, 138, 169, 359
Foligno, family, 307
Fondi, 85, 272
Food, Jewish, 359
Forlì, 122, 131, 133, 147, 149, 157, 175, 212
Formiggini, Angelo Fortunato, 530; family, 376; Moses, 440, 443, 493 n.
Fornovo, 174
Fortis, Abraham, 455
Foscolo, Ugo, 458
Fossano, 135 f., 342, 362, 372, 428, 438, 512
Fossoli, 549
Fossombrone, 321
France, 47, 64, 65, 75, 92, 96, 97, 99, 106, 109, 141, 149, 174, 280, 442 f., 454, 460, 488; expulsions from, 135–6, 137 f., 362; "July Revolution," 455
Frances, Immanuel, 400, 404; Jacob, 400, 404
Franchetti, Alberto, 482; Baron, 484 f.; Judith, 325
Francis I, of Austria, 447, 496
Francis Joseph, of Austria, 471 f.
Franciscans, 153 ff., 158 ff., 162, 165 ff., 249, 266, 274 f.
Franco-Prussian War, 473
Frederick II, Hohenstaufen, emperor, 85, 87, 89, 93 f., 122, 204, 229, 235, 239, 246, 250
Frederick II, of Sicily, 246 f.
Frederick, of Urbino, 119
Fregoso, Ottaviano, 183
French empire, 440, 442–5; invasions of Italy, 279 ff.; loan-bankers, 131; troops, 469, 473; republic, 462
French Revolution, 127, 352, 359, 425–45, 447 f., 456, 484, 491, 495
Friuli, 310, 336, 416, 423
Frizzi, Benedetto, 410, 493 n.
Fulvia, wife of Saturninus, 9
Fundi, 22
Funerals, 26, 82, 384, 414, 453, 550

GAETA, 48, 49, 63, 78, 87, 268, 278
Gaio, Maestro (Isaac ben Mordecai), 147–8, 149
Gaiseric, 37
Galatino, scholar, 287
Galen, 209
Galilee, 14
Gallipoli, 260, 280, 285
Gamaliel II, 15 f.
Gambling, 212 f., 233, 265–6, 370
Garibaldi Battalion, 516–7
Garibaldi, Giuseppe, 462, 469, 473, 519
Gaspar, Fra, 278
Gatti, Abbé Giuseppe, 464
Gaudio (Isaac), 13th century, 239, 246; 14th century, 240
Gaul, Cisalpine, 21
Gedaliah ibn Iacchia, 218, 298
Gelasius I, Pope, 43
Gem merchants, 113, 349
Genoa, 21, 33, 39, 40, 68, 74 f., 84, 86, 110, 135, 169, 175, 179, 183, 189, 218, 309, 344, 350, 416, 421, 445, 453, 491, 538, 542, 544, 546
Gentilomo, firm of, 373
George II, of England, 377
Gerace, 269, 271, 274
German bankers, 130 f.; influences, 143, 150, 151, 182; occupation of Italy, 541–51
Germano-Austrian alliance, 488
Germany, 64 f., 68, 70, 98, 112, 116 f., 118, 123 f.; educational system, 424; emigration from, 277; invasions by, 184, 338–9; Nazi regime, 517–8, 521–51; persecutions in, 137 f., 517–8
Gerousia, 25; *see* Community council
Gerousiarch, 25
Ghetto, 79, 132, 154, 161 f., 186, 246–7, 249, 255, 297–8, 304, 307, 309, 311 f., 314 f., 318, 320 ff., 323–5, 327–8, 320–420, 421, 423–42, 447 f., 450 ff., 456, 459, 461, 466, 468, 470 ff., 479 ff., 487, 489 ff., 493, 495, 501 f., 508, 519, 521, 528, 532 f., 535, 540 ff., 547, 551; *see* Jewish quarter
Ghibellines, 142
Ghiron, Ugo, 482
Giacomo della Marca (Fra Jacopo da Monteprandone), 161, 278
Giambattista d'Este; *see* Alfonso III, of Modena
Gioberti, Vincenzo, 458, 465
Giorgini, Giovanni Battista, 464
Giovanni da Prato, 165 f.
Giovine Italia (Young Italy), movement, 457; periodical, 458
Girgenti, 22, 47, 55, 83, 87, 93, 94 f., 230, 232, 234, 236, 242, 249, 252, 259
Giudecca, 70
Giustiniani, Marcantonio, printer, 226, 290 ff.
Glass manufacture, 375
Gnora Luna, ballad, 412–3, 439, 453
"God-fearers," 17 f.
Goebbels, Joseph, 522
Goldsmiths, 114, 199, 272, 376
Gonars, 336
Gonzaga, Francesco, 174; Guglielmo, 203;

INDEX

house of, 174, 197, 202, 209, 325 ff., 338; Vespasiano, 227
Gorizia, 124, 310, 328, 337, 416, 423 f., 487 f., 497
Gozzo, 83, 151, 230, 234, 257
Gozzoli, Benozzo, 207
Gradisca d'Isonzo, 337, 423 f., 488
Granada, 57, 253; treaty of, 281
Gratian, emperor, 32
Graziadio, craftsman, 199
Graziani, Abraham, 398; Augusto, 483
Greece, 11, 48, 86
Grego, Isaac, 433
Gregory the Great, Pope, 43 ff., 84, 262
Gregory VII, Pope, 97
Gregory IX, Pope, 138
Gregory XIII, Pope, 314, 315–7, 377, 381
Gregory XVI, Pope, 451–2
Grimani, Domenico, Cardinal of S. Marco, 206, 209
Grosso, Niccola (*Il Caparra*), 195
Guarini, Giovanni Battista, 401
Guastalla, 341
Guastalla, Enrico, 452
Gubbio, 143, 168, 175
Guide to the Perplexed, 148–9; commentary by Faraj ben Solomon on, 93
Guido da Cipro, 96 n.
Guilds, Christian, 103, 199, 372, 376; Jewish, 24, 103, 113, 114, 125, 127, 229, 298, 365
Guiscard, Robert, 81, 88; Roger, 81, 88; Sichelgaita, 88 f.
Guizolfi, Zaccarias, 135 n.
Gunpowder manufacturers, 114
"Gymnasium," Jewish, 441

HADRIAN, 18
Hai Gaon, 57, 64, 72, 92
Halakhot Kezubot, 61
Hananel, of Oria, 51
Handicrafts, 68, 86 f., 114, 163, 244, 263, 371 f., 423; *see* Artisans
Handkerchief, 151, 201
Hanukkah, 363
Harun-al-Rashid, caliph, 54
Hasdai ibn Shaprut, 54
Hasmonaeans, 2, 8, 11 f., 14; *see also* under names
Hayim (Khalah), Spanish Jew, 57 f.
Hayyim of Cyprus, 263
Hayyun, Nehemiah, 405
Hazzan, 26
Health, 366, 374–5, 420
Hebraic studies, 59–65, 93 f., 100, 127 f., 203 ff., 208 f., 216, 241–2, 269, 395–6, 495
Hebrew University, Jerusalem, 514, 534
Henry II, of France, 205
Henry IV, of England, 158
Henry VI, emperor, 89
Henry VII, emperor, 141
Henry VIII, of England, 200 f.
Heraclius, 49
Heresy, Christian, 97, 98, 99, 119, 127, 154, 163, 290
Herod, 7, 11, 12; Herodian monarchy, 7
Herzl, Theodor, 519 f.

High Priest, 3
Hillel, 149
Hillel ben Samuel, 147
Hippocrates, 95
Hispalus, Cnaius Cornelius, 3, 4
Historiography, 217 f.
Hitler, Adolf, 517, 524–5
Hiyya ben Abba, 35
Hofer, Andreas, 441
Holidays, Jewish, 46, 111, 116, 198, 356, 362–3, 493; *see* under names
Holy Roman Empire, 66
Homiletics, 217, 242
Honorius, emperor, 35, 36
Honorius II, Pope, 73
Horace, 22, 28
Hospitals, Jewish, 232, 365; public, 450
Hushiel ben Elhanan, 63
Hussites, 153, 163

IBN EZRA, ABRAHAM, 76, 92, 93, 130
Ibrahim, Sicilian ruler, 56
Iglesias, 263
Immanuel of Rome, 119 and n., 120, 130, 140 f., 143 ff., 146, 148, 219, 242, 394; father-in-law of, 142
Immigration, Jewish, to Italy, 22, 23, 82, 116 f., 118, 124, 127 f., 137, 178 ff., 187 ff., 267, 274, 278, 447, 491, 504, 517, 527; prohibited, 527
Immigrants, Jewish, 4 f., 10, 221 f., 334, 344 f., 346–7, 348, 399; from Austria, 527; Balearic Islands, 262; Central Europe, 189, 513; France, 180, 340; Germany, 124 f., 127 f., 180, 189, 221, 262, 347, 474, 517, 527; the Levant, 334, 345, 347, 513, 527; Poland, 347, 527; Portuguese, 180, 186, 281, 285, 299, 334, 338, 346–7; the Provence, 96, 146, 180, 200, 259, 262, 277; Rhodes, 180; Spain, 180, 183, 186, 188 f., 262, 264, 278 f., 283, 285, 334, 338, 346–7; Tripoli, 180
Imola, 70, 72, 201, 218, 221, 298
Index Librorum Prohibitorum, 305, 523
Industrial Revolution, 446
Industry, Jews in, 31, 38, 349, 371–3, 375–6, 415, 423, 449, 486 f., 528
Innocent II, Pope, 73
Innocent III, Pope, 97
Innocent X, Pope, 330
Innocent XI, Pope, 370
Innocentius, bishop, 33
Inquisition, 99, 128, 139, 188, 192 f., 247, 254, 261, 268, 282 f., 290, 292, 299 f., 302 ff., 314 f., 317, 319, 330, 377, 383, 405, 411, 414, 423, 450, 468
Insurance business, 486, 529
Intellectual life, 394–406, 422, 424, 479–83, 490, 495–500, 506–8, 513; *see* Scholars and scholarship
Interlandi, Telesio, 522 f., 526
Intermarriage, 31, 41, 100 n., 287, 505, 523, 528
International Institute of Agriculture, 486
Invasions, French, 184; German, 184, 190 f.; Spanish, 184, 190 f.
Iraq, 57, 58, 60, 63, 64

Iron-workers, 244, 256, 272
Irredentists, 457–8, 487 f.
Isaac of Bologna, 199
Isaac of Marseilles, 238
Isaac of Noyon (Maestro Achino), 200
Isaac al-Fasi, 91
Isaac ben Melchizedek, 91
Isaac ben Mordecai; *see* Maestro Gaio
Isaac di Guglielmo (ben Benjamin), 249
Isaac *Or Zarua*, 77
Isabella, of Spain, 252 ff., 281 f., 290
Isaiah of Trani, 151
Isbili, Isaac, 263
Ishmael Hananiah di Valmontone, 306
Islam, 2, 52, 479, 518; Islamic culture, 92 f.
Isola, 124
Israel, periodical, 500, 508, 513
Israël et l'Humanité, by Elia Benamozegh, 499
Israeli family, of Pieve di Cento, 333
Istria, 117, 124, 191
Italia, L', periodical, 464
Italia del Popolo, periodical, 462
Italian Academy, 510, 533
Italo-Turkish war of 1911, 479, 514
Ivrea, 342, 442

JACOB BONACOSA, 148 n.
Jacopo di Sansecondo, 197
Jacopone da Todi, 146
James I, of England, 396
Jarè, surname, 360
Jason (Joshua) ben Eleazar, 2
Jehiel, grandson of Rabbi Nathan, 78, 106
Jehiel (Vitale) ben Mattathias, of San Miniato, 132
Jehiel of Pesaro; *see* Vitale de' Medici
Jehudah ha-Levi, 497
Jerome, 28
Jerusalem, 1, 2, 5, 6, 9, 11, 12, 13, 14, 22, 37, 50, 60 n., 64, 80, 159 ff., 242, 275, 301, 359, 518–9; spoils from, 17, 20, 59
Jesi, Samuel, 482
Jewellers, 125, 376
Jewish Brigade, 551
Jewish Museum, 514
"Jewish parliaments," Sicily, 233, 249, 286
Jewish quarter, 54, 79, 80, 182 f., 195, 211, 230, 236, 244, 262 f., 266 f., 275, 277, 280, 295, 297, 490; *see* Ghetto
Jewish Relief Committee, 517, 533–4
Jewish state, 3, 15
Jewish Vigilance Committee, 157 ff., 163 f.
Jews, non-Italian, 1, 80, 527, 537, 540; expulsion, 527, 537; *see* Emigrants; Immigrants
Joanna II, of Naples, 159 f., 274–5
Johannes, of Capua, 95
John, King, 241
John XII, Pope, 141 f.
John Hyrcanus, 3
Jonathan ben Moses Finzi (Zinatan di Moiseto), 129
Joseph II, emperor, 422–3, 424
Joseph ha-Cohen, 183, 218

"Joseph Judaeus," 74
Joseph, son of Mattathias, 146
Josephus, Flavius, 7, 12, 14, 16, 23, 60
Joshua, Rabbi, 16
Josippon, 60
Journalism, 486; exclusion from, 535
Judah, physician, 62
Judah ben David; *see* Bonjudes ben Davin (Bonjudes Bondavin)
Judah ben Isaac of Siponto, 79
Judah ben Moses ben Daniel; *see* Leone de Ser Daniel
Judah ben Titus, 35
Judah del Bene, 217
Judah Messer Leon, 203, 217
Judah Romano; *see* Leone de Ser Daniel
Judaism, 2, 4, 5, 9, 10, 12, 14, 15 f., 17, 18, 19, 20, 22, 27 ff., 31 ff., 39, 43 ff., 49, 56, 73, 99, 111 f., 115 f., 164, 187, 192, 209, 213, 215, 218, 221, 241, 242, 245, 251, 253, 258–9, 265–6, 269 f., 282, 288, 290–1, 314, 378, 393, 397, 402, 409, 412, 445, 475, 492–9, 504–8, 515–6, 521, 524, 529, 533, 535, 539, 547
Julian the Apostate, 31 f.
Julius II, Pope, 195
Julius III, Pope, 290, 292 f., 300
Jung, Guido, 510
Jupiter Sabazius, 3 f.
Justinian, 40, 49
Juvenal, 24, 28

KAIROUAN, EMIR OF, 52, 54, 55; rabbis of, 58, 63
Kalila and Dimna, 95
Kalonymus ben Kalonymus of Arles, "the Jew Callo," 96, 146
Kalonymus ben Sabbetai, 92
Kalonymus [Moses ben], 63 f., 69; family of, 70; of Rome, 73
Karaite sectaries, 96
Katzenellenbogen, Meir, 221
Kaufmann, David, 499
Klenau, general, 438
Knights of Malta, 308, 365
Knights of St. John, 350–1
Koran, 242
Küstenland, 446–7

LABOR, FORCED, 540
Laborers, Jewish, 7, 103, 229, 244
Ladislas, of Naples, 273
Lago Maggiore, 543
Lampronti, Isaac, 398–9, 500 n.
Lanciano, 81, 274–5
Landau, Jacob ben Judah, 221
Landholders, Jewish, 46, 56, 68, 70, 86, 130, 154 f., 161, 182, 273, 299, 308, 421, 441, 486, 528, 531
Languages used among Jews in Italy, 28, 80, 82, 147, 216, 222, 287, 347, 349, 358–9, 397, 402, 440, 475, 480, 487, 504, 514–5
Larippa, 146
Latanzi, Giuseppe, 428
Lateran Councils, 177, 289; Third, 97, 104, 297; Fourth, 96 ff., 139, 246
Latis, Israel, 455

INDEX

Lattes, Abraham, 17th century, 342–3; Abraham, rabbi, 19th century, 461, 498; Dante, 508; family, 180
Lavello, 49
Law, civil, 241, 245, 333, 348, 397, 483, 486; commercial, 483; Jewish, 6, 28, 92, 357–8; Jewish contributions to, 14; Jewish sumptuary laws, 369–70; study of, 335–6
Lawyers, Jewish, 539
Lazio, 141
Lazzaro, da Pavia, 202
League of Nations, 518, 522
Learned societies, dismissal from, 528
Lecce, 81, 269, 271, 277, 280, 283, 285
Legends, Jewish, 1, 13, 21 f., 43, 50, 59, 60, 62 f., 69, 72, 74, 86, 128, 142, 192, 359, 389–90, 440
Leghorn (Livorno), 345–50, 351 f., 358, 360, 362 ff., 368–9, 383 ff., 391, 395, 397, 399 f., 404 f., 407, 409, 413, 420, 421 f., 425–6, 435 f., 441 f., 444 f., 447, 453, 455, 457 f., 460, 471, 491 ff., 495, 498–9, 502 f., 513–4, 551
Lemlein, Asher, 191
Lentini, 260
Lenzi, Mario, 208
Leo X, Pope, 167, 197, 206, 292
Leo XII, Pope, 450–1
Leo XIII, Pope, 453
Leone (Judah); see Judah Messer Leon
Leone de Ser Daniel (Judah ben Moses ben Daniel), 95, 148
Leone Ebreo (Judah Abrabanel), 208, 210, 213, 223, 279, 282, 394
Leonora, of Tuscany, 215, 285, 310
Leopold II, emperor, 424–5
Lepanto, 212, 287, 311 f.
Lessing, Gotthold Ephraim, 422
Levant, 81, 112, 123, 149, 187, 261, 299 ff., 306, 310, 318, 330, 346, 376, 399, 404, 419, 452, 514
Levi, Angelo, 455; banking-house of, 456; Benedetto, 498; David, 457–8, 459, 465; Eugenio, 482–3; family of Alessandria, 343; Joseph, 199; Lazzaro, 375–6; Leone, 483; Salamone Vita, 376
Levi-Bianchini, Angelo, 520
Levi-Civita, Tullio, 482, 528
Levies, 141, 177 f., 220, 233, 257–8, 264, 275, 302, 307, 434 f., 438, 447, 449; German, 543; university, 453; war, 280, 427 f., 432, 435; see Taxes
Levi-Perotti, Guistina, 215 n.
Levita, Elias, 191, 208 f., 216, 291
Lévy, Camille, 488
Lewis the Bavarian, 141
Liberalism, 458–73, 475 ff., 494, 516
Liber Continens, by Rhazes, 94 f.
Liberi, Pietro, 391
"Libertines," 5
Libraries, Jewish, 75, 77, 194, 204, 317, 421, 505, 548; Italian, 499, 535
Libya, 520 f., 529, 531, 538
Licinius, emperor, 29
Liguria, 21, 135, 344, 353, 445
Lippiano, 345, 437
Lissa, island of, 210

Liturgy, 50 f., 61, 72, 92, 100, 118, 135, 139, 144, 145 f., 147, 180, 220, 222, 224, 226, 260–1, 314, 334, 361–3, 391, 400, 403, 411, 443, 497, 505–6
Loan-bankers, 85, 103–117, 118 f., 120, 122, 124, 126, 127 ff., 157, 161, 163, 166–76, 178, 182, 184 f., 188 f., 194, 200, 212, 222, 249, 273, 298, 313, 321, 338, 340, 341, 344, 408; see Bankers; Moneylenders
Loan-banks, 103–117, 119, 122, 123, 124, 125, 127 ff., 142, 166–76, 183 ff., 276, 293, 295, 310, 312, 318 f., 320, 322, 334, 336, 341, 343, 370–1, 416; see Banks
Loans to governments, 368, 415
Lodève, bishop of, 396
Lodi, 128, 322–3, 429
Logudoro, 262
Lolli, Eude, 498
Lombardo-Venetian kingdom, 446–7, 458, 466, 496
Lombards, 41, 43, 48, 66, 106, 307
Lombardy, 41, 48, 62, 63, 73, 113, 117, 127, 138, 162, 166, 220, 224, 338, 461 ff., 465 f., 469
Lombroso, Cesare, 483
Longhena, Baldassare, 390
Lopez, Sabatino, 482
Loria, Achille, 483
Louis II, emperor, 68
Louis IX, of France, 98 f.
Louis XII, of France, 281
Louis XVI, of France, 427
Loyola, Ignatius, 290
Lubin, David, 486
Lucca, 63, 68, 70 f., 72, 75 f., 106, 132 f., 169, 175, 309, 344, 442, 450
Lucera, 269, 271
Lucignano, 146
Ludovico, of Piedmont, 161 f.
Lugo, 128, 187, 321, 333, 352, 397, 430, 438, 407, 454, 456, 512, 551
Lullus (Julius), 69
Luna, 47
Luria, Isaac, 403
Lusitanus, Amatus, 202, 300
Luther, Martin, 289
Luzzatti or Luzzatto, surname, 360
Luzzatti, Luigi, 477–8, 479, 483, 486, 489 n.
Luzzatto, Ephraim, 401; Filosseno, 498; Isaac, 401; Moses, 433; Moses Hayyim, 401, 405–6, 410; Samuel David, 496–7, 498 ff., 504, 507; Simone (Simha), 396–7
Lyons, 116, 440 f.

Ma'alot ha-Middot, by Jehiel Anau, 146
Maccabees, Books of, 2; Judas, 2, 3; Jonathan, 3; Simon, 3
Madruzio, Cardinal Cristoforo, 226
Maffoni, G. L., 464
Magino, Meir, 199, 375
Magliabecchi, Antonio, 422
Magna Bibliotheca Rabbinica, by Giulio Bartolocci, 394
Magna Graecia; see South Italy
Mahberet ha-Arukh, by Solomon Parhon, 93
Mahberet ha-Teneh, by Ahitub ben Isaac, 146

INDEX

Mahberot Immanuel, 144
Maimonides, Moses, 83, 93, 147, 148–9
Mainz, 64; archbishop of, 68
Majolica industry, 375–6
Malatesta family, 121; Galeotto, 119; Sigismondo, 209
Malta, 22, 26, 83, 151, 230, 234, 240, 252, 257, 301, 350
Malvano, Giacomo, 478
Manetti, Giannozzo, 204, 209
Manfred, son of Emperor Frederick, 94
Manfredi, poet, 198
Manfredonia, 81, 94, 101
Manin, Daniel, 461 f., 477, 484
Mantegna, Andrea, 174
Mantica, Moses, 372
Mantino, Jacob, 192, 207 f., 213
Mantua, 76, 130 f., 142, 158 f., 164, 169, 173 f., 181 f., 192 f., 197 ff., 202 ff., 209 ff., 213 f., 216–7, 218, 220, 224, 227, 292, 308, 313, 318, 325–8, 338–40, 343–4, 350, 352, 356, 362, 367 ff., 375–6, 377, 382, 385, 389, 391 f., 395, 397, 400, 402 f., 410, 412 f., 419, 423 f., 429 ff., 439 ff., 443, 453–4, 468 ff., 472–3, 483, 493, 495, 498, 502, 504, 552
Manuel da Camerino, 175
Manuel da Gubbio, 143; *see* Immanuel of Rome
Manuel da San Miniato, 204
Manuforte, of Trani, 99 f.
Manuscripts, Hebrew, 204
Manuzio, Aldo, 225, 316
Manzoni, Alessandro, 519
Marcaria, Jacob, 226
Marengo, 440, 444
Margherita, duchess of Savoy, 312–3
Margulies, Samuel Hirsch, 506–7, 520
Maria, Giovanni, 196 f.
Marie of the Provence, queen, 265
Marranos, 101, 186 f., 189, 192, 220, 223, 225, 253, 261, 268, 269–71, 281 f., 288, 299 ff., 314, 317, 332, 334, 338, 340–1, 344, 346–7, 350, 355, 360, 378, 474; *see Neofiti*
Marriage, 82, 503 f.; contracts, 60; restrictions, 447; tax on, 234
Marsala, 55, 230, 236, 248, 250 ff.
Marseilles, 47, 74
Martial, poet, 24
Martin II, king, 236–9, 248, 265
Martin V, Pope, 141, 157 ff., 162, 242, 274
Martini, Archbishop Antonio, 426, 436
Martyrs of Belfiore, 468–9
Marzocco, Il, weekly, 482
Masechet Purim, by Kalonymus ben Kalonymus, 146
Masi, Andrea, 292–3
Massa, 321
Massa Gei Hizzayon, by Benjamin Anau, 145
Massarani, Bezaleel, 318; Tullo, 460, 477, 481
Massarano, Isacchino, 197
Matelica, 116
Matera, 49
Mathematicians, 200, 482–3

Mathia ben Heresh, 17
Mattathias, of Larippa and Norcia, 146; of Lucignano, 146
Matteo di Girgenti, 249
Maurogonato, Isaac Pesaro, 461 f., 468, 477
Maximilian I, emperor, 184
Maximus, 33 f.
Mayence, Ecclesiastical Court at, 206
Mazliah ben Elijah ibn al-Bazak, 57, 92, 232 n., 240 n.
Mazzara, 230, 235
Mazzini, Giuseppe, 457 f., 460, 462, 478, 499, 517
Mazzoli, Gherardo, 303
Meati family, 129; Nathan, 148 n.
Medici, Paolo, 409–10
Medici, de', house of, 134 f., 190, 202, 209, 310, 345; Cardinal, 200; Giuliano, 111; Lorenzino, 200; Lorenzo, 110–1, 134–5, 175, 196, 202, 207, 210, 213; Marie, 378
Medici, de', Vitale (Jehiel of Pesaro), 316
Medicine, 61 f., 93, 94, 95, 113 f., 121, 132, 147 f., 201 f., 207 f., 213 f., 217, 239–40, 263, 298, 316–7, 335, 342, 377, 410, 425, 450, 483, 486
Meir of Padua; *see* Katzenellenbogen, Meir
Melfi, 79, 89
Melli, "Ser" Samuel, 188, 332
Menahem, rabbi, of Rome, 78
Menahem ben Solomon, of Rome, 92
Menahem Corizzi, 60
Menahem of Recanti, 150
Mendelssohn, Moses, 422, 424, 492
Mendes, Gracia (Doña Beatrice de Luna), 215, 301, 308
Menotti, Cesare, 455–6
Meor 'Enayim, by Azariah de' Rossi, 218 f.
Meran, 488
Merchants, Jewish, 4, 5, 7, 23 f., 40, 47, 53, 57 f., 67 f., 70, 71, 75, 84 f., 103, 105, 112 f., 119, 123, 125, 131, 185 f., 188, 229, 270, 272, 301, 330–1, 340–1, 343, 349, 351, 365, 371, 374, 417, 435, 450; Levantine, 185 f.
Meshullam ben Kalonymus, 72
Meshullam Cusi, 223
Messengers, to Italy, 11, 12, 15 f., 17, 35 f., 64, 90, 194, 519; to Palestine, 64
Messianic movements, 8, 10–1, 12, 96, 151, 191, 242–3, 390, 403–6
Mesillat Yesharim, by Luzzatto, 401
Messina, 22, 82, 229, 230, 235 f., 238, 240, 243, 244, 245–6, 247, 250, 252, 254, 255, 256, 260, 351
Mestre, 123, 185
Mesue, book of remedies, 95
Metal-workers, 199
Metternich, Prince, 446
Michel, Solomon, 436
Michelangelo, 195
Michele da Milano, 168
Midrash, 60, 92
Midrash Sekhel Tob, by Menahem ben Solomon, 92
Midrash Talmud Torah, by Jacob Sikilli, 242
Mikdash Me'at, by Moses da Rieti, 219 f.

INDEX

Milan, 21, 29 f., 32, 34, 39, 40, 69, 70, 77, 127 f., 142, 162, 173, 178, 187, 189, 202, 273, 293, 303, 368 f., 322–3, 343, 350, 353, 439 f., 458, 460, 462 f., 469, 482, 488, 491, 502–3, 510, 513, 517, 527, 532, 538, 548; duke of, 126, 129, 131 f., 178, 200, 203
Milan, Five Days of, 460–1
Military service, Jews in, 6, 9, 31, 40, 56, 120, 234, 429, 432, 436, 440, 446 ff., 459–62, 466, 472, 484, 488, 509 f., 528 ff., 541
Mincio, Department of the, 441
Mineo, 248–9, 252
Minghetti, Marco, 477
Min ha-Adomim family, 13
Min ha-Anavim family, 13, 90–1; *see* Anau family
Min ha-Keneset family; *see* De Sinagoga
Min ha-Tapuhim family, 13
Min ha-Zekenim family, 13
Mining, 263
Minz, Abraham, 221; Judah, 221
Mirami, Raphael, 200
Mirandola, 178, 325–6, 339, 341, 383
Mishnah, 91
Mithridates, Flavius, 208
Modena, 68, 70, 110, 129, 169, 170, 172, 176, 182, 183, 187, 189, 211, 320 f., 326, 328, 340–1, 356, 361, 365, 368 f., 371, 376, 385–6, 397 f., 403, 405, 416–7, 425, 429, 438 f., 445, 449–50, 452 f., 455–6, 460, 463, 468 f., 484, 502, 515, 520, 530, 546
Modena, Aaron Berachiah da, 403; Leona da, 391, 396 f., 400; Marco, 202; Pomona da, 214
Modica, 251
Modigliani, Amedeo, 482; socialist leader, 510–1
Modon, Samson Cohen, 400
Modona, Leonello, 498
Molcho, Solomon, 192 f.
Momigliano, Felice, 498
Monastero, 409
Monastero delle Convertite, 379
Moncada, Guglielmo, 207; Raimondo da, 242
Moncalvo, 135–6, 343, 362, 372
Mondolfi, Ludovico, 458
Mondovì, 342
Moneychangers, 119, 125
Moneylenders, 23, 84, 85, 104 ff., 125, 133 f., 136, 154 f., 163, 166 ff., 178, 273; *see* Loan-banks
Moneylending, 103 ff., 130, 165, 182, 187 f., 229, 304, 306, 315, 318, 320; *see* Loan-banks; Pawnbroking
Monferrat, 136, 183, 293, 313, 328, 343, 385, 409, 444
Monnier, General, 435
Monopoli, 280
Monselice, 176, 336
Mons judaicus, 77
Montagnana, 117, 126, 158, 416
Montaigne, 316
Montalcino, 146
Montalto, Elijah, 378
Monte Barroccio, 321

Monte Cassino, abbot of, 210
Monte Cavallo, 432
Montecchio, 129
Montefeltro, 122
Montefiore, 360
Montefiore; family, 347, 407, 457; Sir Moses, 471
Montegiorgio, 77, 86
Monteleone, 280
Montenotte, Battle of, 428
Montepulciano, 134
Monte S. Giuliano, 248, 252
Monte San Savino, 345, 422, 436–7
Monte S. Sepolcro, 169
Monteverde, 26
Monteverdi, Claudio, 197
Monticelli, 341
Monti di Pietà, 166–76, 181, 182, 189, 211, 278, 295, 334, 338, 408, 416, 423; *see* Moneylending
Montpellier, medical school of, 147
Morais, Sabato, 457
Morality, 211
Morocco, 82
Moro di Valle, 299
Morpurgo, Elia, of Gradisca, 18th century, 424; Senator Elia, 20th century, 545; Emilio, 483; Ezechia, 432; family, of Gradisca, 337; firm at Ancona, 373; Giuseppe Lazzaro, 486; Mario, 377; Rachel, 498; Salamone, 481; Salvatore, 431; Samson, 398; surname, 360
Mortara, Edgardo, 471–2; Ludovico, 483, 510; Marco, 498
Moscato, Judah, 217
Moses, Adolph, 469
Moses ben Enoch, 63
Moses ben Halfo, 91
Moses ben Joab, 220
Moses, of Palermo, 95; of Pavia, 63, 69; a second Moses of Pavia, 73; the Spaniard, 58; of Viterbo, 146
Moslem conquests, 52 f., 61, 82; influences, 81–2, 92, 143, 228, 232–3, 234
Mourning, 245
Mozart, Wolfgang, 422
Mufarridsh ibn Salim, "Sultan," 52
Muratori, Lodovico Antonio, 422
Murder libels, 100
Muscovy, grand duke of, 203
Musicians, 114, 196 f., 327, 392, 396, 482
Mussolini, Benito, 509 ff., 517–8, 520, 522, 524, 526, 541 f.; Umberto, 530–1
Mussolino, Benedetto, 519
Mysticism, 50 f., 63, 64, 150 f., 402–6, 496, 499; *see* Cabalism

NACMANI, BANKING-HOUSE, 456
Names, Jewish, 13; *see* Surnames, Jewish
Naples, 8, 22, 40, 44, 46, 48, 52, 62, 66, 79, 87, 93, 95, 96, 100 f., 116, 118, 139, 146, 148, 159 f., 163, 170, 179, 180, 184, 189, 199, 202, 208 ff., 213, 215, 221, 224, 238, 245, 260, 268, 269–88, 289, 299, 351, 403, 434, 440, 450, 455, 484, 491, 502–3, 542
Napoleon I, 428–45, 446, 448 f., 455, 462 f., 476, 484, 494

Napoleon III, 471
Nardo, 285
Naro, 252
Nasas, Sicilian Jew, 46
Nasi, Palestinian, 35
Nasi, Joseph, 190, 215, 308
Naso, 82
Nathan, Ernesto, 478; family, 457, 478
Nathan ben Ephraim of Venosa, 59 f.
Nathan ben Jehiel of Rome, 78, 90 f., 92
Nathan ha-Meati, 148 n.
Nathan of Gaza, 404–5
Nazism, 517–8, 521–51
Negroponte, 96
Neofiti, ("New Christians"), 269–71, 274, 282, 284, 287 f., 314, 346; *see* Marranos
Neppi, Graziadio (Hananel), 442
Nero, 8, 17
Nerva, 15
New Testament, 12, 25, 28, 104, 204; *see* Vulgate
New Year, Jewish, 255, 292, 538
Nicanor, 2
Niccolò da Adria, 96 n.
Niccolò Albergati, 160 f.
Nice, 135, 180, 342, 344 and n., 417, 421, 428, 440, 443, 448, 452 f., 470 n.
Nicholas of Palermo, 247
Nicholas III, Pope, 138, 150 f.
Nicholas IV, Pope, 148, 149
Nicholas V, Pope, 133, 164 f., 166, 201, 204
Nicosia, 230, 232
Ninth of Ab, 301, 311
Nissim, son of Hayim (Khalah), 57 f.
Nizza [Marittima]; *see* Nice
Nizza (Monferrato), 343, 353
Nobile, Umberto, 484–5
Nofet Zufim, by Judah Messer Leon, 217
Nola, 22, 269, 283
Norcia, 121, 146
Normans, 66, 71, 81, 82, 97, 245
Norsa, Daniel, 174 and n.; family, 121, 174 and n., 325; Immanuel, 176; Solomon Jedidiah, 217
North Africa, 48, 52, 64, 74, 260, 261 n., 343, 399; *see* Libya
North Italy, 41 f., 66–73, 74–7, 78 n., 84, 85, 102, 103–52, 157 f., 163, 164, 170 ff., 180, 192, 214, 219, 220, 230, 232, 241 n., 242, 243–4, 249, 252, 272 f., 277 f., 318 f., 325 ff., 329, 333, 337, 344, 359, 361–2, 370, 376, 378, 416, 429, 432, 437 f., 440, 455, 480, 490, 501, 512, 526, 542, 544, 546, 549
Notaries public, 476, 535
Noto, 252
Novara, 136, 162
Novellara, 340
Novi, 183
Numerus clausus in other countries, 514

OATH, JEWISH FORM OF, 80, 369, 476
Occupations, 23 f., 103 f., 114, 164, 262–3, 270, 272, 306, 334, 371–7, 414 ff., 423, 425, 447, 449, 470–1, 485–6, 528–9, 531; *see* under names
Odoacer, 40
Olive-orchards, 68, 86, 137, 298

Olmo, Jacob Daniel, 400
Olper, Samuel, 461, 493
Onorati, Cardinal, 435
Opinione, periodical, 468
Orano, Paolo, 523
Organization for the Relief of Jewish Emigrants (*Delasem*), 517, 533–4, 550
Oria, 13, 22, 26, 49 ff., 52 n., 53, 61, 63
Oriental cults, 18
Orte, 544
Ortona, 224
Orvieto, 120 f., 163, 168, 307, 359
Orvieto, Adolfo, 482; Angiolo, 482
Osimo, 169
Ostia, 21
Ostiana, 340
Ostiglia, 340
Ostiglia, Jonah, 391
Ostrogoths, 40 f., 43
Ostuni, 285
Otranto, 13, 22, 53, 54, 60, 61, 78, 80, 89, 90, 92, 285, 287
Otto II, emperor, 69
Otto III, emperor, 69
Ottolenghi, Abraham Azariah (Bonaiut), 428–9; Adolfo, 546; Donato, 498; family, 438; General Giuseppe, 478 f., 484; Joseph, 221, 303; of Leghorn, 457; surname, 360
Ovid, 27 f.

PACIFICI, ALFONSO, 508; Riccardo, 545–6; surname, 360
Padua, 76, 95, 106 117, 125, 131, 134, 148 n., 157, 158, 161, 162, 166, 169, 175, 176, 184, 185, 194 f., 199, 203, 206, 212, 220 f., 223, 318, 324, 335–6, 337, 357, 363, 365 ff., 371 f., 377–8, 385, 389, 397, 401, 405–6, 408–9, 416, 432, 438, 440, 442, 470, 472–3, 484, 496, 498, 538 f.
Padua, University of, 125, 173, 206, 209, 213, 221, 238, 312, 335–6, 453, 483, 532
Paganini, Nicolò, 412
Paganism, 4, 9, 10, 17, 19, 20, 27 f., 29 f., 31 ff.
Paggi brothers, 455
Pahad Yitzhak, by Isaac Lampronti, 398–9
Palermo, 22, 45, 52, 55, 57 f., 61, 82, 86, 89, 92, 95, 146, 229–30, 232, 234 ff., 243 ff., 251 ff., 257, 259 ff., 491, 542
Palermo, archbishop of, 243
Palestine, 1, 2, 4, 7, 8, 10, 11, 12, 14, 15, 16 f., 18, 19, 22, 23, 24, 29, 30, 35 f., 64, 74, 80, 113, 159 f., 242 f., 286, 307 ff., 403 ff., 415, 508, 518–21, 534; Balfour Declaration, 520; Jewish National Home, 520; mandate, 519 f.; *see* Schools
Palestinian coins, 215
Palestrina, Giovanni, 197
Palmerston, Lord, 519
Paltiel, 53, 57, 79
Panormitano, 105
Pantaleone, 54
Pantelleria, 18, 230, 257
Paoli, General, 350
Paolo Sarpi, 315
Papacy, 1, 42 ff., 67 n., 71, 73 f., 99, 114,

INDEX

141, 157, 164, 177, 296, 315, 454, 473, 533; *see* Church; Vatican; names of Popes
Papal Academy, 533
Papal States, 121, 122, 127, 139 ff., 150, 157, 158, 164 f., 286, 290, 292, 296 ff., 315 ff., 329-33, 345, 348, 361, 368, 370, 377, 381 ff., 408, 411, 413-5, 417 ff., 422, 425 f., 440, 442, 445, 450 f., 454, 456, 459 f., 469
Paper manufacturers, 114, 349
Parente family, 337
Parhon, Solomon, 93
Paris, 442
Parma, 113, 129, 131, 142, 169, 170, 196, 309, 341, 395, 417, 421, 425, 440, 445, 448, 452 f., 469, 499 f.
Parnas; *see Archisynagogus*
Pasquale of Catania, 240
Pasqualigo, deputy, 477
Passover, 16, 171 ff.,191, 355, 392 f., 411, 459, 471
Pasta, Giuditta, 482
Pastimes, 212 f., 233
Pastorino, medallionist, 195
Patriarchate, 35 f.
Paul II, Pope, 386-7
Paul III, Pope, 207 f., 290, 300, 378
Paul IV, Pope, 289-90, 294-8, 299 ff., 304, 319
Paul V, Pope, 326
Paul of Tarsus, 8, 11, 12, 22
Paulus Neofidus, 96 n.
Pavia, 63, 69, 71, 77, 92, 127, 132, 169, 173, 181 f., 213, 221, 304, 322, 359
Pawnbroking, 107, 113, 115, 154, 168, 169, 190, 334, 370-1; see Moneylending
Peasants, Jewish, 46, 86, 308
Peddlers, Jewish, 24, 103, 113, 229, 263, 374, 486, 531, 537
Pedro, King, 246, 264
Pedro de Toledo, 215, 285 f.
Pelation, Roman Jew, 16
Pentateuch, 17 f., 74, 80, 126, 166, 258, 388; printing of, 225; printing of Rashi commentary on, 223; *see* Bible (O. T.)
Pentecost, 28, 142, 190
Pepe, Gabriel, 458
Pepin, 66
Perctarit (Bertarido), king of Lombardy, 41
Periodicals, Jewish, 484, 497, 499-500, 507 f., 513; publication prohibited, 535
Perugia, 120, 129, 138, 146, 159, 168, 175, 199, 213, 218, 307, 318 f., 335, 359, 491 n., 523
Pesaro, 77, 92, 119, 162, 169, 224, 301, 307 f., 321, 331-2, 373, 390, 419, 431-2, 434, 502
Pesaro, Abraham, 462, 512
Pescaro, 72, 81
Pescia, 134
Pesikta Rabbati, 60
Peter of Pisa, 69
Peter, the Apostle, 43
Petit, Solomon, 149
Petra, Cardinal, 411
Petrarch, 143, 211, 215 n., 223, 225, 422
Pfefferkorn, Johannes, 205 f.
Philaster, bishop of Brescia, 33

Philip, emperor, 20
Philip II, king of Spain, 322, 343
Philippson, Abramo, 458
Philo, 12
Philosophia Libera, by Isaac Cardoso, 378
Physicians, Jewish, 23, 61, 85 f., 95, 106, 113 f., 119, 128, 132, 133, 139, 147 f., 156, 158, 162, 163, 164, 183, 188, 200 ff., 207 f., 212, 217, 223 f., 229, 237 f., 239-40, 246, 262-3, 265, 279, 295, 300, 312, 316-7, 327, 335, 361, 377 f., 400 f., 410, 423, 483; women, 214, 240
Physique, Jewish, 360, 420, 487
Piacenza, 169, 170, 182, 309, 341, 425
Piasco, 137
Piattelli family, 13, 91 n.; *see* Delli Mansi
Piave, 488
Piazza, 260
Picho, Azariah, 217, 402
Pico della Mirandola, 205, 206 ff.
Piedmont, 75, 135-6, 161-2, 165, 312, 328, 341-3, 344, 346, 357 ff., 361 f., 371 f., 376, 384, 409, 417, 421, 425, 427 f., 438, 440 ff., 444, 448, 452, 454 ff., 465 ff., 476, 478, 484, 486, 490, 494, 500 f., 512, 516, 543
Piedmontese Constitution of 1848, 465, 467, 469 f.
Pierleoni, Benedict, 73; family, 73, 106; Leo, 73; Piero, 73
Pieve, 187
Pieve di Cento, 307, 333
Pinamonte, Father, 402
Pincherle, Gabriel, 478; family of Gorizia, 337; Leone, 461
Piombino, princes of, 350
Piove di Sacco, 223
Piperno, Ugo, 482
Pirano, 124
Pires, Diego, 223
Pisa, 68, 75, 83, 110, 111, 132, 139, 169, 262, 345 ff., 352, 362, 383, 385, 389, 457, 464, 498, 545 f.
Pistoia, 134, 169
Pitigliano, 345, 437
Pius II, Pope, 174, 177, 202
Pius IV, Pope, 304 f., 357
Pius V, Pope, 305-7, 309 ff., 315, 319
Pius VI, Pope, 414, 418, 429-30, 432, 439
Pius VII, Pope, 450
Pius VIII, Pope, 451
Pius IX, Pope, 459, 462, 464, 468, 470 ff.
Pius XI, Pope, 523, 526, 533
Pius XII, Pope, 543
Plagues, 47, 131, 181, 329-30, 339, 356-7, 377, 380; *see* Black Death
Plato, 205, 208
Playing-cards, makers of, 114, 213
Pliny, 28
Po, Department of the, 444
Poets, Jewish, 23, 50, 59, 60, 64, 91, 106, 116, 121, 138, 143 ff., 164, 190, 194, 197 f., 211, 215, 219-20, 223, 399-401, 403, 405, 412, 422, 457-8, 481, 497-8
Pogroms, 426, 434, 437, 543-9, 551; in Germany, 534, 539-40; *see* Attacks on Jews
Pola, 21, 124

Polacco, Vittorio, 479, 483, 511, 532
Polesine district, 129
Politics, Jews in Italian, 5, 15, 31, 36, 40, 78, 106, 113 f., 163, 239, 246, 279, 425, 427, 429, 431 ff., 440 f., 446 ff., 459, 461–3, 475 ff., 488, 509 ff., 541, 545
Polizzi, 248, 250
Pompeii, 8, 22
Pompey, 4, 6
Pomponesco, 340, 502
Pontremoli, Aldo, 484–5
Popes, 39, 42 f., 66, 72, 73, 97 f., 105, 111, 121, 126, 141, 155, 167, 177, 178, 182, 187, 192, 201 f., 242, 250, 289, 295, 320, 330, 341, 378, 380, 384, 387–8, 407, 417, 473; *see also* under names
Popolo d'Italia, Il, 522
Poppaea, 17
Population, Jewish, 5, 13, 23, 34, 36, 37, 56, 69, 75, 76, 77 ff., 82 f., 115 f., 229–30, 262, 276, 296, 321 ff., 325, 330 ff., 352–3, 407, 419, 442, 447, 484, 488, 501–4, 512 f., 525–6, 534 f., 543, 551 f.
Portaleone, Abraham, son of Guglielmo, 202; Abraham, great-grandson of Guglielmo, 203, 217; family, 202, 327, 377; Guglielmo (Benjamin), 15th century, 202; Guglielmo, 17th century, 377; Lazzaro, 203; Leone da Sommi, 198
Porto, 21
Porto, Allegro, 197
Portobuffolè, 173
Portugal, Inquisition in, 186 f., 190; *see* Immigrants from
Potenza, 549
Pozzuoli, 8, 11, 16, 22, 549
Prato, 134
Prayer book, 147, 224, 441–2, 497, 505
Preziosi, Giovanni, 523
Printing, 114, 190, 223–7, 277, 292, 303 f., 314, 340, 371, 395, 399, 455, 498–9
Privileges granted to Jews, 10, 120, 140, 141, 158, 159, 162, 164, 166, 240
Pro Cultura, Jewish cultural societies, 507
Professions, 371, 375–6, 441, 449, 470, 486, 528–9, 531; *see also* under names
Protestant Reformation, 209, 289; in Germany, 205; *see* Counter-Reformation
Protocols of the Elders of Zion, 523
Provence, 97; *see* Immigrants from
Provenzale, David, 214
Publishing firms, 482, 513
Pugliese, family name, 287; General, 530
Pumbeditha, 92
Purim, 146, 197, 355, 390–1, 392
"Purim Saragossa," 261 n.
Puteoli; *see* Pozzuoli
Puzzamano, Antonio, 206

QUINTILLIAN, 217

RABBINIC WRITINGS, LIBELS AGAINST, 291–2
Rabbinical colleges, 78, 90 ff., 220 ff., 336, 399, 496, 499, 515, 548; *see* Schools; Yeshibot
Rabbis, 1, 11, 26, 60, 116, 145 ff., 213, 222, 232, 265, 285, 293, 333, 336, 360, 366, 369, 377 f., 384, 389, 391, 393, 397 ff., 410 f., 413 ff., 426–7, 441 ff., 452, 454, 492–3, 494, 496–8, 505, 506–7, 513, 515, 524, 536, 545–6; *see* Chief Rabbi
Rabeni, Raphael, 397
Rachel, of Venice, 197
Racialism, 517, 523, 525–6, 527 ff., 533 f., 537, 540 ff.
Ragpickers, Jewish, 125, 365, 373 ff.
Ragusa, 223, 238, 260, 284, 286
Rais of Ragusa, 238
Ramazzini, Bernardo, 374–5
Ramusio, Giovambattista, 192
Rangoni, Guido, 208
Ranza, Citizen, 428
Raphael, painter, 197
Raphael, Mark, 200 f.
Rappa, Jonah, 402
Rashi, 91, 223
Rasseqna Mensile di Israel, La, 513
Rather, bishop, 69
Rationalism, 410
Rattazzi Law, 495, 500, 512
Rattazzi, Urbano, 494 f.
Ravà, surname, 360
Ravenna, 39, 40, 72, 77, 122, 139, 164, 169, 175, 292, 307
Real estate, 154 f., 161, 250, 295, 298, 303 ff., 308, 313, 320, 325, 327, 357–8, 417, 423, 425, 447, 449, 451, 531, 552
Recanati, 77, 119, 150, 165, 169, 302, 359
Reform movement, 443, 445, 489, 492–3
Refugees, relief of, 517, 533–4, 550
Reggio Calabria, 81, 89, 223, 260, 276, 278, 283
Reggio Emilia, 129, 165 f., 169, 172, 173, 176, 187, 211, 303, 320, 328, 340, 352, 369, 380, 383, 386, 398, 403, 405, 421, 429, 438, 441 f., 469, 484, 502
Reggio, Isaac Samuel, 497–8
Regina, 81
Reiner (Reicher), Rabbi Jacob, 214 n.
Rejoicing of the Law, feast of, 392
Religious freedom, 460, 463, 466–7, 468 ff., 473, 475, 478 f.; instruction, 494; persecution, 13, 18; prejudice, 477
Renaissance, 96, 135, 153–227, 242, 291, 318, 394, 397, 406 f., 496, 515
René, of Naples, 163, 238–9
Republic of Italy, 440
Resistance movement against Fascism, 516–7, 548
Restrictions, self-imposed, 157 f.
Retail trade, 486
Reubeni, David, 191–3, 212
Reuchlin, Johannes, 205 f.
Revenues, 128, 131; papal, 83, 88 f., 105 f., 270; *see* Taxes; Dues
Revere, 340, 439
Revere, Giuseppe, 460, 462, 481 f.
Revolt against Rome, 12, 18, 23, 29
Revolutions, Year of, 1848, 460–3, 464–7, 468
Rhazes, Mohammedan physician, 94–5
Rhodes, 515; immigrants from, 180; rabbinical seminary, 515
Ricci, Vincenzo, 466

INDEX

Rienzi, Cola di, 141
Rieti, 359
Rimini, 77, 85, 121 f., 129, 131, 176, 209, 211, 224
Rimos, Moses, 239–40
Risorgimento, 454–73, 476 f., 481, 484, 492, 497, 501 f., 516, 520
Ritual, Jewish, 16, 17 ff., 61, 64, 68, 136, 151, 189, 259, 261 n., 271, 286–7, 288, 300, 308 f., 332, 334, 338, 341, 347, 361–3, 384, 402 f., 409, 414, 428, 443, 492–3, 504 ff., 547, 550
Ritual murder accusations, 170 ff., 183, 198, 247, 337, 388, 410, 413, 453, 471
Riva, Solomon, 214
Riva di Trento, 226–7
Rivarolo, 340
Rivista Israelitica, Florence, 507
Rivista Israelitica, La, Parma, 500
Rivoli, 429
Robert of Anjou, of Naples, 95 f., 141 f., 146, 148, 269 f., 272 f.
Robert, General, 430
Rodrigues, Daniel, 210, 335
Roger I, of Sicily, 88 f.
Roger II, of Sicily, 82, 86, 93, 245
Romagna, 70, 121, 137, 141, 157, **296**, 302, 308, 429 f., 455, 469, 472
Romanelli, Samuel, 400–1
Roman empire, 2, 7–14, 19–37, 40, 49, 67, 425; Fascist, 514, 520
Romanin, Samuel, 481
Romanini, Alfredo, 523
Romano, Benjamin, 241
Romanus Lucapenus, 53
Rome, 1, 4, 5, 7, 9, 11 ff., 16 f., 19 f., 22, 23 ff., 33, 35, 36 f., 39, 41 ff., 44, 45, 47, 48, 50, 52, 59, 60, 66, 69, 71 ff., 77 f., 84, 90, 92, 96, 97, 102, 106 f., 111, 113 f., 116, 117, 118, 120, 121, 126, 127, 138 ff., 143, 145, 147 ff., 156 ff., 177, 179 ff., 187, 188, 190 f., 192, 195, 199 ff., 206, 207 f., 211 ff., 224, 228, 236, 256, 261, 262, 275, 277, 286, 288, 290 ff., 295 ff., 307, 314 ff., 327, 329, 331 f., 345, 352, 353–5, 356 f., 359, 362, 364 f., 367–8, 369 f., 373 ff., 391 ff., 397, 402, 405, 408, 410 ff., 418–9, 426, 429, 432, 434, 440, 442, 444, 450 ff., 456, 459 f., 462 f., 464–5, 470–3, 478, 484, 486 ff., 490–1, 492, 495 f., 498 f., 502–4, 507, 511 ff., 518, 520, 522, 525, 531 f., 535 f., 537, 542 ff., 547–53
Rome-Berlin Axis, 521–41
Romulus Augustulus, 37
Roques, Giuseppe Pardo, 545
Rossano, 61, 80, 89, 269
Rosselli, Carlo, 516–7; family, **457**; Pellegrino, 457
Rothschild, house of, 454; Karl Mayer von, 450 n.; of Paris, 467
Roumania, 478
Rovere, Francesco; *see* Pope Sixtus IV
Rovere, Francesco Maria della, of Urbino, 182, 321; Guidubaldo, 309
Rovighi, Cesare, 484, 499–500
Rovigo, 129 f., 337–8, 371–2, 408–9, 419–20, 433, 442, 453, 472–3, 502

Rovigo, Abraham, **405**
Rubiera, 455
Ruffini, Francesco, 520
Ruschi, Francesco, 391
Russia, 475

Saba, Umberto, 481–2
Sabbatai ben Abraham; *see* **Donnolo**
Sabbataism, 404–6
Sabbatai Zevi, 404–5
Sabbath, 4, 5, 6, 9, 17, 18, 27 f., **43, 44** ff., 111, 151, 198, 213, 273, 313, 338, 343, 383, 393, 451, 475, 506, 521
Sabbionneta, 227, 340, 502
Sabot, Elias, 158, 201, 203
Sacerdote, Alessandro, 441; **Angelo, 511**; Laudadio, *see* Ishmael Cohen; **surname**, 360
Sacristo, Cardinal, 293
Safed, 192, 403
St. Albert of Trapani, 246
St. Francis of Assisi, 154
St. Nilus of Rossano, 61
S. Stafano, Abbess of, 47
Sala, Samuel, 239
Salamone *ebreo*, 147
Salemi, 230
Salerno, 22, 48, 62, 79, **85, 86**, 88 f., 93, 101, 269 f., 455
Saliceti, Citizen, 430
Salom, Abraham, 498; **Dr. Michael, 432**
Salomone, engineer, of Ferrara, 199
Salonica, 192, 224, 261, 287 f., 301, 309, 514
Salsomaggiore, 549
Saltpeter, manufacture of, 199 f.
Saluzzo, 136–7, 342, 512
Samaritans, 7, 39, 44; **alphabet, 217**
Samsam ad-Daulah, 58
Samuel, of Genoa, 74
Samuel, of Otranto, 92
Samuel, of Verona, 151
Samuel ben Hananel, **78 f.**
Samuel ben Jacob, 95
Samuel ibn Nagdela, 57
Sancia, queen, 142
San Daniele, 336, 416
San Germano; *see* **Cassino**
San Gimignano, 134
Sanhedrin, Napoleonic, **442–3**
San Marco, 230, 260
San Marino, 122, 532, **541**
S. Maurizio, order of, 476
San Miniato, 132, 134
S. Salvatore, 409
San Severino, 169
Santa Croce, 170
Santa Lucia, 252
Saracens, 52 f., **55–8, 60, 61, 62, 66, 69**
Saragossa, 150
Saralbo, Joseph, 314
Saraval, Jacob, 397, 410; **Leone Vita, 498**
Sardaigna, surname, 268 n.
Sardi, surname, 268 n.
Sardinia, 9 f., 22, 26, 45, 83, 162, 254, **262–9**, 278, 281, 350, 417, 428, 445, 448, 463, 467, 469, 471, 491 n., 494 f., 537
Sarfatti family, 180; Giuseppe Gallo, **220;**

Joseph (Fra Andrea del Monte), 208, 291–2, 316; Margherita, 510; Samuel (Gallo, "the Frenchman"), 202, 220, 387
Sassari, 262, 266; archbishop of, 266
Sassuolo, 178
Saturninus, senator, 9
Saul, of Venice, 122
Savigliano, 136, 342, 428, 502
Savings banks, 478
Savoca, 251
Savonarola, Girolamo, 133, 190
Savoy, 140, 162, 210, 312, 341–2, 457; duke of, 135 f., 140, 346, 350, 383; house of, 470, 479
Saxons, 69
Scandiano, 178, 340
Scholars and scholarship, 58, 62 ff., 70, 75 f., 78, 81, 90–6, 100, 116, 118, 119, 122, 125, 126, 127 ff., 136, 137, 143 ff., 191, 194–227, 241–2, 269, 272, 323 f., 333, 394–406, 442, 481–4, 496–500, 506–8, 535; see Intellectual life
Schools, Jewish, 59 f., 214, 363–4, 444; Palestinian, 15 f., 35 f., 58, 64, 72, 518; secular, 455; see Education; Rabbinical colleges; Universities; Yeshibot
Sciacca, 230, 233, 235, 252, 260
Scientists, Jewish, 61 f., 199–200, 483
Scot, Michael, 94
Scott, Charles Alexander, 462, 471–2
Sebastiano del Piombo, 197
Secondhand dealers, 113, 125, 185, 296, 334, 372 ff., 415, 455, 486
Segrè, Joshua, 402; Joshua Benzion, 441, 443; Colonel Roberto, 530
Sejanus, 9, 10
Selden, John, 396
Senigallia, 119, 307, 321, 331, 388, 435, 468
Senigallia, Abraham, 428, 438–9
Sepher ha-Teneh, by Ahitub ben Isaac, 242
Serena, Arthur, 485
Sereni, Enzo, 550
"Serfs of the Royal Chamber," Sicily, 232, 235
Sermide, 340, 442, 502
Sermons, forced, 138, 188, 236, 249–51, 265 f., 315–6, 328, 381–2, 385, 414–5, 450, 459
Servadio (Obadiah) of Damascus, 310
Sessa, 269
Seta, Alessandro della, 528
Settlement, Jewish, 1, 2, 4, 5, 7, 8, 9, 10, 13, 14, 20 ff., 42, 44, 48, 54, 67 f., 101 f., 107, 112, 116–37, 138, 141, 142, 146, 154, 163, 170, 183, 185, 228, 269, 285 f., 350, 351–2, 416, 542
Severus, Septimius, 19
Sforno, Obadiah, 205, 208
Sforza, Bianca Maria, 127; Catherine, countess of Imola, 201; Francesco, duke of Milan, 131 f.; Galeazzo, of Milan, 202
Shehita 111, 112, 128, 232, 236, 366, 531
Shekel, 14, 35
Shemariah ben Abraham, 79
Shemariah ben Elijah Ikriti, 96
Shephatiah, poet, 50 f., 52, 60
Shibbole ha-Leket, by Zedekiah Anau, 151

Ship-owners, 85
"Sicilian Vespers" of 1282, 98, 246
Siciliano, Judah, 146, 242
Sicily, 8, 22, 26, 40, 44, 45, 46, 47, 48, 49, 52, 53, 55–8, 66, 71, 81, 82, 83, 84, 87, 89, 93, 98, 101, 139, 140, 151, 160, 164, 209, 212, 214, 228–61, 262 f., 268, 269 f., 275, 280 f., 284, 286, 351, 491 n., 541; expulsion, 178, 278, 537; under Saracen rule, 55–8, 228; Two Sicilies, 288, 296, 341, 351, 445, 469, 491
Sienna, 76 f., 106, 133, 161, 162 f., 169, 175, 195, 212 f., 310 f., 335, 345, 372, 393, 422, 435–6, 437
Sigismund, emperor, 133
Sikilli, Jacob, 242
Silano of Venosa, 50, 60
Silk manufacturers, Jewish, 68, 86 f., 127, 199, 229, 234, 298, 349, 371–2, 375, 416
Silversmiths, Jewish, 114, 229, 376
Simeon ben Johai, 17
Simon of Trent, 171 f.
Sineo, Riccardo, 467
Singers, 197, 482
Singing, teaching of, 196, 327, 377
Siponto, 79, 81, 91
Sirletto, Cardinal, 316
Sixtus IV, Pope, 171 f., 177, 182, 204
Sixtus V, Pope, 199, 317–9, 322, 370, 375, 381
Sixtus of Sienna, 302, 303–4
Slaves, Christian, 31, 39, 41, 46 ff., 259, 265, 267; Jewish, 4 f., 7 ff., 13, 15, 24, 179, 286, 350–1, 365; Moslem, 385; pagan, 31; Roman, 526
Soap-making, 349
Sobieski, Alexander, 386
Social life among Jews, 359, 391 ff., 531
Social relations with Christians, 393–4, 414, 446, 475, 533, 546–7
Soliman of Salerno, 75
Solomon, King, 1
Solomon, Roman Jew, 286
Solomon d'Urbino, 119, 216
Solomon of Anagni, 275
Solomon of Perugia, 146
Solomon "the Babylonian," 72
Soncino, 224
Soncino, Gershom ben Moses, 224 f.; Israel Nathan, 224; Joshua Solomon, 224; press, 224–5
Sonnino, 359
Sonnino, Sidney, 478, 488
Soragna, 341
Sorres, bishop of, 266; diocese of, 262, 266
Sources for history, 3 f., 21, 22, 26, 59, 74 ff., 118, 128, 152, 183, 228–9, 265, 308, 343, 395, 398
South Italy, 2, 13, 20 ff., 36, 41 f., 48, 50–65, 68, 69, 71, 78 ff., 83, 84 ff., 89, 90, 92 ff., 97–102, 116, 117, 137, 159, 163, 164, 177, 204, 228, 234–5, 273, 276, 278 f., 286 ff., 323, 329, 353, 457, 491 n., 540, 542; population, 229–30
Spain, 41, 52, 61, 63, 64, 68, 81, 92, 96, 112, 143, 163, 183, 186 f., 228, 247–8, 252 ff., 268, 322; Almoravide persecutions, 80;

INDEX 573

civil war, 516–7, 530; expulsion, 178, 253–61, 278, 282, 390; Inquisition, 186 f., 190, 253 ff., 290; massacres in, 137, 247–8
Spalato, 210, 335
Spanish influences, 143 ff.
Spezia, 491 n.
Spilimbergo, 336, 416
Spizzichino, surname, 307
Spoleto, 121, 139, 141, 209, 299, 307
Sraffe, Angelo, 483
Steinschneider, Moritz, 499
Stratta, Niccolò, 410
Students, 188, 361; expulsion of, 448–9, 450, 527; see Education; Scholars and scholarship
Stura, Department of the, 444
Suetonius, 11, 15
Sullam, Sarah Coppio, 215, 498
Sulmona, 274, 285
Supino, David, 483; Senator I. B., 481
Suriano, 150
Surnames, Jewish, 13, 287, 307, 359–60, 522, 535; see under names
Svevo, Italo, 482, 532
Sylvester I, Pope, 43 n.
Synagogue, 1, 5, 10, 12, 19, 24–6, 33–4, 40, 43–4, 45–6, 49, 56, 81, 101, 111 f., 121, 153, 161, 163, 179–80, 188 f., 196, 216, 232, 247, 255 f., 259 ff., 276, 287, 290, 294 f., 302, 307 f., 318, 320, 327, 330, 332, 334, 340, 345, 354, 361–3, 366, 383, 389 f., 392, 416 f., 419, 426, 434, 437, 449, 460, 469–70, 474, 479, 489, 491–5, 501–2, 504 ff., 508, 519, 538, 544, 548, 549–51, 552
Syracuse, 22, 37, 49, 55, 83, 234, 241, 243, 247, 248, 252, 260, 261 n., 278
Syria, 2, 6, 75

Tabernacles, feast of, 16, 428
Tacitus, 10
Tagliacozzo, surname, 307
Tagmule ha-Nefesh, by Hillel ben Samuel, 147
Tailors, Jewish, 23, 114, 373 ff., 486
Talmud, 1, 16, 18, 35, 57, 63, 64, 78, 90 ff., 99 f., 128, 136, 138, 142, 151, 163, 164, 194, 205 f., 217, 220 f., 241, 251, 265, 291 ff., 303, 304, 306, 317–8, 319, 333, 382, 394, 397–8, 402 f., 414, 479, 496, 498; printing of, 225; censored edition of, 318
Tanna de-Be Elijahu, 60
Tanners, Jewish, 272
Taormina, 55, 250–1, 252, 260
Taranto, 13, 22, 49, 52, 53, 68, 80, 101, 260, 271, 285, 530
Tasso, Torquato, 223
Tavern-keepers, Jewish, 114, 234
Tax-agents, 85, 129, 272, 263, 376
Taxes, 32, 56, 57–8, 68, 78 ff., 90, 99, 101, 108, 113, 120–1, 125, 140, 158, 178, 180, 230–1, 233–4, 240, 272 ff., 276, 280, 321, 340, 342, 345, 348, 365–8, 382, 408, 418, 425, 447, 449, 494, 512; "beam," 233; birth, 234; capital or income, 366, 368; carnival, 387, 451–2, 459; cheese, 233;
cloth, 233; death, 235, 271; dye, 87, 99; emigration, 255, 408; export, 365, 454; hearth, 368; import, 365; land, 57; loan-banks, 124, 126, 188; marriage, 234; meat, 368; Palestinian schools and religious institutions, 35 f., 58; poll, 56–7, 160, 233, 272, 317; property and capitation, 158, 368, 419; wine, 233, 234, 274; see Dues; Fines; *Fiscus Judaicus*; Levies; Revenues; Tithes; Tolls; Tributes
Teachers, Jewish, 483, 486; exclusion of, 527–8
Telesinus, 43
Temple, Jerusalem, 11, 14, 16, 32, 78, 518–9; tax, 5 f., 9, 12, 14, 16, 35, 518
Terlizzi, 81
Termini, 243, 251
Terni, 121
Terni, Daniel, 398
Terracina, 22, 44, 307
Textile industry, Jews in, 68, 86 ff., 103, 113, 130, 272, 277, 371–3, 389, 407–8, 421, 486
Theater, Jews in, 197 f., 220, 327, 392–3, 400 f., 481 f., prohibition of, 525
Thebes, 86
Theodoric, 39, 40
Theodosian code, 38 f., 41
Theodosius I, 34 f., 70; II, 38 f.
Theudas, Roman Jew, 16, 35
Tiberias, 308, 445
Tiberius, emperor, 8, 9, 10, 262
Tithes, ecclesiastical, 70, 97, 140, 154; see Taxes
Titles of nobility for Jews, 211, 476, 483
Titus, 13, 14, 20, 50, 91
Tivoli, 163 f.
Tivoli, Serafino da, 482
Tobias the physician, 171
Todi, 116, 299
Todros, of Turin, 457
Toledo, 120
Toleranzpatent, 423–4
Tolls, 80, 214, 271, 385; see Taxes
Tommaseo, Niccolò, 458, 463
Torazzo family, 325
Torre, Lelio della, 498
Tortona, 21, 33
Trajan, emperor, 21
Trani, 49, 80, 87, 89 f., 99, 100 f., 151, 269, 270–1, 274, 287
Translators, 90–6, 146 ff., 200, 204 f., 497
Transmontani (Transalpines), 180
Trapani, 230, 232 n., 233, 246, 248, 251
Treblinka, Poland, 549
Trent, 124 f., 171 f., 198, 305
Treves publishing house, 482
Treves, socialist leader, 510–1
Treves de' Bonfili, family, 476; Giuseppe, 441
Treviso, 70, 117, 124, 169, 173, 184, 220, 242
Tributes, 75, 89, 136, 140, 276, 283, 285, 322, 341, 417, 429, 448 f., 456, 469, 471 f.; see Taxes
Trieste, 124, 310, 328, 336–7, 352, 416, 423 f., 443, 446, 462, 470, 473, 486, 487–8,

496, 498, 500, 505, 532, 536, 538, 552; bishop of, 70 n.
Trieste, Gabriel, 440
Trino, 342
Tripoli, 23, 514, 539; immigrants from, 180
Tropea, 280
"True Italians, The" (*I Veri Italiani*), 457
Tunis, 349–50, 503; king of, 94, 239
Turin, 136, 328, 342, 344, 352, 358, 372, 385, 389, 409, 417, 444, 453 f., 460 f., 463, 464 f., 467, 492 f., 494, 502–3, 507, 516, 538 f., 548, 550
Turkey, 260, 301, 307 f., 310, 312, 330
Turks, 166, 177, 193, 311
Tuscans, 124, 125, 130
Tuscany, 111, 132, 141, 157, 176, 179, 182, 201, 215, 308, 310, 345, 384, 410, 424–5, 435–7, 440, 442, 445, 447 f., 453, 459–60, 463, 468 f., 476, 495, 551

UDINE, 117, 124, 169, 182 f., 310, 312, 491 n.
Ullio, of Casale, 313
Umano, 91 n.
Umbria, 116, 120, 137, 139, 143, 161, 163, 168, 209, 296, 299, 307
"Underground" Jews, 546, 550
Union of Italian Jewish Communities, 495, 507, 512–3, 516, 521
Union of Italian Jewish Cultural Societies, 513
United action among Jewish communities, 138
United Italy, 440, 467–70, 473, 476–88, 491, 495
Universities, attendance of Jews at, 160, 213, 240, 447, 459, 466; admission of foreign Jews to, 514; exclusion from 240, 450, 452–3, 455, 527–8; exclusion of foreign Jews from, 527; expulsion from, 448–9
University, Jewish, 216, 240–1
Urban VIII, Pope, 321, 388
Urbino, 108, 119, 121, 169, 182, 199, 202, 204, 210, 242, 292, 299, 301 f., 307 f., 309, 316, 321–2, 331 f., 419, 434
Uscocchi, of Lissa, 210
Usiglio, Angelo, 455–6; Emilio, 455–6, 457
Usque, Abraham, 226; Solomon, 197, 209 f., 223
Usurers, Christian, 109 f., 116, 123, 129, 130, 132, 284 f., 317–8, 371
Usury, 103 ff., 154 f., 161, 167 f., 218, 229, 250, 257, 270, 273 ff., 286, 309, 317–8, 370–1, 444; *see* Loan-banks; Moneylending; *Monti di Pietà*

Valley of Tears, by Joseph ha-Cohen, 183, 218
Vandals, 37, 49
Vannini, Elia, 197
Vannozzo, Francesco di, 128
Vatican, 290, 533, 543; City, 547; Library, 205, 411, 499
Velletri, 471
Venafri, 22, 47, 274
Vendramini family, 371
Venezian, Giacomo, 462

Venice, 21, 47, 67–8, 69–70, 76, 79, 84–5, 117, 122–4, 125, 129–30, 140, 160 f., 166, 171–3, 175 f., 178, 182 f., 184–6, 187, 191 f., 196 ff., 200–1, 206 f., 209 f., 212, 215, 220, 225–6, 273, 280, 290, 292, 297, 303 f., 311 f., 315 f., 322–5, 326–7, 333–5, 336, 341, 346, 350–1, 352, 355 f., 358, 361 f., 365 f., 368 f., 370–1, 373, 375 ff., 382 f., 386, 388 ff., 396 ff., 402, 404, 406 f., 408–9, 415 f., 419, 421, 423, 432–3, 438, 440 f., 443, 445, 458, 461 ff., 466, 468, 470, 472–3, 477, 481, 485 f., 490, 493, 496–7, 498, 500 n., 504, 513–4, 522, 544 ff.
Venosa, 22, 26, 36, 40, 49, 59, 64, 79 f.
Ventura, Rubino, 484
Vercelli, 162, 328, 342, 441, 443, 455, 457, 490, 494, 500
Verona, 69, 71, 76, 92, 130, 136, 147, 151, 162, 169, 173, 184, 199, 220, 323, 338, 352, 355 f., 368, 377 f., 388 f., 391, 413, 416, 419, 432, 438, 441, 470, 472–3, 544, 552
Verona, Guido da, 482
Vesalius, Andreas, 203
Vespasian, 32
Vessillo Israelitico, Il, 500
Viadana, 173, 340, 502
Viareggio, 491 n.
Viccei, Antonio, 386
Vicenza, 162, 169, 173
Vicenzo, apostate, 162
Vico, Giovanni Battista, 422
Victor, Bishop, 45
Vienna, expulsion from, 337
Villefranche, 344, 350
Vineyards, 68, 86, 137, 298, 308
Virdimura, of Catania, 240
Visconti, friar, 170; Giangaleazzo, 127
Visigoths, 37
Vitale, Christian martyr, 22; of Aquila, 275; Benjamin Cohen, 403, 405; Samuel Cohen, 343
Viterbo, 119, 121, 146, 163, 169, 299, 307, 359, 388
Vitta, Emilio, 443
Vittorio Emanuele II, 467, 469 f., 472 f., 477, 484, 499
Vittorio Emanuele III, 479, 486, 520
Vittorio Veneto, 124, 336, 353
Vivante, Vita, 433
Vivanti, Cesare, 483
Vizini, 248
Vo di Este, 549
Voghera, 466
Volterra, 134, 310
Volterra, Vito, 483
Vulgate, 28, 104

WALDENSES, 465
War of Italian Unification, 488
Wars of Liberation, 484
Weaving industry, Jews in, 86 ff., 113, 229, 234, 272
Weddings, Jewish, 244–5, 369–70
Wessely, Naphtali Hart, 424
Wholesale trade, Jews in, 103, 334, 349, 372 f., 415, 422
Widmanstadt, Johanan Albrecht, 208

INDEX

William the Bad of Sicily, 80
William II of the Two Sicilies, 89
Wissenschaft des Judentums, 497
Wolf, Aaron, 391
Wollemborg, Leone, 478
Women, Jewish, 24, 113, 139, 214 f., 219, 229, 245, 364
Woolen industry, Jews in, 338, 371–2
World War I, 488, 491, 500, 514–5, 520
World War II, 535, 536–51

XARCH, GIACOMO, 250

YAKUB IBN KILLIS, 53

Yeshibot, 397–8, 505; *see* Rabbinical colleges; Schools; Universities
Youth Congresses, Jewish, 507, 513–4

ZACUTO, MOSES, 400, 403 f.
Zahalon, Jacob, 377
Zambri the magician, 43 n.
Zante, 335
Zerahiah ben Shealtiel, 148
Zionism, 242–3, 308, 518–21, **534, 536**
Zionist Congress, Italian, 520
Zohar, 205, 208, 303, 403, 405
Zosimus, 49

IT[ALY]

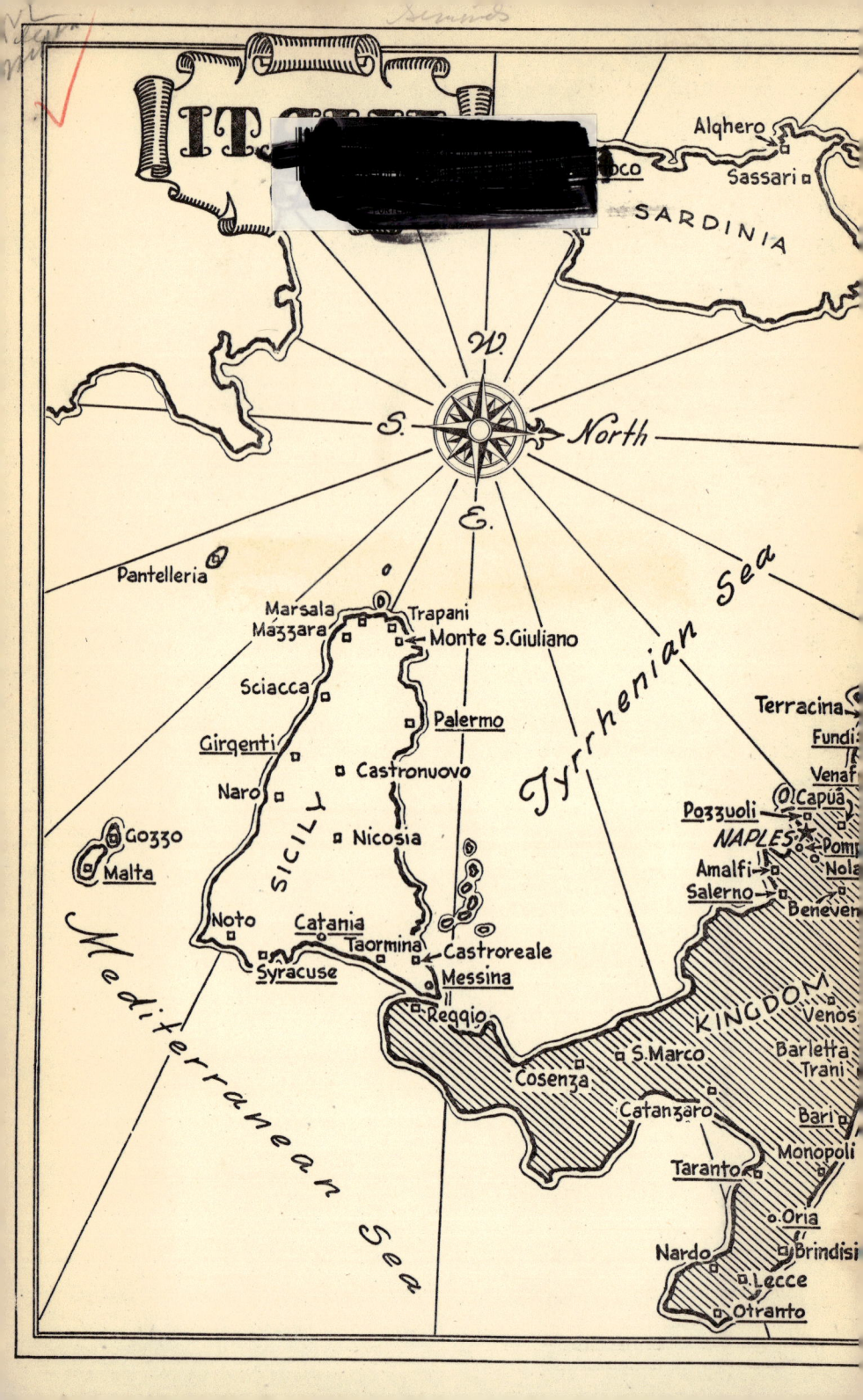

Alghero
Sassari
SARDINIA

N.
S. — North
E.

Pantelleria

Marsala
Mazzara
Trapani
Monte S.Giuliano
Sciacca
Palermo
Girgenti
Castronuovo
Naro
SICILY
Nicosia

Gozzo
Malta

Noto
Catania
Taormina
Castroreale
Syracuse
Messina
Reggio

Tyrrhenian Sea

Terracina
Fundi
Venaf
Pozzuoli
Capua
NAPLES
Pomp
Amalfi
Nola
Salerno
Beneven

KINGDOM
Venos
S.Marco
Barletta
Cosenza
Trani
Catanzaro
Bari
Monopoli
Taranto
Oria
Nardo
Brindisi
Lecce
Otranto

Mediterranean Sea